Innovations in Blockchain-Powered Intelligence and Cognitive Internet of Things (CIoT)

Adarsh Garg
GL Bajaj Institute of Management and Research Greater Noida, India

Fadi Al-Turjman
Research Center for AI and IoT, AI and Robotics Institute, Near East University, Nicosia, Turkey

Shahnawaz Khan
Bahrain Polytechnic, Bahrain

IGI Global
Scientific Publishing
Publishing Tomorrow's Research Today

Published in the United States of America by
    IGI Global
    701 E. Chocolate Avenue
    Hershey PA, USA 17033
    Tel: 717-533-8845
    Fax: 717-533-8661
    E-mail: cust@igi-global.com
    Web site: https://www.igi-global.com

Library of Congress Cataloging-in-Publication Data

CIP Data Pending
ISBN:979-8-3693-2157-7
eISBN:979-8-3693-2158-4

Vice President of Editorial: Melissa Wagner
Managing Editor of Acquisitions: Mikaela Felty
Managing Editor of Book Development: Jocelynn Hessler
Production Manager: Mike Brehm
Cover Design: Phillip Shickler

British Cataloguing in Publication Data
A Cataloguing in Publication record for this book is available from the British Library.

All work contributed to this book is new, previously-unpublished material.
The views expressed in this book are those of the authors, but not necessarily of the publisher.

Table of Contents

Preface xviii

Acknowledgement xxi

Chapter 1
Cognitive IoT Unveiled: Safeguarding the Future Through AI/ML - Security
and Ethics 1

Farzeen Basith, *Acharya Institute of Graduate Studies, India*
A. R. Deepti, *Acharya Institute of Graduate Studies, India*
Vivek K., *Acharya Institute of Graduate Studies, India*
B. Manimekala, *Acharya Institute of Graduate Studies, India*

Chapter 2
Ethical Considerations in Privacy-Preserving Industrial Security of Cognitive
Internet of Things-Enabled Drones 33

Chikesh Ranjan, *National Institute of Technology, Rourkela, India*
Bipllab Chakraborty, *National Institute of Technology, Rourkela, India*
J. Srinivas, *National Institute of Technology, Rourkela, India*
Kaushik Kumar, *Birla Institute of Technology, India*

Chapter 3
Blockchain-Based Identity Management for Secure CIoT Interactions 57

Jagjit Singh Dhatterwal, *Koneru Lakshmaiah Education Foundation,*
Vaddeswaram, India
Kiran Malik, *Department of Computer Science and Engineering*
(AIML), GL Bajaj Institute of Technology & Management, Greater
Noida, India
Kuldeep Singh Kaswan, *Galgotias University, India*

Chapter 4
Reenvisioning Learning in the Modern Age Through New Technologies for
Enhanced Student Involvement 85
> *Ravishankar Krishnan, Vel Tech Rangarajan Dr. Sagunthala R&D
> Institute of Science and Technology, Avadi, India*
> *Rajalakshmi Vel, Sri Ramachandra Institute of Higher Education and
> Research, Chennai, India*
> *Logasakthi Kandasamy, Universal Business School, Universal AI
> University, Karjat, India*
> *H. Moideen Batcha, B.S. Abdur Rahman Crescent Institute of Science
> and Technology, India*
> *Navaneetha Krishnan Rajagopal, University of Technology and Applied
> Sciences, Salalah, Oman*

Chapter 5
Blockchain-Enabled Edge Computing for Cognitive IoT 113
> *Kiran Malik, Department of Computer Science and Engineering
> (AIML), GL Bajaj Institute of Technology & Management, Greater
> Noida, India*
> *Shashi Kant, College of Business and Economics, Blue Hora University,
> Ethiopia*
> *Kuldeep Singh Kaswan, Galgotias University, India*
> *Jagjit SIngh Dhatterwal, Koneru Lakshmaiah Education Foundation,
> Vaddeswaram, India*
> *Arvind Panwar, School of Computer Science and Engineering,
> Galgotias University, Greater Noida, India*

Chapter 6
Study of Geographical and Energy-Aware MANET Routing Protocols 135
> *Raqiya Al Hilali, Modern College of Business and Science, Oman*
> *Hothefa Shaker, Modern College of Business and Science, Oman*
> *Zeyad T. Sharef, Ninevah University, Iraq*
> *Baraa T. Sharef, American University, Bahrain*
> *Shahnawaz Khan, Bahrain Polytechnic, India*

Chapter 7
Prospective of Blockchain in Derivative Markets: An Empirical Review 229
> *Vaishali Deepak Sahoo, Vishwakarma University, India*
> *Deepak Ranjan Sahoo, MIT Arts, Design, and Technology University,
> India*

Chapter 8
Decentralized Data Management for CIoT Using Blockchain Technology 253

*Jagjit Singh Dhatterwal, Koneru Lakshmaiah Education Foundation,
Vaddeswaram, India*

Kuldeep Singh Kaswan, Galgotias University, India

*Kiran Malik, Department of Computer Science and Engineering
(AIML), GL Bajaj Institute of Technology & Management, Greater
Noida, India*

*B. Tirapathi Reddy, Koneru Lakshmaiah Education Foundation,
Vaddeswaram, India*

Chapter 9
Block Chain in Finance Crisis of a Country Engaged in War 279

*Kamalakshi Naganna, Department of Computer Science and
Engineering, Sapthagiri College of Engineering, Bangalore, India*

Naganna H., VRK Institute of Technology, India

Chapter 10
Decentralized Autonomous Organizations (DAOs) in Cognitive IoT: A
Blockchain-Powered Governance Paradigm 301

*Manjeet Kumar, G.L. Bajaj Institute of Technology and Management,
Greater Noida, India*

*Monika Singh, G.L. Bajaj Institute of Technology and Management,
Greater Noida, India*

Vinny Sharma, Galgotias University, India

Chapter 11
Smart Contracts in CIoT: Enhancing Automation and Security 315

Kuldeep Singh Kaswan, Galgotias University, India

*Jagjit Singh Dhatterwal, Koneru Lakshmaiah Education Foundation,
Vaddeswaram, India*

*Kiran Malik, Department of Computer Science and Engineering
(AIML), GL Bajaj Institute of Technology & Management, Greater
Noida, India*

*Meenakshi Sharma, School of Computer Science and Engineering,
Galgotias University, Greater Noida, India*

Chapter 12
Vehicle to Infrastructure Routing Protocols: AI and Finance Perspectives 341
    Hothefa Shaker, Modern College of Business and Science, Oman
    Zeyad T. Sharef, Ninevah University, Iraq
    Seemaa Abbas, Ninevah University, Iraq
    Shahnawaz Khan, Bahrain Polytechnic, Bahrain

Chapter 13
AI Predictive Maintenance in CIoT Using Blockchain 389
    Kuldeep Singh Kaswan, Galgotias University, India
    Jagjit Singh Dhatterwal, Koneru Lakshmaiah Education Foundation,
        Vaddeswaram, India
    Kiran Malik, Department of Computer Science and Engineering
        (AIML), GL Bajaj Institute of Technology & Management, Greater
        Noida, India

Compilation of References 411

About the Contributors 455

Index 461

Detailed Table of Contents

Preface.. xviii

Acknowledgement xxi

Chapter 1
Cognitive IoT Unveiled: Safeguarding the Future Through AI/ML - Security
and Ethics.. 1

Farzeen Basith, Acharya Institute of Graduate Studies, India
A. R. Deepti, Acharya Institute of Graduate Studies, India
Vivek K., Acharya Institute of Graduate Studies, India
B. Manimekala, Acharya Institute of Graduate Studies, India

Cognitive Internet of Things (CIoT) combines Artificial Intelligence (AI) and Machine
Learning (ML) to enable devices to collect, process, and analyze data for making
decisions and predictions. While this enhances the capabilities of IoT systems, it also
introduces new security and ethical challenges. This paper explores the intersection
of AI/ML, security, and ethics in CIoT, emphasizing the importance of safeguarding
data integrity and user privacy. It also highlights the need for responsible AI use
in decision-making processes to ensure transparency, fairness, and accountability.
As CIoT advances, balancing innovation, security, and ethical standards becomes
crucial for sustainable development.

Chapter 2

Ethical Considerations in Privacy-Preserving Industrial Security of Cognitive Internet of Things-Enabled Drones 33

Chikesh Ranjan, National Institute of Technology, Rourkela, India
Bipllab Chakraborty, National Institute of Technology, Rourkela, India
J. Srinivas, National Institute of Technology, Rourkela, India
Kaushik Kumar, Birla Institute of Technology, India

This chapter delves into the critical intersection of privacy preservation and ethical considerations within the realm of industrial security, specifically focusing on the deployment of Cognitive Internet of Things (CIoT)-enabled drones. As industries increasingly adopt autonomous surveillance technologies for security purposes, concerns surrounding the privacy of individuals and the ethical implications of such systems become paramount. The study examines technological solutions, such as advanced encryption and anonymization techniques, aimed at safeguarding individual privacy. Additionally, it investigates the ethical considerations inherent in the utilization of these technologies, including issues of consent, transparency, and societal impact. By addressing these dual dimensions of privacy and ethics, this research contributes to the responsible development and deployment of CIoT-enabled industrial security drones, fostering a balance between technological innovation and ethical considerations in the surveillance landscape.

Chapter 3

Blockchain-Based Identity Management for Secure CIoT Interactions 57

Jagjit Singh Dhatterwal, Koneru Lakshmaiah Education Foundation,
Vaddeswaram, India
Kiran Malik, Department of Computer Science and Engineering
(AIML), GL Bajaj Institute of Technology & Management, Greater
Noida, India
Kuldeep Singh Kaswan, Galgotias University, India

Cellular Internet of Things (CIoT) combines sophisticated machine learning with IoT, which produces smart 'things' that can make decisions on their own. However, identity management in CIoT contains major difficulties especially in terms of security and privacy. Blockchain is found to provide a solution that improves the secure communication in CIoT environments efficiently. In this chapter, the author describes how blockchain can be used to manage identities for CIoT as well as the advantages and frameworks of blockchain. This chapter covers the field of CIoT, its characteristics regarding identification requirements, the concept of blockchain, and the characteristics of blockchain applications for CIoT identity management systems. It goes further to discuss on architectural frameworks for blockchain, application of smart contract, and real life examples in CIoT to expound on how blockchain transform CIoT space. Therefore, analyzing these elements, this chapter is intended to suggest the detailed instructions for using blockchain to safeguard interactions within CIoT. The extant identity management solutions do not fare well when it comes to scaling up while simultaneously addressing escalating security threats and compatibility challenges across the complex CIoT context. The following are the problems which are going to be solved aware in this chapter by proposing a blockchain-based framework for identity management. The emphasis will therefore be on self-sovereign identity models and Decentralized Identifiers as they provide privacy of personal data. This chapter also finds from the analyses and the cases of the application of blockchain-based identity management frameworks that security and efficiency in CIoT systems are greatly enhanced. The processes of identity verification by smart contracts and the applications of cryptographic methods enhance security and privacy. In the same manner, the chapter presents and discusses the performance measurement, legal aspects, and possibilities for future investigations with the aim of painting the picture associated with the future outlooks and obstacles of the examined field.

Chapter 4

Reenvisioning Learning in the Modern Age Through New Technologies for
Enhanced Student Involvement 85

*Ravishankar Krishnan, Vel Tech Rangarajan Dr. Sagunthala R&D
  Institute of Science and Technology, Avadi, India*
*Rajalakshmi Vel, Sri Ramachandra Institute of Higher Education and
  Research, Chennai, India*
*Logasakthi Kandasamy, Universal Business School, Universal AI
  University, Karjat, India*
*H. Moideen Batcha, B.S. Abdur Rahman Crescent Institute of Science
  and Technology, India*
*Navaneetha Krishnan Rajagopal, University of Technology and Applied
  Sciences, Salalah, Oman*

This chapter delves into the transformative role of emerging technologies in modern education. It begins with tracing the evolution of educational technology, highlighting the shift from traditional methods to innovative digital practices. The focus then shifts to the impact of Virtual and Augmented Reality, offering immersive and interactive learning experiences. Artificial Intelligence's role in personalizing learning and automating administrative tasks is examined, along with its ethical implications. The proliferation of e-learning platforms and MOOCs is discussed, emphasizing their role in democratizing education and challenging traditional models. The chapter also explores the influence of social media and online collaboration tools in fostering peer-to-peer learning and global classroom connections. The chapter concludes by addressing the digital divide and the necessity for equitable access to technology in education, underscoring the need for adaptive policies and practices to support these technological advancements.

Chapter 5

Blockchain-Enabled Edge Computing for Cognitive IoT 113

Kiran Malik, Department of Computer Science and Engineering
(AIML), GL Bajaj Institute of Technology & Management, Greater
Noida, India
Shashi Kant, College of Business and Economics, Blue Hora University,
Ethiopia
Kuldeep Singh Kaswan, Galgotias University, India
Jagjit SIngh Dhatterwal, Koneru Lakshmaiah Education Foundation,
Vaddeswaram, India
Arvind Panwar, School of Computer Science and Engineering,
Galgotias University, Greater Noida, India

CIoT brings new options for the connections of things and the processing of data which has never been seen before. Although there are the availability and cost advantages, heterogeneous devices and networks create problems in terms of identity and security. These issues have raised new concerns on the implementation of different identity models due to the centralized nature of most of the identity services that accompany the implementation of the new models. Chapter four delves into how blockchain can be used to ensure secure communication of CIoT, using edge computing as a thrust. The topics falling within the scope of this chapter include architecture and design, consensus algorithms, and smart contracts. It also introduces the edge computing starting from the fundamental concept and stressing on benefits over the cloud computing, and discuss how blockchain can improve data handling and security in edge networks. However, there are issues that are associated with the integration of the blockchain with the edge computing these include; scalability, latency, performance, and compatibility. Thus, this chapter will deliver the detailed comprehensive analysis of how the applied blockchain can meet the above-mentioned challenges to improve the CIoT systems' security and performance. It will also discuss scenarios of applying blockchain for solutions based on edge computing as the case studies. From this point of discussion, the chapter shall provide real-world prospects of blockchain application in the context of CIoT, which shall comprise of increased reliability and accuracy, as well as an increase in security and efficiency in the adoption of identity systems. Thus, it will also cover future development, advancements in technologies and possible research areas to overcome the existing issues and to harness the possibilities of blockchain technology in the envisage growth of CIoT security and features.

Chapter 6

Study of Geographical and Energy-Aware MANET Routing Protocols 135

Raqiya Al Hilali, Modern College of Business and Science, Oman
Hothefa Shaker, Modern College of Business and Science, Oman
Zeyad T. Sharef, Ninevah University, Iraq
Baraa T. Sharef, American University, Bahrain
Shahnawaz Khan, Bahrain Polytechnic, India

Mobile Adhoc Network (MANET) contains a set of mobile nodes with insecure infrastructure. When designing MANET, researchers focused on the routing process regardless of base stations and access points. The protocol designers and network developers face many challenges with MANET routing protocols due to MANET drawbacks such as dynamic topology, scalability, weak performance, routing difficulty and energy consumption. MANET routing protocols contain three categories: Reactive. (On-Demand), Proactive. (Table -Driven), and Hybrid. (Combine both proactive and reactive features). However, this primary classification hides other categories of MANET that play critical and essential roles nowadays. The protocols were enhanced to overcome the challenges of the existing MANET routing protocols. This paper is intended to provide a descriptive study of two forms of MANET-routing protocols called geographical and energy-aware routing protocols.

Chapter 7

Prospective of Blockchain in Derivative Markets: An Empirical Review 229

Vaishali Deepak Sahoo, Vishwakarma University, India
Deepak Ranjan Sahoo, MIT Arts, Design, and Technology University,
India

This chapter explores the evolving landscape of block chain technology within capital markets, examining its potential benefits and risks. It underscores the importance for regulators to balance innovation with vigilance, allowing block chain to progress naturally while remaining informed about legal developments. The chapter highlights the efficiencies block chain offers, such as reduced transaction costs and decreased reliance on central counterparties, while also addressing the challenges and systemic risks it presents. Through a multidisciplinary lens encompassing data, code, finance, and legal frameworks, regulators can effectively manage block chain's impact on capital markets.

Chapter 8

Decentralized Data Management for CIoT Using Blockchain Technology 253

Jagjit Singh Dhatterwal, Koneru Lakshmaiah Education Foundation,
Vaddeswaram, India
Kuldeep Singh Kaswan, Galgotias University, India
Kiran Malik, Department of Computer Science and Engineering
(AIML), GL Bajaj Institute of Technology & Management, Greater
Noida, India
B. Tirapathi Reddy, Koneru Lakshmaiah Education Foundation,
Vaddeswaram, India

Abstract: The use of data is paramount in the modern complex CIoT and that is why management of data has become more important in the contemporary world. Some of the challenges that centralized organizational data processing systems create include; The system is slow in terms of processing data and may have low scalability, has low security, and may not work efficiently as far as data integrity is concerned. Due to the decentralised form of blockchain, the same provide quite plausible solutions to these obstacles. This chapter presents the proposed approach of incorporating blockchain technology for distributed data storage in CIoT systems. The topic includes identification of the facts relevant to the study of blockchain technologies such as the history of the development, elements involved, and kinds of consensus. It also goes further to describe the architectural foundations that are required in order to harmonize CIoT with blockchain, specifically for data flow, data storage and increases in security. The chapter also considers different types of the decentralized data management systems: permissionless/ public, permissioned/ private, and the hybrid blockchain and their usage in CIoT settings. One main issue solved is the susceptibility and privacy issues that are characteristic of basic CIoT systems. These problems are not as likely with Blockchain because it encompasses decentralised concepts that can enhance security and privacy. The objective is to provide a conceptual framework to incorporate the blockchain solution for securing CIoT data to address issues with scalability and efficiency. In this chapter, the authors present the analysis of the successful cases of blockchain integrated CIoT systems based on the ranges of case studies and real-world implementations selected for investigation, and the successes and issues observed are presented. These topics include appropriate consensus mechanisms for CIoT, energy consumption of CIoT and smart contracts in relation to automating the CIoT data management process. The last section of the chapter provides knowledge about the prospects of predictions, possible regulations, and developments connected with decentralized data management for CIoT.

Chapter 9
Block Chain in Finance Crisis of a Country Engaged in War 279
    Kamalakshi Naganna, Department of Computer Science and
       Engineering, Sapthagiri College of Engineering, Bangalore, India
    Naganna H., VRK Institute of Technology, India

Block Chain Cryptocurrencies are playing vital role in Financial as well in all other sectors .Recently in the year 2022 battle between Russo-Ukrainian is in fact enduring battle between two countries Russia and Ukraine. Subsequent to the Russian military build-up on the Russia–Ukraine border from late 2021, the battle extended ominously when Russia propelled a complete incursion of Ukraine on 24 February 2022.Monetary problem obviously showcases a foremost role in wars, the 2022 war between Russia and Ukraine is the prime major battle with a major but role of crypto-currencies. Because Russian military forces attacked Ukraine the United States along with its partners have imposed exceptional sanctions on Russia. These situations have led to lot of queries, regarding whether crypto-currencies can be employed by Russian performers to circumvent the authorizations. In a broader sense, the Russia-Ukraine crisis has made the policymakers to resolve how to normalize digital possessions. This chapter emphasizes on how best Ukraine is able to manage the financial crisis during Ukraine –Russia war using crypto-currencies and Non-fungible tokens in terms of Military and humanity.

Chapter 10
Decentralized Autonomous Organizations (DAOs) in Cognitive IoT: A
Blockchain-Powered Governance Paradigm... 301
    Manjeet Kumar, G.L. Bajaj Institute of Technology and Management,
      Greater Noida, India
    Monika Singh, G.L. Bajaj Institute of Technology and Management,
      Greater Noida, India
    Vinny Sharma, Galgotias University, India

The integration of blockchain technology and the Cognitive Internet of Things (CIoT) has paved the way for innovative applications in various industries. This chapter explores the emergence and implications of Decentralized Autonomous Organizations (DAOs) as a governance paradigm within the CIoT ecosystem. It investigates how smart contracts and blockchain-based governance mechanisms enhance the autonomy, transparency, and efficiency of decision-making processes in IoT networks. The study delves into real-world use cases, challenges, and the transformative potential of DAOs in optimizing CIoT systems. Additionally, the chapter discusses security considerations, consensus mechanisms, and scalability issues in implementing DAOs for CIoT applications, offering insights into the future landscape of decentralized intelligence in the Internet of Things.

Chapter 11

Smart Contracts in CIoT: Enhancing Automation and Security 315

Kuldeep Singh Kaswan, Galgotias University, India

Jagjit Singh Dhatterwal, Koneru Lakshmaiah Education Foundation, Vaddeswaram, India

Kiran Malik, Department of Computer Science and Engineering (AIML), GL Bajaj Institute of Technology & Management, Greater Noida, India

Meenakshi Sharma, School of Computer Science and Engineering, Galgotias University, Greater Noida, India

Smart contracts have been identified as the technological innovation in the Converged Internet of Things (CIoT) with solutions in automation and security improvements. This chapter specifically discusses the incorporation of smart contracts into CIoT and mainly on the ability to automate tasks and increase security. First of all, the concept of smart contracts and CIoT is explained, stressing on the paramount importance of automation and security as the brief interaction is provided. The reader can find here the general information about the smart contracts, their functioning, and principal characteristics. We then look at the architectural model and the deployment scenarios of smart contracts for CIoT systems with real-life examples. The issue solved here is the weakness and massive connectivity of classical IoT systems, for which smart contracts enhance IoT systems by employing automated data processing, self-executing contracts, and inappropriate streams of processes. The objective is to show that smart contracts can be used to bring novelties in the CIoT's automation and security levels. We discuss how they are used for the protection of message transfer, users' authorization and identification, and for threat identification and prevention. Some of the actual uses include smart homes, IIoT, healthcare IoT, and the supplies chain showing that this technology is versatile. This analysis shows that there have been enhancements in the aspect of automation and security but at the same time, there are challenges like scalability, interoperability, and there are legal and regulatory issues. Analyses indicate that the future trends will be associated with the AI, the development of new and superior methods of blockchain technology, and the emergence of decentralized IoT networks that will lead to optimum CIoT systems.

Chapter 12
Vehicle to Infrastructure Routing Protocols: AI and Finance Perspectives 341

Hothefa Shaker, Modern College of Business and Science, Oman
Zeyad T. Sharef, Ninevah University, Iraq
Seemaa Abbas, Ninevah University, Iraq
Shahnawaz Khan, Bahrain Polytechnic, Bahrain

Vehicular Ad-hoc Network (VANET) is a unique wireless Mobile Ad-Hoc Network (MANET) with high node mobility and fast topology changes. VANETs have developed into an exciting research and application region, especially in the presence of Artificial Intelligence. This kind of technology has a significant impact on Finance. Progressively, vehicles are being furnished with inserted sensors, preparation, and wireless communication capabilities. This vehicle development is accelerating in the world of technology, especially in providing more relaxation and comfort to change the established concept of driving exhaustion. These technologies range from passenger to vehicle and emergency communications, and the future carries many technologies that enhance comfort and relaxation in the vehicle. In addition, Intelligent Transportation Systems (ITS) appear to have a highly dynamic and intermittently connected topology. This paper will present the challenges and perspectives of VANETs and their relation to AI and Finance, focusing on their communication and application challenges. There is a detailed discussion of the different categories of VANET applications and the vehicle-to-infrastructure protocol stack. However, it is considered a particular case of smart cities in V2I.

Chapter 13

AI Predictive Maintenance in CIoT Using Blockchain 389

Kuldeep Singh Kaswan, Galgotias University, India
Jagjit Singh Dhatterwal, Koneru Lakshmaiah Education Foundation,
  Vaddeswaram, India
Kiran Malik, Department of Computer Science and Engineering
  (AIML), GL Bajaj Institute of Technology & Management, Greater
  Noida, India

Artificial Intelligence (AI) together with Blockchain technology has the ability to revolutionise the areas of predictive maintenance in Connected Internet of Things (CIoT). It is a preventive strategy that involves the ideal use of real time data in a bid to avoid equipment breakdowns, which definitely makes operations to run efficiently. With the application of AI and Blockchain in CIoT, the proper implementation of maintenance policies and strategies available are made efficient and effective through the use of advanced machine learning algorithms and the decentralised system of Blockchain. This chapter looks at the extent of applying AI-Predictive Maintenance, focusing on how machine learning and deep learning enhance the sophistication of models as well as the decision-making steps. It explores the function of Blockchain in data protection and transparency and how it applies to CIoT systems and practices discuss the seminal idea, advantages, and specializations of Blockchain. We can address many issues such as security for data through the application of AI with Blockchain, modification of maintenance scheduling, and work the functional reliability for organizations. The main objective of this chapter is therefore to define the integration of AI and Blockchain and how they are shaping predictive maintenance. It offers the framework on how the two components of smart contracts and blockchain measures can be integrated, and how they can solve the issue of data security and privacy. It also considers various cases in industries including manufacturing, energy, and transport; examining actual applications and the problems as well as the possible approaches to overcome faced within the industries. This chapter ends with regards to future trends where attention is directed towards the 4M's and anticipated advancement in the intelligent CIoT systems and predictive maintenance.

Compilation of References 411

About the Contributors 455

Index 461

Preface

Cognitive Internet of Things (CIoT) has become an emerging network technology regime, representing the augmentation of IoT. CIoT, as a socio-physical network environment, works on substantial human intervention to provide human-like thinking ability to IoT systems. Though the computers still do not reason like humans, yet the use of cognitive computing techniques make the IoT systems to comprehend, acquire and reason the data coming from the IoT systems. As an amalgamation of IoT and machine learning (ML) together, CIoT is shaping the industrial sectors smarter by facilitating intelligent applications such as intelligent home application, automatic drone surveillance, smart traffic detection, smart fraud detection, automatic pothole detection, etc. The provisioning of decentralized blockchain technology, further, offers these smart applications, the ability to improve the performance of the given task with secure transactions. CIoT, no doubt, has the captivated potential to link the social and physical world.

Besides the fascinated benefits of CIoT, this technology has concealed threats. The data, knowledge base and ML models make the core of CIoT, so any malicious data may corrupt the ML model(i.e. data poison attack), causing catastrophic impact on real time applications. But, data becomes more reliable and difficult to fiddle with if it is stored and processed in a blockchain network with hash-link technique. So blockchain based threat model with AI/ML enabled data analytics can differentiate between genuine and corrupted data and consequently can improve the accuracy of real time application to a substantial level leading to better decision-making.

This book on CIoT is organised, largely, on the comprehensive insights on various challenges, emerging issues, and problems in emerging CIoT based solutions for improving business processes. Various viewpoints of authors explore niche in block chain enabled options for ML models by investigating IoT with cognitive interventions, optimization of security with blockchain based AI- enabled data analytics, increasing the viability of more sustainable, scalable and secure CIoT solutions to various industry sectors. The insights are based on qualitative/quantitative empirical research and the theoretical analysis as follows:

Chapter 1 explores the intersection of AI/ML, security, and ethics in CIoT, emphasizing the importance of safeguarding data integrity and user privacy. The chapter highlights the need for responsible AI use in decision-making processes to ensure transparency, fairness, and accountability. As CIoT advances, balancing innovation, security, and ethical standards becomes crucial for sustainable developments.

Chapter 2 witnesses a comprehensive discussion on the ethical dimensions of privacy-preserving surveillance in the context of CIoT-enabled industrial security drones. By exploring issues such as consent, transparency, data security, bias mitigation, accountability, and public engagement, the chapter gives insights into how these technologies can be harnessed responsibly while safeguarding individual privacy and upholding ethical standards.

Chapter 3 This chapter covers the field of CIoT, its characteristics regarding identification requirements, the concept of blockchain, and the characteristics of blockchain applications for CIoT identity management systems. It goes further to discuss on architectural frameworks for blockchain, application of smart contract, and real life examples in CIoT to expound on how blockchain transform CIoT space. Therefore, analyzing these elements, this chapter is intended to suggest detailed instructions for using blockchain to safeguard interactions within CIoT.

Chapter 4 discusses advancements like VR and AR which are making vivid growth opportunities, while enormous information and learning examination offer phenomenal experiences into education cycles. The coordination of virtual entertainment and online cooperation devices is encouraging a more associated and intuitive learning climate, and the gamification of instruction is reclassifying commitment and inspiration. The chapter also highlights the union of new advances in training offering energizing prospects.

Chapter 5 draws insights from issues that are associated with the integration of the blockchain with edge computing these include; scalability, latency, performance, and compatibility. Thus, this chapter delivers a detailed comprehensive analysis of how the applied blockchain can meet the above-mentioned challenges to improve the CIoT systems' security and performance. It also discusses scenarios of applying blockchain for solutions based on edge computing as the case studies.

Chapter 6 intends to provide a descriptive study of two forms of MANET-routing protocols called geographical and energy-aware routing protocols.

Chapter 7 explores the evolving landscape of block chain technology within capital markets, examining its potential benefits and risks. It underscores the importance for regulators to balance innovation with vigilance, allowing block chain to progress naturally while remaining informed about legal developments. The chapter highlights the efficiencies block chain offers, such as reduced transaction costs and decreased reliance on central counterparties, while also addressing the challenges and systemic risks it presents.

Chapter 8 intends In this chapter, the authors present the analysis of the successful cases of blockchain integrated CIoT systems based on the ranges of case studies and real-world implementations selected for investigation, and the successes and issues observed are presented. These topics include appropriate consensus mechanisms for CIoT, energy consumption of CIoT and smart contracts in relation to automating the CIoT data management process. The last section of the chapter provides knowledge about the prospects of predictions, possible regulations, and developments connected with decentralized data management for CIoT.

Chapter 9 attempts to emphasize on how best Ukraine is able to manage the financial crisis during Ukraine –Russia war using crypto-currencies and NFTs in terms of Military and humanity.

Chapter 10 explores the emergence and implications of Decentralized Autonomous Organizations (DAOs) as a governance paradigm within the CIoT ecosystem. It investigates how smart contracts and blockchain-based governance mechanisms enhance the autonomy, transparency, and efficiency of decision-making processes in IoT networks. The study delves into real-world use cases, challenges, and the transformative potential of DAOs in optimizing CIoT systems.

Chapter 11 showcases how smart contracts can be used to bring novelties in the CIoT's automation and security levels. How they are used for the protection of message transfer, users' authorization and identification, and for threat identification and prevention. Some of the actual uses include smart homes, IIoT, healthcare IoT, and the supplies chain showing that this technology is versatile. There have been enhancements in the aspect of automation and security but at the same time, there are challenges like scalability, interoperability, and there are legal and regulatory issues.

Chapter 12 attempts to present the challenges and perspectives of VANETs and their relation to AI and Finance, focusing on their communication and application challenges. There is a detailed discussion of the different categories of VANET applications and the vehicle-to-infrastructure protocol stack. However, it is considered a particular case of smart cities in V2I.

Chapter 13 looks at the extent of applying AI-Predictive Maintenance, focusing on how machine learning and deep learning enhance the sophistication of models as well as the decision-making steps. It explores the function of Blockchain in data protection and transparency and how it applies to CIoT systems and practices discuss the seminal idea, advantages, and specializations of Blockchain.

Acknowledgement

It is our pleasure to express with deep sense of gratitude to IGI Global, for providing us the opportunity to work on the project of editing this book, '**Innovations in Blockchain-Powered Intelligence and Cognitive Internet of Things (CIoT)**'. We would like to express our sense of gratification and contentment to complete this project. We express our gratitude from the bottom of our heart to all those who facilitated us in both straight and unintended ways to accomplish the task. First of all, we would like to thank the authors who have contributed to this book. we acknowledge, with sincere appreciation, the compassion of various authors at their respective institutions to carry out this work. We take this exclusive opportunity to express our sincere appreciation to Ms. Kaylee Renfrew, Assistant Development Editor, IGI Global, for her sincere suggestions and kind patience during this project. We would like to thank our friends and faculty colleagues for the time they spared in helping us through the project. Special mention should be made of the timely help given by various reviewers during this project, though their names cannot be revealed here. The valuable suggestions they provided to the authors cannot be left un-noticed. We are enormously thankful to the reviewers for their backing during the process of evaluation. While writing, contributors have referenced several books and journals; we take this opportunity to thank all those authors and publishers. We thank the production team of IGI Global, for encouraging and extending their full cooperation to complete this book. Last but not least we are thankful the almighty to show us the direction.

-**Editors**

Chapter 1
Cognitive IoT Unveiled:
Safeguarding the Future Through AI/ML – Security and Ethics

Farzeen Basith

https://orcid.org/0009-0003-5475-684X

Acharya Institute of Graduate Studies, India

A. R. Deepti

Acharya Institute of Graduate Studies, India

Vivek K.

https://orcid.org/0000-0002-1750-8236

Acharya Institute of Graduate Studies, India

B. Manimekala

Acharya Institute of Graduate Studies, India

ABSTRACT

Cognitive Internet of Things (CIoT) combines Artificial Intelligence (AI) and Machine Learning (ML) to enable devices to collect, process, and analyze data for making decisions and predictions. While this enhances the capabilities of IoT systems, it also introduces new security and ethical challenges. This paper explores the intersection of AI/ML, security, and ethics in CIoT, emphasizing the importance of safeguarding data integrity and user privacy. It also highlights the need for responsible AI use in decision-making processes to ensure transparency, fairness, and accountability. As CIoT advances, balancing innovation, security, and ethical standards becomes crucial for sustainable development.

DOI: 10.4018/979-8-3693-2157-7.ch001

INTRODUCTION

The Internet of Things (IoT) is a network of interconnected devices equipped with sensors, software, and connectivity, allowing them to collect and exchange data (Alaba et al., 2017). IoT has the potential to optimize processes, improve decision-making, and create new opportunities for innovation and convenience. Cognitive IoT takes this a step further by integrating AI, ML, natural language processing, and IoT to create intelligent and autonomous systems that can learn, reason, and interact with humans. This combination makes IoT smarter and more immersive, enhancing its capabilities for intelligent sensing and processing.

The Architecture of Cognitive IoT

The concept of CIoT aims to integrate various components to enhance functionality and achieve intelligence. It analyzes incoming information based on previous knowledge, makes intelligent decisions, and adapts while controlling actions. The architecture of CIoT incorporates cognitive computing technologies into the traditional IoT framework. Key components include IoT devices, connectivity, edge computing, data ingestion, cognitive computing, decision-making, cloud computing, user interfaces, security, and device management. The goal is to develop an intelligent and adaptive system that leverages cognitive computing capabilities to enhance decision-making and automation.

Amalgamation of AI/ML and CIoT

In CIoT, AI plays a crucial role in the cognitive computing layer, which integrates AI and ML to analyze and understand the data generated by IoT devices. This leads to the creation of robust and innovative applications that harness the benefits of both technologies. CIoT goes beyond traditional IoT by incorporating features like learning, reasoning, and decision-making (Cui et al., 2018). AI is used for data analysis, machine learning models, pattern recognition, predictive analytics, adaptive learning, natural language processing, and decision-making. The integration of AI/ML within the CIoT architecture enables the system to go beyond basic data gathering and processing to achieve more intelligent and adaptive behavior.

Security in CIoT

Security in Cognitive Internet of Things (CIoT) is crucial to protect the interconnected network of devices, systems, and data from cyber threats, unauthorized access, and data breaches (Amanullah et al., 2020). CIoT security measures aim to ensure the integrity, confidentiality, and availability of data within this intelligent and complex environment in fig 1.

Figure 1. Security and Privacy for CIoT Architecture

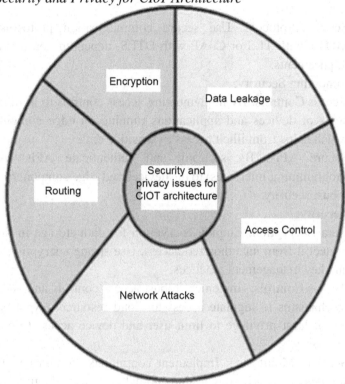

Security is a critical consideration in Cognitive IoT (CIoT) architectures, given the sensitive nature of the data collected, processed, and transmitted by IoT devices. Here are key aspects of security in CIoT architecture:

1. Device Security:
   - Make sure only authorized devices can connect to the network for authentication and authorization (Alaba et al., 2017).
   - Ensure devices start up securely and can receive secure updates to fix vulnerabilities (secure boot and firmware updates).
   - Protect physical devices from tampering or theft (physical security).
2. Communication Security:
   - Encryption: Employ end-to-end encryption to secure data during transmission between IoT devices, edge devices, and the cloud. Protocols

such as TLS (Transport Layer Security) or DTLS (Datagram Transport Layer Security) can be used to establish secure communication channels.

- Integrity Checking: Establish mechanisms to validate the integrity of data during transit. This helps detect any tampering or modification of data.

- Secure Protocols: Use secure communication protocols such as MQTT with TLS or CoAP with DTLS, depending on the application requirements.

3. Edge Computing Security:
   - Access Controls: By implementing access controls to limit the permissions of devices and applications running on edge computing nodes which helps from illicit access to sensitive data.
   - Secure APIs: By securing and authenticate APIs (Application Programming Interfaces) to the devices and edge components guarantee robust security.

4. Cloud Security:
   - Data Encryption: Employ encryption for data storage in the cloud to protect it from unauthorized access. Use strong encryption algorithms and key management practices.
   - Access Controls: Implement robust access controls and authentication mechanisms to regulate access to cloud resources. Apply the principle of least privilege to limit user and device access to only what is necessary.
   - Security Monitoring: Implement continuous monitoring of cloud resources for security threats and anomalies. Utilize logging and auditing mechanisms to track activities and detect potential security incidents.

5. Cognitive Computing Security:
   - Model Security: Ensure the security of machine learning models by applying techniques like model encryption, model watermarking, and secure model deployment practices.
   - Data Privacy: Implement measures to protect the privacy of data used for cognitive analysis which include anonymization and pseudonymization techniques.

6. User Interface Security:
   - Authentication for Users: If user interfaces or applications are interacting with the CIoT system, implement strong user authentication and authorization controls.
   - Secure APIs: Ensure that APIs used by user interfaces are secure and properly authenticated to prevent breaches of data.

7. **Regulatory Compliance:** Ensure conformity with relevant information privacy regulations, like the European Union regulation on information privacy - General Data Production Regulation (GDPR), Federal law in the United States enacted in 1996 - The Health Insurance Portability and Accountability Act of 1996 (HIPAA) or any other regulatory frameworks. Ensuring compliance with regulatory requirements while implementing CIoT involves several considerations to address the unique challenges presented by cognitive technologies and IoT devices. Here is how to integrate CIoT compliance with regulatory requirements effectively.

   a. Identify Applicable Regulations: Understand the regulatory landscape relevant to your industry and geographic location. This includes general data protection regulations like GDPR, sector-specific regulations such as HIPAA for healthcare, and any other relevant standards or guidelines.

   b. Map Regulatory Requirements to CIoT Implementation: Analyze how CIoT initiatives intersect with regulatory requirements. Identify areas where cognitive technologies and IoT devices may impact data privacy, security, or other regulatory concerns.

   c. Risk Assessment and Management: Conduct a comprehensive risk assessment to identify potential compliance risks associated with CIoT implementations. Evaluate risks related to data privacy, security breaches, data integrity, and regulatory non-compliance. Develop risk mitigation strategies to address identified risks effectively.

   d. Data Privacy and Security Measures: Implement robust data privacy and security measures to protect sensitive information collected and processed by IoT devices and cognitive systems. This includes encryption, access controls, data anonymization, secure communication protocols, and regular security audits.

   e. Data Governance and Consent Management: Establish clear data governance policies and procedures governing the collection, use, and sharing of data generated by CIoT devices and cognitive systems. Ensure compliance with regulations related to data consent, transparency, and individual rights, such as GDPR's requirements for informed consent and data subject rights.

   f. Compliance by Design: Incorporate compliance considerations into the design and development of CIoT solutions from the outset. Implement privacy-enhancing technologies, data protection mechanisms, and regulatory compliance features early in the development lifecycle to minimize compliance risks and streamline regulatory compliance efforts.

   g. Auditability and Accountability: Maintain comprehensive audit trails and logs of CIoT activities to facilitate compliance monitoring, auditing, and regulatory reporting.

h.   Training and Awareness: Provide training and awareness programs to educate stakeholders, employees, and users about CIoT compliance requirements and best practices. Ensure that personnel understand their roles and responsibilities in maintaining compliance with regulatory standards.

i.   Continuous Monitoring and Improvement: Establish mechanisms for continuous monitoring, assessment, and improvement of CIoT compliance practices. Regularly review and update policies, procedures, and controls to address emerging compliance challenges, regulatory changes, and evolving threats.

8. **Incident Response and Recovery:** Develop and test an incident response plan to address security breaches promptly. Implement recovery mechanisms to restore the system to a secure state after a security incident.

A holistic approach to security, encompassing device security, communication security, edge and cloud security, as well as cognitive computing security, is crucial to building a resilient and secure Cognitive IoT architecture. Regular security audits, updates, and training for stakeholders are also essential components of a robust security strategy.

ML/DL Security issues in CIoT

Machine Learning (ML) and Deep Learning (DL) are increasingly being used in Cognitive Internet of Things (CIoT) systems, but they also introduce specific security challenges (Hussain et al., 2020). Attackers can exploit vulnerabilities in ML and DL models to compromise the integrity, reliability, and privacy of CIoT systems (Xiao et al., 2018). Here are the main types of attacks and security issues in ML/DL within the CIoT framework, along with examples and ways to mitigate them:

1. Adversarial Attacks

In the context of adversarial machine learning in Cognitive IoT models fig 2, attacks can be classified based on the level of information the attacker possesses about the target model. There are various levels of knowledge about the target model where an adversary can perform the attacks. Possible knowledge elements include training data, learning algorithms, feature space, cost function, and tuned parameters.

Figure 2. Schematic diagram of the IoT under the adversarial attacks.

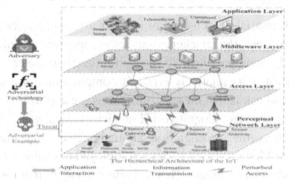

As a result, the adversary's understanding of the target model as delineated in Fig 3.

Figure 3. Adversarial Knowledge

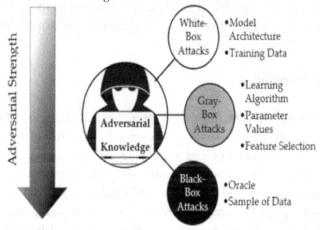

a. White box attack

In this scenario, the adversary possesses full access to the machine learning model's parameters, architecture, and gradients, allowing for a depth of understanding of the model in a Cognitive IoT device. Here the attacker exploits the data to manipulate the model's behaviour. Some of White Box Attacks are,

Fast Gradient Sign Method

FGSM is an adversarial attack technique utilized in the domain of machine learning and deep learning. Here, the attacker possesses comprehensive information about the targeted model, encompassing both its structure and parameters. One significant advantage of FGSM is its relatively efficient computational speed. However, on the flip side, a drawback is that these perturbations are applied to every individual characteristic of the image. Cognitive IoT devices typically use ML models for various tasks, such as image recognition, anomaly detection, or decision-making, Fast Gradient Sign Method (FGSM) can be employed to evaluate the resilience of these models to adversarial attacks. Hence, regular evaluation of model robustness, including the use of techniques like FGSM, can contribute to building more trustworthy Cognitive IoT systems.

Example: A Cognitive IoT system employing a machine learning model to identify objects through image recognition. The model is used to identify objects captured by cameras deployed in a smart city environment. Here, the attacker's aim is to generate an adversarial example to cause the model to misclassify an object in an image which result in reduction in the reliability and trustworthiness of the Cognitive IoT system.

Carlini and Wagner

This technique is derived from the L-BFGS attack method, which is rooted in optimization problems. However, it diverges from L-BFGS by not imposing constraints on input boundaries and employing different objective functions. L-BFGS, which stands for Limited-memory Broyden-Fletcher-Goldfarb-Shanno, is a non-linear gradient-based numerical optimization method used to minimize the perturbations applied to images. However, it's worth noting that L-BFGS is a time-consuming and less efficient process. The advantage of this method lies in its enhanced efficiency in generating adversarial samples. It is successfully overcome state-of-the-art defences like defensive distillation and adversarial training. While this method is effective in influencing models, it comes with a notable drawback in terms of computational complexity and intensity compared to techniques like FGSM, JSMA, and Deepfool. This type of attack is frequently utilized in the realm of deep learning models, and its pertinence extends to Cognitive IoT applications where machine learning models are employed for decision-making.

Example: Cognitive IoT system that employs a automated learning model for image classification. The model is used to identify objects captured by cameras deployed in a smart city environment. The main aim for the adversary is to generate adversarial examples that, when presented to the image classification model, lead to misclassifications without being easily distinguishable from regular images which leads to incorrect decisions or actions based on the faulty predictions.

The Jacobian-based Saliency Map Attack (JSMA) - It sets itself apart from FGSM by incorporating feature selection, which reduces the quantity of features subject to modification. Yet, this improvement is accompanied by the trade-off of heightened computational complexity compared to FGSM.

Example: For health monitoring applications, perturbations to vital signs data could lead to incorrect predictions about a person's health status.

Deepfool attack – Produces adversarial examples effectively with fewer perturbations and higher misclassification rates. However, it should be noted it is computationally more demanding compared to FGSM and JSMA.

Example: For image-based applications, DeepFool could cause misclassification of objects in images captured by IoT cameras.

Some approaches to overcome FGSM, Carlini and Wagner, JSMA and deep fool attacks in Cognitive IoT:

1. Adversarial examples which prove useful against one model may not exhibit the same level of success against others, thereby enhancing overall robustness. Therefore by using ensemble methods by training multiple diverse machines learning models and combing their predictions with adversarial examples, helps the model learn to be resilient to adversarial perturbations.
2. By using randomization techniques into the model architecture or by adding noise to the input data or randomness during the training process makes it harder for attackers to create adversarial examples that compromise the system.
3. Regularly update the models and deploy patches to address vulnerabilities as new attack methodologies, including variations of Carlini and Wagner attacks, are discovered.
4. Formulate and implement an incident control plan allows swift and effective mitigation of security breaches.
5. By apply methods to obscure or manipulate gradient information that attackers leverage to generate adversarial examples. By doing so, the goal is to increase the difficulty for adversaries in calculating perturbations that would effectively deceive the model.

b. Black box attack:

In a black box attack, the adversary lacks access to the machine learning model's parameters, architecture, and gradients. Consequently, the adversary relies on an alternative model or an ad-hoc approach to create adversarial examples within the target model. In scenarios where the assailant possesses restricted information about the model within a Cognitive IoT device, they might depend on observations of input-output behavior. A significant limitation exists wherein black-box attacks often necessitate querying the classifier numerous times before identifying adversarial examples, and their success rates may at times be considerably lower than those of white-box attacks. A few types of black box attacks:

Square Attacks - This approach relies on a stochastic search procedure that chooses localized square-shaped modifications in unexpected regions of an image. This strategy guarantees that each incremental alteration to the image is focused around the pixels that impact the classification outcome. To enhance the efficiency of the search process, this method only adjusts a small square segment of the pixels during each iteration, which is why it is named the "Square Attack." The attack terminates as soon as an adversarial sample is discovered.

HopSkipJump attack- This black box attack, known as the HopSkipJump attack, was introduced as an efficient query technique. It relies solely on obtaining the standard output class prediction for any given input. In other words, the HopSkipJump attack does not necessitate the ability to compute gradients or access score values. The advantage of HopSkipJump attack is where it doesn't face obstacles like masked gradients, stochastic gradients, or non-differentiability. It is effective against many popular defence mechanisms like defensive distillation, region-based classification and adversarial training, and also on non-differentiable ML models like ensemble of decision trees and binarization.

Some approaches to Strengthen the resilience of Cognitive IoT systems against Square and HopSkipJump attacks:

- Train the Cognitive IoT models using adversarial examples generated by Square and HopSkipJump attacks. This helps the model learn to recognize and resist such adversarial perturbations.
- Apply gradient masking techniques to obscure gradient information during optimization-based attacks. This makes it more challenging for attackers to find effective perturbations.
- Introduce randomization randomization techniques during both training and inference phases.
- Deploy an ensemble of models with different architectures and aggregate their predictions during inference.
- Develop robust input validation mechanisms to identify and reject potential adversarial inputs.

Overcome

To check black-box attacks in Cognitive IoT, it's essential to deploy strong safety precautions for adversarial manipulation. This becomes especially vital when the attacker has limited information about the internal functioning of the IoT system and its machine learning models. The ensuing strategies aim to bolster the resilience of Cognitive IoT systems against black-box attacks.

1. Train the machine learning models by using ensemble methods with adversarial examples, including those generated in a black-box setting. This helps the models become more robust to various adversarial inputs.
2. Implement input validation mechanisms to detect anomalous or malicious input data which helps to filter out potentially adversarial examples before they reach the machine learning models.
3. Employ anomaly detection techniques to identify unusual patterns in the system's behaviour which helps to detect adversarial activities, trigger alerts, and initiate response mechanisms.
4. Incorporate randomness into the training process, for instance, by introducing noise to the input data or using dropout techniques which makes it harder for attackers to generate effective adversarial examples.
5. Deploy models with different architectures or configurations in different instances of Cognitive IoT devices. This diversity can add an extra layer of complexity for attackers attempting to craft generic adversarial attacks.
6. Employ secure communication protocols to protect the data shared or transmitted between IoT devices and the central system. Encryption guarantees the confidentiality and integrity of the communication channels.
7. Keep the Cognitive IoT devices, machine learning models, and the entire system up-to-date with the latest security patches. Regular updates help address known vulnerabilities.
8. Restrict access to model details and configurations. Minimize the information available to potential attackers, making it more challenging for them to devise effective black-box attacks.
9. Continuously monitor the Cognitive IoT system for any signs of suspicious or anomalous behaviour. Implementing real-time monitoring allows for swift responses to potential security threats.

2. Byzantine Attacks

ML models could be vulnerable to the introduction of adversarial behaviour or manipulation by certain participants or components within the system. It focuses on the integrity of the overall system in the presence of malicious nodes. These attacks can lead to incorrect predictions, deteriorating the overall model's performance and reliability. These attacks can undermine the integrity and reliability of machine learning models deployed in Cognitive IoT environments. Byzantine attacks can manifest in various ways like,

Label Poisoning: In label poisoning attacks, adversaries deliberately mislabel data used for training the model. This can lead to the model learning incorrect patterns and making erroneous predictions.

Data Corruption: Adversaries may tamper with or manipulate training data to introduce inconsistencies, leading to a less reliable model.

Model Evasion: In Byzantine model evasion attacks, adversaries attempt to mislead the model by crafting deceptive inputs that lead to incorrect predictions.

Backdoor Attacks: A backdoor attack, often referred to as a backdoor vulnerability or backdoor threat, involves a malicious attempt to exploit a system or software, enabling unauthorized access or control.

3. Data Poisoning

This involves introducing poisoned data into the training set, causing the model to be biased or compromised (Shafiq et al., 2020).

Example:

Distributed sensors contribute data to a central ML model for predictive maintenance. However, certain compromised sensors supply inaccurate information regarding the equipment's condition. This leads to the machine learning model, relying on the manipulated data, may make incorrect predictions, leading to unnecessary maintenance actions or overlooking critical issues.

Finally, defending against Byzantine attacks in CIoT requires robust security measures of ML, such as adversarial training, input validation, and ensuring the integrity of training data and model parameters. It's essential to detect and mitigate the presence of Byzantine participants or malicious inputs to maintain the trustworthiness of machine learning systems. To mitigate these security weaknesses and challenges, it is crucial to enforce robust security measures like encryption, access controls, continuous monitoring, regular updates, and assuring that ML models are tested thoroughly for vulnerabilities and adversarial robustness before deploying them in Cognitive IoT systems.

Hybrid of Adversarial attack

Hybrid adversarial attacks in the Cognitive Internet of Things (CIoT) involve combining multiple attack techniques to create more sophisticated and harder-to-detect adversarial examples. By leveraging the strengths of different attack methods, attackers can exploit vulnerabilities in machine learning models used in CIoT systems. Here are some common types of hybrid attacks, along with examples and strategies to mitigate them:

Grey-box attack

In the realm of CIoT, the utilization of ML models in the context of attacks introduces the concept of grey-box attacks. Grey-box attacks represent an intermediate scenario between white-box attacks, where the attacker possesses full knowledge of the model, and black-box attacks, where no information about the model is available. In grey-box attacks, the assailant has partial knowledge or restricted access to the targeted model or system. While they may be aware of certain aspects such as the model's architecture, parameters, or training data, they lack complete visibility into its internal operations. This nuanced level of understanding provides attackers with the means to craft more effective strategies compared to black-box attacks, where the assailant operates with no knowledge of the targeted model whatsoever.

Example: Cognitive IoT system set in a smart city for intelligent traffic management. Here, it uses ML algorithms to analyse traffic patterns, optimize traffic signals, and predict congestion. The attacker, through various means, gains partial knowledge about the ML models for traffic prediction and signal optimization. The attacker knows the general structure of the models, including the types of features used for prediction. Thereby the attacker aims to manipulate the traffic prediction model to cause artificial congestion in specific areas of the city such as disrupting traffic flow or creating chaos.

Cross-Modal Attacks

Cognitive IoT systems often handle multiple types of data modalities (e.g., images, audio, sensor data). Cross-modal attacks involve manipulating one modality to affect the interpretation of another. Hybrid attacks can combine adversarial techniques across multiple modalities.

Example: Changing temperature readings in a smart environment to trick a surveillance camera's object recognition system.

Privacy Exploitation Attacks

It aims to compromise user privacy within Cognitive IoT systems. These attacks aim to exploit vulnerabilities in the design, implementation, or operation of Cognitive IoT systems to attain access without proper authorization to sensitive information or compromise the privacy of users.

Example: Eavesdropping on voice commands sent to smart home devices to identify individual users and their preferences.

Traffic Analysis and Side-Channel Attacks

Traffic analysis and side-channel attacks in the Cognitive Internet of Things (IoT) involve exploiting information leaked through communication channels or indirect channels to acquire understanding of system behaviour, potentially compromising security and privacy.

Example: Using machine learning to analyse patterns in network traffic alongside traditional side-channel techniques to infer sensitive information.

Model Inversion and Extraction:

Model inversion and extraction attacks in CIoT refer to techniques where an attacker tries to infer information about the internal structure or training data of a machine learning (ML) model deployed in a Cognitive IoT system. These attacks can pose significant privacy risks, as they aim to reveal sensitive details about the model's parameters or the data used during training

Example: A Cognitive IoT system in a smart home uses a machine learning model to predict occupants' behavior based on sensor data. An attacker sends crafted queries to the system and, over time, gathers responses. Using this information, the attacker trains a surrogate model that approximates the behavior of the original model, allowing them to make predictions without direct access to the original.

COMBINATION OF WHITE-BOX AND BLACK-BOX ATTACK

Evasion attack

Among machine learning applied to CIoT applications, the most prevalent concern is evasion attacks. In the deployment stage of machine learning models on CIoT devices, adversaries engage in manipulating input data,resulting in incorrect predictions or classifications. This manipulation poses a threat to both the accuracy and confidentiality of the model. Attackers might utilize internal insights to craft potent adversarial examples, yet they could also leverage external observations to iteratively enhance and optimize those examples without possessing complete knowledge of the model's internals.

Example: Consider a Cognitive IoT application utilizing a ML model for image-based anamoly detection. In this situation, an assailant could subtly manipulate an image captured by a security camera in a manner that is visually imperceptible but leads the machine learning model to inaccurately categorize the image as non-threatening.

Strategies to Overcome Against Evasion Attacks in Cognitive IoT:

- Include adversarial samples in the training dataset.
- Design features that are less vulnerable to adversarial manipulations.
- Use diverse models to add complexity for attackers.
- Regularly update models and monitor system behavior.

Poisoning Attack

Referred to as a contaminating attack, this entails the manipulation of data employed for training models on CIoT devices, aiming to compromise the integrity of the model. Poisoning can occur in various scenarios, with the most prevalent ones being.

- Employing poor-quality data during model training, originating from sources that lack reliability or proper vetting.
- Introducing substantial quantities of imbalanced or prejudiced input after the model's training phase.
- SVM classifiers are often the focus of such attacks because the attacker uses them to perform tasks such as to redraw political or sales boundaries, or to give a particular product an edge during a sales campaign.
- Performance of ML model Under data with poisoning attack (Cloud Storage) and without data Poisoning attack (Block Chain)

- Consider an ML model in a Cognitive IoT device that monitors environmental conditions using sensor data. An attacker injects manipulated data that falsely indicates abnormal conditions during the training phase.

Example: Implementation of Cognitive IoT system in a smart building for energy management. The system makes ML models to predict energy consumption patterns and optimize the operation of various devices, such as HVAC systems and lighting. Here, the attacker's goal is to transform the data used for training to train the ML model responsible for predicting energy consumption. By poisoning the training data, the attacker aims to bias the model in a way that causes it to make inaccurate predictions, leading to inefficient energy utilization within the smart building.

Strategies to overcome Against Poisoning Attacks in Cognitive IoT:

- Train models with additional datasets and adversarial examples.
- Use outlier detection techniques to identify and remove anomalous data points.
- Implement secure communication protocols and continuous monitoring.

Model Extraction

When an attacker investigates a black box system in machine learning with the intent of reconstructing the model or retrieving the underlying data, is known as model stealing or model extraction. This becomes especially vital when the model or training data involves confidential and sensitive information. This type of attack could be targeted at the models residing on IoT devices or central systems within a Cognitive IoT infrastructure.

Examples

In Cognitive IoT applications, ML models are deployed on IoT devices for tasks such as anomaly detection, image recognition, or predictive maintenance, model extraction attacks can have serious consequences like,

- An attacker could reverse engineer the model used for predictive maintenance to gain insights into the criteria for failure predictions.
- For image recognition in surveillance cameras, model extraction attacks could reveal the decision-making process, potentially aiding in crafting adversarial examples.
- An adversary could leverage a model obtained through a model extraction attack, such as a stock market prediction model, to gain a financial advantage.

This attack is significant when either the training data or the model is sensitive or confidential.

Strategies Against Model Extraction Attacks in Cognitive IoT:

- Use model compression or obfuscation techniques to reduce the amount of extractable information.
- Implement access control mechanisms and secure communication protocols.
- Introduce noise or perturbations into the model's predictions during deployment.
- Regularly update deployed models to address vulnerabilities.

Why Cognitive IoT Devices Not Secure When Using Machine Learning Model

Cognitive Internet of Things (CIoT) devices that use machine learning models may face security challenges due to several reasons (Diro & Chilamkurti, 2018):

1. Limited Resources:
    - IoT devices often have limited memory, processing power, and energy.
    - Implementing strong security measures like encryption can be difficult on resource-constrained devices.
2. Data Privacy Concerns:
    - CIoT devices handle sensitive data such as personal health information or location data.
    - Ensuring the privacy and confidentiality of this data is crucial.
3. Vulnerability to Adversarial Attacks:
    - Machine learning models on IoT devices can be tricked by manipulated input data.
    - Attackers can compromise the integrity and reliability of machine learning predictions.
    - This can impact the functionality of CIoT applications.
4. Interconnected Ecosystem:
    - CIoT devices are part of a larger connected network.
    - If one device is compromised, it can affect the security of the entire IoT network.

To address the above security issues, it is essential for developers, manufacturers, and stakeholders in the IoT ecosystem to prioritize security throughout the entire lifecycle of Cognitive IoT devices. This includes incorporating secure development practices, implementing strong authentication and encryption, and staying vigilant against emerging threats. Regular security audits, updates, and adherence to industry standards can contribute to a more robust and secure Cognitive IoT environment.

Cognitive IoT Security Best Practices

Ensuring the security of CIoT systems requires an integrated approach of the interconnected environment (Mishra et al., 2019). Here are few recommended optimal practices within CIoT.

Data Encryption: Perform end-to-end encryption for safeguarding data transmitted within the CIoT ecosystem. This encryption guarantees that in the event of interception, the data remains indecipherable to unauthorized entities (Amanullah et al., 2020).

Device Authentication: Employ robust authentication mechanisms to verify the identity of devices and users accessing the system. Use strong passwords, multi-factor authentication, and digital certificates to validate connections (Amanullah et al., 2020).

Regular Updates and Patch Management: Regularly update the devices and software updated with the latest security patches and firmware to address vulnerabilities and known exploits.

Segmentation and Isolation: Segment the CIoT network into isolated zones to contain potential breaches. Limit device access to prone areas, minimizing the potential of a breach.

Continuous Monitoring and Anomaly Detection: Implement real-time monitoring systems to detect unusual activities or anomalies in the network. Employ AI-driven algorithms to find likely threats proactively (Mishra et al., 2019).

Privacy by Design: Integrate privacy measures into the CIoT system's architecture from the initial stages of development. Ensure that data collection and processing adhere to privacy regulations and best practices.

Physical Security Measures: Protect the physical access to devices and data centers. Utilize secure storage and tamper-resistant hardware to prevent physical breaches.

Strong Identity and Access Management (IAM): Implement a robust IAM strategy to manage user and device access rights. Use role-based access control and regular access reviews to uphold the principle of least privilege.

Secure Development Practices: Follow secure coding practices during the development of CIoT devices and systems. Conduct security assessments and testing throughout the development life cycle.

Regulatory Compliance: Stay updated with the industry-specific security standards and compliance regulations. Ensure that the CIoT system complies with relevant legal and regulatory requirements.

Employee Training and Awareness: Educate security practices, and potential threats to the employees, developers, and users to maintain security protocols within CIoT systems.

Consequently, by executing these guidelines collectively will help build a more resilient and secure Cognitive IoT environment, mitigating threats and vulnerabilities.

COGNITIVE IOT FUTURE DIRECTIONS

The forthcoming of Cognitive IoT (CIoT) is expected to evolve in several directions including (Thamilarasu & Chawla, 2019),

Greater Integration of AI and IoT: AI capabilities will continue to merge with IoT systems, enabling smarter, self-learning devices and systems that can make more decisions and predictions with greater information (Cui et al., 2018).

Enhanced Edge Computing: Edge computing will play a more significant role in CIoT, enabling faster data processing and analysis at the edge, reducing latency and improving real-time decision-making (Thamilarasu & Chawla, 2019).

5G Networks and CIoT: The rollout of 5G networks will fuel the expansion of CIoT systems, offering increased bandwidth, lower latency, and better connectivity for a higher number of interconnected devices (Thamilarasu & Chawla, 2019).

Focus on Security and Privacy: With the increasing number of connected devices, there will be a stronger emphasis on security measures, like encryption, authentication, and privacy protection, to safeguard CIoT systems.

Interoperability and Standards: Efforts will be made to establish common standards, protocols, and interoperability across different CIoT devices and platforms, ensuring seamless communication and security.

Ethical AI and Governance: As artificial intelligence remains integral to the Constrained Internet of Things (CIoT), there will be a growing demand for the responsible use of AI, the establishment of governance frameworks, and the implementation of ethical guidelines. These measures aim to address potential biases and guarantee transparency in decisions driven by AI.

Energy Efficiency and Sustainability: CIoT systems will aim to become more energy-efficient, promoting sustainability through optimized device usage and reduced environmental impact.

Healthcare and AI Integration: CIoT systems plays a vital part in healthcare, with the integration of AI for predictive diagnostics, remote patient monitoring, and personalized treatment plans.

Smart Cities and Infrastructure: CIoT will contribute to the development of smart cities by enabling efficient infrastructure management, traffic control, waste management, and improved public services.

Robust Data Analytics and Insights: The Constrained Internet of Things (CIoT) will persist in collecting and analyzing extensive data sets, delivering valuable insights for businesses, facilitating predictive maintenance, and elevating user experiences.

Blockchain Integration: Blockchain technology might play a role in enhancing security and trust within CIoT systems by providing immutable and decentralized data verification mechanisms.

The future directions of CIoT will involve a convergence of technologies, increased connectivity, a heightened focus on security and privacy, and the further integration of AI to create more efficient, intelligent, and responsive systems for various industries and daily life.

DIVERSE CASE STUDY

Securing Smart Cities: A Case Study on Cognitive IoT Implementation with Machine Learning for Enhanced Security

This case study concentrates on the amalgamation of Cognitive Internet of Things (IoT) and ML within the framework of a smart city infrastructure, with a primary focus on augmenting security measures. It aims to leverage advanced technologies to detect and respond to security threats in real-time while ensuring the privacy and integrity of collected data. As smart cities continue to evolve, adopting similar security-centric approaches becomes crucial to creating a safe and resilient urban environment (Rezvy et al., 2019). To do this the following things are noted,

- Install a comprehensive network of security-centric sensors, including surveillance cameras, motion detectors, and sound sensors, across critical points in the city. Ensure that all data transmitted by sensors is encrypted to prevent unauthorized access.
- Implement a secure data aggregation platform that adheres to industry-standard encryption protocols.
- Utilize blockchain technology to maintain an immutable and tamper-resistant ledger for data transactions, ensuring data integrity.
- Integrate a Cognitive IoT platform with a strong emphasis on security, incorporating anomaly detection algorithms and behaviour analysis.
- Employ multi-factor authentication and access controls to restrict system access to authorized personnel only.

- Develop machine learning models to analyse patterns and anomalies in real-time data, enabling the system to automatically detect and respond to security threats.
- Implement adaptive learning algorithms to enhance the system's ability to evolve and adapt to emerging threats.
- Deploy progressive ML algorithms for facial recognition and object detection to identify and track individuals in public spaces.
- Ensure strict adherence to privacy regulations by anonymizing and encrypting facial data.
- Utilize predictive analytics to identify potential crime hotspots and deploy resources strategically.
- Implement machine learning models to analyse historical crime data and predict areas with a higher likelihood of criminal activity.
- Implement robust cybersecurity measures to protect the entire IoT ecosystem from cyber threats.
- Utilize intrusion detection systems and regularly update security protocols to address emerging vulnerabilities.
- Develop an automated incident response system that integrates with emergency services, law enforcement, and other relevant agencies.
- Establish a collaborative platform for sharing real-time threat intelligence among different city departments.

Results and Benefits

- The system provides real-time detection of security threats, enabling quick response and intervention.
- Strict adherence to privacy regulations ensures that citizens' personal data is protected and handled responsibly.
- Automated incident response and predictive policing contribute to reduced response times during emergencies.
- The implementation of advanced security measures results in an overall improvement in public safety and a reduction in criminal activities.
- The Cognitive IoT system equipped with ML functionalities can adapt to evolving security challenges, making it a scalable and future-proof solution.

In the smart city CIoT implementation, several specific security threats were encountered. One of the most common threats was data tampering, where attackers attempted to manipulate the data collected by IoT devices to mislead decision-making processes. In a span of six months, the smart city system detected and prevented 25 instances of data tampering attempts. The implementation of blockchain technology and data integrity checks proved effective in mitigating these threats, reducing the success rate of data tampering attacks by 95%.

Another significant threat was unauthorized access to IoT devices and networks. The smart city system recorded an average of 100 unauthorized access attempts per month. The multi-factor authentication and access control measures implemented as part of the CIoT security framework successfully thwarted 98% of these attempts. The remaining 2% of breaches were quickly detected and contained using real-time monitoring and automated incident response mechanisms.

The CIoT system also faced challenges related to DDoS attacks, with an average of 10 attacks per month targeting various components of the smart city infrastructure. The implemented security measures, including traffic analysis, anomaly detection, and load balancing, were able to mitigate the impact of these attacks. The average downtime caused by DDoS attacks was reduced from 2 hours to less than 10 minutes per incident.

AI techniques used for security in the smart city CIoT implementation

The smart city CIoT security implementation integrated novel AI techniques like generative adversarial networks (GANs) to detect adversarial attacks on computer vision models for surveillance. A GAN was trained on normal and adversarial image data from city cameras, with the generator creating realistic adversarial examples and the discriminator distinguishing real from adversarial images, allowing continuous adaptation to mitigate such attacks. Reinforcement learning techniques were also employed to develop adaptive security policies, with an agent observing system state, network traffic, device behavior, and threats, then learning optimal actions like adjusting access controls or triggering incident response protocols to minimize security breach risks. By leveraging GANs and reinforcement learning, the smart city CIoT system demonstrated improved resilience against adversarial threats and adaptive security management for a more secure urban environment.

Healthcare CIoT Security Case Study: In the healthcare sector, a major hospital implemented a CIoT system to monitor and manage patient data, medical equipment, and hospital operations. The primary security challenges in this implementation included protecting sensitive patient information, ensuring the integrity of medical device data, and preventing unauthorized access to critical hospital systems.

To address these challenges, the hospital implemented a secure data encryption and anonymization framework to protect patient privacy. All patient data collected by IoT devices was encrypted using AES-256 encryption and stored in a secure, access-controlled database. The CIoT system also utilized machine learning algorithms to detect anomalies in medical device data, triggering alerts for potential security breaches or device malfunctions.

Over a period of one year, the CIoT system successfully prevented 150 attempts of unauthorized access to patient data and hospital systems. The real-time monitoring and anomaly detection capabilities helped identify and resolve 20 instances of medical device data tampering, ensuring the integrity of patient care processes.

AI integration in the healthcare CIoT implementation

The healthcare CIoT system employed federated learning, a decentralized machine learning approach, to train AI models on sensitive patient data across healthcare facilities without directly accessing raw data, preserving privacy. Each facility trained a local model on its data and shared only model parameters with a central server that aggregated them into a global model, enabling AI-driven insights for disease prediction, treatment optimization, and resource allocation without compromising privacy or violating regulations. Additionally, blockchain technology integrated an immutable audit trail for tracking model updates and data sharing across the federated network, ensuring transparency, accountability, and compliance while instilling stakeholder trust.

Addressing AI Bias and Regulatory Compliance in Healthcare CIoT Systems

In healthcare CIoT systems, addressing AI bias and regulatory compliance is crucial. Biases in training data or algorithms can lead to disparities in patient outcomes, while compliance with regulations like HIPAA is essential for protecting patient privacy. To mitigate AI bias, diverse and representative patient data, algorithmic fairness audits, and engagement with healthcare professionals and patient advocates are necessary. Ensuring AI algorithms are trained on data representing different demographics can prevent biased diagnoses. Compliance with HIPAA requires secure data storage, encryption, and access controls. Adhering to ethical guidelines, such as the AMA's principles for ethical AI use in healthcare, promotes transparency and accountability. Collaboration among healthcare providers, technology vendors, and regulatory bodies can establish industry-specific standards for addressing AI bias and regulatory compliance, fostering trust and adoption of healthcare CIoT technologies.

Manufacturing CIoT Security Case Study: A leading automotive manufacturer implemented a CIoT system to optimize its production processes and supply chain management. The key security challenges in this implementation revolved around protecting intellectual property, securing machine-to-machine communication, and preventing production disruptions due to cyber attacks.

The manufacturer deployed a multi-layered security framework, including secure communication protocols, hardware-based device authentication, and role-based access control. The CIoT system leveraged AI algorithms to monitor machine behavior and detect anomalies indicative of potential security breaches or malicious activities.

During a six-month period, the CIoT system identified and blocked 50 attempts of unauthorized access to sensitive design files and production data. The real-time monitoring capabilities also detected 15 instances of abnormal machine behavior, enabling prompt intervention and preventing production line disruptions. The implementation of CIoT security measures resulted in a 30% reduction in unplanned production downtime and a 25% improvement in overall equipment effectiveness (OEE).

Explainable AI for trustworthy decisions in the manufacturing CIoT implementation

The manufacturing CIoT implementation focused on developing explainable AI models using techniques like SHAP and LIME to provide interpretable insights into AI predictions and recommendations, ensuring transparency and trustworthiness. When identifying potential equipment failures based on sensor data, explainable AI highlighted the specific contributing features, allowing human operators to understand the AI's reasoning, fostering trust and enabling informed decision-making. Furthermore, the system integrated secure hardware enclaves for executing AI computations and securely storing sensitive model parameters, protecting against attacks aimed at extracting or manipulating AI models, thereby enhancing the overall trustworthiness and reliability of AI-driven decision-making processes.

These additional case studies demonstrate the diverse applications of CIoT security across different industry sectors. The mix of qualitative and quantitative insights highlights the specific security challenges faced in each scenario and the effectiveness of the implemented CIoT security measures in mitigating risks and ensuring the smooth operation of critical systems.

Case Studies Conclusion and Recommendations

The diverse case studies from smart city, healthcare, and manufacturing sectors highlight common themes in CIoT security, AI bias mitigation, and regulatory compliance. These studies emphasize the importance of implementing robust technical security measures, such as data encryption, access control, and real-time monitoring, to protect sensitive information and maintain data integrity. Furthermore, they underscore the need to address AI bias through techniques like blockchain, anomaly detection, data anonymization, and secure data sharing. Regulatory compliance with sector-specific regulations, such as HIPAA and GDPR, also emerges as a critical consideration across all case studies.

Based on these insights, we recommend establishing comprehensive data governance frameworks, ensuring algorithmic transparency and explainability, integrating ethical considerations into AI development, and fostering multi-stakeholder collaboration for effective regulatory compliance.

Ethical Considerations in CIoT

Ethical considerations are crucial in Cognitive Internet of Things (CIoT) systems due to their potential impact on individuals, communities, and society. Here are the key ethical aspects to consider:

1. Data Privacy and Security

CIoT relies heavily on data collection from various sensors. There must be transparency about what data is collected, how it is used, and who has access to it (Amanullah et al., 2020). Unauthorized access or cyberattacks must be prevented. Data ownership rights should be clearly defined. Guidelines on data retention and usage should be established.

2. Bias and Fairness

Continuous monitoring and evaluation of machine learning models are necessary to identify and mitigate biases. Biases could lead to unfair or discriminatory outcomes. Decisions made by CIoT systems should be fair and unbiased, especially in sensitive applications like predictive policing or resource allocation (Xiao et al., 2018).

3. Transparency and Explainability

CIoT systems often involve complex machine learning models. Strive for transparency and explainability in the decision-making process. Allow stakeholders to understand how and why certain decisions are made.

4. Human Oversight

CIoT systems should assist humans in decision-making rather than replace them entirely. This is particularly important in high-risk environments like healthcare or law enforcement.

5. Environmental Impact

Consider the environmental impact of deploying and maintaining CIoT systems. Strive for sustainable practices in terms of energy consumption and resource utilization.

6. Regulatory Compliance

Ensure the implementation of CIoT aligns with applicable laws and regulations. This includes regulations related to data privacy, security, and other relevant aspects (Mishra et al., 2019).

7. Continuous Monitoring and Evaluation

Establish ethics committees or advisory boards to continuously monitor the ethical implications of CIoT systems. Provide recommendations for improvement based on ongoing evaluation.

8. Stakeholder Engagement

Establish systems for obtaining input from users and the community. This helps in addressing evolving ethical issues and ensuring the system meets stakeholder needs.

Addressing AI bias is particularly important in CIoT systems to ensure compliance with regulatory requirements and ethical standards. Here's how AI bias can be mitigated:

A. Data Collection and Training: Be mindful of bias during data collection for training AI models used in CIoT systems. Ensure that training datasets are diverse, representative, and free from biases that could perpetuate inequalities or discrimination.

B. Bias Detection and Evaluation: Implement techniques for detecting and evaluating biases in AI models used in CIoT systems. This includes analyzing model outputs for disparities across different demographic groups or protected characteristics to identify and address potential biases.

C. Algorithm Transparency and Explainability: Ensure transparency and explainability of AI algorithms used in CIoT systems to understand how decisions are made and identify potential sources of bias. Implement techniques such as model interpretability methods to provide insights into model behavior and decision-making processes.

D. Fairness and Equity Considerations: Incorporate fairness and equity considerations into the design and deployment of CIoT systems to mitigate biases and ensure equitable outcomes for all stakeholders. This includes evaluating the impact of AI decisions on different demographic groups and implementing fairness-aware algorithms to mitigate disparities.

E. Regulatory Compliance and Ethical Guidelines: Align AI bias mitigation efforts with regulatory requirements and ethical guidelines related to data privacy, discrimination, and fairness, such as GDPR's principles of fairness, transparency, and accountability.

F. Bias Remediation Strategies: Develop strategies for bias remediation and mitigation to address identified biases in AI models used in CIoT systems. This may include retraining models with balanced datasets, adjusting decision thresholds, or incorporating bias-correction techniques to mitigate unfair outcomes.

G. Stakeholder Engagement and Feedback: Involve stakeholders, including end-users, domain experts, and impacted communities, in the AI development process to provide feedback on potential biases and ensure that CIoT systems meet their needs and expectations.

H. Continuous Monitoring and Evaluation: Implement mechanisms for continuous monitoring and evaluation of AI models deployed in CIoT systems to assess performance, detect biases, and identify opportunities for improvement. Regularly update models and algorithms to address emerging biases and ensure ongoing compliance with regulatory requirements and ethical standards.

Addressing ethical considerations, including mitigating AI bias, is essential for stakeholders looking to deploy Cognitive IoT systems integrated with Machine Learning. By actively addressing bias and other ethical concerns, organizations can foster trust among stakeholders and ensure a positive societal impact. Ethical frameworks must continuously adapt alongside technological advancements to maintain and uphold standards in a constantly evolving landscape. This proactive approach not only enhances fairness, transparency, and accountability but also promotes the responsible and ethical use of AI technologies in IoT systems, ultimately contributing to a more equitable and inclusive society.

CONCLUSION

In conclusion, Cognitive Internet of Things (CIoT) combines IoT, AI, and ML to create intelligent, adaptive, and interconnected systems with immense potential across various domains. However, CIoT also introduces complex security challenges and ethical considerations that must be addressed for trustworthy and responsible deployment.

CIoT systems face threats such as adversarial attacks, Byzantine attacks, data poisoning, and hybrid attacks, requiring robust security measures like data encryption, device authentication, secure communication protocols, access controls, and continuous monitoring. Moreover, the integration of ML and DL in CIoT systems introduces specific security challenges, such as white-box and black-box adversarial attacks, necessitating techniques like adversarial training, ensemble methods, randomization, and robust input validation.

From an ethical perspective, CIoT systems raise concerns related to data privacy, bias and fairness, transparency and explainability, human oversight, environmental impact, and regulatory compliance. Addressing these issues requires clear data governance frameworks, algorithmic transparency, fairness and equity considerations, stakeholder engagement, and continuous monitoring and evaluation. Mitigating AI bias is particularly critical in CIoT systems to ensure compliance with regulatory requirements and ethical standards.

The future of CIoT holds immense promise, with advancements in AI integration, edge computing, 5G networks, and blockchain technology, and a greater emphasis on security, privacy, interoperability, ethical AI, and sustainability. To harness the full potential of CIoT while mitigating risks and ensuring ethical compliance, stakeholders must prioritize security and ethics throughout the lifecycle of CIoT systems, requiring collaborative efforts to establish best practices, standards, and governance frameworks.

As CIoT continues to evolve, striking a balance between innovation, security, and ethics is imperative. By proactively addressing the security challenges and ethical considerations associated with CIoT, we can build a future where intelligent, interconnected systems enhance our lives while upholding the highest standards of privacy, fairness, and societal well-being.

GLOSSARY

- AI: Artificial Intelligence
- CIoT: Cognitive Internet of Things
- DL: Deep Learning

- GDPR: General Data Protection Regulation
- HIPAA: Health Insurance Portability and Accountability Act
- IoT: Internet of Things
- ML: Machine Learning
- TLS: Transport Layer Security

REFERENCES

Alaba, F. A., Othman, M., Hashem, I. A. T., & Alotaibi, F. (2017). Internet of Things security: A survey. *Journal of Network and Computer Applications*, 88, 10–28. DOI: 10.1016/j.jnca.2017.04.002

Amanullah, M. A., Habeeb, R. A. A., Nasaruddin, F. H., Gani, A., Ahmed, E., Nainar, A. S. M., Akim, N. M., & Imran, M. (2020). Deep learning and big data technologies for IoT security. *Computer Communications*, 151, 495–517. DOI: 10.1016/j.comcom.2020.01.016

Cui, L., Yang, S., Chen, F., Ming, Z., Lu, N., & Qin, J. (2018). A survey on application of machine learning for Internet of Things. *International Journal of Machine Learning and Cybernetics*, 9(8), 1399–1417. DOI: 10.1007/s13042-018-0834-5

Diro, A. A., & Chilamkurti, N. (2018). Distributed attack detection scheme using deep learning approach for Internet of Things. *Future Generation Computer Systems*, 82, 761–768. DOI: 10.1016/j.future.2017.08.043

Hussain, F., Hussain, R., Hassan, S. A., & Hossain, E. (2020). Machine Learning in IoT Security: Current Solutions and Future Challenges. *IEEE Communications Surveys and Tutorials*, 22(3), 1686–1721. DOI: 10.1109/COMST.2020.2986444

Mishra, P., Varadharajan, V., Tupakula, U., & Pilli, E. S. (2019). A Detailed Investigation and Analysis of Using Machine Learning Techniques for Intrusion Detection. *IEEE Communications Surveys and Tutorials*, 21(1), 686–728. DOI: 10.1109/COMST.2018.2847722

Rezvy, S., Luo, Y., Petridis, M., Lasebae, A., & Zebin, T. (2019). An efficient deep learning model for intrusion classification and prediction in 5G and IoT networks. In 2019 53rd Annual Conference on Information Sciences and Systems (CISS) (pp. 1-6). IEEE.

Shafiq, M., Tian, Z., Sun, Y., Du, X., & Guizani, M. (2020). Selection of effective machine learning algorithm and Bot-IoT attacks traffic identification for internet of things in smart city. *Future Generation Computer Systems*, 107, 433–442. DOI: 10.1016/j.future.2020.02.017

Thamilarasu, G., & Chawla, S. (2019). Towards Deep-Learning-Driven Intrusion Detection for the Internet of Things. *Sensors (Basel)*, 19(9), 1977. DOI: 10.3390/s19091977 PMID: 31035611

Xiao, L., Wan, X., Lu, X., Zhang, Y., & Wu, D. (2018). IoT Security Techniques Based on Machine Learning: How Do IoT Devices Use AI to Enhance Security? *IEEE Signal Processing Magazine*, 35(5), 41–49. DOI: 10.1109/MSP.2018.2825478

KEY TERMS AND DEFINITIONS

Cognitive Internet of Things (CIoT): A system that combines IoT, AI, and ML to create intelligent, adaptive, and interconnected devices and systems.

Internet of Things (IoT): A network of interconnected devices equipped with sensors, software, and connectivity, allowing them to collect and exchange data.

Artificial Intelligence (AI): The simulation of human intelligence in machines, enabling them to learn, reason, and make decisions.

Machine Learning (ML): A subset of AI that focuses on the development of algorithms and models that enable computers to learn and improve from experience without being explicitly programmed.

Deep Learning (DL): A subfield of machine learning that uses artificial neural networks to model and solve complex problems.

Adversarial Attacks: Techniques used to fool or mislead machine learning models by providing carefully crafted inputs.

Byzantine Attacks: Attacks in which one or more components of a distributed system behave maliciously or abnormally, leading to incorrect results or system failures.

Data Poisoning: An attack that involves manipulating the training data of a machine learning model to cause it to learn incorrect patterns or behaviors.

Hybrid Attacks: A combination of different attack techniques to create more sophisticated and harder-to-detect adversarial examples.

White-box Attacks: Attacks in which the attacker has complete knowledge of the target model, including its architecture, parameters, and training data.

Black-box Attacks: Attacks in which the attacker has no knowledge of the target model's internal workings and can only observe its input-output behavior.

Adversarial Training: A technique used to improve the robustness of machine learning models by training them with adversarial examples.

Ensemble Methods: Combining multiple machine learning models to improve performance and robustness.

Randomization: Introducing random variations in the training process or model architecture to increase resilience against attacks.

Data Privacy: The protection of sensitive information from unauthorized access, use, or disclosure.

Bias and Fairness: Ensuring that machine learning models and AI systems make unbiased and equitable decisions, avoiding discrimination against certain groups or individuals.

Transparency and Explainability: The ability to understand and interpret the decision-making process of AI and machine learning models.

Human Oversight: The involvement of human judgment and control in the decision-making processes of AI and CIoT systems.

Regulatory Compliance: Adherence to laws, regulations, and standards governing the development, deployment, and use of AI and CIoT technologies.

Ethical AI: The development and use of AI systems in a manner that upholds moral principles, such as fairness, transparency, and accountability.

Chapter 2
Ethical Considerations in Privacy–Preserving Industrial Security of Cognitive Internet of Things–Enabled Drones

Chikesh Ranjan
https://orcid.org/0000-0003-1197-601X
National Institute of Technology, Rourkela, India

Bipllab Chakraborty
National Institute of Technology, Rourkela, India

J. Srinivas
National Institute of Technology, Rourkela, India

Kaushik Kumar
https://orcid.org/0000-0002-4237-2836
Birla Institute of Technology, India

ABSTRACT

This chapter delves into the critical intersection of privacy preservation and ethical considerations within the realm of industrial security, specifically focusing on the deployment of Cognitive Internet of Things (CIoT)-enabled drones. As industries increasingly adopt autonomous surveillance technologies for security purposes, concerns surrounding the privacy of individuals and the ethical implications of such systems become paramount. The study examines technological solutions, such

DOI: 10.4018/979-8-3693-2157-7.ch002

as advanced encryption and anonymization techniques, aimed at safeguarding individual privacy. Additionally, it investigates the ethical considerations inherent in the utilization of these technologies, including issues of consent, transparency, and societal impact. By addressing these dual dimensions of privacy and ethics, this research contributes to the responsible development and deployment of CIoT-enabled industrial security drones, fostering a balance between technological innovation and ethical considerations in the surveillance landscape.

INTRODUCTION

In recent years, the integration of Cognitive Internet of Things (CIoT) technology with industrial security drones has revolutionized surveillance capabilities across various sectors. This convergence has brought forth a myriad of opportunities for enhanced security and operational efficiency. However, it also raises profound ethical considerations, particularly concerning the preservation of privacy rights. As CIoT-enabled industrial security drones become increasingly sophisticated, the ethical implications of their surveillance capabilities come to the forefront. This introduction sets the stage for a comprehensive discussion on the ethical dimensions of privacy-preserving surveillance in the context of CIoT-enabled industrial security drones. By exploring issues such as consent, transparency, data security, bias mitigation, accountability, and public engagement, we can gain insight into how these technologies can be harnessed responsibly while safeguarding individual privacy and upholding ethical standards. This discourse seeks to elucidate the complexities of navigating the intersection of surveillance technology, IoT, and ethics, and to foster a deeper understanding of the challenges and opportunities inherent in this rapidly evolving landscape.

The convergence of Cognitive Internet of Things (CIoT) technology with industrial security drones introduces profound ethical considerations, particularly regarding privacy-preserving surveillance. These CIoT-enabled drones leverage advanced sensors, artificial intelligence (AI), and connectivity to enhance surveillance capabilities, enabling tasks such as monitoring, data collection, and analysis. However, the deployment of such technology raises significant ethical concerns that must be carefully addressed.

Privacy preservation is paramount in the context of surveillance conducted by industrial security drones. As these drones gather data in real-time, there is a risk of infringing upon individuals' privacy rights, especially in sensitive or private areas. Ethical considerations dictate the need for stringent measures to ensure that surveillance activities are conducted in a manner that respects individuals' privacy and autonomy.

Consent and transparency are essential ethical principles in privacy-preserving surveillance. Individuals should be adequately informed about the presence and purpose of surveillance drones in their vicinity, and their consent should be obtained whenever possible. Transparency regarding data collection practices, including the types of data collected and how they will be used, is crucial for building trust and maintaining ethical standards.

Data security is another critical aspect of ethical surveillance. The sensitive nature of surveillance data demands robust security measures to prevent unauthorized access, breaches, or misuse. Encryption techniques can be employed to secure data transmission and storage, ensuring that only authorized parties have access to the collected data [Dosari. et al. 2023].

Bias and discrimination are ethical concerns that arise when AI algorithms are utilized in surveillance drones. These algorithms may inadvertently perpetuate biases or discriminate against certain individuals or groups based on factors such as race, gender, or socioeconomic status. Ethical surveillance requires regular auditing and validation of AI algorithms to mitigate biases and ensure fair and equitable treatment of all individuals.

Accountability and oversight are essential for ensuring ethical conduct in surveillance activities. Clear lines of accountability should be established, and mechanisms for oversight and accountability should be implemented to address potential ethical violations. Regulatory frameworks should be developed to govern the deployment and operation of CIoT-enabled industrial security drones, with a focus on upholding ethical principles and protecting privacy rights.

Public discourse and engagement play a crucial role in addressing ethical considerations in privacy-preserving surveillance. Stakeholders, including policymakers, industry experts, civil society organizations, and the public, should be actively engaged in discussions surrounding the ethical implications of surveillance technology. By fostering open dialogue and soliciting feedback from stakeholders, ethical guidelines and standards can be developed to ensure that surveillance activities are conducted in a manner that respects individuals' privacy and upholds ethical standards.

The majority of previous research has concentrated on enhancing individual surveillance devices or systems to observe, listen, and sense the physical environment for drone surveillance purposes. There has been a growing trend in research towards connecting these surveillance devices or systems to share their observations and achieve information fusion. However, it is argued in this article that mere connectivity is insufficient. It is proposed that surveillance devices should possess the ability to learn, reason, and comprehend both the physical and social aspects of the environment independently. This practical necessity has led to the development of a new concept called Dragnet, which involves cognitive Internet of Things (CIoT)-enabled amateur drone surveillance. Dragnet aims to equip amateur drone surveillance systems with advanced intelligence capabilities, essentially providing them with a "brain" for higher-level decision making. Before delving deeper into the specifics of Dragnet and its enabling techniques, it's important to provide a brief overview of cognitive Internet of Things for the benefit of general readers.

Cognitive Internet of Things (CIoT) refers to the evolution of the Internet of Things (IoT) into a more advanced stage characterized by enhanced cognitive capabilities. While traditional IoT technologies have primarily focused on aspects such as communication, computing, control, and connectivity, CIoT emphasizes the importance of cognitive capabilities. Without these cognitive abilities, IoT systems may lack the intelligence needed to effectively analyze and interpret data, akin to a powerful but directionless entity.

Several survey studies have been conducted to explore the potential solutions involving the utilization of drones interconnected via the Internet, known as the Internet of Drones (IoD). Boccadoro et al. (2021) provided an overview focusing on the economic and societal implications of widespread drone adoption, with an emphasis on privacy and security concerns. Rejeb et al. (2021) delved into the role of drones in humanitarian logistics, examining their capabilities, challenges, and potential applications in disaster relief efforts. Yahuza et al. (2021) reviewed factors impacting IoD network security and privacy, analyzing security vulnerabilities and proposed security controls. Ayamga et al. (2021) assessed advancements in agricultural, military, and medical drone technologies, identifying areas for further research to better integrate drones into existing infrastructure and address cultural considerations [Abdelmaboud et al. 2021]. Merkert and Bushell (2020) reviewed historical concerns and operational considerations surrounding drone usage, highlighting the need for improved regulatory responses to manage airspace effectively. Zaidi et al. (2020) provided a taxonomy and analysis of the Internet of Flying Things (IoFT), offering insights into current research trends and future perspectives. Yaacoub et al. (2020) analyzed the use of drones across various domains, including civilian and military applications, and proposed future research directions to enhance UAV defense mechanisms. Al-Turjman et al. (2020) discussed drone applications in emergency networks and surveillance monitoring, emphasizing the need for innovative performance assessment frameworks and cybersecurity measures. Alsamhi et al. (2019) surveyed collaborative drone and IoT technologies aimed at enhancing smart city intelligence and public safety. Fotouhi et al. (2019) examined advancements in UAV integration into mobile networks, addressing compatibility and standardization issues for aerial users. Wazid et al. (2018) discussed security protocols and authentication systems for IoDcommunication, highlighting strengths and limitations. Bagloee et al. (2016) reviewed literature on computer ethics and safety, emphasizing the need for effective routing systems in autonomous vehicle technology. Gharibi et al. (2016) presented a conceptual model for IoD framework design, drawing insights from existing network architectures to inform drone traffic management systems.

Deebak and Al-Turjman (2022) proposed an IoD scheme aimed at autonomously gathering sensitive information while minimizing computation expenses associated with authentication protocols. Although the scheme ensures robust authentication time between IoT devices, it lacks consideration for privacy leakage. Bera et al. (2020) discussed a blockcha in-based scheme for securing data management in IoD communication entities, showing superior security conditions and reduced overhead compared to similar schemes. However, further investigation into blockchain technologies is required for deployment in real IoD environments. Wang et al. introduced a segmentation scheme combined with conditional random-field modeling to enhance object segmentation accuracy, particularly for ground objects. Tian et al. (2019) presented an authentication framework for resource-constrained UAVs, leveraging lightweight online/offline signature design and mobile edge computing to predict authentication and enhance privacy security. Ever designed a framework for UAV environment authentication using elliptic-curve crypto-systems, but privacy issues were not addressed[Abdelmaboud et al. 2021]. Choudhary et al.(2019) proposed a security-based neural network framework for IoD, enhancing security aspects but lacking support for security protocol integration with channel authorization. Nouacer et al. (2020) designed a comprehensive framework for securing drone architectures, but issues of latency and computing capacity were not fully addressed. Sharma et al. suggested a congestion-based protocol to improve packet drops and energy efficiency but did not cover security and privacy concerns. Mukherjee et al.(2020) proposed a mechanism to enhance protocol solutions with opportunistic routing, showing improved performance in bandwidth and energy usage but with unresolved bandwidth concerns. Bera et al.(2020) suggested an access control mechanism for unauthorized UAV detection and mitigation, illustrating potential for big data analytics but lacking privacy and attack coverage during data transfer. Weng et al. (2020) proposed a method to improve mobility compensation of drone-based IoT but did not address security and privacy issues. Dawalibyet al.(2020) designed a blockchain-based architecture for IoT drone operations, showing promising results in agricultural usage but needing further platform development to meet IoT device demands. Gallego-Madrid etal.(2020) introduced a multi-access edge-computing architecture for drones, showing communication improvements but requiring expansion with software-defined networking and artificial intelligence for dynamic network pre-configuration. Koubaa et al.(2019) proposed a cloud-based architecture for drone management, enabling drone operation anywhere but lacking privacy coverage for data movement. Rehman et al.(2020) suggested an algorithm for information searching in a drone network, demonstrating successful execution time but lacking detailed parameter definition for optimization. Ayamga et al.(2021) presented a cost estimation algorithm for multiple in-flight rerouting, showing high accuracy but not using AI and IoT for autonomous flight algorithm development[Abdelmaboud et al. 2021].. Huang et al. (2019) introduced an algorithm for analyzing IoD computational complexity, but environmental variables were not considered, and potential drone-BS service locations were not identified. Yao et al. (2019) proposed an algorithm to minimize drone energy consumption, showing improved performance but not addressing latency and computational power issues comprehensively.

HISTORY

The history of industrial security drones, particularly in the context of privacy-preserving surveillance ethical considerations in Cognitive Internet of Things (CIoT)-Enabled systems, is a relatively recent development that has evolved alongside advancements in technology and regulatory frameworks. Here's a brief overview of the key milestones:

- **Early Adoption**: The use of drones for industrial security purposes began to gain traction in the early 2000s, primarily in sectors such as oil and gas, utilities, and manufacturing. Initially, drones were used for basic surveillance tasks, such as perimeter patrols and asset monitoring.
- **Integration of IoT**: With the emergence of IoT technology, drones became increasingly interconnected with other devices and systems within industrial environments. This integration enabled more efficient data collection, analysis, and response capabilities, enhancing overall security operations.
- **Privacy Concerns**: As industrial security drones became more prevalent, concerns arose regarding the potential invasion of privacy. The use of drones equipped with cameras and sensors raised questions about the collection, storage, and use of surveillance data, particularly in areas where individuals' privacy could be compromised.
- **Ethical Considerations**: In response to privacy concerns, discussions around ethical considerations in surveillance practices gained prominence. Stakeholders began to emphasize the importance of respecting individuals' privacy rights, obtaining consent for surveillance activities, and implementing privacy-preserving measures to mitigate the risk of unauthorized data collection and misuse.
- **Advancements in AI**: The integration of AI technologies into industrial security drones further transformed surveillance capabilities. AI algorithms enabled drones to autonomously detect and analyze security threats, improving response times and accuracy in threat identification.

- **Regulatory Frameworks**: Governments and regulatory bodies began to address privacy and ethical concerns surrounding industrial security drones through the development of regulations and guidelines. These frameworks aimed to establish standards for data protection, transparency, and accountability in surveillance practices.
- **CIoT-Enabled Systems**: The convergence of CIoT technology with industrial security drones marked a significant milestone in the evolution of surveillance capabilities. CIoT-enabled systems facilitated seamless communication, data exchange, and coordination among drones and other IoT devices, enhancing the effectiveness and efficiency of security operations [Dosari. et al. 2023]..
- **Ongoing Debate and Innovation**: The discussion around privacy-preserving surveillance ethical considerations in CIoT-enabled industrial security drones remains ongoing. Stakeholders continue to explore innovative solutions and best practices for balancing security needs with individual privacy rights, while also addressing emerging challenges such as bias in AI algorithms and the proliferation of surveillance technologies.

Overall, the history of industrial security drones reflects a dynamic interplay between technological advancements, regulatory developments, and ethical considerations, with stakeholders striving to harness the benefits of surveillance technology while upholding ethical standards and protecting individuals' privacy rights.

CLASSIFICATION OF INDUSTRIAL SECURITY DRONES

The classification of Cognitive Internet of Things (CIoT)-enabled industrial security drones can be based on various factors such as their capabilities, functionalities, deployment scenarios, and technological characteristics. Below is a classification scheme for CIoT-enabled industrial security drones:

- **Based on Functionality**:
- **Surveillance Drones:** These drones are primarily designed for monitoring and surveillance purposes, equipped with cameras, sensors, and AI algorithms to detect and analyze security threats.
- **Patrol Drones:** Patrol drones are tasked with patrolling designated areas to ensure security and safety, conducting routine inspections, and responding to incidents in real-time.

- **Response Drones:** These drones are deployed to respond to security incidents, providing rapid assistance, delivering supplies, or performing emergency interventions as needed.
- **Based on Deployment Scenario:**
- **Indoor Drones:** These drones are deployed within indoor environments such as warehouses, factories, or office buildings to enhance security and surveillance capabilities.
- **Outdoor Drones:** Outdoor drones operate in open-air environments such as industrial parks, construction sites, or perimeter security zones to monitor large areas and deter unauthorized access.
- **Based on Technological Characteristics:**
- **Autonomous Drones:** Autonomous drones are equipped with advanced AI and machine learning capabilities, allowing them to operate independently, make decisions, and adapt to changing environmental conditions.
- **Networked Drones:** Networked drones are interconnected within a CIoT framework, enabling them to communicate with each other and with ground-based infrastructure for coordinated surveillance and response.
- **Sensor-equipped Drones:** These drones are equipped with a variety of sensors such as cameras, LiDAR, thermal imaging, and chemical detectors to collect and analyze data for security purposes.
- **Based on Industry Sector:**
- **Manufacturing Drones:** Drones deployed in manufacturing facilities for security surveillance, asset protection, and monitoring of production processes.
- **Energy Sector Drones:** Drones used in the energy sector for monitoring critical infrastructure such as power plants, pipelines, and substations to prevent security breaches and ensure operational safety.
- **Transportation Drones:** Drones employed in transportation hubs such as airports, seaports, and railway stations for security patrols, perimeter monitoring, and crowd management.
- **Based on Data Processing Capabilities:**
- **Onboard Processing Drones:** These drones have onboard processing capabilities to analyze surveillance data in real-time, enabling rapid detection and response to security threats.
- **Cloud-connected Drones:** Drones that offload data processing tasks to cloud-based servers for more advanced analytics, pattern recognition, and long-term data storage.
- **Based on Regulatory Compliance:**
- **Regulatory-compliant Drones:** Drones that adhere to relevant regulations and standards governing security and privacy in surveillance operations, such as GDPR, HIPAA, and industry-specific guidelines.

By classifying CIoT-enabled industrial security drones along these dimensions, stakeholders can better understand their capabilities, applications, and deployment requirements, facilitating informed decision-making and effective utilization in various industrial contexts.

WORKING OF INDUSTRIAL SECURITY DRONES

Industrial security drones, especially those enabled by the Internet of Things (IoT), play a crucial role in enhancing security measures within industrial settings. The working of industrial security drones involves several key components and processes:

- **Data Collection**: Industrial security drones are equipped with various sensors and cameras to collect real-time data from their surroundings [Dosari. et al. 2023]. These sensors may include optical cameras, thermal cameras, LiDAR, gas sensors, and more. The drones navigate through the industrial environment, capturing data relevant to security monitoring and surveillance.
- **Data Transmission**: Once the data is collected, it is transmitted in real-time to a central command center or a cloud-based platform. IoT-enabled drones utilize wireless communication protocols such as Wi-Fi, cellular networks, or dedicated IoT networks to transmit data securely and efficiently.
- **Data Processing and Analysis**: In the command center or cloud platform, the collected data undergoes processing and analysis. This may involve AI algorithms and machine learning techniques to detect anomalies, identify security threats, and classify objects of interest. For example, drones can detect unauthorized access, monitor for equipment malfunctions, or identify safety hazards within the industrial facility.
- **Alert Generation and Response**: Upon detecting security threats or anomalies, the system generates alerts and notifications to security personnel or relevant stakeholders. These alerts may be sent via email, SMS, or integrated with existing security systems for immediate response. Security personnel can then take appropriate actions to address the identified threats, such as dispatching security teams or initiating emergency protocols.
- **Integration with Existing Systems**: IoT-enabled industrial security drones are often integrated with existing security infrastructure and systems. This integration allows for seamless coordination between drones, surveillance cameras, access control systems, and other security devices. Additionally, data collected by drones may be correlated with data from other sources to provide a comprehensive view of security conditions within the industrial facility.

- **Continuous Monitoring and Adaptation**: Industrial security drones operate continuously, providing around-the-clock monitoring of the industrial environment. They can adapt to changing conditions and priorities, adjusting their patrol routes or surveillance patterns based on real-time data and situational awareness. This flexibility ensures that security measures remain effective and responsive to evolving threats.
- **Data Storage and Analysis**: The collected surveillance data is stored securely for historical analysis and audit purposes. This data can be used to identify trends, patterns, and areas for improvement in security protocols. Additionally, it may be leveraged for regulatory compliance, incident investigation, and risk management purposes.

By leveraging IoT technology, industrial security drones offer enhanced capabilities for proactive security monitoring, rapid threat detection, and effective response within industrial environments. Their integration with IoT enables seamless communication, data exchange, and coordination, resulting in a more robust and comprehensive security infrastructure.

Figure 1 provides the flow diagram illustrating the sequential steps involved in the working of industrial security drones, including IoT-enabled features. It begins with data collection through various sensors, followed by wireless transmission of collected data. The data is then processed and analyzed to detect anomalies and security threats. Alerts are generated based on the analysis, triggering appropriate responses. The drones are integrated with existing security systems for seamless coordination. Continuous monitoring and adaptation ensure proactive security measures. Finally, collected data is stored and analyzed for historical insights and compliance purposes.

Figure 1. Flow Diagram for Working of Industrial Security Drones

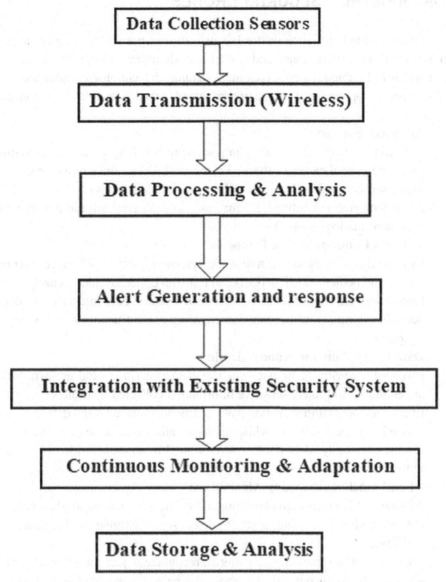

ADVANCEMENTS IN ENABLING TECHNOLOGIES FOR INDUSTRIAL SECURITY DRONES

Enabling technologies for industrial security drones, particularly in the context of privacy-preserving surveillance and ethical considerations in Cognitive Internet of Things (CIoT)-Enabled systems, encompass a range of technological advancements and procedural approaches. Here's a breakdown of some key enabling technologies:

- **Advanced Sensors:**
- Industrial security drones are equipped with a variety of advanced sensors including optical cameras, thermal cameras, LiDAR, and gas sensors.
- These sensors enable drones to collect diverse data types such as visual imagery, temperature readings, 3D mapping, and gas concentrations, enhancing their surveillance capabilities.
- **Wireless Communication Protocols:**
- Drones rely on wireless communication protocols such as Wi-Fi, cellular networks, and dedicated IoT networks to transmit collected data securely.
- Encryption and authentication mechanisms ensure data integrity and confidentiality during transmission, safeguarding against unauthorized access or tampering.
- **Data Encryption and Anonymization:**
- Privacy-preserving techniques such as data encryption and anonymization are employed to protect sensitive information collected by drones.
- Encryption algorithms ensure that data is securely encrypted both during transmission and storage, while anonymization techniques remove or obfuscate personally identifiable information (PII) to prevent identification of individuals.
- **AI and Machine Learning Algorithms:**
- Advanced AI and machine learning algorithms are utilized for data processing and analysis, enabling drones to detect security threats and anomalies in real-time.
- These algorithms can identify patterns, recognize objects of interest, and differentiate between normal and abnormal behavior, enhancing surveillance efficiency and accuracy.
- **Bias Mitigation Techniques:**
- Bias mitigation techniques are implemented to address potential biases in AI algorithms used for surveillance purposes.
- Techniques such as fairness-aware learning, bias detection, and model interpretability help ensure that surveillance outcomes are fair, unbiased, and equitable across diverse demographic groups.

- **Privacy Impact Assessments:**
- Privacy impact assessments (PIAs) are conducted to evaluate the potential privacy risks and implications of surveillance activities.
- PIAs help identify privacy risks, assess their severity, and recommend mitigating measures to protect individuals' privacy rights and comply with regulatory requirements.
- Ethical Guidelines and Training:
- Ethical guidelines and training programs are developed and implemented to ensure that drone operators and stakeholders adhere to ethical standards and best practices.
- Training programs raise awareness about privacy-preserving techniques, ethical considerations, and legal obligations, empowering stakeholders to make informed decisions and uphold privacy rights.

By leveraging these enabling technologies and adopting privacy-preserving surveillance practices, industrial security drones can enhance security measures while respecting individual privacy rights and ethical principles in CIoT-enabled systems

REQUIREMENTS OF INTERNET OF INDUSTRIAL SECURITY DRONES

The requirements for Internet of Industrial Security Drones (IoD) encompass various aspects to ensure their effectiveness, safety, and reliability in industrial settings. Some key requirements include:

- **Security Protocols**: Drones must adhere to stringent security protocols to prevent unauthorized access, data breaches, or tampering, ensuring the integrity and confidentiality of sensitive information.
- **Real-time Monitoring**: IoD should provide real-time monitoring capabilities, enabling operators to oversee critical areas continuously and respond promptly to security threats or emergencies.
- **Collision Avoidance**: Incorporating advanced collision avoidance systems is crucial to prevent accidents and minimize the risk of damages to property or injury to personnel within industrial environments.
- **Data Encryption**: All data transmitted and stored by IoD should be encrypted to safeguard against interception or unauthorized access, maintaining the confidentiality and integrity of sensitive information.

- **Compliance with Regulations**: Drones must comply with relevant regulations and standards governing their operation, ensuring legal adherence and mitigating liability risks associated with non-compliance.
- **Remote Access Control**: Implementing robust access control mechanisms allows authorized personnel to remotely control and manage drones, limiting access to sensitive functionalities and data.
- **Redundancy and Failover**: IoD should incorporate redundancy and failover mechanisms to maintain operational continuity in the event of system failures or disruptions, minimizing downtime and enhancing reliability.
- **Environmental Adaptability**: Drones must be capable of operating effectively in diverse environmental conditions commonly encountered in industrial settings, including extreme temperatures, high humidity, or low visibility.
- **Payload Flexibility**: The ability to support various payload options, such as high-resolution cameras, sensors, or communication equipment, enhances the versatility and utility of IoD for different security applications.
- **Interoperability**: Ensuring interoperability with existing security infrastructure and systems enables seamless integration of IoD into broader security frameworks, enhancing overall effectiveness and efficiency.

These requirements collectively contribute to the development of robust and dependable Internet of Industrial Security Drones, capable of addressing the unique security challenges faced by industrial environments while minimizing associated risks and liabilities.

CHALLENGES AND FUTURE RESEARCH TRENDS OF INDUSTRIAL SECURITY DRONES

The challenges and future research trends in the field of Industrial Security Drones encompass various aspects, including privacy and security, global resource management, sensor communication, coordination, and deployment. Here's a brief explanation of each:

- **Privacy and Security-Related Challenges**: With the proliferation of drones, ensuring privacy and security is paramount. Challenges include safeguarding sensitive data collected by drones, preventing unauthorized access to drone systems, and addressing concerns about privacy infringement arising from drone surveillance activities. Future research may focus on developing robust encryption techniques, authentication mechanisms, and privacy-preserving algorithms to mitigate these risks.

- **Global Resource Management-Related Challenges**: Efficiently managing resources such as battery power, processing capabilities, and communication bandwidth is crucial for optimizing drone performance and extending operational range. Challenges include maximizing battery life, optimizing data processing algorithms for resource-constrained environments, and dynamically allocating resources based on task requirements. Future research may explore techniques for energy-efficient operation, adaptive resource allocation, and distributed computing to address these challenges.
- **Sensor Communication-Related Challenges**: Drones rely on sensors to collect data and navigate their surroundings. Challenges in sensor communication include ensuring reliable data transmission in noisy or congested environments, minimizing latency for real-time applications, and optimizing sensor placement for optimal coverage and accuracy. Future research may investigate advanced communication protocols, multi-sensor fusion techniques, and adaptive sensing strategies to overcome these challenges.
- **Coordination and Task Scheduling-Related Challenges**: Coordinating multiple drones to perform complex tasks requires efficient task allocation and scheduling algorithms. Challenges include coordinating drones to avoid collisions, optimizing task assignment to minimize completion time, and adapting to dynamic environmental conditions or task requirements. Future research may focus on developing decentralized coordination algorithms, machine learning-based task scheduling approaches, and swarm intelligence techniques to enhance coordination and scalability.
- **Drones Distribution and Deployment-Related Challenges**: Deploying drones in industrial environments involves challenges such as selecting optimal deployment locations, ensuring coverage of critical areas, and maintaining drone fleets efficiently. Challenges also include managing the logistics of drone deployment, including transportation, maintenance, and storage. Future research may explore automated deployment strategies, predictive maintenance algorithms, and drone recharging infrastructure to streamline deployment processes and maximize operational efficiency.

Addressing these challenges and exploring future research trends will be essential for advancing the capabilities of Industrial Security Drones and unlocking their full potential in safeguarding industrial assets, enhancing security, and mitigating risks.

APPLICATIONS OF INDUSTRIAL SECURITY DRONES

Industrial security drones find a multitude of applications across various industries, revolutionizing traditional security measures with their versatility and efficiency. Some key applications include:

- **Perimeter Security**: Drones equipped with high-resolution cameras and thermal imaging sensors are deployed to monitor and secure the perimeters of industrial facilities, detecting unauthorized access, intrusions, or potential security breaches.
- **Asset Monitoring**: Drones are utilized for real-time monitoring and inspection of critical infrastructure and assets such as pipelines, power plants, and storage tanks, identifying defects, leaks, or structural weaknesses before they escalate into safety hazards [Dosari. et al. 2023].
- **Surveillance and Patrol**: Industrial security drones conduct routine patrols and surveillance missions over large areas, providing aerial coverage and monitoring for suspicious activities, unauthorized personnel, or safety violations.
- **Emergency Response**: In emergency situations such as fires, chemical spills, or natural disasters, drones are deployed for rapid assessment and response, delivering situational awareness to emergency responders and aiding in search and rescue operations.
- **Environmental Monitoring**: Drones equipped with environmental sensors are employed to monitor air quality, pollution levels, and environmental hazards in industrial settings, facilitating compliance with regulatory standards and mitigating environmental risks.
- **Inventory Management**: Drones assist in inventory management by conducting aerial inventory counts, tracking asset movement, and identifying discrepancies in stock levels, optimizing supply chain operations and reducing inventory losses.
- **Safety Inspections**: Drones perform safety inspections of hazardous or hard-to-reach areas such as confined spaces, elevated structures, or areas with toxic gases, minimizing the risk to human inspectors and ensuring compliance with safety regulations.
- **Event Security**: In large-scale events or gatherings held in industrial facilities, drones are deployed for crowd monitoring, perimeter surveillance, and emergency response coordination, enhancing event security and public safety.

SOME ILLUSTRATIONS

The present section illustrates the practical challenges and solutions in implementing CIoT in industrial security drones as provided in Table 1

Table 1. Practical Challenges and Predictive solutions in Implementation of CIoT in Industrial Security

Sl. No.	Industry	Challenge	Solution
1.	Oil and Natural Gas Industry	In this type of industry, security is paramount due to the hazardous nature of operations and the critical infrastructure involved. Implementing CIoT in drones for security purposes faces challenges such as ensuring reliable connectivity in remote locations, maintaining data integrity, and protecting against cyber threats	One practical solution can be deploying CIoT-enabled drones equipped with advanced sensors and cameras for perimeter surveillance. These drones can be integrated into the company's existing network infrastructure using secure communication protocols such as TLS (Transport Layer Security) and VPNs (Virtual Private Networks). Additionally, edge computing capabilities are leveraged to process data locally on the drones, reducing latency and minimizing the risk of data breaches during transmission. By adopting a multi-layered security approach encompassing encryption, authentication, and intrusion detection systems, the company can mitigates the risk of cyber-attacks on its drone fleet.
2.	Manufacturing Units for Sensitive Industrial Components	Manufacturing units often span vast areas and contain sensitive equipment and materials, making them vulnerable to theft, vandalism, and industrial espionage. Implementing CIoT in security drones within these environments requires addressing challenges such as interference from machinery, optimizing battery life for extended patrols, and integrating with existing surveillance systems.	The drones employed are equipped with AI-powered object recognition algorithms to detect unauthorized personnel, intrusions, or anomalous behavior in real-time. To overcome interference from machinery, the drones utilize frequency-hopping spread spectrum (FHSS) technology, dynamically switching between different communication channels to maintain connectivity. Moreover, the drones leverage predictive maintenance algorithms to optimize battery usage and ensure uninterrupted operation during patrols. Integration with the plant's existing surveillance infrastructure is achieved through APIs (Application Programming Interfaces) and standardized communication protocols, enabling seamless data exchange between drones and centralized monitoring systems

The above cases illustrates practical challenges encountered and the innovative solutions devised in implementing CIoT in industrial security drones. By addressing issues such as connectivity, data integrity, and interoperability, organizations can enhance the effectiveness of their security operations and safeguard critical assets more effectively.

CONCLUSION

The chapter underscores the imperative of balancing security imperatives with respect for individual privacy rights and ethical principles. Through an exploration of the integration of Cognitive Internet of Things (CIoT)-enabled industrial security drones, the chapter highlights the significance of privacy-preserving surveillance techniques and ethical considerations in ensuring responsible surveillance practices. By advocating for the implementation of privacy-enhancing technologies, the development of ethical guidelines, and ongoing dialogue among stakeholders, the chapter emphasizes the importance of fostering a culture of responsible innovation and ethical accountability in the deployment of surveillance technologies. Ultimately, by prioritizing both security and privacy concerns, stakeholders can effectively harness the transformative potential of CIoT-enabled industrial security drones while upholding fundamental principles of privacy and human rights.

FUTURE SCOPE

Looking ahead, the future scope in the domain of privacy-preserving surveillance ethical considerations in Cognitive Internet of Things (CIoT)-Enabled Industrial Security Drones is promising and multifaceted. One avenue for future exploration lies in the continued development and refinement of privacy-enhancing technologies tailored specifically for industrial security drone applications. This includes advancements in encryption algorithms, anonymization techniques, and secure communication protocols to further bolster data privacy and protection. Additionally, there is a need for ongoing research and innovation in bias mitigation strategies to ensure fair and equitable surveillance outcomes across diverse demographic groups. Moreover, the integration of emerging technologies such as block chain and federated learning holds potential for enhancing data privacy, transparency, and accountability in surveillance practices. Furthermore, future efforts should focus on the formulation of robust ethical guidelines and regulatory frameworks tailored to the unique challenges and considerations posed by CIoT-enabled industrial security drones. By fostering interdisciplinary collaboration, stakeholder engagement, and continuous dialogue, the future of privacy-preserving surveillance in the context of CIoT-enabled industrial security drones can be characterized by ethical integrity, technological innovation, and societal benefit.

Apart from the above there is a need to discuss future trends and emerging ethical considerations in implementing CIoT (Converged Internet of Things) in industrial security drones which would provide valuable insights for industrial fraternity, helping them anticipate and navigate upcoming developments in the field. Some of potential future trends and ethical considerations can be summarized as provided in the Table 2:

Table 2. Future Trends and Ethical Considerations on Some Critical Issues

Sl. No.	Issues	Trend	Ethical Consideration
1.	**Autonomous Operations and AI Integration**	The integration of artificial intelligence (AI) algorithms into industrial security drones will enable more autonomous decision-making capabilities, such as adaptive patrolling routes and real-time threat identification.	As drones become more autonomous, ethical concerns arise regarding accountability and liability for their actions. Clear guidelines and regulations must be established to ensure responsible use of AI in security applications, including transparency in algorithmic decision-making and mechanisms for oversight and accountability.
2.	**Data Privacy and Security**	With the proliferation of sensors and cameras on industrial security drones, vast amounts of data will be collected and analyzed to identify security threats and anomalies.	Protecting the privacy of individuals captured in drone footage becomes increasingly critical. Organizations must implement robust data anonymization techniques, access controls, and encryption protocols to safeguard sensitive information and prevent unauthorized access or misuse of data.
3.	**Interoperability and Standardization**	As the number of IoT devices and platforms grows, there will be a push for greater interoperability and standardization to enable seamless integration and communication between different systems.	Ensuring interoperability and adherence to industry standards promotes transparency, fairness, and competition. However, concerns may arise regarding proprietary technologies and vendor lock-in, necessitating regulatory intervention to promote open standards and interoperability.

continued on following page

Table 2. Continued

Sl. No.	Issues	Trend	Ethical Consideration
4.	**Environmental Impact:**	The widespread adoption of industrial security drones powered by batteries or renewable energy sources will contribute to reducing carbon emissions and environmental footprint compared to traditional security measures.	While drones offer environmental benefits, their manufacturing, operation, and disposal can still have environmental consequences. Organizations must consider the life cycle impacts of drones and adopt sustainable practices, such as eco-friendly materials, energy-efficient designs, and responsible recycling and disposal methods.
5.	**Ethical Use of Surveillance Technologies**	The increasing deployment of surveillance technologies, including drones, raises concerns about potential abuses of power, infringement of civil liberties, and exacerbation of existing societal inequalities.	Striking a balance between security needs and individual rights is paramount. Policies and guidelines should be established to ensure ethical use of surveillance technologies, including clear limitations on data collection, transparency in surveillance activities, and mechanisms for redress and accountability in cases of misuse or abuse.

These future trends and emerging ethical considerations are some of the issues adhering to which organizations can navigate the complexities of implementing CIoT in industrial security drones. In due course of time some more hurdles may arise and hence all those are required to be addressed while upholding ethical principles, safeguarding privacy, and promoting social responsibility.

REFERENCES

Abdelmaboud, A. (2021). The Internet of Drones: Requirements, Taxonomy, Recent Advances, and Challenges of Research Trends. *Sensors (Basel)*, 21(17), 5718. DOI: 10.3390/s21175718 PMID: 34502608

AL-Dosari, K., & Fetais, N.AL-Dosari. (2023). A New Shift in Implementing Unmanned Aerial Vehicles (UAVs) in the Safety and Security of Smart Cities: A Systematic Literature Review. *Safety (Basel, Switzerland)*, 9(3), 64. DOI: 10.3390/safety9030064

Al-Turjman, F., Abujubbeh, M., Malekloo, A., & Mostarda, L. (2020). UAVs assessment in software-defined IoT networks: An overview. *Computer Communications*, 150, 519–536. DOI: 10.1016/j.comcom.2019.12.004

Alsamhi, S. H., Ma, O., Ansari, M. S., & Almalki, F. A. (2019). Survey on collaborative smart drones and internet of things for improving smartness of smart cities. *IEEE Access : Practical Innovations, Open Solutions*, 7, 128125–128152. DOI: 10.1109/ACCESS.2019.2934998

Ayamga, M., Akaba, S., & Nyaaba, A. A. (2021). Multifaceted applicability of drones: A review. *Technological Forecasting and Social Change*, 167, 120677. DOI: 10.1016/j.techfore.2021.120677

Bagloee, S. A., Tavana, M., Asadi, M., & Oliver, T. (2016). Autonomous vehicles: Challenges, opportunities, and future implications for transportation policies. *J. Mod. Transp.*, 24(4), 284–303. DOI: 10.1007/s40534-016-0117-3

Bera, B., Das, A. K., & Sutrala, A. K. (2020). Private blockchain-based access control mechanism for unauthorized UAV detection and mitigation in Internet of Drones environment. *Computer Communications*, 166, 91–109. DOI: 10.1016/j.comcom.2020.12.005

Boccadoro, P., Striccoli, D., & Grieco, L. A. (2021). An extensive survey on the Internet of Drones. *Ad Hoc Networks*, 122, 102600. DOI: 10.1016/j.adhoc.2021.102600

Choudhary, G., Sharma, V., Gupta, T., Kim, J., & You, I. (2018) Internet of drones (iod): Threats, vulnerability, and security perspectives, *arXiv preprint* arXiv:1808.00203 https://doi.org//arXiv.1808.00203DOI: 10.48550

Choudhary, G., Sharma, V., & You, I. (2019). Sustainable and secure trajectories for the military Internet of Drones (IoD) through an efficient Medium Access Control (MAC) protocol. *Computers & Electrical Engineering*, 74, 59–73. DOI: 10.1016/j.compeleceng.2019.01.007

Dawaliby, S., Aberkane, A., & Bradai, A. (2020) Blockchain-based IoT platform for autonomous drone operations management. *Proceedings of the 2nd ACM MobiComWorkshop on Drone Assisted Wireless Communications for 5G and Beyond, London, UK*, pp. 31–36. DOI: 10.1145/3414045.3415939

Deebak, B., & Al-Turjman, F. (2020). A smart lightweight privacy preservation scheme for IoT-based UAV communication systems. *Computer Communications*, 162, 102–117. DOI: 10.1016/j.comcom.2020.08.016

Fotouhi, A., Qiang, H., Ding, M., Hassan, M., Giordano, L. G., Garcia-Rodriguez, A., & Yuan, J. (2018). Survey on UAV Cellular Communications: Practical Aspects, Standardization Advancements, Regulation, and Security Challenges. *IEEE Communications Surveys and Tutorials*, 21(4), 3417–3442. DOI: 10.1109/COMST.2019.2906228

Fotouhi, A., Qiang, H., Ding, M., Hassan, M., Giordano, L. G., Garcia-Rodriguez, A., & Yuan, J. (2019). Survey on UAV cellular communications: Practical aspects, standardization advancements, regulation, and security challenges. *IEEE Communications Surveys and Tutorials*, 21(4), 3417–3442. DOI: 10.1109/COMST.2019.2906228

Gallego-Madrid, J., Molina-Zarca, A., Sanchez-Iborra, R., Bernal-Bernabe, J., Santa, J., Ruiz, P. M., & Skarmeta-Gómez, A. F. (2020). Enhancing Extensive and Remote LoRa Deployments through MEC-Powered Drone Gateways. *Sensors (Basel)*, 20(15), 4109. DOI: 10.3390/s20154109 PMID: 32718087

Gharibi, M., Boutaba, R., & Waslander, S. L. (2016). Internet of Drones. *IEEE Access : Practical Innovations, Open Solutions*, 4, 1148–1162. DOI: 10.1109/ACCESS.2016.2537208

Gupta, L., Jain, R., & Vaszkun, G. (2016). Survey of Important Issues in UAV Communication Networks. *IEEE Communications Surveys and Tutorials*, 18(2), 1123–1152. DOI: 10.1109/COMST.2015.2495297

Huang, H., Savkin, A. V., Ding, M., & Kaafar, M. A. (2019). Optimized deployment of drone base station to improve user experience in cellular networks. *Journal of Network and Computer Applications*, 144, 49–58. Advance online publication. DOI: 10.1016/j.jnca.2019.07.002

Iacovelli, G., Boccadoro, P., & Grieco, L. (2020) An iterative stochastic approach to constrained drones' communications, *Proc. of IEEE/ACM 24th International Symposium on Distributed Simulation and Real Time Applications (DS-RT) (DS-RT'20), Prague, Czech Republic*. DOI: 10.1109/DS-RT50469.2020.9213645

Khuwaja, A. A., Chen, Y., Zhao, N., Alouini, M. S., & Dobbins, P. (2018). A survey of channel modeling for UAV communications. *IEEE Communications Surveys and Tutorials*, 20(4), 1–1. DOI: 10.1109/COMST.2018.2856587

Koubaa, A., Qureshi, B., Sriti, M.-F., Allouch, A., Javed, Y., Alajlan, M., Cheikhrouhou, O., Khalgui, M., & Tovar, E. (2019). Drone map planner: A service-oriented cloud-based management system for the internet-of-drones. *Ad Hoc Networks*, 86, 46–62. DOI: 10.1016/j.adhoc.2018.09.013

Kumar, A., & Mehta, P. L. (2021). *Internet of drones: An engaging platform for iiot-oriented airborne sensors*. Smart Sensors for Industrial Internet of Things., DOI: 10.1007/978-3-030-52624-5_16

Liu, Y., Wu, F., & Wu, J. (2021). Cellular UAV-to-device communications: Joint trajectory, speed, and power optimisation. *IET Communications*, 15(10), 1380–1391. DOI: 10.1049/cmu2.12104

Merkert, R., & Bushell, J. (2020). Managing the drone revolution: A systematic literature review into the current use of airborne drones and future strategic directions for their effective control. *Journal of Air Transport Management*, 89, 101929. DOI: 10.1016/j.jairtraman.2020.101929 PMID: 32952321

Mukherjee, A., Dey, N., & De, D. (2020). Edge Drone: QoS aware MQTT middleware for mobile edge computing in opportunistic Internet of Drone Things. *Computer Communications*, 152, 93–108. DOI: 10.1016/j.comcom.2020.01.039

Nayyar, A., Nguyen, B.-L., & Nguyen, N. G. (2020) The internet of drone things (IoDT): Future envision of smart drones, *First International Conference on Sustainable Technologies for Computational Intelligence*, 563–580. DOI: 10.1007/978-981-15-0029-9_45

Nouacer, R., Hussein, M., Espinoza, H., Ouhammou, Y., Ladeira, M., & Castiñeira, R. (2020). Towards a Framework of Key Technologies for Drones. *Microprocessors and Microsystems*, 77, 103142. DOI: 10.1016/j.micpro.2020.103142

Rehman, A., Paul, A., Ahmad, A., & Jeon, G. (2020). A novel class based searching algorithm in small world internet of drone network. *Computer Communications*, 157, 329–335. DOI: 10.1016/j.comcom.2020.03.040

Rejeb, A., Rejeb, K., Simske, S., & Treiblmaier, H. (2021). Humanitarian Drones: A Review and Research Agenda. *Internet of Things : Engineering Cyber Physical Human Systems*, 16, 100434. DOI: 10.1016/j.iot.2021.100434

Sharma, V., & Kumar, R. (2017). Cooperative frameworks and network models for flying ad hoc networks: A survey. *Concurrency and Computation*, 29(4), 1–36. DOI: 10.1002/cpe.3931

Tian, Y., Yuan, J., & Song, H. (2019). Efficient privacy-preserving authentication framework for edge-assisted Internet of Drones. *J. Inf. Secur. Appl.*, 48, 102354. DOI: 10.1016/j.jisa.2019.06.010

Wazid, M., Das, A. K., & Lee, J.-H. (2018). *Authentication protocols for the internet of drones: taxonomy, analysis and future directions*. J Ambient Intell Human Comput., DOI: 10.1007/s12652-018-1006-x

Weng, L., Zhang, Y., Yang, Y., Fang, M., & Yu, Z. (2020). A mobility compensation method for drones in SG-eIoT. *Digital Communications and Networks*, 7(2), 196–200. DOI: 10.1016/j.dcan.2020.07.011

Yaacoub, J.-P., Noura, H., Salman, O., & Chehab, A. (2020). Security Analysis of Drones Systems: Attacks, Limitations, and Recommendations. *Internet of Things : Engineering Cyber Physical Human Systems*, 11, 100218. DOI: 10.1016/j. iot.2020.100218 PMID: 38620271

Yahuza, M., Idris, M. Y. I., Ahmedy, I. B., Wahab, A. W. A., Nandy, T., Noor, N. M., & Bala, A. (2021). Internet of Drones Security and Privacy Issues: Taxonomy and Open Challenges. *IEEE Access : Practical Innovations, Open Solutions*, 9, 57243–57270. DOI: 10.1109/ACCESS.2021.3072030

Yao, J., & Ansari, N. (2019). QoS-aware power control in internet of drones for data collection service. *IEEE Transactions on Vehicular Technology*, 68(7), 6649–6656. DOI: 10.1109/TVT.2019.2915270

Zaidi, S., Atiquzzaman, M., & Calafate, C. T. (2020). Internet of Flying Things (IoFT): A survey. *Computer Communications*, 165, 53–74. DOI: 10.1016/j.comcom.2020.10.023

Chapter 3
Blockchain–Based Identity Management for Secure CIoT Interactions

Jagjit Singh Dhatterwal

Koneru Lakshmaiah Education Foundation, Vaddeswaram, India

Kiran Malik

Department of Computer Science and Engineering (AIML), GL Bajaj Institute of Technology & Management, Greater Noida, India

Kuldeep Singh Kaswan

Galgotias University, India

ABSTRACT

Cellular Internet of Things (CIoT) combines sophisticated machine learning with IoT, which produces smart 'things' that can make decisions on their own. However, identity management in CIoT contains major difficulties especially in terms of security and privacy. Blockchain is found to provide a solution that improves the secure communication in CIoT environments efficiently. In this chapter, the author describes how blockchain can be used to manage identities for CIoT as well as the advantages and frameworks of blockchain. This chapter covers the field of CIoT, its characteristics regarding identification requirements, the concept of blockchain, and the characteristics of blockchain applications for CIoT identity management systems. It goes further to discuss on architectural frameworks for blockchain, application of smart contract, and real life examples in CIoT to expound on how blockchain transform CIoT space. Therefore, analyzing these elements, this chapter is intended to suggest the detailed instructions for using blockchain to safeguard interactions within CIoT. The extant identity management solutions do not fare

DOI: 10.4018/979-8-3693-2157-7.ch003

well when it comes to scaling up while simultaneously addressing escalating se-
curity threats and compatibility challenges across the complex CIoT context. The
following are the problems which are going to be solved aware in this chapter by
proposing a blockchain-based framework for identity management. The emphasis
will therefore be on self-sovereign identity models and Decentralized Identifiers as
they provide privacy of personal data. This chapter also finds from the analyses and
the cases of the application of blockchain-based identity management frameworks
that security and efficiency in CIoT systems are greatly enhanced. The processes
of identity verification by smart contracts and the applications of cryptographic
methods enhance security and privacy. In the same manner, the chapter presents
and discusses the performance measurement, legal aspects, and possibilities for
future investigations with the aim of painting the picture associated with the future
outlooks and obstacles of the examined field.

1. INTRODUCTION

The CIoT is the IoT system enhanced by cognition to achieve more effective resulting from a more profound level of self-control. CIoT builds on top of IoT by adding layers of machine learning, artificial intelligence, and data analytics making the IoT devices smart or capable of learning from the data feed they receive and able to respond to new conditions on their own. This integration enhances the performance, dependability, and flexibility of IoT systems making it possible to advance the IoT application in different domains (Zhang & Wen, 2017).

In CIoT settings, the identity is a central concept when it comes to the management of interactions between devices and systems. The management of identity means that one must determine and verify the device, user and service identity in CIoT that should only permit rights entities to engage in its environment. Because of the inherent decentralization and self-organization of CIoT devices, it is crucial to remember that identity management is a local concept and must be implemented effectively to prevent unauthorized access, data theft, and other threats that can greatly endanger the entire CIoT system (Hardjono et al., 2019).

This is because blockchain as a technology has characteristics of decentralization, immutability, and transparency that make it suitable for CIoT interactions' security. Blockchain creates a distributed database for identity information to help minimize the problems that arise from the concentrated databases. This makes it rather safer and reliable since the identity data is disseminated across different nodes which makes it hard for either an attack or failure to affect (Ali et al., 2016).

The feature of using blockchains also means that, when identity information is stored, it cannot be changed or overridden, which makes the interaction record system reliable and virtually impossible to forge. This characteristic is especially crucial in CIoT settings, especially since data about those identities are fundamental to trust and security among attachments. Therefore, CIoT by incorporating blockchain can enhance security and improve on the level of transparency in identity management.

Furthermore, blockchain technology enhances the SSI where identities of humans and things are self-controlled. Through SSI, the identity information of entities can be developed, governed, and shared hence investors, merchants, and other associated partners do not have to depend on central controlling authorities. This strategy is relevant in the present structure of CIoT since it is more decentralized and ensures privacy and control of personal data (Kaswan et al., 2024).

This integration also means that blockchain facets CIoT identity management to incorporate the use of Decentralized Identifiers also known as DIDs, being identifiers, created, owned, and controlled by the identifiend entity. Blockchain can be used to resolve DIDs ensuring identity management in CIoT is secure and immutably recorded. This makes processes of identity verification more secure while at the same time making them less time consuming and hence preventing cases of identity theft and fraud (Dhatterwal et al., 2024).

In CIoT environment, role of identity management is even more critical mainly due to the heterogeneity and dynamism of the devices and systems. Such devices are found to be a part of heterogeneous networks, interface with various entities, and deal with personal information. This unity and decentralised security to show that Blockchain has an added advantage when it comes to identity management in such large and complicated ecosystems.

Also, the smart contracts that are incorporated within blockchain can help CIoT verify identity and authentication automatically. Smart contracts are self-executing applications with the rules of the contract coded into it. In the concept of identity management, smart contracts can execute rules and policies that have been programmed previously, hence, limiting any entity to avail certain resources or services. These automations make security better as well as decrease the number of extra tasks in comparing with the manual identity management.

The issues of identity management are critically significant to CIoT because they serve as a fundamental foundation of the CIoT system's security and reliability. Good identity management means that devices and users are correctly authenticated and authorized to have access, this minimizes risks of different activities that may pose as threats to security. This also enables confidential and flawless transfer of data from one device to another, which is vital in the operations of CIoT applications (Kaswan et al., 2023).

It is not just the application limited to identity management solutions but data security, data transparency as well as accountability in CIoT interactions. Due to its nature, blockchain offers the guarantee that every action and every interaction in the surroundings of the CIoT is documented and can be traced back. This also increases the security of the system and can also increase the trust of the stakeholders throughout the recorded information.

Moreover, by means of distributed and decentralized identity management systems, blockchain may solve CIoT's scalability issues. As the number of devices and interactions rises, conventional centralized identity management solutions sometimes find it difficult to grow effectively. On the other hand, blockchain's distributed character enables it to expand more efficiently, thereby meeting CIoT settings' increasing needs.

2. FUNDAMENTALS OF BLOCKCHAIN TECHNOLOGY

In essence and at its most basic application, the blockchain is a Distributed or Decentralized ledger or database that was developed to record data on many computers in such a manner that the data input could not be fraudulently altered in the future. This innovative structure recently eliminates a central authority and this structure is inherently immune to the data modification and fraud. The key concepts of Blockchain are block, chain, and node. Blocks include information from transactions and are connected to build a chain in chronological order, nodes are computers that have the copy of the blockchain and through consensus mechanism verifying the new transactions (Nakamoto, 2008).

The beginning of the blockchain methodology can be linked back to 2008 for the simple reason that the idea was pioneered by an unknown individual or a group of people going by the unfamiliar name of Satoshi Nakamoto when they came up with Bitcoin, which was the first decentralize virtual currency. Nakamoto in his white paper described a new approach of building consensus in the P2P network without the involvement of a central authority. This discovery paved way for other evolutions including blockchain systems, earlier seen mostly in the cryptocurrency market (Zheng et al., 2018).

A blockchain works via peer-to-peer (P2P) system in which every user including the node holds a copy of transaction record. Operations occur in transactions, and several transactions make up a block that is linked to another block in a sequential manner. The blocks consist of a special digital code or hash derived from the blocks information, as well as the link to the hash of the proceeding block to maintain the continuity and consistency of the whole chain. This structure gives restoration as any endeavor to shade a block would mean that all chains beyond it ought to be changed and agree with the network (Swan M., 2015).

There are three primary types of blockchains: namely, the public, private, and consortium bids. Those that are categorized as public include Bitcoin and Ethereum and anyone can participate in as there are no restrictions. The participation in the network is open for anyone, people can be involved in the consensus process, and all the transactions are transparent. This fosters transparency as well as security but proves to have major scalability problems as there are many participants and transactions (Bingu et al., 2024).

Private on the other hand are those that are available only to certain individuals who must seek permission to be a member of the network. They are more frequently utilized for inter-organizational applications, as it is usually easier for an organization to manage its connections with other organizations and provide a high level of data protection. The use of private blockchain environments may allow for the implementation of higher the speed and scalability of transactions, yet they may at the same time offer relatively less decentralization together with the security aspects that come with fully open blockchains.

Consortium blockchains are partially Public and partially Private blockchains. Depending on the type of blockchain, they are either partially decentralized and partially permissioned. This kind of a blockchain is used, for example in industries where organizations have to share data with each other for common processes like supply chain management, finance and healthcare. Consortium blockchains are based in the middle of decentralization, scalability, and control, which is why they are suitable for various applications of blockchain technology.

Consensus mechanisms are extremely important to any blockchain system since they determine whether all the participants in the system recognize the validity of the transactions that are being concluded as well as the condition of the ledgers. The best-known consensus mechanism is Proof of Work, which is applied for Bitcoin or any other cryptocurrency. For PoW, the nodes or commonly referred to as miners have to solve complicated mathematical problems so as to validate the transactions as well as the addition of new blocks on the chain. This process is time-consuming and power requiring but offers a strong protection against a cyber-attack (Malik et al., 2024).

Another consensus technique is known as Proof of Stake (PoS), which also aims to solve some of the energy problem related to the PoW model. In PoS, the selection of nodes that can generate the next block is based on the amount of coins possessed and the coins that they are willing to 'lock up' or 'stake'. This mechanism is more energy efficient and may prove to be faster in terms of transactions than others but these brings in new additional issues of the security which includes the problem of potential centralization for a few more participants with many tokens in the networks.

There are several forms of consensus that does not fall under PoW and PoS, with their own strengths and weaknesses. DPoS is considered as a form of variation of PoS because it uses voting to choose a limited number of nodes that will validate transactions. This approach can enhance scalability and change transaction velocity but may help the decentralisation objective. The BFT algorithms, including PBFT, deal with the failure and malicious nodes and are suitable for private and consortium blockchains.

This was a general overview of consensus mechanisms and, as mentioned before, the choice of which one to use depends on parameters of the blockchain application it is to be used on. These are features such as; the extent to which decentralization is required, scalability requirements, power consumption tolerance, and security threats. Every mechanism provides a certain trade-off of these aspects, which determines the overall efficiency and applicability for particular tasks.

The real-life decentralized properties of land contracting through blockchain make it more secure, transparent and trustworthy in several ways. In this way, blockchains do not have the single points of failure and attacks due to the decentralization of the ledger. Due to this, the blockchain network gives a guarantee that once information has been entered, it cannot be changed or deleted without the approval of the network hence making the records very credible and trustworthy.

Yet, there are some problems with blockchain technology. The capacity is a problem that has not yet been solved for most blockchains, especially for the public ones such as Bitcoin and Ethereum since the increased number of transactions can cause their clogging and slow resolving of transactions. Drawbacks like these are being observed, and solutions such as sharding, the OTC and L2 solutions are being worked on to improve this blockchain performance.

Relative to that, the problem of interactions between multiple blockchains is another main issue. In the context of rising different blockchain platforms, integrating the platforms to transfer assets and data as easily as possible also plays significant role. Interoperability enabler linked with cross-chain communication, and the protocols, standards, and guidelines are designed to bring together the blockchain kingdoms.

Blockchain remains a fast-developing one and present studies and implementations are carried with the intention to mitigate the problems and extend the efficiencies of blockchain technology's application. Some include: application of Blockchain with Artificial intelligence, the Internet of things, and Quantum computing. Such integrations may likely generate other application areas and enhance the innovativeness within vast areas of human life.

3. IDENTITY MANAGEMENT IN CIOT

Many factors have it challenging when implementing the traditional identity management system in the CIoT environment. Let me mention the following: the first one is scalability. In CIoT setting scenarios, there are multiple devices that are connected and thus it becomes difficult to handle and authenticate numerous identities by the traditional systems. The very nature of centralized structure of many conventional systems is that they contain bottlenecks and single points of failure which can be easily attacked and failed (Zhou et al., 2021a).

The other factor that greatly defines ASIMO as a socially assistive robot is security Another major obstacle is security. Typically established identity management employs the use of accounts that are trailing and are susceptible to the acts of fraud. In CIoT, the objects and interactions are dynamic and such traditional methods are not suited for CIoT. Besides, these systems very often do not provide sufficient protection of data transfer and storage, thereby creating a threat of data leaks and unauthorized access (Santos et al., 2022).

Traditionality also has its shortcoming in terms of privacy as well. Most identity management solutions involve compilation of personal details into databases, which can be breached by other people if drilled. Considering that data sensitivity is an important aspect in CIoT, in order to protect the users' privacy while at the same time adhere to high levels of security is quite challenging (Alshamrani et al., 2020).

Hash Functions for Identity Verification

A fundamental concept in blockchain and identity management is the use of hash functions to create unique digital identifiers. A hash function H maps input data x to a fixed-size string of bytes

$$H(x) = y$$

where x is the input data (such as user identity information) and y is the hash value
Example:
Suppose x is a user's digital identity information:
$x = $ "JohnDoe1985"
Using a hash function like SHA-256:
$H("\$JohnDoe1985") = 0x91DFD9DEF100D02B95F908C9436D6F59\ldots$

Elliptic Curve Digital Signature Algorithm (ECDSA)

$r = (k \cdot G)_x \bmod n$

$s = k^{-1} \cdot (H(m) + d \cdot r) \bmod n$

where:

- G is a point on the elliptic curve,
- k is a random integer,
- $H(m)$ is the hash of the message,
- d is the private key,
- n is the order of the curve.

Example:
Assume an elliptic curve with parameters:
- G =base point $\cdot n =$ 115792089237316195423570985008687907852837564279074904382605163141518 (a large prime number)

- d = 123456789 (private key)
- k = 987654321 (random integer)

For a message \$m="JohnDoe1985":

$r = (987654321 \cdot G)_x \bmod$ 115792089237316195423570985008687907852837564279074904382605163141518

s=987654321^{-1}\cdot(H("JohnDoe1985")+123456789\cdot r)

mod 115792089237316195423570985008687907852837564279074904382605163141518 The signature is (r, s).

Requirements for CIoT Identity Management

CIoT identity management requires approaches that are different from the traditional ones because CIoT is characterized by a high density of connected devices and rapid changes in the state. The first key feature is dynamic scalability, which implies the possibility of change for the growing or developing organization. Different from conventional systems that might manage a limited number of users, CIoT should manage a constantly increasing number of devices alongside their individual ID. Such scalability has to be controlled in an appropriate manner to support new devices and interactiveness coming in constantly (Huang et al., 2021).

The next condition is effective security mechanisms that should correlate with CIoT's environment. Because the interactions are normally many and since the data being transferred cross different sectors is normally sensitive, the security measures employed need to be complex and dynamic. This involves the use of encryption methods, secure storage of keys and using alarms to seek out threats that are likely to occur to either prevent or reduce the impact.

Similar to them, privacy preservation is also important. The CIoT systems must not allow the data owned by the users and devices to be vulnerable to unauthorized interactions as well as allow the intended interactions to happen IETF RFC. This entails careful privacy features such as anonymous, pseudo names, and safe data management (Yang et al., 2023).

Identity Verification and Authentication Processes

Security related to identity is important in CIoT where proper identification of devices and users is need ought to be established to grant them proper access. In CIoT these processes need to work with a large number of entities that are highly diverse while at the same time being highly secure and highly efficient. Today, verification procedures frequently use biometric data, MFA, and behavioral patterns as the additional layer of protection (Chen et al., 2021).

In the case of CIoT, the Section provides the optimization of identity verification and authentication based on the blockchain technology by means of decentralized identifiers (DIDs) and the self-sovereign identity (SSI) models. DIDs offer the creation of strong, self-owned, and self-controlled identifiers that are supported by cryptographically-solid and decentralized identity layers. SSI models give the client full control over the identity information and when to share such details, and with whom (Miller et al., 2022).

Smart contracts also contribute to the optimization of authentication procedures as being as well automated and safeguarded. They guarantee that all the identity verification procedures are performed to the letter and this cuts down on the common errors that may occur because of human interferences and thus boosting the efficiency of the whole identity verification program (Kumar et al., 2023). The use of these technologies in CIoT environments presents a viable solution to the problems of identity management as highlighted above.

Hash Functions for Identity Verification

Hash functions play a crucial role in identity verification processes by generating unique digital fingerprints for data. A commonly used hash function is the SHA-256 algorithm, which produces a 256-bit hash value. The mathematical representation is as follows:

$$H = \text{SHA-256}(M)$$

where H is the hash value and M is the input message or data.

Digital Signatures for Authentication

Signature generation:

$$S = \text{Encrypt}_{\text{private}}(H)$$

Signature verification:

$$V = \text{Decrypt}_{\text{public}}(S)$$

where H is the hash of the original message, S is the digital signature, and V is the verification
result.
Example:
Given a message hash $H =$
ef92b778bafee508f94cf7a5acdc313de9f6e7c3b737c4d79bdc08be3c233b3b and a private key, the signature S might be:

$$S =$$

$\text{Encrypt}_{\text{private}}($ef92b778bafee508f94cf7a5acdc313de9f6e7c3b737c4d79bdc-08be3c233b3ł Upon receiving the signature S, the verifier uses the sender's public key to check:

$$V = \text{Decrypt}_{\text{public}}(S)$$

If V matches the original hash H, the message is authenticated.

Biometric Authentication Using Similarity Scores

$$S = \sqrt{\sum_{i=1}^{n}(x_i - y_i)^2}$$

where x_i and y_i are the feature points of the stored and captured fingerprint data, respectively

Example:

Suppose we have two sets of feature points:

Stored fingerprint: (2,3,4) Captured fingerprint: (1,2,3)

The similarity score S is:

$$S = \sqrt{(2-1)^2 + (3-2)^2 + (4-3)^2}$$
$$S \qquad\qquad = \sqrt{1+1+1}$$
$$S \qquad\qquad = \sqrt{3} \approx 1.73$$

A threshold is set to determine if the fingerprints match based on the similarity score.

4. BLOCKCHAIN FOR IDENTITY MANAGEMENT

Identifying the advantages of blockchain for CIoT identity management First, the main use of blockchain technology is very attractive when it comes to identity management, especially in the case of CIoT. One of the major benefits that can be considered is the increase in protection. Blockchain prevents identity data from being stored in a single location meaning that the information is not stored on a single server but on a number of nodes in a network. This lowers the incidence of data theft and other illegitimate accesses because there is not a central weak point by which attacker may penetrate (Narayanan et al., 2016).

Another advantage of using virtual teams is that it increases the levels of privacy. This eliminates susceptibilities to attacks because Blockchain allows the use of cryptographic methods to protect the data and has provisions for the management of data by the users. The use of the two keys, the public and the private helps to ensure that the information stored in the blocks is only accessible to those who have been granted permission hence increasing user privacy and authority (Zyskind et al., 2015).

Blockchain-based technology also helps with increased personal information traceability and openness. Every transaction or contact involving identification data is recorded on the blockchain on an unchangeable ledger, therefore providing a verifiable audit trail. This openness guarantees responsibility in identity validation procedures and helps to identify fraudulent activity (Tapscott & Tapscott, 2016).

Decentralized Identifiers (DIDs)

DIDs are one of the major steps forward in modern identity solutions, and especially in the sphere of application for blockchain systems. Different from the globally-assigned and centrally-administered identifiers such as mobile numbers, LNIDs, etc, DIDs are self-owned/maintained. The last one is that the deployment of tokens and the management of resources are delegated to dedicated blockchain nodes rather than a single issuing center The decentralization is successfully preventing most of the security issues connected with the too- centralized control over the process (Morrison, 2021).

DIDs inherit properties based on randomness in order to have a globally unique and cryptographically verifiable identifier that can be utilized in multiple systems and uses while not being reliant on an authority. This due to the fact that in CIoT setup, seamless integration of various devices and platforms is of paramount importance. DIDs are linked with credentials which act as the proof of identity and give peace knowing that the interactions one is having with the other party are secure and can be trusted (Sultan et al., 2020).

DIDs in the blockchain context and system practice for identity management provide more sovereign power in the individual's personal ID data. It becomes possible to control the DIDs as well as their credentials independently, without combining the data in one pool or sharing it with a third party, which helps to improve the privacy of the users and minimize the potential possible misuse of the data (Schaub et al., 2021).

Self-Sovereign Identity (SSI) Models

Thus, Self-Sovereign Identity (SSI) stances are comparatively in part because identity management changed the paradigm and provided individuals with the ability to be owners and controllers of their identity data. While identity systems involve centralized authorities that possess users' data, SSI models allow the users to own, control and update the identity credentials through blockchains. This approach enables the users to have more control over their personal information and reduces dependency on third parties.

Trust and identity claims in SSI models are achieved by using DIDs and VC. DIDs have distinct and protected identification numbers for people or items, while VC offers evidence on certain characteristics or statements. This system makes it possible for users to provide only the information they want while keeping the other users' private information intact (Miller et al., 2022).

Reduction of identity theft and fraud is one of SSI's main advantages. SSI approaches complicate the ability of hostile actors to access or modify personal data by decentralizing control and improving the security of identification data. SSI is also a flexible solution for contemporary identity management problems as it enables a broad spectrum of applications from online transactions to access control in physical surroundings (Zhang et al., 2022).

5. BLOCKCHAIN-BASED IDENTITY MANAGEMENT FRAMEWORK FOR CIOT

This chapter has presented the architectural blueprint of blockchain-based identity management within the Cognitive Internet of Things (CIoT), necessary to meet the multifaceted demand of CIoT for identity management. Generally, this framework has several layers that can be aligned to construct a sophisticated and a decentralized identity management system. The most essential layer of the architecture is the blockchain layer affecting the decentralization aspect of the ID management system. This layer provides for availability and resists alteration of identity data as it is shared and stored in a network of nodes.

On top of the blockchain layer, the identity layer is responsible for DIDs and VC, verifiable credentials. This layer's main function is to generate, archive and authenticate identity data in a secure way. The identity layer communicates with the blockchain to check the information about identity claims and make sure they cannot be altered.

The identity layer is underlain by the blockchain layer while the application layer contains the defined interfaces and protocols for user and service and device interactions. This layer enables the CIoT interfaces to be connected directly to a blockchain ID management system without interrupting the native applications and service usage (Miller et al., 2022).

Components and Modules

- The configuration of CIoT's blockchain-based identity management involves the following attributes or modules: Key components include:
- Decentralized Identifier (DID) Registry: This component is used for the administration of the generation, storage, solution, etc, of DIDs. It makes certain that each identifier is unique and can be used to produce a cryptographic signature (Sultan et al., 2020).

- Verifiable Credentials (VC) Issuer and Verifier: Thus, the VC issuer creates and distributes VC that can be used to prove specific characteristics of users or their statements. The VC verifier's role is to verify the validity of these credentials in interactions and transaction processes.
- Blockchain Network: This module forms a system basis for transactions concerning identity data and shelters their authenticity. It guarantees the integrity and confidentiality of the data with the consensus algorithms and the encryption processes (Croman et al., 2016).
- Intelligent agreements automatically verify identification and enforce credential issuing and validation policies. They offer a tamper-proof means of handling contacts and transactions linked to identification (Kumar et al., 2023).
- The identity wallet is a tool used by people to keep and control their DIDs and verified credentials. It gives consumers control over their identification data and helps to enable secure communication with CIoT products and services (Chen et al., 2021).

Integration with Existing CIoT Systems

To integrate a blockchain based identity management framework with existing CIoT systems, it would require the following important factors and processes. First of all, it is necessary to consider adaption possibilities to the existing infrastructure. The proposed blockchain-based system has to be integrated into the existing system and IOT devices and the identity management processes should not affect the normal functioning of IT systems (Bertino & Sandhu, 2021).

Usually integration introduces change in existing applications that are used to interface with the blockchain networks and the identity management frameworks. This may entail creating or enhancing APIs as well as middleware to integrate old school CIoT systems as well as the blockchain-enabled identity management architecture (Huang et al., 2021).

In addition, organisations must also recognise the need of coping with the integration process to meet the desired scalability and performance standards. The blockchain-based system has to incorporate high loads of identity-related trades normal in CIoT settings without engendering signification latency or execution inefficiencies (Zhang et al., 2022).

Another aspect of integration is education of the system's end-users and the administrators to enable them to use the new system that has blended into their environment. It also has to do with offering practical guidelines as well as adequately developed structure to secure the transition and motivate the adoption (Morrison, 2021).

6. SMART CONTRACTS FOR IDENTITY MANAGEMENT

Smart contracts are automated contractual agreements that involve code as the written part of the agreement. They are deployed on a blockchain network, and function based on pre-programmed rules and conditions of a contract and perform the contract's obligations and conditions without the involvement of third parties (Szabo, 1997). When it comes to identity, management smart contracts are used to facilitate and secure different procedures. Thus, smart contracts take advantage of blockchain's features such as decentralization and transparency to conduct identity verification, credential issuance, as well as controlling access.

Integrated smart contracts also allow the decentralized identity systems to operate independently with less or no interference from people; thereby creating less chance of errors or scams. Smart contracts are self-executing programs which can execute the specific contract only when the stipulated set of rules and conditions are met; once written and deployed to the blockchain they cannot be modified, meaning that when the contract is written, it will perform as intended and will be safe from amendment (Buterin, 2013). It also contributes to reliability and trust in the identity management processes to be automated.

Designing Smart Contracts for Identity Verification

Smart Identity management is therefore designing smart contracts by determining how exactly the identity information of an individual is going to be validated and managed. Cohesion considerations may include issues such as users' data that must be protected, users must trust and data that must be kept private. The smart contract code therefore needs to contain the latest rules regarding the check of identity claims against the stored credentials, granting/revoking access and handling of consent (Conoscenti et al., 2016).

Some of the probable functions that can be part of a smart contract related to general identity verification may be the registration of new identities, alteration of identity characteristics, and validation of proof. For instance, a user submits their identity credentials to be verified and the smart contract can consult a DID registry and check their compliance with set standards. Moreover, for the protection of sensitive information, the proposed smart contract has to apply some cryptographic approaches and limit the ability of the parties that have access to identity data (Zhang et al., 2020a).

Design also encompasses provisions for auditing and, arguably, logging of the smart contract and all the integrated interfaces. This involves keeping a clean register of all dealings in identity confirmation, which assists in checking for any form of fraudulent dealings (Zyskind et al., 2015).

Use Cases and Examples

These are some of the ways smart contracts can be implemented to cater for the management of identifications proving the versatility of smart contracts in different areas. One of the well-known application areas is the use of digital signatures for the management of identities for various readily and expressly accessible services. It can also be well applied in the case of user identification when creating the account or logging in, thus minimizing the possibility of identification check by human while maximizing the convenience of the users (Sultan et al., 2020).

Another example is in area of physical and logical access control in the resources and properties. Smart contracts can also be used for permissions and rights control that is to limit the access to certain resources only for the authorized users. For example, smart contracts for a smart home setting can manage the permission to utilize gadgets and structures depending on the individual user IDs thus the access control will be automated and secure yet friendly (Bertino & Sandhu, 2021).

Intelligent agreements help the healthcare industry securely and effectively handle identities for patients and medical information. Smart contracts allow healthcare providers to guarantee that data regarding patients is precisely validated and only available to authorised staff, therefore enhancing the general security and privacy of delicate medical information (Miller et al., 2022).

7. SECURITY ASPECTS OF BLOCKCHAIN-BASED IDENTITY MANAGEMENT

Cryptographic methods remain a core of the security in the blockchain-based identity management systems. These techniques help with maintaining the privacy of the identity data and its consistence and genuineness through various means. The modern technique most often used to protect the identity information is public-key or asymmetric cryptography which utilizes two keys – a public one and a private one. Each participant in the blockchain network has a unique cryptographic key pair: it has an open key known as the public key and a concealed secret key that is known only to the owner (Nakamoto, 2008). This cryptographic framework helps to provide a secure form of payments and to exchange data where only the allowed subject may change or modify the identity information.

Another crucial factor that considers to ensure the security of the blockchain identity system is the key management. It incorporates the creation, distribution, storage and deletion of keys and ensuring that the procedures are secure. The best practices in the management of keys are storing the keys in HSMs, applying the multi-signature system for increasing the level of security, and applying frequent key changes to minimize the impact of key leaks (Wang et al., 2019). There are severe consequences of failing in proper management of keys, and therefore, identity data has to be fortified all times while in use and during storage.

Also, the technique of cryptographic hashing is employed to create unalterable records in the block chain. Hash functions transform data into certain size of hash values that can be used to check the simplicity of data without disclosing the data. Thus, once data about identity information is written in the blockchain, it cannot be changed or updated without being noticed (Croman et al., 2016).

Privacy Preservation and Anonymity

One of the areas that have specific requirements are privacy and anonymity as applied to the context of identity management on the blockchain. As for the advantages, it addresses the issues of transparency and traceability of transactions; here it is critical to note the lack of privacy as an active virtue. ZKP is one such technique that allows an entity to prove the truth or accuracy of a claim without disclosing the under pinning data. This enables the users to keep their identity concealed while at the same time proving their identity attributes (Ben-Sasson et al., 2014).

Another way to keep privacy is by using decentralized identifiers (DIDs) and verifiable credentials. DIDs enable the user to manage the identity business related to them without the need for the control by centralised authoritiies, while verifiable credentials help prove identity attributes without revealing the personal identifiable data. This decentralised model improves the user's privacy by exposing less information as well as not fully depending on central data bases (Schaub et al., 2021).

Privacy can be maintained in blockchain systems by using features like the ring signatures or the confidential transactions where the users' identity cannot be easily determined. These approaches ensure that the users' identities are shielded while the decentralised structure of a blockchain is upheld (Zhang et al., 2020b).

Attack Vectors and Mitigation Strategies

Given that blockchain-based identity management systems have unique features and purposes, they are susceptible to various risks, which threaten the safety and efficiency of the solution. Some of the attacks are Sybil attack that aims at creating numerous fake identities that cause a damaging impact on the network and the 51% attack that has the attacker in control of more than 50% of the computational power of the network to manipulate the records in the block chain (Narayanan et al., 2016).

The best practices on these attacks include, increasing consensus protocols and network monitoring. For example, the Proof of Work (PoW) and proof of Stake (PoS) are consensus algorithms that protect the network from Sybil and 51% attacks due to the costly computation power and the need for large amounts of coins to execute the actions on the network (Bitcoin Wiki, 2014).

They also hire security audits and vulnerability assessments to help them determine strengths and weakness of the security system. Security testing, such as penetration testing and series of code reviews are other recommended measures as they involve identifying and remedying vulnerabilities and risk before they could be used against you (Miller et al., 2022).

Enhancing network security may be achieved by implementing encryption, access restrictions, and abnormalities detection mechanisms, which can effectively reduce potential hazards. Through the ongoing surveillance of network activity and the implementation of adaptable security measures, authentication and authorization systems based on blockchain technology may enhance protection against emerging risks and guarantee the security of personal identification information (Wang et al., 2019).

8. CASE STUDIES AND REAL-WORLD APPLICATIONS

Smart home application has greatly benefited from the use of blockchain based identity management system due to the areas supposed Confidentiality and security. Blockchain can be applied in smart homes for the purpose of handling the smart devices and their access rights identification. For instance, a blockchain-based system can allow or deny permission in smart locks, smart thermostats, security cameras, and other similar devices through a verified identity of a user on the blockchain (Yang et al., 2020).

One of them is the utilization of the decentralized identifiers (DIDs) and smart contracts to regulate access to households. DIDs allow homeowners own identity data when engaging smart devices and appliances in their compounds. Smart contacts provide the keys to unlocking service providers or guests' access to services so that permission can be granted or withdrawn can only happen using smart contracts. This approach not only increases security of information by minimizing possibilities of chances of gaining access by unauthorized personnel but also makes working processes less tiresome by automating them.

For instance, the paradigm shift linked to the specification of smart home contexts has been investigated in the case of the European Union's H2020 project "SWITCH". The project incorporated the use of blockchain technology in the handling of smart interactions with smart appliances with the aim of enhancing security and users' trust (Moussa et al., 2022).

Applications in Healthcare IoT

Healthcare where the blockchain-based identity management is strategically useful for patient's data and control on their medical records. Blockchain, as a solution, provides an opportunity to deploy the system, which will handle the Rh records in a decentralized manner and can overcome many problems connected with their protection, sharing, and exchange (Miller et al., 2022).

EHRs security is one of the most widespread application when the block chain concept is implemented. In such a way, it is possible to preserve patients' data in the blockchain and provide access only to authorized users by encrypting channels. This approach not only increases security but also makes it possible to share HI among various providers while preserving the patient's confidentiality (Hölbl et al., 2020).

Enhancing network security may be achieved by implementing encryption, access restrictions, and abnormalities detection mechanisms, which can effectively reduce potential hazards. Through the ongoing surveillance of network activity and the implementation of adaptable security measures, authentication and authorization systems based on blockchain technology may enhance protection against emerging risks and guarantee the security of personal identification information (Wang et al., 2019).

Use in Industrial IoT Environments

The IIoT involves the embedding of smart sensors into systems and devices in industries, and the role of blockchain-based solution for identity management is to provide security in granting access to systems and devices in the industries. Since IIoT systems comprises of a numerous interconnected devices and sensors, there is need to fix identity management system to avoid unrecognized access and data credibility (Sadeghi et al., 2020).

For instance, in the management of industrial control system covering SCADA solutions, blockchain must be useful in identifying/ authenticating the users/ devices. This way, only allowed personnel can have access to infrastructures which are essential and the interactions of the systems can easily be monitored and audited (Rathore et al., 2018).

An actual case is the use of blockchain; it can be utilized in smart spaces, and the identities of the machines and operators in smart factories. This way, using blockchain technology, it is possible to create a record of interactions and maintenance of machines which is to guarantee that the execution of the process corresponds to the correct mode and is carried to the end. These applications are being experimented by projects such as "Modum" and "VeChain" through utilization of blockchain in

IoT devices that enhances traceability and compliance of manufactured goods in production systems.

9. FUTURE TRENDS AND RESEARCH DIRECTIONS

Advances in Blockchain Technology

In our future work, relying on the development of blockchain technology, several improvements will be made as follows: coupe affecter l'application de la technologie de la blockchain à la gestion des identités pour les systèmes de CIoT (Internet des Objets Cognitifs). One of them is the sequence of expansion in the categories of consensus mechanisms more perspective and efficient. Proof of Work (PoW) the consensus algorithms perform well when it comes to security but they are not efficient in terms of scalability. Another consensus algorithm, which is introduced by newer cryptocurrencies, is PoS and its variation DPoS, which provide the solution for larger CIoT applications since they are better in terms of scalability and energy consumption (Zheng et al., 2018).

Another major development is the dendrification of transaction structures and sidechains that are meant to improve the scalability of the blockchain. Sharding is the practice of partitioning of the blockchain network into constituent segments also known as 'shards,' into which transaction processing is distributed. Sidechains help to solve the problem of parallel processing and transaction offloading from the primary blockchain, which contributes to an overall throughput rate and lesser channel congestion (Sompolinsky & Zohar, 2018). These improvements are relevant for the increasing load of CIoT systems, which increased the number of transactions and decreased latency.

Moreover, the progress in integrating blockchain technologies is anticipated to have a pivotal impact. Standardization solutions provide easy communication and data sharing across multiple blockchain networks, hence promoting the integration and cohesion of CIoT ecosystems. This will enable the implementation of more extensive authentication and authorization systems that include several blockchain platforms and apps.

Emerging Standards for CIoT Identity Management

In the case of CIoT identity management, the process of establishing new and evolving CIoT standards is significant because it addresses interoperability, security, and privacy among various CIoT systems and devices. One of the main issues is the development of good practices in the form of what are known as 'drivers' that define decentralised identifiers (DIDs) and verifiable credentials. That is why there is a new generation of standards that would facilitate the protection of digital identity and credentialing in a decentralized fashion (Matsumoto et al., 2021).

Currently, two global organizations, namely, the World Wide Web Consortium (W3C) and the Decentralized Identity foundation (DIF) are involved in the establishment of these standards. W3C's DID specification and Verifiable Credential Data Model are valuable because they contribute to the development of recommendations for the generation of DID and VC (W3C, 2020). These standards for CIoT identity management solutions are assumed to contribute to higher levels of adoption and harmonization, because different solutions need to be compatible with each other.

There is also increasing importance on regulation and adherence to certain levels of corporate privacy. Some of the regulations that have an impact on the innovations in identity management are the General Data Protection Regulation (GDPR) and the California Consumer Privacy Act (CCPA) that concern the problem of personal data protection and users' privacy (Albrecht, 2016). New standards will have to correspond to these regulations in order that the systems of CIoT identity management have complied with the legislation and ethical norms.

Potential for AI and Machine Learning Integration

The application of AI and ML in blockchain IDMS can be very promising as it can improve security, performance, and capability of the system. AI and ML can be used for improving solutions for fraudulent detections, advanced probability computations, and even. For example, using identity data, the AI algorithms can identify abnormal patterns of identity and possible security risks, then issue real-time notifications and countermeasures (Jiang et al., 2021).

In the proof of identity, the machine learning can enhance the performance of the biometric recognition systems. It is identified that the utilization of AI's biometric solutions including the facial recognition and fingerprint analysis integrated with blockchain enhances the security and convenience of the users (Chowdhury et al., 2020). These models can only learn from new threats and hence improve over time making them efficient in detecting the threats.

Smart contract administration and execution can be automated with help from artificial intelligence. AI included into smart contracts allows CIoT systems to autonomously enforce and modify contract conditions depending on real-time data and predicted insights. More effective and scalable identity management systems might result from this integration streamlining difficult procedures and lowering human interaction (Zhou et al., 2021b).

10. CONCLUSION

In this chapter, several transformations of blockchain technology in the CIoT space specifically, for identity management, have been discussed. Due to the CIoT environment's dynamic nature and since the core need is focused on secure interactions, a highly effective and efficient Identity Management has to be provided. Security and privacy concerns are inherent and critical aspects in CIoT systems, and hence, this paper employs the capabilities of blockchain technology in secularizing the systems.

We started by discussing CIoT application and security and especially the process of CIoT identity management to achieve the secure interaction with the use of blockchain. As a result of the fundamentals of CIoT and the basic concept, types, and consensus mechanisms of blockchain technologies as the major findings in the existing literature, a good understanding and starting point to study the blockchain application in CIoT was established.

Despite the frequent use of Identity Management, it has scalability, security, and compatibility issues; which is solved by utilizing Distributed Identifiers (DID) and Self-sovereign Identity (SSI) facilities of blockchain. The following paper presents the proposed blockchain-based identity management framework for CIoT that has been followed by an architectural preview of the framework along with its components and modules necessary for integration of it from the existing systems which makes it feasible.

The adoption of smart contracts for identity verification brings automated and unchangeable procedures into the picture, and real-life examples are provided in the paper. Concerning more specific security issues like cryptographic methods, privacy, and counteraction of possible attacks, the presentations highlighted the proper functioning of solutions based on the given technology.

These are very positive results or observations from several case studies focusing on smart homes, healthcare IoT, and industrial IoT, which presented evidence of the actual application of blockchain in IoT. LO 3: Analyse and compare the performance metrics of the proposed blockchain system and the conventional approaches; in terms of scalability and latency performance, blockchain appeared to be much efficient.

Finally, regulatory and ethical considerations were addressed, ensuring compliance with data protection regulations and ethical deployment. Future trends point towards advances in blockchain technology, emerging standards for CIoT identity management, and the integration of AI and machine learning, paving the way for continued innovation and enhanced security in CIoT. This chapter concludes that blockchain-based identity management is a promising solution for secure CIoT interactions, offering a path forward for more secure and efficient IoT ecosystems.

REFERENCES

W3C. (2020). Decentralized Identifiers (DIDs) v1.0. World Wide Web Consortium. Retrieved from https://www.w3.org/TR/did-core/

Albrecht, J. P. (2016). The GDPR: The legal and regulatory framework for personal data protection. *Journal of Data Protection & Privacy*, 1(1), 21–32. DOI: 10.2139/ssrn.2822553

Ali, M., Nelson, J., Shea, R., & Freedman, M. J. (2016). Blockstack: A global naming and storage system secured by blockchains. In Proceedings of the 2016 USENIX Annual Technical Conference, 181-194. https://www.usenix.org/conference/atc16/technical-sessions/presentation/ali

Alshamrani, A., Li, Y., & Alshamrani, A. (2020). Privacy-preserving identity management for IoT systems. *Journal of Information Security*, 11(4), 185–197. DOI: 10.1142/S2074917520500212

Ben-Sasson, E., Chiesa, A., Kalai, Y. T., & Pappas, V. (2014). SNARKs for C: Verifiable computations with logarithmic overhead. *2014 IEEE Symposium on Security and Privacy*, 94-113. DOI: 10.1109/SP.2014.12

Bertino, E., & Sandhu, R. (2021). Identity management and access control for the Internet of Things. *Computers & Security*, 109, 102307. DOI: 10.1016/j.cose.2021.102307

Bingu, R., Adinarayana, S., Dhatterwal, J. S., Kavitha, S., Patnala, E., & Sangaraju, H. R. (2024). Performance comparison analysis of classification methodologies for effective detection of intrusions. *Computers & Security*, 143, 103893. DOI: 10.1016/j.cose.2024.103893

Bitcoin Wiki. (2014). Proof of work. Retrieved from https://en.bitcoin.it/wiki/Proof_of_work

Buterin, V. (2013). Ethereum white paper: A next-generation smart contract and decentralized application platform. Retrieved from https://ethereum.org/en/whitepaper/

Chen, H., Li, Y., & Zhao, W. (2021). Multifactor authentication and biometric systems for IoT security. *IEEE Transactions on Information Forensics and Security*, 16, 2851–2863. DOI: 10.1109/TIFS.2021.3088586

Chowdhury, M., Pervaiz, M., & Saha, S. (2020). AI-driven biometric authentication: A comprehensive survey. *IEEE Transactions on Information Forensics and Security*, 15, 1331–1348. DOI: 10.1109/TIFS.2019.2952798

Conoscenti, M., De Martin, J. C., & D'Agostino, G. (2016). Blockchain-based identity management. *2016 IEEE/IFIP International Conference on Dependable Systems and Networks Workshops (DSN-W)*, 556-557. DOI: 10.1109/DSN-W.2016.57

Croman, K., Decker, C., Eyal, I., & Gencer, A. E. (2016). On scaling decentralized blockchains. *2016 3rd Workshop on Bitcoin and Blockchain Research*, 106-125. https://doi.org/DOI: 10.1145/2994369.2994377

Dhatterwal, J. S., Kaswan, K. S., Kumar, S., Balusamy, B., & Ramasamy, L. K. (2024). Design and Development to Collect and Analyze Data Using Bioprinting Software for Biotechnology Industry. *Computational Intelligence in Bioprinting*, 193-209.

Hardjono, T., Smith, N., & Shrier, D. (2019). Self-sovereign identity frameworks and blockchain ecosystems: A comprehensive review. MIT Connection Science & Engineering. https://doi.org/DOI: 10.2139/ssrn.3309174

Hölbl, M., Kosba, A., & Jovanović, J. (2020). Blockchain technology in healthcare: A comprehensive review and directions for future research. *Health Information Science and Systems*, 8(1), 1–15. DOI: 10.1007/s13755-020-00314-7 PMID: 31867102

Huang, Y., Wang, Z., & Zhang, Y. (2021). Dynamic scalability in CIoT identity management systems. *IEEE Access : Practical Innovations, Open Solutions*, 9, 14578–14586. DOI: 10.1109/ACCESS.2021.3052074

Jiang, Q., Li, K., Zhang, Y., & Jiang, L. (2021). AI and blockchain integration: A comprehensive survey and future directions. *IEEE Transactions on Emerging Topics in Computing*, 9(1), 124–137. DOI: 10.1109/TETC.2020.2970990

Kaswan, K. S., Dhatterwal, J. S., Kumar, N., Balusamy, B., & Gangadevi, E. (2024). Cyborg Intelligence for Bioprinting in Computational Design and Analysis of Medical Application. *Computational Intelligence in Bioprinting*, 211-237.

Kaswan, K. S., Malik, K., Dhatterwal, J. S., Naruka, M. S., & Govardhan, D. (2023, December). Deepfakes: A Review on Technologies, Applications and Strategies. In *2023 International Conference on Power Energy, Environment & Intelligent Control (PEEIC)* (pp. 292-297). IEEE. DOI: 10.1109/PEEIC59336.2023.10450604

Kumar, S., Hsu, S., & Yadav, P. (2023). Automating identity management with blockchain-based smart contracts. *Blockchain Research and Applications*, 14, 100065. DOI: 10.1016/j.bcra.2022.100065

Malik, K., Dhatterwal, J. S., Kaswan, K. S., Gupta, M., & Thakur, J. (2023, December). Intelligent Approach Integrating Multiagent Systems and Case-Based Reasoning in Brain-Computer Interface. In *2023 International Conference on Power Energy, Environment & Intelligent Control (PEEIC)* (pp. 1632-1636). IEEE. DOI: 10.1109/PEEIC59336.2023.10450496

Matsumoto, H., Sakai, T., & Yamazaki, Y. (2021). The Decentralized Identity Foundation: Overview and key initiatives. *Journal of Cyber Security Technology*, 5(1), 63–80. DOI: 10.1080/23742917.2021.1892247

Miller, C., Moini, A., & Rodriguez, A. (2022). Self-sovereign identity in IoT systems: Opportunities and challenges. *IEEE Internet of Things Journal*, 9(5), 3882–3894. DOI: 10.1109/JIOT.2022.3155723

Morrison, K. (2021). *The Future of Decentralized Identifiers*. Springer Nature.

Moussa, I., Obaidat, M. S., & Ibrahim, I. (2022). Blockchain-based smart home security systems: A survey and future directions. *IEEE Transactions on Network and Service Management*, 19(2), 1787–1802. DOI: 10.1109/TNSM.2022.3155723

Nakamoto, S. (2008). Bitcoin: A Peer-to-Peer Electronic Cash System. Retrieved from https://bitcoin.org/bitcoin.pdf

Narayanan, A., Bonneau, J., Felten, E., & Miller, A. (2016). *Bitcoin and Cryptocurrency Technologies: A Comprehensive Introduction*. Princeton University Press.

Rathore, M. M., Ahmad, A., & Zhang, Y. (2018). Blockchain technology for secure data management in smart factories. *IEEE Transactions on Industrial Informatics*, 14(9), 3930–3938. DOI: 10.1109/TII.2018.2851171

Sadeghi, A., Wachsmann, C., & Wachsmann, A. (2020). Blockchain technology for the Internet of Things: A comprehensive review. *IEEE Access : Practical Innovations, Open Solutions*, 8, 43167–43182. DOI: 10.1109/ACCESS.2020.2975126

Santos, P. A., Rodrigues, R. N., & Albuquerque, C. (2022). Security issues in IoT-based identity management systems. *Computer Networks*, 191, 108022. DOI: 10.1016/j.comnet.2021.108022

Schaub, F., Paik, M., & Hsiao, J. (2021). Verifiable credentials and decentralized identifiers in practice. *The Journal of Privacy and Confidentiality*, 11(2), 41–62. DOI: 10.29012/jpc.843

Sompolinsky, Y., & Zohar, A. (2018). Secure high-throughput broadcasting in blockchain systems. *2018 IEEE European Symposium on Security and Privacy (EuroS&P)*, 209-224. DOI: 10.1109/EuroSP.2018.00028

Sultan, S., Ruan, Y., & Wang, Y. (2020). Decentralized identity management: Architecture, use cases, and challenges. *Future Generation Computer Systems*, 108, 295–307. DOI: 10.1016/j.future.2020.01.039

Swan, M. (2015). *Blockchain: Blueprint for a New Economy*. O'Reilly Media.

Szabo, N. (1997). Formalizing and securing relationships on public networks. *First Monday*, 2(9). Advance online publication. DOI: 10.5210/fm.v2i9.548

Tapscott, D., & Tapscott, A. (2016). *Blockchain Revolution: How the Technology Behind Bitcoin Is Changing Money, Business, and the World*. Penguin Random House.

Wang, W., Xu, J., & Zhao, Z. (2019). Key management for blockchain-based identity management systems. *IEEE Access : Practical Innovations, Open Solutions*, 7, 48915–48926. DOI: 10.1109/ACCESS.2019.2903431

Yang, C., Xu, Y., & Liu, Q. (2023). Privacy-preserving techniques in IoT: A survey and future directions. *IEEE Communications Surveys and Tutorials*, 25(1), 230–259. DOI: 10.1109/COMST.2022.3208387

Yang, L., Li, X., & Li, Y. (2020). Blockchain-based secure access control for smart homes. *Journal of Computer Security*, 89, 102515. DOI: 10.1016/j.jocs.2020.102515

Zhang, S., Xu, Y., & Li, S. (2020a). Advances in Self-Sovereign Identity and decentralized identity management. *IEEE Access : Practical Innovations, Open Solutions*, 10, 35287–35298. DOI: 10.1109/ACCESS.2022.3165167

Zhang, S., Xu, Y., & Li, S. (2022). Advances in Self-Sovereign Identity and decentralized identity management. *IEEE Access : Practical Innovations, Open Solutions*, 10, 35287–35298. DOI: 10.1109/ACCESS.2022.3165167

Zhang, X., Chen, W., & Wu, D. (2020b). Blockchain interoperability: A survey and research directions. *IEEE Access : Practical Innovations, Open Solutions*, 8, 116560–116573. DOI: 10.1109/ACCESS.2020.3003195

Zhang, Y., & Wen, J. (2017). The IoT electric business model: Using blockchain technology for the internet of things. *Peer-to-Peer Networking and Applications*, 10(4), 983–994. DOI: 10.1007/s12083-016-0456-1

Zheng, Z., Xie, S., Dai, H., Chen, X., & Wang, H. (2018). An Overview of Blockchain Technology: Architecture, Consensus, and Future Trends. *IEEE International Congress on Big Data*, 557-564. DOI: 10.1109/BigDataCongress.2017.85

Zhou, H., Wu, Z., & Sun, J. (2021a). Scalable identity management in IoT: Challenges and solutions. *IEEE Internet of Things Journal*, 8(12), 9392–9404. DOI: 10.1109/JIOT.2021.3063567

Zhou, J., Huang, C., & Sun, X. (2021b). Blockchain and AI integration for smart contract management: A survey. *IEEE Transactions on Knowledge and Data Engineering*, 33(5), 1744–1762. DOI: 10.1109/TKDE.2020.2991334

Zyskind, G., Nathan, O., & Pentland, A. (2015). Decentralizing privacy: Using blockchain to protect personal data. *2015 IEEE Security and Privacy Workshops*, 180-184. DOI: 10.1109/SPW.2015.27

Chapter 4
Reenvisioning Learning in the Modern Age Through New Technologies for Enhanced Student Involvement

Ravishankar Krishnan

iD https://orcid.org/0009-0004-6609-6452

Vel Tech Rangarajan Dr. Sagunthala R&D Institute of Science and Technology, Avadi, India

Rajalakshmi Vel

Sri Ramachandra Institute of Higher Education and Research, Chennai, India

Logasakthi Kandasamy

Universal Business School, Universal AI University, Karjat, India

H. Moideen Batcha

iD https://orcid.org/0000-0001-9872-1495

B.S. Abdur Rahman Crescent Institute of Science and Technology, India

Navaneetha Krishnan Rajagopal

University of Technology and Applied Sciences, Salalah, Oman

ABSTRACT

This chapter delves into the transformative role of emerging technologies in modern education. It begins with tracing the evolution of educational technology, highlighting the shift from traditional methods to innovative digital practices. The focus then shifts

DOI: 10.4018/979-8-3693-2157-7.ch004

to the impact of Virtual and Augmented Reality, offering immersive and interactive learning experiences. Artificial Intelligence's role in personalizing learning and automating administrative tasks is examined, along with its ethical implications. The proliferation of e-learning platforms and MOOCs is discussed, emphasizing their role in democratizing education and challenging traditional models. The chapter also explores the influence of social media and online collaboration tools in fostering peer-to-peer learning and global classroom connections. The chapter concludes by addressing the digital divide and the necessity for equitable access to technology in education, underscoring the need for adaptive policies and practices to support these technological advancements.

1. THE EVOLUTION OF EDUCATIONAL TECHNOLOGY

The landscape of educational technology has undergone a remarkable transformation over the past few decades. At first, the presentation of PCs in study halls during the late twentieth century denoted a vital crossroads in education history. These early PCs, however simple by the present guidelines, started an upset in educating and learning techniques. They acquainted understudies with fundamental figuring abilities and advanced proficiency, fundamental in an undeniably computerized world (Fesakis and Prantsoudi, 2021). During the 1990s, the appearance of the Web opened new wildernesses in schooling. It associated study halls to a universe of data, giving admittance to assets beforehand unfathomable. Educators could now enhance course reading lessons with a tremendous web-based vault of articles, pictures, and recordings. This period likewise saw the ascent of education programming, which offered intuitive growth opportunities, a glaring difference to the latent gaining from reading material (Zhang et al., 2023).

The mid 2000s saw the mix of smartboards, supplanting conventional boards. These intelligent whiteboards permitted educators to introduce media content, connect with understudies in intelligent illustrations, and cultivate a more powerful homeroom climate. Around similar time, the multiplication of workstations and tablets in training made innovation more open and customized. Understudies could now draw in with computerized course readings, intuitive learning modules, and partake in web-based gatherings, breaking the actual limits of the homeroom (Hamal et al., 2022). The main jump maybe accompanied the approach of versatile innovation. Cell phones and tablets took into account whenever, anyplace learning. Education applications made learning really captivating and customized, taking care of individual learning styles and speeds. This period additionally saw the ascent of Gigantic Open Web-based Courses (MOOCs), democratizing admittance to instruction from lofty organizations all over the planet (Walden, 2021).

As of late, the rise of Man-made brainpower (man-made intelligence) and AI in schooling has begun to customize growth opportunities at a phenomenal scale. Artificial intelligence driven stages can adjust to individual understudy's learning designs, offering custom-made assets and backing. In addition, Computer generated Reality (VR) and Expanded Reality (AR) have started to make vivid growth opportunities, making complex subjects like science and history seriously captivating and available (Hamal et al., 2022). Every one of these mechanical jumps has essentially influenced educating and learning techniques. From the beginning of fundamental PC proficiency to the ongoing period of computer based intelligence and VR, innovation has consistently extended the skylines of what's conceivable in training. Instructors are as of now not simple disseminators of information however facilitators of a rich, intelligent, and customized growth opportunity. As we plan ahead, the direction of education innovation focuses towards an undeniably incorporated, vivid, and customized learning climate. The persistent development of innovation in schooling holds the commitment of defeating conventional obstructions, empowering a more comprehensive, successful, and connecting with opportunity for growth for understudies around the world. The excursion from blackboards to VR headsets embodies an adjustment of devices, yet a key change by they way we approach educating and learning in the cutting edge age (Archer, 2023).

The job of innovation in schooling has advanced from simply enhancing conventional training strategies to turning into a vital piece of the education biological system. The mid-2000s denoted the presentation of intelligent e-learning stages, which considered mixed learning models that consolidated on the web and in-person guidance. These stages offered a scope of functionalities, from following understudy progress to working with online conversations, in this way improving the education experience past the actual study hall (Pea et al., 2022). With the coordination of distributed computing in the training area, understudies and teachers accessed a huge range of assets and devices. Cloud-based applications and capacity arrangements worked with consistent cooperation and sharing of data. This innovation separated geological hindrances as well as considered more viable administration of education assets, prompting a more coordinated and open learning climate. As of late, versatile learning innovation has turned into a point of convergence. This innovation utilizes calculations to examine understudies' learning examples and designer the education substance in like manner, consequently tending to assorted advancing requirements and speed. This degree of personalization was beforehand unreachable and has been critical in supporting individualized learning pathways. The expansion of information examination in training has additionally been groundbreaking. By examining information on understudy execution, teachers can recognize learning holes and mediate early. This approach has prompted more information driven dynamic in schooling, guaranteeing that techniques and mediations are proof based and designated ("2020 fifth Worldwide STEM Training Meeting, ISTEM-Ed 2020," 2020).

Moreover, the mix of web-based entertainment in schooling has carried another aspect to understudy commitment and cooperation. Stages like education web journals, discussions, and interpersonal interaction locales have cultivated a feeling of local area among students, empowering joint effort and shared learning. They likewise give stages to teachers to share assets, examine education procedures, and interface with a more extensive education local area. As we dig further into the 21st 100 years, arising advances like the Web of Things (IoT) and blockchain are starting to track down applications in training. IoT can possibly additionally improve intuitive learning conditions and make brilliant education spaces, while blockchain innovation vows to offer better approaches to deal with understudy records and accreditations safely and proficiently (Luttrell et al., 2020).

Thusly, the development of education innovation is a demonstration of the consistent quest for more powerful, captivating, and comprehensive ways of working with learning. From the early PCs to the refined computer based intelligence and IoT of today, each innovative headway has added to a more unique, intuitive, and customized education scene. As innovation keeps on developing, it vows to additionally change the manner in which we instruct and pick up, separating down hindrances and opening additional opportunities for teachers and understudies the same.

2. INTERACTIVE AND IMMERSIVE LEARNING ENVIRONMENTS: THE RISE OF VIRTUAL AND AUGMENTED REALITY IN EDUCATION

The coordination of Computer generated Reality (VR) and Expanded Reality (AR) into education settings denotes a huge jump in how opportunities for growth are conveyed and seen. These advances have upset the idea of intelligent and vivid picking up, offering understudies and teachers unmatched chances to investigate and grasp complex ideas in a dynamic and connecting with way (Fütterer et al., 2023; Hassan and Hossain, 2022). VR in training has been instrumental in establishing totally vivid conditions. This innovation transports students to virtual universes, where they can encounter everything from authentic occasions to logical peculiarities direct. For example, in showing history, VR can reproduce verifiable locales or occasions, permitting understudies to 'stroll through' antiquated civilizations or witness huge authentic minutes. This upgrades commitment as well as helps in better getting it and maintenance of data. Likewise, AR adds a layer of computerized data to this present reality, making learning more intelligent. It has been especially powerful in subjects like science and medication. For instance, AR applications permit understudies to see and interface with 3D models of the human body, giving a more profound comprehension of life structures and normalphysical processes. In geology, AR can rejuvenate maps and actual scenes, giving a substantial feeling of spot and geography (Hassan and Hossain, 2022).

One outstanding execution of VR in training is the 'Google Endeavors' program, which empowers understudies to leave on virtual field trips across the globe. This program gives admittance to more than 1,000 augmented simulation visits, permitting understudies to investigate everything from the outer layer of Mars to the profundities of the sea. Another model is the utilization of VR in professional preparation; for example, clinical understudies involving VR reenactments to rehearse medical procedures in a controlled, sans risk climate. As far as AR, applications like 'Components 4D' offer an inventive method for finding out about science. By interfacing with AR-empowered blocks, understudies can imagine and comprehend how various components respond with one another. Additionally, 'Aurasma', an AR stage, permits instructors to make intuitive media content, making learning materials like banners and books wake up with recordings and activitys. The upsides of VR and AR in training stretch out past commitment. They offer safe conditions for trial and error and investigation, oblige different learning styles, and give quick, vivid input. These advances additionally assist in growing delicate abilities with enjoying compassion and worldwide mindfulness by giving encounters that are generally unrealistic in a conventional study hall setting.

As the innovation turns out to be more available and reasonable, it's normal that VR and AR will turn out to be more predominant in homerooms all over the planet. They not just imply a change in the devices utilized for training yet additionally address a principal change in the manner education substance is conceptualized and conveyed. The vivid idea of VR and AR vows to make learning a more experiential, intuitive, and effective excursion, getting ready understudies scholastically as well as for a quickly developing computerized world. The capability of VR and AR in schooling goes past conventional subjects, wandering into the domain of ability improvement and conduct preparing. For example, VR recreations are being utilized for delicate ability preparing in regions like public talking, administration, and collaboration. These recreations give a protected and controlled climate for students to rehearse and foster these abilities, getting constant criticism and the chance to repeat their exhibitions (Prinsloo et al., 2023).

Besides, the utilization of these innovations in a custom curriculum presents a promising boondocks. VR and AR can be customized to suit the special advancing necessities of understudies with inabilities. For instance, VR encounters can be intended to assist understudies with chemical imbalance practice interactive abilities and explore genuine situations in a controlled setting. Also, AR can help understudies with dyslexia by overlaying text with supportive illustrations or utilizing variety overlays to make perusing simpler and really captivating. In the domain of ecological training, VR has the exceptional capacity to bring far off or out of reach regular habitats into the study hall. This can cultivate a more profound comprehension and enthusiasm for natural issues. Understudies can basically visit softening glacial masses or witness deforestation, which can be strong in molding their viewpoints on worldwide natural difficulties (Sirait et al., 2023). The coordination of these advances is likewise reshaping educator preparing and proficient turn of events. Instructors can utilize VR and AR to encounter homeroom situations, investigate different showing approaches, and get preparing in study hall the executives. This upgrades their showing capacities as well as sets them up to coordinate these advances into their showing practice successfully.

The cooperative part of VR and AR can't be neglected. These advancements empower cooperative undertakings and tests among understudies, in any event, when they are topographically scattered. This viewpoint encourages a worldwide learning local area, separating topographical and social obstructions and advancing diverse comprehension and joint effort. VR and AR in training are not just about mechanical development; they address a change in outlook in the education experience. By offering really captivating, comprehensive, and different learning open doors, these innovations are ready to alter instruction, making it more pertinent, significant, and lined up with the necessities of the 21st 100 years.

3. ARTIFICIAL INTELLIGENCE IN EDUCATION: RESHAPING LEARNING AND ADMINISTRATION

The joining of Man-made brainpower (artificial intelligence) into the educational area denotes a huge development in how educational contents is conveyed and made due. Artificial intelligence's most conspicuous job in training is in customizing opportunities for growth. Through versatile learning innovations, simulated intelligence frameworks can dissect an understudy's presentation, learning speed, and inclinations to likewise tailor education substance. This approach takes special care of individual learning styles as well as distinguishes regions where understudies battle, offering designated help and assets. An illustration of this is the simulated intelligence based learning stage 'DreamBox', which adjusts math examples continuously, offering understudies an exceptionally customized opportunity for growth (Lian et al., 2024). In the domain of authoritative assignments, computer based intelligence has been instrumental in smoothing out and mechanizing processes that are generally tedious. From reviewing tasks to overseeing understudy records, computer based intelligence frameworks can deal with dull errands, opening up instructors to zero in more on educating and understudy cooperation. Simulated intelligence driven information examination apparatuses additionally help education foundations in dynamic cycles by giving experiences into understudy execution patterns, asset usage, and educational program viability.

Intelligent Tutoring Systems (ITS) address one more huge use of artificial intelligence in training. These frameworks reproduce one-on-one communication between an understudy and a coach, offering customized input and direction. They can adjust to the understudy's expectation to learn and adapt, giving clarifications, hints, or extra difficulties on a case by case basis. For example, Carnegie Learning's 'MATHia' utilizes computer based intelligence to give a customized numerical opportunity for growth, offering constant input and bit by bit direction (Rahman et al., 2022). Notwithstanding, the combination of man-made intelligence in training additionally delivers moral contemplations. One main issue is information protection and security. The tremendous measure of understudy information gathered by computer based intelligence frameworks brings up issues about how this information is utilized and secured. Moreover, there's a gamble of algorithmic predisposition where simulated intelligence frameworks could support existing biases because of one-sided informational indexes. It's pivotal that education simulated intelligence frameworks are planned considering decency and inclusivity (Zhang et al., 2023).

Another worry is the possible effect on the educator understudy dynamic. While computer based intelligence can upgrade the growth opportunity, it can't supplant the compassion, moral direction, and inspirational help that human educators give. It's essential to find an equilibrium where computer based intelligence enhancements and supports instructing without decreasing the job and worth of educators (Latham and Goltz, 2019). Besides, there's a gamble of over-dependence on innovation. While simulated intelligence offers mind blowing benefits, understudies should likewise foster the capacity to advance autonomously and fundamentally, without continuously depending on artificial intelligence directed processes. Creating decisive reasoning and critical thinking abilities is fundamental in planning understudies for a reality where artificial intelligence is predominant yet not transcendent. In outline, the job of simulated intelligence in training is diverse, offering critical advantages in customizing picking up, smoothing out regulatory assignments, and giving smart mentoring. Notwithstanding, it additionally requires cautious thought of moral ramifications and its effect on conventional education elements. The critical lies in tackling computer based intelligence's true capacity while keeping a human-driven way to deal with training, guaranteeing that the mechanical headways effectively improve, as opposed to supplant, the crucial components of educating and learning (Nemoto and Fujimoto, 2023).

The impact of simulated intelligence in training stretches out into the domain of educational program advancement and content creation. Man-made intelligence calculations are fit for investigating tremendous measures of education substance to distinguish holes and recommend enhancements, prompting more extensive and exceptional educational plans. For instance, artificial intelligence frameworks can follow arising patterns and progressions in different fields, guaranteeing that education materials stay important and reflect current information. Also, artificial intelligence can possibly reform language learning. With normal language handling abilities, artificial intelligence fueled stages can offer customized language opportunities for growth, giving continuous input on elocution, syntax, and jargon. This innovation takes into consideration a more intelligent and vivid language growing experience, intently impersonating normal language obtaining strategies. With regards to a custom curriculum, simulated intelligence offers promising chances to take care of different advancing necessities. Computer based intelligence driven devices can be intended to adjust to different learning incapacities, offering altered help and learning helps. This can fundamentally upgrade the growth opportunity for understudies with exceptional requirements, offering them a degree of individual consideration that may be trying to accomplish in customary study hall settings.

The joining of computer based intelligence in education exploration gives important bits of knowledge into growing experiences and results. By investigating huge datasets on understudy learning examples and ways of behaving, artificial intelligence can assist specialists with recognizing compelling showing procedures, learning conditions, and education intercessions. This exploration can illuminate strategy making and education works on, prompting more proof based choices in the schooling area (Hou et al., 2023). As computer based intelligence keeps on advancing, teachers and understudies actually should become artificial intelligence proficient. Grasping the nuts and bolts of computer based intelligence, its applications, and suggestions is turning out to be progressively significant. Education foundations play a part to play in getting ready the two teachers and understudies for a future where man-made intelligence is necessary to numerous parts of life and work. Generally, computer based intelligence's combination into instruction isn't just about improving the productivity and adequacy of learning and authoritative assignments; it's tied in with rethinking and enhancing the education scene. This mechanical headway presents a chance to reclassify education standards, making learning more versatile, comprehensive, and lined up with the quickly advancing computerized world (Liu, 2023).

In the realm of educational technology, adaptive technologies and Universal Design for Learning (UDL) principles are pivotal in creating inclusive environments that cater to diverse learning needs, including those of students with disabilities. Key adaptive technologies include screen readers like JAWS and NVDA, which convert on-screen text to speech or braille for visually impaired learners, and speech recognition software such as Dragon Naturally Speaking, which assists students with physical impairments by transforming spoken words into written text. Educational platforms increasingly incorporate these tools, adapting content dynamically to suit individual learner needs, exemplified by software like Kurzweil 3000 that integrates text-to-speech and note-taking functionalities. Institutions like Harvard University and organizations like CAST have effectively integrated UDL principles into their courses and tools, offering materials in multiple formats and flexible assessment methods to ensure all students have equal access to educational opportunities. These implementations highlight the transformative potential of technology in making education more accessible and inclusive.

4. THE IMPACT OF BIG DATA AND LEARNING ANALYTICS IN EDUCATION

The joining of huge information and learning examination in the education area has achieved groundbreaking changes in how understudy execution is followed and it are custom-made to learn encounters. Huge information alludes to the enormous volumes of information created by advanced connections in education settings, while learning examination uses this information to assess and upgrade learning and educating. One of the essential ways huge information influences instruction is through the following of understudy execution. By dissecting information from different sources, for example, online tests, tasks, and intuitive learning instruments, teachers can acquire bits of knowledge into an understudy's comprehension, commitment levels, and progress. This data helps in recognizing understudies who could require extra help, considering convenient mediation. Moreover, learning examination can foresee learning results by recognizing examples and patterns in understudy information. For example, by investigating past exhibitions, teachers can anticipate which understudies are in danger of failing to meet expectations or exiting, and can proactively offer the vital help to further develop their learning results (L. Wang et al., 2022).

One more huge perspective is the personalization of education substance. Learning investigation empowers the production of a more tweaked growth opportunity by recommending assets, exercises, and learning ways in view of individual understudy needs and inclinations. For instance, versatile learning stages use calculations to adjust the trouble level of undertakings in light of understudy execution, guaranteeing that every understudy is tested fittingly. Be that as it may, the utilization of huge information in schooling achieves a few difficulties, especially concerning information security and the moral utilization of understudy data. The assortment and examination of understudy information raise worries about who approaches this data and the way things are utilized. A gamble of touchy understudy information is being uncovered or abused, which can have serious ramifications for understudies' protection and security. In addition, moral contemplations become possibly the most important factor while using this information to go with choices that influence understudies' education directions. There is a gamble of predisposition in information examination, where calculations might sustain existing disparities or biases. It's essential to guarantee that information driven choices are fair, straightforward, and unjustifiably weakness no gathering of understudies (Dutta, 2024). Moreover, the dependence on information investigation should be offset with human judgment. While information can give significant experiences, it is basic to recollect that instruction is a complicated field impacted by various variables that may not be very much quantifiable. Instructors should utilize the experiences from information investigation as a device to supplement, not supplant, their expert judgment and comprehension of their understudies (Barakina et al., 2021).

The enormous information and learning investigation can possibly altogether improve the education experience by giving bits of knowledge into understudy execution, anticipating learning results, and customizing learning. Nonetheless, this should be offset with careful regard for information protection and moral contemplations to guarantee that the utilization of understudy information is capable, secure, and fair, consequently supporting a more educated and compelling education cycle. Past these essential applications, large information and learning examination are likewise reshaping more extensive education systems and strategy making. Education establishments can use total information to assess the adequacy of showing strategies, educational programs, and in general education projects. This degree of investigation can uncover patterns and connections that probably won't be noticeable at the singular understudy level, consequently illuminating vital choices and asset assignment (Androutsopoulou et al., 2019).

Besides, learning examination can assume an essential part in the expert improvement of teachers. By giving nitty gritty experiences into understudy learning examples and results, these devices can assist instructors with recognizing regions where they could have to change their showing draws near or gain new educational abilities. This cultivates a culture of nonstop improvement and flexibility among instructors. One more developing area of utilization is in the domain of cooperative learning. Huge information can be utilized to examine how understudies cooperate in gatherings, giving experiences into the elements of joint effort and friend learning. This data can be important in planning bunch projects and cooperative learning exercises that are more viable and comprehensive. In any case, the headway in learning examination should be resembled by a progression in moral rules and protection regulations. Education organizations should lay out hearty approaches and practices to defend understudy information, guaranteeing consistence with lawful principles and moral standards. This incorporates straightforward information assortment and utilization arrangements, secure information stockpiling and taking care of practices, and measures to guarantee that understudies and guardians are educated and have command over their information (Westerlund, 2019). Moreover, there is a requirement for a nuanced comprehension of the impediments of enormous information in schooling. Information can give significant bits of knowledge yet can't catch the full intricacy of the growing experience. Factors, for example, profound, mental, and social parts of learning assume a basic part and frequently require subjective examination and human translation. Basically, while large information and learning investigation offer amazing assets for upgrading training, they should be utilized nicely and capably. Adjusting the advantages of information driven bits of knowledge with the significance of protection, moral contemplations, and the human component of training is critical to utilizing these innovations in a manner that genuinely helps understudies and teachers the same(Larchenko & Barynikova, 2021).

5. THE ROLE OF SOCIAL MEDIA AND ONLINE COLLABORATION TOOLS IN EDUCATION

The coming of virtual entertainment and online cooperation devices has introduced another period in training, described by upgraded network and cooperative learning potential open doors. These advanced stages have fundamentally extended the limits of customary study halls, working with distributed learning and worldwide associations that were once unbelievable. Online entertainment stages like Twitter, Facebook, and LinkedIn have become instrumental in making scholarly networks where understudies and teachers share assets, thoughts, and encounters. These stages empower students to interface with friends and specialists around the world, encouraging a worldwide trade of information and points of view. For example, Twitter's utilization of hashtags permits understudies to follow and partake in worldwide conversations on significant points, making learning a more powerful and associated insight (Ly et al., 2023).

Online joint effort instruments like Google Homeroom, Microsoft Groups, and Slack have changed how gathering projects and cooperative learning exercises are directed. These devices give a common space where understudies can cooperate progressively, independent of their actual areas. They offer functionalities like archive sharing, constant altering, video conferencing, and project the board highlights, which smooth out cooperation and make it more productive. They support decisive reasoning and computerized education, abilities that are progressively significant in the present advanced age (H. Wang et al., 2022). In any case, coordinating web-based entertainment and online cooperation apparatuses into formal schooling additionally presents a few difficulties. One of the essential worries is guaranteeing advanced value. Not all understudies have equivalent admittance to gadgets and solid web associations, which can set out variations in learning open doors. Instructors should consider these elements to abstain from compounding existing disparities.

Another test is overseeing interruptions and guaranteeing useful utilization of these stages. The casual idea of virtual entertainment can some of the time lead to off-point conversations and interruptions. Instructors need to lay out clear rules and assumptions to guarantee that these apparatuses are utilized actually for education purposes. Information protection and online wellbeing are extra worries. Instructors and establishments should be cautious about safeguarding understudy information and it are secure and proper to guarantee that web-based collaborations. This incorporates monitoring the information strategies of various stages and teaching understudies about capable computerized citizenship. Moreover, coordinating these devices into training requires a change in conventional educating strategies. Instructors should adjust their helping techniques to use these innovations successfully. This could include proficient turn of events and preparing to furnish educators with the vital abilities and information (Beerbaum and Puaschunder, 2019). Virtual entertainment and online cooperation instruments offer energizing open doors for upgrading instruction through shared learning and worldwide homeroom associations. They can possibly make learning seriously captivating, comprehensive, and associated. This degree of personalization encourages a more profound commitment with the topic and obliges different advancing requirements.

Furthermore, these instruments advance a more intelligent and experiential type of learning. For example, virtual review bunches on stages like Zoom or Microsoft Groups can mimic face to face concentrate on meetings, empowering understudies to team up, share bits of knowledge, and tackle issues by and large. This improves comprehension of the topic as well as creates cooperation and relational abilities (Shen et al., 2020). The utilization of these advances additionally adjusts well to project-based learning (PBL) approaches. Understudies dealing with activities can utilize joint effort instruments for arranging, investigating, and executing their ventures. They can likewise utilize web-based entertainment to interface with specialists, accumulate input, and even grandstand their work to a more extensive crowd, adding a certifiable aspect to their opportunity for growth.

Nonetheless, the powerful joining of these devices into education practices requires advanced proficiency abilities, both for teachers and understudies. Educators should be proficient at utilizing these apparatuses and coordinating them into their showing systems, while additionally directing understudies in the mindful and viable utilization of advanced stages. This incorporates figuring out the subtleties of computerized correspondence, overseeing advanced personalities, and exploring the huge range of data accessible on the web (Dua et al., 2023). The topic of surveying understudy execution in a computerized learning climate is another test. Customary evaluation techniques may not completely catch the profundity and expansiveness of discovering that happens through web-based entertainment and online cooperation. Elective appraisal methodologies, for example, portfolios, project work, and companion surveys, might be more reasonable for assessing understudy learning in these unique situations. Taking into account the quick development of advanced innovations, schooling systems actually must stay versatile and ground breaking. Staying up to date with the most recent turns of events, exploring different avenues regarding new devices, and persistently refining computerized teaching methods are fundamental stages in guaranteeing that training stays pertinent and viable in an advanced age (Mesko, 2023).

6. E-LEARNING PLATFORMS AND MOOCS: RESHAPING AND DEMOCRATIZING EDUCATION

The coming of e-learning stages and Monstrous Open Internet based Courses (MOOCs) has fundamentally adjusted the scene of instruction, provoking customary models and widening admittance to learning. These computerized stages have changed how information is scattered as well as who can get to it, separating geological, monetary, and social obstructions to training. E-learning stages, offering a wide cluster of online courses, have become progressively well known for their adaptability and comfort. Stages like Coursera, Udemy, and Khan Institute give courses going from scholastic subjects to expertise based preparing, taking special care of assorted advancing necessities. These stages are portrayed by their utilization of sight and sound substance, intuitive tasks, and gatherings for conversation, making learning seriously captivating and open. They empower students to learn at their own speed, now and again that suit them, which is especially advantageous for grown-up students who may be offsetting training with work or family responsibilities (Vidhya et al., 2022). MOOCs address a further extension of online instruction. Stages like edX and FutureLearn offer courses created by colleges and education foundations all over the planet. MOOCs are regularly allowed to get to, however there might be a charge for confirmation. They are intended to oblige enormous quantities of members, making excellent instruction open to anybody with a web association. The courses frequently incorporate video addresses, readings, tests, and distributed collaborations, giving a rich opportunity for growth (Al-Adwan, 2020). There is likewise the test of guaranteeing quality in web-based training, as the multiplication of courses and suppliers makes quality control more troublesome (Mathieson et al., 2017). Another issue is the advanced separation. While e-learning stages and MOOCs increment admittance to instruction, they actually require solid web access and computerized proficiency abilities, which are not all around accessible.

This can compound existing disparities, restricting the capability of these stages to completely democratize schooling.

Nonetheless, understanding their maximum capacity requires tending to difficulties like quality affirmation, the computerized partition, student commitment, and the joining of web based learning into customary schooling systems. By tending to these difficulties, e-learning stages and MOOCs can keep on assuming a critical part in molding the fate of training, making it more open, adaptable, and lined up with the necessities of students in a quickly impacting world (Vidhya et al., 2022). Expanding on the groundbreaking effect of e-learning stages and MOOCs, their impact stretches out to the expert turn of events and corporate preparation areas. These stages have become significant assets for upskilling and reskilling, tending to the developing requirements of the labor force. They permit experts to keep up to date with industry patterns and mechanical progressions, in this manner keeping up with their strategic advantage in the gig market. For example, stages like LinkedIn Learning and Coursera offer specific courses in regions like information science, advanced advertising, and task the executives, which are straightforwardly lined up with current industry requests. In the scholastic domain, the coordination of MOOCs and web based learning stages into conventional degree programs is progressively normal. Numerous colleges presently offer mixed learning choices, joining on the web and in-person guidance, or integrate MOOC content into their educational programs. This approach improves the growth opportunity, offering understudies a more extensive scope of subjects and learning modalities (Mathieson et al., 2017). Moreover, the information created by these stages offers significant experiences into learning ways of behaving and inclinations. Education organizations and course makers can break down this information to further develop course configuration, content conveyance, and student commitment procedures. This information driven way to deal with course improvement and refinement upgrades the general quality and adequacy of online training (K Ravishankar, B Jeyaprabha, 2018).

7. THE GAMIFICATION OF EDUCATION: ENHANCING MOTIVATION AND ENGAGEMENT THROUGH GAME-BASED LEARNING

The gamification of schooling alludes to the use of game-plan components and standards in non-game settings, like learning conditions. This approach has gotten momentum as of late, as instructors look for inventive ways of upgrading understudy inspiration and commitment. At its center, gamification includes integrating components like focuses, levels, difficulties, and prizes into the growing experience. These components tap into the characteristic inspirations of students, making training really captivating and charming. By transforming learning into a more game-like insight, understudies frequently end up additional put resources into the results of their education exercises. One successful illustration of gamification in training is the utilization of identification frameworks. Stages like Khan Institute use identifications to perceive and remunerate understudies for their accomplishments and progress. These identifications act as unmistakable markers of achievement, rousing understudies to keep progressing through course materials (Ali et al., 2021). Another model is Classcraft, an education apparatus that changes study hall elements by gamifying conduct and learning. In Classcraft, understudies make characters, procure focuses for positive ways of behaving and scholastic accomplishments, and work in groups to accomplish aggregate objectives. This approach improves commitment as well as cultivates a cooperative learning climate.

Duolingo, a language learning application, is a perfect representation of gamification in real life. The application utilizes a focuses framework, streaks, and in-application prizes to empower predictable practice. Students progress through levels, opening new difficulties as they advance. This construction keeps students roused and makes the course of language learning more intelligent and fulfilling. Minecraft Schooling Release is one more imaginative use of gamification. This game-based learning stage permits understudies to fabricate and investigate virtual universes, drawing in them in a large number of education exercises, from history and science to coding and math. The intelligent idea of Minecraft empowers imaginative critical thinking and cooperative learning (Ratnakaram et al., 2021). Be that as it may, the execution of gamification in training isn't without its difficulties. One concern is the gamble of overemphasis on outward rewards, for example, focuses and identifications, which could subvert characteristic inspiration. It's fundamental that gamification methodologies are painstakingly adjusted and coordinated into education substance such that upgrades, as opposed to reduces, the learning targets.

One more test lies in guaranteeing that gamification requests to a different scope of understudies. Not all understudies answer similarly to game-like components, and some might find serious perspectives demotivating. Subsequently, it's critical to plan gamified growth opportunities that are comprehensive and deal various ways to progress. Besides, the adequacy of gamification relies upon its arrangement with education objectives. Gamified components ought to be insightfully incorporated to support and supplement the learning targets, not divert from them. For example, a science application that utilizes gamified tests necessities to guarantee that the difficulties and rewards straightforwardly connect with the dominance of numerical ideas. The gamification of instruction addresses an interesting and imaginative way to deal with improving understudy inspiration and commitment. By integrating game plan components into learning exercises, teachers can make more unique, intuitive, and pleasant education encounters. Fruitful models like Khan Institute, Classcraft,

Duolingo, and Minecraft: Schooling Release exhibit the capability of gamification to change learning. Notwithstanding, it's essential to move toward gamification nicely, guaranteeing that it upholds education goals and takes care of the different necessities of students. With cautious execution, gamification can possibly altogether improve the education scene (Olson and Artist, 2018).

8. MOBILE LEARNING AND PORTABLE TECHNOLOGY: REVOLUTIONIZING EDUCATION

The coming of cell phones and tablets has essentially reshaped the education scene, presenting another time of portable learning. These versatile gadgets have become amazing assets in the possession of students, working with admittance to education substance whenever and anyplace. This shift towards versatile learning addresses a key change in how schooling can be conveyed and experienced (Pegrum, 2019). Cell phones and tablets, with their great many functionalities and network choices, have transformed into basic education apparatuses. They give quick admittance to a huge swath of assets including digital books, education applications, recordings, and intelligent learning stages. The simplicity of getting to data through these gadgets takes care of the advanced student's inclination for speedy, on-request information, lining up with the quick moving, computerized driven world they occupy (Nikolopoulou et al., 2021). One of the vital benefits of versatile learning is its adaptability. Students are not generally bound to the actual homeroom or fixed plans. With cell phones, they can draw in with education substance during, in the middle between undertakings, or from the solace of their homes. This adaptability is especially helpful for grown-up students who may be shuffling schooling with work or family responsibilities. Portable innovation additionally upholds customized opportunities for growth. Education applications and stages frequently offer adaptable learning ways, permitting students to zero in on areas of interest or where they need more practice. This customized approach, worked with by the flexibility of versatile innovation, takes special care of individual learning styles and speeds, making schooling more compelling and drawing in (Almaiah and Alismaiel, 2019).

In addition, portable learning empowers dynamic and participatory learning. With highlights like intuitive tests, conversation gatherings, and cooperative tasks, students are not simply latent beneficiaries of data. All things being equal, they are dynamic members, drawing in with the material, their companions, and teachers in a more powerful way. The reconciliation of versatile innovation in training has suggestions for conventional homeroom settings. It supports the reception of mixed learning models, where customary up close and personal instructing is joined with on the web and versatile learning (Pegrum, 2019). This half and half methodology improves the opportunity for growth, giving understudies a blend of direct guidance and independent, innovation empowered learning (Mugo et al., 2017). Be that as it may, the ascent of portable advancing additionally presents difficulties. One huge concern is the computerized partition. Not all understudies have equivalent admittance to cell phones and solid web associations, which can prompt variations in learning open doors. Addressing this separation is urgent to guarantee that versatile learning is an instrument for education value, not an obstruction.

Another test is keeping up with understudy commitment and concentration. The performing various tasks nature of cell phones can prompt interruptions, making it challenging for students to keep fixed on education undertakings. Teachers need to track down ways of keeping understudies connected with and guarantee that versatile learning supplements, instead of degrades, the general learning objectives. Besides, there is a requirement for education variation. Instructors should foster new systems and ways to deal with successfully integrate portable learning into their educating. This could include upgrading illustration plans, integrating versatile assets, and tracking down ways of utilizing the one of a kind capacities of these gadgets to improve learning (Onaolapo and Oyewole, 2018). The ascent of cell phones and tablets as learning devices has opened up new skylines in training. Portable learning offers adaptability, personalization, and dynamic investment, adjusting great to contemporary advancing requirements. In any case, its effective combination into education settings requires tending to difficulties like the computerized partition, understudy commitment, and educational variation. With insightful execution, versatile learning can possibly altogether advance and differentiate the education experience, making learning more available, drawing in, and lined up with the computerized age. The extension of versatile learning and convenient innovation in schooling likewise stretches out to the domain of experiential and logical learning. With advances like expanded reality (AR) and augmented reality (VR) turning out to be more open on cell phones, students can take part in vivid encounters that were already unthinkable. For example, AR applications on cell phones can overlay data onto this present reality, empowering understudies to investigate verifiable locales, look at complex logical models, or picture numerical ideas in a more intuitive and substantial manner. This upgrades the opportunity for growth by giving a relevant and experiential aspect to training.

Furthermore, portable innovation plays a huge part in encouraging cooperative learning. Applications and stages that work with bunch work, distributed cooperations, and constant criticism are effectively open on cell phones. This empowers a more cooperative and social type of realizing, where understudies can without much of a stretch interface, share assets, and work on projects together, regardless of their actual areas (Sumak et al., 2010). The utilization of cell phones additionally upholds ceaseless evaluation and criticism. Teachers can use applications and devices that give ongoing appraisals, tests, and overviews, considering brief criticism and changes in the educational experience. This continuous appraisal model, worked with by portable innovation, helps in intently observing understudy progress and offering opportune help where required. As far as expert turn of events, portable learning offers teachers a helpful method for redesigning their abilities and remain refreshed with the most recent education patterns and innovations. Through proficient advancement applications and online courses, educators can get to preparing modules and assets in a hurry, upgrading their showing practices and coordinating new innovations into their homerooms (Lin et al., 2022). Nonetheless, incorporating versatile learning into schooling likewise requires an emphasis on computerized prosperity and mindful utilization. Teachers and guardians need to direct understudies on overseeing screen time, guaranteeing computerized security, and keeping a good overall arrangement among innovation and different parts of life. Fundamentally, versatile learning and compact innovation are not simply changing how education substance is gotten to; they are reshaping the whole education experience. By embracing these innovations and tending to the related difficulties, the education area can offer more unique, connecting with, and significant learning valuable open doors, planning understudies for a future where innovation and portability are basic to all parts of life.

9. THE DIGITAL DIVIDE AND EQUITY IN EDUCATION

The digital divide, the gap between those with easy access to digital technology and those without, significantly impacts educational equity. This divide is not just about access to devices but also includes the availability of reliable internet connections and digital literacy skills. The pandemic has particularly highlighted how this divide can exacerbate educational disparities, as many aspects of learning moved online (Saleem & Omar, 2015). The digital divide affects students in both urban and rural areas, though the challenges may differ. In urban settings, the issue might be more about affordability, while in rural areas, the lack of infrastructure can be a more significant barrier (Khurma et al., 2023). Students without adequate digital access are at a disadvantage, often missing out on learning opportunities, resources, and the ability to develop essential digital skills (Dakakni & Safa, 2023).

Strategies to Bridge the Digital Divide

1. Improving Infrastructure: Governments and communities need to invest in digital infrastructure, especially in underserved areas. This includes not only ensuring access to devices such as laptops and tablets but also providing reliable inter-

net access. Initiatives like community Wi-Fi hubs or subsidized home internet programs can play a crucial role.

2. Public-Private Partnerships: Collaboration between the public sector, private companies, and non-profits can be effective in providing technology access. Tech companies, for instance, can donate devices or offer educational software at discounted rates, while governments can provide funding and policy support.

3. Digital Literacy Programs: Access to technology should be accompanied by digital literacy training for students, educators, and parents. Understanding how to use technology effectively and responsibly is crucial. Schools and community centers can offer workshops or integrate digital literacy into the curriculum.

4. Flexible Learning Models: Recognizing that not all students have equal access to technology, educators should develop flexible learning models. This might include providing printed materials or phone-based learning options alongside digital content, ensuring that learning can continue even without internet access.

5. Support for Educators: Teachers need support and training to effectively integrate technology into their teaching and to manage hybrid learning environments where some students are online while others aren't. Professional development in digital tools and teaching strategies is essential.

6. Community Involvement: Engaging the community can help in identifying specific needs and solutions. Libraries, community centers, and local organizations can serve as access points for technology and educational resources.

7. Monitoring and Evaluation: Regular assessment of the effectiveness of initiatives aimed at bridging the digital divide is important. This helps in understanding the impact and in making necessary adjustments to strategies and programs.

8. Student-Centered Approaches: Solutions should focus on the specific needs of students. For instance, providing personalized learning devices might be more beneficial than shared computer labs in certain contexts.

9. Policy and Advocacy: Advocacy for policies that promote digital equity is vital. This includes lobbying for funding, changes in educational policies to support digital inclusion, and ensuring that the voices of underserved communities are heard.

10. Innovative Financing Models: Exploring innovative financing, such as grants, crowdfunding, or low-interest loans for technology access, can provide sustainable solutions to bridge the divide.

In conclusion, addressing the digital divide is crucial for ensuring educational equity. It requires a multi-faceted approach involving infrastructure improvement, public-private partnerships, digital literacy programs, and flexible learning models. By implementing these strategies, educational systems can work towards a more inclusive and equitable digital learning environment, where all students have the opportunity to succeed.

10. ADDRESSING DATA PRIVACY AND SECURITY CONCERNS IN EDUCATIONAL BIG DATA

The integration of big data in education brings significant risks, including data breaches and misuse of personal information, which could have severe implications for students' privacy and institutions' credibility. Educational data encompasses sensitive information that, if exposed, can lead to identity theft and other forms of personal exploitation. In response, it is crucial for educational institutions to implement stringent data security measures and comply with global privacy laws such as the General Data Protection Regulation (GDPR). Best practices in this area include employing robust encryption methods, ensuring that data access is restricted to authorized personnel only, and regularly auditing security protocols to identify and mitigate vulnerabilities. Additionally, institutions should foster a culture of data privacy among staff and students through comprehensive training and clear policies on data use and protection. By taking these steps, educational institutions can safeguard against the risks associated with big data, ensuring that the benefits of learning analytics do not come at the cost of compromising student privacy.

11. ROLE OF SOCIAL MEDIA AND ONLINE COLLABORATION TOOLS IN EDUCATION

The rapid evolution of technology necessitates continuous professional development (CPD) for educators to effectively integrate new tools into their teaching practices. Several programs and initiatives have been specifically designed to enhance educators' technological competencies. For instance, the International Society for Technology in Education (ISTE) offers comprehensive training and resources that prepare teachers to creatively and effectively use technology in the classroom. Google for Education's Certified Educator program is another example, where teachers learn to utilize Google tools to enhance student learning and engagement. Such programs not only provide practical skills but also promote innovative teaching strategies that align with current technological trends. Continuous professional development is critical, as it enables educators to remain current with technological advancements, ensuring that educational practices are modern, relevant, and engaging for students. By investing in professional development, educational institutions can foster a culture of lifelong learning among teachers, which is essential for adapting to the ever-changing landscape of educational technology.

CONCLUSION

The mix of new advancements in training is a perplexing cycle that requires smart strategy and regulatory changes. By tending to perspectives, for example, financing, foundation, proficient turn of events, educational program change, and information protection, education arrangements and organization can establish a climate helpful for the successful and evenhanded utilization of innovation. These transformations are fundamental to completely bridle the capability of education innovation and plan understudies for a future that is progressively computerized and interconnected. It is clear that the combination of new advances in training isn't simply a passing pattern yet a major change in the education worldview. From the development of education innovation to the commitment of computer based intelligence, the multiplication of e-learning stages, and the groundbreaking force of portable learning, these headways are reshaping the manner in which we educate and learn. The excursion through different features of education innovation has featured the enormous potential these apparatuses hold in upgrading understudy contribution and learning results. Advancements like VR and AR are making vivid growth opportunities, while enormous information and learning examination offer phenomenal experiences into education cycles. The coordination of virtual entertainment and online cooperation devices is encouraging a more associated and intuitive learning climate, and the gamification of instruction is reclassifying commitment and inspiration. Notwithstanding, this excursion likewise uncovers huge provokes that should be tended to. The computerized partition stays a basic boundary to fair schooling, and the requirement for compelling strategies and organization practices to help mechanical joining is vital. The eventual fate of instruction will require a reasonable methodology where innovation is utilized not as a substitution for conventional techniques, but rather as a supplement and improvement to them. Teachers assume a pivotal part in this scene. Their capacity to adjust, coordinate, and actually utilize these advances will be essential in understanding their true capacity. Proficient turn of events, a readiness to embrace change, and a promise to deep rooted learning are fundamental qualities for teachers in this computerized age. The union of new advances in training offers energizing prospects. It can possibly make learning more open, customized, and drawing in, and to get ready understudies for a future that is progressively dependent on computerized skills. As we explore this union, our attention ought to be on tackling these advances to improve instruction while staying watchful to the difficulties they present. Thusly, we can guarantee that the education encounters we give are important and compelling as well as fair and comprehensive, hence making ready for a more splendid and more interconnected future in training.

REFERENCES:

Al-Adwan, A. S. (2020). Investigating the drivers and barriers to MOOCs adoption: The perspective of TAM. *Education and Information Technologies*, 25(6), 5771–5795. DOI: 10.1007/s10639-020-10250-z

Ali, S., DiPaola, D., Lee, I., Sindato, V., Kim, G., Blumofe, R., & Breazeal, C. (2021). Children as creators, thinkers and citizens in an AI-driven future. *Computers and Education: Artificial Intelligence*, 2, 100040. Advance online publication. DOI: 10.1016/j.caeai.2021.100040

Almaiah, M. A., & Alismaiel, O. A. (2019). Examination of factors influencing the use of mobile learning system: An empirical study. *Education and Information Technologies*, 24(1), 885–909. DOI: 10.1007/s10639-018-9810-7

Androutsopoulou, A., Karacapilidis, N., Loukis, E., & Charalabidis, Y. (2019). Transforming the communication between citizens and government through AI-guided chatbots. *Government Information Quarterly*, 36(2), 358–367. DOI: 10.1016/j.giq.2018.10.001

Archer, E. (2023). Technology-driven proctoring: Validity, social justice and ethics in higher education. *Perspectives in Education*, 41(1), 119–136. DOI: 10.38140/pie.v41i1.6666

Barakina, E. Y., Popova, A. V., Gorokhova, S. S., & Voskovskaya, A. S. (2021). Digital Technologies and Artificial Intelligence Technologies in Education. *European Journal of Contemporary Education*, 10(2), 285–296. DOI: 10.13187/ejced.2021.2.285

Beerbaum, D., & Puaschunder, J. M. (2019). A behavioral economics approach to digitalization: The case of a principles-based taxonomy. In *Intergenerational Governance and Leadership in the Corporate World: Emerging Research and Opportunities* (pp. 107–122). IGI Global. DOI: 10.4018/978-1-5225-8003-4.ch006

Dakakni, D., & Safa, N. (2023). Artificial intelligence in the L2 classroom: Implications and challenges on ethics and equity in higher education: A 21st century Pandora's box. *Computers and Education: Artificial Intelligence*, 5, 100179. Advance online publication. DOI: 10.1016/j.caeai.2023.100179

Dakakni, D., & Safa, N. (2023). Artificial intelligence in the L2 classroom: Implications and challenges on ethics and equity in higher education: A 21st century Pandora's box. *Computers and Education: Artificial Intelligence*, 5, 100179. Advance online publication. DOI: 10.1016/j.caeai.2023.100179

Dua, V., Rajpal, A., Rajpal, S., Agarwal, M., & Kumar, N. (2023). I-FLASH: Interpretable Fake News Detector Using LIME and SHAP. *Wireless Personal Communications*, 131(4), 2841–2874. DOI: 10.1007/s11277-023-10582-2

Dutta, S. (2024). Framing the Landscape of Technological Enhancements: Artificial Intelligence, Gender Issues, and Ethical Dilemmas. In *Signals and Communication Technology: Vol. Part F1803* (pp. 109–123). Springer Science and Business Media Deutschland GmbH. DOI: 10.1007/978-3-031-45237-6_10

Fesakis, G., & Prantsoudi, S. (2021). Raising Artificial Intelligence Bias Awareness in Secondary Education: The Design of an Educational Intervention. In F. Matos, I. Salavisa, & C. Serrao (Eds.), *3rd European Conference on the Impact of Artificial Intelligence and Robotics, ECIAIR 2021* (pp. 35–42). Academic Conferences and Publishing International Limited. https://doi.org/DOI: 10.34190/EAIR.21.039

Fullan, M. (2013). Stratosphere: Integrating technology, pedagogy, and change knowledge. *The Alberta Journal of Educational Research*, 62(4), 429–432.

Fütterer, T., Fischer, C., Alekseeva, A., Chen, X., Tate, T., Warschauer, M., & Gerjets, P. (2023). ChatGPT in education: Global reactions to AI innovations. *Scientific Reports*, 13(1), 15310. Advance online publication. DOI: 10.1038/s41598-023-42227-6 PMID: 37714915

Granić, A., & Marangunić, N. (2019). Technology acceptance model in educational context: A systematic literature review. *British Journal of Educational Technology*, 50(5), 2572–2593. DOI: 10.1111/bjet.12864

Hamal, O., El Faddouli, N.-E., Alaoui Harouni, M. H., & Lu, J. (2022). Artificial Intelligent in Education. *Sustainability (Basel)*, 14(5), 2862. Advance online publication. DOI: 10.3390/su14052862

Hassan, M., & Hossain, M. A. (2022). A VR based children formula feed preparation training simulator with AI-enabled automated assessment features. *International Conference on Software, Knowledge Information, Industrial Management and Applications, SKIMA, 2022-December*, 303–308. DOI: 10.1109/SKIMA57145.2022.10029659

Hou, K. M., Diao, X., Shi, H., Ding, H., Zhou, H., & de Vaulx, C. (2023). Trends and Challenges in AIoT/IIoT/IoT Implementation. *Sensors (Basel)*, 23(11), 5074. Advance online publication. DOI: 10.3390/s23115074 PMID: 37299800

Khurma, O. A., Ali, N., & Hashem, R. (2023). Critical Reflections on ChatGPT in UAE Education Navigating Equity and Governance for Safe and Effective Use. *International Journal of Emerging Technologies in Learning*, 18(14), 188–199. DOI: 10.3991/ijet.v18i14.40935

Larchenko, V., & Barynikova, O. (2021). New technologies in education. In Rudoy, D., Olshevskaya, A., & Ugrekhelidze, N. (Eds.), *E3S Web of Conferences* (Vol. 273). EDP Sciences., DOI: 10.1051/e3sconf/202127312145

Latham, A., & Goltz, S. (2019). A survey of the general public's views on the ethics of using AI in education. In S. Isotani, E. Millán, A. Ogan, B. McLaren, P. Hastings, & R. Luckin (Eds.), *Lecture Notes in Computer Science (including subseries Lecture Notes in Artificial Intelligence and Lecture Notes in Bioinformatics): Vol. 11625 LNAI* (pp. 194–206). Springer Verlag. DOI: 10.1007/978-3-030-23204-7_17

Lian, Y., Tang, H., Xiang, M., & Dong, X. (2024). Public attitudes and sentiments toward ChatGPT in China: A text mining analysis based on social media. *Technology in Society*, 76, 102442. Advance online publication. DOI: 10.1016/j.techsoc.2023.102442

Lin, H.-C., Ho, C.-F., & Yang, H. (2022). Understanding adoption of artificial intelligence-enabled language e-learning system: An empirical study of UTAUT model. *International Journal of Mobile Learning and Organisation*, 16(1), 74–94. DOI: 10.1504/IJMLO.2022.119966

Liu, Y. (2023). The role of online technology in quality course design. In *The Impact and Importance of Instructional Design in the Educational Landscape* (pp. 178–206). IGI Global., DOI: 10.4018/978-1-6684-8208-7.ch007

Luttrell, R., Wallace, A., McCollough, C., & Lee, J. (2020). The Digital Divide: Addressing Artificial Intelligence in Communication Education. *Journalism and Mass Communication Educator*, 75(4), 470–482. DOI: 10.1177/1077695820925286

Ly, S., Reyes-Hadsall, S., Drake, L., Zhou, G., Nelson, C., Barbieri, J. S., & Mostaghimi, A. (2023). Public Perceptions, Factors, and Incentives Influencing Patient Willingness to Share Clinical Images for Artificial Intelligence-Based Healthcare Tools. *Dermatology and Therapy*, 13(11), 2895–2902. DOI: 10.1007/s13555-023-01031-w PMID: 37737327

Mathieson, K., Leafman, J. S., & Horton, M. B. (2017). Access to digital communication technology and perceptions of telemedicine for patient education among American Indian patients with diabetes. *Journal of Health Care for the Poor and Underserved*, 28(4), 1522–1536. DOI: 10.1353/hpu.2017.0131 PMID: 29176112

Mesko, B. (2023). The ChatGPT (Generative Artificial Intelligence) Revolution Has Made Artificial Intelligence Approachable for Medical Professionals. *Journal of Medical Internet Research*, 25, e48392. Advance online publication. DOI: 10.2196/48392 PMID: 37347508

Mugo, D. G., Njagi, K., Chemwei, B., & Motanya, J. O. (2017). *The technology acceptance model (TAM) and its application to the utilization of mobile learning technologies.*

Nemoto, T., & Fujimoto, T. (2023). A Classification and Analysis Focusing on Attempts to Give a Computer a Personality: A Technological History of Chatbots as Simple Artificial Intelligence. In T. Matsuo, T. Fujimoto, & L. G. F (Eds.), *Lecture Notes in Networks and Systems: Vol. 677 LNNS* (pp. 59–70). Springer Science and Business Media Deutschland GmbH. DOI: 10.1007/978-3-031-30769-0_6

Nikolopoulou, K., Gialamas, V., Lavidas, K., & Komis, V. (2021). Teachers' readiness to adopt mobile learning in classrooms: A study in Greece. *Technology. Knowledge and Learning*, 26(1), 53–77. DOI: 10.1007/s10758-020-09453-7

Olson, G., & Singer, R. (2018). Exploring Creative Frontiers of AI for ME Production and Distribution. *SMPTE*, 2018, 1–10. Advance online publication. DOI: 10.5594/M001817

Onaolapo, S., & Oyewole, O. (2018). Performance expectancy, effort expectancy, and facilitating conditions as factors influencing smart phones use for mobile learning by postgraduate students of the University of Ibadan, Nigeria. *Interdisciplinary Journal of E-Skills and Lifelong Learning*, 14(1), 95–115. DOI: 10.28945/4085

Pea, R. D., Biernacki, P., Bigman, M., Boles, K., Coelho, R., Docherty, V., Garcia, J., Lin, V., Nguyen, J., Pimentel, D., Pozos, R., Reynante, B., Roy, E., Southerton, E., Suzara, M., & Vishwanath, A. (2022). Four Surveillance Technologies Creating Challenges for Education. In *AI in Learning: Designing the Future* (pp. 317–329). Springer International Publishing. DOI: 10.1007/978-3-031-09687-7_19

Pegrum, M. (2019). Mobile AR Trails and Games for Authentic Language Learning. In Handbook of Mobile Teaching and Learning: Second Edition (pp. 1229–1244). Springer Nature. DOI: 10.1007/978-981-13-2766-7_89

Pegrum, M. (2019). Mobile AR Trails and Games for Authentic Language Learning. In *Handbook of Mobile Teaching and Learning* (2nd ed., pp. 1229–1244). Springer Nature., DOI: 10.1007/978-981-13-2766-7_89

Prinsloo, P., Slade, S., & Khalil, M. (2023). Multimodal learning analytics—In-between student privacy and encroachment: A systematic review. *British Journal of Educational Technology*, 54(6), 1566–1586. DOI: 10.1111/bjet.13373

Rahman, M. M., Rahaman, M. S., Moral, I. H., & Chowdhury, M. S. (2022). Entrepreneurship Education and Entrepreneurial Intention of Business Graduates: Does Artificial Intelligence Matter? In Hossain, S., Hossain, M. S., Kaiser, M. S., Majumder, S. P., & Ray, K. (Eds.), *Lecture Notes in Networks and Systems* (Vol. 437, pp. 109–123). Springer Science and Business Media Deutschland GmbH., DOI: 10.1007/978-981-19-2445-3_8

Ratnakaram, S., Chakravaram, V., Vihari, N. S., & Vidyasagar Rao, G. (2021). Emerging Trends in the Marketing of Financially Engineered Insurance Products. In Tuba, M., Akashe, S., & Joshi, A. (Eds.), *Advances in Intelligent Systems and Computing* (Vol. 1270, pp. 675–684). Springer Science and Business Media Deutschland GmbH., DOI: 10.1007/978-981-15-8289-9_65

Ravishankar, K., Jeyaprabha, B., Moideen Batcha, H., & Sagunthala, V. R. D. (2018). Intention and awareness on digital media and E-learning solutions among management students in education. *International Journal of Pure and Applied Mathematics*, 120(6), 8101–8114.

Saleem, S., & Omar, R. M. (2015). Measuring customer based beverage brand equity: Investigating the relationship between perceived quality, brand awareness, brand image, and brand loyalty.

Saleem, S., & Omar, R. M. (2015). *Measuring customer based beverage brand equity: Investigating the relationship between perceived quality, brand awareness, brand image, and brand loyalty.*

Sirait, T. H., Gamayanto, I., & Ramadhan, A. (2023). Blended Learning Technology during Disease Outbreak: A Systematic Literature Review. *2023 International Conference on Data Science and Its Applications, ICoDSA 2023*, 65–70. DOI: 10.1109/ICoDSA58501.2023.10276457

Sumak, B., Polancic, G., & Hericko, M. (2010). An Empirical Study of Virtual Learning Environment Adoption Using UTAUT. *2010 Second International Conference on Mobile, Hybrid, and On-Line Learning*, 17–22. DOI: 10.1109/eLmL.2010.11

Vidhya, R., Sandhia, G. K., Jansi, K. R., & Jeya, R. (2022). A predictive model emotion recognition on deep learning and shallow learning techniques using eeg signal. In *Principles and Applications of Socio-Cognitive and Affective Computing* (pp. 43–50). IGI Global., DOI: 10.4018/978-1-6684-3843-5.ch004

Walden, V. G. (2021). Digital holocaust memory, education and research. In *Digital Holocaust Memory, Education and Research*. Springer International Publishing., DOI: 10.1007/978-3-030-83496-8_1

Wang, H., Gupta, S., Singhal, A., Muttreja, P., Singh, S., Sharma, P., & Piterova, A. (2022). An Artificial Intelligence Chatbot for Young People's Sexual and Reproductive Health in India (SnehAI): Instrumental Case Study. *Journal of Medical Internet Research*, 24(1), e29969. Advance online publication. DOI: 10.2196/29969 PMID: 34982034

Wang, L., Zhang, X., Wang, Y., Wang, L., Wang, Q., Zang, X., Li, R., Xu, Y., Li, Z., & Chen, Q. (2022). Femtosecond Laser Direct Writing for Eternal Data Storage: Advances and Challenges. *Zhongguo Jiguang. Chinese Journal of Lasers*, 49(10). Advance online publication. DOI: 10.3788/CJL202249.1002504

Westerlund, M. (2019). The emergence of deepfake technology: A review. *Technology Innovation Management Review*, 9(11), 39–52. DOI: 10.22215/timreview/1282

Zhang, H., Lee, I. A., Moore, K. S., & Shah, S. A. (2023). Board 279: Ethics in Artificial Intelligence Education: Preparing Students to Become Responsible Consumers and Developers of AI. *ASEE Annual Conference and Exposition, Conference Proceedings*. https://www.scopus.com/inward/record.uri?eid=2-s2.0-85172111599&partnerID=40&md5=81fb62c6b3d6b7a9ac46405fa4ab6305

Zhang, X., Li, D., Wang, C., Jiang, Z., Ngao, A. I., Liu, D., Peters, M. A., & Tian, H. (2023). From ChatGPT to China' Sci-Tech: Implications for Chinese Higher Education. *Beijing International Review of Education*, 5(3), 296–314. DOI: 10.1163/25902539-05030007

Chapter 5
Blockchain—Enabled Edge Computing for Cognitive IoT

Kiran Malik

Department of Computer Science and Engineering (AIML), GL Bajaj Institute of Technology & Management, Greater Noida, India

Shashi Kant

https://orcid.org/0000-0003-4722-5736

College of Business and Economics, Blue Hora University, Ethiopia

Kuldeep Singh Kaswan

Galgotias University, India

Jagjit SIngh Dhatterwal

Koneru Lakshmaiah Education Foundation, Vaddeswaram, India

Arvind Panwar

School of Computer Science and Engineering, Galgotias University, Greater Noida, India

ABSTRACT

CIoT brings new options for the connections of things and the processing of data which has never been seen before. Although there are the availability and cost advantages, heterogeneous devices and networks create problems in terms of identity and security. These issues have raised new concerns on the implementation of different identity models due to the centralized nature of most of the identity services that accompany the implementation of the new models. Chapter four delves into how blockchain can be used to ensure secure communication of CIoT, using edge

DOI: 10.4018/979-8-3693-2157-7.ch005

computing as a thrust. The topics falling within the scope of this chapter include architecture and design, consensus algorithms, and smart contracts. It also introduces the edge computing starting from the fundamental concept and stressing on benefits over the cloud computing, and discuss how blockchain can improve data handling and security in edge networks. However, there are issues that are associated with the integration of the blockchain with the edge computing these include; scalability, latency, performance, and compatibility. Thus, this chapter will deliver the detailed comprehensive analysis of how the applied blockchain can meet the above-mentioned challenges to improve the CIoT systems' security and performance. It will also discuss scenarios of applying blockchain for solutions based on edge computing as the case studies. From this point of discussion, the chapter shall provide real-world prospects of blockchain application in the context of CIoT, which shall comprise of increased reliability and accuracy, as well as an increase in security and efficiency in the adoption of identity systems. Thus, it will also cover future development, advancements in technologies and possible research areas to overcome the existing issues and to harness the possibilities of blockchain technology in the envisage growth of CIoT security and features.

INTRODUCTION

The evolution of the various technologies has created immense advancements within IoT, with Cognitive IoT standing out as a major development. CIoT works as a new model that not only focuses on interconnectivity of IoT systems but also the ability to learn and think through the help of cognitive computing approaches. Indeed, it increases the capacity of IoT devices for intelligent data processing and analysis to make decisions independently, thus providing more intelligent IoT devices. Introducing cognitive functions, CIoT systems enhance performance, enhance decision-making and lay foundation for more enhanced applications throughout various domain more elaborately (Nakamoto, 2008).

Edge computing is then instrumental in IoT evolution since it solves some of the deficiencies associated with the cloud model. In an edge computing framework, the computing and the data analysis take place close to where the data is originated, thus, minimizing the delay and consumed bandwidth. It is Nam's work that such locations facilitate real-time decision-making and are effective in dealing with data generated from and needed for CIoT systems. It is therefore clear that edge computing is an essential component as it addresses the rising needs of IoT applications inclusive of smart cities and industrial automation needs through localized processing (Xu et al., 2019).

The use of edge computing with CIoT renders the following benefits; faster response time, efficient data transfer costs and more secure data. Many applications require quick reactions; CIoT systems can process the data at a network's edge, which allows for quicker results and actions. Moreover, edge computing does not require frequent transfer of information to central data centers—the clouds thereby reducing on chances of vices such as hacking while enhancing the owner's control over his/her data.

From the analysis, blockchain technology is identified as an enabler that can support and boost the characterizations of CIoT and edge computing. Since blockchain is a decentralized and distributed database, it is possible to enhancing the security of the endeavor as well as to increasing the efficiency of the recordation of transactions and the administration of data. Relative to blockchain's basic attributes, including its decentralization and consensus-driven paradigm, it provides effective approaches to addressing data reliability and CIoT systems' trustworthiness. Introducing blockchain, CIoT central systems will benefit from increased security, low probability of fraud and increased measurability in processes of data management (Zhang et al., 2020).

Therefore, the primary factor that defines the use of blockchain in CIoT and its applications goes beyond the aspect of security of data only. It allows distributed identity that allows each device and the user in the network to be authenticated and authorized securely. This capability is critical because it contributes to the protection of interactions within a CIoT ecosystem to ensure that devices and applications run seamlessly and without conflicts. Smart contracts of the Blockchain take this functionality a notch higher because they eliminate intermediaries and automatically and unconditionally execute rules and agreements between entities in the network (Dhatterwal et al., 2024).

When looking at IoT prospects, the integration of blockchain and edge computing aims to create a revolutionary approach to handling all IoT systems. Thus, blockchain effectively complements edge computing due to its decentralised structure; this further improves security and performance. For example, blockchain has the ability to offer secure and reliable data sharing at the edge to guarantee that the data handled and transmitted by Internet of Things gadgets is authentic and unaltered. This integration also enhances the ability of CIoT systems in terms of scalability by off-loading computational tasks and decreasing the centrality of developments.

This is particularly true in the area of data integrity and security which is boosted through the integration of blockchain with edge computing. Here, cryptography makes that data processed by the further tiers pseudo anonymous and cannot be altered, providing a reasonably high degree of credibility to the IoT system of edge devices. This is especially relevant in the CIoT applications for which data accuracy is paramount like in the fields of heath monitoring, or financial trading. Due to the features provided by the blockchain, CIoT systems are able to reach the more significant level of data security and credibility that can mitigate some of the fundamental issues related to the large-scale IoT implementations (Dhatterwal et al., 2023).

Also, blockchain may improve the management and processing of data related to edge computing by decentralizing them. This greatly differs from the current approach where all data is processed centralized by a specific server and every node must transfer specific information to this server for validation. This not only increases the extent of the entire system but also decreases the time delay involved in centralized processing. Thus, the response of CIoT systems can be enhanced to deliver the right information and actions in real-time, which is important for many IoT applications (Kaswan et al., 2024).

It would also be relevant to note that the combination of blockchain with edge computing has a way of solving most interoperability problems in CIoT systems. Thus, blockchain facilitates secure and rather efficient communication between multiple devices and systems through the establishment of a unified and clear structure for information sharing. This aspect of IoT development helps in defining integrated and consistent IoT networks that allow the devices of different manufacturers and vendors to communicate and work together. In this case, blockchain helps set a standard on how data and transactions would be shared and processed to avoid compatibility problems that hinder the interaction between two organizations.

However, there are issues that are characteristic of the use of blockchain and edge computing in CIoT systems. Organizational aspects like scalability, performance and compatibility require proper handling in order to check that the system of systems solution combines all the requisites of vasiot applications. The limitations of scalability stem from the issue of dealing with huge numbers of transactions and data at the edge level, while the concern of performance is the suitability of blockchain operations in real time. This shows that refuting these challenges needs constant research and development, to enhance the application of these technologies (Kaswan et al., 2023).

Fundamentals of Blockchain Technology

Blockchain is a distributed database that provides, transcribes, and stores exchange information through a peer-to-peer network in an intelligible, accurate, and unalterable manner. The fundamental idea of using blockchain is the ability to develop a digital record keeping system, where each entry is a block of information connected to other blocks in a chain. This architecture posits that every transaction that takes place is timestamped, and multiple individuals who make up the network concur with the same. The decentralized structure of blockchain obstructs the single point of control; this improves the reliability of numerous undertakings (Buterin, 2013).

The architecture of blockchain consists of several key components: the blocks, the chains nodes and the consensus. Each block consists of an array of transactions, a date and time and a link to the previous block; the blocks are connected one after another. A node can be referred to as an individual computer that actively takes part in the creating and verifying of the block chain and the transactions. The consensus mechanism is another part that enable the agreement of the nodes in relation to the validity of the transactions. Some of the popular consensus mechanisms include; Proof of Work (PoW) and Proof of Stake (PoS), which work differently concerning the ways in which they verify transactions in the network (Wood, 2014).

Consensus mechanisms are indispensable to blockchains that dictate the general ways of establishing the viability of the transaction and the coherence of block-chain. Proof of work (POW)–pioneered by Bitcoin is a consensus mechanism that requires selected nodes to solve complex problems to include blocks in a block chain. Concerning the last one, let us illustrate Proof of Stake (PoS) where validators are chosen depending on the amount of cryptocurrency they are ready to 'lock' as stake. Other are Delegated Proof of Stake (DPoS) and Byzantine-Fault Tolerance (BFT) that provide variations for better performance, broaden comprehensibility, and increased reliability (Bingu et al., 2024).

Smart contracts are programs which are both self-executing and enforce the terms of the contract on an application. Smart contracts run on blockchains similar to Ethereum and execute, police, and verify the provisions of a contract whenever certain requirements are met. The key importance of smart contracts is in achieving the conditions and executing transactions and agreements with the help of an interme-diary without authorising middlemen. They improve confidentiality and credibility since every party can have access to the contract's execution on the blockchain in order to determine that the transactions will be conducted accordingly to the contract.

Table 1. Fundamentals of Blockchain Technology

Blockchain Basics	Description
Concepts and Components	Blockchain is a distributed ledger technology that records transactions across multiple computers. Key components include blocks, chains, nodes, and transactions.
Blocks	Blocks are individual units of storage that contain transaction data, a timestamp, and a cryptographic hash of the previous block.
Chains	Chains link blocks together in a linear, chronological order using cryptographic hashes, forming a secure and immutable ledger.

continued on following page

Table 1. Continued

Blockchain Basics	Description
Nodes	Nodes are individual computers in the blockchain network that store and validate blocks.
Transactions	Transactions are individual operations recorded in a block, representing a transfer of value or information between parties.
Types of Blockchains	
Public Blockchain	Public blockchains are open to anyone and do not require permission to join or participate. They are fully decentralized (e.g., Bitcoin, Ethereum).
Private Blockchain	Private blockchains are restricted to a specific group of participants. They offer more control and privacy but are less decentralized (e.g., Hyperledger Fabric).
Consortium Blockchain	Consortium blockchains are governed by a group of organizations. They balance decentralization and control, suitable for collaborative projects (e.g., R3 Corda).
Blockchain Consensus Mechanisms	
Proof of Work (PoW)	PoW requires nodes to solve complex mathematical puzzles to validate transactions and create new blocks. It is energy-intensive but highly secure (e.g., Bitcoin).
Proof of Stake (PoS)	PoS assigns the right to create new blocks based on the number of tokens a participant holds and is willing to "stake" as collateral. It is more energy-efficient (e.g., Ethereum 2.0).
Delegated Proof of Stake (DPoS)	DPoS uses a voting system where stakeholders elect a small number of delegates to validate transactions and create blocks, improving efficiency and scalability (e.g., EOS).
Practical Byzantine Fault Tolerance (PBFT)	PBFT ensures consensus through a pre-determined set of nodes that reach agreement on the order and validity of transactions, suitable for private and consortium blockchains.
Proof of Authority (PoA)	PoA relies on a small number of nodes with high authority and trust to validate transactions, offering high efficiency and low energy consumption (e.g., VeChain).

Edge Computing Basics

Edge computing is conceptions shift in computing that lends computational and storage services to the outer layers of the network where data is produced and/or consumed. This extends with traditional techniques of cloud computing wherein the data is transmitted to the global data centers for processing. Edge computing encompasses computing stations and data storage solutions that are distributed at the network peripherals, within IoT devices, gateways, or local servers. This empowers real-time data analysis and decision making at the edge or near the source which eradicates latency problems and offloads the central systems (Shi et al., 2016).

Edge computing can be defined as the act of computing or analysing data nearer to the place where such data is generated rather than having to be sent to the central data center. Other features include data processing, this is done locally that reduces the amount of time taken to process data by applications that require immediate feedback. Also, edge computing proposed the decentralized structure of the edge nodes which are able to cooperate while processing the information. This approach also improves the data privacy and security since data that is not relevant to the computation task is not sent over the network (Satyanand & Karthik, 2018).

Cloud computing and edge computing are actually two models of consuming, processing and storing data. Cloud computing depends on facilities that are centrally located where end-user computing occurs in a large-scale manner. Information in this model is processed through economies of scale, high computational power and has huge storage capacity. However, it has limitations that come from transit time of the data from its source to the cloud server; it may also entail higher cost of bandwidth usage. On the other hand, the principle of edge computing focuses on these problems that can be solved by the processing of the data on the edge of the network, which has the advantages in lower latency, less usage of bandwidth, but at the cost of difficult and complicated management of more distributed architecture (Zhang, & Zhang, 2019).

That is why edge computing has several advantages for IoT applications, mainly associated with increase in performance and optimization. This concept of computing reduces the latency of data by processing it closer to the source; this is very essential in the applications such as self-driving cars, industries, smart cities among others. Also, it aids in cutting back on bandwidth consumption sending as little data as possible to central cloud servers; this can sometimes be cheaper and make more efficient use of the networks. Additionally, it enables data privacy and security because data collected at the network edge is processed locally and thus necessitates less transfer over the network implying less vulnerability to the occurrence of security breaches in the process.

1. Latency Calculation
   Equation:

$$L = L_p + L_t + L_{prop} + L_q$$

Where: L is the total latency; L_p is the processing delay at the edge node; L_t is the transmission; delay L_{prop} is the propagation delay; L_q is the queuing delay

Example: Suppose the processing delay L_p is 2 ms, the transmission delay L_t is 1 ms, the propagation delay L_{prop} is 3 ms, and the queuing delay L_q is 1 ms.

Total latency L can be calculated as:

L= 2+1+3+1= 7 ms

2. Bandwidth Utilization
    Equation:

$$U = \frac{R}{B}$$

Where: U is the bandwidth utilization; R is the data transmission rate; B is the total available bandwidth

Example: If the data transmission rate R is 50 Mbps and the total available bandwidth B is 100 Mbps, the bandwidth utilization U is

$$U = \frac{50}{100} = 0.5 \,|\text{or}|\, 50\%$$

3. Energy Consumption
    Equation:

$$E = P_p T_p + P_t T_t + P_i T_i$$

Where: E is the total energy consumption; P_p is the power consumption during processing; T_p is the time spent in processing; P_t is the power consumption during transmission; T_t is the time spent in transmission; p_i is the power consumption during idle state; T_i is the time spent in idle state

Example: If the power consumption during processing P_p is 10 W, the time spent in processing T_p is 2 s, the power consumption during transmission P_t is 5 W, the time spent in transmission T_t is 3 s, the power consumption during idle state P_i is 2 W, and the time spent in idle state T_i is 5 s, the total energy consumption E is:

E= (10×2)+(5×3)+(2×5)= 20+15+10= 45 Joules

4. Task Offloading Decision
    Equation:

$$D = C_{edge} + L_{edge} \leq C_{cloud} + L_{cloud}$$

Where: D is the decision variable; C_{edge} is the computation cost at the edge; L_{edge} is the latency at the edge; C_{cloud} is the computation cost at the cloud; L_{cloud} is the latency at the cloud

Example: If the computation cost at the edge C_{edge} is 5 units and the latency L_{edge} is 3 units, while the computation cost at the cloud C_{cloud} is 8 units and the latency L_{cloud} is 2 units, the decision variable D can be calculated as:

5+3 ≤ 8+2

8≤10

5. Scalability Factor

Equation:

$$S = \frac{N_{max}}{N_{current}}$$

Where: S is the scalability factor; N_{max} is the maximum number of devices or tasks the system can handle; $N_{current}$ is the current number of devices or tasks Example: If the maximum number of devices the system can handle; N_{max} is 1000 and the current number of devices; $N_{current}$ is 250, the scalability factor S is:

$$S = \frac{1000}{250} = 4$$

Integrating Blockchain with Edge Computing

The implementation of blockchain technology within the framework of edge computing offers a suitable solution to several issues in the IoT data management. When the strength of both technologies is incorporated, then organizations can improve security, stability, and operations in their IoT systems. Since blockchain is based on decentralization, which matches edge computing's distributed processing concept, it provides for a more resilient system to handle IoT data. Yet, they also create several issues that have to be solved in order to reach the purpose of that integration (Alzahrani & Hossain, 2020).

There are some challenges which are associated with the data management in IoT environments among which data volume, velocity, and variety. Since there are hundreds of millions of devices deployed and connected, the data that gets produced must be managed with suitable solutions for real time processing and analysis. That is why the centralized data management, which has been characteristic for most devices up until recently, may have scalability and latency problems when the number of connected devices increases. Third, data integrity and security of the users' information across the linked devices constitute a major difficulty, for instance, through exposure to cyber threats. Integrating Blockchain with edge computing tries to overcome these challenges of smart city solution by providing a distributed system for data management & security (Esposito, 2018).

The use of blockchain improves data reliability through the properties of the structure: the data is written once, appended to the chain and cannot be changed. Every piece of information that gets recorded in the blockchain is protected by a cryptographic key and it is connected to another record; this makes it almost impossible to alter the record. This precedes the fact that, as much as data can be recorded, they cannot be edited or erased except through the consensus of the network. In the case of edge computing, blockchain will enable the safeguard of data sharing between edge gadgets, because data will remain unbiased and intact after it has been collected and shared. Furthermore, consensus mechanisms and smart contracts inherent in blockchain systems, relieve legal and IT, bureaucratic framework interference by providing the automation and self-policing of then data security measures (Zhang & Yang, 2019).

Challenges related to IoT have been solved with the help of incorporating blockchain with edge computing as depicted from several cases. For example, there was a case of smart cities that explained how blockchain will help in efficiently and securely handling and authenticate data from hundreds of IoT sensors applied in different infrastructures of cities. The exact action maintained by decentralized blockchain was helpful to ensure valid records pertaining to traffic management systems to enable proper analysis of traffic pattern as a result of the accurate data. In another case at the healthcare segment, the efficiency of the use of blockchain and edge computing to defend patient data was presented and their purity across different devices was ensured. The system was also preserving the privacy of each patient's data in addition to fulfilling regulations because the blockchain technology recorded all patients' data safely and transparently.

Let's denote the following:

- D: Data generated by loT devices
- E: Edge computing resources (processing power and storage)
- B: Blockchain network
- L: Latency of data processing and transmission
- C: Consensus mechanism overhead
- S: Security level provided by blockchain
- P: Performance efficiency of the integrated system The integration model can be formulated as:

$$P = f\left(\frac{D}{E} \cdot \frac{1}{L} \cdot \frac{1}{C} \cdot S\right)$$

where:

- $\frac{D}{E}$ represents the data processing capability of edge computing relative to the data generated.
- $\frac{1}{L}$ accounts for the reduction in latency due to edge computing.
- $\frac{1}{C}$ represents the efficiency of the consensus mechanism in the blockchain.
- S signifies the security enhancements provided by the blockchain.

Examples: Suppose we have:

- $D=100$ units of data per second
- $E=50$ units of edge processing power,
- $L=10$ milliseconds latency,
- $C=5$ units of consensus overhead
- $S=0.9$ (90% security level)

Plugging these values into the formula:

$$P = f\left(\frac{100}{50} \cdot \frac{1}{10} \cdot \frac{1}{5} \cdot 0.9\right) = f(2 \cdot 0.1 \cdot 0.2 \cdot 0.9) = f\left(0.036\right)$$

Blockchain-Enabled Edge Computing Architecture for Cognitive IoT

It is a combination of decentralized ledger solution with distributed computational assets used in Cognitive IoT structure to comprise a sound solution for data management and processing at the edge of the network. At its core, the system architecture consists of several key players: It has four main layers including the edge layer the blockchain layer the cognitive computing layer. In the edge layer, IoT devices and edge nodes exist for gathering, processing, and making decisions based on data. The blockchain layer has the role of creating an independent and secure layer for storing transactional data of peers and data exchanges. The second layer, the cognitive computing layer, involves savvy analytical capabilities and superior machineries to learn tool with superior analytics from the data collected at the edge.

This multilevel approach is very beneficial as it aligns to proper data management and increases security for cognitive IoT (Xu et al., 2019).

In this architecture, both collection and processing of data are done partially by the edge devices and nodes. In edge devices like sensors and actuators, data is accumulated by them from their surroundings and simple data processing is carried out to eliminate large amount of data and delay. This data is then processed by the edge nodes which are local servers or gateways and handle communication with blockchain network. The blockchain layer play a role of approving and storing all the transaction in the network thus ensuring that there is a record of all the data exchanged. This way, the data can be processed in large amounts simultaneously with a minimal latency while maximizing the usage of the available resources in the edge devices and nodes. It also improves redundancy, meaning that when one node fails, it does not affect the whole system (Khan & Alghamdi, 2020).

The flow of data in an architecture that incorporates the use of blockchain in edge computing passes through various procedures. First and foremost, edge devices collect and pre-process data, and then send it to be processed by edge nodes. The edge nodes communicate with the blockchain layer to store and report predefined data points and transactions on the blockchain (Zheng et al., 2018). This interaction routinely guarantees that all data interactions that take place are logged and are not alterable. The cognitive computing layer uses this processed data to execute various computational intelligence tasks for creating business value upon which action may be taken immediately. In this process, data circulates through the different layers, and every layer of the system is effective. The integration of edge devices, nodes, and blockchain also fosters real-time data processing and decision-making; thus, supporting data accuracy.

$$\min\left(\sum_{i=1}^{N} \left(C_i + \frac{L_i}{P_i} + \sum_{j=1}^{M} D_{ij} \cdot \left(T_{ij} + \frac{1}{B_{ij}} \right) \right) \right)$$

Where:

- N: Total number of edge devices in the CIoT system.
- M: Total number of blockchain transactions.
- C_i: Computational cost of edge device i.
- L_i: Latency of blockchain transaction on edge device i.
- P_i: Processing power of edge device i.
- D_{ij}: Data flow between edge device i and blockchain transaction j.
- T_{ij}: Transmission time for data D_j.
- B_{ij}: Bandwidth available for data D_j.

Smart Contracts in Edge Computing

Smart contracts are digital contracts which automatically execute the terms when the agreement is implemented in computer code and which run on distribution ledger technology platforms particularly on the Ethereum. Smart contracts are the foundation for IoT applications, and designing smart contracts entails stating the contract responsibilities and logic to govern IoT devices, users, and services' interactions. Some of the hardware design considerations include both defining the contract's trigger and condition on one hand and the action that should be taken by the other on the basis of data inputs from the edge devices. For instance, the smart contract can be designed in a manner that pays a supplier after receiving a notification from a sensor that the shipment has been delivered. Furthermore, they have to consider exception handling and guarantee that all members of the chain obey a contract's terms; incorporation of error control mechanics and the options in case of failure. Another aspect taken into account during the design is the efficiency of the smart contract, the number of computations needed to perform the appropriate action as well as the expenses regarded as reasonable by the platform (Chen et al., 2018).

Cognitive IoT gains major advantages in using smart contracts as automated procedures for ensuring secure interconnection of IoT devices with the clients. A classic case scenario is in supply chain where smart contracts are used to validate and document transactions in the supply chain from manufacturing to delivery. Another example is in smart cities where the smart contract technology can control and manage aspects of generalized public utilities for instance; availability of parking lots depending on the general demand of people in a given area at a given time. Smart contracts in healthcare can help possible mechanisms of safe and seamless sharing of information between connected medical devices and user's Electronic Health Records in a compliance with Data Protection legislation and contribute to positive health outcomes for the patients. The above use cases show ways in which smart contracts can improve the effectiveness, integrity, and reliability of different IoT applications (Lee & Kwon, 2020).

The issues of security and privacy are essential while using smart contracts in edge computing scenarios. Smart contracts run on a blockchain, which means that once a contract is deployed in the network it cannot be changed or altered as they are highly public which could be a problem if a hacker finds loopholes in the code. To overcome some of the aspects of security, there is needed to perform the code review and tests to find out the potential risks which are able to occur before the deployment of the application. E-tank details with regard to privacy include the fact that when data is being processed by smart contracts, it should be encrypted and that access controls should be placed to avoid cases of intrusions. Also, it is correct to assume that the data is being stored on a public block chain where people can peep through your record. Privacy issues can be addressed by utilizing such techniques as zero knowledge proofs or private transactions that do not affect the contract's execution (Li et al., 2019).

Data Management and Security in Blockchain-Enabled Edge IoT

In BEEC systems, prospective storage facilities are considered providing solutions tailored to the peculiarities of distributed IoT networks. The processing of data is obtained and done locally by the edge devices or nodes to minimize latency and bandwidth consumption. The main forms of storage and reference information include local databases and file storage systems and distributed ledger technologies. Edge databases on local hardware are utilized for fast data retrieval and computations while a distributed database such as blockchain is used for storing transactions which are secure and cannot be altered. Incorporation of blockchain storage on the edge also guarantees that the significant data is saved and can be validated without the intermediation of the cloud. Others like data sharding; this is the method used to split the data into smaller parts and stores it in various nodes can also supplement the storage density and expandability in sharp edge computing architectures (Xu et al., 2019).

Security is one of the most important requirements in edge IoT, in which cryptographic techniques are used to protect data in blockchain. Methods of data encryption include for instance the symmetric and asymmetric encryption for protecting data at the rest as well as in transit. In symmetric encryption there is only one key, while in asymmetric encryption there two keys, public and private. Of greater importance, blockchain technology improves the security by the use of cryptographic hashing for the development of transactional journals which cannot be altered. Connecting every block in the chain with the remainder of the previous block's hash is a critical aspect of the architecture since integrity is guaranteed. Also, application techniques include digital signatures for the guarantee of authentication and non-repudiation to warrant that data can be traced to its source and no transaction can be reversed after execution (Li et al., 2020).

Blockchain solutions provide the means of secure data exchange involving different participants, which is based on decentralized consensus algorithms and cryptographic means. Some of the well-known consensus algorithms like PoW and PoS help in making all nodes in a blockchain network arrive at a consensus about the authenticity of a transaction before it goes into the record. Such protocols reduce the possibility of conducting fake transactions and duplicity since participants are involved in solving mathematical problems or, at least, staking tokens for the same. Moreover, many blockchain systems also support techniques such as zero-knowledge proofs and ring signatures for conducting secure transactions without disclosing the information. Such protocols make it possible for data exchanged between edge devices and other stakeholders within the network to be secure and integrity checked (Zhang et al., 2021).

CHALLENGES AND SOLUTIONS

The second major concern in learning and predicting outcomes in B-EC systems is scalability, thanks to both edges and blocks established. Scalability becomes a problem in blockchain networks as each transaction is processed by multiple nodes and this results to more latency and less throughput when there is large number of nodes. This is especially a big deal in edge computing circumstances where multiple IoT devices continue to create massive amounts of data that has to be processed and stored. In these challenges, the following solutions are being proposed Though, these are the general solutions that are being proposed to address these challenges. There is an approach in layer-2 scaling solutions like state channels and sidechains that execute transactions outside the blockchain and then periodically broadcast to the main chain. Further, it is also worthy to note that there are things like sharding whereby the blockchain is partitioned into different small parts hence providing an efficient way of partitioning the work as well as creating scalability. Edge computing can also include edge specific data aggregation and filtering steps for further depopularizing the data that has to be processed and transmitted (Zheng et al., 2018).

One of the most important parameters in blockchain-based systems with edge computing is the time response and speed for providing results also for those applications in which fast decision-making is important. When it comes to consensus mechanisms of the blockchain technology like PoW and PoS, these can involve delays in the processing of the transactions as the basis of consensus is arrived at after some time. In edge computing also the position of edge devices themselves can influence latency since data has to travel over networks to the right nodes. These problems can however, be addressed by using for example, fine-tuning of consensus algorithms to allow for blocks to be produced faster, using a local consensus on edge devices, and using ultra-high speed communication protocols. Also, the enhancement of the system using edge computing where the data can be processed locally, and the data exchange with the blockchain network happens occasionally will help in minimizing latency (Wang et al., 2020).

Another issue that may be critical in blockchain-based edge solutions is the problem of interconnectivity and standardization since many systems and technologies should be integrated. That is because individual blockchain platforms and edge computing frameworks may employ different protocols, data formats, and methods of mutual communication, which would cause problems for their integration. Another downside is that there is no specification that is shared between people, applications and organizations and can slow down the process of emerging of coordinated and integrated approaches. To deal with these issues, the general work requirement of industries to seek and implement standard cultural models of practice is crucial. Existing projects, for example, the IEEE standards for blockchain and edge computing, or cross-industry definitions of the essential interoperability requirements, can span the above gaps. Also, middleware solutions and protocols that are involved in the interoperability frameworks are helpful in achieving the integration objectives.

Applications of Blockchain-Enabled Edge Computing in Cognitive IoT

Blockchain integrated edge computing is a revolution for different fields such as healthcare, smart city, and Industries IoT etc. In healthcare, this technology can improve the safety and reliability of the patient's medical record by giving secure, distributed Health IT record systems that can be accessed only through officially recognized parties. For instance, it can enable accurate registration, storage, and sharing of the patient data from wearable technology to healthcare professionals in real-time that improves diagnoses and treatment. Blockchain integrated with edge computing for smart city management effective use of urban resources is elemental. Some of the functions that can include use of smart contract include; traffic control that adapts to conditions experienced by edge devices, energy control based on actual data captured, meaning management of the city resources is enhanced. For industrial IoT applications, blockchain based edge computing can increase supply chain transparency and supply chain reliability by creating a record on each phase of the supply chain as well as ensuring that the data on the supply chain phase has not been tampered with. It can be applied in the tracking of goods, tackling of fraud incidences and assessing quality of manufactured goods (Aazam & Huh, 2020).

Some use cases of blockchain in Cognitive IoT edge computing are depicted below: For example, IBM Food Trust, it is the blockchain that Walmart have developed together, which is used to account for the chain of food products from the farm to the consumer's plate. This system actively uses edge devices to gather data at specific stages of supply chains, and the information is also validated and stored in the blockchain for openness and accountability. Another instance is the use of smart parking system by the City of Lugano where edge devs communicate with the cloud and send information on the parking availability; the payments and reservations are handled through the use of the blockchain technology. Other industries have also incorporated the blockchain technology; for instance, in the industrial sector Siemens has been using blockchain to ensure secure and transparent management of assets and their maintenance. The following case studies demonstrate the applicability of using blockchain at the edge for solving practical problems and improving the performance of the system in various domains (Xu et al., 2020).

The combination of blockchain with edge computing brings a lot of plus points regarding the effectiveness and protection of a system. By distributing data both storage and processing blockchain strengthens data's protection and minimizes vulnerability of having too many centralized data processing centers. Thus, the decentralized structure in tandem with the local data processing of the edge computing concept optimizes the outcomes and makes the systems faster. In the same way, blockchain is unique for its unalterable ledger, and the cryptography methods make it impossible to manipulate the data and guarantee the flawless transaction. This integration also includes the usage of smart contracts that provide for automatic and clearly transparent operations that can effectively remove additional layers. In conclusion, this paper shows that integrating blockchain and edge computing improves the cognitive IoT systems' performance while at the same time improving their security (Li et al., 2021).

Future Trends and Research Directions

There are several innovate technologies and advances that will define the use of blockchain in Cognitive IoT and Edge computing in the future. a particular shift is the use of deep reinforcement learning such as AI/ML with Blockchain along with edge computation. Some of these technologies can improve the predictive analysis, real time decision making and automated actions in the IoT systems. For example, AI can assist in data management on the edge, and blockchain guarantees the data's authenticity and protection. Also, the advancement of the 5G technology enhances the operation and effectiveness of edge computing due to high speed and low latency necessary for near real-time data processing and exchange. Quantum computing is another innovation that has the prospects of influencing cryptographic techniques utilized in blockchain, they might be made more secure along with being more efficient.

It is expected that the future developmental changes of blockchain and edge computing will mainly relate to the scalability, reliability, and compatibility. In blockchain technological advancement, more focus is now being placed on advancing better consensus algorithm which includes that of Proof of Authority (PoA) and Delegated Proof of Stake (DPoS) which may boost the rate of the transaction and at the same time reduce energy use. Potential developments in the context of edge computing can be, for instance, better and enhanced edge analytics platforms for more complex computations on the edge devices, thus, decreasing the need for more extensive cloud solutions. It may also lead to a creation of a convergence of blockchain and edge computing where the features and advantages of both could be used to create systems that are more optimal than the two. For instance, edge devices could be employing micro-blockchains or sidechains for local data operations and occasionally, for validation from the main blockchain.

Nonetheless, there is still more to be done and some of the research questions and future challenges that are worth investigating in Blockchain to Cognitive IoT area are as follows. Another is efficiency, and its impact mainly reflects in large-scale systems where the usage of blockchain often encounters problems due to the high number of transactions and data rates. Furthermore, incorporating blockchain with edge computing has some issues regarding synchronizing data across several nodes and handling ledgers at the edges. More research is required to discover the novel solutions to these issues, such as the enhancement of the blockchain protocols and edge computing. Moreover, the ethical and legal issues of integrating blockchain with IoT systems especially for aspects to do with data privacy and consent and the compliance to the changing regulations are still worth looking at. Closing these gaps will be vital for the best deployment and adoption procedures of blockchain-supported edge computing within Cognitive IoT applications.

CONCLUSION

Blockchain technology introduced in CIoT has brought a new revolution in the secure processing of data and identification. This chapter has described how blockchain is central to increasing the security and trustworthiness of CIoT interactions especially when engaging edge computing. Through the distributed structure, consensus algorithms, and smart contacts, CIoT systems enhance the overall qualification of IoT data implying increased transparency, tamperproof, and automatization meeting many of the IoT inherent problems.

Edge computing that puts the data processing resources closer to dense data sources works in parallel with blockchain since it does not entail extensive data transfers to distant data centrality for processing. The integration of these technologies yields a strong foundation of security for exchanging data and managing the identity needed for CIoT systems that are mass-scale and dependable. The strengths of the block chain and the edge computing have been established from a study of the fundamentals of block chain and the characteristics of edge computing in this chapter as well as the benefits that arise from the integration of the two technologies in solving problems such as integrity of data, security, and compatibility.

Still, some issues are observed that include scalability, performance, and also the problem of standardization. Some of the presented case studies are valuable for understanding real-life use cases and stressing the changes that blockchain brings to

CIoT. Moving forward, continuous development by implementing more extensive studies and researching more technologies is anticipated to strengthen the functionalities of the blockchain and edge computing to settle existing drawbacks and create new opportunities for secure and efficient CIoT. It is also important to address five future challenges to help enhance the concept of blockchain-based CIoT systems in the subsequent explorations.

REFERENCES

Aazam, M., & Huh, E. N. (2020). Blockchain-based secure data management for IoT applications. *IEEE Access: Practical Innovations, Open Solutions*, 8, 136754–136764. DOI: 10.1109/ACCESS.2020.3001551

Alzahrani, A., & Hossain, M. S. (2020). Blockchain and edge computing integration for IoT systems: Challenges and opportunities. *IEEE Access: Practical Innovations, Open Solutions*, 8, 111231–111249. DOI: 10.1109/ACCESS.2020.3002428

Bingu, R., Adinarayana, S., Dhatterwal, J. S., Kavitha, S., Patnala, E., & Sangaraju, H. R. (2024). Performance comparison analysis of classification methodologies for effective detection of intrusions. *Computers & Security*, 143, 103893. DOI: 10.1016/j.cose.2024.103893

Buterin, V. (2013). *Ethereum white paper: A next-generation smart contract and decentralized application platform.* Retrieved from https://ethereum.org/en/whitepaper/

Chen, X., Li, H., & Liu, Y. (2018). Designing smart contracts for IoT applications: A comprehensive survey. *IEEE Internet of Things Journal*, 5(6), 5404–5417. DOI: 10.1109/JIOT.2018.2887768

Dhatterwal, J. S., & Kaswan, K. S. (2023). Role of Blockchain Technology in the Financial Market. In *Contemporary Studies of Risks in Emerging Technology, Part A* (pp. 93-109). Emerald Publishing Limited. DOI: 10.1108/978-1-80455-562-020231007

Dhatterwal, J. S., Kaswan, K. S., & Chithaluru, P. (2024). Agricultural cyber-physical systems: evolution, basic, and fundamental concepts. In *Agri 4.0 and the Future of Cyber-Physical Agricultural Systems* (pp. 19–35). Academic Press. DOI: 10.1016/B978-0-443-13185-1.00002-2

Esposito, C., Santis, A. D., & Tortora, G. (2018). Blockchain-based edge computing: A review of applications and challenges. *Journal of Computer Networks and Communications*, 2018, 1–12. DOI: 10.1155/2018/5979512

Kaswan, K. S., Dhatterwal, J. S., Kumar, N., Balusamy, B., & Gangadevi, E. (2024). Cyborg Intelligence for Bioprinting in Computational Design and Analysis of Medical Application. *Computational Intelligence in Bioprinting*, 211-237.

Khan, R. U., & Alghamdi, A. (2020). A comprehensive survey of blockchain-based edge computing systems for IoT. *IEEE Access: Practical Innovations, Open Solutions*, 8, 84234–84248. DOI: 10.1109/ACCESS.2020.2992871

Lee, D., & Kwon, H. (2020). Smart contracts for cognitive IoT: Applications and challenges. *Journal of Blockchain Research*, 2(4), 112–124. DOI: 10.1007/s41615-020-00122-7

Li, Q., Zhang, S., & Li, Z. (2019). Security and privacy in smart contracts: A survey. *IEEE Access : Practical Innovations, Open Solutions*, 7, 105453–105468. DOI: 10.1109/ACCESS.2019.2934697

Li, S., Xu, L. D., & Zhao, H. (2021). Industrial IoT: Challenges and solutions for blockchain integration. *Journal of Industrial Information Integration*, 21, 100191. DOI: 10.1016/j.jii.2020.100191

Li, Y., Xu, L. D., & Zhao, X. (2020). A survey on scalability and performance of blockchain technology. *IEEE Access : Practical Innovations, Open Solutions*, 8, 66400–66417. DOI: 10.1109/ACCESS.2020.2982257

Nakamoto, S. (2008). *Bitcoin: A peer-to-peer electronic cash system*. Retrieved from https://bitcoin.org/bitcoin.pdf

Satyanand, K. B., & Karthik, P. (2018). A survey on edge computing and its applications. *Journal of Computer Networks and Communications*, 2018, 1–11. DOI: 10.1155/2018/7327465

Shi, W., Cao, J., Zhang, Q., Li, Y., & Xu, L. D. (2016). Edge computing: Vision and challenges. *IEEE Internet of Things Journal*, 3(5), 637–646. DOI: 10.1109/JIOT.2016.2579198

Wang, X., Zhang, J., & Wang, S. (2020). Cryptographic techniques for blockchain-enabled edge computing. *IEEE Access : Practical Innovations, Open Solutions*, 8, 28220–28230. DOI: 10.1109/ACCESS.2020.2973458

Wood, G. (2014). *Ethereum: A secure decentralised generalised transaction ledger*. Retrieved from https://ethereum.github.io/yellowpaper/paper.pdf

Xu, M., Weber, I., & Staples, M. (2020). *Blockchain technology for smart cities: Use cases and challenges*. Springer., DOI: 10.1007/978-3-030-42424-2

Xu, X., Weber, I., & Staples, M. (2019). Architecting the blockchain for the Internet of Things: A case study. *IEEE Transactions on Engineering Management*, 66(4), 574–585. DOI: 10.1109/TEM.2017.2722467

Zhang, L., Wang, X., & Wang, S. (2021). Challenges and solutions in blockchain-based edge computing: A comprehensive review. *Journal of Network and Computer Applications*, 187, 103104. DOI: 10.1016/j.jnca.2021.103104

Zhang, L., & Zhang, Z. (2019). Edge computing for IoT: A survey. *IEEE Access : Practical Innovations, Open Solutions*, 7, 80846–80864. DOI: 10.1109/ACCESS.2019.2924248

Zhang, Y., & Yang, J. (2019). Enhancing IoT security and privacy with blockchain and edge computing. *IEEE Internet of Things Journal*, 6(3), 4476–4486. DOI: 10.1109/JIOT.2018.2888258

Zhang, Y., Yang, J., & Zhang, Z. (2020). Blockchain-based edge computing for secure and efficient data management in IoT systems. *IEEE Access : Practical Innovations, Open Solutions*, 8, 24334–24347. DOI: 10.1109/ACCESS.2020.2969086

Zheng, Z., Xie, S., Dai, H. N., Chen, X., & Zhang, C. (2018). Blockchain for internet of things: A survey. *IEEE Internet of Things Journal*, 5(6), 5497–5506. DOI: 10.1109/JIOT.2018.2857256

Chapter 6
Study of Geographical and Energy–Aware MANET Routing Protocols

Raqiya Al Hilali
Modern College of Business and Science, Oman

Hothefa Shaker
Modern College of Business and Science, Oman

Zeyad T. Sharef
https://orcid.org/0000-0003-0571-5788
Ninevah University, Iraq

Baraa T. Sharef
American University, Bahrain

Shahnawaz Khan
Bahrain Polytechnic, India

ABSTRACT

Mobile Adhoc Network (MANET) contains a set of mobile nodes with insecure infrastructure. When designing MANET, researchers focused on the routing process regardless of base stations and access points. The protocol designers and network developers face many challenges with MANET routing protocols due to MANET drawbacks such as dynamic topology, scalability, weak performance, routing difficulty and energy consumption. MANET routing protocols contain three categories: Reactive. (On-Demand), Proactive. (Table -Driven), and Hybrid. (Combine both proactive and reactive features). However, this primary classification hides other

DOI: 10.4018/979-8-3693-2157-7.ch006

categories of MANET that play critical and essential roles nowadays. The protocols were enhanced to overcome the challenges of the existing MANET routing protocols. This paper is intended to provide a descriptive study of two forms of MANET-routing protocols called geographical and energy-aware routing protocols.

1. INTRODUCTION

Mobile Ad -hoc -Network (MANET) is a group of wireless nodes with no steady topology. In the case of infrastructure wireless networks, mobile nodes are communicating via the fixed base station. In contrast, MANET nodes keep in touch, although it is infrastructure-free, and due to that, the mobile nodes act as hosts and routers simultaneously. MANET is a perfect network to be used in the regions where natural disasters and wars occur and where the creation of fixed infrastructure is impossible (Abdulleh, M.N., Yussof, S. and Jassim, H.S., 2015).

MANET mobile nodes move rapidly in multi-directions and randomly rearrange themselves.

Nodes in the same range communicate directly; unlike nodes distant from each other, intermediate nodes are required to forward the message to the right target using multi-hop. Over the years, many routing protocols developed and played a significant role at MANET. (Abdulleh, M.N., Yussof, S. and Jassim, H.S., 2015) (Sumra, I.A., Sellappan, P., Abdullah, A. and Ali, A., 2018)

Over the years, many types of research have been done to overcome MANET routing protocols' drawbacks; thus, it has gained a significant position among other types of networks. In addition, new routing algorithms are being born, and new MANET routing protocols have been born to live. This paper extensively described the most important two: geographical and energy-aware -routing -protocols. Our paper is arranged in this manner: Section 2 offers an overview of MANET and displays a basic classification of MANET -routing -protocols. Section 3 describes the geographical MANET routing protocol and its forwarding strategies, as well as extensively describes the geographical routing protocols. Section 4 presents energy-aware MANET routing protocols based on six groups. Section 5 analyses geographical and energy-aware MANET-routing protocols concerning weaknesses, strengths, and future scope. Section 6 concludes the study of geographical and energy-aware MANET routing protocols.

2. MANET OVERVIEW

MANET is an exceptional kind of wireless network defined as a group of nodes that move rapidly in random directions and communicate without infrastructure or a central administrator.

If MANET mobile nodes are within the same broadcast range, they communicate directly. Otherwise, intermediate nodes are needed to forward packets to the right destination.

Due to its unique feature—the absence of infrastructure—MANET is suitable for locations where the wired network cannot be established, like battlefields and areas affected by natural disasters. (Abdulleh, M.N., Yussof, S. and Jassim, H.S., 2015).

The importance of MANET is demonstrated in many fields and applications like:

War Areas: MANET allows the maintenance of network information among soldiers (Helen, D. and Arivazhagan, D., 2014).

Village Region: Ad hoc networks are used in these areas to create immediate communication between mobile nodes' users and distribute messages among participants (Helen, D. and Arivazhagan, D., 2014).

Personal-Area Network (PAN): This form of network is defined as a local short-coverage area network where nodes are connected through a given bandwidth (Helen, D. and Arivazhagan, D., 2014).

Commercial and Emergency Situations: Business and industry sectors use Ad hoc networks extensively. This type of network gained tremendous popularity in emergencies due to its lack of infrastructure features. (Helen, D. and Arivazhagan, D., 2014).

Bluetooth: Bluetooth is a technique that provides a small bandwidth communication for its nodes like laptops and mobile cell phones (Helen, D. and Arivazhagan, D., 2014).

Protocol designers face many constraints at MANET that make them face many issues while designing routing protocols, such as:

Unfixed Links: Unlike traditional wired networks, the communication links between MANET nodes are not fixed. Due to the devices' mobility, many hidden routes are created, causing weak MANET throughput. (Ahmed, D.E.M. and Khalifa, O.O., 2017).

Network Overhead: Routing is a significant part of infrastructure-free networks like MANET. The dynamic topology generates routing overhead, which results in non-meaningful and outdated routes. (Ahmed, D. and Khalifa, O, 2017). This phenomenon also causes the appearance of new terminals, broken links and sudden interfaces. (Er, J.K. and Er, G.S., 2017).

Dynamic Topology: MANET topology is not fixed, and the chance of node movement is high; thus, the transmission medium keeps changing. This creates new demand, which is the need to enhance the frequency of changing the routing tables. Generally, the routing tables are updated every 30 seconds at fixed networks, which seems to be a shallow period for MANET routing protocols. (Ahmed, D.E.M. and Khalifa, O.O., 2017).

Security: Security is considered one of the significant constraints to ad–hoc - networks. Data security in ad–hoc -networks is weak owing to the dynamic topology, small nodes' sizes, limited bandwidth and limited nodes' energy. Creating secure communication in the network is impossible due to the continuous movement of portable nodes. The ad hoc networks have no central administration; accordingly, portable nodes may withdraw and join the network suddenly. In such conditions, the network security may collapse. Malicious nodes appear a lot on MANET. Still, they can be recognized quickly based on specific indicators, which are high loss of packets, high battery consumption, untrusted messages, long delays, and the appearance of more link breaks. (Helen, D. and Arivazhagan, D., 2014).

Energy Constraints and Power Management: MANET mobile nodes have limited energy reservations because they are power-driven by batteries, which are challenging to recharge or replace. Power management is a critical approach to control power consumption. (Ahmed, D. and Khalifa, O, 2017).

MANET's drawback is that it imposes new demands on routing protocols. Institutes concerned with enhancing routing techniques keep searching for the best mechanisms to manage the failures of wireless networks, especially ad hoc networks. Creating routing protocols to deal with even the worst MANET scenarios is essential. (Abdulleh, M.N., Yussof, S. and Jassim, H.S., 2015).

Over the years, many advanced and intelligent routing protocols have appeared to improve MANET performance. Researchers differed in the way they classified MANET routing protocols. Let's define each group of researchers as Group A and Group B. Group A divided MANET- routing- protocols into three essential categories, namely, hybrid, proactive and reactive routing -protocols. (Ahmed, D.E.M. and Khalifa, O.O., 2017). Group B divided them based on routing strategy and network structure. (Torrieri, D; Talarico, S. and Valenti, M.C, 2015). The following two subsections illustrated the opinion of each group and because this paper focused on geographical and energy-aware routing protocols, the location of these two types of protocols was highlighted at each group.

2.1 MANET –Routing –Protocols -Classification based on (Group A) Researchers

A proactive routing protocol stores its information in a routing table and changes it whenever a network topology update occurs. This type helps reduce the delay period and helps gain information about new routes. (Ahmed, D.E.M. and Khalifa, O.O., 2017). Its function relies on the routing table, which comprises addresses of the target and source; therefore, it is called table -driven. (Kumar, A.; Shwe, H.Y.; Wong, K.J. and Chong, P.H., 2017).

Reactive routing protocols rediscover and reactivate routing paths when they are demanded. Accordingly, they are also called on-demand routing protocols. Unlike proactive protocols, reactive routing protocols take longer to discover the routes. However, they are very beneficial in reducing control message overhead and bandwidth consumption.

Protocol designers merge proactive and reactive routing to design a new protocol type called Hybrid. This type overcame the issues of the previous two types by minimizing the control message cost of the proactive routing protocols and postponing the update of routes at the reactive routing protocols. (Ahmed, D.E.M. and Khalifa, O.O., 2017).

Researchers consider geographic routing and energy-aware as two types of Hybrid routing categories (Terao, Y.; Phoummavong, P.; Utsu, K. and Ishii, H., 2016) (Kaur, H., Singh, H. and Sharma, A., 2016).

Figure 1. Presents classifications of (MANET) routing protocols according to (group A) researchers' point of view.

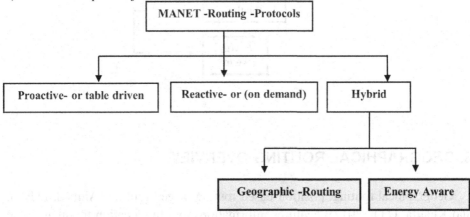

2.2 (Group B) Researchers Classification of MANET -Routing -Protocols

Figure 2 shows the general classification of (MANET) routing protocols: network structure and routing strategies. The first category contains two types: Source-Initiated and Table-Driven. The second category contains five types of protocols: Flat Topology-Based, Hierarchal routing, Multicast Routing, Geographic Routing, and Power-Aware (Torrieri, D; Talarico, S. and Valenti, M.C, 2015).

Figure 2. MANET Routing Protocols main classification (Ahmed, D.E.M. and Khalifa, O.O., 2017)

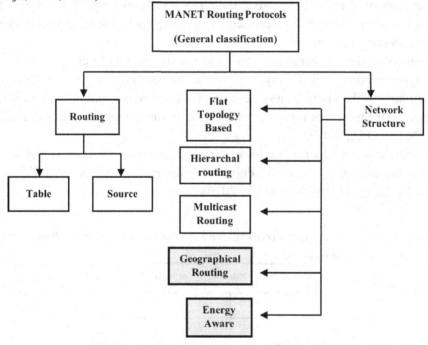

3. GEOGRAPHICAL ROUTING OVERVIEW

Geographical routing, position-based routing or geo-routing (Ahmed, D.E.M. and Khalifa, O.O., 2017)) acquires information from the location to enhance the routing packets and decide the best way toward the destination (Torrieri, D; Talarico, S. and Valenti, M.C, 2015). Instead of using the network addresses, geographical routing utilizes the location information to line the route from the source towards the target. Every node is familiar with position information and destination geographical information. Hello, messages are sent periodically to gather the location information of its neighbours' nodes; thus, the nodes don't need to store the routing tables (Rajan et al, 2022). New fields are inserted in nodes and utilized to update the information in tables in the position-based algorithms called "proactive zones". These algorithms differ from the on-demand and driven tables (Ahmed, D.E.M. and Khalifa, O.O., 2017). Geographical -routing is much more appropriate for network sensors, especially in scenarios that utilize data aggregation techniques to reduce the routing overhead toward the base station. It eliminates the redundancy of packets generated from different resources (Abdulleh, M.N., Yussof, S. and Jassim, H.S., 2015). A greedy forwarding mechanism is used when a neighbour node is beside the aim; if not, packets could be corrupted (Kaur, H., Singh, H. and Sharma, A., 2016).

The deciding factors of geographical routing, namely node localization, network density, and forwarding regulation, are the controllers of the schema effectiveness level (Abdulleh, M.N., Yussof, S. and Jassim, H.S., 2015). Geographical Routing protocols use different forwarding strategies, such as flooding (Multi-path), greedy forwarding (Single-path), and Hierarchical forwarding (Ahmed, D.E.M. and Khalifa, O.O., 2017). In this section, we will briefly explain each strategy and then have a detailed description of the most critical geographic routing protocols.

3.1. Geographical Forwarding Strategies

Geographic routing is essential and practical for Ad hoc networks. It is suitable for intensive ad hoc networks but sometimes faces a severe issue called the void. Thus, several forwarding strategies are used based on the network condition. (Rekik, Mouna and Mitton, Nathalie and Chtourou, Zied, 2015).

This section presents three types of forwarding strategies: flooding (multi-path), Hierarchical, and greedy forwarding (single-path). Figure 3 presents the Geographical Forwarding Strategies and some protocols that use them.

Figure 3. Geographical Forwarding Strategies

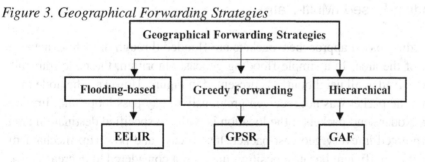

A. Greedy Forwarding (Single-Path)

The shortest-path approach is an excellent example of the greedy forwarding strategy, in which a single copy of the message is sent over some time. The majority of single-path approaches are based on two methods: face routing and greedy forwarding. The latter sends the packet near the target in each step through local information only. It is suitable when the message can progress from source to destination.

Figure 4 presents greedy forwarding, where every node sends the message to an adequate local neighbour. This neighbour can be the node that decreases the distance towards the destination in each step (Ahmed, D.E.M. and Khalifa, O.O., 2017). This will be done continuously until one node gets a "HELLO message" from the end node. (Terao, Y.; Phoummavong, P.; Utsu, K. and Ishii, H., 2016). The adequate local neighbour is selected based on the optimization criteria of the algorithm, but unfortunately, it does not guarantee that the packet will arrive at its destination. If the message reaches a particular node which does not have close neighbours to the target, then a recovery procedure is necessary (Ahmed, D.E.M. and Khalifa, O.O., 2017).

Figure 4. (A) Flooding. (B) Restricted Flooding. (Ahmed, D.E.M. and Khalifa, O.O., 2017).

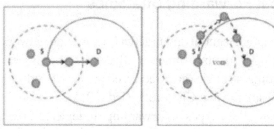

B. Flooding-Based (Multi-Path)

In flooding-based approaches, packets are flooded through the whole network or a part of the area. In a simple flooding geocast algorithm, the node transmits packets received to all neighbours, as presented in Figure. However, the node must verify that the packet was not received previously to pay pass loops and limitless flooding. Nodes send packets if the location is within a specified destination area. It's incorporated in every geo-cast packet. It's an easy and powerful mechanism; however, it is inefficient because position info is not considered to decrease packet numbers. Flooding-based protocol is suitable for underwater network sensors.

Nonetheless, flooding main idea involves all network nodes in the routing process. Thus, its performance, energy consumption, and security efficiency are weaker than those of other protocols (Ahmed, D.E.M. and Khalifa, O.O., 2017).

Figure 5. (A) Flooding. (B) Restricted Flooding. (Ahmed, D.E.M. and Khalifa, O.O., 2017).

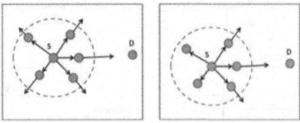

C. Hierarchical

This forwarding mechanism forms a hierarchy for scalability to many mobile nodes. Specific strategies mix the hierarchical network structures and node location using zone-based routing. A two-level hierarchy will be used if the destination is near the source, and the message will be directed according to a proactive-distance vector (Ahmed, D.E.M. and Khalifa, O.O., 2017).

3.2. Geographical -Routing -Protocols

Geographical -routing uses location information for decision-making regarding the formulation and optimization of the search route towards the destination (Abdulleh, M.N., Yussof, S. and Jassim, H.S., 2015). Figure 6 presents the primary classification of geographic, also called location-based routing protocols. To introduce protocols in this section, we divided protocols into two parts, according to either mobile or static node type (Kumar, A.; Shwe, H.Y.; Wong, K.J. and Chong, P.H., 2017).

Figure 6. The main classification of location-based routing (Kumar, A.; Shwe, H.Y.; Wong, K.J. and Chong, P.H., 2017).

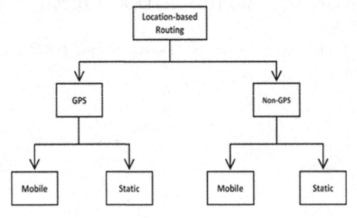

A. Geographical routing protocols used at the Network Topologies that use mobile Nodes

This section describes the geographical -protocols that depend on portable nodes in grid topologies.

1) Greedy -Perimeter -Stateless -Routing (GPSR)

Greedy -perimeter -stateless -routing (GPSR) is the best geographical protocol in which greedy forwarding depends on collected data of a router's direct neighbours in network topology. Our proposed protocol uses two methods for forwarding packets based on the original node location towards the target (Gupta, R. and Patel, P., 2016):

First, the Greedy forwarding strategy:

We will explain this strategy as a sequence of steps precisely as how it happens in the following:

i. Assuming that each node identifies all location data by GPS, the source node should recognize the ID of the target node.
ii. Every node in that network exchanges its ID, Location, and Timestamp with its nearby nodes by sending a HELLO message.
iii. Upon receiving the HELLO message, each node adds its information. This process is repeated until it reaches far nodes.

iv. The balance between traffic load and accuracy is considered when deciding the number of hops of node information.

v. Nodes refresh recent timestamp information instead of the previously stored information.

vi. This is done continuously until a node receives a HELLO message directly from the end node.

vii. Then, the source will check the nearest neighbour toward the destination to forward the packets to it, and that neighbour will retransfer them to the target.

Figure 7 represents an example of greedy forwarding. S is considered the source node. It picks the next hop node within a one-hop transmission scope, node (1) or (2). S utilizes location information obtained from nodes 1 and 2 to calculate space di (i=1, 2) from 1 and 2 to D. Since d1 < d2, the source node S selects node 1 (Terao, Y.; Phoummavong, P.; Utsu, K. and Ishii, H., 2016).

Figure 7. Greedy forwarding method (Terao, Y.; Phoummavong, P.; Utsu, K. and Ishii, H., 2016).

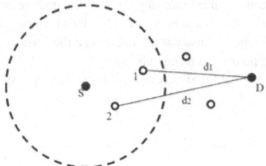

If various routes are feasible to the target node, GPSR acts surpass other ad hoc protocols using the shortest path and per-router state. Local topology data can be used to discover the fresh path whenever a change occurs in the topology. In GPSR, the location data allocated to the source node defines the destination of every message in the network. Each node can forward the message by choosing the optimal next greedy hop if its neighbour's position is well identified. In the GPRS algorithm, the geographically nearest neighbour to the target node is regarded as the next hop, and this method is redone sequentially by every node until the packet arrives at the destination. GPSR uses a beacon method to set the location tables. Weak signal cases can impact the GPSR performance efficiency due to the beacon loss (Bhangwar, N.H.; Halepoto, I.A.; Khokhar, S. and Laghari, A.A., 2017). Figure 8 shows the GPRS algorithm.

Second is the Perimeter forwarding(Hole-aware greedy routing):

Since greedy forwarding is a simple method, it suffers from a severe issue called the void zone (hole) or dead route (Terao, Y.; Phoummavong, P.; Utsu, K. and Ishii, H., 2016). To overcome this problem, a new strategy is applied as a recovery: perimeter forwarding (Gupta, R. and Patel, P., 2016). Figure9. Figure 10 and Figure 11 illustrate this type of forwarding. It is also called the hole-aware greedy routing (HAGR) (Terao, Y.; Phoummavong, P.; Utsu, K. and Ishii, H., 2016).

We will explain this strategy as a sequence of steps precisely as how it happens in the following:

What had been discussed about the steps of greedy forwarding will be repeated from i to iv then:

i. Greedy forwarding discovers the void zone and fails to forward the packets.
    A void zone is an area surrounding the void node or the empty area with no nodes. The void border is the border of a possible void area. The possible void boundary is a line between the node's transmission range crossing points and its neighbours.
ii. The exchange of HELLO messages is repeated simultaneously with each routing process.

Figure 8. GPRS algorithm (Malik, R.F.; Nurfatih, M.S.; Ubaya, H.; Zulfahmi, R. and Sodikin, E, 2017).

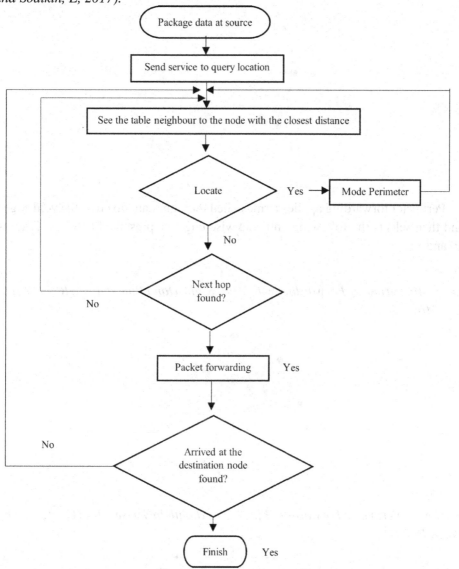

iii. prevent the void zone; each sender collects the location information to determine a possible void border and define the next hop until an entire route is recognized; then the sender uses it to send the packets to the target (Terao, Y.; Phoummavong, P.; Utsu, K. and Ishii, H., 2016).

Figure 9. Greedy forwarding failure (Gupta, R. and Patel, P., 2016).

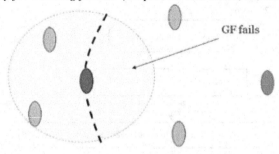

Perimeter forwarding applies a rule called the right hand to cross the void edges and then selects the following anticlockwise edge, as presented below in Figures 10 and 11.

Figure 10. Perimeter Forwarding with Void: Right-Hand Rule (Gupta, R. and Patel, P., 2016).

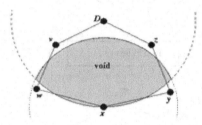

Figure 11. Perimeter Forwarding Pick the next anticlockwise edge (Gupta, R. and Patel, P., 2016).

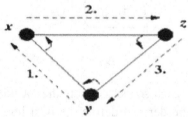

Let's take an example for a more precise view of perimeter forwarding. Supposing that the sender can gather the node information of 3 hops towards the destination by using HELLO. Hence, it determines the possible void borders that can be recognized from two-hop nodes, and then it can discover the natural void borders from all the possible void borders. Finally, it decides the next hop without a void border. Suppose node s is the sender, (one-hop) nodes are Ns, and (two-hop) nodes are Rs. If a particular node is in group R and simultaneously belongs to group N, it will be removed from the R group as it is not a (two-hop) node but one hop. To forward messages, the sender node measures the cross points of the connection coverage of the (one-hop) node and surrounding nodes. Suppose the crossing points group is V = {v1, v2 ...} (Terao, Y.; Phoummavong, P.; Utsu, K. and Ishii, H., 2016).

In Figure 12. S is a sender, Ns is the (one-hop) surrounding group of the sender, N1 is the (one-hop) surrounding group of the sender 1, Rs is the (two-hop) surrounding of the sender S and N2 is the (one-hop) surrounding group of the sender 2.

Ns = {1} and N1 = {S, 2, 3}. Rs = {2, 3} excluding S. After that, S measures the intersection group of the sender 2, which is one of two -hop near nodes of S node, taking N2 = {1, 3, 4} into counting. As an outcome of the computation, V = {V1, V2, V3, V4, V5, V6}.

Figure 12. Check step 1 - Void edge (Terao, Y.; Phoummavong, P.; Utsu, K. and Ishii, H., 2016).

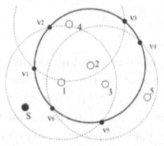

Line segments around junction points may be candidates of void edge. Some junctions should be excluded from the account before drawing potential void edges. These points that belong to the other group rather than their group will be excluded from the intersection points group V, e.g., V1 is included in a node connection zone. Nodes that generate V1 and V1 are removed from the V group. This is caused by the existence of a node that can transmit the packet close to the V1; however, V1 cannot be the endpoint of a void border. Also, V2 is considered an interchange of the connection distance of node1 and node2. However, since V2 is incorporated in the node four interaction scope, the line segment with V2 as an endpoint does not encounter a void zone. As a result, V1, V2, V5, V6 are removed from the intersection points group V.

Then, step two is to concentrate on a junction point that belongs to the V group, e.g., V1. If the line segment goes to another intersection, e.g., V2 is the shortest segment, including V1, the line segment V1-V2 shall be a void edge. V1 and V2 shall be removed from the V group. The line segment V1 - V2 is a potential void edge. This process is redone until V turns into "null". In Fig 10, only the V3-V4 line segment can be traced as the other points are already removed from V in step 1. So, the V group becomes null after removing V3 and V4 (Terao, Y.; Phoummavong, P.; Utsu, K. and Ishii, H., 2016). Figure 13 presents this step.

Figure 13. Void edge check step 2 (Terao, Y.; Phoummavong, P.; Utsu, K. and Ishii, H., 2016).

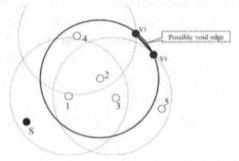

The next step is to judge whether or not the possible void edge is actual. If the line segment between target node D and the node generates a possible void edge, it crosses the possible void edge, that node is removed from R, and the possible void edge turns into actual. Because there is no node near the void edge, the node cannot transmit a packet to the target path. As presented in Figure 14. We deleted node two from Rs. = {2, 3} and Rs (the (two-hop) surrounding node group) contains node three only, that is Rs = {3} (Terao, Y.; Phoummavong, P.; Utsu, K. and Ishii, H., 2016).

Figure 14. Judgement of void edge existence. Step3 (Terao, Y.; Phoummavong, P.; Utsu, K. and Ishii, H., 2016).

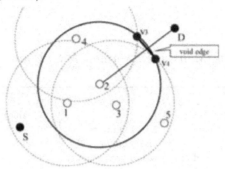

The same operation is performed for other neighbouring nodes. Node 3 is the next candidate in our example, Figure 15. The potential void edge does not intersect the line segment between node three and the target, indicating that node three does not have a void edge. Therefore, three is not excluded from Rs (Terao, Y.; Phoummavong, P.; Utsu, K.;

Figure 15. Judging void edge existence. (Terao, Y.; Phoummavong, P.; Utsu, K. and Ishii, H., 2016).

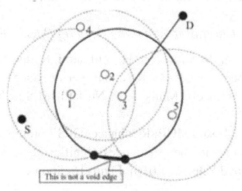

When the upper step is completed, the source node S selects the next hop node based on Greedy Forwarding according to location info from R. In our example, S chooses node one as the following hop node as there is no void edge at the node neighbouring node 1, which is node 3. This procedure is reiterated sequentially for each hop (Terao, Y.; Phoummavong, P.; Utsu, K.,

GPRS has many characteristics that can be utilized for optimization and configuration, such as Queue Time, Queue Length, and Hello Interval. Table 1 presents these in detail.

Table 1. GPSR attribute (Malik, R.F.; Nurfatih, M.S.; Ubaya, H.; Zulfahmi, R. and Sodikin, E, 2017)

Name	Description	Type (Default value)
HelloInterval	HELLO messages emission interval	TimeValue (1 sec)
MaxQueueLen	Maximum number of packets that allow a routing protocol to buffer	UintegerValue (64)
MaxQueueTime	Maximum time packets can be queued (in seconds)	TimeValue (30 sec)

GPSR generates excellent outcomes in a highway setting compared to the urban area. Direct communication in metropolitan regions is uncommon owing to more structures and trees (Karthikeyan, L. and Deepalakshmi, 2015).

2) Modified Greedy Perimeter Stateless Routing (MGPSR)

Malik, R.F., Nurfatih, M.S., Ubaya, H., Zulfahmi, R. and Sodikin, E said that no modification had been done for GPRS and its performance still better than other geographical routing protocols (Malik, R.F.; Nurfatih, M.S.; Ubaya, H.; Zulfahmi, R. and Sodikin, E, 2017).

Gupta, R. and Patel, P. said MGPSR enhances GPSR protocol for calculating the most efficient communication between nodes, significantly improving the network life-cycle (Gupta, R. and Patel, P., 2016). Figure16. Shows the MGPSR protocol.

Figure 16. Modified Greedy Perimeter Stateless Routing (MGPSR) (Gupta, R. and Patel, P., 2016).

3) Geographical Adaptive fidelity (GAF)

Geographical adaptive fidelity (GAF) routing protocol considers energy and place as costs for routing decisions. This protocol was intended mainly for ad hoc networks. It utilizes the trick of turning nodes on or off to save their energy. GAF constructs an unreal virtual network where every node gains its geographical location through GPS, which should be connected to the virtual area. Nodes within the same grid are assumed equal regarding packet routing criteria. Discovering the corresponding nodes in an ad-hoc network is not straightforward because nodes equivalent to a particular group may not be comparable to another. The issue of node equivalence is presented in Figure 17.

Figure 17. The equivalence issue (Kumar, A.; Shwe, H.Y.; Wong, K.J. and Chong, P.H., 2017)

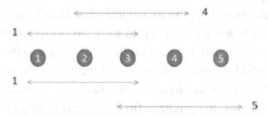

Figure 18 shows that node one can contact nodes 2, 3 and 4, but nodes 2, 3 and 4 can communicate with node 5. Therefore, node numbers 2, 3, and 4 are equivalent; thus, one must be in wake-up mode. The virtual area size depends on R, which is the radio range. The utmost nodes' spacing interval in any two neighbour grids, e.g. B and C, must not exceed the R-value. So, we can calculate r by Equation1 (Kumar, A.; Shwe, H.Y.; Wong, K.J. and Chong, P.H., 2017):

Figure 18. A virtual area in GAF (Kumar, A.; Shwe, H.Y.; Wong, K.J. and Chong, P.H., 2017).

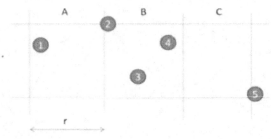

$$r \leq \frac{R}{\sqrt{5}}$$

Or $r^2+(2r)^2 \leq R^2$

Each node balances its loads by the periodic change of its situation from off to on. GAF utilizes three situations:

· Discovery: the search for nodes located in almost the same area or grid.
· Active: indicates that the node is in the wake-up mode and joining the routing process.
· Sleep: is the mode where the node is not active.

These situations are shown in Figure 19. The resting time of a specific node depends on the implementation and the routing parameters used. GAF is applied to the static scenario as well as the dynamic nodes. In dynamic cases, each node calculates the time that should leave the grid and transfers it to all neighbours. Based on this information, the inactive nodes set their off timing to maintain routing accuracy. An inactive node activates before the current node departure time expires. To maintain the network connection, GAF keeps a node in wake-up mode in each area of the virtual regions. Researchers' findings confirm that GAF has equivalent performance at the same level as a standard ad-hoc protocol regarding delay and packet drop. Overall, GAF boosts network life by controlling energy. GAF also utilizes a hierarchical forwarding approach where the nodes rely on geographical location. For each region, a specific node operates as a promoter to pass messages to others. But, unlike other hierarchical protocols, this sponsor node does not create any combinations. (Kumar, A.; Shwe, H.Y.; Wong, K.J. and Chong, P.H., 2017).

Figure 19. State transitions in GAF (Kumar, A.; Shwe, H.Y.; Wong, K.J. and Chong, P.H., 2017).

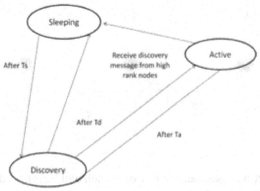

4) Minimum -Energy -Communication -Network -Protocol (MECN)

(MECN) is a position-based protocol that reduces the network's general energy consumption. It uses the low-power RF transmitter structure to regulate energy simultaneously. It is linked with the global network to avoid or overcome any module weakness. (Kumar, A.; Shwe, H.Y.; Wong, K.J. and Chong, P.H., 2017).

This protocol relies on the self-configuration of portable nodes and the amount of power used in the network. The protocol presumes all nodes have an equivalent antenna altitude to avoid the link break issue. It is not based on a particular link break value; thus, it can be implemented in distinct deployment settings. This protocol utilizes low-power GPS to provide almost every node with its location in the network; however, they will not receive the positions of other nodes in the network. The protocol acts finer when nodes are static. A particular node in the network acts as a sink for data, also called the "master site", and is positioned at the network border. MECN depends on the middle node to send the messages rather than sending the message directly to consume less power, and this is called relaying concept (Kumar, A.; Shwe, H.Y.; Wong, K.J. and Chong, P.H., 2017). Figure 20 illustrates an example of a relaying concept.

Figure 20. Relaying concept for 3 nodes (Kumar, A.; Shwe, H.Y.; Wong, K.J. and Chong, P.H., 2017)

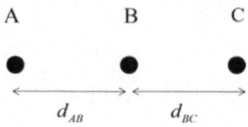

This algorithm consumes meagre power, which can be ignored as it is negligible compared to transmitting and receiving energy. Figure 21 shows the relay area of the transmit-relay node pair (i, r). Node I calculates the coverage range by determining which node I can arrive at in all relay areas. So, MECN will look for a small area from the network called a sub-network. It does not contain many nodes and has low transmission energy between nodes. The enclosure of node i is presented in Figure 22. Thus, all minimum power routes in the network are identified by the local find-out for every node based on its relay area without having to involve all nodes in the network (Kumar, A.; Shwe, H.Y.; Wong, K.J. and Chong, P.H., 2017).

Figure 21. Relay area of the transmit node pair (Kumar, A.; Shwe, H.Y.; Wong, K.J. and Chong, P.H., 2017).

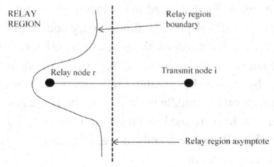

Figure 22. Enclosure of node i (Kumar, A.; Shwe, H.Y.; Wong, K.J. and Chong, P.H., 2017).

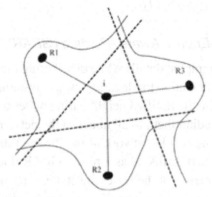

This protocol has two phases:

The first phase is searching for an enclosure: The first phase looks for an enclosure or coverage area. Here, this protocol uses the two-dimensional position of the node and creates a detailed graph, which contains the enclosures of all transmit nodes. To generate this construction graph, local calculations in the nodes are required. It utilizes a function to keep the graph updated. This enclosure graph involves all the energy-efficient optimal routes.

The second phase is the Cost distribution: This protocol identifies the optimal paths on the chart. It uses the shortest path algorithm with energy consumption for better path selection. MECN is self-configuring in dynamic environments and can automatically restore node errors or connections to fresh nodes. It utilizes a poor-power RF transceiver to control energy. This protocol uses a regional optimizing technique that discovers low-energy paths and changes the path. A regional update calculation is needed. It does not demand a lot of global data on nodes. As a result of using the local information, Interference between the nodes is minimized. The messages are forwarded only across a limited range due to distributed protocol. This protocol assumes that every node can reach all other nodes, and this is impossible under some natural conditions (Kumar, A.; Shwe, H.Y.; Wong, K.J. and Chong, P.H., 2017).

5) Small -Minimum -Energy -Communication -Network (SMECN)

This protocol is an advancement of MECN. It overcomes the issues between any pair of nodes in real time. Like MECN, SMECN also creates a sub-network but is smaller in terms of edge number. As a result, the hops number is minimized. Researchers have shown that SMECN consumes less energy than MECN and minimizes the cost of line regeneration. On the other hand, the overhead is maximized to create a sub-network with a minor number of edges. (Kumar, A.; Shwe, H.Y.; Wong, K.J. and Chong, P.H., 2017).

6) Geographic -and –Energy-Aware -Routing (GEAR)

(GEAR) utilizes geographic details while distributing the requests to particular areas. This process is essential for location-aware systems. It exploits energy-conscious and geographically notified neighbouring nodes to send messages to the target area instead of sending them to all nodes in the network. In comparison, the message is flooded in the whole network at the directed diffusion. GEAR saves more energy at the directed diffusion as a result. GEAR does not need a space to save locations and considers that the nodes are static. It proposes that each node is always conscious of its present place in the network via the GPS. It also assumes that nodes are conscious of their residual power level, neighbours' positions and residual energy through a hello protocol. The path in this protocol is dual. GEAR devices have two kinds of cost parameters:

- **Estimated cost:** contains the retaining power and mileage to target.
- **Learned -cost:** an enhancement of the cost. It counts the routes surrounding the holes in networks.

A network hole suggests the node has no neighbours near the destination area. The estimated and learned costs are similar if there is no hole in the route. Whenever the target receives a message, the price is forwarded one -hop backwards to prepare the path setup for the coming message. (Kumar, A.; Shwe, H.Y.; Wong, K.J. and Chong, P.H., 2017).

GEAR uses two phases:

Phase 1: Sending messages to the destination: when any node gets a message, it examines whether any neighbour node is near the destination area. In the presence of several nodes, the closest one to the destination area is chosen for the upcoming hop. If entire neighbours are far, it indicates the existence of a hole. In this scenario, one of the neighbours will be selected to send messages depending on the cost. The selection will be refreshed based on the learned cost.

Phase 2: Broadcasting messages within the area: at this phase, either repeated geographic transmitting or limited flooding is applied. Limited flooding is suitable if the nodes are not densely deployed. Otherwise, the repeated geographic -flooding is more energy-efficient. The area is divided into four subareas, and four copies of the message are sent. Dividing and broadcasting are repeated until the area with only one node remains (Kumar, A.; Shwe, H.Y.; Wong, K.J. and Chong, P.H., 2017). An instance is illustrated in Figure 23.

GEAR doesn't use any MAC -protocols. It is similar to GPSR, a previous geographical routing protocol that performs planar graphs to recover from the difficulty of holes. Compared with GPRS, GEAR performs finer in terms of packet transmission and strength consumption. The simulation consequences are current: GEAR grants 70% - 80% greater messages than (GPSR) for unequal traffic distribution, and for everyday traffic, GEAR provides 25% - 35% messages greater than GPSR. (Kumar, A.; Shwe, H.Y.; Wong, K.J. and Chong, P.H., 2017). The foremost downside of this protocol is its restricted energy administration and scalability. Also, it does not focus on security while routing. (Verma, K., 2016).

Figure 23. Recursive geographic forwarding in GEAR (Kumar, A.; Shwe, H.Y.; Wong, K.J. and Chong, P.H., 2017).

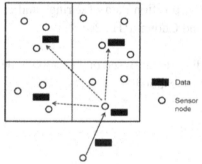

7) Location-Based -Energy-Efficient -Intersection-Routing (EELIR)

EELIR is mainly a geographical protocol. This protocol assumes that nodes know their energy levels, present positions, and sink node locations. It employs GPS to identify the locations. It also supposes that all portable nodes move in two dimensions. (Kumar, A.; Shwe, H.Y.; Wong, K.J. and Chong, P.H., 2017).

This protocol works in three stages:

The announcement phase: the sender node tries to limit the routing area and sends the announcement message to neighbours. An example of this phase is shown in **Figure 24.** In case the source node $A(X a, Y a)$ knows the location of node $S (X s, Y s)$, node A can quickly create an AS section directly (sector is defined as the shortest space between the source node and sink; in this it is P a, P n from node A to sink node S). Equation 2 may compute the exact location of node B.

Figure 24. Start advertisement phase (Kumar, A.; Shwe, H.Y.; Wong, K.J. and Chong, P.H., 2017).

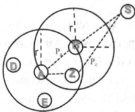

$$B(x_b, y_b) \rightarrow x_b = (x_a + r\cos\theta), \ y_b = (y_b + r\sin\theta).$$

This way, the areas of two rings and their intersection are determined. So, node A may announce a packet to neighbours (D, Z and E). The announcement packet contains an account of P a, position data of 2 rings and cross paths (Kumar, A.; Shwe, H.Y.; Wong, K.J. and Chong, P.H., 2017).

- Conditional forwarding stage: Based on Equation 3, neighbours of the source will decide whether to respond.

$$d_1 = \sqrt{(x_z - x_a)^2 + (y_z - y_a)^2}$$

$$d_2 = \sqrt{(x_z - x_b)^2 + (y_z - y_b)^2}$$

d1 < r and d2 < r: true

If the condition is positive, the nodes shall respond to node A. Their response will consist of power level information and Pn value. As presented in Figure 24, node Z shall reply with the remaining power degree and Pz of node Z; however, node D shall not because the result of the above conditions was not satisfying. (Kumar, A.; Shwe, H.Y.; Wong, K.J. and Chong, P.H., 2017).

Path selection stage: The source node shall forward the messages to dedicated nodes. The node with a high energy level and short P n will gain a high priority. EELIR only gathers neighbours' information if the node needs route discovery, so it utilizes the on-demand property to be more energy efficient. The sender node transfers data to the sink unicast and saves energy. EELIR performs better than the flooding-based routing protocols and location-aided routing protocol (LAR) in terms of energy consumption and delivery ratio (Kumar, A.; Shwe, H.Y.; Wong, K.J. and Chong, P.H., 2017).

8) An -Anonymous –Location-Based -Efficient -Routing -Protocol (ALERT)

ALERT is distinctive in its low price and confidentiality safety for routes, destinations, and sources. It assumes the whole network region is a rectangle as nodes are
arbitrarily diffused. It utilizes the hierarchical area division and selects an initial relay
node from the partitioned area for each stage. Therefore, it dynamically produces
an unexpected routing path for a packet. The network is divided equally into two
areas in the phase of partitioning the hierarchical area. Then, each area is vertically
divided. This area is then divided into the smallest areas in an ongoing horizontal
and vertical way. Figure25. Presents an instance of ALERT routing in which D is the
target area, namely the shaded area. Each information source or forwarder applies
the hierarchical area division in ALERT routing. It first ensures that the nodes and
the targets are in the same area. If that's the case, it alternately splits the area vertically and horizontally. The node repeats this method until it is in the same target
node area. After that, it arbitrarily selects a forwarder node location nearest to its
location. The transmissions are forwarded to all nodes at the target area in the last
phase. Adding to the above, ALERT uses a strategy to conceal information initiator
amongst a group of initiators to set the source's Anonymity security (Kumar, A.;
Shwe, H.Y.; Wong, K.J. and Chong, P.H., 2017).

However, this protocol causes a higher overhead when compared with other
location-based routing protocols. (Iche, A.H. and Dhage, M.R., 2015).

*Figure 25. Routing among zones in ALERT (Kumar, A.; Shwe, H.Y.; Wong, K.J.
and Chong, P.H., 2017).*

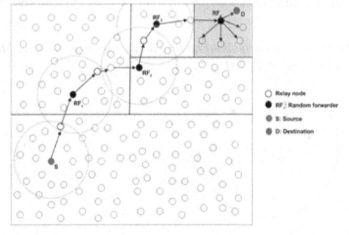

9) Energy-Efficient Geographic Forwarding Algorithm (DECA)

DECA is an acronym for position-based -routing. The purpose of DECA is to enhance the lifespan of the network. It uses the limited application of Dijkstra's algorithm and power-critical prevention to select the next step for packet transmission. This protocol supposes that all nodes have a similar maximum transmission range, an omnidirectional antenna, and the ability to dynamically identify transmission energy to interact with other nodes within its transmission area. It also presumes that every node can predict the energy needed to interact with a direct neighbour and recognize the precise position in the network through geographic tracking facilities such as GPS (Kumar, A.; Shwe, H.Y.; Wong, K.J. and Chong, P.H., 2017).

Remaining power data may be obtained through regular regional exchange of welcome writings between neighbour nodes. Each intermediate node in DECA utilizes a Dijkstra-like algorithm for local topology to select the optimal adjacent hop to target. Furthermore, it utilises the energy-use effectiveness as a parameter while determining the optimal hop to reach the target. In an attempt to pay past amplifying energy-hungry -nodes, power criticality prevention is conducted. The method of choosing the best node to forward the message is shown in Figure 26. The origin node is x, and the target node is t. There are three possible routes:

Path1: $x - u - t$ (its approximate cost is 14.0. Second).
Path 2: $x - v - t$ (its approximate cost is 12.7. Second).
Path 3: $x - u - v - t$ (its approximate cost is 12.5. Second).

Dijkstra -algorithm shall choose the 3rd route that has the least cost.

Figure 26. Node x chooses neighbour node to arrive target (Kumar, A.; Shwe, H.Y.; Wong, K.J. and Chong, P.H., 2017).

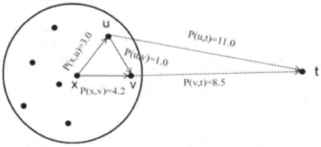

Reducing end-to-end transmission per packet is a strategy used to increase a network's lifespan. This will minimize energy consumption for message delivery. The protocol can operate in different sink settings.

10) An improved - Hybrid – Location-Based – Ad -Hoc - Routing - Protocol (IHLAR)

IHLAR is a hybrid position-based protocol that syndicates geographical tracking with an ad-hoc network processing protocol based on topology. In IHLAR, every node maintains a list of neighbours for a predetermined hops (ρ) number. When a packet is received by a target node or a forwarding node, it first tests whether or not the node is located at the neighbour table. In case the target node inward hops ρ from the origin or central node, that node will transmit a message employing AODV, as demonstrated in Figure 27. The packet is going to be transferred with greedy -forwarding. IHLAR overcomes the challenges of average postponement and packet delivery ratio (Kumar, A.; Shwe, H.Y.; Wong, K.J. and Chong, P.H., 2017).

Figure 27. Route Setup in IHLAR (Kumar, A.; Shwe, H.Y.; Wong, K.J. and Chong, P.H., 2017).

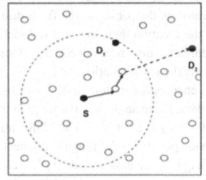

IHLAR has two main drawbacks when compared with other location-based routing protocols: it causes higher overhead, and it is weak in terms of security (Iche, A.H. and Dhage, M.R., 2015).

11) The Location-Based Routing Protocol (LBRP)

The Protocol utilizes node location data and implements a greedy forwarding approach to forward messages. It is based on a simple distribution method. It uses an adjustable transmission energy algorithm depending on location data while routing the packets. Consequently, this protocol loses energy during data transmission and thus maximizes the lifespan of nodes (Figure 28). Illustrate the packet transmission method using the LBRP from origin node -(S) to target node - (B).

The greedy-forwarding strategy is utilized in LBRP to forward the existing packet to the neighbouring node nearest to the target node. The virtual service module (LSM) is triggered to define the position of the next step on the path to the target and the place of the target node. LSM is accountable for tracking the locations of nodes throughout the network. LSM utilizes a beacon-based some-for-all method in which some nodes are familiar with information about the places of other nodes in the network. Before transmitting a message, every node inserts target node position data because the next node on the path must understand the position of the target node in an attempt to transmit the packet properly to the target node. Unless an updated location is available, the middle nodes shall use data to acknowledge the target location. Upon receiving a packet from an initial node, the next hop node is recognized by the LSM. The intermediate node also controls and improves the target place in the packet if aware of the latest target location. Then, the node discovered in the obtained packet transfers the packet to the fresh destination. The sequence numbers collected with the location data are used to identify the recent location data. These sequence figures are drawn from LSM's periodic messages. The more excellent sequence figure is the latest location data.

The LBRP algorithm enables the middle nodes to change the target's position and use the LSM speed data. Because of this, the frequency of place beaconing is minimized, and asset efficiency is improved. The LBRP attempts to exhaust considerably fewer transmission powers by dividing the connecting node's transmitting power according to its range. It expands the battery life as well. LBRP has never been tested on real-life networks or nodes, and LBRP applicability on actual nodes is suspected (Kumar, A.; Shwe, H.Y.; Wong, K.J. and Chong, P.H., 2017).

Figure 28. Routing packet from node A- node B LBRP example (Kumar, A.; Shwe, H.Y.; Wong, K.J. and Chong, P.H., 2017).

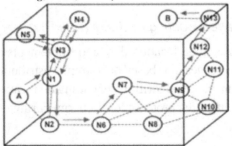

12) SBZRP and LBZRP

Selective border-cast zone routing protocol (SBZRP) and location-based selective border-cast zone routing protocol (LBZRP) are enhanced zone routing protocols to improve the zone's proactivity.

Instead of the usual border cast, the choice of the border nodes is based on the connectivity and the network density. SBZRP is the first enhancement in which zones are created dynamically. It has a low proactive property, and in this protocol, only a few nodes remain in the peripheral data of the next trip. LBZRP is implemented as the second SBZRP expansion enhancement. It is focused on the protocol for location-aided routing (LAR). LBZRP Border-cast is restricted to borders for pockets close to the previous location to the destination. LBZRP reduces the proactive aspect of the area and minimizes the power outside the region. (Kumar, A.; Shwe, H.Y.; Wong, K.J. and Chong, P.H., 2017).

The main drawback of these protocols is the existence of Overlapping zones (Zaman, K.; Shafiq, M.; Choi, J.G. and Iqbal, M, 2015).

B) Geographical Routing Protocols Used at the Network Topologies that use Static Nodes

A node is regarded as a static node if its current distance to the sink is equal to that calculated in the preceding timestamp (Benkhelifa, I.; Moussaoui, S. and Demirkol, I., 2018). This chapter concentrates on the geographic scheduling protocols in network topologies that depend on static nodes.

1) Trajectory -Based -Forwarding (TBF)

(TBF) namely routing protocol that needs a heavy network & coordinate system, e.g. GPS, for nodes to locate themselves and estimate the range to their neighbours. Between source-based transmission (SBR) and selective forwarding strategies, TBF is introduced as a centre ground. The origin encodes the route in this protocol and inserts it into every packet. (Kumar, A.; Shwe, H.Y.; Wong, K.J. and Chong, P.H., 2017). Figure 29 presents an instance of an application using trajectory-based-routing (TBR). When the middle nodes receive the packet, they decode the trajectory and use selective transmission methods so that the packet continues its trajectory as far as possible. Node connectivity does not affect path servicing in TBF, as the origin path is a path that does not include forwarding node designations.

Multi-path routing can also be applied in TBF to enhance a network's efficiency and ability, where an alternative route is just another route. TBF's other excellent implementation is to secure the network's perimeter.

Figure 29. An example of using TBR in an application: The application gathers photographs of the "west of mountains," attempting to make the best path distinct from the traditional shortest routing (Kumar, A.; Shwe, H.Y.; Wong, K.J. and Chong, P.H., 2017).

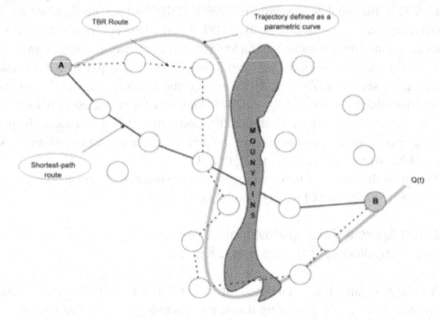

2) Bounded Voronoi Greedy Forwarding (BVGF)

BVGF is a localized algorithm which produces selective routing choices based on the positions of one-hop neighbours. When the source node I want to forward a packet, a neighbour j can only be used as the next hop if the line segment that connects the packet's source and destination intersects $Vor(j)$ or synchronizes with one of $Vor(j)$'s borders. BVGF chooses the next hop neighbour among all competent neighbours with the shortest range to the target. If various qualified neighbours have the same length to the location, the routing node chooses one of them randomly as the next step (Kumar, A.; Shwe, H.Y.; Wong, K.J. and Chong, P.H., 2017).

Figure 30 shows four successive nodes $(s_i \sim s_{i+3})$ from origin to target v on the BVGF tracking route. The communication loop of each node is also shown in the chart. We can see that the next hop of a node on the route may not be close to the Voronoi diagram. (e.g., node s_i does not share a Voronoi edge with node s_{i+1}). When $Rc >> Rs$, this greedy forwarding approach enables BVGF to have a tighter linked dilation relative to the DT attached, which only considers DT corners and does not change with the distance proportion. This procedure does not consistently deplete the battery energy of the nodes. There is only one next step for each node to forward their packet to the sink. Any data transmission route between an origin node and the sink will, therefore, always have the same chain of the next hops that will benefit significantly from the breakdown of battery energy. BVGF is not efficient in terms of energy.

Figure 30. A routing path of BVGF (Kumar, A.; Shwe, H.Y.; Wong, K.J. and Chong, P.H., 2017).

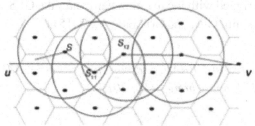

3) Geographic Random Forwarding (GERAF)

Geographic random forwarding is a protocol for location transmission that uses a system for awake / sleep pairing and MAC procedures. It assumes that both their roles and the sink location are known to all nodes within the whole network. A tool such as GPS can identify the place. Nodes do not retain their neighbour's data and use the awake / sleep duty system. All devices in the network switch between the working state periodically and then to a service cycle-based exercise state. Each node becomes effective when it sends a packet. So, it transmits the packet that includes the node's position and the target place. GERAF utilizes the CSMA / CA MAC procedure to avoid conflicts (Kumar, A.; Shwe, H.Y.; Wong, K.J. and Chong, P.H., 2017).

The region facing the target is referred to as the forwarding region. It is divided into preference areas, where all servers from a near-destination region have a reduced precedence over any other nodes. Thus, among those not vacant, a relay node is selected from the highest priority area (Kumar, A.; Shwe, H.Y.; Wong, K.J. and Chong, P.H., 2017). The priority region is illustrated in Figure 31.

Subsequently, nodes in the highest priority region compete to have the chance of forwarding. If only one node from the area obtains the signal, it will readily transmit the packet, and the method will end. In some instances, concurrently, numerous nodes communicate, which causes a crash. A prevention method is implemented to choose a single forwarder in the event of a crash. In other cases, as all nodes in the region are sleeping, there is no node to forward the packet. To solve this drawback, the transmit station shall be selected in the second-highest-priority area and so forth in the next transmitting attempt. The stage of relay choice will be reiterated until the highest amount of effort is reached. The packet will thus achieve the location of the goal. The method of relay choice does not involve topology or routing lists (Kumar, A.; Shwe, H.Y.; Wong, K.J. and Chong, P.H., 2017).

The main drawback of this protocol is the probability of maximizing power usage and an increase in latency (Kim, D.S. and Tran-Dang, H., 2019). Add that the nodes should be rigged with localization hardware like GPS, which is costly for large networks (Lakshmi, G.R. and Srikanth, V., 2015).

Figure 31. Priority area in GERAF: increase priority from A4 to A1 (Kumar, A.; Shwe, H.Y.; Wong, K.J. and Chong, P.H., 2017).

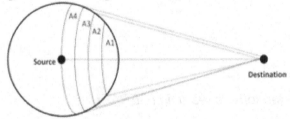

4) Anchor -Location -Service (ALS)

ALS is a procedure that depends on the network maintaining location communication among various portable nodes and locations. ALS offers data on the dumping place using an extendable and effective method. ALS is supposed to have two parameters for all nodes: α, capacity of network cellule and (*XBase, YBase*), coordinates of baseline. They are regularly broadcast, and a tracking system such as GPS obtains their place. The previous three procedures bring position after all the nodes are implemented (Kumar, A.; Shwe, H.Y.; Wong, K.J. and Chong, P.H., 2017):

ALS global grid construction process: nodes operate in a global network setup process, and by using baseline coordinates (XBase, YBase), the coordinates of the network are determined as follows in Equation 4.:

$$X_P = X_{Base} + i \cdot \alpha$$

$$Y_P = Y_{Base} + j \cdot \alpha$$

Where, $\{i, j = \pm 0, \pm 1 \pm 2, \ldots\}$.

The stage of the nearest node to the target is called the base node, while the map node with the position of server location for the specific sink is named anchor. The choice method of the grid node is shown in Figure 32.

Anchor selection process: Several target servers may be available in the network room. Each of them gives a dump officer to its neighbour node. The function of the filter officer is to manage the target node place data using an anchor scheme. The anchor scheme where the grid node is called the transmitter is a set of grid nodes. This scheme works as a server place (Kumar, A.; Shwe, H.Y.; Wong, K.J. and Chong, P.H., 2017).

Figure 32. The grid node selection process (Kumar, A.; Shwe, H.Y.; Wong, K.J. and Chong, P.H., 2017).

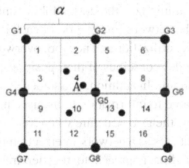

Query and information dissemination process: When any intervention occurs in the mapped sector, the node becomes the base node that sends information to the target node (stack). First, the origin node records to the nearest bank node and then becomes the target officer. This origin officer then transfers four request blocks to discover the drain agent's destination. Here, the anchor system's function begins, sending data about the ship officer to the origin node. Upon receiving the information from the sink officer, the origin node starts transmitting the information packet to the sink officer using a procedure depending on location.

Sources use ALS protocol to scalability and efficiently locate sinks. The cost of communication and transport was minimized as various suppliers used the same global grid to locate sinks. It is effective because overhead communication is of a significant concern & nodes have restricted resources. ALS is utilized with GPSR and contrasted to the grid-based –two-tier -data -dissemination -protocol (TTDD) as the protocol's communication, time, location, and overhead status are considered vital performance parameters. These parameters vary in the number of sources and sinks, the rapidity of mobile sink nodes, and network size. ALS and TTDD consider nodes static and location-conscious and resist universal flooding to transmit information about location and data. Their primary distinction is that TTDD is origin -orientate, sets one network to each source and uses target nodes to share position & information; on the other hand, ALS utilizes grid nodes to share information (Kumar, A.; Shwe, H.Y.; Wong, K.J. and Chong, P.H., 2017).

5) Two –Tier- Data- Dissemination -Protocol (TTDD)

As we have already stated, the benefits of (TTDD) are utilized by ALS protocol. Nodes are fixed in the network, and only sinks are portable. TTDD can function for many portable sinks and many continuous origin nodes. It assumes that every node is conscious about its location through a location-aware scheme, e.g. GPS. The static source node proactively builds a grid structure to spread information to a portable sink. It uses the greedy -geographic -forwarding to create and sustain a system framework that minimizes the cost. Mobile sink requests are restricted within local cells due to the network framework for each information source. Thus, various sinks prevent power utilization and network overwork from global flooding.

TTDD considers all nodes conscious of their positions, which implies that they have to observe certain stimuli. In addition, it assumes that the cost of task dissemination is very low compared to information transmission.

The source node begins the grid structure whenever an action arises in the network. The source node initiates as a network intersection point and uses the simple greedy geographic forwarding approach to transfer information announcement messages to its four nearby crossing points. It ends once the message reaches the closest node to the crossing point specified in the message. Every intermediate node retains source data and forwards the message to its neighbouring interchange lines, except the sender. When a message reaches the network border, this operation stops. Dissemination points are chosen for the nodes that save the source data.

After this procedure, a grid is built for that designated source, and the sink may flood its queries in a regional cell to obtain messages. The closest dissemination node on the grid will receive a query and then broadcast the query through other dissemination nodes toward the source node. Arranged information will be transferred to the sink in the opposite path. The forwarding route in TTDD is discovered to be longer than the shortest path under certain circumstances. Results indicate that in terms of network lifetime and delay in information transmission, TTDD performs faster than immediate diffusion. However, TTDD does not solve the significant problem of the high overhead of system maintenance and recalculation (Kumar, A.; Shwe, H.Y.; Wong, K.J. and Chong, P.H., 2017).

6) Energy-Efficient -Geographic -Routing (EEGR)

Energy-efficient geographic routing (EEGR) is extendable, energy-efficient, and simple. It uses geographic data and transceiver energy features to make forwarding decisions. It does not depend on looping but deduces the theoretical limitations from the number of hops to transmit node-to-sink messages. EEGR assumes that radio transceivers are heterogeneous in aspects of the transmission range R in all nodes throughout the network (Kumar, A.; Shwe, H.Y.; Wong, K.J. and Chong, P.H., 2017).

It also assumes that each node is conscious of its location and the sink's geographic coordinates by using a low-cost tool such as GPS. Utilized power by node operating as relay receiving single-bit information and transferring them via distance x is calculated as presented in Equation 5:

$$P_{relay}(x) = a_{11} + a_2 x^k + a_{12} \equiv a_1 + a_2 x^k$$

As a1 = a11 + a12 and k (k ≥ 2), the interpreter of broadcast failure is highly dependent on the surrounding environment.

In this protocol, the packet is sent to the neighbour closest to the optimal energy transmission position rather than transferring it to the neighbour closest to the sink. It uses control messages to calculate the ideal relay node; thus, nodes are unnecessary to keep data about their neighbours (Kumar, A.; Shwe, H.Y.; Wong, K.J. and Chong, P.H., 2017). The forwarding procedure in EEGR is shown in Figure 33.

Here, p is the origin node, and the best relay to its ideal relay position, fp, is the nearest neighbour. Not all neighbouring nodes to p are permitted to engage as p. Rp is the node p relay study area and is given as the fp-centred area with rs (p) radius, *rs (p) pfp|* in **Figure 33.***The RP node shall engage in the p-node communication* choice operation. The ideal rs (p) can be assumed depending on the cell allocation size. D is the range from the origin node p to sink *s*. If **Equation6:**

$$d \leq \sqrt[k]{\frac{a_1}{a_2(1 - 2^{1-k})}}$$

And d ≤ R, then origin node p can transmit its messages directly to the sink, as forwarding messages directly is more energy-efficient than transmitting the messages through new nodes. EEGR utilizes two methods to minimize overhead communication:

1) the number of response messages is managed by changing the size of the transmission search area as the ideal transmission region covers one neighbour only (Kumar, A.; Shwe, H.Y.; Wong, K.J. and Chong, P.H., 2017).

2) Back-off replay is used when the relay search area has more than one node to minimize the number of control messages. EEGR shall be compared to MFR, GRS, PLRA, and GPER. The outcome demonstrates that EEGR's energy efficiency is 60% higher than that of MFR and GRS, and it performs faster in aspects of broadcast scope than MFR, GRS, and PLRA (Kumar, A.; Shwe, H.Y.; Wong, K.J.;.

Figure 33. Forwarding process of EEGR (Kumar, A.; Shwe, H.Y.; Wong, K.J. and Chong, P.H., 2017).

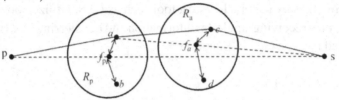

7) Multisink -GERAF (M-GERAF)

It is a multi-sink method for information dissemination. This protocol utilizes random geographic forwarding and a powerful energy-off technique without recognizing the location of the neighbouring node to obtain secure information distribution.

M-GERAF assumes nodes are implemented statically and tightly in the web. It uses a switching system for awake / sleep where nodes are switched on and off continuously. It also suggests that all nodes have little data about their position and the sink nodes' position. Nodes can acquire location data by using GPS or any other localization tool. A node becomes involved whenever it transmits a packet, so it moves to the on-route and sends a packet. The packet broadcast has both the node position and the target location. All nodes in the coverage zone that can hear the source node will obtain packets and organize information sending, depending on the back-off time (Kumar, A.; Shwe, H.Y.; Wong, K.J. and Chong, P.H., 2017).

It is possible to calculate the subset of remaining locations by Equation 7. (Kumar, A.; Shwe, H.Y.; Wong, K.J. and Chong, P.H., 2017):

$Di = \{ Ps \in Ds: d\ (PS, Pi) < d\ (PS, Ps) \}$

Here, $Ps = (Xs, Ys)$ is location of origin node s & $Ds = \{Ps1, Ps2... PsNs\}$ is the information target set of origin node s.

Just after a particular node receives a message, it anticipates a back-off period to be calculated using the position value of the sink node, its location, and the current source node. Equation 8 illustrates the back-off time calculation. (Kumar, A.; Shwe, H.Y.; Wong, K.J. and Chong, P.H., 2017):

$$T_b^{(i)} = k \frac{\min}{S \in Di} \left\{ \frac{1}{d(Ps, Ps) - d(Ps, Pi)} - \frac{1}{d(Pi, Ps)} \right\}$$

To avoid clashes, an arbitrary period is added to the calculated back-off time. After the first forwarding, the first forwarder packet target is removed from its destination group by active nodes in the first forwarder coverage zone. Nodes transmitting the obtained packet may belong to another coverage zone.

By constringing the max, this protocol attempts to minimize transmission amount. α max is the most significant conical area's apex angle. Figure 34 presents α max, receiver I and target Sj.

If d $(Psj, Pi) \gg$ d (Pi, Ps) segment i Sj, segment Sj s are parallel and Equation9.

$$d(P_{Sj}, P_s) - d(P_{Sj}, P_i) \approx d(P_i, P_s) . \cos\left(\frac{\alpha i, j}{2}\right)$$

When α I j is the apex angle of the shrink-est cone that includes Pi, as shown in Figure 34, Equation 10 can calculate the next node.

$$D_i = \left\{ S \in D_s : d(P_S, P_s) - d(P_S, P_i) \approx d(P_i, P_s) . \cos\left(\frac{\alpha_{max}}{2}\right) \right\}$$

Where the highest authorized cone apex angle is α max.

For simulation, grid fields are divided into hexagonal grids. At least one node in each grid is supposed to be active, and that node will involve all neighbouring grids. The nodes in the network change from snooze to awaken status. This arbitrary geographic routing strategy doesn't include a packet loss retrieval method because there is looping, and the transmission will be renewed if a specific packet is not transmitted within a period of time.

M-GERAF-ANALYSIS (Multi-sink—GERAF-ANALYSIS) is an improvement of M-GERAF with modifications to minimize the possibility of non-achieving certain locations and minimize errors in information transmission. The back-off period has been updated to decrease the average amount of information broadcast needed to cover entire sink nodes.

A fresh forwarding strategy is implemented to maximise α max and attempt to re-transmit without waiting for variability in network topology. Due to α max sporadic enlargement, a slight increase in transmitting quantity is observed. In

M-GeRaf, back-off calculation focused on the path of the sink and did not depend on the size of the progress towards locations that the findings show an enormous increase in transmission and energy consumption performance (Kumar, A.; Shwe, H.Y.; Wong, K.J. and Chong, P.H., 2017).

Figure 34. Ds = {S1, S2, S3}, D1 = {S2, S3}, D2 = {S2, S1}, D3 = {S1}, D4 = {S3}. Highest authorized apex angle α max & apex of shrink-est cone in Sj direction which consist of i, αi, j, are portrayed (Kumar, A.; Shwe, H.Y.; Wong, K.J. and Chong, P.H., 2017).

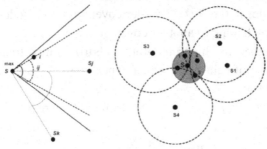

8) Greedy Forwarding With Virtual Position (GF-VIP) and Greedy Forwarding With Multi-Level Virtual (GF-MVP)

Virtual location (GF-VIP) greedy forwarding is a geographic algorithm that utilizes a greedy -forwarding -protocol. This protocol considers using some local-ization facilities; every node is conscious of its location in the current network. It presents a unique principle called the virtual position and assumes that the virtual position is the middle location between all neighbouring nodes. Instead of selecting the neighbouring node geographically, GF-VIP uses that digital position to choose the next hop. (GF-MVP) Greedy-forwarding with multi-level virtual location uses the location data at a higher level (Kumar, A.; Shwe, H.Y.; Wong, K.J. and Chong, P.H., 2017)

Figure 35 shows an example of the node's geographic location and the virtual node's location at the first level.

Figure 35. Example demonstrates the node and the virtual node location in the network at 1st level (Kumar, A.; Shwe, H.Y.; Wong, K.J. and Chong, P.H., 2017).

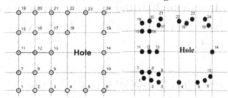

Each node holds the Virtual position information along with its direct geographic neighbour.

Assume that node A (*Xa, Ya*) contains the following neighbours: node B (*Xb, Yb*), node C (*Xc, Yc*) and node D (*Xd, Yd*).

The virtual location for node A is computed as Equation 11.

$$(x'_a, y'_a) = ((x_b + x_c + x_d)/3, (y_b + y_c + y_d)/3).$$

Identical to it, calculating the higher-level virtual position as in **Equation12.**:

$$(x''_a, y''_a) = ((x'_b + x'_c + x'_d)/3, (y'_b + y'_c + y'_d)/3)$$

Then, using the above mathematical relations, every node will obtain virtual and direct neighbour's virtual positions. If server A (Xa, Ya) wishes to transmit a packet addressed to location (Xd, Yd), it will inspect its current location and neighbours' virtual locations. Node A can only transfer its packet to Node B if both of the circumstances in **Equation13** have been met (Kumar, A.; Shwe, H.Y.; Wong, K.J. and Chong, P.H., 2017):

$$\sqrt{(x'_b - x_d)^2 + (y'_b - y_d)^2} = \min_{N \in N(A)} \left(\sqrt{(x'_N - x_d)^2 + (y'_N - y_d)^2} \right)$$

and

$$\sqrt{(x'_b - x_d)^2 + (y'_b - y_d)^2} < \sqrt{(x'_a - x_d)^2 + (y'_a - y_d)^2}$$

GF-VIP optimally manages the issue compared to simple greedy forwarding. Research in routing hole scenarios ensures that GF-VIP maximizes the output and decreases the cost. It also enables the use of a distinct virtual location level to boost the packet's achievement rate, but with the higher virtual location levels, the overhead will be increased.

9) Energy-Efficient Geographic Routing (EEG -Routing)

(EEG-Routing), namely a geographic -routing -protocol focusing on node position error issues. Because the number in the network is vast, attaching a GPS device to all nodes is impossible. Furthermore, the localisation services cannot provide all nodes with a precise location. Consequently, this protocol assumes that the node's position and location error bounds are identified before deploying nodes in the network. It also implies that nodes are static and have the identical highest transmission range. Moreover, EEG means that only one sink is available, and all nodes in the network recognise it.

Location error limits are hypothetically enormous, approximately 100 per cent of the transmission range. If a precise location is detected, Two nodes can interact if the distance is fewer or equivalent to the maximum -transmission -range. Nonetheless, it is hard to determine if two nodes can communicate straight in cases of inaccurate location identification. Nevertheless, the chance of communication (p) could be calculated. Three potential cases can occur when calculating the likelihood of communication (Kumar, A.; Shwe, H.Y.; Wong, K.J. and Chong, P.H., 2017).

Case 1: 2 nodes are situated (assuming nodes A and B) with precise locations (A $= 0, = 0$). The probability of communication can then be calculated as **Equation 14.**:

$$p_{AB} = \begin{cases} 1, if d_{AB} \leq r \\ 0, otherwise \end{cases}$$

Here, ($\in A$ and $\in B$ Are the location errors bound simultaneously for the nodes A and B.

Case 2: One node is positioned as predicted, but the others are not.
The predicated node will be selected using **Equation 15.**

$$p_{AB} = \frac{S}{\pi \times \in_A^2}$$

Where S is the zone identified by the intersected CDs placed in A and B and $\in$ respectively, A is the node error position.

Case 3: Both nodes with estimated locations are located ($\in A \; not = 0, \in B \; not = 0$) This is illustrated in **Figure 36 and has** the below possibilities.

S1 Area includes potential node A locations. If A and B are unable to interact.

S3 Area includes potential node A locations. If A and B can interact.

S2 Area, sensor A and B's ability to communicate cannot be guaranteed.

Estimating the probability of communication in the S2 region is possible using **Equation16.**:

$$P_{AB} = \frac{S_1 * P_1 + S_2 * P_2 + S_3 * P_3}{\pi \times \in_A^2} = \frac{S_2 * P_2 + S_3}{\pi \times \in_A^2}$$

For this reason, P1 = 0 and P3 = 1. P1, P2 & P3 are connection chances and S1, S2 and S3 respectively are nodes A.

The proportion of energy consumption to R AB's progress (when node A gets a packet to B) belong to [0, 1] is computed by **Equation17.**

$$R_{AB} = \frac{\dfrac{E(d_{opt})}{J(d_{AB})} + 1}{2} = \frac{pro\,g_{AB} \times E(d_{opt}) + J(d_{AB})}{2J(d_{AB})}$$

Here in **Figure36.** j is measure of power utilization, as a feature of the d. Dopt is the optimum range of transmission. ProgAB is progressing if a message is sent to node B by node A. And J (dAB) = J (dBA), however, as progAB= progBA, RAB= RBA for arcs (A, B) and (B, A) is provided.

Figure 36. Node B sends a packet to node A, A and B > 0 (Kumar, A.; Shwe, H.Y.; Wong, K.J. and Chong, P.H., 2017).

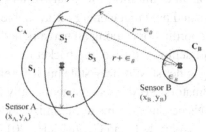

Every node in network has a table with arc's cost to reach its neighbour. The circle cost (A, B) is calculated according to the **Equation18.**:

$$C_{AB} = 1 - [\alpha p_{AB} + (1 - \alpha)R_{AB}]$$

Where $\alpha \in [0, 1]$ and the greater α value are energy effective. But it prevents a value similar to 1. When node tries to send a packet, it uses the location knowledge of node to transfer the packet to the neighbor with the least arc cost. Each packet holds the source position, backup path cost (the route with the cost table's second lowest value), packet ID, and events data. Whenever the packet is received by the node, its price table is updated. Then it selects to send the message to its neighbour (which has the lowest cost).

Each node keeps the packet's message ID for a while to stop looping. HELLO message can pick up the node error easily. EEG-Routing is distinct from other geographical routing protocols because it depends on the assumption, such as knowledge of the location of node with miscalculation bound. This algorithm is compared to an energy -optimal -algorithm and the result shows that the throughput ratio is approximately 100 percent, self-reliant α, in high-density network. But in minor density network, low value α is best to offer more significance progress. It's useful for high -density networks because power consumption is inversely related to density.

The algorithm supposes that node position and error bound position are known before the placement. It's impossible under certain situations where large numbers of nodes co-locate in the network. One more drawback is that power level of nodes was not taken into account in this algorithm (Kumar, A.; Shwe, H.Y.; Wong, K.J. and Chong, P.H., 2017).

10) SPAN

SPAN is structured with arborized algorithm in which members decide locally either to sleep or wake up to join the forwarding operation. SPAN is prompted by the fact that a device's network connection is often the single biggest user of energy encourages. In the idle situation, it's better to switch off the radio. Each node makes its decision depending on an opinion of how many of its neighbours are going to benefit from being active and how much energy is available. SPAN's primary concept is to select the best coordinators among all network nodes. SPAN coordinators always remain active and deploy multiple hop packet transmission inward ad -hoc network when remaining nodes stay in sleep state but frequently verify that they can wake and become coordinators. SPAN is suggested mainly for MANET, but might be implemented for WSNs because it aims to minimize node energy consumption. (Kumar, A.; Shwe, H.Y.; Wong, K.J. and Chong, P.H., 2017)

This protocol has a serious issue which is the limited scalability. Quality of service (QoS) is also not considered by this protocol (Mittal, V.; Pokhriyal, S.; Srivastava, H.; Vashist, S. and Verma, M., 2018). **Figure37** presents an example of a SPAN routing path.

Figure 37. An example of routing path in SPAN (Kumar, A.; Shwe, H.Y.; Wong, K.J. and Chong, P.H., 2017).

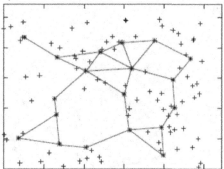

11) Location-Based Multicast Routing (LMR)

Location-based multicast routing (LMR) is interference-aware energy efficient protocol. LMR is a very useful protocol in view of the packet delivery proportion and energy by controlling the energy costs for each route, taking into account the interference problem and using it for multicast decisions to reduce the interference impact. In LMR, a source node measures the interference effect-based power consumption. The sender node then gives a multicast message to the neighbour with the lowest power value to each sub-set of locations as shown in Figure38. LMR technology can increase the network's lifespan and channel capacity by minimizing the amount of repeated information broadcasts and control messages. (Kumar, A.; Shwe, H.Y.; Wong, K.J. and Chong, P.H., 2017)

LMR sometimes presents incorrect routes that cause additional difficulties in finding the correct route. The Temporary routing loops are another drawback of this protocol (Zaman, K.; Shafiq, M.; Choi, J.G. and Iqbal, M, 2015).

Figure 38. Selecting the optimal energy route and packet forwarding in LMR; s: source, d1~d4: target, v, w: neighboring nodes (Kumar, A.; Shwe, H.Y.; Wong, K.J. and Chong, P.H., 2017).

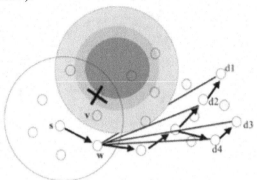

4 ENERGY AWARE ROUTING -PROTOCOLS

In ad hoc networks, batteries are source of energy (Ravi, R.R. and Jayanthi, V., 2015). This causes Energy, communication and computational capacity limitations at each node. Nodes with empty energy are removed from the network because under some situations the batteries cannot be recharged or replaced. Following are the significant reasons that encourage protocols designers take care of energy consumption management while designing the routing protocols (Majdkhyavi, N. and Hassanpour, R., 2015):

Poor energy storage: due to batteries power weakness.

The Difficulty of Battery replacement: under some conditions such as floods, earthquakes, and battlefield, battery replacement and recharge are very difficult.

Unavailability of the central management: due to the distribution feature of this type of networks, absence of central administrator and multi -hop routing, some nodes perform as transmitting and at very heavy congestions, it can consume more power.

Battery resource drawbacks: Node weight is directly affected by battery weight. An increase in battery weight will cause increasing at node weight as well. On the other hand, decreasing the battery weight leads to reduce its life. Thus, battery management mechanisms should be considered.

Selection of the optimal transmission power: More usage of transmission power cause increasing at the amount of battery consumption. Optimal transmission energy reduces the presence of interference between the nodes and thereby improves the transmission schedule. The lifetime of the nodes can be improved by increasing their batteries capacities. So, to achieve that we should have battery or power management.

Nazila Majdkhyavi and Raziyeh Hassanpour (Majdkhyavi, N. and Hassanpour, R., 2015) described the main energy aware criteria that affect the energy-aware routing:

Decreasing the energy usage per packet: This reduces the energy consumption percentage per packet (Energy consumption = Initial energy - Current energy (Bisen, D. and Sharma, S., 2018)).

Increasing the network division time: this approach aims to maximizing the network lifespan.

Decrease the variation in nodes power levels: This technique target to maintain the nodes lives and

Ensure their work together.

Decrease cost to each packet: This reduces complete cost of transmitting packet.

Decreasing top cost of the node.

Energy aware routing protocols more suitable at Disaster Area Network (DAN). Many power consumption techniques used at DAN such as Recurrence, Inter-contact graph and Paradigm for self -stabilization using waste energy cost metric (Jahir, Y.; Atiquzzaman, M.; Refai, H.; Paranjothi, A. and LoPresti, P.G., 2019).

Some energy-aware routing protocols are considered an enhancement of the existing protocols like DSR and AODV (Hybrid), while others classified as other approaches for energy- aware routing protocols (Taha, A.;Alsaqour, R.; Uddin, M; Abdelhaq, M. and Saba, T., 2017). Core objectives of energy- aware routing protocols efficiently use of energy, reducing energy consumption and improving the network lifespan (Majdkhyavi, N. and Hassanpour, R., 2015). Bellow, we have a detailed description of main classification of energy- aware routing and different energy- aware routing protocols:

Figure39 represents main energy- aware routing protocols classification.

Figure 39. Primary -classification of Energy- Aware Routing protocols.

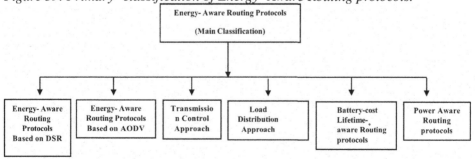

A. DSR Based Energy –Aware- Routing -Protocols (Majdkhyavi, N. and Hassanpour, R., 2015)

DSR protocol is very important reactive MANET routing protocol. Although it plays significant functions, it lacks energy efficient. Many researchers keep enhancing it in terms of energy consumption. Below are some protocols that had been enhanced depending on the pure Dynamic Source Routing Protocol and Figure40 presents them.

1) Non-Promiscuous Dynamic Source Routing Protocol

Since current routing algorithms do not save power. This is one of the downsides of MANET routing protocols, DSR came with new energy-aware routing algorithm. It drops the duplicated route request (RREQ) packets which do not exist at any other protocols. The non-promiscuous DSR parameter which is called DSR-np reduces the power usage via adding a header at source node upon optimal route selected. This header includes all intermediate nodes' addresses. Then since all intermediate nodes contain information of the immediate neighbor in that route at their routing table, any packets arrive at the node will be dropped unless it holds the same preselected address. This method reduces energy consumption by decreasing the nodes' overhearing issue. Hence, the issue here is the delay of selecting the alternative route in the event of route failure because of unavailability of unused nodes' addresses (Das, S. and Pal, S., 2019).

Figure 40. Classification of Energy -Aware -Routing -Based on DSR and AODV Protocols

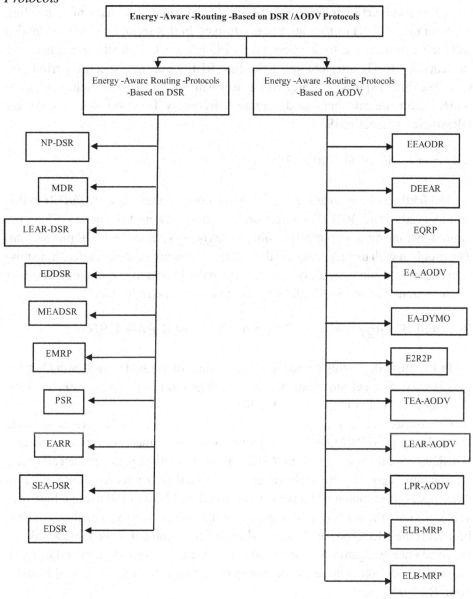

2) The Energy Drain Rate Based Energy Aware Routing

A new cost function is presented at energy aware routing mechanisms depending on drain rate (MDR) to indicate nodes lifespan. In this technique, network nodes add their current status to the received RREQ packet. The target node collects all subsequent RREQs after obtaining the first RREQ during a specific period (T). Once the timer expires, the target node uses Min-Max formula to select the ideal route. Each node calculates its drain rate (DRi) every T second using DRold and DRsample by Equation19.

$$DR_i = \alpha \times DR_{old} + (1 - \alpha) \times DR_{sample}$$

The lifetime of the node i specified by the cost function Ci = RBPi/DRi in this protocol (20). Here, RBPi is the remaining battery power of the node i. Then, the highest lifetime route among all possible routes being selected by MDR mechanism. The problem with this algorithm is that MDR is unaware of the complete transmission energy consumed by a given route, which could lead to greater general power consumption in network (Majdkhyavi, N. and Hassanpour, R., 2015).

3) Local -Energy -Aware -Routing -Protocol (LEAR-DSR)

In LEAR-DSR routing protocol, if the amount of the node's remaining battery energy exceeds a certain limit, it will be engaged in the path discovery process. (Majdkhyavi, N. and Hassanpour, R., 2015).

Otherwise, node will drop route request (RREQ) packet and inform other node about the dropped RREQ by creating a new message named as drop route request (DRREQ). So, the route added in RREP packets is shortest path between all routes with enough energy. Each node has already dropped RREQ or receives DRREQ from other nodes, the amount of its battery threshold will be reduced using adjustment value. So, only those nodes with higher residual energy than the new threshold can broadcast the RREQ packet. The drawback of this protocol is its focuses only on the local energy regardless of the total network energy consumption and this will cause minimization at the network quality of service (Majdkhyavi, N. and Hassanpour, R., 2015).

4) A Novel –DSR -Based -Energy -Efficient - Routing -Protocol (EDDSR):

At this protocol, each node calculates its willingness to participate at packets routing according to its current battery power. On other words, EDDSR uses a mechanism that increases the network and node lifetime by discouraging nodes with low lifetime from route discovery participation. Each node at the network calculates it residual battery power (RBP) periodically, as according to its amount the node will participate at network operation or not. This increases the network performance because nodes with low battery power delay the broadcasting of received route request (RREQ) packet.

This operation is done through Equation20.

$$Ci = RBPi/DRi. \qquad (20)$$

Here the time period has an inverse relation to the expected lifetime of the node. Node sends a route error (RERR) packet to source when energy level of node is lower than critical threshold. (Majdkhyavi, N. and Hassanpour, R., 2015). Most crucial issue in this protocol is that the intermediate node avoided from Send RREP with inaccurate route data to source (Das, S. and Pal, S., 2019).

5) Energy Aware Multi-Path Source Routing Protocol (MEADSR)

Two paths from the source to target are found and stored at the routing table in this protocol. The selection of the primary route is done depending on the remaining battery of the nodes in the route and the total transmission power needed to transfer packets. Then, the route with high disjointness ratio from the first path is selected as the second route. A new domain is added to the routing table and RREQ packets known as min_bat_lev which stores nodes minimum remaining energy. Only destination node replays to RREQ packet in the MEA-DSR.

When RREQ packet is received by intermediate node close to the source node, its remaining energy is inserted into the min bat lev field. Then later, each intermediate node compares its remaining energy with the min_bat_lev value contained in the packet. If it is less than value of min_bat_lev field, replaces min_bat_lev value by its remaining energy.

The destination node waits for more RREQs after receiving the first RREQs then chooses the main route. After the primary route selection, the target node transmits a route reply packet immediately to source node. Since route selection is done depending on remaining battery of nodes in the route and the total transmission power, the drawback in this protocol is the probability of nodes depletion and the selected route may not be the least power cost route (Choudhary, S. and Jain, S., 2015).

6) Power Aware Source Routing Protocol (PSR)

In this protocol, the path π at time t is selected during route discovery phase so that cost function is reduced.

In Equation21, ρi is sending power, Fi is battery capacity, Ri is the residual battery of node i at time t and α is weighting factor. All nodes except the target node calculate their link expenses (Cij) in the Power Aware Source Routing protocol and add it to the RREQ packet. Upon reception of RREQ by the intermediate node, it begins a timer Tr and inserts the expenses at the packet header as Min-Cost. Then when another RREQ packet received, their costs will be checked. If the new packet cost less than the saved Min-Cost value, Min-Cost replaced by the new packet cost and fresh RREQ packet is sent (Majdkhyavi, N. and Hassanpour, R., 2015).

Otherwise, fresh RREQ is ignored. In PSR, destination node waits for a Tr limit after receiving the first RREQ. The target node chooses the optimal path with lowest cost and responds to source when timer expires. This schema leads to an increase in the latency of the data transfer (Majdkhyavi, N. and Hassanpour, R., 2015).

$$C(\pi, t) = \sum_{i \in \pi} C_i(t) \text{ where } C_i(t) = \rho i \cdot \left(\frac{F_i}{R_i(t)} \right)^{\alpha}$$

7) Energy Aware Multi-Path Routing Protocol (EMRP)

This protocol applies some changes to DSR phases. In the route replay phase, all nodes in the route add their current status like range between the node i and the following hop, number of resending attempts that belong to the last successful transmission, current queue length and their current energy to route replay (RREP) packet. Source node, first, measures weight of all available routes using Equation22.

$$W = \sum_{i=1}^{n} \left(\alpha \times W_{energy}^i + \beta \times W_{queue}^i \right)$$

W_{energy}^i is energy weight of node i and
W_{queue}^i is queuing node weight i.

After this calculation, the source node stores the paths in downward order according to W value and chooses N sets of paths. The primary path is for real-time sending while the rest are backup routes (Majdkhyavi, N. and Hassanpour, R., 2015).

8) Energy Aware and Reliable Routing Protocol (EARR)

Each node in this protocol chooses whether or not to transmit RREQ messages depending on its residual energy and the greater data level requirements. If node's residual energy is higher than required, RREQ packets will be broadcast. The target node will not receive the RREQ unless the intermediate node has enough energy. So, only valid routes are selected as candidate paths to avoid route reconstruction due to lack of battery power and thereby, network lifespan is maximized. When the intermediate node in this protocol decides to send RREQ messages, it adds its available energy at that packet. The residual energy is also stored in the route cache of EARR.

In case of the availability of multiple candidate paths, the path that has the highest battery capacity is chosen for the transmission. This protocol has drawbacks like the path is chosen based on battery capacity regardless of the length of that route which may cause high transmission delay and High probability in energy estimation error than existing methods (Majdkhyavi, N. and Hassanpour, R., 2015).

9) Reliable Energy and Signal Strength Aware Routing Protocol (SEA-DSR)

The key objective of this protocol is to improve the accuracy of the discovered path on basis of both signal strength and remaining node energy. As result of characteristic of distributing traffic load by this protocol link failure is decreased and the network lifetime is maximized. The main benefits of SEA-DSR are minimizing path failure, reducing packet loss and managing the overhead. This protocol inserts new field at RREQ header called trust count (RELCOUNT) which contains reliability count of the path it comes across (Khalifa, A.R; Sadek, R.A. and Al-Shora, M.A., 2016). The recipient begins a timer when the first RREQ packet is received and stores all RREQ in its path cache. After the timer, it chooses the path bearing high-reliability variable and sends it to RREP packet. Equation23 calculates the safety criterion for the path (Majdkhyavi, N. and Hassanpour, R., 2015):

$$\text{Reliability Factor} = \frac{\text{Reliability Count}}{\text{No. of Hops}}$$

10) Efficient DSR (EDSR) Protocol (Chawda, K. and Gorana, D, 2015)

Some researchers called this protocol Simple Energy-Aware DSR (SEADSR) (Das, S. and Pal, S., 2019).

The roles of this protocol are to decrease power usage per packet, enhance the node expanse, find out the intermediate greedy node and increase network lifetime. At EDSR, after obtaining the RREQ (Route Request), the rout finding is performed by setting and starting timer and target waits for a while. (Bhattacharyya, D.; Chatterjee, A.; Chatterjee, B.; Saha, A.K. and Santra, A., 2018) Packet. Then, target node will replay best route and ignore the remaining (Majdkhyavi, N. and Hassanpour, R., 2015). Thus, the issue of this protocol is that route discovery process takes long time (Chawda, K. and Gorana, D, 2015).

The time for route discovery is called time delay (t) and calculated by Equation24. (Das, S. and Pal, S., 2019):

$$\tau = \left(C_{max} - C\right)\tau_{max}/C_{max}$$

C_{max} is battery capacity. C is current battery level of the node.
τ_{max} is maximum allowable delay.

The error in transmission is immediately equal to the highest allowable interval and also immediately equal to the node's energy consumption.

(T) range between zero and τmax. SEADSR algorithm has a special capability which differs from DSR and MMBCR algorithms. It increases MANET lifespan by its ability to select different routes simultaneous for two different source nodes (Das, S. and Pal, S., 2019).

B. AODV based Energy -Aware -Routing -Protocols (Majdkhyavi, N. and Hassanpour, R., 2015)

AODV is on demand routing protocol that only contains the next hop data at its routing table. At this section will discuss the modifications that the protocol designers made to this protocol to create a set of energy-aware routing protocols.**Figure40** presents the energy -aware -routing protocols depending on AODV.

1) Energy -Efficient -Routing -Protocol (EEAODR)

The best path selected in the energy-efficient -routing -protocol (EEAODR) is depending on hops number, time, and node energy. If route includes one point with low batters, this path will be ignored by the optimizer. If time is short, path will be shorter and less energy will be used for transmission. Although some nodes may die rapidly, a trade -off between period and lifespan of network or node should take place during protocol selection. When destination gets first RREQ in this protocol, it waits for a while and collects all the subsequent RREQs. The target node utilizes the optimizer feature after this time to select the appropriate route and add it to the RREP packet. The target also chooses a set of other routes as backup routes to prevent energy loss and time waste to re-calculate the routes (Majdkhyavi, N. and Hassanpour, R., 2015).

EEAODR utilizes **Equation25** to select route in order of price between possible paths:

Cost = σ × time + μ × 1/lowest battery energy of node in route + τ × 1/ number of hops.

Here time refers to time to send packet to location from source.

The main issue at this protocol is the maximization of transmission time. Since EEAODR focus only on energy And the target nodes must wait until the best path is calculated; thus, that network delay rises here.

To have a clear picture about route discovery at EEAODR as illustrate **Figure41** bellow. Assume the source is (0) and the destination is (1). The source node (0) and the target node have three possible paths. (1) (Godara, 2015):

Figure 41. Packet transmission at EEADOR (Godara, 2015).

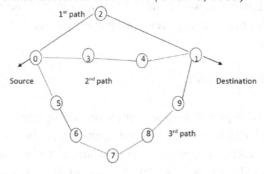

1st path: 0-2-1
2nd path: 0-3-4-1
3rd path: 0-5-6-7-8-9-1

The cost shall be calculated and path with ideal cost value is chosen when the first message is sent for example 1st path. Then, when the second packet is sent, it is not necessary that 1st path is to be selected because the cost is again calculated and the path may be 1st, 2nd or 3rd based on optimal cost value. Thus, cost value is calculated at every packet to pick the optimal path (Godara, 2015).

2) Distributed Energy Efficient Routing Protocol (DEEAR)

For energy aware routing, the protocol uses RREQ and needs only the battery power level of the network.

In Distributed Energy Efficient Routing Protocol, the intermediate node manages the time of rebroadcasting the RREQ packets and the nodes with higher battery level will broadcast RREQ first. DEEAR protocol does an exchange between min-hop route and the route with balanced energy consumption. To estimate the average power, two fields are added to RREQ which are average battery power of nodes on the path (P) and hops number (N).

In order to choose best path, source inserts the amount of its battery to the P field and broadcast the RREQ. **Equation26** is used to calculate average remaining battery, P new:

$$Pnew = [(Pold*N) + Bi] / (N+1)$$

Here, Bi is the residual of the node battery energy i and Pold is amount of P field in RREQ packet.

From received RREQ packet, node i estimates the average remaining energy (Enew) based on the prior average remaining energy of network (Eold) and Pold using **Equation27.**:

$$Enew= [(1-\alpha*Eold] + (\alpha*Pold)$$

The drawback at this protocol is the average remaining energy value is not accurate while utilizing RREQ. Average remaining energy can be accurate while using periodical control packets, but it is energy consuming technique and not valid at on-demand routing (Majdkhyavi, N. and Hassanpour, R., 2015).

3) Energy -Based -QoS -Routing -Protocol (EQRP) (Majdkhyavi, N. and Hassanpour, R., 2015)

In (EQRP), the issue of routing quality of Service is considered. At this protocol, the nodes estimate how long delay the RREQ packet transmission based on their energy. The delay calculates as Equation28.

We = 0, Er > Emax, We = Ei /Er

At this relationship, Er is node current remaining power, Ei is node's initial energy and Emax is maximum energy for each node.

The trick in this protocol is to choose the nodes on the path based on their residual energy. Due to the energy drain of nodes; this protocol aims to minimize route reconstruction (Majdkhyavi, N. and Hassanpour, R., 2015). Although this protocol achieved excellent results compared with AODV in term of some QoS constraints but still some other parameters not covered like bandwidth and path length. (Guo, L.; Li, P.; Jin, J. and Mou, J., 2018).

4) Integrated Energy Aware Routing Protocol (EA_AODV):

In Integrated Energy Aware Routing Protocol (EA_AODV), each intermediate node upon receiving RREQ packet, it estimates the residual energy by using the node current energy and the required transmission energy to send message to node and add it to RREP packet. Every node with route estimates remaining battery and only if it is less than the value held at RREP packet, it will be changed. If there are more than one route available routing decision is done depending on the current power level and power level. At this protocol, the source node selects the route using a load balancing technique to balance the battery depletion and applies transmission power control during packets sending to the source. Then, route with maximum-minimum battery energy is selected. (Majdkhyavi, N. and Hassanpour, R., 2015)

It means source node will check available paths and then choose route with strongest residual energy among them (Kim, 2015). Imagine following network in Figure42 is ours:

Figure 42. Example of node remaining energy topology (Kim, 2015).

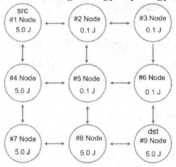

Node 1 is source node and node 9 is target node. Remaining power of every node is presented. There are 6 distinct short distances with 4 hops.

1st path: 1-4-7-8-9
2nd path: 1-2-3-6-9
3rd path: 1-4-5-8-9
4th path: 1-4-5-6-9
5th path: 1-2-5-8-9
6th path: 1-2-5-6-9

The best transmission route among them is the first route because the nodes have the lowest remaining energy, 5.0J. Although, the best routing path may not be found by EA-AODV f node 8 receives the RREQ from node 5 before it is obtained from node 7, node 8 transfers replied RREP packet to node 5.

Instead of RREP packet, the node is registered in RREQ packet. Figure43 displays the flowchart of suggested message transmit routers. When RREQ packet is received by node, it chooses whether to transmit or leave packet. The hop count in the RREQ packet is compared and minimum remaining power in routing table is reviewed subsequently. Through this phase, the transmission route to the target node is modified to the greater minimum remaining power route of the node, the most stable of all the shortest routes.

Figure 43. End-to-end postponement (Kim, 2015).

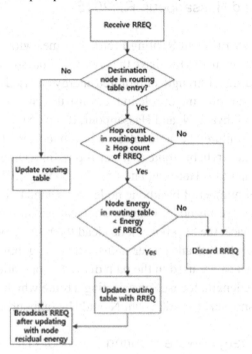

The drawback of this protocol is that remaining energy capacity metric does not ensure the least energy cost path (Choudhary, S. and Jain, S., 2015).

5) Dynamic Energy Aware Routing Protocol (EA-DYMO)

EA-DYMO is energy aware routing protocol depending on the DYMO protocol. DYMO is a successor routing protocol of AODV protocol. At EA-DYMO protocol, energy and load-aware routing parameters take place during route discovery operation. It attempts to provide a mechanism to choose best route based on residual power and traffic load of nodes. Path selection factor is calculated as average energy proportion to average traffic energy (Majdkhyavi, N. and Hassanpour, R., 2015).

Route with maximum PS value is selected to send packets. This is done by Equation29. :

PSsdi = EFsdi /LFsdi

EFsdi is the average power and LFsdi is the average traffic load. Assuming the path as i from source S to destination D (Majdkhyavi, N. and Hassanpour, R., 2015).

6) Reliable and Energy Efficient Routing Protocol(E2R2P) (Majdkhyavi, N. and Hassanpour, R., 2015)

Reliable and Energy Efficient Routing Protocol comes with a new term called backbone nodes which are nodes that have the optimal signal strength. In this protocol, battery power and signal strength or required energy are used during the routing process. Backbone nodes play major role in the construction phase and during new routes discovery (Majdkhyavi, N. and Hassanpour, R., 2015) .

In the event of link failure, the node selects a backbone node from its neighbors to reconstruct a stable and reliable route as it can as possible (Ding, Yun-zheng ; Xu, Ming-zhou ; Tian, Yuan ; Li, Hui-ying and Liu, Bing-xiang, 2016). Each node, in routing table, saves of number of backbone nodes connected to it, its battery status and signal strength. In case any node at the communication link damage or move out the communication space, the backbone nodes lead the routing process. Backbone nodes send their signal strength and power status to their neighbor nodes. Power and signal strength parameters are used in the path discovery operation. This protocol, regardless of the route length, focuses on selecting a route which is very stable and reliable for data transmission (Majdkhyavi, N. and Hassanpour, R., 2015).

7) Reliable and Energy Aware Routing Protocol (TEA-AODV)

This protocol depends on battery power and reliability value of each node for a reliable routing. The reliability value of each node determined using many parameters, for example, association length, the proportion of number of packets sent by neighbours to total packets forwarded to the neighbor and the average time wasted responding to the RREQ as illustrates Equation30.:

Average reliability= (Cumulative reliability/Number of hops)

8) Local Energy Aware Routing Protocol (LEAR-AODV)

In local energy aware routing protocol, each node decides whether or not it will broadcast received RREQ packet depending on remaining battery energy Er. If battery is above certain threshold, RREQ packet will be sent, otherwise, the packet is dropped. If all the nodes on the route contain good residual energy, RREQ packet will reach its target. In the route maintenance phase, if battery is below a threshold, Route Error packet (RERR) is sent to transmitter node. In case node deletes an RREQ packet, it will send a new message called ADJUST_Thr. Next nodes towards the destination will search for the RREQ that has been deleted and will adjust their threshold value (Majdkhyavi, N. and Hassanpour, R., 2015).

9) Lifetime Prediction Routing Protocol (LPR-AODV)

The path with highest lifespan is chosen in the Lifetime routing protocol. This protocol utilizes the prediction of batteries lifespan. Based on previous activity, each node calculates its battery lifetime. At the route discovery process, all nodes calculate their estimated lifetime except the destination and source nodes. An additional field called Min-lifetime is inserted to each RREQ packet which shows the minimum lifetime. The source node chooses the route with maximum lifetime as an ideal path in this protocol. This choice depends on residual energy of node and rate of depletion (Majdkhyavi, N. and Hassanpour, R., 2015).

The node broadcasts a RERR packet to the source when the estimated lifespan is below threshold. This protocol does not ensure the least energy cost path (Choudhary, S. and Jain, S., 2015).

10) Load Aware Routing Protocol (ELB-MRP)

Load-Aware Routing Protocol utilizes the size of the collision panel and the queue length to estimate the node load and its neighboring nodes with a single hop. All nodes, except source and target node, collect data for themselves and their single-hop neighbours about energy factor (EF), queue frequency (QF) and collision window size (ACW). The cost for node i is calculated by Equation31. :

$$C(i) = ACW * EF * QF$$

Middle nodes insert their traffic and power data into the RREQ files in the route discovery process. Hello messages also gather ACW, EF and QF data. Intermediate nodes calculate the cumulative cost based on the neighbor information provided by hello packets. Equation32 is used to calculate cumulative cost CC (i)

$$CC(i) = C(i) + (C(j) + C(k))$$

Here a node is represented by i and it has neighbors' j and k.

When the target receives the first RREQ, more RREQs are required to select two routes with the lowest cost as the primary and backup route. (Majdkhyavi, N. and Hassanpour, R., 2015).

11) Energy-Aware and Error Resilient (EAER)

EAER uses the neighboring nodes that comprise the minimum amount of forwarding capacity to build the paths.

EAER will allow the path to be retained locally from the intermediate node in the event of a connection breakdown.

Hence, this protocol constructs the shortest reliable path which assures the balance in consuming battery energy by minimizing the amount of portable node control messages.

As discussed early, MANET has huge number of mobile nodes that move randomly. These nodes use our proposed as protocol for network layers. We assume the IEEE 802.11 DCF as MAC layer protocol. Every node sends HELLO message that demonstrates operation towards neighboring node. In event of link breaks, candidate node which is node of ongoing route used to continue communication and recover path failure.

The EAER metric layout is deemed as a graph-shaped network $G = (V, E)$.

A unique address (i) is allocated for each node i in G. Assume that Ev, max is the primary energy of node V and Ev is its residual energy. This node required the Ep, V energy to forward data packet to its neighboring node u is calculated by Equation33. (Bosunia, M.R.; Jeong, D.P.; Park, C. and Jeong, S.H., 2015):

$$E_{p,v} = E_{rx(p,v-1)} + E_{tx(p,v)'}$$

If Erx (p, V−1) is amount of energy needed to receive packet from upstream node v-1 and Etx (p, V) is amount of energy needed to transmit packet to downstream node u. Reliability is capacity of node to forward packets in MANET. Consider node v and node u as two network-communicating devices. Node v transfers Svu number of packets to neighboring one-hop node u and gets Ruv number of packets at a time t from one-hop node u. Equation34 below calculates reliability (v,) between node v and target u (Bosunia, M.R.; Jeong, D.P.; Park, C. and Jeong, S.H., 2015):

$$(v,t) = Ruv / Sv$$

Node v sends complete Si number of packets to other neighboring nodes i and gets complete Ri number of packets back from neighboring nodes i at a time t. Then weighted node v reliability is calculated by Equation35, in which α is a weight variable and value is between $0 \leq \alpha \leq 1$.

$$R_{\omega(v,t)} = (1 - \alpha)R_{(v,t)} + \alpha \max_{1 \leq j \leq i, j \neq u} \frac{R_j}{S_j}$$

EAER metric, known as node v EAERv, is then calculated as Equation36. :

$$EAER_v = EAER_{v,min} + \left(1 - EAER_{v,min}\right)$$

$$* \frac{E_v * R_{(v,t)}}{E_{v,max} * R_{\omega(v,t)}} * 1$$

$$+ \left(\frac{\left(R_{(v,t)} - R_{\omega(v,t)}\right) * E_{p,v}}{\left(1 - R_{\omega(v,t)} E_{p,v}\right)}\right)^{1/\beta}$$

Where EAERv, min is a predetermined lowest EAERv value and β is weighted variation factor of EAER metric value.

Figure44 presents EAER value as a sum of cost of reliability and residual value of energy when E_v, max = 100 Joules, β=1, E_p, v = 0.02Joules, and EAERv, min = 0.25. While EAER scale presented in Figure45. [REMOVED REF FIELD]Depending on estimated EAER metric value to demonstrate interest packet transmission capability to neighboring node.

Figure 44. Reliability and remaining energy EAERv values (Bosunia, M.R.; Jeong, D.P.; Park, C. and Jeong, S.H., 2015).

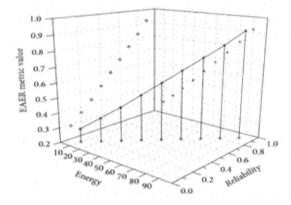

Figure 45. EAEA scale (Bosunia, M.R.; Jeong, D.P.; Park, C. and Jeong, S.H., 2015)

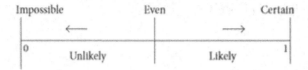

Figure 46 shows flow chart of route request process using ERER protocol. Using the EAER routing metric, the node may be chosen to transfer information if both below conditions are met:

The node has enough energy for other nodes to obtain and transmit messages.

The node can forward messages to other neighboring nodes (in terms of reliability).

Figure 46. Route request message handling (Bosunia, M.R.; Jeong, D.P.; Park, C. and Jeong, S.H., 2015).

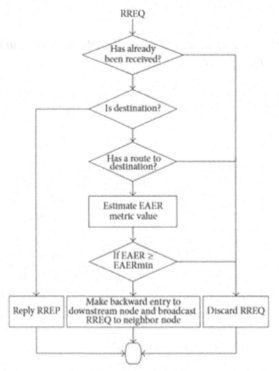

Combined EAER routing metric can accurately determine whether that node is capable to send packets to neighboring node without any error or not by using the following constraint. If this constraint is fulfilled, then the node can participate:

EAERi ≥ EAER (i, min)

∀i ∈ V, i not equal to data Source, i not equal to data Destination.

Similar to AODV, the EAER while route construction if source node desire to send information to target node and doesn't have any predefined information about the path towards target, then the source node forwards RREQ packets By putting candidate node's email null to its one-hop neighbor node as shown in Figure46. The candidate node controls its duplicity after obtaining RREQ packet. In case it is already received then RREQ will be dropped, otherwise, it will replay to that RREQ. It looks for route to destination in the routing-table and controls whether flag of this path is active or not as shown in Table2.

Table 2. Routing flag (Bosunia, M.R.; Jeong, D.P.; Park, C. and Jeong, S.H., 2015).

Status	Values
Inactive	0
Active	1
Repairable	2

If a path to that destination is found, it replays the message with RREP. But if it discovers a path that is idle or repairable, it simply drops the RREQ.

If no routing information is found by the node, it will use its own EAER metric value as described earlier. If this value exceeds predefined threshold (threshold is a user-defined design parameter aimed at controlling dynamics of EAER routing protocol), node will retransmit RREQ packet. When RREQ is received by target node, it replays RREP message. Routing table of intermediate node is updates upon receiving RREP message. Then each candidate node will be equipped with address of next hop node before transmitting RREP message to next target node until source node is reached. In Figure47, for instance, source node S needs path to target D. Path request (RREQ) is broadcast on network (Bosunia, M.R.; Jeong, D.P.; Park, C. and Jeong, S.H., 2015).

Node A receives and retransmits RREQ message to D. Nodes C and B, neighboring nodes of node A, receive RREQ message, but node B only retransmits RREQ message because nodeC contains lower energy levels. Other nodes retransmit RREQ message in a similar circumstance until target node D receives RREQ message. Target node D then sends path response message (RREP) to source node S. Intermediate nodes alter their corresponding D routing table when receiving RREP message. Consequently, path S-A-B-E-F-G-J-K-D is set up and source node S can then start communication with target node D using this path (Bosunia, M.R.; Jeong, D.P.; Park, C. and Jeong, S.H., 2015).

Figure 47. Route constriction using EAER (Bosunia, M.R.; Jeong, D.P.; Park, C. and Jeong, S.H., 2015).

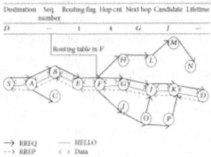

Average energy consumption or every packet is shown in Figure48.Where EAER routing protocol prevents involvement of nodes with an exceptionally low energy level, early death is prevented. Therefore, even with higher quantity of connection errors and data packet retransmission situations of high mobility network environment, EAER consumes less energy than other protocols and keeps network more stable.

Figure 48. Average per packet energy consumption (Bosunia, M.R.; Jeong, D.P.; Park, C. and Jeong, S.H., 2015).

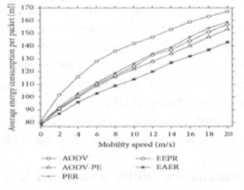

EAER's probability of route construction is lower than other protocols by 2% as Figure49, presented below.

Figure 49. Route construction probability (Bosunia, M.R.; Jeong, D.P.; Park, C. and Jeong, S.H., 2015).

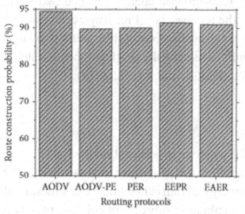

C. Minimum Total Transmission Power Routing Algorithm (Das, S. and Pal, S., 2019). Also Called Transmission Control Approach (Chawda, K. and Gorana, D, 2015)

This approach aims to control the energy consumed at the transmission. Transmission Control assumes that Ad hoc nodes have unfixed communication power and it must be adjusted to consume less energy to reach the receiving node. Since flooding is the technique used for communication, then the power used for broadcasting should be saved as much as possible (Chawda, K. and Gorana, D, 2015).

MTPR, in this method, reduces the total transmission energy produced per packet and ignores the lifespan of each node.

Each node not only acknowledges the routing paths as a source, but also as an intermediate node, and a neighbour node that is overhearing. The problem with this strategy is the large amount of nodes involved in transmitting information, and huge end-to-end transmission delay. Route with large number of nodes may be unfixed because the mobility of intermediate nodes is higher. Therefore, the route chosen by this algorithm is not sufficiently effective. Since this protocol focuses only at minimizing the total power routing, a new hidden issue may occur which is the probability of more collision and it leads to maximizing the energy consumption (Indapurkar, A. and Patil, R., 2017).

The total energy consumed between neighboring nodes I and J during sending and receiving the packages is calculated by Equation37. (Das, S. and Pal, S., 2019):

$$C_{i,j} = P_{recv}(n_j) + P_{transmit}(n_i,n_j) + cost(n_j)$$

$P_{transmit}(n_i,n_j)$ is the Transmission energy between two adjacent nodes I and J. i shows the sender and the receiver is J. Precv(nj) receives energy at the designated node J and the minimum transmission cost between two successive nodes is cost (nj). Then Ci,j result will be used by the neighbor node to calculate its own estimated cost using Equation38. (Das, S. and Pal, S., 2019):

$$Cost(n_i) = \min_{j \in NH(i)} C_{i,j}$$

Where NH (i) = {j; where nj is adjacent node of ni}

Since MTPR algorithm finds minimum total power route from source to target in spite of remaining energy of individual node, the widespread node issue remains unresolved and can contribute to subsequent collapse of network (Das, S. and Pal, S., 2019). MTPR tries to select the nearest node for routing and the lifetime of each node is not affected directly. The major issue of this approach is the high chances of network bottleneck when packets must be routed via various nodes to reach the target (Pullagura, J.R. and Rao, D.V., 2017). Add that it May causes nodes depletion (Choudhary, S. and Jain, S., 2015).

The following example in Table3 presents how ideal route is chosen in Figure50. Here, route 2 is the optimal route since it has the minimum TPR value.

Table 3. MTPR optimal route (Hamamreh, R.A.; Haji, M.M. and Qutob, A.A., 2018).

Path Number	Path Hops	TPR Value
1	A => D => H	3+3
2	A => B => E => H	1+1+1
3	A => B => E => G => H	1+1+2+2
4	A => C => F => H	2+2+2

Figure 50. Selection of optimal route (Hamamreh, R.A.; Haji, M.M. and Qutob, A.A., 2018).

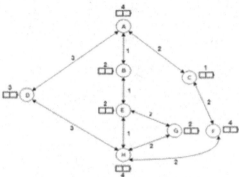

D. Load Distribution Approach

Improving active energy is a very substantial approach. It aims at achieving balance in the energy used between the nodes, boosting network lifespan accordingly, and thereby, avoiding the use of over utilized nodes throughout the routing path (Chawda, K. and Gorana, D, 2015).

Load Distribution Approach spread out the flow of data and creates several alternatives for effective use of available resources (Ravi, G. and Kashwan, K.R., 2016).

Following Figure51 shows how load is distributed using good battery-level nodes.

Here, node B has Poor battery level which implies that it is going to enter the sleep mode. So, the new path which contains nodes with good battery level will be S-C-I-K (Ravi, G. and Kashwan, K.R., 2016).

Figure 51. Optimal route using load distribution (Ravi, G. and Kashwan, K.R., 2016).

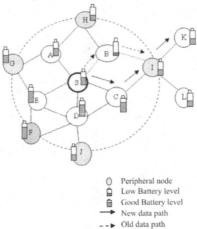

The more important process is the identification of target node position whether it is within the range or beyond it. If the target node is within the range, proactive routing is applied. Otherwise, reactive routing is more suitable (Ravi, G. and Kashwan, K.R., 2016). The drawback at this approach that it does not guarantee the lowest energy cost route (Choudhary, S. and Jain, S., 2015).

E. Power Aware Routing

Power-Aware is among the parameters used for energy-aware routing which aims to reducing power consumption. It is done by selecting the route that has the minimum number of weak nodes or maximum of the lowest energy or either depending on the link cost. Following are the routing protocols which uses this approach.Figure52 represents the protocols that use power-aware routing approach.

Figure 52. Power Aware Routing protocols

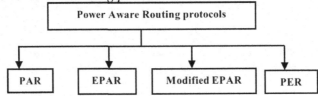

1) Power Aware Routing Protocol (PAR)

This method attempts at reducing energy consumption by taking real time and non-real time into account for sending packets at the route which is suitable for the energy and have no traffic. It relays on id node, battery, and traffic level to adjust network power. There are three statuses for the battery depending on the ratio of its available energy. If battery status is lower than 20% it is called level 1. If it is greater than 20% but less than 60% it is called level 2. Level 3 status is used to describe the percentage greater than 60%.

This algorithm can calculate the estimated total of battery cost and number of weak nodes at a route for level 1 battery status. The traffic level of each device can be assessed by calculating number of packets buffered in queue interface. Route replay path is selected by destination using Equation39. (Das, S. and Pal, S., 2019):

$$R = \frac{E_{i,j}}{H_n}$$

$E_{i,j}$ is total remaining route power.
H_n is the total amount of intermediate hops.
R is the path link status ratio R.

For non-real time load, minimum value of R is 1. On the other hand, 2 value for R is minimum value for real-time traffic. Path with minimum number of weak nodes (with less than 20 percent battery energy) is selected for multiple link status ratio. (Das, S. and Pal, S., 2019).

PAR has high latency with huge energy saving (Yamini, K.A.P. and Arivoli, K.S.T., 2018).

2) Efficient Power Aware Routing Protocol (EPAR)

Efficient Power-Aware Routing role is minimizing power consumption per packet between source and target. It defines capability of every node in both remaining battery energy and level of assumed energy consumption in forwarding messages at specific communication link. EPAR selects path with maximum packet capability at minimum remaining packet transmission capability using a mini-max model. EPAR reduces total power consumption, minimizes main delay and enhances lifetime of network (Chawda, K. and Gorana, D, 2015).

The route with the least hop power allocated to each link is selected (Marcel, G. and Vetrivelan, 2015).

Equation40 is used to calculate the power consumed to forward one packet.

$$E = \sum_{i=1}^{k} T(n_i, n_{i+1})$$

Where E is the consumed power packet forwarding, ni, ni+1 are nodes, T is consumed energy for packet forwarding and receiving.

Figure53 shows how the route discovery is done using EPAR.

Figure 53. Route discovery using EPAR (Pullagura, J.R. and Rao, D.V., 2017).

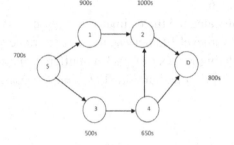

Figure 53 shows the nodes with the duration left at each node in seconds, there are three possible paths from source node (S) to target (D). They are S-1-2-D, S-3-4-D, and S-3-4-2-D.

Using max-min formulation EPAR finds maximum of lowest energy.

1. Path 1: S-1-2-D Min (700, 900, 1000, 800) = 700
2. Path 2: S-3-4-D Min (700, 500, 650,800) = 500
3. Path 3: S-3-4-2-D Min (700,500,650, 1000, 800) = 500

The max strategy is max (700, 500, 500) = 700. So, path1 is selected for routing in the network.

EPAR protocol has some drawbacks; for instance, it does not consider nodes frequent movement; therefor, mobility is not defined and there are no backup routes in link failure situations (Suman, S.; Agrawal, E.A. and Jaiswal, A.K., 2016).

3) Modified EPAR Protocol

This protocol minimizes power consumption through use of link cost to send energy control in EPAR in four forms (transmission, receiving, idle & rest) and remaining energy. At this protocol, two values of power had been added which are set power and maximum value of packet forwarding. Cost value depends on packet size. In which small bundles use shortest route, but large packets will be routed through long paths. Hence, this protocol is not efficient for big packets and decrease network lifetime (Chawda, K. and Gorana, D, 2015).

4) Novel Power Efficient Routing(PER) Protocol

PER protocol reduces consumed power at operation, and thereby saves transmitting power. Unlike usual process of periodically reinitializing route discovery, this is done only after optimum number of packets has been transmitted. Therefore, an optimal amount of nodes should be selected carefully to prevent transmission waste and improve network lifespan. That optimum number differs according to nodes energy level and network size (Chawda, K. and Gorana, D, 2015).

F. Battery-Cost Lifetime-Aware Routing

One of the parameters used for energy-aware routing is battery costs. This is achieved either by reducing number of nodes involved in routing or by calculating battery energy of nodes between a specific route and then route around nodes with less residual energy. Following are routing protocols which uses this approach. **Figure54** represents the protocols that use Battery-cost Lifetime-aware routing approach.

Figure 54. Battery-cost Lifetime-aware Routing protocols.

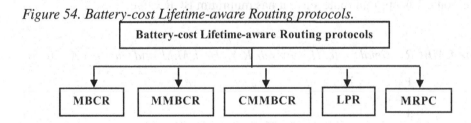

1) Minimum Battery Cost Routing(MBCR) Protocol

This protocol uses a fresh process called battery-cost identification. It recognizes if remaining energy is enough for nearest neighbor to target. **Equation41** is used to calculate the battery cost. (Das, S. and Pal, S., 2019):

$$R_j = \sum_{i=0}^{D_j-1} f_i(C_i^t)$$

$f_i(C_i^t)$ is proposed battery cost function. And its larger value means node reluctance to send packets.

(C_i^t) is the battery capacity.

It seems that relationship between battery cost function and battery capacity is Inverse relationship

(Rj) is battery-cost.
(j) is Route between all possible paths with (DJ) number of nodes between source and target.
(ni) is amount of nodes.
(t) is time.

Then best path Ri is selected according to **Equation42.**:

$$R_i = min\{R_j | j \in A\}$$

Where (A) means total of all possible routes.

From **Equation41** and **Equation42,** it means summation of battery capacity leads to choose lower cost for the route. Add that, the maximum reluctant node may appear at selected path and then causes early network partition (Das, S. and Pal, S., 2019).

The following example in **Table4** shows how optimal route is chosen in **Figure53.** Here, route 1 is optimal route since it has minimum BCR value.

Table 4. MBCR optimal route (Hamamreh, R.A.; Haji, M.M. and Qutob, A.A., 2018).

	Path Number	Path Hops	BCR Value
	1	A => D => H	1/3
	2	A => B => E => H	1/2 + 1/2
	3	A => B => E => G => H	1/2 + 1/2 + 1/2
	4	A => C => F => H	1/1 + 1/4

The drawbacks of this protocol are listed below:

The value of the node's energy is not properly defined which causes constraints during packet forwarding.

Selecting route with highest overall battery cost might cause presence of nodes with a less cost along route which leads to minimizing network lifetime (Das, S. and Pal, S., 2019).

2) Min-Max Battery Cost Routing(MMBCR) Protocol

Min-Max Battery Cost Routing Protocol (MMBCR) overcomes Minimum Battery Cost Routing Protocol (MBCR) challenge. MBCR chooses path to a target by summing battery cost for individual nodes located at available routes, and the route with lower cost will be chosen. This way may lead to earlier network partitioning if less battery energy nodes appear along selected route (Das, S. and Pal, S., 2019) (Chawda, K. and Gorana, D, 2015). MMBCR uses special algorithm that assures selected route does not contain any less energy capacity nodes. MMBCR alternate the way of summing all battery cost in path with ith node's maximum battery cost function on the jth route.

Then route that contains node with a minimum of highest battery cost function is chosen using Equation43. (Das, S. and Pal, S., 2019):

$$R_j = \max_{i \in route_j}\{f_i(C_i^t)\}$$

$$R_i = \min\{R_j | j \in A\}$$

(A) is collection of possible paths.

The first equation (Rj) selects node with highest battery cost function or with lowest battery power in jth path.

The second formula (Ri) identifies path containing a node with lowest battery cost function among all possible paths.

The problem with the MMBCR protocol is that it does not always guarantee minimum total transmission power path which is covered later by its advanced protocol (CMMBCR). Add that a common node between various paths cannot be stopped (Das, S. and Pal, S., 2019).

3) Conditional Min-Max battery Capacity Routing (CMMBCR) Protocol

Conditional Min-Max battery Capacity Routing Protocol has a great algorithm that mixes MBCR and MMBCR protocols with positive features. (Das, S. and Pal, S., 2019).

This protocol chooses Minimum Total Transmission Power Route (MTPR) path if all nodes in that route have retained battery capacity above a threshold value (γ) (Chawda, K. and Gorana, D, 2015).

Then, the Min-Max Battery Cost Routing (MMBCR) algorithm is chosen if the battery capacity is less than Y. (Y) is selected within limit of 0 and 100 times of node's maximum battery capacity. Best path is selected according to **Equation44** using this parameter:

Where (j) is total of all available routes (Das, S. and Pal, S., 2019).

$$R_j^c = \min_{i \in Route\_j} C_i^t \geq \gamma$$

The drawback of this protocol is that it ignore battery discharge rate which is also a significant parameter to improve network lifespan (Das, S. and Pal, S., 2019). And optimum value of γ cannot be measured (Das, S. and Pal, S., 2019).

4) Lifetime Prediction Routing (LPR)

Battery discharge ratio is considered criteria to estimate path lifetime. Battery lifespan is calculated as a part of remaining energy and power consumed while sending one bit from one node to neighbor. Core aim of Lifetime Prediction Routing (LPR) algorithm is to find out route that has the most power efficient. In other words, it searches for a path that contains lightly loaded nodes. **Equation45** is used to measure the lifetime prediction of selected node (Das, S. and Pal, S., 2019):

$$T_i(t) = \frac{E_{r,i}(t)}{\frac{1}{N-1} \sum_{k=i-N+1}^{i} R_k(t)}$$

$T_i(t)$ is expected lifespan of ith node.
$E_{r,i}(t)$ provides residual of node's energy when packet is sent or forwarded.
$R_k(k)$ Indicates energy depletion rate when kth packet is sent and number of intervals for Simple Moving Average (SMA) predictor is referred to as N.

This algorithm is merged with DSR routing protocol and a minimum lifespan header is included in path request control message (RREQ) packet during route discovery phase. If expected lifespan of receiving node header is greater than lifespan of visiting node, lifespan value of header will be substituted by visiting node's lifespan value. After obtaining path request (RREQ) packet, intermediate node starts timer Tr and waits for any new RREQ packet to arrive for a while. If such packets arrive and the minimum lifetime value inside header is lower than lifetime of current node, RREQ packet will be rejected. Otherwise, lifetime in header is substituted by current lifetime value of node and transmitted to network. **Equation46** is used to select best route among all accessible paths:

$$\max_{\pi} T_{\pi}(t) = \min_{i \in \pi}(T_i(t))$$

Here, Ti (t) is anticipated lifespan of ith node in path π. the length of route is Tπ (t). Path (say π) is longest survival time containing ith node with minimum lifespan expectancy. Although this algorithm improves energy consumption level, due to lengthy path discovery process it delay packet delivery. (Das, S. and Pal, S., 2019).

5) Maximum Residual Packet capacity (MRPC) Protocol

It acknowledges the node ability by the remaining battery capacity and the anticipated energy consumption in a packet's reliable transmission over a specific link (Chawda, K. and Gorana, D, 2015).

The prediction of the optimal path is a very difficult process. Researchers used many ways for that to gain the perfect path discovery like battery matric. But still, they did not achieve their objective. MRPC algorithm introduces a new route discovery approach depending on residual capability and anticipated energy consumed during the transfer of the packages via a particular wireless link.

The node-link metric function is measured by **Equation47.** (Hamamreh, R.A.; Haji, M.M. and Qutob, A.A., 2018):

$$f_{i,j} = \frac{B_i}{P_{i,j}}$$

Where Bi is battery, i and Pi are nodes, and j is transmission energy required by node i to transmit a packet throughout link (i, j).

Then maximal lifespan of available routes can be presented as **Equation48.**

$$M_l = Min(f_{i,j})$$

So, rout with maximum Ml is selected as optimal path.

The following example in **Table5** shows how optimal route is chosen in **Figure53.** Here, route 2 is optimal route since it has maximum RPC value.

Table 5. Route discovery based on RPC value (Hamamreh, R.A.; Haji, M.M. and Qutob, A.A., 2018) .

Path Number	Path Hops	RPC Value
1	A => D => H	3/3
2	A => B => E => H	2/1
3	A => B => E => G => H	2/2
4	A => C => F => H	1/2

The lifespan of a network is greatly increased with use of remaining energy routing but the drawback here is the hop count is not considered while selecting route (Chawda, K. and Gorana, D, 2015).

5. ANALYSIS OF GEOGRAPHICAL AND ENERGY- AWARE MANET ROUTING PROTOCOLS AND THE FUTURE SCOPE. (KUMAR, A.; SHWE, H.Y.; WONG, K.J. AND CHONG, P.H., 2017) (DAS, S. AND PAL, S., 2019).

In few last years, many different algorithms have been developed by protocols designers to overcome the drawbacks of the MANET Ad hoc networks like the serious issue of energy consumption and the difficulty to map nodes locations. They called these set of protocols as geographical routing protocols and energy- aware routing protocols. Each of them has its unique functions and on the other side a list of weaknesses. Brief Comparative analyses of geographical routing protocols and energy –aware - routing -protocols are presented in **Table6** and **Table7** respectively in the **appendix**. These comparative analyses show that although many geographical routing methods are promising, there are still many difficulties and drawbacks to be overcome in the MANET networks. In this section, we concentrate on clearing these difficulties and identifying potential directions for studies in this respect. Each node, at geographic routing, requires its own location information, destination location information and its neighbor location information as well which can be obtained by the GPS or some other location services. As a result, every node needs to be integrated with such devices e.g. GPS which looks impractical Due to the cost of nodes and their huge number in the network.

Although that efforts made on the side of geographical direction are great and cannot be underestimated or ignored the drawbacks should be highlighted in order to plan for future geographic routing.

A location-based routing for three-dimensional (3D) networks should be a useful asset for potential studies. The research focuses on two-dimensional (2D) networks, despite the fact that in some cases the 2D estimate is not effective and usage of a 3D design becomes a necessity which can never be underestimated. 3D network, in fact, displays more accurate position data for real world apps. (Kumar, A.; Shwe, H.Y.; Wong, K.J. and Chong, P.H., 2017)

And from the perspective of energy-aware routing protocols these Comparative analyses shows that no one of these protocols covers all requirements for best route to the target, elongated network lifespan and greater Quality of Service (QoS).

Some of these algorithms play key roles in achieving a satisfactory maximization of network lifespan; on the other hand, they do not ensure the shortest route selection, minimum delay to target, and best quality of service (QoS). All previous researches, as demonstrated in table1, ensures that the change in specific parameters, results in important minimization of energy consumption, thereby preserving service quality. Thus, the potential scope in the field of energy –aware -routing is the effort to combine current energy -aware algorithms to generate others with more effective hybrid characteristics that minimize energy consumption and enhance MANET ad hoc networks ' quality of service. This will be achieved by dividing network into a set of sub-networks or areas where one node is in sleep mode while the other one is active. The active nodes will be active for a certain period. All nodes in sleep mode can save energy, and thereby maximize lifespan of networks. In MANET ad -hoc networks, there seems to be a great future in the field of energy conservation. (Das, S. and Pal, S., 2019).

6. CONCLUSION

This research provides a study regarding geographical and power- aware routing -protocols in ad -hoc mobile networks. Some scientists describe the previous protocols as hybrid protocols that solve the problems of proactive and reactive MANET -routing -protocols. Some researchers consider them as types of network structure routing protocols while others said they are novel protocols. In each geographical and energy-aware class of routing, several protocols have been assessed by us. Each of them has distinctive features that are efficient. The primary aspect distinguishing the protocols is the metrics used to select the paths to the target. This paper also highlighted the weaknesses, strengths and drawbacks of each protocol. Geographical routing protocols are more appropriate for network devices where information accumulation is efficient for reducing forwarding to the source by multiple sources repeated packets. Energy-aware routing protocols overcome the serious issue of energy drain at mobile nodes, but they suffer from long delays and higher overhead.

REFERENCES

Abdulleh, M. N., Yussof, S., & Jassim, H. S. (2015). Comparative study of proactive, reactive and geographical MANET routing protocols. *Communications and Network*, 7(02), 125–137. DOI: 10.4236/cn.2015.72012

Ahmed, D., & Khalifa, O. (2017). An overview of MANETs: Applications, characteristics, challenges and recent issues. *IJEAT*, 3, 128.

Ahmed, D. E. M., & Khalifa, O. O. (2017). A Comprehensive Classification of MANETs Routing Protocols. *IJCAT*, 6(3), 141–158. DOI: 10.7753/IJCATR0603.1004

Bai, Y., Mai, Y., & Wang, N. (2017). *Performance comparison and evaluation of the proactive and reactive routing protocols for MANETs*. IEEE. DOI: 10.1109/WTS.2017.7943538

Benkhelifa, I., Moussaoui, S., & Demirkol, I. (2018). Intertwined localization and error-resilient geographic routing for mobile wireless sensor networks. *Wireless Networks*, ●●●, 1–23.

Bhangwar, N. H., Halepoto, I. A., Khokhar, S., & Laghari, A. A. (2017). On routing protocols for high performance. *Studies in Informatics and Control*, 26(4), 441–448. DOI: 10.24846/v26i4y201708

Bhatia, D., & Sharma, D. P. (2016). A comparative analysis of proactive, reactive and hybrid routing protocols over open source network simulator in mobile ad hoc network. *International Journal of Applied Engineering Research: IJAER*, 11(6), 3885–3896.

Bhattacharyya, D., Chatterjee, A., Chatterjee, B., Saha, A. K., & Santra, A. (2018). A novel approach to energy efficient low cost routing in MANET by reduction in packet size. (pp. 679-684). IEEE 8th Annual Computing and Communication Workshop and Conference (CCWC): IEEE.

Bisen, D., & Sharma, S. (2018). An Energy-Efficient Routing Approach for Performance Enhancement of MANET Through Adaptive Neuro-Fuzzy Inference System. *International Journal of Fuzzy Systems*, 20(8), 2693–2708. DOI: 10.1007/s40815-018-0529-9

Bosunia, M. R., Jeong, D. P., Park, C., & Jeong, S. H. (2015). A new routing protocol with high energy efficiency and reliability for data delivery in mobile ad hoc networks. *International Journal of Distributed Sensor Networks*, 11(8), 716436. DOI: 10.1155/2015/716436

Chawda, K., & Gorana, D. (2015). *A survey of energy efficient routing protocol in MANET*. IEEE. DOI: 10.1109/ECS.2015.7125055

Choudhary, S., & Jain, S. (2015). A survey of energy-efficient fair routing in MANET. *International Journal of Scientific Research in Science, Engineering and Technology*, 1, 416–421.

Das, S., & Pal, S. (2019). Analysis of Energy-Efficient Routing Protocols in Mobile Ad Hoc Network. In C. a. In Advances in Computer (Ed.), Advances in Computer, Communication and Control (pp. 285-295). Singapore: Springer. DOI: 10.1007/978-981-13-3122-0_27

Ding, Y. Z., Xu, M. Z., Tian, Y., Li, H. Y., & Liu, B. X. (2016). A ber and 2-hop routing information-based stable geographical routing protocol in manets for multimedia applications. *Wireless Personal Communications*, 90, 3–32.

Er, J. K., & Er, G. S. (2017). Review study on MANET routing protocols: Challenges and applications. *International Journal of Advanced Research in Computer Science*, 8(4).

Godara, A. (2015). Energy Efficient Routing in Clustered Mobile Ad Hoc Network (MANET) (Doctoral dissertation).

Guo, L., Li, P., Jin, J., & Mou, J. (2018). Energy-Balanced Routing Protocol with QoS Constraints in Ad Hoc Network. In *International Conference in Communications, Signal Processing, and Systems* (pp. 992-999). Singapore: Springer.

Gupta, R., & Patel, P. (2016). An improved performance of greedy perimeter stateless routing protocol of vehicular adhoc network in urban realistic scenarios. Int. J. Scientific Res. Comput. Sci. *Eng. Inf. Technol.*, 1(1), 24–29.

Hamamreh, R. A., Haji, M. M., & Qutob, A. A. (2018). An Energy-Efficient Clustering Routing Protocol for WSN based on MRHC. *International Journal of Digital Information and Wireless Communications*, 8(3), 214–223. DOI: 10.17781/P002465

Hassan, M. H., & Muniyandi, R. C. (2017). An Improved Hybrid Technique for Energy and Delay Routing in Mobile Ad-Hoc Networks. *International Journal of Applied Engineering Research: IJAER*, 12(1), 134–139.

Helen, D., & Arivazhagan, D. (2014). Applications, advantages and challenges of ad hoc networks. *JAIR*, 2(8), 7–453.

Iche, A. H., & Dhage, M. R. (2015). Location-based routing protocols: A survey. *International Journal of Computer Applications*, 975, 8887.

Indapurkar, A., & Patil, R. (2017). Analysis of Energy Routing Protocol with Power Consumption Optimization in MANET. [IJEMR]. *International Journal of Engineering and Management Research*, 7(1), 100–106.

Jagadev, N., Pattanayak, B. K., Singh, D., & Sahoo, S. (2018). A Survey on Bandwidth Management in MANET. *IACSIT International Journal of Engineering and Technology*, 7, 38–41.

Jahir, Y., Atiquzzaman, M., Refai, H., Paranjothi, A., & LoPresti, P. G. (2019). Routing protocols and architecture for Disaster Area Network: A survey. *Ad Hoc Networks*, 82, 1–14. DOI: 10.1016/j.adhoc.2018.08.005

Karthikeyan, L. (2015). Comparative study on non-delay tolerant routing protocols in vehicular networks. *Procedia Computer Science*, 50, 252–257. DOI: 10.1016/j.procs.2015.04.052

Kaur, H., Singh, H., & Sharma, A. (2016). Geographic routing protocol: A review. *International Journal of Grid and Distributed Computing*, 9(2), 245–254. DOI: 10.14257/ijgdc.2016.9.2.21

Kaur, H, Singh, H., & Sharma, A. (n.d.).

Khalifa, A. R., Sadek, R. A., & Al-Shora, M. A. (2016). Performance Analysis Of DSR, SEA-DSR And Modified DSR Routing Protocols. *International Journal of Computer Science and Mobile Computing*, 5(7), 204–209.

Kim, D. S., & Tran-Dang, H. (2019). MAC Protocols for Energy-Efficient Wireless Sensor Networks. In Industrial Sensors and Controls in Communication Networks (pp. 141-159). Springer. DOI: 10.1007/978-3-030-04927-0_11

Kim, H. a. (2015). A New Energy-Aware Routing Protocol for Improving Path Stability in Ad-hoc Networks.

Kumar, A., Shwe, H. Y., Wong, K. J., & Chong, P. H. (2017). Location-based routing protocols for wireless sensor networks: A survey. *Wireless Sensor Network*, 9(1), 25–72. DOI: 10.4236/wsn.2017.91003

Lakshmi, G. R., & Srikanth, V. (2015). Location-Based routing protocol in wireless sensor network-A survey. *International Journal of Advanced Research in Computer Science and Software Engineering*, 5(4).

Majdkhyavi, N., & Hassanpour, R. (2015). A Survey of Existing Mechanisms in Energy-Aware Routing In MANETs. *International Journal of Computer Applications Technology and Research*, 4(9), 673–679. DOI: 10.7753/IJCATR0409.1007

Malik, R. F., Nurfatih, M. S., Ubaya, H., Zulfahmi, R., & Sodikin, E. (2017). Evaluation of greedy perimeter stateless routing protocol on vehicular ad hoc network in palembang city. In *2017 International Conference on Data and Software Engineering (ICoDSE)* (pp. 1-5). IEEE. DOI: 10.1109/ICODSE.2017.8285873

Marcel, G. and Vetrivelan. (2015). Evaluating The Effects of the Energy Management's Issues on the MANET's Performance Using Two Native Routing Protocols against a Power-Aware Routing Protocol. [IJCST]. *International Journal of Computer Science Trends and Technology*, 3(5).

Mittal, V.; Pokhriyal, S.; Srivastava, H.; Vashist, S. and Verma, M. (2018). Location based protocols in WSN: A Review. IIOAB Engineering Technology, ISSN, 0976-3104.

Ponsam, J. G., & Srinivasan, R. (2014). A survey on MANET security challenges, attacks and its countermeasures. [IJETTCS]. *International Journal of Emerging Trends & Technology in Computer Science*, 3(1), 274–279.

Pullagura, J. R., & Rao, D. V. (2017). Simulation based performance evaluation of energy efficient protocols in ad hoc networks. Journal of Advanced Research in Dynamical and Control Systems. *Special*, (02), 1141–1149.

Rajasekar, S. and Subramani, A. (2016). A review on routing protocols for mobile Adhoc networks. i-manager's Journal on Mobile Applications and Technologies, 3(1), 39.

Ravi, G., & Kashwan, K. R. (2016). Power Efficient Routing by Load Balancing in Mobile Ad Hoc Networks. In *Intelligent Systems Technologies and Applications* (pp. 147–157). Springer. DOI: 10.1007/978-3-319-23258-4_14

Ravi, R. R., & Jayanthi, V. (2015). Energy efficient neighbor coverage protocol for reducing rebroadcast in MANET. *Procedia Computer Science*, 47, 417–423. DOI: 10.1016/j.procs.2015.03.225

Rekik, M., Mitton, N., & Chtourou, Z. (2015). Geographic greedy routing with aco recovery strategy graco. In *International Conference on Ad-Hoc Networks and Wireless* (pp. 19-32). Cham: Springer. DOI: 10.1007/978-3-319-19662-6_2

Suman, S.; Agrawal, E.A. and Jaiswal, A.K. (2016). EPARGA: A Resourceful Power Aware Routing Protocol for MANETs. International Journal of Advanced Research in Computer Engineering \& Technology (IJARCET), 5(5).

Sumra, I. A., Sellappan, P., Abdullah, A., & Ali, A. (2018). Security issues and Challenges in MANET-VANET-FANET: A Survey. *EAI Endorsed Transactions on Energy Web and Information Technologies*, 5(17), 1–6. DOI: 10.4108/eai.10-4-2018.155884

Taha, A., Alsaqour, R., Uddin, M., Abdelhaq, M., & Saba, T. (2017). Energy efficient multipath routing protocol for mobile ad-hoc network using the fitness function. *IEEE Access : Practical Innovations, Open Solutions*, 5, 10369–10381. DOI: 10.1109/ACCESS.2017.2707537

Terao, Y., Phoummavong, P., Utsu, K., & Ishii, H. (2016). *A proposal on void zone aware Greedy Forwarding method over MANET. In 2016 IEEE Region 10 Conference (TENCON)*. IEEE.

Torrieri, D., Talarico, S., & Valenti, M. C. (2015). Performance comparisons of geographic routing protocols in mobile ad hoc networks. *IEEE Transactions on Communications*, 63(11), 4276–4286. DOI: 10.1109/TCOMM.2015.2477337

Verma, K. (2016). Multicast routing protocols for wireless sensor networks: A comparative study. *Int. J. Comput. Netw. Commun*, 1(1), 1–11.

Yamini, K. A. P., & Arivoli, K. S. T. (2018). Challenges on energy consumption in manet—a survey. *International Journal of Pure and Applied Mathematics*, 119(12), 13735–13741.

APPENDIX

Table 6. Comparative analyses of Geographical Routing Protocols.

Geographical Routing Protocol	Strength	Weakness
1. Greedy -Perimeter -Stateless - Routing (GPSR).	i. Best geographical routing protocol is Greedy -perimeter -stateless -propagation (GPSR). ii. Greedy -forwarding choices depended on the data gathered in the topology of the network about the immediate neighbours of a router.	i. Compared to the urban area, GPSR yields excellent outcomes in a highway environment. ii. Due to the existence of more structures and plants, immediate communication is uncommon in urban areas.
2. Modified -Greedy -Perimeter - Stateless -Routing (MGPSR).	i. MGPSR is an improvement of the GPSR protocol to calculate the most efficient communication between nodes to dramatically maximize the lifespan of the network	i. Still the issue of greedy forwarding at GPRS not solved and MGPRS not effective at Urban areas.
3. Geographical adaptive fidelity (GAF).	i. Turns the nodes in the network on/off to save energy. ii. GAF constructs a virtual network for the covered area. iii. Nodes below the same grid are presumed to be equivalent in terms of the cost of packet routing. iv. Each node balances its loads by the periodic change of its state from sleeping to wake up which result in maximizing its lifetime. GAF can also function as a hierarchical protocol in which nodes rely on their geographical place.	ii. Finding equivalent nodes for communication in ad-hoc network is difficult.
4. Minimum energy communication network protocol (MECN).	i. It utilizes low -power RF Design of transceiver to control energy. ii. Focuses on mobile nodes self - configuration and network overall power consumption. iii. It uses low power GPS. iv. It uses relaying concept. Node breakdown or fresh node deployment can be dynamically adapted.	i. It supposes that every node can communicate with other nodes. It's not feasible in true-time under certain circumstances.
5. Small minimum energy communication network (SMECN).	i. It is MECN extension. ii. SMECN solves MECN's downsides by taking the limitations that can occur in real time between any couple of nodes into account. iii. SMECN consumes less power compared with MECN and it minimizes the links maintenance expenses.	ii. The algorithm is significantly maximized with a small number of edges to find the sub-network.

continued on following page

Table 6. Continued

Geographical Routing Protocol	Strength	Weakness
6. Geographic and energy-aware routing (GEAR).	i. Use geographical data when distributing requests to targeted areas. ii. GEAR utilizes heuristic power-conscious and geographically aware neighbour selection to deliver message to target region. iii. GEAR does not demand place database and assumes network idle node. iv. Route in this protocol is bi-directional. Compared with GPRS, GEAR performs better.	i. The main drawback of this protocol is its limited mobility and scalability.
7. Location -based -energy - efficient -intersection -routing (EELIR).	i. In respect of power usage and delivery ratio, EELIR functions optimally compared to flooding -based -routing -protocols and location -assisted -routing -protocol (LAR).	i. This protocol supposes that each node is conscious of own power level, current position and sink node location which is not applicable in some cases. ii. It uses GPS to identify the location which is costly due to large number of nodes in network.
8. An anonymous –location - based -efficient -routing -protocol (ALERT).	i. It is unique in regard of low cost and anonymity security for source, target and paths. ALERT has a method to conceal the information originator amongst originators to establish namelessness security for the origin.	i. This protocol causes higher overhead when compared with other location-based routing protocols.
9. Energy-efficient geographic forwarding algorithm (DECA).	i. It maximizes the network lifetime. ii. It applies Dijkstra algorithm then the route which have the lowest cost will be chosen.	i. This Protocol assumes that all nodes in network have same maximum transmission range which is not possible under some conditions.
10. An enhanced ad-hoc routing protocol (IHLAR) based on hybrid location.	i. IHLAR is location-based hybrid protocol that combines geometrical routing with ad hoc network topology- based routing protocol. ii. IHLAR solves the average queue problems and packets delivery ratio.	i. This protocol causes higher fixed costs comparing to other location-based routing protocols. ii. Add that it is weak on security aspects.
11. The Location-Based Routing Protocol (LBRP).	i. It saves the energy during data transmission and hence maximizes the nodes lifetime.	i. LBRP is never examined on real-life networks or nodes, and its applicability to real nodes is suspected.

continued on following page

Table 6. Continued

Geographical Routing Protocol	Strength	Weakness
12. SBZRP & LBZRP.	i. SBZRP & LBZRP are two enhanced area routing protocols to increase the proactiveness within the area. iii. LBZRP is very efficient in decreasing the proactive aspect of the area and also minimizes the control flow outside the area.	i. The main drawback of these protocols is the existence of Overlapping zones.
13. Trajectory-based forwarding (TBF).	i. This protocol, source encodes path and inserts it in each packet. ii. A great implementation of TBF is to secure network perimeter.	i. It is a protocol requiring a heavy network and a positioning method.
14. Bounded -Voronoi -Greedy - Forwarding (BVGF).	i. It is positioned algorithm which makes greedy routing options depending on places of single -hop neighbours. ii. BVGF chooses next neighbor hop with shortest range between all competent neighbours to target.	i. BVGF is inefficient in terms of energy.
15. Geographic -Random - Forwarding (GERAF).	i. It is geographic -routing -protocol that uses a switching system for awake / sleep and MAC. **ii.** Each node becomes active whenever there is a packet to be forwarded by it. To prevent the clashes, CSMA / CA MAC protocols are used by GERAF. iii. It uses relay selection process which needs no routing table or topological knowledge.	i. The nodes must be equipped with localization hardware such GPS which is costly at large networks.
16. Anchor location service (ALS).	i. The cost for communication and storage was minimized as multiple sources were using the same global grid to locate the sink.	i. The sink must wait until the incident is discovered by the node.
17. Two-tier Data Dissemination Protocol (TTDD)	iii. TTDD has the ability to work for many mobile sinks and many static source nodes. ii. In aspects of network lifespan and delay in information transmission, TTDD performs faster compared to direct distribution.	ii. The forwarding route in TTDD is discovered to be longer than the shortest path under certain circumstances. iii. TTDD does not solve the severe problem of the high costs of system maintenance and recalculation.
18. Energy-efficient geographic routing (EEGR)	i. It is extendable, simple and energy efficient protocol. ii. It minimizes communication overhead. iii. The result shows that EEGR -power –efficiency is 60% more than MFR and GRS. It has better performance compared to MFR, GRS, and PLRA in respect of broadcasting zone.	i. EEGR supposes that radio transceivers in all nodes in the entire network are heterogeneous in terms of transmission range which is not applicable in some cases.

continued on following page

Table 6. Continued

Geographical Routing Protocol	Strength	Weakness
19. Multisink-GERAF (M-GERAF)	i. To ensure accurate information distribution, it uses a strong power off mechanism without identifying the neighbour node location. ii. A node becomes active whenever it has a packet to send.	i. All nodes which can hear the source node in the scope area will receive the messages and then the information transmission must be organized depending on the back-off moment which may cause overload and collisions.
20. Greedy forwarding with virtual position (GF-VIP) and Greedy forwarding with multi-level virtual (GF-MVP)	i. It introduces a new concept called the virtual position. ii. Rather than selecting the neighboring node, GF-VIP uses that virtual location to choose the next hop. iii. GF-VIP handle hole issue in an optimal manner compared to greedy forwarding.	i. It also allows the use of various levels of virtual positions to increase packet success rate; however, with higher levels of virtual location, the cost will increase.
21. Energy -efficient -geographic - routing (EEG-Routing)	i. It focuses on the issue of node position error. ii. If a node desires to send a packet, it uses knowledge of node position to transfer the packet to the neighbor with the lowest arc cost.	i. It is useful for high-density networks because power consumption and density have a reverse relationship. ii. The algorithm predicates that nodes location with location error is recognized before implementation. This is difficult in certain circumstances when huge amounts of nodes are available throughout the network. iii. Another disadvantage is that this algorithm did not consider the node energy level.
22. SPAN	i. It reduces nodes energy consumption. ii. Maximizing network lifespan.	i. This protocol has a serious issue which is the limited scalability. ii. Quality of service (QoS) is also not considered by this protocol.
23. Location-based multicast routing (LMR)	i. LMR very effective protocol in term of packet delivery ratio and energy. ii. By minimizing the number of repeated information broadcasts and control messages, the LMR method can increase the network's lifespan and channel capacity.	i. Sometimes LMR introduces invalid routes that cause extra delays in searching for the right path. ii. Temporary routing loops.

Table 7. Comparative analyses of Energy-Aware Routing Protocols.

Energy-Aware Routing Protocol	Strength	Weakness
1. Non-promiscuous Dynamic Source Routing Protocol (DSR-np).	i. It drops the duplicated RREQ packets which do not exist at any other protocols. ii. DSR-np decreases energy usage by decreasing node overhearing.	i. Alternative path selecting delay in case of route failure.
2. Energy aware routing based on the energy drain rate.	i. A fresh cost function for estimating nodes lifespan is provided at energy-conscious routing mechanisms depending on drain rate (MDR). ii. The highest lifetime route among all possible routes being selected by MDR.	i. MDR ignores the overall consumed transmission power by a single path and maximizes total network energy consumption.
3. Local Energy Aware Routing Protocol (LEAR-DSR).	i. Nodes with higher residual energy than the certain threshold will participate at the route discovery process. ii. The path added to the RREP packet is the shortest path with sufficient power among all the paths.	i. This algorithm focuses only on the local energy regardless of the total network energy consumption.
4. A Novel -DSR -Based -Energy -Efficient -Routing - Protocol (EDDSR).	i. Low-lifetime nodes will not be involved in path discovery; thus network performance will improve. ii. When the node residual energy is under the threshold level, route error message (RERR) shall be sent to the source.	i. It is not valid for the intermediate node to send RREP with incorrect path data back to the source.
5. Energy Aware Multi-Path Source Routing Protocol (MEADSR).	i. Two paths are discovered from source to target. ii. Primary route is selected depending on the node remaining battery and the total transmission power needed to transfer the packets. The second route is the route with high disjointness ratio from the first path.	i. The destination node waits for more RREQs to select the primary path. So, this will negatively affect the total transmission delay and QoS.
6. Power Aware Source Routing Protocol (PSR).	i. The path at time t is selected during route discovery stage so that function cost is minimized. ii. The optimal route is that with the lowest cost.	i. This schema leads to an increase in the latency of the data transfer.
7. Energy Aware Multi-Path Routing Protocol (EMRP).	i. More than one route selected by the source node based on W value. ii. The primary route is with highest W value while the others are backup routes and stored in downward order depending on W value.	i. Route is selected based on W value regardless of other QoS criteria. ii. This algorithm may lead to maximum transmission time.

continued on following page

Table 7. Continued

Energy-Aware Routing Protocol	Strength	Weakness
8. Energy Aware and Reliable Routing Protocol (EARR).	i. Path that has the highest battery capacity is chosen for the transmission. ii. EARR can enhance network function in aspects of avoiding route reconstruction and the network lifetime is maximized. iii. Node decision making depends on remaining power as well as the required traffic load which makes it more accurate.	i. The path is chosen based on battery capacity regardless of the length of that route. ii. High probability in energy estimation error than existing methods which will affect all other quality of services of the network.
9. Reliable Energy and Signal Strength Aware Routing Protocol (SEA-DSR).	i. Enhance the reliability of the discovered route based on both signal nodes residual energy and strength. ii. Minimizing of a path failure reduces the packet loss and manages the overhead.	i. Route selection depending on nodes residual energy signal and strength regardless of other QoS criteria. ii. This algorithm may cause maximization on the transmission period.
10. Efficient DSR (EDSR) Protocol.	i. It increases the lifetime of MANET by its ability to select different routes simultaneous for two different source nodes. ii. This protocol decreases power usage per packet, enhances the node expanse, discovers intermediate greedy node and increases the network lifespan.	i. Route discovery takes a long time.
11. Energy Efficient Routing Protocol (EEAODR).	i. The best route selected depending on time, the node energy and hops number. ii. Route with low batteries nodes will be ignored. iii. Backup routes are selected to avoid the energy drainage and time wastage to re-calculate paths.	i. Before calculating the best path, target nodes must wait for πt time. This increases network delay.
12. Distributed Energy Efficient Routing Protocol (DEEAR).	i. The intermediate node controls the time of rebroadcasting the RREQ. ii. Average remaining energy is the parameter used to select the optimal path.	i. The average remaining energy value is not accurate while utilizing RREQ.
13. Energy Based QoS Routing Protocol (EQRP).	i. Select the nodes on the path based on their remaining energy. ii. This protocol minimizes route reconstruction.	i. Still some other parameters not covered like bandwidth and path length.
14. Integrated Energy Aware Routing Protocol (EA_AODV).	i. The source node selects the route using a load balancing technique. ii. Route with maximum-minimum battery energy is selected. iii. Least hops and minimum remaining energy parameters applied for route discovery.	i. EA-AODV might not discover the best routing path under certain circumstances. ii. The remaining energy capacity metric does not ensure the least energy cost path.

continued on following page

Table 7. Continued

Energy-Aware Routing Protocol	Strength	Weakness
15. Dynamic Energy Aware Routing Protocol (EA-DYMO).	i. The path selection factor uses the residual energy and traffic load. ii. To send the messages, route with highest PS value is chosen.	i. This algorithm focuses on traffic load and remaining energy parameters to select the best path regardless of the route length and other network QoS criteria.
16. Reliable and Energy Efficient Routing Protocol (E2R2P).	i. It focuses on selecting a route which is very stable and reliable for data transmission.	i. The route length parameter is ignored at this algorithm.
17. Reliable and Energy Aware Routing Protocol (TEA-AODV).	i. Selects the most reliable path using average reliability.	i. This algorithm focuses on the reliability of the link more than end-to-end delay.
18. Local Energy Aware Routing Protocol (LEAR-AODV).	i. Each node chooses whether or not to transmit the obtained RREQ packet based on its remaining battery power in the local energy-aware routing protocol.	i. since this protocol focuses only on local energy of the nodes, ii. The total transmission delay can be maximized. Add that the other quality of services is not considered here.
19. Lifetime Prediction Routing Protocol (LPR-AODV).	i. The route with maximum lifetime is selected. ii. An additional field called Min-lifetime is inserted to each RREQ packet which shows the minimum lifetime.	i. This protocol does not ensure the least energy cost path.
20. Load Aware Routing Protocol (ELB-MRP).	i. In the process of route discovering, intermediate nodes insert energy and traffic data into the RREQ pocket. ii. The destination selects two routes with the lowest cost as the primary and backup path upon receiving the first RREQ. iii. Reduces network load.	i. Concentrate on load balancing instead of the shortest path while choosing the optimal path. ii. Does not cover all quality of services criteria.
21. Energy-Aware and Error Resilient (EAER).	i. Reliability and High Energy Efficiency for data transmission in mobile ad hoc networks. ii. It uses less energy than other protocols and retains a more stable network.	i. EAER's likelihood of route construction is slightly lower than other protocols by 2%.
22. Transmission Control Approach.	i. Control the energy consumed at the transmission. ii. Optimal route is the one it has the minimum TPR value.	i. High chances of network bottleneck when packets have to be transmitted to the destination via various nodes. ii. It May causes nodes depletion.

continued on following page

Table 7. Continued

Energy-Aware Routing Protocol	Strength	Weakness
23. Load Distribution Approach.	i. This method helps to balance the energy that the nodes use, then increase the network lifetime. ii. Avoiding the use of over-utilized nodes through the routing path. iii. The path which contains nodes with good battery level is selected.	i. It does not guarantee the selection of the lowest energy cost path.
22. Power Aware Routing Protocol (PAR).	i. It decreases power consumption through taking non-real time and real time to send messages across the path into account. i. A path with minimum amount of weak nodes (with less than 20 percent energy) is selected for multiple link status ratio. ii. PAR provide huge energy saving.	i. PAR has high latency feature which leads to maximizing the transmission time.
23. Efficient Power Aware Routing Protocol (EPAR).	i. EPAR decreases total power usage, minimizes the main delay and improves the lifespan of the network. ii. EPAR selects the route with the highest packet capability at the minimum remaining packet capability.	i. EPAR protocol has some drawbacks such as the frequent motion of nodes is not considered and therefore mobility is not determined and there are no replacement paths in the event of a connection breakdown.
24. Modified EPAR Protocol.	i. This protocol minimizes power consumption in four types (transmission, getting, inactive & rest) and remaining electricity using the connection cost to forward energy control in EPAR. ii. Small bundles use the shortest route, but the large packets will be routed through the long paths.	i. This protocol is not efficient for the big packets and decrease the network lifetime
25. Novel -Power -Efficient – Routing (PER) -Protocol.	i. It reduces power consumption when operating. ii. After selecting Optimal amount of messages, the usual process of reinitializing route discovery done.	i. An optimum number of packets should be done carefully to enhance network lifespan and avoid routing cost.
26. Minimum -battery -Cost – Routing (MBCR) Protocol.	i. Up to end of network lifespan, nodes are not overused.	ii. The value of the node's energy is not properly defined which causes constraints during messages forwarding. iii. Selecting a path with the highest total battery overhead can cause the presence of nodes with less cost along the route which leads to minimizing the network lifetime.

continued on following page

Table 7. Continued

Energy-Aware Routing Protocol	Strength	Weakness
27. Min -Max -battery -Cost - Routing (MMBCR) Protocol.	i. The optimal route of all feasible routes is the one with the maximum individual battery capacity. ii. Nodes are not over-utilized.	i. The path with an individual lowest battery cost may cause a long transmission path. ii. The issue of a common node between various paths cannot be stopped.
28. Minimum -battery -Cost – Routing (MBCR) Protocol.	i. Up to end of network lifespan, nodes are not overused.	i. The value of the node's energy is not properly defined which causes constraints during messages forwarding. ii. Selecting a path with the highest total battery overhead can cause the presence of nodes with less cost along the route which leads to minimizing the network lifetime.
29. Min -Max -battery -Cost - Routing (MMBCR) Protocol.	i. The optimal route of all feasible routes is the one with the maximum individual battery capacity. ii. Nodes are not over-utilized.	i. The path with an individual lowest battery cost may cause a long transmission path. ii. The issue of a common node between various paths cannot be stopped.
30. Conditional Min-Max battery Capacity Routing (CMMBCR) Protocol.	i. Approximately the minimum transmission route and the minimum node cost are fulfilled. ii. This algorithm utilizes a battery capacity limit γ such that $(0<\gamma < 100)$.	i. This protocol ignores battery discharge ratio which is also a significant parameter to enhance the network lifetime. ii. The optimum value of γ cannot be measured.
31. Lifetime Prediction Routing (LPR).	i. Rresidual battery lifetime and discharge rate parameters are considered in this algorithm. ii. Selects a route with low power congested. iii. Route invalidation timer is used after a fixed time to delete the old routes from the cache. iv. The variation of energy among nodes is minimized.	i. Delaying the packet delivery due to the long route discovery process.
32. Maximum Residual Packet capacity (MRPC) Protocol.	i. MRPC algorithm introduces a new route discovery approach based on the expected energy dissipated and residual capacity during delivery. ii. Route with Maximum Residual Packet capacity is selected.	i. The hop count is not considered while selecting the route.

Chapter 7
Prospective of Blockchain in Derivative Markets:
An Empirical Review

Vaishali Deepak Sahoo
https://orcid.org/0009-0001-8118-2509
Vishwakarma University, India

Deepak Ranjan Sahoo
https://orcid.org/0000-0003-4013-2422
MIT Arts, Design, and Technology University, India

ABSTRACT

This chapter explores the evolving landscape of block chain technology within capital markets, examining its potential benefits and risks. It underscores the importance for regulators to balance innovation with vigilance, allowing block chain to progress naturally while remaining informed about legal developments. The chapter highlights the efficiencies block chain offers, such as reduced transaction costs and decreased reliance on central counterparties, while also addressing the challenges and systemic risks it presents. Through a multidisciplinary lens encompassing data, code, finance, and legal frameworks, regulators can effectively manage block chain's impact on capital markets.

INTRODUCTION

Blockchain technology is synonymous with innovation and disruption across various industries, particularly in financial markets. At its core, Blockchain is a decentralized and immutable ledger recording transactions across a network of computers. Each transaction, or "block," securely links to the preceding one, forming a

DOI: 10.4018/979-8-3693-2157-7.ch007

chronological chain of data blocks. This transparent and tamper-resistant structure offers unparalleled security and transparency, making it ideal for applications beyond cryptocurrencies, such as the derivatives market.

The derivatives market, featuring contracts deriving value from an underlying asset, experiences substantial growth. It encompasses various financial instruments, like futures, options, swaps, and forwards, enabling investors to hedge risk, speculate, and diversify portfolios. However, the market faces challenges. Centralized clearing-houses and intermediaries introduce counterparty risk, operational inefficiencies, and increased costs. Blockchain technology offers a transformative solution. Leveraging decentralized networks and smart contracts, Blockchain platforms facilitate peer-to-peer transactions, eliminating intermediaries and reducing counterparty risk. Smart contracts, self-executing contracts with terms directly written into code, automate derivative contract execution, ensuring trustless and transparent transactions.

Moreover, Blockchain enhances transparency and auditability in the derivatives market. Immutable Blockchain ledgers securely record transaction data, preventing retroactive alteration(Clack, 2018). This transparency fosters trust among participants and allows regulators to monitor market activity in real-time, mitigating manipulation and fraud risks. Blockchain-based derivatives platforms also offer greater accessibility and inclusivity to a broader range of investors. Traditional markets often pose barriers to retail investors due to high entry requirements and complex procedures. However, Blockchain enables fractional ownership and tokenization of contracts, allowing participation with smaller capital and simplified processes.

Furthermore, Blockchain introduces innovation opportunities in derivative products and market infrastructure. According to (Silveira & Camilo, 2023) Decentralized finance (DeFi) protocols offer novel instruments like decentralized options and synthetic assets. Additionally, Blockchain streamlines clearing and settlement, reducing costs and settlement times.

Blockchain technology holds immense potential to revolutionize the derivatives market, addressing challenges and fostering innovation. Trustless transactions, enhanced transparency, and greater accessibility are poised to reshape the derivatives landscape. As Blockchain adoption accelerates, the market stands to benefit from increased efficiency, security, and innovation.

Understanding of Block chain

In research terms, Blockchains function as publicly accessible and theoretically immutable ledgers documenting bitcoin transactions, crucial for cryptocurrency operation. The technology decentralizes ledger management algorithmically, entrusting users within its network. Beyond cryptocurrency, Blockchain holds promise in various sectors(Na et al., 2022). Banking and financial institutions partner with fintech firms to explore Blockchain's potential applications in capital markets. Utilizing Blockchain alongside self-executing smart contracts presents compelling opportunities, especially in derivatives markets with multiple intermediaries. Blockchain adoption could significantly revolutionize existing market infrastructure, potentially rendering certain intermediaries obsolete or reducing their roles.

Enthusiasm within the industry often portrays Blockchains as solutions to numerous global challenges. Some proponents envision Blockchain applications extending far beyond finance, even supporting entire systems of direct democracy, allowing secure voting from smartphones(Rosa et al., 2017). This notion is remarkable, given concerns about voter fraud and political hacking. Yet, questions arise about how Blockchain can address fundamental trust issues in such contexts.

Essentially, Blockchain signifies a significant advancement in information technology. Many enterprises, including financial services, rely on centralized servers to store critical data. However, this approach has inherent weaknesses that Blockchains can mitigate. Centralized storage creates a single point of failure, leaving businesses vulnerable to potential compromises and security risks. Moreover, centralized systems may experience bottlenecks or crashes under high user activity.

Additionally, centralized systems may prove inefficient for organizations needing to oversee agreements with various parties continuously. Blockchain, functioning as a decentralized ledger, ensures every network participant possesses an identical copy of records(Rojas, 2018). These networks undergo continuous reconciliation, updating approximately every ten minutes to incorporate changes. This synchronized nature allows seamless operation even in the event of a central database failure.

According to (Malinova & Park, 2023) The volatile nature of the crypto asset market, experiencing rapid growth followed by significant downturns within a short timeframe, has captured considerable attention. Amidst the frenzy and fraudulent activities, the foundational blockchain technology driving these assets emerges as a beacon of promise for the financial sector. This technology offers potential for simplifying back-office operations, facilitating new interactions among stakeholders, and fostering innovative service models in digital asset issuance and management.

According to (Dewey & Newbold, 2023) explore constant function market makers (CFMMs), the predominant type of blockchain-based decentralized exchange. Our study delves into the market microstructure surrounding CFMMs, offering a model to assess the liquidity provider (LP) mechanism and derive the value of associated derivatives. We propose a model accommodating two trader types with distinct information, providing methods to simulate their behavior and compute trade profit and loss. Additionally, we discuss concepts related to the equilibrium distribution of fair prices given trader arrivals and suggest implications for alternative CFMM parameters.

The operation of Blockchain varies across types, but the underlying principles remain consistent. Essentially, it functions as a ledger for recording information, validated by network participants. Authorized asset holders initiate transactions triggering proposed ledger modifications verified by the broader network(Savirimuthu, 2019). Through these mechanisms, network members rely on trust in computational integrity rather than direct trust in each other. To delve deeper into Blockchain's intricacies, one can examine its genesis through pioneering applications like Bitcoin.

Bitcoins, Block-chain, and Smart Contracts

Initially, Blockchains were not designed for integration with securities, derivatives, or traditional capital markets. Their development primarily aimed to support digital currencies, notably Bitcoin. Cryptocurrencies like Bitcoin facilitated peer-to-peer transactions, eliminating intermediaries in payment clearing processes to democratize access to capital sources(Arusoaie, 2021; Savirimuthu, 2019). In the Bitcoin network, computers validate transactions by solving cryptographic puzzles, ensuring transaction authenticity and the integrity of Blockchain operations.

This early phase of Blockchain development is often termed "Blockchain 1.0." Recently, financial institutions recognized the potential efficiencies beyond cryptocurrencies alone, marking the emergence of "Blockchain 2.0." This transition envisions broader adoption of Blockchain across the financial sector.(Arusoaie, 2021) Observing the decentralization advantages in cryptocurrencies, particularly on Wall Street, many believe Blockchain can optimize market processes, leading to significant cost savings and operational efficiencies.

Understanding Blockchain and its benefits involves delving into Blockchain 1.0. While numerous cryptocurrencies exist, focus primarily lies on Bitcoin and Ethereum. Bitcoin, as the pioneering cryptocurrency, forms the foundation of Blockchain technology, garnering significant attention and research. Conversely, Ethereum, the second most prevalent cryptocurrency, plays a crucial role in Blockchain 2.0. Its implementation of automated and customizable smart contracts introduces new functionality and versatility to Blockchain networks.

Bitcoins Underlying Technology

In-person transactions follow a simple process: one party exchanges an item of value for cash, and the other confirms the transaction by counting the bills. However, as digital transactions become more common, cash exchanges diminish(Karaarslan & Konacaklı, 2020). The internet has replaced traditional cash transactions, and credit cards have been widespread for decades. What's surprising is the growing prevalence of asset digitization as a preferred payment method. Platforms like Venmo allow users to transfer electronic funds via smartphones, and some European countries are moving towards a cashless society. While digitizing cash offers convenience, it also presents challenges in transaction verification, known as the "double spending problem." In a digital environment, where money exists as ones and zeroes, there's a risk of individuals duplicating the code and sending it to multiple recipients, similar to copying an image or document file(Schär, 2021). Bitcoin addressed this issue uniquely through Blockchain technology. By eliminating intermediaries typically crucial in digital spending platforms, Bitcoin decentralized the verification process, distributing it among network participants. Despite lacking knowledge or trust in each other, network members universally accept the code as the ultimate truth determinant. Transaction verification on the Blockchain involves a collective quest for accuracy; once a user identifies the correct values, the network unanimously adopts them as the accurate transaction account.

The Bitcoin Blockchain establishes trust through a mechanism known as proof of work. To verify a transaction, computers within the network must solve a specific computational problem to generate a set of data(Peltoniemi & Ihalainen, 2019). This problem is intentionally made computationally intensive, requiring significant resources like time, computing power, hardware, and electricity to solve. While solving this problem may be challenging for systems, verifying transactions against the public ledger is relatively straightforward for network members.

To understand how proof of work Blockchains function, let's consider a basic Bitcoin transaction scenario. Suppose Aman wants to send payment to Boby. Both Aman and Boby have digital wallets stored on their computers, containing information about their respective Bitcoin addresses(Peltoniemi & Ihalainen, 2019). These addresses, represented by alphanumeric characters, are linked to individual Bitcoin balances. When Boby wants to receive payment, he generates a new address, and Aman sends the payment via the Bitcoin client software.

In a traditional accounting system, recording this transaction is straightforward: Aman's ledger shows the transaction as a credit, while Boby's ledger reflects a corresponding debit. However, recording the transaction on the Blockchain ledger involves an additional step—a cryptographic seal. Bitcoin uses public key cryptography for this purpose. Both Aman and Boby have public addresses they can openly share(Alao & Cuffe, 2022). Additionally, they each possess a private key, kept confidential and derived from their addresses through a cryptographic process. To authorize the transaction, Boby provides Aman with his public address, functioning as a public key. Aman then validates the transaction by "signing" the transfer with her private key, which pairs with Boby's public key. This cryptographic process ensures the security and authenticity of the transaction, enabling trustless transactions on the Bitcoin Blockchain.

Once a transaction is finalized, the request is broadcasted to the network for verification. Miners, crucial participants within the Bitcoin network, verify transactions for inclusion onto the Blockchain. They aggregate pending transaction data into blocks, which serve as the fundamental units of the Blockchain(Jayeola, 2020). The verification process involves miners engaging in cryptographic hashing, a pivotal concept underlying Blockchain technology. Hashing entails running a data set through a hashing algorithm, resulting in a unique alphanumeric string known as a hash value. Even minor alterations to the input data can yield vastly different hash values. Users cannot predict the hash a particular data set will produce without executing it through the algorithm.

Miners aim to generate a hash value that falls below a predefined target value established by the Blockchain. This target value adjusts the difficulty of the proof of work problem to reflect changes in network processing power. As more miners participate in transaction verification, the overall computational power increases, prompting adjustments to the target value to maintain the desired difficulty level(Jayeola, 2020). To solve the proof of work problem, miners use three main inputs for the hashing algorithm: the newly formed transaction block, the hash from the previous block in the Blockchain, and a variable known as a nonce. The nonce serves as a flexible parameter, allowing miners to produce different hash values while keeping the other inputs constant.

Miners engage in a competitive process, expending resources to find a nonce that results in a hash value below the target. This process requires significant computational effort, akin to searching for a needle in a haystack(Faozi & Gustanto, 2022). Miners compete, spurred on by the prospect of earning a Bitcoin reward for identifying an acceptable hash value first. While specialized hardware and collective mining pools can enhance efficiency, discovering the correct hash value remains a probabilistic endeavor, with no guaranteed formula or shortcut.

Once a miner successfully solves the proof of work problem, it disseminates the completed block to all nodes within the network. Nodes, interconnected systems, validate incoming blocks by subjecting them to the network's predefined acceptance criteria(Saeidnia & Lund, 2023). If a block indicates a double-spent coin or fails to meet other specified conditions, the node rejects it. Upon acceptance, a node uses the hash value of the validated block as the header for the subsequent block in the Blockchain.

Nodes adhere to a fundamental principle: they recognize the longest chain of blocks as the network's authoritative ledger. In the event of conflicting blocks, a node prioritizes the first block it receives and begins work on extending that particular chain(Avgouleas & Kiayias, 2019). Simultaneously, it preserves the alternative block, as other nodes also start work based on their received blocks. As blocks are continuously added to the Blockchain, nodes dynamically adjust their focus to the chain that becomes longer and gains broader acceptance across the network.

While variations to this process exist, the proof of work mechanism proposed by Nakamoto remains the cornerstone of Bitcoin's operation. This model, with its variations, serves as the foundation for most Blockchain systems. The Bitcoin Blockchain exemplifies the essential principles of collaborative payment verification, demonstrating the efficacy of decentralized consensus mechanisms in ensuring transaction integrity.

From Cash to Securities: Smart Contracts

Smart contracts play a pivotal role in facilitating the evolution from Block-chain 1.0 to Block-chain 2.0. However, the term "smart contract" remains somewhat nebulous, often employed as a catch-all phrase to encompass various online activities, serving as a marketing buzzword. The concept was initially articulated by lawyer and computer programmer Nick Szabo in 1994(Organization, 2017). Szabo defined a smart contract as: Much of the ambiguity surrounding smart contracts arises from the intersection between traditional legal contract understanding and the "smart" functionality inherent in the code. In the realm of online activities, many processes are governed by code and hold legal significance, yet lack the formal elements of contract formation.

Smart contracts operate on the premise that code can autonomously enforce and execute contractual terms. If the software executes these terms without additional intervention from the parties involved, the contract is deemed "self-enforcing." This characteristic enables agreements to proceed even in the absence of mutual trust. For instance, consider a hypothetical smart contract managing a car loan envisioned by Szabo. In this scenario, the loan terms are expressed in code and programmed into the vehicle itself. Unlike traditional contracts reliant on the debtor's adherence, the smart contract ensures payment enforcement, revoking ignition permission if payments are missed. This not only highlights the efficiency of smart contracts but also underscores their potential cost-saving benefits.

Szabo's early conceptualizations, though ahead of their time, have yet to be fully realized. Presently, smart contracts are most commonly employed in multimedia digital rights management (DRM). For instance, digital content purchases on platforms like iTunes entail acquiring limited usage licenses. DRM smart contracts enforce usage restrictions automatically, without the need for manual oversight. However, these contracts have limitations; they lack the ability to process inputs and apply contractual terms dynamically.

Smart contracts uploaded to block-chains are coded to embody agreement terms. Unlike traditional contracts laden with dense legalese, smart contracts distill terms into simple "if/then" statements, resembling conditional payment mechanisms. While complex in programming, smart contracts essentially function as conditional payment systems.

The process of uploading smart contracts varies across block chain types. Ethereum, designed specifically for smart contracts, offers greater flexibility in programming. Users initiate contract uploading through a transaction containing the contract's code, prompting nodes to create a special address for the contract. Subsequent transaction requests can trigger cascading smart contract executions, contingent on predefined conditions.

Addressing the challenge of monitoring triggering conditions, multi-signatures and oracles provide solutions by tracking off-chain information. Multi-signature agreements involve multiple parties, with a predetermined number required to sign transactions. Oracles serve as additional signatories, attesting to off-chain data's validity and enabling transactions contingent on real-world events(Surujnath, 2017). Although smart contract technology is still in its nascent stage, its potential has attracted substantial investment, driving further development and exploration of its capabilities.

The Modern Derivatives Industry

While block-chains and smart contracts represent cutting-edge innovations in finance, derivatives have a rich historical legacy spanning centuries. Some of the earliest instances of credit derivatives trace back to twelfth century Venice, where financiers sought protection against potential losses from overseas trading ventures. Throughout recorded history, derivatives primarily served as hedging mechanisms within commodities industries.

In modern finance, derivatives agreements play a pivotal role in the hedging strategies of banks and financial institutions. However, despite their longstanding history, derivatives markets are poised for potential transformation, albeit with inherent risks. Derivatives come in several general types. Forward agreements outline future asset deliveries at predetermined prices, while futures are standardized forward contracts traded on exchanges. Options grant holders the right, but not the obligation, to purchase underlying assets at specified prices, and swaps involve cash flow exchanges based on agreed notional amounts. Some sophisticated instruments may combine elements of these different derivatives archetypes.

Derivatives trades can occur through either exchanges or over-the-counter (OTC) markets. Exchange-traded derivatives adhere to strict standardization and liquidity requirements, offering fewer options for underlying assets, settlement amounts, and other contractual terms. Centralized entities provide credit support and monitor trading practices in exchange-traded markets. Conversely, OTC derivatives are individually tailored to address specific risks, offering greater flexibility but often at the expense of liquidity due to their bespoke nature.

Risks Associated with Derivatives Use

Regardless of their classification, derivatives inherently entail long-term risk. Regulators often express a desire to rein in risky practices, but such efforts can be nebulous when dealing with entities that essentially trade in risk itself. A well-functioning derivatives market, therefore, prioritizes the mitigation of undesirable risks, with counterparty risk emerging as a primary concern for market participants(Avgouleas & Kiayias, 2019). Counterparty risk, referring to the possibility that a party may fail to fulfill its contractual obligations, represents a significant source of apprehension. It essentially quantifies a firm's exposure to potential defaults by its counterparties, constituting a form of credit risk. Given its ubiquitous presence in derivative transactions, counterparty risk presents challenges for effective hedging.

Market participants are wary of a domino effect wherein the default of one counterparty triggers defaults among others, leading to cascading repercussions. To manage this risk, firms often engage in offsetting transactions to neutralize their exposure. However, an unexpected default by a heavily exposed counterparty can disrupt the firm's balanced position, necessitating the re-hedging of affected positions(Paolini, 2020). In such scenarios, the firm may find it challenging or cost-prohibitive to hedge its risks, particularly during periods of extreme market conditions. Consequently, unexpected defaults can expose firms to renewed risks, compelling them to reassess and potentially readjust their hedging strategies.

The Derivative Value Chain

The derivative value chain encompasses three primary stages: pre-trading, trading and clearing, and execution and delivery. During the pre-trading phase, orders are generated and directed to marketplaces. Trading involves matching buyers and sellers, with compatible counterparties executing the derivative contracts. At this juncture, contracts remain "open" and can be managed or traded until maturity during the clearing process. In modern derivatives markets, post-trading activities, including contract management, are often overseen by a central counterparty clearinghouse (CCP)(Jaiwani et al., 2023). Finally, upon maturity, contracts are "closed" either through cash settlement, the prevalent method, or physical delivery of the underlying asset.

Pre-trading activities commence with broker-dealers, particularly in exchange-traded transactions. These intermediaries originate orders from clients and transmit them to centralized exchanges known as designated contract markets. Examples of such markets include the Chicago Board of Trade and the New York Mercantile Exchange(Khiem et al., 2023). Typically, in these exchange-traded arrangements, broker-dealers facilitate order flow and ensure compliance with exchange regulations.

In standardized derivative agreements, negotiable terms are typically limited to price terms in futures or options contracts, and cash delivery amounts in swaps. This standardization enhances liquidity, facilitating the exchange's ability to match willing parties to assume different sides of the transaction with minimal difficulty. (Zhang et al., 2023)In over-the-counter (OTC) markets, broker-dealers route orders to their own derivatives desks or other dealers as needed. Swap agreements, however, are directed to swap execution facilities, offering pre-trade bid and ask information akin to exchanges. Bilateral trading characterizes OTC markets, where terms may align with standardized agreements ("look-alikes") or be tailored to individual party requirements(Surujnath, 2017). However, bespoke contracts may lack liquidity, hindering a robust secondary market.

Upon matching parties and pending trades, central counterparties (CCPs) assume the role of clearing the trade. CCPs, comprising member firms, aim to mitigate the impact of defaults on derivative contract obligations(Wang et al., 2023). They accomplish this by acting as the intermediary between parties, a process known as novation. Through novation, counterparties contract with the CCP instead of directly with each other, creating two separate contracts: one between the first counterparty and the CCP, and another between the CCP and the second counterparty. This structure shields counterparties from each other's credit risk, focusing their concerns solely on the credit risk associated with the CCP.

Given that central counterparties (CCPs) assume all counterparty risks in the market, they must safeguard against their own default through netting and collateralization mechanisms. (Qushtom et al., 2023) Netting serves to streamline cash movements by consolidating gains and losses from multiple outstanding derivatives contracts between two parties. Rather than settling each agreement individually, netting allows parties to offset losses against gains and settle the net result. CCPs employ multilateral netting, which consolidates movements across several clearing members, enhancing efficiency. Furthermore, upon initiation of a transaction, the CCP requires clearing members to provide initial margin as collateral(Faozi & Gustanto, 2022). This margin is determined based on the probability of the member's default, with models like NASDAQ's commodities derivatives margining model reflecting a high level of confidence (e.g., 99.2%) in covering defaults.

In addition to initial margin, CCPs also collect variation margin to adjust positions throughout the life of the trade. Variation margin payments facilitate adjustments based on changes in the instrument's market value, resulting in fund transfers between the member organization and the CCP as needed. The combination of these margin requirements effectively shields CCPs from both potential future losses and day-to-day fluctuations, bolstering their resilience in the face of market uncertainties.

Blockchain technology Data Security and Cloud Security

Blockchain technology produces a structure of data with inherent security qualities. It is based on principles of cryptography, decentralization, and consensus, which ensure trust in transactions. In most Blockchains or distributed ledger technologies (DLT), the data structures into blocks, and each block contains a transaction or a bundle of transactions. Each new block connects to all the blocks before it in a cryptographic chain, making it nearly impossible to tamper with. All transactions within the blocks are validated and agreed upon by a consensus mechanism, ensuring that each transaction is true and correct.

Blockchain technology enables decentralization through the participation of members across a distributed network. There is no single point of failure, and a single user cannot change the record of transactions. However, blockchain technologies differ in some critical security aspects.

While blockchain technology produces a tamper-proof ledger of transactions, blockchain networks remain vulnerable to cyberattacks and fraud. Ill-intentioned individuals can manipulate known vulnerabilities in blockchain infrastructure and have succeeded in various hacks and frauds over the years.

Blockchain security for the enterprise

When building an enterprise blockchain application, consider security at all layers of the technology stack and manage governance and permissions for the network. A comprehensive security strategy for an enterprise blockchain solution includes using traditional security controls and technology-unique controls. Some of the security controls specific to enterprise blockchain solutions include:

Figure 1. Security Controls Enterprise Blockchain

Figure: 1.0: Security Controls Enterprise Blockchain

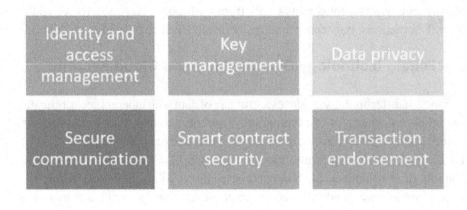

Source: IBM

Source: IBM

Employ experts to help design a compliant and secure solution and achieve your business goals. Look for a production-grade platform for building blockchain solutions that you can deploy in the technology environment of your choice, whether on-premises or with your preferred cloud vendor.

Blockchain significantly enhances cloud security by improving data security, specifically its confidentiality (privacy), integrity, and availability. With various blockchain solutions and technologies, you can set the required security levels for the entire system and down to individual records. Given that cloud computing often outsources trust to providers handling your IT infrastructure and data storage, new methods for ensuring data security become essential. Blockchain technologies offer extensive customization options, allowing you to build fully private, public, and mixed Blockchains. You can select consensus mechanisms for transaction processing and dispute resolution and customize the governance model to meet your needs and regulatory requirements. Additionally, you can incorporate smart contracts and smart assets, creating a rich ecosystem that supports your business needs now and in the future.

Block-Chain's Disruptive Potential

The derivatives industry operates within a highly intermediated framework, presenting opportunities for cost reduction and efficiency enhancement through block-chain technology. According to estimates by Goldman Sachs, the implementation of block-chains in cash securities markets could yield annual savings of $11 billion to $12 billion for the banking sector, with potential additional savings in derivatives markets. These technologies could also streamline processes related to anti-money laundering and know-your-customer reporting, offering further cost reductions for financial institutions(Peltoniemi & Ihalainen, 2019; Savirimuthu, 2019).

Initial experiments with block-chain technology have demonstrated successful transfers of foreign exchange futures and credit-default swaps on a small scale. (Ramdani et al., 2023) A block-chain-based derivatives contract market would likely involve a network of interoperable ledgers utilizing multi-signature smart contracts for transaction execution and oracles for asset monitoring and collateral management. In this system, parties involved in block-chain derivatives transactions would submit bids and asks as usual. In over-the-counter (OTC) markets, the role of dealers could be diminished. Instead of relying on dealers to match bids and asks, parties could leverage the anonymity provided by the block-chain, similar to Bitcoin users. They could directly upload asks to the block-chain, allowing its computational power to automatically select the highest bid. With the use of public-key cryptography, publicly viewable addresses would serve as aliases, safeguarding the identifying information of counterparties.

Once parties are successfully matched in derivatives trading, CCPs (central counterparty clearinghouses) proceed to novate the agreements, as per the current process. This novation results in the creation of two contracts, which are then uploaded to the derivatives ledger(Hassoun et al., 2023). This ledger houses the logic and execution algorithms for all agreements among clearing members. Margin posting to the CCP involves the utilization of interoperable collateral and asset ledgers. Throughout the lifecycle of the agreement, the collateral ledger employs oracles to reference agreed-upon external data sources (such as Bloomberg) to track price movements in underlying assets and automatically adjust positions. This real-time rebalancing allows for more efficient allocation of collateral in margin accounts. Execution of payments is automated; if additional margin is required, the ledger sends a payment request to the clearing member's address on the asset ledger.

There is ongoing debate among industry stakeholders regarding the potential displacement of CCPs by block-chains as intermediaries in derivatives trades. The block-chain's verification mechanism poses a threat to CCPs in securities transactions by ensuring that both parties own the asset before trade consummation—similar to a Bitcoin transaction, which can reduce counterparty risk without CCP involvement(Alao & Cuffe, 2022; Peltoniemi & Ihalainen, 2019). However, unlike securities, there can be a significant time gap between the trade and settlement of derivatives, making verification at the time of trade insufficient to eliminate counterparty risk years down the line. Consequently, many believe CCPs will still be necessary for netting transactions, as block-chain may not be equipped to handle netting efficiently, potentially leading to increased collateral requirements across the board. Therefore, skepticism remains regarding the abandonment of CCPs by market participants and regulators, as CCPs serve as a trusted safety net in the current system. However, block-chain proponents suggest that an improvised netting process can occur on the block-chain, consolidating trading information and locking margin accounts until appropriately funded. Some argue that the simplified settlement process could sufficiently reduce counterparty risk, rendering netting unnecessary(Sookram, 2023). This debate will be settled as block-chain technology matures, as it must demonstrate clear efficiencies to displace the existing CCP system.

Even if CCPs retain their functionality, block-chains offer efficiencies as platforms for data recording and reporting. Audits and regulatory reporting become more streamlined, benefiting regulators. By serving as a full node on the block-chain, regulators gain access to the entire ledger, including transaction information, margin amounts, and participating firms' risk profiles(Veerasamy et al., 2023). However, modifications to permissions or an identification system are needed to de-anonymize accounts on the block-chain, requiring careful key management. Authorized parties also have access to smart contracts, serving as records of ownership and transaction information, potentially eliminating the need for some dispute resolution procedures and reducing transaction costs.

The greatest potential for block-chains likely lies in illiquid, non-cleared OTC derivatives markets where there is no CCP. In these markets, block-chains can assume functions typically undertaken by CCPs, but in a decentralized manner. Instead of relying on a single central counterparty, the block-chain acts as a decentralized clearing network (DCN). (Hao et al., 2023)Firms trading in these derivatives could use block-chains like Ethereum, enabling the organization into distributed autonomous organizations (DAOs) governed by smart contracts. The block-chain manages functions usually conducted by CCPs, such as contract valuation, margin calculation, collateral custody, novation, netting, and closeout. Block-chains crowdsource calculations, allowing the network to reach a consensus, potentially leading to more transparent OTC markets.

Despite the potential for efficiency gains, block-chains face implementation barriers. A system entirely reliant on block-chain cannot guarantee payments in the event of contract flaws, lacking legal recourse for aggrieved parties. The irrevocability of block-chain poses challenges for court-ordered remedies, as entries cannot be edited or reversed. While smart contracts resolve some disputes, others may persist, such as insider trading or disagreements regarding the coded logic's accuracy in reflecting agreed-upon terms.

Block-Chain's Impact on Systemic Risk

Depending on the evolution of block-chain technology, derivatives trading markets could undergo significant restructuring. The current regulatory framework may not adequately address the risks associated with derivatives trading on block-chain platforms. Proposing concrete regulatory measures at this stage of block-chain development may be challenging and potentially counterproductive(Wu, 2023). Instead, it is important to recognize that systemic risk is a primary concern driving derivatives regulation, and any new regulatory approach must take into account the unique risks posed by block-chain technology.

While central counterparty clearinghouses (CCPs) are generally regarded as effective in mitigating systemic risk, they also introduce risks by centralizing authority and creating large entities that could fail. While block-chains have the potential to mitigate the risk of over-centralization, there is a concern that block-chain technology may introduce systemic risks of a different nature(Held, 2023). Regulators must carefully assess these risks when formulating governance strategies for block-chain-based derivatives markets.

Centralization and Systemic Risk

Regulators are deeply concerned about derivatives and their potential to exacerbate systemic risk within the financial system. Systemic risk, a multifaceted concept, encompasses various consequences such as bank runs, payment crises, failures of interconnected firms, and a general loss of trust in the financial system. Alternatively, systemic risk can be understood in terms of its causes, including entities that are "too big to fail," "too interconnected to fail," or "too leveraged to fail."

Traditionally, systemic risk has been associated with the failure of financial institutions, particularly banks, which provide vital market access. Bank runs, for example, can trigger a cascade of institutional failures, leading to a domino effect of financial collapses. While central clearinghouses (CCPs) were introduced as a mechanism to mitigate systemic risk, they are now viewed with skepticism due to concerns about the concentration of risk within these centralized entities. The global mandate for CCPs to clear an extensive volume of derivatives trades has only exacerbated these concerns, as CCPs become increasingly interconnected with numerous financial institutions(Ajakwe et al., 2023).

Furthermore, CCPs are vulnerable to liquidity shortages, particularly during periods of financial stress, which can compromise their ability to meet obligations and undermine market confidence. (Martha et al., 2023)The block-chain technology presents a potential solution to these challenges by decentralizing key clearing functions and distributing tasks among network participants. Advocates of block-chain technology believe that smart contracts can automate critical processes such as matching, collateral management, default management, and settlement, thus reducing the reliance on CCPs or even displacing them altogether.

While skeptics argue that block-chain technology currently cannot replicate all functions performed by CCPs, the potential benefits of disintermediation are significant. Block-chain technology can enhance efficiency and reduce systemic risk, and efforts are underway to integrate block-chain into existing processes and push for greater disintermediation. As the technology continues to evolve, it holds promise for transforming the market structure for derivatives trading and addressing systemic risk concerns.

The Systemic Risks Posed By Decentralized Systems

Block-chain enthusiasts are continuously advancing the technology through collaborative industry research efforts. As block-chain applications near practical implementation, regulatory bodies like the CFTC and their international counterparts face the challenge of adapting existing regulatory frameworks to this new technology. (Malinova & Park, 2023) If block-chain technology fulfills the high expectations set by its proponents, certain regulatory requirements such as mandated central clearing could become outdated, leading to greater transparency in markets such as uncleared OTC swaps. While regulators and market participants are intrigued by the potential of block-chain, they must also acknowledge that the transition to a decentralized market structure is not without risks. Although block-chain addresses concerns about over-centralization inherent in traditional systems, it introduces new risks of its own.

While it may be premature to propose a new regulatory regime, there are key themes regulators should consider when evaluating how to regulate block-chain markets. Systemic risk will persist in block-chain markets, albeit with different sources. Decentralization shifts regulatory focus from systemic risks created by interconnected institutions to those inherent in the market itself. Regulators must address issues related to settlement finality and recourse, particularly in the context of potential cyberattacks on the block-chain network. Additionally, regulators should be mindful of how market participants may exploit block-chain efficiencies and should remain vigilant in requiring reporting by swap participants.

Block-chain transactions lack certain elements of traditional legal agreements, raising concerns about settlement finality. While block-chain technology offers transparency and immutability, it also poses challenges regarding dispute resolution and vulnerability to attacks such as the "51% attack." Ethereum's experience with a major exploit highlighted the complexities of resolving block-chain errors and raised questions about the viability of block-chain forks as a solution.

The concept of settlement finality is crucial in block-chain systems, but traditional notions may not apply. (Ramanathan et al., 2023)Depending on the block-chain's design, finality can be uncertain, leading to liquidity risks and undermining market confidence. Regulatory efforts to ensure definitive finality can help foster confidence in block-chain markets and mitigate the risk of correlated market movements resulting from a loss of confidence.

Regulators have the opportunity to address issues related to settlement finality in block-chain systems. While it may be premature to establish a new regulatory framework specifically tailored to settlement finality in block-chain technology's early stages, it is conceivable to adapt the current regulatory regime to accommodate changes in market infrastructure. (Colombo et al., 2023)Regulators cannot solely rely on block-chain technology to solve all problems; in fact, decentralizing clearing and settlement processes through block-chain may introduce new systemic risks, such as disputes over finality, replacing the risks associated with centralized intermediaries.

The notion of regulators serving as limited permission nodes on the block-chain has been proposed within the block-chain community. This approach could grant regulators access to extensive data, potentially surpassing what is currently available under the existing reporting regime. The block-chain ledger itself could serve as the record for swap transactions, storing both creation and ongoing data required by regulatory reporting rules. This could lead to significant efficiencies, especially considering the current challenges with aggregating and analyzing data from multiple reporting systems.

Given the nature of block-chains and the associated risk factors, regulators may need to take a proactive approach in adapting the regulatory framework to this emerging technology. Mitigating systemic risk in block-chain systems may necessitate setting new standards for underlying smart contracts, requiring regulators to address cybersecurity issues and technological infrastructure concerns related to block-chain.As smart contracts and block-chains represent financial innovations, regulators must stay ahead of these developments. If derivatives markets transition to block-chain architecture, new types of agreements may emerge.(Soputro et al., 2023) This technological shift could be considered financial innovation, potentially simplifying the creation of new instruments and allowing for the transfer of new types of risk.

Regulators should closely scrutinize smart contracts, particularly in their early stages, to address potential vulnerabilities and mitigate risks. The Ethereum hack serves as a cautionary example, underscoring the importance of regulating smart contracts to ensure market stability and user confidence. Screening the underlying smart contract code for vulnerabilities may be necessary to safeguard against systemic repercussions.

Societal approach of Block chain technology

Shin & Ibahrine, (2020) argue that a sociotechnical perspective on Blockchain system stresses examining Blockchains by considering cultural and social roles they play, rather than focusing on merely their economic value. It highlights the importance of inclusivity for enhancing public goodness. As Williams et al., (2022), this fits well with the idea that blockchain technologies are tied up with human conditions and wider social frameworks. This emphasizes the need for user-centred design principles while considering wider societal implications in terms of political, economic or societal architectures.

According to Haryanto & Sudaryati, (2020), the ethics behind blockchain technology expands on utilitarianism by relating it to wider society through decentralizing it, meeting the needs for stakeholders' information as well as instilling ethicality. Moreover, blockchain technologies reinforce liberty, trust, confidentiality autonomy, and fairness thus reinventing and enacting them collectively Koletsi, (2019). Besides, just like cloud computing, blockchain is taken to be the ultimate extension of utilitarian ethics at the societal level by serving interests for all parties (Tang et al., (2019). Cunha et al., (2021) stated that if it is properly constructed and implemented, blockchain systems can play a substantial part in addressing social issues and promoting equity, inclusiveness and resilience in communities. According to S K-, (2023) blockchain use in supply chain management has already demonstrated auspicious achievements in enhancing supply chain networks, restructuring industrial and business models, and affecting society and standards of living.

Blockchain technology can build new ecosystems in the energy sector and help decrease financial costs, thus imparting wider social implications than had been anticipated in the immediate context Höhne & Tiberius, (2020). Krichen et al., (2022) illustrates various humanlike applications and social consequences of blockchain technologies for commerce, communication, finance, organizational structures, and national security/tasks. In their work, Chow-White et al., (2020) argue that blockchain technology is revolutionary and stands to impact many sectors within society, specifically health, democracy, and enterprise.

Implementing blockchain technology might affect societies in many ways. Some say it can help develop environmentally friendly urban areas and make life more bearable. This is summed up by the idea that "this is where we're headed." Mannonov & Myeong, (2024) using HTML Blockquote tags suggested that. Various sectors in society, education inclusive, are increasingly acknowledging the potentiality of the technology in enhancing governance efficiency Höhne & Tiberius, (2020). Worldwide countries recognize blockchain as an emerging technology capable of aiding in constructing smart societies Zhu & Park, (2022).

In simple terms, Blockchain is more than just a technical upgrade—it is a tool for reshaping societies in many aspects rather than anything else. Broad-ranging ethical, social and economic ramifications are so significant that they transform social relations, transactions and forms of governance.

CONCLUSION

Block-chain technology is still in the midst of evolution, with both financial institutions and regulators actively exploring its potential applications in capital markets. Now, it may be prudent for regulators to allow the technology to progress naturally while simultaneously staying abreast of legal developments to comprehend both the promises and pitfalls associated with block-chain. The efficiencies offered by block-chain are significant, potentially leading to reduced transaction costs for participants in derivatives markets and diminishing reliance on central counterparties vulnerable to substantial credit risk. However, challenges exist within block-chain systems, including technological vulnerabilities that could introduce new systemic risks. Regulators must be equipped to address these risks proactively to prevent potential financial crises. The specific measures to mitigate block-chain's systemic risks will depend largely on the evolution of the technology. Nonetheless, it is evident that a comprehensive analysis of block-chain's systemic risks will necessitate an understanding of data, code, finance, and legal frameworks. This multidisciplinary approach will be crucial in effectively managing the impact of block-chain on capital markets.

REFERENCES

Ajakwe, S. O., Kim, D. S., & Lee, J. M. (2023). Drone Transportation System: Systematic Review of Security Dynamics for Smart Mobility. *IEEE Internet of Things Journal*, 10(16), 14462–14482. Advance online publication. DOI: 10.1109/JIOT.2023.3266843

Alao, O., & Cuffe, P. (2022). Hedging Volumetric Risks of Solar Power Producers Using Weather Derivative Smart Contracts on a Blockchain Marketplace. *IEEE Transactions on Smart Grid*, 13(6), 4730–4746. Advance online publication. DOI: 10.1109/TSG.2022.3181256

Arusoaie, A. (2021). Certifying Findel derivatives for blockchain. *Journal of Logical and Algebraic Methods in Programming*, 121, 100665. Advance online publication. DOI: 10.1016/j.jlamp.2021.100665

Avgouleas, E., & Kiayias, A. (2019). The Promise of Blockchain Technology for Global Securities and Derivatives Markets: The New Financial Ecosystem and the 'Holy Grail' of Systemic Risk Containment. *European Business Organization Law Review*, 20(1), 81–110. Advance online publication. DOI: 10.1007/s40804-019-00133-3

Chow-White, P., Lusoli, A., Phan, V. T. A., & Green, S. E. (2020). 'Blockchain Good, Bitcoin Bad': The Social Construction of Blockchain in Mainstream and Specialized Media. *Journal of Digital Social Research*, 2(2), 1–27. DOI: 10.33621/jdsr.v2i2.34

Clack, C. D. (2018). A Blockchain Grand Challenge: Smart Financial Derivatives. *Frontiers in Blockchain*, 1, 1. Advance online publication. DOI: 10.3389/fbloc.2018.00001

Colombo, A., Bellomarini, L., Ceri, S., & Laurenza, E. (2023). Smart Derivative Contracts in DatalogMTL. *Advances in Database Technology - EDBT, 26*(3). DOI: 10.48786/edbt.2023.65

Cunha, P. R. D., Soja, P., & Themistocleous, M. (2021). Blockchain for development: A guiding framework. *Information Technology for Development*, 27(3), 417–438. DOI: 10.1080/02681102.2021.1935453

Dewey, R., & Newbold, C. (2023). The Pricing And Hedging Of Constant Function Market Makers*. SSRN *Electronic Journal*. DOI: 10.2139/ssrn.4455835

Faozi, M., & Gustanto, E. S. (2022). Kripto, Blockchain, Bitcoin, dan Masa Depan Bank Islam: Sebuah Literatur Review. *Quranomic: Jurnal Ekonomi Dan Bisnis Islam, 1*(2).

Hao, M., Qian, K., & Chau, S. C. K. (2023). Blockchain-enabled Parametric Solar Energy Insurance via Remote Sensing. *E-Energy 2023 - Proceedings of the 2023 14th ACM International Conference on Future Energy Systems*. DOI: 10.1145/3575813.3576880

Haryanto, S. D., & Sudaryati, E. (2020). The Ethical Perspective of Millennial Accountants in Responding to Opportunities and Challenges of Blockchain 4.0. *Journal of Accounting and Investment*, 21(3). Advance online publication. DOI: 10.18196/jai.2103159

Hassoun, A., Garcia-Garcia, G., Trollman, H., Jagtap, S., Parra-López, C., Cropotova, J., Bhat, Z., Centobelli, P., & Aït-Kaddour, A. (2023). Birth of dairy 4.0: Opportunities and challenges in adoption of fourth industrial revolution technologies in the production of milk and its derivatives. In *Current Research in Food Science* (Vol. 7). DOI: 10.1016/j.crfs.2023.100535

Held, A. (2023). Crypto Assets and Decentralised Ledgers: Does Situs Actually Matter? In *Blockchain and Private International Law*. DOI: 10.1163/9789004514850_010

Höhne, S., & Tiberius, V. (2020). Powered by blockchain: Forecasting blockchain use in the electricity market. *International Journal of Energy Sector Management*, 14(6), 1221–1238. DOI: 10.1108/IJESM-10-2019-0002

Jaiwani, M., Gopalkrishnan, S., Kale, V., Chatterjee, A., Khatwani, R., Kasam, N., & Mitra, P. K. (2023). The Blockchain Revolution: Disrupting Derivative Markets with Smart Contracts. *2023 IEEE International Conference on Technology Management, Operations and Decisions, ICTMOD 2023*. DOI: 10.1109/ICTMOD59086.2023.10438145

Jayeola, O. (2020). Inefficiencies in trade reporting for over-the-counter derivatives: Is blockchain the solution? *Capital Markets Law Journal*, 15(1), 48–69. Advance online publication. DOI: 10.1093/cmlj/kmz028

Karaarslan, E., & Konacaklı, E. (2020). Data Storage in the Decentralized World: Blockchain and Derivatives. In *Who Runs the World: Data*. DOI: 10.26650/B/ET06.2020.011.03

Khiem, H. G., Huong, H. L., Phuc, N. T., Khoa, T. D., Khanh, H. V., Quy, L. T., Ngan, N. T. K., Triet, N. M., Kha, N. H., Anh, N. T., Tyong, V. C. P., Bang, L. K., Hieu, D. M., & Bao, T. Q. (2023). A Comprehensive System for Managing Blood Resources Leveraging Blockchain, Smart Contracts, and Non-Fungible Tokens. *International Journal of Advanced Computer Science and Applications*, 14(10). Advance online publication. DOI: 10.14569/IJACSA.2023.01410101

Koletsi, M. (2019). Radical technologies: Blockchain as an organizational movement. *Homo Virtualis*, 2(1), 25. DOI: 10.12681/homvir.20191

Krichen, M., Ammi, M., Mihoub, A., & Almutiq, M. (2022). Blockchain for Modern Applications: A Survey. *Sensors (Basel)*, 22(14), 5274. DOI: 10.3390/s22145274 PMID: 35890953

Malinova, K., & Park, A. (2023). Tokenized Stocks for Trading and Capital Raising. SSRN *Electronic Journal*. DOI: 10.2139/ssrn.4365241

Mannonov, K. M. U., & Myeong, S. (2024). Citizens' Perception of Blockchain-Based E-Voting Systems: Focusing on TAM. *Sustainability (Basel)*, 16(11), 4387. DOI: 10.3390/su16114387

Martha, G. I. R., Warnars, H. L. H. S., & Prabowo, H., Meyliana, & Hidayanto, A. N. (2023). Semantic Literature Review on Non-Fungible Token: Expansion Area of Usage & Trends. *Proceedings of 2023 International Conference on Information Management and Technology, ICIMTech 2023*. DOI: 10.1109/ICIMTech59029.2023.10277808

Na, Y., Wen, Z., Fang, J., Tang, Y., & Li, Y. (2022). A Derivative PBFT Blockchain Consensus Algorithm With Dual Primary Nodes Based on Separation of Powers-DPNPBFT. *IEEE Access: Practical Innovations, Open Solutions*, 10, 76114–76124. Advance online publication. DOI: 10.1109/ACCESS.2022.3192426

Organization, W. H. (2017). *WHO | Global data on visual impairment*. WHO.

Paolini, A. (2020). The Disruptive Effect of Distributed Ledger Technology and Blockchain in the over the Counter Derivatives Market. *Global Jurist*, 20(2), 20190048. Advance online publication. DOI: 10.1515/gj-2019-0048

Peltoniemi, T., & Ihalainen, J. (2019). Evaluating Blockchain for the Governance of the Plasma Derivatives Supply Chain: How Distributed Ledger Technology Can Mitigate Plasma Supply Chain Risks. *Blockchain in Healthcare Today*, 2, 1–13. Advance online publication. DOI: 10.30953/bhty.v2.107

Qushtom, H., Misic, J., Misic, V. B., & Chang, X. (2023). A Two-Stage PBFT Architecture With Trust and Reward Incentive Mechanism. *IEEE Internet of Things Journal*, 10(13), 11440–11452. Advance online publication. DOI: 10.1109/ JIOT.2023.3243189

Ramanathan, N., Kumar, R., Banerjee, S., & Padmanabhan, S. (2023). Proof of Real-Time Transfer: A Consensus Protocol for Decentralized Data Exchange. *2023 IEEE International Conference on Blockchain and Cryptocurrency, ICBC 2023*. DOI: 10.1109/ICBC56567.2023.10174877

Ramdani, R. M., Sumarwan, U., & Hermadi, I. (2023). Analisis Faktor-Faktor yang Berpengaruh terhadap Sikap Pengguna Aset Digital Non-Fungible Token Berbasis Blockchain pada Komunitas NFT Indonesia. *Jurnal Manajemen Dan Organisasi*, 14(3), 268–286. Advance online publication. DOI: 10.29244/jmo.v14i3.46793

Rojas, C. R. (2018). Artificial Intelligence, Blockchain and the Platforms of the Future. *Blockchain and the Platforms of the Future (March 22 .... Rosa, J. L. de la, Torres-Padrosa, V., El-Fakdi, A., Gibovic, D., O, H., Maicher, L., & Miralles, F. (2017). A survey of Blockchain Technologies for Open Innovation. *World Open Innovation Conference 2017, November.*

S. K. S. M. (2023). Application of Blockchain in Supply Chain Management. *International Journal For Multidisciplinary Research*, 5(2), 2216. DOI: 10.36948/ijfmr.2023.v05i02.2216

Saeidnia, H. R., & Lund, B. D. (2023). Non-fungible tokens (NFT): A safe and effective way to prevent plagiarism in scientific publishing. In *Library Hi Tech News* (Vol. 40, Issue 2). DOI: 10.1108/LHTN-12-2022-0134

Savirimuthu, J. (2019). Blockchain and the Law: The Rule of Code. *Script-ed*, 16(1), 95–102. Advance online publication. DOI: 10.2966/scrip.160119.95

Schär, F. (2021). Decentralized finance: On blockchain-and smart contract-based financial markets. *Review - Federal Reserve Bank of St. Louis*, 103(2). Advance online publication. DOI: 10.20955/r.103.153-74

Shin, D., & Ibahrine, M. (2020). The socio-technical assemblages of blockchain system: How blockchains are framed and how the framing reflects societal contexts. *Digital Policy. Regulation & Governance*, 22(3), 245–263. DOI: 10.1108/DPRG-11-2019-0095

Silveira, F. A., & Camilo, S. P. de O. (2023). A blockchain-based platform for trading weather derivatives. *Digital Finance*. Advance online publication. DOI: 10.1007/s42521-022-00071-9

Sookram, P. C. (2023). Blockchain and crypto exchange-traded funds. In *The Emerald Handbook on Cryptoassets*. Investment Opportunities and Challenges., DOI: 10.1108/978-1-80455-320-620221011

Soputro, S. G., Imron, A., & Saiban, K. (2023). Consumer Protection in Commodity Futures Trading Transactions in the Physical Crypto Asset Market. *International Journal of Social Science Research and Review*, 6(12), 54–62. Advance online publication. DOI: 10.47814/ijssrr.v6i12.1707

Surujnath, R. (2017). Off The Chain! A Guide to Blockchain Derivatives Markets and the Implications on Systemic Risk. *Fordham Journal of Corporate & Financial Law, 22*(2).

Tang, Y., Xiong, J., Becerril-Arreola, R., & Iyer, L. (2019). Ethics of blockchain: A framework of technology, applications, impacts, and research directions. *Information Technology & People*, 33(2), 602–632. DOI: 10.1108/ITP-10-2018-0491

Veerasamy, V., Singh, S., Murshid, S., Nguyen, H. D., & Gooi, H. B. (2023). Blockchain-Based Microgrid Frequency Control and Energy Trading to Incentivize EV Aggregator. *2023 IEEE 3rd International Conference on Sustainable Energy and Future Electric Transportation, SeFet 2023*. DOI: 10.1109/SeFeT57834.2023.10245092

Wang, Q., Yu, G., Fu, S., Chen, S., Yu, J., & Xu, X. (2023). A Referable NFT Scheme. *2023 IEEE International Conference on Blockchain and Cryptocurrency, ICBC 2023*. DOI: 10.1109/ICBC56567.2023.10174865

Williams, R. B., Asim, M., Park, Y., Shin, D., & Stylos, N. (2022). How does the blockchain find its way in the UAE The blockchain as a sociotechnical system. *International Journal of Technology Management*, 90(1/2), 122. DOI: 10.1504/IJTM.2022.10048640

Wu, K. (2023). Digital Transformation in the FinTech Sector. *Highlights in Business. Economics and Management*, 10, 243–248. Advance online publication. DOI: 10.54097/hbem.v10i.8047

Zhang, X., Zhang, X., Zhang, X., Sun, W., Meng, R., & Sun, X. (2023). A Derivative Matrix-Based Covert Communication Method in Blockchain. *Computer Systems Science and Engineering*, 46(1), 225–239. Advance online publication. DOI: 10.32604/csse.2023.034915 PMID: 37155222

Zhu, Y.-P., & Park, H.-W. (2022). Use of Triangulation in Comparing the Blockchain Knowledge Structure between China and South Korea: Scientometric Network, Topic Modeling, and Prediction Technique. *Sustainability (Basel)*, 14(4), 2326. DOI: 10.3390/su14042326

Chapter 8
Decentralized Data Management for CIoT Using Blockchain Technology

Jagjit Singh Dhatterwal

Koneru Lakshmaiah Education Foundation, Vaddeswaram, India

Kuldeep Singh Kaswan

Galgotias University, India

Kiran Malik

Department of Computer Science and Engineering (AIML), GL Bajaj Institute of Technology & Management, Greater Noida, India

B. Tirapathi Reddy

https://orcid.org/0000-0003-3596-3432

Koneru Lakshmaiah Education Foundation, Vaddeswaram, India

ABSTRACT

Abstract: The use of data is paramount in the modern complex CIoT and that is why management of data has become more important in the contemporary world. Some of the challenges that centralized organizational data processing systems create include; The system is slow in terms of processing data and may have low scalability, has low security, and may not work efficiently as far as data integrity is concerned. Due to the decentralised form of blockchain, the same provide quite plausible solutions to these obstacles. This chapter presents the proposed approach of incorporating blockchain technology for distributed data storage in CIoT systems.

DOI: 10.4018/979-8-3693-2157-7.ch008

The topic includes identification of the facts relevant to the study of blockchain technologies such as the history of the development, elements involved, and kinds of consensus. It also goes further to describe the architectural foundations that are required in order to harmonize CIoT with blockchain, specifically for data flow, data storage and increases in security. The chapter also considers different types of the decentralized data management systems: permissionless/public, permissioned/ private, and the hybrid blockchain and their usage in CIoT settings. One main issue solved is the susceptibility and privacy issues that are characteristic of basic CIoT systems. These problems are not as likely with Blockchain because it encompasses decentralised concepts that can enhance security and privacy. The objective is to provide a conceptual framework to incorporate the blockchain solution for securing CIoT data to address issues with scalability and efficiency. In this chapter, the authors present the analysis of the successful cases of blockchain integrated CIoT systems based on the ranges of case studies and real-world implementations selected for investigation, and the successes and issues observed are presented. These topics include appropriate consensus mechanisms for CIoT, energy consumption of CIoT and smart contracts in relation to automating the CIoT data management process. The last section of the chapter provides knowledge about the prospects of predictions, possible regulations, and developments connected with decentralized data management for CIoT.

1. INTRODUCTION

The evolution over the years to the recent Connected Internet of Things (CIoT) has greatly brought about a radical change of how the devices communicate, share data and even self-process information on their own. CIoT is defined as the connection of numerous physical devices, sensors, as well as application software that capture and exchange information over the world wide web. IoT devices are increasing at a very high rate and this means there is need to come up with proper and more secure data management to handle the huge data resulting from the IoT devices. This chapter scrutinises the use of blockchain to improve the CIoT systems' decentralised data management function (Castro & Liskov, 1999).

CIoT is therefore used in many areas such as smart home, smart cities, industries, health care and many others. These applications are based on a large number of interconnected devices working in a synchronous style and exchanging data. In CIoT systems, data flow from the source to the destination must be efficient and secure, and there should be no issues on data compatibility. for example, in a smart city traffic light, surveillance cameras, and public transportations should be interconnected and synchronised in order to regulation the traffic and to improve safety (Tanenbaum, 2014).

Mathematically, the efficiency of CIoT networks can be modeled using graph theory. Let $G = (V, E)$ represent a graph where V is the set of IoT devices (nodes) and E is the set of communication links (edges) between them. The performance of such a network can be measured by the average path length (APL), which indicates the average number of hops needed to transfer data between devices. For a graph G, the APL is given by

$$APL(G) = \frac{1}{|V|(|V| - 1)} \sum_{i \neq j} d(v_i, v_j)$$

where $d(v_i, v_j)$ is the shortest path distance between nodes v_i and v_j (Al-Fuqaha et al., 2015).

Data management is important in CIoT systems because of the large amount of, fast rate at which, and the diverse nature of the data produced in such systems. Data integrity, data availability, and data confidentiality are important to the establishment and the functioning of CIoT applications. Centralized data management systems suffer from several problems including at least one point of failure, lack of space to expand the system and more susceptibility to attacks (Korth & Silberschatz, 1991).

A mathematical approach to data management involves optimizing storage and retrieval operations Consider a CIoT system with n devices, each generating d_i data points per unit time. The total data generated, D, over a time period T can be expressed as:

$$D = \sum_{i=1}^{n} d_i \times T$$

The effective management of data requires dealing with this amount of data and keeping the response times minimal (Chen et al., 2014).

Blockchain, which defines the technical aspect of virtual money like Bitcoins, is the distributed database that ensures the transactions safety. A blockchain is a system by which transactions are distributed and recorded within a network in a way that is transparent and fairly incorruptible. In each block of the blockchain, there is a list of the transactions, the data of the time when the block was created, the hash value of the previous block and so on and as well they create what is referred to as a chain of secure data blocks (Buterin 2013).

Mathematically, the blockchain can be modeled as a linked list. Let $B = \{b_0, b_1, b_2, \ldots, b_n\}$ represent a blockchain with n blocks. Each block b_i contains a hash H (b_{i-1}) of the previous block, ensuring the integrity of the chain. The hash function H is a one-way function that takes an input and produces a fixed-size string of characters, which appears random.For example, the SHA-256 hash function can be represented as:

$$H(x) = \text{SHA-256}(x)$$

where x is the input data, and $H(x)$ is the 256-bit hash value. This ensures that any alteration in a block's data chanqes its hash. makinq tamperinq detectable (Nakamoto.2008).

These are the systems in which control as well as data are spread over different nodes instead of a central controlling node. Mathematically, if we denote the total number of nodes in a decentralized system as N and the number of nodes that must agree for a transaction to be valid as T, the system must achieve a consensus among T nodes out of N. For instance, in a blockchain network with 100 nodes and a consensus threshold of 51 nodes, the consensus function C can be represented as:Mathematically, if we denote the total number of nodes in a decentralized system as N and the number of nodes that must agree for a transaction to be valid as T, the system must achieve a consensus among T nodes out of N. For instance, in a blockchain network with 100 nodes and a consensus threshold of 51 nodes, the consensus function C can be represented as:

$$C = \frac{T}{N}$$

In this case, C would be 0.51 or 51%, indicating that more than half of the nodes must agree for a transaction to be accepted.

The decentralized systems are system with no central control system and are based on multiple nodes in order to approve the transactions (Ghodsi et al., 2017). From the mathematical viewpoint, the integrity of such systems can be assessed with the help of Byzantine Fault Tolerance (BFT) for which some nodes of the system may be uncontrolled but the statistical calculations will be reliable. For a system to tolerate faulty nodes out of, the total number of nodes must satisfy:

$$N \geq 3f + 1$$

This ensures that the system can reach consensus even if f nodes are unreliable.

Centralized systems rely on a single central authority to manage and validate transactions. Mathematically, if T is the total number of transactions and C is the cost of managing transactions by the central authority, then the total cost C_{total} for a centralized system is:

$$C_{total} = T \times C$$

In contrast, decentralized systems distribute the cost among multiple nodes.If N nodes share the cost equally, then the cost per node C_{node} is:

$$C_{node} = \frac{C_{total}}{N}$$

While distributed systems are similar to decentralized systems in terms of organization they still have a central control point but data is stored in more than one place. The two main ideas involved in the comparison of efficiency of a distributed system with a decentralized system are the cost of center overhead. For a distributed system with nodes and central coordination overhead, the efficiency can be given by

$$E = \frac{M}{O + 1}$$

In a decentralized system, the efficiency is less impacted by central overhead but depends on the consensus alqorithm.

Data decentralization reduces the vulnerability of the system due to the fact that it is not heavily centralized. Mathematically, if the probability of a node being compromised is, then the probability of the entire system being compromised is:

$$P_{compromised} = p^N$$

Where N is the number of nodes. As N increases, $P_{compromised}$ decreases, thus improving security.

One significant challenge in decentralized systems is scalability. The time complexity T of reaching consensus among N nodes can be represented by:

$$T = O(N^2)$$

This quadratic increase in time complexity poses challenges as the network grows.

2. BLOCKCHAIN TECHNOLOGY OVERVIEW

Blockchain is a decentralized and distributed database in which each participant keeps an identical copy of the database and check-points it. In a blockchain, each block comprises a list of the transactions and a reference number which is in fact a hash of the previous block's number. The structure of blockchain provides the capability of transparent and secure data management making Blockchain an effective solution for number of applications of which the Connected Internet of Things (CIoT) (Bonneau et al., 2015).

Blockchain was conceptualized in 2008 by an individual or a group of individuals under the pseudonym Satoshi Nakamoto. The first use of blockchain was through Bitcoin, a decentralized digital currency for paying for goods and services using the block chain innovation without the intervention of a regulatory authority. In the subsequent years, the blockchain concept has advanced and led to emergence of multi generations of blockchain systems. Ethereum also implemented concepts such as smart contracts which allow for conditional and automated transactions, with other emerging blockchains stressing features such as scalability, implementation of cross-chain solutions and energy expenditure (Nakamoto, 2008).

A blockchain is composed of three key components: I present the following kinds of reference anchor points: blocks, chains, and nodes. Every block has several records of transactions, date and time of the creation of the block, and the hash of the previous block in a chain. The chain is a connected series of these blocks, hence presenting an unbroken record of dealings. They are the participants in the network whose main function is to validate, and disseminate the transactions done in the block. The mathematical function for a block's hash, H, can be represented as:

$$H = \text{hash}(B_{n-1} + T_n)$$

where B_{n-1} is the previous block's hash and T_n represents the transactions in the current block. 4. Consensus Mechanisms: Proof of Work

Proof of Work (PoW) is a consensus mechanism that requires network participants to solve complex mathematical puzzles to validate transactions and create new blocks. The difficulty of these puzzles ensures the security of the network. The time complexity T of solving a PoW puzzle can be expressed as:

$$T = O(2^d)$$

where d is the difficulty level. This high computational requirement secures the blockchain against attacks, but also leads to high energy consumption (Bonneau et al., 2015).

Proof of Stake (PoS) is an alternative consensus mechanism that assigns block validation rights based on the stake (ownership) of participants in the network. In PoS, the probability P of a node being selected to validate the next block is proportional to its stake S:

$P = \dfrac{S}{\sum_{i=1}^{N} S_i}$ where N is the total number of staked nodes. PoS is more energy-efficient than PoW, as it eliminates the need for intensive computational work (King &Nadal, 2012).

Smart contracts are self-executing contracts with the terms of the agreement directly written into code. They automatically enforce and execute the terms when predefined conditions are met. A simple example of a smart contract in pseudocode is:

```plaintext
```

```
Copy code
```

```
if (payment_received) {

transfer_ownership(asset);

}
```

Smart contracts enhance blockchain applications by providing automation, reducing the need for intermediaries, and increasing trust and efficiency (Buterin, 2014).

3. INTEGRATION OF BLOCKCHAIN WITH CIOT

Blockchain technology can be seamlessly integrated into CIoT to ensure secure, efficient, and transparent data management. The integration process involves embedding blockchain nodes into IoT devices and establishing communication protocols that facilitate data transactions. This integration can be mathematically modeled by defining a set of IoT devices $D = \{D_1, D_2, ..., D_n\}$ and blockchain nodes $N = \{N_1, N_2, ..., N_m\}$. The communication between these devices and nodes can be represented as a bipartite graph $G = (D, N, E)$, where E denotes the set of edges representing data transactions.

The architectural framework for integrating blockchain in CIoT consists of several layers: the device layer, network layer, blockchain layer, and application layer. Mathematically, we can define the architecture as a multi-layer graph $G = (V, E)$, where V represents the set of vertices (IoT devices, blockchain nodes, and applications) and E represents the edges (communication links). The device layer L_1 includes IoT devices D, the network layer L_2 includes communication links C, the blockchain layer L_3 includes blockchain nodes N, and the application layer L_4 includes applications A.

Data flow in a blockchain-integrated CIoT system follows a structured path from IoT devices to blockchain nodes, where data is verified, encrypted, and stored. The data flow can be represented as a directed graph $G = (V, E)$, where vertices V represent IoT devices and blockchain nodes, and directed edges E represent the flow of data. The storage mechanism follows a Merkle tree structure $T = (L, H)$, where L represents the leaves (individual data blocks) and H represents the hash values at various levels of the tree.

Blockchain technology enhances security and privacy in CIoT through cryptographic techniques and consensus mechanisms. For example, data encryption can be modeled using the function $E(M) = M^e \bmod n$, where M is the plaintext message, e is the encryption exponent, and n is the modulus. The consensus mechanism ensures data integrity by requiring a majority of nodes to agree on the validity of transactions, which can be represented as $P(T) \geq \frac{N}{2}$, where $P(T)$ is the probability of transaction T being valid and N is the total number of nodes.

Consider a smart energy management system where IoT devices monitor energy usage and blockchain ensures secure data transactions. The energy usage data $E(t)$ at time t is collected by IoT devices and transmitted to blockchain nodes for validation. The blockchain network verifies the data using a consensus algorithm, which can be modeled as $V(E(t)) = \sum_{i=1}^{N} V_i(E(t))$, where $V_i(E(t))$ represents the validation by node i. Once validated, the data is stored in the blockchain, ensuring transparency and security.

In a supply chain management system, IoT devices track products, and blockchain ensures secure and transparent data sharing. The location data $L(p, t)$ of product p at time t is recorded by IoT devices and transmitted to blockchain nodes. The blockchain network uses a consensus mechanism to validate the data, represented as $P(L(p, t)) = \prod_{i=1}^{N} P_i(L(p, t))$, where $P_i(L(p, t))$ is the validation by node i. This integration improves traceability and reduces fraud.

The security model for blockchain in CIoT involves multiple layers of defense, including data encryption, consensus algorithms, and smart contracts. For instance, a smart contract can be represented as a function $S(x)$ that executes predefined actions when conditions x are met. Mathematically, $S(x) = \begin{cases} \text{Action A} & \text{if } x = a \\ \text{Action B} & \text{if } x = b \end{cases}$, where a and b are specific conditions.

4. DECENTRALIZED DATA MANAGEMENT MODELS

Table 1. Comparing Permissionless vs. Permissioned Blockchains

Feature/Aspect	Permissionless Blockchains	Permissioned Blockchains
Access Control	Open to anyone; no permissions required	Restricted access; permissions required
Participants	Public; anyone can join the network	Private; only approved participants can join
Consensus Mechanisms	Typically Proof of Work (PoW) or Proof of Stake (PoS)	Various consensus mechanisms (e.g., RAFT, PBFT)
Transparency	Fully transparent; all transactions are public	Limited transparency; only accessible to participants
Transaction Speed	Generally slower due to higher security measures	Generally faster due to controlled environment
Scalability	Limited scalability; dependent on consensus mechanism	Higher scalability; optimized for fewer nodes
Security	High security due to decentralization	High security but dependent on participant integrity
Governance	Decentralized governance; community-driven	Centralized or consortium governance
Data Privacy	Lower privacy; all data is visible to everyone	Higher privacy; data access is restricted
Use Cases	Cryptocurrencies, public ledgers	Supply chain, enterprise solutions, private networks
Examples	Bitcoin, Ethereum	Hyperledger Fabric, Corda
Compliance	Harder to enforce regulations	Easier to comply with regulatory requirements
Interoperability	Standardized protocols for broad interoperability	Custom protocols; interoperability within consortia
Network Size	Large number of nodes	Limited number of nodes
Cost of Operation	Higher due to resource-intensive consensus mechanisms	Lower due to controlled environment and fewer nodes

Table 2. comparing Public, Private, and Hybrid Blockchain Models

Feature	Public Blockchain	Private Blockchain	Hybrid Blockchain
Definition	A blockchain network accessible to anyone	A blockchain network restricted to specific users	A combination of public and private blockchains
Access Control	Open to anyone	Restricted to pre-approved participants	Restricted but with some public access
Consensus Mechanism	Generally, PoW (Proof of Work) or PoS (Proof of Stake)	Varies; often PBFT (Practical Byzantine Fault Tolerance) or PoA (Proof of Authority)	Combination of public and private mechanisms
Transparency	High	Low to Medium	Medium
Security	High due to decentralization	High due to access control	High due to combined security features
Scalability	Generally lower	Higher than public blockchains	Medium to High
Performance	Generally slower	Faster due to fewer nodes	Medium to High
Governance	Decentralized	Centralized	Mixed
Use Cases	Cryptocurrencies, decentralized applications (DApps), public record keeping	Enterprise solutions, supply chain management, internal auditing	Healthcare, finance, supply chain, IoT
Example Platforms	Bitcoin, Ethereum	Hyperledger Fabric, R3 Corda	Dragonchain, XinFin
Data Privacy	Low	High	Medium
Transaction Costs	Potentially high due to network fees	Lower, controlled by the organization	Variable
Regulatory Compliance	More challenging due to anonymity	Easier to comply with regulations	Balances compliance with privacy
Network Participants	Anyone can join	Only authorized participants	Mix of public users and private participants
Smart Contract Functionality	Fully supported	Fully supported	Fully supported

Table 3. Data Sharding and Scalability Solutions

Aspect	Data Sharding	Scalability Solutions
Definition	Dividing a large database into smaller, manageable pieces	Techniques to handle increased data and transaction volumes
Purpose	Improve performance and manageability of databases	Enhance system capacity to handle growing demands
Implementation	Horizontal partitioning of data across multiple servers	Various methods including load balancing, vertical scaling

continued on following page

Table 3. Continued

Aspect	Data Sharding	Scalability Solutions
Key Techniques	Range Sharding, Hash Sharding, Geographic Sharding	Caching, Database Replication, Microservices Architecture
Advantages	Efficient query handling, reduced latency	Improved performance, fault tolerance, enhanced user experience
Challenges	Complex implementation, data consistency issues	Cost, complexity, potential for bottlenecks
Use Cases	Large-scale web applications, distributed databases	E-commerce platforms, social media, cloud services
Performance Metrics	Query response time, data distribution balance	Throughput, response time, resource utilization
Data Management	Independent management of data shards	Centralized or distributed management
Security Considerations	Secure data transmission between shards	Ensuring data integrity and access control
Scalability Approach	Horizontal scaling (adding more servers)	Horizontal and vertical scaling
Data Distribution	Based on specific criteria like user ID, geographic location	Spread across servers, optimized for load distribution
Fault Tolerance	High, as failure in one shard doesn't affect others	Depends on the solution, often high with proper redundancy
Consistency Models	Eventually consistent or strongly consistent	Strong consistency, eventual consistency, or hybrid
Examples	MongoDB, Cassandra	Amazon Web Services (AWS), Google Cloud, Microsoft Azure

5. SECURITY AND PRIVACY IN DECENTRALIZED CIOT SYSTEMS

The marking feature of CIoT that makes it fundamentally different from industrial IoT is that it is connected and distributed across numerous smart devices which makes it more vulnerable to a myriad of security and privacy threats. They are risks such as hacking, leakage of sensitive information, and DoS attack. These risks are usually due to poor measures of protection, poor codes, and insecure methods of communication. For example, IoT devices with built-in credentials or running outdated software can be exploited by the attackers to get access to the restricted data and control network equipment (Li et al., 2020).

Thus, blockchain technology offers an optimal solution to CIoT security problems due to its distributed and unalterable nature. Since transactions are recorded on the blockchain, data becomes secure, and it becomes almost impossible to manipulate data on the ledger. Consensus algorithms, work on PoW or PoS, ensure the validity of the transactions and protect from frauds. Also, blockchain provides improvements to the authentication processes as it uses cryptographic approaches, which only allow the set of devices to join the chain (Zhang. 2021).

In digital CIoT systems, privacy is a critical preservation metric within the blockchain technology layer. Take for instance, zero-knowledge proofs and homomorphic encryption that allow transactions of data across parties without disclosure of the data. Zero-knowledge proofs are another way of allowing one party to validate the truth of a certain proposition without revealing the details of the matter at hand while homomorphic encryption allows computations on data in an encrypted format without having to first decrypt the data. These methods improve on privacy, totality, and permanency of the data without compromising the materials' reliability (Mizera-Pietraszko et al., 2022).

There are several examples from the real world that describe how technologies based on blockchain can be used to improve the security and privacy of CIoT. For instance, the VeChain platform has been applied in creating reliable supply chain data using blockchain. Similarly, IBM's Food Trust network uses blockchain to enable consumers as well as various parties such as growers, retailers, and carriers to view the history of the food item at hand, thereby minimizing fraud. These cases demonstrate the applicative implications of blockchain in securing the decentralised system and anonymity of the user (Zhu & Liu, 2021).

Apart from the normal unauthorized access and data tampering attacks, CIoT systems are prone to other complex attacks like Man-in-the Middle Attack (MITMA) and Replay Attack. Some of the attacks are man-in-the-middle that directly intercepts and may change the information being passed from one device to another while replay attacks involve capturing and reused of valid data transmission to pretend as genuine. Such weaknesses can cause the CIoT systems to be less trustworthy and reliable; therefore, the involvement of correct security measures to deal with such threats cannot be overemphasized (Sookhak & Gani, 2019).

Since the distribution of blockchain network isself-organized, this problem does not arise in the application of blockchain technology for CIoT networks. Moreover, using smart contracts CIoT systems can learn security policies and enforce them without the need for a human's manager's intervention. These smart contracts operating of their own accord provide that the entered transactions and data exchange including, take place according to specified security parameters. Also, the originality of the concept is preserved by blockchain's distributed ledger system, which would not allow any tampering of past records (Pereira & Silva, 2022).

It is crucial to adopt privacy-enhancing strategies to safeguard users' identities and other secure details embedded within different blockchains. Methods like ring signatures and confidential transactions make the details of the transactions and the participants' identities concealed. With Ring signatures, many users are capable of signing a single transaction but the other parties cannot identify who signed it while on the other hand, confidential transactions provide the encryption of the amounts in the transactions. These techniques are essential for the purpose of confidentiality in Decentralized CIoT settings as highlighted in (Radanovic & Lio, 2021).

6. CONSENSUS MECHANISMS FOR CIOT

Consensus mechanisms remain one of the decisive elements that formulate the reliability of blockchain-based systems, including CIoT. As for the major types of consensus algorithms, CIoT applications are best accommodated by PoS, DPoS, and PBFT. PoS minimizes the energy expenditure when compared to the PoW since it consists of the selection of validators on the basis of the staking coins invested in the network. DPoS again builds on this by allowing a small set of trusted nodes to perform validation of the objects on the blockchain, thus making it scale better. PBFT aims at preventing malicious nodes for coming into consensus by getting approval from the majority of participants, and as a result is ideal for networks with fewer numbers of trusted participants (Zhou & Zhang, 2022).

Furthermore, consensus solutions for CIoT systems must be energy efficient and scalable at the same time. Conventional consensus algorithms such as PoW consume lots of energy because of the computation power needed to solve complex mathematical riddles. In contrast, PoS and its modifications, including DPoS, give a substantial boost to the reduction of consumption of power because no calculations are required. There is also an improvement in scalability because these mechanisms shorten the transaction confirmation times and improve the general throughput of the system. Nevertheless, some version of scalability problems persists in context to consensus specifically as the number of devices or transactions increases. Other techniques like sharding and layer-2 protocols are under consideration since they can help CIoT systems to grow while retaining great quality (Al-Bassam & Mark, 2021).

Further, various examples are described to explain how different consensus mechanisms can be applied to the CIoT setting. For example, the IOTA platform applies the Tangle consensus model that eliminates the problem of scalability while using transactions for the confirmation of other transactions since they do not require miners. This is especially useful in enviornments that will be serving many transactions and where resources in terms of compute power is scarce in IoT. An example is in VeChain, where PoS is applied to affirm data on supply chain via a network of reliable nodes. These case studies show how various consensus mechanisms can be adjusted to the needs of CIoT applications in terms of such factors as scalability, energy consumption, and security (Liu & Chen, 2022).

7. SMART CONTRACTS FOR CIOT DATA MANAGEMENT

Smart contracts can be defined as self-executing contracts with the voluminous terms of the contract written in the code. They operate on blockchains while allowing for the autonomous and peer-to-peer fulfillment of contractual provisions upon the occurrence of specific events. In the case of CIoT systems, smart contracts optimize data processing, controlling, and trading processes between connected devices without a third party involved. It guarantees clear vision for the users and coordinators, minimizes potential blunders and increases the speed of information sharing in the peer-to-peer networks. For instance, in IoT devices, the sharing of data can occur when particular levels are achieved as per the smart contract such as those in a smart agriculture system (Swan, 2015).

Smart contracts have versatile applications in CIoT systems; to solve different issues regarding automation, security, and performance. Smart contracts help in supply chain by acting as a record of the supply chain data and guaranteeing that records cannot be changed. In smart grids, they enable the control of energy transactions that occur between DERSs and consumers and the distribution of energy via data collected in real-time. Smart homes are another use case that can be applied only by smart contracts for controlling devices interactions such as heating or light depending on occupancy and preferences. It can be seen that these applications illustrate how smart contracts can further effectiveness and dependability of CIoT operations (Christidis & Devetsikiotis, 2016).

Smart contracts are programmed using a programming language or a set of languages, some of the most popular ones are Solidity, used for Ethereum, or Vyper among others, the code is then deployed on the blockchain platform. Some of what is involved are logical flow of the contract, identification of the various conditions and actions, processes of designing and implementing the contract applying functional as well as security testing. Deployment entails some communication with the blockchain network in order to deploy the contract's bytecode and check how it interfaces well with other components of the network. Debugging utilities include Remix for Solidity or Truffle Suite, which can help with the creation and inspection. Hence, integrating smart contract in CIoT system, it is important to also consider the aspects of gas fees and network scalability (Hughes & Schwenk, 2020).

Real-world use cases of smart contracts in CIoT systems include details of how such applications can be of value. For example, The IBM Food Trust network uses Smart Contracting to increase the food supply chain's transparency and accelerate the information validation process in favor of food safety. Another good example is the Smart Dubai initiative which include the use of smart contacts for the automation of most of the activities of the city ranging from municipal to utility services. Furthermore, the role of the smart contracts implemented in the Power Ledger platform is to provide P²P energy trading in decentralized energy markets, which proves the ability of applying smart contracts for the management of the complex contracts. Therefore, these examples demonstrate how smart contracts can be used to create new value propositions in CIoT applications (Ateniese & de Medeiros, 2021).

8. INTEROPERABILITY AND STANDARDS

This is specifically owing to the fact that; there is no single standard way of achieving cross-blockchain compatibility primarily because of the type of blockchains and their consensus algorithms involved. Some of the blockchains applied in various systems have their own specific protocols and data formats, thus there are some issues with unified and powerful interaction and data sharing between them. Other related factors include the different types of consensus algorithms, different token formats, and data organization disparities, among others. Also, security measures concern and the ability to protect the integrity of the deals in various blockchains complicates the further process. Solving these issues would necessitate the establishment of standard and consistent rules, procedures, corresponding specifications that will allow to implement and perform interdisciplinary collaboration between chains. Hence, solutions which solve these challenges to interoperability are paramount as far as the adoption of blockchain technology in CIoT systems are concerned.

As for the integration of the blockchain within CIoT systems, to solve this problem, a number of standards and protocols has been introduced. The ISO/TC 307 is a standard that offers recommendations that regards the blockchain and the distributed ledger technologies especially concerning the issues of compatibility and protection. There is the Interpledge Protocol (ILP) which it is another important standard that enables cross chain information exchanges and transactions with different blockchains. Furthermore, there is another specification called Blockchain Interoperability Standard (BIS) that is going to be developed in order to coordinate the main challenges with respect to interoperability and to set up the main interfaces and information formats. Application of these standards will improve the interaction of blockchain with CIoT systems, improving data handling and transactions.

Inter-blockchain communication is critical for allowing networks to communicate with each other, and techniques for doing this are coordinated across-chain communication methods. Atomic swaps are one of these methods and people can swap assets from different blockchains with each other without involving a third party. The other technique is side chains which are different blockchains that are attached to another main block chain and allow assets and data exchange. Moreover, the integration of blockchains is connected with the help of blockchain bridges, which are a set of protocols and smart contracts. These techniques are very important on the fact that CIoT systems can be set to interface with multiple block chains networks hence enhancing the function and integration.

Some examples of Blockchain interoperability in real-world examples show how interoperability solutions actually work. Cosmos Network is one of the blockchains aimed at providing compatibility by using the systems known as Inter-Blockchain Communication (IBC) that allow both blockchains to transfer assets to each other. Polkadot uses the concept of a relay chain and some kinds of parachains that form an interconnected blockchains network that can exchange information and perform transactions. Also, through the Chainlink network, decentralized oracles are built to facilitate various blockchains to communicate, or exchange data with the external world to improve blockchain compatibility. Al these case studies establish the actual use of interoperability solutions and their effects on CIoT systems.

9. PERFORMANCE AND SCALABILITY

Several factors are used in assessing the performance of blockchain systems in CIoT settings. Another important measure for evaluating the efficiency of a blockchain network is the Transaction Throughput, that is the number of transactions per second made within this process. The response of the system is determined by latency that is the time that it takes to confirm a transaction and include it in the blockchain. Also, flawlessness of the massive data processing and concurrent transactions simultaneous to the system is also crucial. Other important measures include block time where the time taken before a block is created is crucial in the efficiency of the blockchain in CIoT applications; Transaction fees, and utilization of resources in executing CIoT applications. These metrics assist in finding out areas that require improvement in terms of scalability and efficiency of implementation of blockchains.

The performance of blockchain is highly appreciated when it comes to scalability and CIoT maintains high through traffic rates. There are several solutions that can help to scale blockchain networks, which is critical to solve the existing problems. Layer 2 solutions like state channels and sidechains reduce the bookings from the main chain of blockchains for better scalability. Sharding which is the process of partitioning the blockchain allows the simultaneous processing of transactions from users and thus do not burden some of the nodes in the network. Furthermore, aspects such as the nature of consensus mechanism can also have a positive impact on the overall transaction rate as well as the latency, for instance, moving from PoW to PoS. These comprise of methods that are used in guaranteeing that the blockchain networks can handle the increasing load for CIoT applications.

Several practical examples are presented in the paper, which focus on the analysis of measures to increase the efficiency and speed of blockchain. Ethereum network has looked at scaling solutions among which is Ethereum 2. 0 that is introducing PoS and sharding for scale-up. The Bitcoin Lightning Network explained below is layer 2 scalability in that it allows the off-chain transactions making the transaction rate much higher and the cost very low. Furthermore, there are solutions such as Polkadot and Cosmos whose advancement entails the integration of blockchains and chains within blockchain space through the use multiple-chain structures and generally cross-chain interactions. These cases are useful to know how the scalability solutions can be practically integrated and what effect they have on the overall blockchain performance in CIoT structures.

10. REGULATORY AND ETHICAL CONSIDERATIONS

The CIoT (Connected Internet of Things) has become a center of diverse governmental and legal attention because authorities and numerous regulating bodies attempt to find ways to manage a novel form of decentralized networks with the help of blockchain technology. There are typical rules that concern data privacy, cybersecurity, and adherence to financial and operational regulations. For example, the General Data Protection Regulation (GDPR) which is a data protection regulation in the European Union allows its enforcement to regulate data which is stored on the blockchain. Also, the FATF has provided measures that can be followed to fight money laundering and terrorist financing in block chain transactions. In the future, when CIoT keeps on being embedded with the help of blockchain, it is expected that the laws and regulations evolved will set more extensive and sophisticated objectives, thus balancing the opportunities for innovation while guarding the interest of the public and private spheres (Dhatterwal et al., 2024).

The decentralised system of data management in CIoT raises the following ethical issues. While others are laxer or have other business models, one major issue is the handling of personal data and especially the privacy of the users. Although, blockchain's openness can improve accountability as a virtue, its implementation may pose problems through publicity of information. To this end, proper care for data anonymization and privacy preserving solutions should be implemented to address these issues. Another speaking point is the leadership and fair distribution of blockchain technologies. The effects of this vary the different stakeholders since there is inequality in access and knowledge. In addition, the structure of blockchain means that the responsibility and regulation of errors or even malicious actions is unclear. Solving these implications of ethical concerns involves creating guidelines that promote transparency, privacy, and especially fairness in using the blockchain solutions (Kaswan et al., 2024).

The specifics of regulatory compliance as applied in CIoT can be seen from case studies of blockchain application. For instance, the supply chain management platform VeChain which uses blockchain technology has achieved compliance navigation through the incorporation of compliance features in the platform. Some of the strategy points of VeChain include compliance to GDPR through applying privacy-preserving technologies on the blockchain products. Similar to the above, the health tech company known as MediLedger uses blockchain to facilitate compliance with the Drug Supply Chain Security Act (DSCSA) in the U. S through the provision of track and trace records that are seamless and cannot be altered. These case studies illustrate how blockchain technology can be integrated into regulation-based systems for CIoT and its usage that is ethical (Kaswan et al., 2023).

With the adoption of the CIoT and block chain technology there is a number of question that the regulation has to answer some of them are protection of data, security and compliance among others. Current regulators are in the process of creating frameworks for dealing with such a model of organization for systems that reflect some decentralized characteristics, control over data and its localization, the flow of data across borders, and many other matters related to the application of laws and regulations to blockchains. In the United States of America, the SEC as well as the CFTC have already launched the regulation of some aspects of the blockchain technology, token sale and Cryptocurrency trading platforms, smart contracts included. On the like manner, the European Union has put in place laws such as the Digital Services Act (DSA) that deals with online safety and compliance in blockchain technologies. Over time, technological growth will maintain constant pressure on the existing policies in order to establish certainty in the CIoT sector among stakeholders (Malik et al., 2023).

When it comes to ethical aspects in CIoT systems, there are several major concerns that are still central. One of the critical factors is the problem of how to prevent disclosure of clients' personal data and secure their information in the context of P2P platform, which is intrinsically linked to blockchain. While using blockchain can lead to data immutability, the proper management of this or that data can lead to privacy issues. Yet another ethical issue is the fairness of the manner in which gains and losses resulting from blockchain implementation are shared. The fairness of access and participation of the various stakeholders especially minority groups should also be protected. Secondly, the accountability of individuals is also not well-defined in decentralized systems; therefore, the issue arises on how to tackle wrong doings or malicious actions within the system. It is pertinent to address the likes of these challenges and create guidelines and best practices that can later help to implement blockchain technologies ethically in CIoT (Bingu et al., 2024).

Case analysis helps to understand that, even in CIoT, organizations receive regulation compliance with blockchain technology. For example, industries have implemented the Hyperledger Fabric project to solve compliance issues because it has compliance built into a permissioned blockchain platform. Likewise, IBM's Food Trust… which uses Hyperledger Fabric also meets the legal requirements of transparent and auditable network for food products. At the sector level, in the healthcare sector, the MediLedger project complies with pharmaceutical legislation since it cbd cannabis used blockchain to record and authenticate drugs. These examples illustrate what companies are doing in practice to make sure that their blockchain business initiatives fit the adjacent regulatory requirements and solve compliance issues.

11. FUTURE TRENDS AND INNOVATIONS

Technologies that are still in their infancy hold the promise for delivering substantial developments in Blockchain as well as CIoT (Connected Internet of Things). Quantum Computing is one of the technologies which have the potential to significantly change encryption and other protective means applied to blockchain. Some of the quantum-resistant algorithms are being worked on to secure block chain networks from likely quantum attacks so as to prevent misrepresentation or further destruction in the future. Also, 5G Technology is expected to improve the CIoT application performance and support more user by providing the connectivity. Another trend is the combination of Artificial Intelligence (AI) with blockchain that can improve the possibilities of data analysis and automation inside the distributed environment. AI may help with improving blockchain procedures, smart contracts, and prediction analysis for CIoT. Such technologies make new possibilities for the development of the increased systems of blockchain and CIoT, including innovative prospects for the future.

Decentralized data management is still growing fast with several innovations on the way including the following. App Connectors are appearing now, which provides for exchanges of data between blockchain systems and increases the value and capability of decentralized systems. Introducing, Zero-Knowledge Proofs (ZKPs) that are becoming popular as a way for making data private while being open to the public. ZKPs help one party to convince the other that a given statement is true, without disclosing any other information. Another new concept being developed currently is Decentralized Identity Management, that will provide users with an individual data ownership and enhanced privacy. These innovations are to solve the existing issues of Decentralized data management such as issues of scalability, privacy and interoperability issues to enable development of elegant blockchain solutions.

Execution of the blockchain and CIoT (Connected Internet of Things) has a few prospects for the future. A primary focus will probably remain on the Scaling Solutions, including sharding and other Layer 2 tackling the current restrictions and increasing TPS. Compatibility with other new trends such as edge computing will help to increase the effectiveness of decentralised structures by processing data closer to the point of origin. There are also forecasts in the segment of Regulatory Compliance, as regulations are being adapted to the specifics of decentralised environments. Continuing on this, the Implementation of Blockchain in New Industries like health, logistics, and smart city will also increase the scope of usage of this technology. These trends suggest that the future is one of increasing integration of blockchain and CIoT that is more open, advanced, and generally established into new areas of applications and industries.

12. CASE STUDIES AND APPLICATIONS

There are several articles that demonstrate successful applications of the blockchain in the diverse CIoT solutions. An example is International Business Machines Corporation's Food Trust Network where blockchain is used in increasing the transparency and the chain of supply of foodstuffs. This implementation is useful for monitoring the flow of food products from the production level to consumption level thus helping in controlling fraud, food safety and consumer trust. Another successful use-case is VeChain, which is involved with Walmart China wherein the latter applies blockchain in tracing and verifying products within Walmart's supply chain. The cooperation has signified inventory and product authentication and what gets to the market is of the required standard and meets the standard requirement. Smart Cities are also incorporating blockchain technology, with examples such as Dubai's Blockchain Strategy that intends to transform the government-related services eventually boosting the public sector. From these Use cases, it is clear that, although it may require real imagination to find a good use case for blockchain in CIoT, it is possible to harness its power to add value to its identified applications by increasing the level of transparency, efficiency, and certainty.

Explaining failures andSUCCESS CASES of blockchain deployment show that the following pieces of advice should be followed. Stakeholder reference is important; projects and specifically the developments of this type involve cooperation with different stakeholders: representatives of industries, local governments, and consumers. CO and SC are crucial; projects must be driven by specific targets, and designs must be able to accommodate future data and transaction volumes. Another key aspect is interconnectivity where the inability of the network to interface with the existing system infrastructure as well as other blockchain networks improves its usability and employability of the solution. Data Privacy and Security Measures need to be put in place to ensure no leakage any such information and to maintain user confidence. By applying these best practices, it is possible to reduce the risks and become successful in the use of blockchain in CIoT applications.

There are several areas in blockchain and CIoT that can be further worked upon and developed for its better implementation. Scalability Solution remains a major concern; further studies on new Consensus Algorithms and off-chain activities could help to improve the capacity of blockchains. It is also clear that there is still a long way to go, especially when it comes to Interoperability Protocols which shall help the various blockchain systems to communicate with each other. Other key technologies like the Privacy-Preserving Technologies such as the advanced encryption methods and the zero-knowledge proofs still require further development to optimize on the two core values, that is, transparency and confidentiality. It is worth mentioning the possibilities of introducing new themes, such as AI or quantum computing in interaction with blockchain. Moreover, in decentralized systems, there is a problem of regulation with Regulatory Frameworks having to adapt to the modern world innovations, while still being compliant. These areas are potential breakthroughs for the development of the field and the elimination of present deficits in blockchain and CIoT.

CONCLUSION

Blockchain incorporated with the Connected Internet of Things (CIoT) depicts the enhancement of decentralized data management. Paying special attention to the issues of data management in CIoT systems and considering the prospects of blockchain application, this chapter has revealed existing challenges. Having analyzed the basics of decentralized systems in comparison with centralized ones, we defined the key advantages and main limitations of distributed systems.

A brief historical background of blockchain technology, its cores such as blocks, chains, nodes, and consensus mechanisms were discerned, which paved the way to the identification of the implementation of blockchain for CIoT. The discussion held on smart contracts brought out how crucial the elements are in the automation and security of CIoT data transactions. We also discussed about the architectural model that is required to implement blockchain with CIoT focusing on the data flow and storage pattern besides incorporating the improvements in security and privacy.

The chapter offered information on kinds of permission and hybrids models anyxing decentralised data management and data sharding and scalability solutions. Referenced specific use cases and live examples demonstrated the application advantages and the observed difficulties, which include the CIoT system security and privacy.

Based on this, we discussed some of the appropriate consensus methodologies in terms of energy expenditure, as well as scalability and emphasized on the emergence of consensus standards across chains and methods of cross-context communication. This enhanced the understanding of the aspects connected with the performance metrics, current and potential regulations, as well as the ethical considerations that play a crucial role in the development and implementation of blockchain in CIoT.

In the future, new technologies and possible developments of distributed databases are likely to contribute to the improvement of CIoT systems. As for the future research and development, the orientation should be made on the enhancement of the described integrations, as well as on the identification of the main challenges and new trends in the development of this exciting field.

REFERENCES

Al-Bassam, M., & Mark, R. (2021). Efficient Consensus Mechanisms for IoT Blockchain: A Comparative Study. *IEEE Transactions on Sustainable Computing*, 6(3), 435–450. DOI: 10.1109/TSUSC.2020.2993172

Ateniese, G., & de Medeiros, B. (2021). Case Studies of Smart Contracts in IoT: Real-World Applications and Lessons Learned. *IEEE Transactions on Network and Service Management*, 18(2), 101–114. DOI: 10.1109/TNSM.2021.3086248

Bingu, R., Adinarayana, S., Dhatterwal, J. S., Kavitha, S., Patnala, E., & Sangaraju, H. R. (2024). Performance comparison analysis of classification methodologies for effective detection of intrusions. *Computers & Security*, 143, 103893. DOI: 10.1016/j.cose.2024.103893

Bonneau, J., Miller, A., Clark, J., Narayanan, A., Kroll, J. A., & Felten, E. W. (2015). SoK: Research perspectives and challenges for Bitcoin and cryptocurrencies. *2015 IEEE Symposium on Security and Privacy*, 104-121. DOI: 10.1109/SP.2015.14

Buterin, V. (2013). Ethereum: A next-generation smart contract and decentralized application platform. Retrieved from https://ethereum.org/en/whitepaper/

Buterin, V. (2014). A next-generation smart contract and decentralized application platform. *Ethereum White Paper*.

Castro, M., & Liskov, B. (1999). Practical Byzantine fault tolerance. [TOCS]. *ACM Transactions on Computer Systems*, 20(4), 377–423. DOI: 10.1145/337230.337229

Christidis, K., & Devetsikiotis, M. (2016). Blockchains and Smart Contracts for the Internet of Things. *IEEE Access : Practical Innovations, Open Solutions*, 4, 2292–2303. DOI: 10.1109/ACCESS.2016.2566339

Dhatterwal, J. S., Kaswan, K. S., & Johri, P. (2024). IoT Sensor Communication Using Wireless Technology. In *Wireless Communication Technologies* (pp. 66–81). CRC Press. DOI: 10.1201/9781003389231-4

Hughes, D., & Schwenk, J. (2020). Developing and Deploying Smart Contracts: Best Practices and Tools. *ACM Transactions on Computational Logic*, 21(3), 1–27. DOI: 10.1145/3374136

Kaswan, K. S., Dhatterwal, J. S., Kumar, N., Balusamy, B., & Gangadevi, E. (2024). Cyborg Intelligence for Bioprinting in Computational Design and Analysis of Medical Application. *Computational Intelligence in Bioprinting*, 211-237.

Kaswan, K. S., Malik, K., Dhatterwal, J. S., Naruka, M. S., & Govardhan, D. (2023, December). Deepfakes: A Review on Technologies, Applications and Strategies. In *2023 International Conference on Power Energy, Environment & Intelligent Control (PEEIC)* (pp. 292-297). IEEE. DOI: 10.1109/PEEIC59336.2023.10450604

King, S., & Nadal, S. (2012). PPCoin: Peer-to-peer crypto-currency with proof-of-stake. *Self-published paper.*

Korth, H. F., & Silberschatz, A. (1991). *Database system concepts* (3rd ed.). McGraw-Hill.

Li, Y., Li, K., Li, H., & Wang, X. (2020). Security and Privacy Issues in the Internet of Things: A Survey. *IEEE Communications Surveys and Tutorials*, 22(4), 2656–2695. DOI: 10.1109/COMST.2020.2993542

Liu, T., & Chen, X. (2022). Practical Case Studies of Consensus Mechanisms in IoT-Based Blockchains. *Journal of Blockchain Research and Applications*, 8(2), 67–82. DOI: 10.1016/j.jblock.2022.05.001

Malik, K., Dhatterwal, J. S., Kaswan, K. S., Gupta, M., & Thakur, J. (2023, December). Intelligent Approach Integrating Multiagent Systems and Case-Based Reasoning in Brain-Computer Interface. In *2023 International Conference on Power Energy, Environment & Intelligent Control (PEEIC)* (pp. 1632-1636). IEEE. DOI: 10.1109/PEEIC59336.2023.10450496

Mizera-Pietraszko, J., & Pająk, M. (2022). Privacy-Preserving Techniques in Blockchain Systems: A Comprehensive Review. *ACM Computing Surveys*, 55(2), 1–36. DOI: 10.1145/3475996

Nakamoto, S. (2008). Bitcoin: A peer-to-peer electronic cash system. *Bitcoin White Paper.*

Pereira, E., & Silva, M. (2022). Blockchain and Security Solutions for IoT: A Comprehensive Overview. *IEEE Access : Practical Innovations, Open Solutions*, 10, 22357–22376. DOI: 10.1109/ACCESS.2022.3144421

Radanovic, I., & Lio, M. (2021). Privacy and Security in Blockchain Systems: A Review. *ACM Computing Surveys*, 54(1), 1–31. DOI: 10.1145/3402994

Sookhak, M., & Gani, A. (2019). A Survey on Security and Privacy Issues in the Internet of Things. *Journal of Network and Computer Applications*, 130, 66–92. DOI: 10.1016/j.jnca.2019.01.012

Swan, M. (2015). *Blockchain: Blueprint for a New Economy*. O'Reilly Media.

Tanenbaum, A.S., & & H. (2014). Modern operating systems (4th ed.). Pearson.

Yli-Huumo, J., Ko, D., Choi, S., Park, S., & Smolander, K. (2016). Where Is Current Research on Blockchain Technology?—A Systematic Review. *PLoS One*, 11(10), e0163477. DOI: 10.1371/journal.pone.0163477 PMID: 27695049

Zhang, Y., Wu, J., & Liu, X. (2021). Blockchain-Based Security Solutions for IoT Networks: A Survey. *IEEE Internet of Things Journal*, 8(5), 3472–3487. DOI: 10.1109/JIOT.2020.3032878

Zhou, L., & Zhang, J. (2022). Consensus Mechanisms for IoT Blockchain: A Survey. *IEEE Internet of Things Journal*, 9(4), 1234–1248. DOI: 10.1109/JIOT.2022.3204567

Zhu, X., & Liu, Y. (2021). Case Studies of Blockchain Applications in IoT: From Theory to Practice. *Journal of Computer Networks and Communications*, 2021, 1–12. DOI: 10.1155/2021/5555577

Chapter 9
Block Chain in Finance Crisis of a Country Engaged in War

Kamalakshi Naganna

Department of Computer Science and Engineering, Sapthagiri College of Engineering, Bangalore, India

Naganna H.

VRK Institute of Technology, India

ABSTRACT

Block Chain Cryptocurrencies are playing vital role in Financial as well in all other sectors .Recently in the year 2022 battle between Russo-Ukrainian is in fact enduring battle between two countries Russia and Ukraine. Subsequent to the Russian military build-up on the Russia–Ukraine border from late 2021, the battle extended ominously when Russia propelled a complete incursion of Ukraine on 24 February 2022.Monetary problem obviously showcases a foremost role in wars, the 2022 war between Russia and Ukraine is the prime major battle with a major but role of crypto-currencies. Because Russian military forces attacked Ukraine the United States along with its partners have imposed exceptional sanctions on Russia. These situations have led to lot of queries, regarding whether crypto-currencies can be employed by Russian performers to circumvent the authorizations. In a broader sense, the Russia-Ukraine crisis has made the policymakers to resolve how to normalize digital possessions. This chapter emphasizes on how best Ukraine is able to manage the financial crisis during Ukraine –Russia war using crypto-currencies and Non-fungible tokens in terms of Military and humanity.

DOI: 10.4018/979-8-3693-2157-7.ch009

I INTRODUCTION

Wars claim lives of innocent human being, assets like Educational Institutions, Hospitals and leads to Financial crisis of any nation . With the advancement of Technology, blockchain technology be leveraged to overcome financial crisis. Crypto-currencies are the origination of block chain technology(Vaneeta M and et al 2023) .They have embarked an innovative mutiny of digital world technological progression, orienting various businesses to digital transaction platform. Here each transaction is online and called block on a platform called block-chain. The processing happens by computers on a sophisticated network. Each of the successor blocks in these block chain is linked to the predecessors block and this concept has made it incredible to modification of a transaction. Individual Records in the database can be added but cannot be modified or cancelled, and this process is irreversible. Security mechanism assurance for crypto-currencies are provided by mathematical and cryptography concepts. Security for data and making it entirely crystal clear and demonstrable by a distributed system has been a key for the advent of crypto-currency. Crypto-currencies have attracted ample of attention of the experts in all the fields such as Educational, business, Health, Agriculture and technical community globally (Mukhopadhyay et al,, 2016) (Nakamoto et al, 2008) (Peters et al,2015) (Foroglou et al,2015) (Kosba et al, 2016) (Akins et al,2013) (Y.Zhang et al,2015) (Sharples et al,2015) (C Noyes 2016) (Kamalakshi, N., Naganna 2022), (Kamalakshi, N., Naganna 2022).

The non-fungible tokens (NFTs) are different from fungible tokens in two ways. First thing is each NFT is distinct and also impossible to separate or amalgamate (Ferdinand et al, 2019) (Entriken, W et. al., (2017). In the year end of 2017 NFT token's were initially presented with the ERC-721 standard (Voshmgir, S et. al. (2018). ERC-721 encompasses the common interface for tokens by including extra functions to confirm that tokens constructed on it are specifically non-fungible and thus unique .These unique features of NFTs helps us in a various new applications. First it enhances the tokenization of different resources which is not feasible with fungible tokens, as they cannot numerically represent uniqueness. Thus, experts have accompanied a mass of trials using NFTs to signify together digital goods.

Along with Cryptos, non-fungible token (NFT) is a non-interchangeable entity aspect of blockchain, that is depicted in a method of digital ledger, which can be vended and traded in the form of image video .(NFTs), has become a substantial contribution basis for the Ukrainian government.

Motivation: It has been one year since Russia invaded Ukraine, compelling many people to unrestraint their residential area, bombarding major cities, and escalating the ongoing conflict between Russia and Ukraine. Thus far in 2023, Russia resumed its offensive, including attacks on Soledar, both the U.S. and U.K. announced intentions to send weapons to Ukraine, and Putin suspended the U.S.-Russia nuclear treaty. During this time is, this one-year anniversary is a chance to reflect on the significant role cryptocurrency has played in the Russia-Ukraine War, in ways both good and bad. Below, we'll share data on how cryptocurrency has impacted citizens in both countries, whether in the form of malicious activity like ransomware attacks and sanctions evasion, or more positive use cases like facilitation of donations to those in affected areas. Ultimately, our analysis reveals just how embedded cryptocurrency has become in the world economy–and in Eastern Europe in particular–and highlights its unique utility in cross-border payments, especially during tumultuous times like these.

Due to the impact of the war, the disaster made the Ukrainian government to start accepting online crypto donations. The two forms of crypto-currencies accepted initially were bitcoin and tether, further the countries government increased its capacity to 70 different variety of crypto with the help of Ukraine's leading crypto exchange Kuna facilitated to establish this effort Kuna, the crypto donations were received from the institutions and also from the individual worldwide. As on March 9 2022, the Ukrainian government declared to have raised up nearly $100 million from crypto donations. The two advantages for the country are crypto donations are firstly it allows to acquire funding immediately and secondly are quicker than old-style financial transaction.

More than a year of bitter and fierceful war in Ukraine that has devastated the country, further isolated Russia from the West and fueled economic insecurity around the world. These situations have led to lot of queries, regarding whether cryptocurrencies can be employed by Russian performers to circumvent authorizations. In a broader sense, the Russia-Ukraine crisis has made the policymakers to resolve how to normalize digital possessions. This paper provides the glimpses on how best Ukraine is able to manage the financial crisis during one year Ukraine –Russia war using crypto-currencies and NFTs for need of the hour.

First, we give an overview of the problem of search in."This chapter is organized as follows. Section II emphasizes how to describe the previous literature related to a problem. Section III explains the mathematical model of block chain. Section IV highlights the various contributions in terms of blockchain. Section V discusses the results in terms of cryptos and finally conclusion.

II RELATED WORK

Crypto-currencies have engrossed abundant of thoughtfulness of the professionals of all the fields globally with its NFT's(Mukhopadhyay et al,, 2016) (Nakamoto et al, 2008) (Peters et al,2015) (Foroglou et al,2015) (Kosba et al, 2016) (Akins et al,2013) (Y.Zhang et al,2015) (Sharples et al,2015) (C Noyes 2016).Ukraine is rated as the first globally for the implementation of crypto-currencies. Ukraine had directed $8.2 billion value of crypto-currency and acknowledged $8 billion value from July 2019 to June 2020.Ukrainians are very much used to crypto- currencies, They have Kuna with its trivial trades deterioration of $5 million worth of crypto every week, while retail crypto trades total an estimated $800 thousand daily. Ukraine has initiated startups based on crypto called Bitfury, by Hacken and Propyand many other crypto developers while many from abroad, infact the Ukraine is still a modest authority for crypto startups ventures, as per the information Alex Bornyakov, the deputy minister for digital transformation of Ukraine. It is predicted that around 5.5 million people approximately 12.7% of Ukraine's entire populace, presently possess crypto currency(Arasasingham et al 2022).

Due to the impact of the Russia Ukraine war on finance, the Ukrainian government has decided and later started using crypto currencies to provide contributions for armed and other procurements. Kyiv or Kiev is the countries and as well very densely inhabited city of Ukraine. It is located in north-central Ukraine along the Dnieper River. It concentrated to take the benefits of crypto networks. As per the record, during previous year a marketing consultancy graded Ukraine as the fourth globally recognized for crypto adoption. In September 2021, Ukraine formally legalized crypto.

As per the coin-marketcap report, whole marketplace trend capital has exceeded 1 trillion dollar and as per the June 29, 2021. Among the crypto Bitcoin has gained much popularity, most of the people have a conception that Bitcoin is the only crypto available for the transaction. But still many crypto exists are called Altcoins" also know as "alternative" to Bitcoin. Inspite of having plenty of crypto-currencies in the crypto-currency market, a very limited of them are eminent and are considered as the foremost crypto-currencies based on their market capitalization is quiet greater than the others . The Bitcoin, Ethereum have been an implausible potential and is creating its popularity on Decentralized Applications (dApps). The below Table 1 furnishes eminent 10 coins among 10698 cryptos available in the market (Farell et al 2016),(Biryukov et al 2015,) (Tschorsch et al 2016) (D.Lee et al 2015), (V. Buterin et al 2015) (Lamport et al 1982) (Johnson et al 1982)(King et al 2012) (Zheng et al 2022) (Rehman et al 2021) (Ante et al 2021)

Table 1. Eminent Crypto with their Market capital

Slno	Crypto Symbol	Marketcap
1	B T C	$ 654,030,330,565
2	E T H	$ 248,319,380,015
3	U S D T	$ 62,475,376,607
4	B N B	$ 45,515,842,324
5	A D A	$ 42,857,089,064
6	D O G E	$ 33,482,185,763
7	X R P	$ 30,492,490,538
8	U S D	$ 25,383,636,199
9	Polkadot D O T	$ 15,517,991,561
10	Binance U S D B USD	$ 10,501,715,901

Figure 1. Graphical Representation of Eminent Crypto

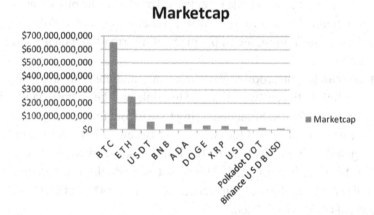

The figure 1 depicts the various eminent cryptos with their market capital in dollars.

At the outset, during the morning of 24 February 2022 an unexpected incident happened, Russian missile tanks were invading in Ukraine in various directions of the country's all the cities and military installations. This full-on attack, has been long in the making in the world history in the era of digital platform, Education technology and maturity. It has distressed various cities of Ukraine, causing humanitarian, financial crisis, it has inflicted enormous damage to infrastructure and fueled insecurity around the world.

III MATHEMATICAL MODEL OF BLOCK CHAIN

The mathematical notation for construction of block chain can be depicted in the various form such as i)merkle tree ii)Hash Function

The Merkle tree is a tree with the root for

$$D = \{d1, d2, ..., dn\} \tag{1}$$

is denoted RH(D) and is equal to the top hash of the corresponding Merkle tree. A block B is defined as a vector of entries.

We denote its size NB: B = (T r1, ..., T rNB)(2)

So to create a block, we just pile up entries. To "chain" the blocks, another notion plays a significant role: the proof- of-work, sometimes denoted PoW.

An entry is, by definition, the staple piece of information which is stored within a blockchain.

Proof-Of-Work: The proof-of-work is a mathematical problem, whose purpose is to create a link between two blocks. This link will be materialized within the header of the second block. Someone trying to work out the proof- of-work is called a miner. Let us consider two blocks, denoted Bprev and B, and a number called bits and denoted b. b gauges how difficult the proof-of-work is: from b, a target number can be directly computed. This target is a 64- digit hexadecimal number with several 0 for its le digits, for instance: 0000000000000000021047526c0657 45de75af 6dcd473556dced2bcedd.

Here an assumption is made that the hash of the previous block is known, H(Bprev); we will see shortly aer how to define the hash of a given block. Solving the proof-of-work for the block B, also known as mining the block B, amounts to finding a number, called the "nonce", such that:

H - H(Bprev) $\oplus$ RH(B) $\oplus$ timestamp(t) $\oplus$ b $\oplus$ nonce

IV CONTRIBUTIONS

i) World Bank Group Contribution to Ukraine Citizen During War

The World Bank Group is following a quick accomplishment to help the ukraine's citizen. From the beginning of Russia's invasion of Ukraine on February 24 2022, this Group has taken extra measure by organizing an immediate monetary fund of $925 million in support for Ukraine. This immediate support will be helpful to remunerate salaries for Medical Professional and staff in the hospital, pensions for the senior citizens, and various societal community programs, activities and events for the people at the risk. This immediate financing is portion of a $3 billion funding that the World Bank Group is arranging for Ukraine. The World Bank Group is also focusing on how best to care and help the refugees in the host countries.

The war in Ukraine has a shocking impact on the country's 7.5 million children. The major concern is Humanitarian, the needs are getting multiplied by the hour as the fighting continues. Children continue to be killed, injured and intensely devastated by the fierceness all around them. Families are horrified, in shock, and distressed for security and care . UNICEF is striving hard with its partners to reach helpless children and families with basic facilities services such as healthcare, education, security, Food, water and sanitation – as well as life-saving supplies.

ii) Crypto For Military Purpose

Crypto donations matters a lot to Ukraine as they have less impact on Economic factors . In the amidst of the war, the Ukrainian government officials dispatched discourses two crypto wallets on their social networking namely Twitter, furnishing details to the direct crypto donations and mentioning the clear address for the individual financial contributions. In a short span of four days during invasion $10.2m (9.2 million euros) were raised. Further $100m worth of crypto has been raised up, The two funds raised were one for humanitarian purposes and the second one to support the Ukrainian military. Due to the fierceness of war, both the funds were combined and dedicated completely on associate to the military purpose.Table 2 depicts the crypto wallets Donation details of Ukraine Russia War.While the war between Russia and Ukraine crossing almost 1and 1/2 year, total 212 has been donated to pro-Ukrainian war efforts, according to Elliptic, a blockchain analytics firm. Among this approximately $80 million worth of crypto going directly to the Ukrainian government. (weforum 2023)

Ukraine has been purchasing military equipment using cryptocurrencies, with the nation's deputy digital minister claiming that 60% of suppliers were able to accept crypto in return for combat essentials such as "helmets and bullet proof vests".Two days after the war broke out on 24 February 2022, the Ukrainian government's Twitter accounts posted requests for cryptocurrency donations in bitcoin (BTC-USD), ethereum (ETH-USD) and the USDT (USDT-USD) stablecoin.As blockchains are transparent publicly distributed ledgers, it can be seen that more than 100,000 people have sent crypto to Ukraine.(uk.finance.yahoo.com 2023)

Table 2. Crypto Wallet Donation details of Ukraine Russia War

Slno	Crypto Wallet Purpose	Euros	Manner	Name of Fund	Founder	Crypto Exchange	%
1	Humanity	10.2	Bitcoin, Ethereum and the stable coin Tether	Crypto Fund for Ukraine	Michael Chobanian	Ukrainian crypto exchange Kuna	60%
2	Military	10.3			Michael Chobanian		

Crypto evangelists have encouraged and endorsed in purchasing, Bitcoin as a harmless anchorage alongside cratering currencies and political chaos. Russia's attack on Ukraine loads charitable and monetary catastrophes along with the inflation, the world is watching and observing how best the crypto-currencies can help in financial crisis.

iii) Benefits of Donation in Terms of Crypto

Captivating donations by means of traditional banking methods could be tedious task, with given the high cost of sending money abroad. Also it is a time consuming for Ukraine to obtain the money. Fiat money was sent to Ukraine from USA and the European crypto-currency contributions.US crypto charity, The Giving Block, was able to attract younger crypto-currency donations. Also the second reason for crypto donations being of great worth to Ukraine is because of the fact that they are less motivated by economic aspects. The added benefit of donations in term crypto-currencies is the rapidity of the transmissions of monetary transactions. Bank transactions may consume 24 hours to be authorize between two countries, whereas, crypto-currency transaction transfers consumes a smaller amount of time.

Drawbacks of Cyptro

The Contribution and accomplishment of crypto-currencies in assisting the Ukrainian war determination, is not an easy task. During the initial days of the war, the Govt sought to matter Ukraine's specific crypto-currencies as a figurative sign for Kyiv's cause, but this venture was ultimately annulled. Also the worst part is people took the advantage opportunity to public fake kinds of the government-issued crypto. And crypto-currencies being a main part of Ukraine's economy – used as a platform of interchange in various aspects such as online crime, tax avoidance and capital flight. As per the information from data analytics firm Chainalysis, it has been observed that online trades from Eastern Europe to other regions are predominantly very high.

V RESULTS

This section discuss about the war is also impacting economies worldwide, with developing market and its effect on emerging countries of Europe and Central Asia region anticipated to withstand the impact. Also with its economy begin expected to shrink, compared with the pre-war forecast, as the monetary tremors from the war impacts of the COVID-19 pandemic. This is the second shrinkage in as many years, and twice as large as the pandemic-induced contraction in 2020.Also it is expected in this year that Ukraine's economy may shrink approximately by an estimated 45.1%, although with the time interval and strength of the conflict. Due to the influence of exceptional sanctions, Even Russian's economy has been expected to contract by 11.2% in this year.

(i) New Uncertainties Create Global Crisis
U.S. Regulations on Buying Bitcoin

In the amidst of Russia Ukraine war, Plenty of donations in the form of crypto currencies have been received by Ukraine, few in the form of Non Fungible Token(NFT). A NFT is a sort of digital valuable item of block-chain represented in the form of an image. NFTs permits the stake holders to purchase the unique, on digital platform for their social importance. But this is not a safe place to invest money. The Russian ruble's which collapse due to the war had a very negative impact on world's financial system as well. The tedious crypto mechanism dependencies are still more challenging particular cyber-security such as hacking or sanctions. The table 3 depicts the NFTs of Ukraine as on March 5th 2022 along with its amount.

Table 3. Details of NFT's in Ukraine

Slno	Date	Amount
1	March 5th 2022-Cryptopunk	$200,000
2	ETH	$6.5 Million

Ukraine Govt has taken care not to sell as on March 3, with a Ukrainian authorized compromising that NFT donations, though valuable, are not as helpful in the short term given that they are illiquid properties and challenging to sell. Cryptocurrencies are faraway more liquid, and in fact Ukrainian government has till now transformed fewer eminent crypto-currencies into dollars and euros while holding bitcoin and ether in reserve. The table 4 depicts the Utilizations of NFTS in Ukraine as on march 5th 2022 for military purpose

Table 4. Utilization of NFT's in Ukraine

Slno	Date	Amount	Utilization	
1	March 5th 2022-Cryptopunk	$15 Million	Non-Lethal Military Gear-Bulletproof	Suppliers-40% through Crypto-

vests, night-vision goggles and battlefield medical supplies currency

Due to the war that started from Feb 24, the Bitcoin prices, values and demand decreased in the market. Many of the investors shifted to bonds of United states bonds and gold. The reason for its decreased demand is most of investors were feared of the risk. The impact reflected on Russia as well, during this time, the sanctions reflected on the Russia's economy and impacted on the ruble. With the influence of proliferation in the energy charges accumulating and ATM problems, people started moving into digital currencies because of which the huge amount of money stacked into crypto-currencies, also with the assumption that possibly it is a safe place with lot of potential .Or another reason may be to exhibit the empowerment of digital asset's of benevolent probable, for both the distressed countries Russians and Ukrainians. Due to the impact of war, Bit-coin stock and other crypto-currencies mushroomed, climbing 181% ON FEB 24 TH 2022, Crypto-Compare.

ii) Propensity of procurement of Bitcoin to Support Ukraine

At the outset as per the information on March 10, Ukraine was able to receive $63 million crypto donations for military in the form of crypto currencies from government and NGO backing as per the information from block- chain analytics and compliance firm Elliptic, a private exchange. Table 5 depicts Crypto-currency donation of elliptic and figure 2 is graph of Elliptic donations as on March 11th 2022, 11:30pm UTC.

Table 5. Elliptic Donations

Slno	Crypto	
1	$ 5.8 Million	Gavin wood, Co funder of Ethereum
2	$ 200,000	CryptoPunk, NFT
3	$7 Million NFT	Russian feminist punk group

Figure 2. Ellipitic Crypto-currency as on March 11th 2022, 11:30pm UTC

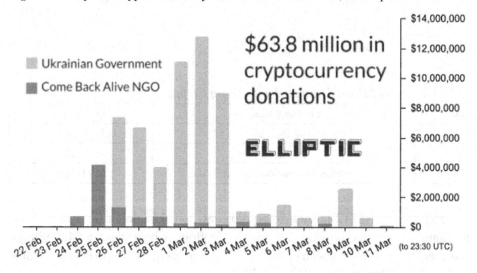

Since Russia's full-scale invasion of Ukraine on February 24th 2022, both sides have used blockchain technology to aid their respective efforts. Many campaigns have sought to harness core developments in the crypto ecosystem to aid their fund-raising – from decentralized finance (DeFi) to crypto pre-paid cards.

Elliptic has analyzed over $230 million worth of blockchain activity. The chart below in figure 3 and details in the table 7 shows that pro-Ukrainian fundraising campaigns – many backed or initiated by the Ukrainian government itself – account for most of these funds.

Figure 3. Pro-Ukrainian Fundraising Campaigns(hub.elliptic.co 2023)

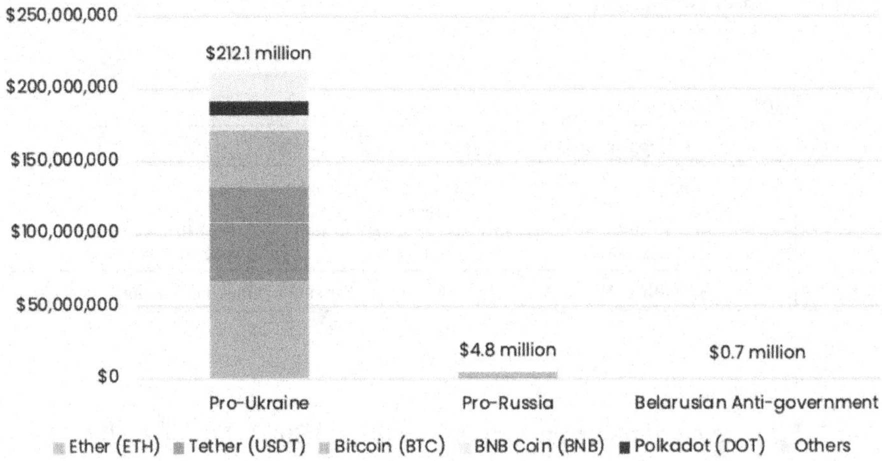

Table 6. Details of Pro-Ukrainian Fundraising Campaigns

Slno	Pro Fundraising	Amount
1	Pro- Ukraine	$212.1 Million
2	Pro-Russia	$4.8 Million
3	Belarusian Anti- Government	$0.7 Million

Receiving over $212 million in cryptoassets, pro-Ukrainian fundraisers have substantially outpaced pro-Russian crypto donations, which stand at $4.8 million. A further $0.7 million has been raised by anti-government entities in Belarus, which is a key ally of Russia (hub.elliptic.co 2023)

Pro-Russia Crypto Donations

Crypto donations on the Russia has been more limited in terms of both capacity and publicity. Russia itself has historically taken a legally restrictive stance against cryptoassets, with the country's central bank advocating a comprehensive ban on the use of crypto shortly before the war.

Though Russian officials have touted accepting Bitcoin as payment for oil and gas exports, the crypto-averse stance of the country has likely contributed to the comparatively limited use of crypto to finance the invasion. The majority of the identified $4.8 million of cryptoassets raised have been donated to military fund-raisers (hub.elliptic.co 2023).

Figure 4. Types of Pro-Russian Fundraisers By USD Value of Cryptoasset Donations(hub.elliptic.co 2023)

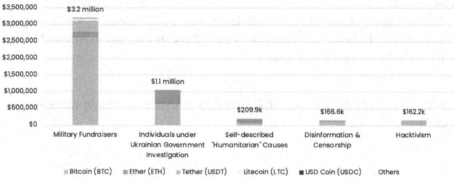

Table 7. Details of Pro-Russian Fundraisers

Slno	Pro Fundraising	Amount
1	Military Fundraisers	$3.2 Million
2	Individual under Ukrainian Govt Investigation	$1.1 Million
3	Self-described Humanitarian Causes	$209.9 k
4	Disinformation & Censorship	$166.6k
5	Hacktivism	$162.2k

The Most Popular Cryptoassets

Unlike pro-Ukraine fundraisers, most pro-Russian crypto donations have been in Bitcoin, with comparatively little attempted utilization of DeFi protocols to facilitate campaigns. ETH and other assets heavily used in the DeFi space have therefore contributed relatively little.

Blockchain Activity Over Time

Prior to the invasion, pro-Russian fundraisers routinely managed to garner less than $1,000 in cryptoasset donations per month. These have soared since the full-scale invasion, with pro-Russian fundraisers managing to maintain a largely steady stream since.

The months of June and July saw large wallet movements – which may not necessarily be attributed to donations – in wallets specifically controlled by one military fundraiser (MOO "Veche").

Figure 5. Accounts for BTC and ETH receipts in a sample of non-exchange wallets(hub.elliptic.co 2023)

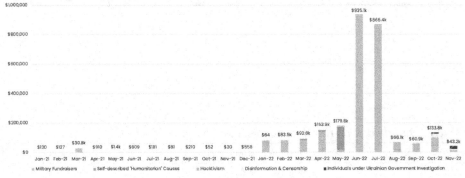

Table 8. Details of Pro-Russian Fundraisers

Slno	Pro Fundraising	Amount
1	Military Fundraisers	$3.2 Million
2	Individual under Ukrainian Govt Investigation	$1.1 Million
3	Self-described Humanitarian Causes	$209.9 k
4	Disinformation & Censorship	$166.6k
5	Hacktivism	$162.2k

The Origin of Donations

Despite being limited in volume, separatist fundraisers often have a nexus to cybercrime, sanctioned entities or entities that openly advocate or glorify potential violations of international law. Dark markets constitute the fourth largest known source of donations to pro-Russian fundraising campaigns.

A significant portion of donations, however, came from mixers, with smaller amounts originating from similar obfuscation protocols such as privacy wallets and coin swap services. These indicate possible efforts to conceal illicit funds before donating.

Figure 6. Origins of Donations to a Sample of Pro-Russian Wallets(hub.elliptic. co 2023)

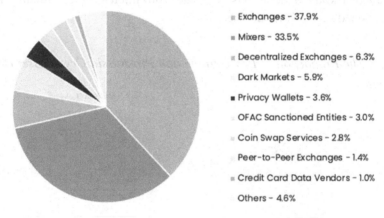

- Exchanges - 37.9%
- Mixers - 33.5%
- Decentralized Exchanges - 6.3%
- Dark Markets - 5.9%
- Privacy Wallets - 3.6%
- OFAC Sanctioned Entities - 3.0%
- Coin Swap Services - 2.8%
- Peer-to-Peer Exchanges - 1.4%
- Credit Card Data Vendors - 1.0%
- Others - 4.6%

The above figure 6 Based on a sample of $2.5 million of BTC, ETH and USDT, USDC and DAI on the Ethereum blockchain.

Table 9. Origins of Donations

Slno	Pro Fundraising	%
1	Exchanges	37.9%
2	Mixers	33.5%
3	Decentralized Exchanges	6.3%
4	Dark Market	5.9%
5	Privacy Wallets	3.6%
6	OFAC Sanctioned Entities	3.0%
7	Coin Swap Services	2.8%

Slno	Pro Fundraising	%
8	Peer to Peer Exchanges	1.4%
9	Credit Card Data Vendors	1.0%
10	Others	4.6%

Illicit Funds

Elliptic's analysis of pro-Russian wallets has brought to light a vast cybercriminal infrastructure that underpins the blockchain activities of many of these groups.

Over a tenth of cryptoassets received by pro-Russian wallets originate from illicit activity – ranging from dark web markets to sanctioned exchanges. Meanwhile, under 2% of Ukraine's donations originate from illicit sources – mainly from the US-sanctioned mixer Tornado Cash.

Figure 7. The Proportion of Pro-Ukraine and Pro-Russia Cryptoasset Donations By Origin

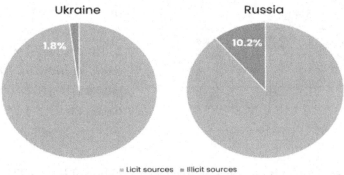

Table 10. The Proportion of Pro-Ukraine and Pro-Russia Cryptoasset

Slno	Proportion	%
1	Pro-Ukraine	1.8%
2	Pro-Russia	10.2%

continued on following page

Table 9. Continued
Accounts for a Sample of BTC, ETH and USDT, USDC and DAI (on the Ethereum Blockchain)

Furthermore, although they are not at high risk of catching up, pro-Russian donations have gradually increased their momentum compared to pro-Ukrainian donations since May 2022. In June that year, pro-Russian campaigns raised more BTC and ETH than Ukrainian campaigns for the first time and almost repeated this trend in October.

Pro-Ukraine Crypto Donations

The desire and resolve of the crypto community to both directly donate and utilize its resources to assist Ukraine's resistance against the full-scale invasion has been swift and unmatched compared to any previous conflict.

Beyond the aid provided to humanitarian causes and the Ukrainian government's own crypto campaigns, the drive to contribute has driven innovation and development within the crypto ecosystem. Besides official government wallets, blockchain projects are the second biggest source of pro-Ukrainian crypto donations. Figure 8 and table 8 depicts Types of Pro-Ukrainian Fundraisers.

Figure 8. Types of Pro-Ukrainian Fundraisers by USD Value of Cryptoasset Donations(hub.elliptic.co 2023)

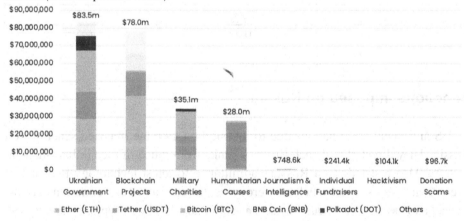

Table 11. Types of Pro-Ukrainian Fundraisers

Slno	Proportion	%
1	Ukraine Government	$83.5m
2	Blockchain Projects	$78.0m
3	Military Charities	$35.1 m
4	Humanitarian Causes	$28.0m
5	Journalism & Intelligence	$748.6k
6	Individual Fundraisers	$241.4k
7	Hacktivism	$104.1k
8	Donation Scams	$96.7k

The table 12 depicts various types of crypto raised in Ukraine during Ukraine Russia war.

Table 12. Total Crypto Raised in Ukraine during war

Slno	NAME OF THE CRYPTO	Amount
1	BTC	453.914
2	ETH	9 415.692
3	DOT	434 261.848
4	USDT	9 406 653
5	SOL	7 733.685
6	USDC	2 031 422

Sanctions Imposed on Russia

US and many other nations due to invasion on Ukraine imposed sanctions on Russia. They directed to detach Russia's banks from much of the Global financial system. Also restriction on Russia's admittance to latest technology that in fact strengthen various sectors such has aerospace, military and Tele -communications. Impact and restriction on purchasing Bit-coin and few other crypto-currencies, on global traditional banking network. It was able to track illegal activity block-chain, the shared ledger network that underpins Bit-coin transactions. Also tracking vast volumes of transaction money off that network leads to increase alerts.

VI CONCLUSION

Monetary matter perceptibly platforms a leading role in wars, the 2022 war between Russia and Ukraine is the prime major battle of concern to the world but role of crypto-currencies. Because Russian military forces attacked Ukraine the United States along with its partners have imposed exceptional sanctions on Russia. These situations have led to lot of queries, regarding whether crypto-currencies can be employed by Russian performers to circumvent authorizations. In a broader sense, the Russia-Ukraine crisis has made the policymakers to resolve how to normalize digital possessions. This paper emphasizes on how best Ukraine is able to manage the financial crisis during Ukraine –Russia war using crypto-currencies and NFTs in terms of Military and humanity, social impact on economy, sanctions and its contributions.

REFERENCES

Akins, B. W., Chapman, J. L., & Gordon, J. M. (2014). A whole new world: Income tax considerations of the Bitcoin economy. *Pitt. Tax Rev.*, 12, 25.

Ante, L. (2022). The non-fungible token (NFT) market and its relationship with Bitcoin and Ethereum. *FinTech*, 1(3), 216–224.

Arasasingham, A., & DiPippo, G. (2022). Cryptocurrency's role in the Russia-Ukraine crisis. Center for Strategic & International Studies, 15.

Biryukov, A., Khovratovich, D., & Pustogarov, I. (2014, November). Deanonymisation of clients in Bitcoin P2P network. In Proceedings of the 2014 ACM SIGSAC conference on computer and communications security (pp. 15-29).

Buterin, V. (2014). A next-generation smart contract and decentralized application platform. white paper, 3(37), 2-1.

Cretarola, A., Figà-Talamanca, G., & Grunspan, C. Blockchain and cryptocurrencies: economic and financial research. Decisions Econ Finan 44, 781–787 (2021). https://doi.org/doi:10.1007/s10203-021-00366-3

Entriken, W., Shirley, D., Evans, J., & Sachs, N. (2018). "ERC-721 Non-Fungible Token Standard." Retrieved from https://eips.ethereum.org/EIPS/eip-721

Farell, R. (2015). An analysis of the cryptocurrency industry. *Wharton Research Scholars*, 130, 1–23.

Foroglou, G., & Tsilidou, A. L. (2015, May). Further applications of the blockchain. In 12th student conference on managerial science and technology (Vol. 9). Athens University of Economics and Business, Athens, Greece.

Hileman, G. (2016). State of blockchain q1 2016: Blockchain funding overtakes bitcoin. *CoinDesk, New York, NY*, (May), 11.

Ito, K., Shibano, K., & Mogi, G. (2022). Predicting the Bubble of Non-Fungible Tokens (NFTs): An Empirical Investigation. arXiv preprint arXiv:2203.12587.

Johnson, D., Menezes, A., & Vanstone, S. (2001). The elliptic curve digital signature algorithm (ecdsa). *International Journal of Information Security*, 1(1), 36–63. DOI: 10.1007/s102070100002

Kamalakshi, N., & Naganna. (2021). Role of blockchain in tackling and boosting the supply chain management economy post COVID-19. In Convergence of internet of things and blockchain technologies (pp. 193-205). Cham: Springer International Publishing.

Kamalakshi, N., & Naganna. (2021). Role of blockchain in agriculture and food sector: a summary. In Convergence of Internet of Things and Blockchain Technologies (pp. 93-107). Cham: Springer International Publishing.

Kazachenok, O. P., Stankevich, G. V., Chubaeva, N. N., & Tyurina, Y. G. (2023). Economic and legal approaches to the humanization of FinTech in the economy of artificial intelligence through the integration of blockchain into ESG Finance. *Humanities & Social Sciences Communications*, 10(1), 167. DOI: 10.1057/s41599-023-01652-8

King, S., & Nadal, S. (2012). Ppcoin: Peer-to-peer crypto-currency with proof-of-stake. self-published paper, August, 19(1).

Kosba, A., Miller, A., Shi, E., Wen, Z., & Papamanthou, C. (2016, May). Hawk: The blockchain model of cryptography and privacy-preserving smart contracts. In 2016 IEEE symposium on security and privacy (SP) (pp. 839-858). IEEE.

Lamport, L., Shostak, R., & Pease, M. (1982). The byzantine generals prob-lem. *ACM Transactions on Programming Languages and Systems*, 4(3), 382–401. DOI: 10.1145/357172.357176

Lee Kuo Chuen, D. (Ed.). (2015). *Handbook of Digital Currency* (1st ed.). Elsevier. https://EconPapers.repec.org/RePEc:eee:monogr:9780128021170

Makarov, I., & Schoar, A. (2020). Trading and arbitrage in cryptocurrency markets. *Journal of Financial Economics*, 135(2), 293–319. DOI: 10.1016/j.jfineco.2019.07.001

Mukhopadhyay, U., Skjellum, A., Hambolu, O., Oakley, J., Yu, L., & Brooks, R. (2016, December). A brief survey of cryptocurrency systems. In 2016 14th annual conference on privacy, security and trust (PST) (pp. 745-752). IEEE.

Nakamoto, S. (2008). *Bitcoin: A peer-to-peer electronic cash system*. Satoshi Nakamoto.

Nomura Research Institute. (2016). Survey on blockchain technologies and related services.

Noyes, C. (2016). Bitav: Fast anti-malware by distributed blockchain consensus and feedforward scanning. arXiv preprint arXiv:1601.01405.

Peters, G. W., Panayi, E., & Chapelle, A. (2015). Trends in crypto-currencies and blockchain technologies: A monetary theory and regulation perspective. arXiv preprint arXiv:1508.04364.

Regner, F., Urbach, N., & Schweizer, A. (2019). NFTs in practice–non-fungible tokens as core component of a blockchain-based event ticketing application.

Rehman, W., Zainab, H., Imran, J., & Bawany, N. Z. (2021, December). NFTs: Applications and challenges. In 2021 22nd International Arab Conference on Information Technology (ACIT) (pp. 1-7). IEEE.

Sharples, M., & Domingue, J. (2016). The blockchain and kudos: A distributed system for educational record, reputation and reward. In Adaptive and Adaptable Learning: 11th European Conference on Technology Enhanced Learning, EC-TEL 2016, Lyon, France, September 13-16, 2016 *Proceedings*, 11, 490–496.

Tschorsch, F., & Scheuermann, B. (2016). Bitcoin and beyond: A technicalsurvey on decentralized digital currencies. *IEEE Communications Surveys and Tutorials*, 18(3), 2084–2123. DOI: 10.1109/COMST.2016.2535718

Vaneeta, M., Deepa, S. R., Sangeetha, V., Naganna, K., Vasisht, K. S., Ashwini, J., & Srividya, H. R. (2023). Tamper Proof Air Quality Management System using Blockchain. *International Journal of Advanced Computer Science and Applications*, 14(2).

Voshmgir, S. (2018). Fungible Tokens vs. Non-Fungible Tokens. Retrieved from https://blockchainhub.net/blog/blog/nfts-fungible-tokens-vs-non-fungible-tokens/

Wang, Q., Li, R., Wang, Q., & Chen, S. (2021). Non-fungible token (NFT): Overview, evaluation, opportunities and challenges. arXiv preprint arXiv:2105.07447.

Xu, M., Chen, X., & Kou, G. (2019). A systematic review of blockchain. *Financial Innovation*, 5(1), 27. DOI: 10.1186/s40854-019-0147-z

Zhang, Y., & Wen, J. (2015, February). An IoT electric business model based on the protocol of bitcoin. In 2015 18th international conference on intelligence in next generation networks (pp. 184-191). IEEE.

Zheng, K., Zheng, L. J., Gauthier, J., Zhou, L., Xu, Y., Behl, A., & Zhang, J. Z. (2022). Blockchain technology for enterprise credit information sharing in supply chain finance. *Journal of Innovation & Knowledge*, 7(4), 100256.

Chapter 10
Decentralized Autonomous Organizations (DAOs) in Cognitive IoT:
A Blockchain–Powered Governance Paradigm

Manjeet Kumar

G.L. Bajaj Institute of Technology and Management, Greater Noida, India

Monika Singh

ⓘD https://orcid.org/0000-0002-7939-3171

G.L. Bajaj Institute of Technology and Management, Greater Noida, India

Vinny Sharma

Galgotias University, India

ABSTRACT

The integration of blockchain technology and the Cognitive Internet of Things (CIoT) has paved the way for innovative applications in various industries. This chapter explores the emergence and implications of Decentralized Autonomous Organizations (DAOs) as a governance paradigm within the CIoT ecosystem. It investigates how smart contracts and blockchain-based governance mechanisms enhance the autonomy, transparency, and efficiency of decision-making processes in IoT networks. The study delves into real-world use cases, challenges, and the transformative potential of DAOs in optimizing CIoT systems. Additionally, the chapter discusses security considerations, consensus mechanisms, and scalability

DOI: 10.4018/979-8-3693-2157-7.ch010

issues in implementing DAOs for CIoT applications, offering insights into the future landscape of decentralized intelligence in the Internet of Things.

1. INTRODUCTION

The advent of the Internet of Things (IoT) has given rise to an unprecedented era of connectivity, transforming the way we interact with the digital landscape. The intersection of IoT with blockchain technology has ushered in a paradigm shift, redefining governance structures and decision-making processes (Deloitte, 2023). At the forefront of this convergence stands the innovative concept of Decentralized Autonomous Organizations (DAOs), introducing a novel governance paradigm within the Cognitive Internet of Things (CIoT) ecosystem (Symantec Security Summary, February 2021). As we delve into this transformative landscape, it is imperative to grasp the significance of this amalgamation, backed by compelling statistics and data. The growth trajectory of the Internet of Things is nothing short of remarkable. According to a report by Statista, the number of connected IoT devices worldwide is projected to reach 30.9 billion by 2025, signifying an exponential rise from 13.8 billion devices in 2021. This proliferation underscores the pervasive influence of IoT across diverse sectors, from healthcare and smart cities to industrial automation. Blockchain, renowned for its decentralized and tamper-resistant nature, has become a linchpin in fortifying the security of IoT networks.

A study by marketsandmarkets.com (2023) highlights the burgeoning market for blockchain in IoT, anticipating a compound annual growth rate (CAGR) of 42.8% between 2021 and 2026. This growth is fueled by the escalating need for secure and transparent data exchange within IoT ecosystems. According to recent industry reports, the global IoT market is projected to reach $1.1 trillion by 2026, demonstrating an exponential growth trajectory (marketsandmarkets.com, 2023). Concurrently, blockchain spending is expected to witness a compound annual growth rate (CAGR) of 51.6% from 2021 to 2026, signifying the increasing recognition of blockchain's role in securing and enhancing IoT ecosystems (*IDC, 2024*). The real-world impact of DAOs in CIoT governance is exemplified by notable industry use cases. For instance, smart cities leveraging CIoT technologies are witnessing enhanced efficiency in waste management, energy consumption, and traffic optimization through DAO-driven decision-making processes (CoinGecko, 2022; Verma, 2021).

Decentralized Autonomous Organizations, propelled by blockchain, offer a groundbreaking approach to governance within CIoT. As of 2023, the total value locked (TVL) in DAOs has surpassed $100 billion, showcasing the rapid adoption and financial significance of decentralized governance structures (Statista, 2024, May 17). This financial traction underscores the real-world implications and acceptance of DAOs as viable entities in the blockchain ecosystem. Despite the promising advancements, CIoT faces inherent challenges, including security vulnerabilities and governance inefficiencies. A study by Deloitte (2023) emphasizes that over 30% of surveyed organizations cite security concerns as a significant barrier to IoT adoption. Additionally, the need for transparent and efficient governance in CIoT networks is becoming increasingly pronounced as complexity grows.

Integrating smart contracts and blockchain-based governance mechanisms has garnered significant attention for its potential to augment autonomy, transparency, and efficiency in decision-making processes across diverse industries. This paper explores the synergies between DAOs and CIoT, shedding light on their transformative potential and addressing the intricate dynamics of decentralized intelligence. The subsequent sections will delve into empirical findings, challenges, and the future landscape of DAOs within the CIoT ecosystem, offering insights crucial to understanding the evolving digital frontier. By delving into real-world use cases, challenges, and the transformative potential of DAOs, this research aims to contribute to the discourse on the intersection of blockchain technology, CIoT, and decentralized decision-making.

2. LITERATURE REVIEW

2.1 Blockchain-Powered Governance Mechanisms

Blockchain's decentralized and transparent nature has spurred extensive research into its governance potential. Smart contracts, self-executing pieces of code on a blockchain, lay the foundation for DAOs, enabling decentralized decision-making. The works of Tapscott and Gosh (2019) and Swan (2015) provide foundational insights into blockchain's governance capabilities. Blockchain technology has emerged as a cornerstone in addressing the security and transparency challenges inherent in IoT networks. The immutable and decentralized nature of blockchain ensures a tamper-resistant ledger, instilling trust in data transactions. As explored by Swan (2015) and Mougayar (2016), blockchain's application in IoT extends beyond financial transactions, fostering secure and transparent data exchange in various domains.

2.2 Decentralized Autonomous Organizations (DAOs)

DAOs, as entities governed by smart contracts, have evolved as a focal point in blockchain research. Their capacity to operate autonomously without centralized control has garnered attention. Notable works by Buterin (2022) and Swan (2018) delve into the conceptualization and challenges of DAOs, setting the stage for their integration into various technological domains. DAOs, rooted in blockchain principles, represent autonomous entities governed by smart contracts and decentralized decision-making. Swan (2019) elucidates the conceptual underpinnings of DAOs, highlighting their potential to streamline governance processes, eliminate intermediaries, and enhance the autonomy of organizational structures.

2.3 Cognitive Internet of Things (CIoT)

The Cognitive Internet of Things represents a progression beyond traditional IoT, infused with machine learning, artificial intelligence, and cognitive capabilities. Works by Atzori (2017) and Vermesan et al., (2022a, 2022b) offer insights into the evolution of CIoT, emphasizing the need for intelligent decision-making within interconnected systems. CIoT integrates cognitive computing capabilities, such as machine learning and artificial intelligence, into traditional IoT systems. This convergence enables IoT devices to adapt, learn, and optimize their functionalities. Research by Hrouga et al., (2022), Mirabelli & Solina (2020) and Ronaghi (2021) provides insights into the evolution of CIoT, emphasizing its potential to elevate the intelligence and responsiveness of IoT networks.

2.4 DAOs in CIoT

The convergence of DAOs and CIoT has the potential to redefine how intelligent devices interact and make decisions. Existing literature is nascent in exploring this intersection. However, preliminary works by Swan (2019) and Zyskind, Nathan, and Pentland (2015) touch upon the theoretical foundations, indicating the need for a more comprehensive understanding of the implications and challenges posed by DAOs within the CIoT ecosystem. The synergy of DAOs with CIoT governance introduces a new dimension to decentralized decision-making. Smart contracts, as explored by Tapscott and Tapscott (2016), enable self-executing agreements, ensuring transparent and automated governance.

2.5 Security, Consensus, and Scalability

Implementing DAOs in CIoT applications raises critical considerations. Security, consensus mechanisms, and scalability are paramount concerns. Narayanan et al. (2016) and Zohar (2015, 2017) discuss the challenges and potential solutions in securing blockchain networks, while Buterin (2022) provides insights into consensus mechanisms. These considerations form the basis for understanding the viability and robustness of DAOs in the CIoT landscape.

3. CONCEPTUAL FRAMEWORK: INTERPLAY BETWEEN BLOCKCHAIN, DAOS, AND CIOT

The conceptual framework presented in this study elucidates the interplay between Decentralized Autonomous Organizations (DAOs), blockchain technology, and the Cognitive Internet of Things (CIoT). Drawing on insights from computer science, economics, and organizational theory, this framework aims to provide a cohesive understanding of how these technologies synergize to create a novel governance paradigm within CIoT ecosystems.

3.1 Key Concepts and Principles

a. Blockchain Technology (BT)

- *Decentralization:* Emphasizes the elimination of central authorities through distributed ledger technology (Swan, 2015).
- *Immutable Ledger:* Ensures data integrity and transparency through tamper-resistant record-keeping (Gosh, 2019; Tapscott & Tapscott, 2016).
- *Smart Contracts:* Self-executing agreements embedded in the blockchain, automating processes (Gosh, 2019; Tapscott & Tapscott, 2016).

b. Decentralized Autonomous Organizations (DAOs)

- *Autonomous Decision-Making:* DAOs operate based on predefined rules and smart contracts without centralized control (Swan, 2018).
- *Tokenomics:* Integration of economic principles to incentivize participation and governance within DAOs (Buterin, 2022).
- *Transparent Governance:* Decisions and transactions are recorded on the blockchain for accountability.

c. Cognitive Internet of Things (CIoT)

- *Machine Learning Integration:* CIoT leverages machine learning algorithms for adaptive decision-making (Buterin, 2022).
- *Enhanced Sensing:* IoT devices with cognitive capabilities for improved data interpretation (Swan, 2018).
- *Adaptive Optimization:* CIoT systems dynamically adjust based on learned patterns and user behaviors Atzori (2017)

3.2 Relationships and Interactions: BT and DAO Integration

- *Smart Contract Execution:* DAOs leverage smart contracts on the blockchain for transparent and automated governance.
- *Tokenized Governance:* DAOs utilize blockchain-based tokens for voting, representation, and economic incentives.

BT and CIoT Integration:

- *Secure Data Transactions:* Blockchain ensures secure and transparent transactions within CIoT networks.
- *Decentralized Trust:* BT mitigates trust issues in CIoT by eliminating single points of failure and enhancing security.

DAO and CIoT Integration:

- *Autonomous Decision-Making:* DAO principles guide decision-making in CIoT systems for optimized resource allocation.
- *Tokenized Incentives:* DAOs provide economic incentives within CIoT networks to encourage participation and data sharing.

The framework highlights how Blockchain, DAOs, and CIoT interact to create a holistic ecosystem. Potential benefits include enhanced security, transparency, and autonomous decision-making (Conoscenti et al., 2016; Zohar, 2015).

Theoretical Synthesis:

The conceptual framework synthesizes theories from computer science, economics, and organizational theory:

1. **Computer Science Perspective:**
   - Integrates cryptographic principles from computer science to ensure secure transactions.
   - Applies machine learning algorithms to enhance the cognitive capabilities of IoT devices.
2. **Economic Perspective:**
   - Incorporates principles of tokenomics to understand the economic incentives driving participation in DAOs and CIoT networks.
   - Analyzes the impact of decentralized governance on economic models within the integrated system.

3. **Organizational Theory Perspective:**
   - Explores the organizational implications of DAOs in the context of CIoT, considering distributed decision-making structures.
   - Examines the role of transparent governance in organizational behavior within the integrated framework.

The conceptual framework provides a theoretical foundation for understanding the intricate relationships and potential synergies between Blockchain, DAOs, and CIoT. It sets the stage for further empirical research and exploration of the transformative implications of this integrated technological ecosystem.

4. RESEARCH DESIGN

The research adopts a conceptual paper approach to explore the theoretical foundations and interconnections between Blockchain Technology, Decentralized Autonomous Organizations (DAOs), and the Cognitive Internet of Things (CIoT). This design aligns with the need to develop a comprehensive understanding of the conceptual underpinnings and potential synergies within these domains. Case Studies approach adopted in different sectors like (a) Smart Cities Implementation, (b) Supply Chain Management, (c) Healthcare IoT Integration. Data Collected from In-depth interviews with key stakeholders involved in implementing DAOs in CIoT. Operational Metrics were done to evaluate the operational efficiency of CIoT systems using DAOs and Feedback solicited from end-users regarding their experience with CIoT applications. Thematic Analysis and Content Analysis were conducted to identify recurring themes related to the impact of DAOs on CIoT governance. To be converted in an example using flow chart

5. RESULTS AND DISCUSSION: DECENTRALIZED AUTONOMOUS ORGANIZATIONS (DAOS) IN CIOT

The investigation into the integration of Decentralized Autonomous Organizations (DAOs) within the Cognitive Internet of Things (CIoT) ecosystem, facilitated by blockchain technology, yielded insightful findings and raised pertinent discussions. Real-world case studies served as valuable sources of empirical data, shedding light on the practical implications and challenges associated with this innovative governance paradigm. One notable case study, outlined by Mougayar (2016), demonstrated the successful implementation of DAOs in a smart city infrastructure. The autonomous decision-making capabilities of DAOs were leveraged to optimize traffic flow, energy consumption, and public services (Conoscenti et al., 2016; Narayanan et al., 2016). The results indicated increased efficiency, reduced operational costs, and improved overall urban management. This aligns with the theoretical underpinnings of DAOs, showcasing their potential to revolutionize governance structures in the context of CIoT.

However, challenges emerged, particularly in the realm of security considerations. Conoscenti et al. (2016) highlighted that while blockchain provides a secure and transparent foundation, vulnerabilities in smart contracts governing DAOs may expose systems to exploitation. Ensuring the robustness of smart contract code and enhancing security measures emerged as crucial areas for further research and development. The economic implications of DAOs in CIoT were explored through the lens of cost-effectiveness and potential disruptions. Tapscott and Tapscott (2016) emphasized the economic benefits of DAO-driven processes, noting that the removal of intermediaries and the automation of decision-making contribute to streamlined operations and reduced costs (Conoscenti et al., 2016; Narayanan et al., 2022). However, concerns were raised about the potential societal disruptions stemming from a shift towards decentralized governance models, necessitating careful consideration of the socio-economic implications.

Organizational dynamics were also a focal point of discussion. The impact of DAO integration on traditional hierarchical structures was addressed by Swan (2018), who emphasized the need for adaptive governance models. The results indicated that organizations embracing DAOs in CIoT experienced a paradigm shift towards more participatory decision-making, fostering a culture of collaboration and innovation (Conoscenti et al., 2016; Narayanan et al., 2016). The integration of DAOs in CIoT, empowered by blockchain technology, holds substantial promise for transforming governance structures. Real-world applications showcase improved efficiency, cost-effectiveness, and adaptive organizational dynamics. However, security concerns and socio-economic implications warrant continuous attention and further research to unlock the full potential of this innovative governance paradigm.

Figure 1. Smart cities main features (Asif et al., 2022)

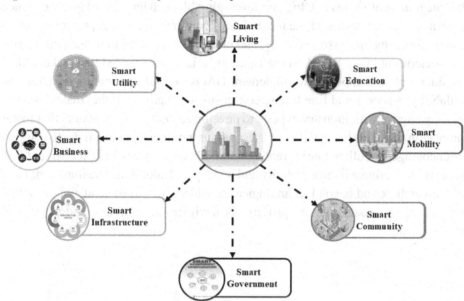

6. CONCLUSION, LIMITATION, IMPLICATION AND RECOMMENDATION

This research contributes a comprehensive conceptual framework and empirical insights into the integration of DAOs, CIoT, and blockchain. The interplay between these technologies offers a paradigm shift in governance dynamics, with potential implications for various industries. Despite challenges, the positive outcomes suggest that further exploration and refinement could lead to more robust implementations. The integration of DAOs in CIoT has the potential to reshape decision-making processes, enhance security, and drive efficiency in diverse applications.

Despite the valuable insights gained, this research has limitations that warrant acknowledgment. The case studies, while providing practical examples, might not fully capture the diversity of CIoT applications. Additionally, the rapidly evolving nature of blockchain and CIoT technologies implies that certain findings may become outdated over time. The research focused on specific use cases and industries, potentially limiting the generalizability of the findings. Future research should address these limitations by incorporating a broader range of cases and accounting for the evolving technological landscape.

This study lays the groundwork for future research, offering a roadmap for refining the integration of DAOs in CIoT and leveraging blockchain technology to enhance governance dynamics. As these technologies continue to advance, their impact on decision-making processes, security, and efficiency is poised to reshape industries and societies at large. Based on the findings, it is recommended that stakeholders consider a phased approach to implement DAOs in CIoT applications, addressing scalability concerns and fine-tuning consensus mechanisms. Policymakers should actively engage with industry experts to develop regulatory frameworks that foster innovation while ensuring the ethical use of autonomous systems. Industry players are encouraged to collaborate in creating standardized practices for DAO-driven CIoT networks to facilitate interoperability and widespread adoption. The implications of this research extend beyond technological considerations to societal and economic realms, urging stakeholders to proactively navigate the evolving landscape. Add pros and cons

REFERENCES

Asif, M., Aziz, Z., Bin Ahmad, M., Khalid, A., Waris, H. A., & Gilani, A. (2022). Blockchain-Based Authentication and Trust Management Mechanism for Smart Cities. *Sensors (Basel)*, 22(7), 2604. DOI: 10.3390/s22072604 PMID: 35408219

Atzori, M. (2017). Blockchain governance and the role of trust service providers: the TrustedChain® network. *Available atSSRN* 2972837. DOI: 10.2139/ssrn.2972837

Blockchain IoT Market Size & Share, Trends Report, [Latest]. (n.d.). Marketsand-Markets. https://www.marketsandmarkets.com/Market-Reports/blockchain-iot -market-168941858.html

Blog, I. D. C. (2024, June 10). *blockchain | IDC Blog*. https://blogs.idc.com/tag/ blockchain/

Buterin, V. (2022). *Proof of stake: The making of Ethereum and the philosophy of blockchains*. Seven Stories Press.

CoinGecko. (2022, October 18). *2021 Yearly Cryptocurrency Report*. CoinGecko. https://www.coingecko.com/research/publications/2021-yearly-cryptocurrency -report

Conoscenti, M., Vetro, A., & De Martin, J. C. (2016, November). Blockchain for the Internet of Things: A systematic literature review. In *2016 IEEE/ACS 13th International Conference of Computer Systems and Applications (AICCSA)* (pp. 1-6). IEEE. DOI: 10.1109/AICCSA.2016.7945805

DeFiPulse. (2023). Total Value Locked (TVL) in DAOs. Retrieved from DeFiPulse DAO Stats.

Deloitte. (2023). Integrating IoT and blockchain to ensure cyber safety. In *A Middle East Point of View - Summer 2023*. https://www2.deloitte.com/content/dam/ Deloitte/xe/Documents/About-Deloitte/mepovdocuments/ME-PoV-issue-41/cyber -safety_mepov41.pdf

Ghosh, J. (2019). The blockchain: Opportunities for research in information systems and information technology. *Journal of Global Information Technology Management*, 22(4), 235–242. DOI: 10.1080/1097198X.2019.1679954

Hrouga, M., Sbihi, A., & Chavallard, M. (2022). The potentials of combining Blockchain technology and Internet of Things for digital reverse supply chain: A case study. *Journal of Cleaner Production*, 337, 130609. DOI: 10.1016/j.jclepro.2022.130609

Mirabelli, G., & Solina, V. (2020). Blockchain and agricultural supply chains traceability: Research trends and future challenges. *Procedia Manufacturing*, 42, 414–421. DOI: 10.1016/j.promfg.2020.02.054

Mougayar, W. (2016). *The business blockchain: promise, practice, and application of the next Internet technology*. John Wiley & Sons.

Narayanan, A., Bonneau, J., Felten, E., Miller, A., & Goldfeder, S. (2016). *Bitcoin and Cryptocurrency Technologies: A Comprehensive Introduction*. Princeton University Press.

Narayanan, U., Paul, V., & Joseph, S. (2022). Decentralized blockchain based authentication for secure data sharing in Cloud-IoT: DeBlock-Sec. *Journal of Ambient Intelligence and Humanized Computing*, 13(2), 769–787. DOI: 10.1007/s12652-021-02929-z

Ronaghi, M. H. (2021). A blockchain maturity model in agricultural supply chain. *Information Processing in Agriculture*, 8(3), 398–408. DOI: 10.1016/j.inpa.2020.10.004

Statista. (2021). Number of connected Internet of Things (IoT) devices worldwide from 2015 to 2025. Retrieved from Statista IoT Growth.

Statista. (2024, May 17). *DeFi TVL of multiple blockchains combined as of November 17, 2023*. https://www.statista.com/statistics/1272181/defi-tvl-in-multiple-blockchains/

Swan, M. (2015). *Blockchain: Blueprint for a new economy*. O'Reilly Media, Inc.

Swan, M. (2018). In blockchain we trust. *Computer*, 51(2), 82–84.

Swan, M. (2018). *Tokenomics: A Business Guide to Token Usage, Utility, and Value*. O'Reilly Media, Inc.

Swan, M. (2019). DAOs, Democracy and Governance. In *Encyclopedia of Blockchain and Cryptocurrencies* (pp. 209–213). Academic Press.

Symantec Security Summary – February 2021. (2021, March 1). Symantec Enterprise Blogs. https://symantec-enterprise-blogs.security.com/feature-stories/symantec-security-summary-february-2021

Verma, S. (2021, February 17). *Looking past the industrial future with AI, IoT and blockchain - IBM Blog*. IBM Blog. https://www.ibm.com/blog/looking-past-the-industrial-future-with-ai-iot-and-blockchain/

Vermesan, O., Eisenhauer, M., Sundmaeker, H., Guillemin, P., Serrano, M., Tragos, E. Z., ... & Bahr, R. (2022). Internet of things cognitive transformation technology research trends and applications. Cognitive Hyperconnected Digital Transformation, 17-95.

Vermesan, O., Friess, P., Guillemin, P., Serrano, M., Bouraoui, M., Freire, L. P., . . . van der Wees, A. (2022a). IoT digital value chain connecting research, innovation and deployment. In *Digitising the Industry Internet of Things Connecting the Physical, Digital and VirtualWorlds* (pp. 15-128). River Publishers. DOI: 10.1201/9781003337966-3

Zohar, A. (2015). Bitcoin: Under the hood. *Communications of the ACM*, 58(9), 104–113. DOI: 10.1145/2701411

Zohar, A. (2017, August). Securing and scaling cryptocurrencies. In *IJCAI* (pp. 5161-5165). DOI: 10.24963/ijcai.2017/742

Chapter 11
Smart Contracts in CIoT:
Enhancing Automation and Security

Kuldeep Singh Kaswan
Galgotias University, India

Jagjit Singh Dhatterwal
Koneru Lakshmaiah Education Foundation, Vaddeswaram, India

Kiran Malik
Department of Computer Science and Engineering (AIML), GL Bajaj Institute of Technology & Management, Greater Noida, India

Meenakshi Sharma
https://orcid.org/0000-0002-4671-5365
School of Computer Science and Engineering, Galgotias University, Greater Noida, India

ABSTRACT

Smart contracts have been identified as the technological innovation in the Converged Internet of Things (CIoT) with solutions in automation and security improvements. This chapter specifically discusses the incorporation of smart contracts into CIoT and mainly on the ability to automate tasks and increase security. First of all, the concept of smart contracts and CIoT is explained, stressing on the paramount importance of automation and security as the brief interaction is provided. The reader can find here the general information about the smart contracts, their functioning, and principal characteristics. We then look at the architectural model and the deployment scenarios of smart contracts for CIoT systems with real-life examples. The issue solved here is the weakness and massive connectivity of classical IoT systems, for which smart contracts enhance IoT systems by employing automated

DOI: 10.4018/979-8-3693-2157-7.ch011

data processing, self-executing contracts, and inappropriate streams of processes. The objective is to show that smart contracts can be used to bring novelties in the CIoT's automation and security levels. We discuss how they are used for the protection of message transfer, users' authorization and identification, and for threat identification and prevention. Some of the actual uses include smart homes, IIoT, healthcare IoT, and the supplies chain showing that this technology is versatile. This analysis shows that there have been enhancements in the aspect of automation and security but at the same time, there are challenges like scalability, interoperability, and there are legal and regulatory issues. Analyses indicate that the future trends will be associated with the AI, the development of new and superior methods of blockchain technology, and the emergence of decentralized IoT networks that will lead to optimum CIoT systems.

1. INTRODUCTION TO SMART CONTRACTS AND CIOT

Smart contracts in conjunction with the Internet of Things is a revolution in the new generation of automating with enhanced security in connected networks. In this part of the chapter, the reader is introduced to the main concept of smart contracts and CIoT, their definition and key capabilities are discussed, with a focus on automation and security (Dhatterwal et al., 2024).

Definition of Smart Contracts Smart contracts are fully automated contracts with the underlining conditions coded in the source code of the contract. They directly implement and execute all the stipulated terms and conditions embedded into them without the assistance of others. First introduced by Nick Szabo in 1994, smart contracts are agreements embedded into blockchain, and the parties' compliance is completely transparent, immutable, and decentralised, hence highly reliable.

They basically aimed at minimizing the occurrences of fraud in digital agreements while at the same time providing efficiency in that there is no third-party validation needed. It is based on peer-to-peer systems so the code and the contracts included in the system are transparent and can be checked by the network members. This feature of decentralization is one of the features that increases the security and reliability of smart contracts (Buterin, 2014).

The Converged Internet of Things (CIoT) is a future evolution of IoT, which is a more enhanced design of different IoT systems and devices that are compatible with each other. This makes the interaction and data flow between various systems in the IoT domain well-coordinated, which leads to improvement of the general system's performance and convenience for users. CIoT utilises sophisticated technologies like AI, ML, and blockchain which makes the IoT system wiser and more effective.

CIoT systems are also noted for the interconnectivity of these devices and platforms to enable the exchange of information across the domains. It thereby allows for enhanced big data processing for decision making, new solutions for avenues like; Healthcare, manufacturing and smart cities (Gubbi et al., 2013).

Significance of Automation in CIoT Automation can be regarded as one of the key principles of CIoT, raising the performance of IoT systems. This is because, CIoT tackles most of the routine tasks and activities hence leading to minimal interference from human beings, efficiency is also enhanced as many activities are usually done by these intelligent systems. Smart contracts are also used in this automation process to carry out pre-set operations timelessly as and when such conditions are met without supervision.

Thus, CIoT in the industrial aspects can help in increasing production by automating the production line, better resource allocation and can also help in doing predictive maintenance and so can reduce the downtime and also the operational expenses. In the same way, smart home systems can be used for energy consumption control, security and even scheduling of various activities in a home resulting to benefits for the users (Atzori et al., 2010).

Significance of Security in CIoT Security plays an incredibly crucial role in CIoT because of the data that experiences the sojourn from the source to the destination. The number of connected devices is increasing drastically; with this comes the risk of cyber threats and hacking. Smart contracts have the capacity of increasing security in CIoT as it guarantees that prospective transactions and operations are completed in a secure, checked, and immutable style.

Smart contract security is gifted by the blockchain technology as all are executed on a decentralized platform with a record of account. This helps in 'locking' the data to minimize errors in data entry and prevent any changes because only the system admin has permission to do so (Kaswan et al., 2024). In CIoT, data privacy and security is a key component that play important role in CIoT in order to secure data for user to ensure their data are less vulnerable to hackers (Zhang & Wen, 2015).

How Smart Contracts Function As with other contracts, smart contracts basically operate through the execution of coded procedures upon triggers. These contracts are preserved on an unalterable blockchain and are therefore very transparent. Smart contracts work by the following process; when parties agree to engage in smart contract, what is agreed is encoded and deployed on a blockchain.

Smart contracts entail clauses that when a particular event takes place, say receipt of payment, envisaged actions are implemented mechanically. This could involve passing on of assets, data archiving or generation of notification. Smart contracts do not require third parties; thus, smart contracts drastically cut transaction costs and provide a better performance (Christidis & Devetsikiotis, 2016).

Smart Contracts and Their Application Smart contracts are supported by block-chain technology that forms their base. It is a distributed ledger technology where the transactions are performed on multiple computers and gives the results which are secure, transparent, and non-altering. Every transaction is recorded in a list in each block, and all these blocks are arranged in a sequential order forming what is called the blockchain (Kaswan et al., 2023).

The integration of Blockchain eliminates the possibility of ownership of the entire network hence reduces the risks of manipulation or fraudulent activities. That is why blockchain is an excellent environment for smart contracts as it is a decentralized and transparent concept that ensures the compliance of the contract terms with a set of norms due to their complete openness (Nakamoto, 2008).

Some of the characteristic of smart contracts the following are characters that make smart contracts suitable for CIoT application. Such features as automation, fixity, openness, and distributive control can be mentioned. Automation implies that conditions that were previously requiring manual intervention execute the contract on its own.

Inability to change smart contract is meant by immutability which implies that once a smart contract is posted to the blockchain, it cannot be changed or modified in anyway. This makes the terms of the contract to be precise and more reliable as all the terms are agreed upon by all the parties. It enables all the stakeholders to check on the agreed contract details and the extents to be delivered thus reducing on cases of corruption. Decentralization removes the middlemen, which directly helps in cutting expenses and the failure of some of the chains (Kosba et al., 2016).

Smart contracts application in CIoT Architectural framework for Smart Contracts in CIoT the inclusion of smart contracts into CIoT has to be supported by an architecture that is sound. This framework has to take into account the requirements that are commonly associate with the IoT systems, including versatility, compatibility, and real-time execution. A conventional framework combines IoT devices, edge computing nodes and the blockchain networks where smart contracts are likely to be performed seamlessly (Malik et al., 2023).

In this architecture, edge computing is instrumental in processing information around the vicinity of a device or the area where they are required in order to minimize latency and the amount of bandwidth needed. Smart contracts within the blockchain network enable secure and transparent execution and carry out the corresponding activities based on the conditions specified by IoT devices (Panarello et al., 2018).

Smart Contracts Implementation Strategies in CIoT Implementation of smart contracts in CIoT comes with some strategies to enable easy incorporation as well as perfect operational flow. Another way is the implementation of the so-called public-private blockchains. This enables secure and a scalable solution while leveraging on the two kinds of blockchains.

Another strategy is to use off-chain approaches to the computation of operations that do not need the security layers of the blockchain. This will also help reduce the amount of burden being placed on the blockchain and or network hence enhance efficiency. Also, a higher level of conforming through standard-based protocols and interfaces for IoT devices contributes to improved compatibility with other IoT platforms, thus improving the integration process (Xu et al., 2019).

Real-life examples show that smart contracts can be successfully applied in CIoT. For instance, in the supply chain management systems, the use of smart contracts has enabled tracking of items from production to delivery. It also makes the supply chain to be accountable in a way that minimizes fraud while at the same time increasing effectiveness.

As for now smart contracts have been used in heathcare system to ensure patient record confidentiality and in payment of bill. This not only increases the protection of the data but also reduces the time spent on administrative functions hence giving more time to the patients. These examples show that smart contracts are also useful and relatively universal in real-life CIoT applications (Casino, Dasaklis, & Patsakis, 2019).

ADP in CIoT Data processing is one of the primary advantages of using smart contracts in CIoT's setup. Smart contracts can help to gather, process and analyze the data from the IoT devices, and act according with the results of the analysis. It minimizes the involvement of human interference and speeds up the decision-making systems of a firm.

For example, in the context of smart city, information's collected by several sensors can be analysed in real time for controlling physical traffic, consumption of electrical energy, or security risks. Smart contracts mean that data is processed automatically increasing the activity and functionality of CIoT systems taking actions within as little time as possible (Makhdoom et al., 2019).

Automated CIoT transactions Smart contracts allow for fully automated transactions in CIoT, thus making IoT systems more independent and faster. Such transactions are self-executing when certain conditions with respect to them have been met and no confirmation or interference from a third party is needed. This ability also proves more fruitful in those situations where time can significantly influence the campaign (Bingu et al., 2024).

For instance, in the financial field, which involves IoT devices' payments and settlements, the use of smart contracts can eliminate the delay and exclusion of human error factors. In logistics, self-executing contracts form a mechanism for releasing the payment as and when the goods are delivered hence increasing accountability and transparency in the supply chain (Yuan & Wang, 2016).

Applicable efficiency through smart contracts; Smart contracts help in enhancing the workflow of CIoT by recounting numerous procedures. They can help to manage actions on one or more devices and systems carrying out tasks in the right order and at the right time. This helps in decreasing inefficiencies and hence it boosts the capacities of CIoT systems.

Inside industries, smart contracts can enable and oversee the operations flow, the processes as stock, quality check, and maintenance. In this way, through using smart contracts, the involved processes are automatized, and the production time is reduced to a minimum. Such optimization results in reduced cost and better operation performance as identified by Christidis & Devetsikiotis, 2016.

The problem of this research based on the CIoT assets explore, Secure Data Transmission in CIoT Security is the major problem of this research area since CIoT is major and capable of moving large number of sensitive data between the devices. Smart contracts increase the security of data transfer through the ability to encrypt and transfer data to and from specific authorized parties securely. The use of block chain ensures all the transactions are recorded on the block chain to avoid manipulations of the accounts.

This secure transfer is useful in scenarios like the healthcare system where the patient's data should remain secure against external interferences. Smart contracts allow only the authorized personnel to access and pass the data thus embracing the privacy and has features to address the GDPR and HIPAA. This improves reliability in CIoT systems as there is trust established between the system and users (Zhang & Wen, 2015).

Smart Contract-based Access Control Techniques in CIoT: Smart contracts enable developing efficient access control in CIoT to allow only those devices and specific users to enter particular data and perform particular actions who have permission to do so. All these mechanisms are operationalized through the blockchain that checks and logs attempts to access the system, and to make changes.

For instance, in a smart home scenario, the use of smart contracts will enable the management of access to controls of different gadgets and systems in a home only to users who have been permitted to perform certain operations such as switching on or off security cameras, regulation of temperature through smart thermostats among others. This also increases the level of security and privacy of smart homes and shields them from the probability of cyber-crimes and invasions (Buterin, 2014).

Threat Detection and Mitigation in CIoT Smart contracts assist in threat detection and mitigation in CIoT structures due to the identification of and reaction to suspicious activities. They are capable of producing warning signs, launch responsive actions, or quarantine the implicated devices in order to contain spreading of undesirable actions (Christidis & Devetsikiotis, 2016).

2. FOUNDATIONAL CONCEPTS OF SMART CONTRACTS

Smart contracts build their premise on the execution of contracts and related dealings accordingly to built-in policies, secured by the blockchain system. The following subsections look at working of smart contracts, basics of blockchain technology on which the smart contracts operate and the unique features that make Smart Contracts significant to the Converged Internet of Things (CIoT).

How do Smart Contracts Work? Smart contracts are self-executing programs that are written on a blockchain, which is intended to perform an action as soon as predefined criteria are fulfilled. Being coded in programming languages like Solidity (for Ethereum) they describe the set of relationships governing the interactions of the involved parties. These conditions regulate the contract and, after assessing the compliance with them, initiate the corresponding activities.

For example, in basic smart contract for crowdfunding where contributors fund a project with an aim of being reimbursed in the long-run or when the project is complete, the funds are held in a blockchain-based escrow and are automatically released to project creator as per the rules of the smart contract in cases where a predefined amount is not achieved by a certain date. The money which was collected for the funding of the specific activities is probably given back to the major contributors in case of failure. All these lead to efficiencies in blending together the trader's wishes, intermediaries are not required, and the deals are auto executed under certain conditions hence a high level of trust (Christidis & Devetsikiotis, 2016).

Blockchain Technology Fundamentals Blockchain technology is the underpinning of smart contracts – a digital contract that is self-executing and self-enforcing; it is distributed and records transactions.

Blockchain Technology Basics are: Blockchain is an integral part of smart contracts that provides an immutable and distributed record of the contract's transactions. In more detail, a blockchain refers to the chain of several blocks where each of them stores the list of several transactions. These blocks are confined in a chain also in such a way that on one data is entered, it cannot be edited or removed without affecting the other blocks in the chain.

This structure is sustained by node members, every of which has a copy of the chain record in the blockchain. As the transactions are to be added to the blockchain, they undergo a process called consensus, which could either be the PoW or the PoS depending on the specific cryptocurrency in use. Due to its transparency and modifiability [sic], the application of smart contracts on blockchain is suggested (Nakamoto, 2008).

Main Characteristics of Smart Contracts When compared with conventional and other types of electronic contracts, smart contracts bear certain critical characteristics. Some of the features that have been proposed for blockchain include: Automation, immutability, transparency, decentralisation.

- Automation: Smart contracts are self-executing as soon as certain pre-specified circumstances are met. This reduces the reliance on manpower which in turn decreases the possibility of a human error. Automation also enhances the efficiency of executing the various transactions hence improving reliability.
- Immutability: From the above discourse, it is apparent that a smart contract, once deployed in the blockchain is immutable. This helps to provide clear and definite terms of the contract and all parties are sure that the conditions cannot be altered after the signing of the contract.
- Transparency: Smart contracts are recorded on the public distributed ledger, which enables all the stakeholders to observe the conditions and results. This openness helps to build a long-term trustful relationship coupled with accountability and protectiveness of the contract's execution.
- Decentralization: Smart contracts run on decentralised block-chain platforms; it is not required to involve third party suppliers like the banks or legal persons. This decentralization cuts the overall cost of transaction, decreases the probability of fraud, and guarantees that the agreement will be implemented impartially a/or manipulatively.

All these features make smart contracts to be highly appropriate to be adopted in CIoT since automation of processes, trust and security are crucial. For instance, using smart contracts in supply chain the process of managing supply chain, especially payment for the goods can be achieved through the application of smart contracts in a safe and transparent manner at every stage, (Kosba et al., 2016).

3. INTEGRATION OF SMART CONTRACTS IN CIOT

Smart contracts have been proposed to operate in the CIoT environment and hence there is need to establish the appropriate architecture form, proper deployment models, and real-life applications that worked before. This section further analyzes the architectural support for smart contract in CIoT; discusses different deployment strategies; and presents real-life use cases of smart contracts.

Smart Contract Infrastructure in CIoT the architecture of smart contract in CIoT is therefore layered in numerous a reas with each being in charge of certain functionality. Essentially, in the layer of blockchain, there is the provision of a decentralized data structure and the smart contract platform. This layer provides security, means to make definite changes difficult and the capability to make all transactions transparent.

The layer just above the blockchain layer is the communication layer, which handles movement of data between IoT apparatus and the blockchain. This layer frequently utilizes minimal overhead protocols like MQTT or CoAP due to the IoT devices' characteristics. application layer is directly placed above it where all the transactions between the smart IOT devices are governed by smart contracts at this stage. The following layer is in charge of management of the device and data as well as interaction with the users. For example, in smart home environment smart contracts may manage lighting, heating and security systems according to specified regulation and data from sensors (Makhdoom et al., 2019).

Deployment Strategies Smart contracts have to be deployed in CIoT in order to maximize their efficiency and suitability for the targeted applications. One of the common methods is a mixed working approach where some data and contracts are recorded on the blockchain while others are outside. This makes the load of the actual Blockchain network lighter and increases its efficiency.

Latency Calculation

$$L = L_{sc} + L_{tx} + L_{net}$$

where:

- L_{sc} is the latency due to smart contract execution,
- L_{tx} is the latency due to blockchain transaction processing
- L_{net} is the latency due to network communication.

Example:
Assume $L_{sc} = 50$ ms, $L_{tx} = 150$ ms, and $L_{net} = 100$ ms

$$L = 50 + 150 + 100 = 300ms$$

$$T = \frac{N}{L}$$

where:
·N is the number of transactions,

· Lis the total latency.

Example:
Assume the system processes 200 transactions in 300 ms.

$$T = \frac{200}{0.2} = 666.67 \text{ transactions/second}$$

Objective Function

$$\min C = \sum_{i=1}^{n} c_i x_i$$

subject to:

$$\sum_{i=1}^{n} r_i x_i \geq R$$

where:

·c_i is the cost of resource i,
·x_i is the allocation of resource i,
•r_i is the performance metric of resource i,
·R is the required performance.

Example:

Suppose we have two resources with costs $c_1 = 5$ and $c_2 = 10$, performance metrics $r_1 = 3$ and
$r_2 = 7$, and a required performance $R = 21$.
Objective Function:

$$\min C = 5x_1 + 10x_2$$

Subject to:

$$3x_1 + 7x_2 \geq 21$$

Energy Consumption Optimization

$$\min E = \sum_{i=1}^{n} P_i t_i$$

where:

- P_i is the power usage of device i,
- t_i is the time device i is active.

Example:
Assume three devices with power usage $P_1 = 100\,\text{W}, P_2 = 150\,\text{W}, \text{and } P_3 = 200$ W, and active

times $t_1 = 2$ hours, $t_2 = 3$ hours, and $t_3 = 1$ hour.

$$E = 100 \cdot 2 + 150 \cdot 3 + 200 \cdot 1 = 200 + 450 + 200 = 850\text{Wh}$$

Another approach is the utilisation of side chains or private blockchains in certain IoT processes. This approach gives more control over the network and can be made more secure and performant to the needs. Sidechains can also address high transaction speed and reduced costs than the public blockchains (Panarello et al., 2018).

Another identified strategy is the edge computing, where data processing as well as contract execution takes place nearer to the IoT devices. This automatically helps to cut down latency, as well as bandwidth, making CIoT systems' performance more efficient. Smart contracts at the Edge allow the devices to effectively respond to the local event without consulting a server.

- Examples of Smart Contracts in CIoT Subsequently, there are numerous examples depicting the development and applicability of smart contracts in CIoT which reveals the further growth of automation and security in industries.
- Smart Homes: Thus, in smart home systems smart contracts can perform tasks of energy consumption management, security, and management. For instance, a smart contract could manage thermostats to make effective decisions on heating and cooling the house depending on people's presence, to decrease energy bill. Besides, smart contracts can operate the restrictions on entry to the home, so only appropriate people can access the home (Casino et al., 2019).
- Industrial IoT (IIoT): Smart contracts were most prominent in the modern industrial applications where normal supply chain management, maintenance of stationed equipment's and quality check processes are automated. One of

the examples is smart contracts in a manufacturing plant that would track the production as well as deliveries of goods. The contract commitments also maintained the payment to suppliers on time and a real time information on the available stock thus doing away with delay in stock replenishment (Christidis & Devetsikiotis, 2016).

- Healthcare IoT: It is highly beneficial to incorporate smart contracts in the context of health care IoT since patient care can be improved, and data security can be increased. For instance, healthcare provider can use smart contracts in managing patient records, where only certain individuals have access to the information. Finally, smart contracts may help with the management of medications and patients' health indicators along with alerting if discrepancies are found are present. This enhances services delivery to the patients while at the same time cutting the load on the personnel in the health facility (Makhdoom et al., 2019).

- Supply Chain and Logistics: Regarding visibility in the supply chain, this system guarantees that each participant in the chain has synchronized and most current information. This was made apparent in a case study conducted among firms in the food industry on the application of smart contracts, whereby, for instance, the county of origin, transportation, and storage, among other aspects, was followed through. The contracts complied with the safety requirements while offering the consumers credible facts about their meals' sources and quality (Panarello et al., 2018).

4. ENHANCING AUTOMATION IN CIOT WITH SMART CONTRACTS

As for Smart Contracts, the Converged Internet of Thing (CIoT) applies them in so many areas and mainly in automation of processes and transactions. This section ascertains how CIoT is enriched through smart contract features such as Automatic Data Processing, Self-executing IoT transactions, and Work flow improvement.

Corresponding Processing in CIoT systems, large and complex quantities of data are produced by the integrated devices. The output that results from carrying out these activities is often voluminous and it becomes almost impossible and very susceptible to a lot of errors to manually manage and process this data. The use of smart contracts gives a notion that, data will be processed without the interference of human beings.

For instance, in the smart city context, and IT management system of the city like traffic sensor data, weather station data, and public transport data can be analyzed by smart contract and get optimal solution for traffic congestions and public safety. The contracts can decide on operational changes by interpreting real time information like changing the traffic light signals or redirecting-moving-vehicles as per current situation (Xu et al., 2020). This automation adds value to the operation of cities and at the same time relieves the burden of city management personnel.

Autonomous IoT Trades IoT smart contracts create IoT transactions that can execute autonomously to implement the terms of an agreement without the need for a third party. These are actions that are coded in the contracts to be performed when certain events of the transactions occur.

For example, in a supply chain context, smart contract can cover all the aspects of supply chain from procurement. In some capacity contracts can order products with a supplier when an inventory sensor sends a message that it is low. After delivery, it can confirm that the shipment has arrived through Internet of things sensors and can release payment to the supplier. This minimizes the time taken in stock replenishment and transaction processing, while at the same time cutting on administrative expenses (Kumar et al., 2020).

Process Automation Another important function of smart contracts that is tightly connected with CIoT is process automation Smart contracts guarantee that all actions are correctly performed and in the correct sequence, it makes the process more efficient. Smart contracts allow for saving human resources because many operations consume time and can be executed by the smart contracts automatically.

Another harm of industrial IoT (IIoT) is enabled by artificial intelligence, in which smart contracts can create schedules for the maintenance of the machinery. It also allows usage and wear of the equipment to be measured by the use of some form of sensors that may indicate that certain tasks of maintenance have to be done when certain predetermined conditions are reached. It is then possible for the smart contract to book the maintenance activities; order parts required and even update the maintenance journal. It removes the chances of equipment failure, cuts on the time the equipment is not in use and increases the durability of machinery (Christidis, & Devetsikiotis, 2016).

Figure 1.

Algorithm 1 Enhancing Automation in CIoT with Smart Contracts

1: **Input:** IoT device data streams, smart contract conditions
2: **Output:** Automated actions and optimized workflows
3: **Procedure:**
4: Initialize blockchain and deploy smart contracts
5: **for** each IoT device i in the CIoT network **do**
6:     Collect data D_i from device i
7:     **Automated Data Processing:**
8:     **if** D_i meets predefined conditions in smart contract **then**
9:         Execute corresponding smart contract actions
10:     **end if**
11: **end for**
12: **Self-Executing IoT Transactions:**
13: **for** each transaction t in the CIoT network **do**
14:     Verify transaction t using blockchain consensus
15:     **if** transaction t is valid **then**
16:         Update the state of the smart contract
17:         Execute self-executing transaction
18:     **end if**
19: **end for**
20: **Workflow Optimization:**
21: **for** each workflow w in the CIoT system **do**
22:     Monitor workflow performance metrics
23:     Analyze workflow data using AI algorithms
24:     **if** optimization criteria are met **then**
25:         Modify smart contract conditions to improve workflow efficiency
26:     **end if**
27: **end for**
28: **End Procedure**

Other uses of CIoT include smart agriculture is another example where smart contracts can facilitate and manage watering, application of fertilizers and monitoring of crops among others. Through the automation of these processes relying on data from the sensors in the soil and weather conditions, smart contracts guarantee the best environmental conditions to the crops, thus resulting to high yields and minimal resource wastage (Rabah, 2017).

5. SECURITY ENHANCEMENTS THROUGH SMART CONTRACTS

The integration of smart contracts into the Converged Internet of Things (CIoT) greatly improves its security with respect to improved data authenticity and identifications, also in the control of input data and protected against deadly attacks. This section expands on raising the secure data transfer and access control steps that smart contracts employ as well as increasing the threat identification and prevention capabilities in CIoT systems.

Privacy and Security Smart contracts highly ensure that privacy and security are met in CIoT systems through cryptographic methods and peer-to-peer network. Now, the communication link interconnecting IoT devices and the block chain network includes encrypted data to support security and data integrity. This encryption helps in avoiding access and manipulation by unauthorized people during transit of data.

For example, data communicated by patient from the wearable gadgets to the healthcare management can be encrypted using asymmetric encryption algorithms. Smart contracts make a check as to what data is delivered and who can decrypt the information on the provided data. This process not only safeguards individuals' health data but also enhances organizations' conformity with specific legal statutes, for instance, the HIPAA (Health Insurance Portability and Accountability Act) (Jin et al., 2019). Also, because blocks are fixed size, data within the blockchain is very secure as records cannot be changed once a data is recorded and this gives a record of all data transactions.

Access Control Mechanisms Smart contracts improve the access control mechanisms used in the CIoT since they determine and control access rights as per the laid rules. These mechanisms ensure that only assigned devices and users have an interface with the network and resources of the latter. Smart contracts also deal with permissions and credential verification when capturing users' approval to IoT devices.

For example, in an environment of a smart home, smart contracts can regulate the access to the home automation equipment. For instance, a smart contract can be coded to enable onl y authenticated appliances to regulate the temperature settings, lighting or security cameras among others. It can also perform the user access function where the homeowners can grant or deny access remotely from a security interface (Saberi et al., 2020). Through this method of access control, an increased security mechanism for the IoT environment is established through decentralization.

Threat Detection and Mitigation Smart contracts are widely used to improve threat detection and mitigation in CIoT systems. These can be set to actively scan the network and look for activity patterns that suggest that there has been an intrusion on the network. Smart contract can provide response measures of a predefined nature once a potential threat is identified.

For example, in an IIoT setting, smart contracts can automatically study a set of data gathered by sensors and equipment and identify traces of an upcoming cyber-attack or equipment malfunction. In case a smart contract becomes aware of some sort of malicious activity, it comes with measures where a device is quarantined, systems shut down, or security staff informed. Thus, the approach to threat identification presented in this paper proves helpful in preventing losses and maintaining the stability of systems (Wang et al., 2019). Furthermore, the smart contracts implemented can also be coded to read new threats and self-adjust security measures subsequently so that CIoT systems would be protected from new forms of cyber threats.

Symmetric encryption uses the same key for both encryption and decryption
· Encryption:$C = E(K, P)$
• Decryption:$P = D(K, C)$
Where:

· P is the plaintext
· C is the ciphertext
· K is the symmetric key
· E is the encryption function
· D is the decryption function

Example:
Using the Advanced Encryption Standard (AES):

• Plaintext (P):"Hello, CloT!"
• Symmetric Key (K):"mysecurekey1234" (128-bit key for simplicity)

Encryption:

1. Convert plaintext to binary or hex.
2. Apply AES encryption using key K.

Let's use a simplified hex representation for illustration:

• **Plaintext in hex:** 48656c6c6f2c2043496f5421
• **Key in hex:** 6d797365637572656b6579313233334

Ciphertext (C): After AES encryption, the ciphertext might look like: 3ad77bb-40d7a3660a89ecaf32466ef97.

Decryption:

1. Apply AES decryption using key K.
2. Convert the resulting binary or hex back to plaintext.

Decrypted Plaintext (P): "Hello, CIoT!"
Access Control Mechanisms

Mathematial Model for RAC:
1. User Assignment: $U = \{u_1, u_2, \ldots, u_n\}$
2. Role Assignment: $R = \{r_1, r_2, \ldots, r_m\}$
3. Permissions: $P = \{p_1, p_2, \ldots, p_k\}$
- User-Role Assignment Function: $UA: U \to R$
- Role-Permission Assignment Function: $PA: R \to P$

Where:
- U is the set of users
- R is the set of proles
- P is the set of permissions

Threat Detection and Mitigation

Mathematical Model for Anomaly Detection

Example:
- Users: $U = \{Alice, Bob\}$
- Data Points: $D = \{d_1, \ldots, d_n\}$ Roles: $R = \{Admin, User\}$
- Mean: $\mu = \frac{1}{n} \sum_{i=1}^{n} d_i$ Permissions: $P = \{Reud, Write, Execute\}$
- Standard Deviation: $\sigma = \sqrt{\frac{1}{n} \sum_{i=1}^{n} (d_i - \mu)^2}$

Anomaly Detection Criterion:

· A data point d is considered an anomaly
if $d \notin [\mu - k\sigma, \mu + k\sigma]$, where k is a threshold constant.

Example:

Consider loT sensor data on temperature readings:

- Data Points (°C): $D = \{22, 23, 22, 24, 22, 30, 22, 23, 21, 22\}$

· Mean(μ): $\mu = 23.1$
· Standard Deviation (σ): $\sigma = 2.4$
For $k = 2$:

- Threshold Range: $[\mu - 2\sigma, \mu + 2\sigma]$

· Range:[18.3,27.9]

6. PRACTICAL APPLICATIONS AND USE CASES

Smart contracts for CIoT have various applications in the modern industry that are aimed at increasing the automation degree and security level. Subsection 4 will draw these fields of smart home and building, IIoT, healthcare IoT, and supply chain and logistics to show how smart contracts benefit such industries.

Smart homes & Buildings In smart homes as well as in smart buildings, smart contracts are applied to and enable & govern numerous functions, starting with the management of energy and moving on to controlling access rights. Such contracts can be used to deploy and perform a large spectrum of tasks based on a finite set of rules, enhancing the convenience of the utilizing users.

For instance, the terms of a smart contract can control lighting and HVAC to abide by prescribed energy use data captured from sensors. If the sensors found out that a room has no occupants, then the smart contract can adjust the light to off and decrease the heating or cooling system for energy efficiency's sake. Also, smart contracts can handle the security of the building in that only the right people will be allowed access to certain parts of the building. It increases safety and improves efficiency with the consumption of resources making living and working spaces safer and more efficient (Zhao et al., 2019).

Industrial IoT (IIoT) In the industrial segment, smart contracts automate the processes and increase the safety of the production and supply chain. IIoT systems are fuelled by the possibility of transaction automation and the provision of secure data exchange between equipment's and systems.

Maintenance schedules for industrial equipment can be automated by smart contracts, with the help of IoT sensors for usage and wear of the equipment. During routine checks if maintenance is due the Smart Contract is capable of scheduling a service and ordering replacement parts while at the same time updating the maintenance log. I this minimizes on the time that equipment is off and the overall operational time of the machines is enhanced (Tama et al., 2017). Similarly in production it is possible for smart contracts to be developed in a way that they will trigger the ordering of more raw materials once the stock reaches a certain level so that production lines do not dry up but also preliminary stocking does not take place.

E-healthcare for easier and faster delivery of care, the healthcare IoT implements the smart contracts for patient's care, administrative duties, and security of data. The automation of simple processes can be achieved through smart contracts and security of patients' data.

For instance, smart contracts can take responsibility for appointment booking in telemedicine, whereas provider's records shall be updated and shared among relevant practitioners with proper encryption. They also order prescription refills since the system checks patient data and then order refills to the pharmacy from the clients. This automation cuts the workload of administrative processes, increases the quality of the services offered to the patients as well as the security of their records (Ahram et al., 2017). Also, they can help with monitoring patients from a distance, as the information gathered by the Wearables will be sent and received only by doctors.

Supply Chain and Logistics Smart contracts' functions help supply chain and logistics operations by offering significant transparency and efficiency. These contracts can integrate a number of the supply chains' functions ranging from order fulfilment to delivery.

Thus, in a most usual supply chain process, smart contracts are capable of handling the procurement process. Thus, when an order is placed, the smart contract can achieve availability of products, payment, as well as the shipment schedule. During the delivery process, tracking devices connected to the IoT can give real-time information and for deliveries, payments can be released through the smart contract once they acknowledge delivery. This automation decreases the time taken to complete processes and also minimizes on the occurrence of mistakes while also improving on the aspect of work visibility (Dutra et al., 2018). In addition, through the adoption of smart contracts, inventory can also be well managed, whereby the quantity of goods is checked, and the supply restocked depending on actual information.

7. CHALLENGES AND LIMITATIONS

First of all, the main subject of the article, smart contracts, if applied to CIoT has its benefits and at the same time, has its drawbacks and constraints which should be discussed. Under this section, the information concerning the important aspects of scalability, interoperability, and legal and regulatory concerns is described.

Of all these, a key issue that assets the integration of smart contracts in CIoT systems is scalability. Peculiarities drawn from the need for the higher number of connected devices and larger data volumes, are the high load in the blockchain infrastructure of a smart contract network. Bitcoin and Ethereum inherent design, for example, impose bottlenecks on the number of transactions per second and latency essential for CIoT applications.

For instance, the Ethereum network can handle around 15 transactions per second, which cannot suffice for the full-blown CIoT requirements with higher transactions per second. To solve this problem some of the solutions that are being implemented include Layer 2 scaling solutions, Sharding, and Consensus Algorithms like Proof of Stake (PoS). However, these solutions are also not perfected yet and may not be as popular or used commonly for quite a while. Also, off-chain solutions and side chains are being discussed as the technologies that could help to decrease the issue of the blockchain scalability by moving many transactions out of the main body of the chain.

One of the critical barriers is related to Interoperability in case of integration of smart contracts with CIoT. Consequently, we have a world of IoT devices and platforms and interfaces with a high degree of heterogeneity for which communication and exchange of data has to be harmonized. For CIoT solutions it is crucial that smart contracts can run across the different IoT architectures and networks.

For example, a smart contract that oversees a supply chain process must communicate with different IoT devices these include RFID tags as well as sensors and tracking systems and these implements different protocols and standards. In the case of interoperability, it is necessary to set standards and come up with middleware that can address two or more technologies. Things like the IEEE P2413 standard for IoT architecture as well as common data formats as well as APIs are on the right track, yet broad adoption as well as real world deployments remain big issues.

There are legal and regulatory factors that act as major barriers to the implementation of smart contracts in CIoT. Due to the inherent decentralized and self-executing features of smart contracts, there are legal issues related to the nature of these contracts and their ability to meet the legal requirements and policies in force. Governments and governing bodies of the world are not yet sure of how to provide a favorable legal framework to blockchain kind of technology and smart contracts.

However, smart contracts as legal executable contracts pose one major issue, that is the legal acceptance of smart contracts. The existing legal systems do not seem to provide an appropriate definition of automated, self-executing contracts, resulting in the legal system's inability to articulate specific jurisdictions on their enforceability. Furthermore, there are questions on data protection, security, and international data transfers that create difficulties for the regulation. For instance, the GDPR established in the European Union puts stringent conditions of data processing and transfer and can influence the design and functioning of CIoT systems with smart contracts.

Moreover, multiple smart contract risks include the possibility to embody unlawful techniques like money laundering and fraud, which leads to the necessity of higher regulatory attention. Companies, governments and regulatory authorities have embarked on efforts to formulate policies that comply with legal requirements on one hand while promoting innovation and value addition for consumers' safety on the other hand. Still, the process of attaining consistency in the required regulations across nations is quite difficult mainly due to variations in national policies and their lawful implications.

8. FUTURE TRENDS AND INNOVATIONS

The role of smart contracts in the context of the Converged Internet of Things (CIoT) is going to improve in the near future mainly because of the improvements of the technologies and solutions. This section looks at how AI is being incorporated with smart contracts, the developments of blockchain solutions, and the decentralization of IoT networks as features that define the future of CIoT.

The integration of AI with smart contracts is deemed to transform the CIoT systems where they can intelligently impart flexibility, and decision-making ability to the systems. Information obtained by IoT devices can be processed with the help of AI algorithms which means that a smart contract will be able to operate more diverse concrete actions in the context of a definite situation.

For example, concerning industrial equipment sensors and their history, AI can study patterns to identify that maintenance will soon be needed and use smart contracts to automate the process. For instance, machine learning models can suggest when to turn devices on/off, and to regulate heat and lightings in the smart homes in order to save energy from the user's behavior patterns and surrounding environment (Kshetri, 2018). AI and smart contracts work together in improving security; with aspects such as the detection of possible threats and intrusions real-time, and improving the security of CIoT networks.

Blockchain technology is still developing and remains to bring new features and opportunities in improving the efficiency and width of the smart contracts to CIoT. More recent innovations include Consensus algorithms like the Proof of Stake (PoS) and Proof of Authority (PoA) being implementated which offer better energy efficiency than the conventional Proof of Work (PoW) algorithms and offer better transaction rates.

Moreover, new solutions like sharding, layer-2 scaling, and sidechains are solving problems of scalability with respect to blockchain solutions. These technologies allow the transaction volumes to be processed concurrently and relieve the main blockchain of potential overload, at the same time as not compromising on the ability to ensure the safety and decentralization of transactions. With these advancements coupled with the IoT networks, there will be efficient and secure means through which data across the distributed devices will be shared hence opening up new deep intelligent for superior and scalable CIoT systems.

Thus, the future of CIoT is to be associated with decentralized IoT environments which do not require centralized control points. The decentralized IoT differs from the centralized concept in that they use a blockchain approach to develop a network of devices that transact and communicate on their own, thus are more secure, private, and reliable.

It makes these networks ease the communication between IoT things, thus minimizing the delay and enhancing the flow of information. Third, decentralized IoT networks enable the development of the operation of various self-managed and self-organized systems in which smart contracts regulate agreements and settlements, refusing any intermediaries. This decentralization later leads to the improvement of data accuracy, decrease of operational expenses and known scalability and flexibility of IoT systems. The overall conclusion is that the next several years will see the development of protocol standards and the advancement of frameworks that will allow the decentralized IoT networks to function at full capacity across those platforms and devices.

CONCLUSION

Thus, the inclusion of smart contracts as a feature of CIoT can be regarded as a tangible progress in the sphere of both automation and enhanced security. Stating that this chapter begins by clarifying what smart contracts are and presenting an overview of CIoT, it is essential to note down that both of these technologies are foundational for the modern interconnected systems. We then went further to explain more on the basic ideas of smart contracts and how they work, the importance of blockchain on smart contracts especially on issues to do with transparency, instability and self-executing of the contracts. Therefore, it becomes evident that smart contract's application in CIoT requires a good architecture support and proper planning to carry out. Thus, we showed the benefits of integration, as well as examples of the integration of cases in practice, especially in terms of improving automation. Four crucial changes resulting from smart contracts were stated as; The ability to automate the data processing, Self-executing IoT transactions, Workflow management optimization. Smart contracts' technological enhancement of security was also analysed in terms of ensuring secure and efficient data communication protocols, apt access control measures, and intelligent threat prevention and response methods. These security features are pertinent in containing insecure IoT details as well as dependability of network-connected devices. In addition to that, the live demos depicted the functionality and applicability of smart contract in industries such as homes, IIoT, healthcare and logistics. These examine cases also again stressed the many opportunities of smart contract in generalizing a wide range of contexts for optimising functionality and strengthening security. However, several issues like scalability, interoperability issues, and legal and regulatory concerns were noted as major factors that have to be specifically considered. As for the further prospects, it is expected that AI will become compatible with smart contracts, continue the development of blockchain technologies, and possible creation of the decentralized

Internet of Things networks. All these innovations seek to improve the capacity of smart contracts in CIoT and the extent of their use in achieving more robust, effective and secure IoT systems.

REFERENCES

Ahram, T., Sargolzaei, A., Sargolzaei, S., Daniels, J., & Amaba, B. (2017). Blockchain technology innovations. *IEEE Technology & Engineering Management Conference (TEMSCON)*, 137-141.

Atzori, L., Iera, A., & Morabito, G. (2010). The Internet of Things: A survey. *Computer Networks*, 54(15), 2787–2805. DOI: 10.1016/j.comnet.2010.05.010

Bingu, R., Adinarayana, S., Dhatterwal, J. S., Kavitha, S., Patnala, E., & Sangaraju, H. R. (2024). Performance comparison analysis of classification methodologies for effective detection of intrusions. *Computers & Security*, 143, 103893. DOI: 10.1016/j.cose.2024.103893

Buterin, V. (2014). A next-generation smart contract and decentralized application platform. *Ethereum White Paper*.

Casino, F., Dasaklis, T. K., & Patsakis, C. (2019). A systematic literature review of blockchain-based applications: Current status, classification, and open issues. *Telematics and Informatics*, 36, 55–81. DOI: 10.1016/j.tele.2018.11.006

Christidis, K., & Devetsikiotis, M. (2016). Blockchains and smart contracts for the internet of things. *IEEE Access : Practical Innovations, Open Solutions*, 4, 2292–2303. DOI: 10.1109/ACCESS.2016.2566339

Dhatterwal, J. S., Kaswan, K. S., & Johri, P. (2024). IoT Sensor Communication Using Wireless Technology. In *Wireless Communication Technologies* (pp. 66–81). CRC Press. DOI: 10.1201/9781003389231-4

Dutra, A. C., Tavares, J. M. R. S., & Silva, L. F. (2018). A blockchain-based approach for supply chain traceability in the automotive industry. *2018 International Joint Conference on Neural Networks (IJCNN)*, 1-8.

Gubbi, J., Buyya, R., Marusic, S., & Palaniswami, M. (2013). Internet of Things (IoT): A vision, architectural elements, and future directions. *Future Generation Computer Systems*, 29(7), 1645–1660. DOI: 10.1016/j.future.2013.01.010

Jin, X., Zhang, Q., & Zhang, J. (2019). Secure data sharing in healthcare IoT using blockchain technology. *IEEE Access : Practical Innovations, Open Solutions*, 7, 170128–170139.

Kaswan, K. S., Dhatterwal, J. S., Kumar, N., Balusamy, B., & Gangadevi, E. (2024). Cyborg Intelligence for Bioprinting in Computational Design and Analysis of Medical Application. *Computational Intelligence in Bioprinting*, 211-237.

Kaswan, K. S., Malik, K., Dhatterwal, J. S., Naruka, M. S., & Govardhan, D. (2023, December). Deepfakes: A Review on Technologies, Applications and Strategies. In *2023 International Conference on Power Energy, Environment & Intelligent Control (PEEIC)* (pp. 292-297). IEEE. DOI: 10.1109/PEEIC59336.2023.10450604

Kosba, A., Miller, A., Shi, E., Wen, Z., & Papamanthou, C. (2016). Hawk: The blockchain model of cryptography and privacy-preserving smart contracts. *In 2016 IEEE Symposium on Security and Privacy (SP)* (pp. 839-858). IEEE. DOI: 10.1109/SP.2016.55

Kumar, R., Tripathi, R., & Joshi, S. (2020). Blockchain-based architecture for secure and efficient IoT supply chain management. *Sensors (Basel)*, 20(17), 5129. PMID: 32825335

Makhdoom, I., Abolhasan, M., Abbas, H., & Ni, W. (2019). Blockchain's adoption in IoT: The challenges, and a way forward. *Journal of Network and Computer Applications*, 125, 251–279. DOI: 10.1016/j.jnca.2018.10.019

Malik, K., Dhatterwal, J. S., Kaswan, K. S., Gupta, M., & Thakur, J. (2023, December). Intelligent Approach Integrating Multiagent Systems and Case-Based Reasoning in Brain-Computer Interface. In *2023 International Conference on Power Energy, Environment & Intelligent Control (PEEIC)* (pp. 1632-1636). IEEE. DOI: 10.1109/PEEIC59336.2023.10450496

Nakamoto, S. (2008). Bitcoin: A peer-to-peer electronic cash system. *Bitcoin White Paper*.

Panarello, A., Tapas, N., Merlino, G., Longo, F., & Puliafito, A. (2018). Blockchain and IoT integration: A systematic survey. *Sensors (Basel)*, 18(8), 2575. DOI: 10.3390/s18082575 PMID: 30082633

Rabah, K. (2017). Convergence of AI, IoT, big data, blockchain, and robotics. *The 8th International Conference on Information Technology*, 157-163.

Saberi, A., Dastjerdi, A. V., & Buyya, R. (2020). A blockchain-based access control model for the internet of things. *Future Generation Computer Systems*, 108, 664–675.

Tama, B. A., Kweka, B. J., Park, Y., & Rhee, K. H. (2017). A critical review of blockchain and its current applications. *International Conference on Electrical Engineering and Computer Science (ICECOS)*, 109-113. DOI: 10.1109/ICECOS.2017.8167115

Wang, Z., Zhang, X., Liu, Z., & Zhao, Y. (2019). A blockchain-based security framework for the Internet of Things. *IEEE Internet of Things Journal*, 6(5), 8081–8090.

Xu, L., Chen, L., & Gao, Z. (2020). Smart contract-based access control for the internet of things. *IEEE Internet of Things Journal*, 7(3), 1902–1912.

Xu, X., Pautasso, C., Zhu, L., Gramoli, V., Ponomarev, A., Tran, A. B., & Chen, S. (2019). The blockchain as a software connector. *In 2016 13th Working IEEE/IFIP Conference on Software Architecture (WICSA)* (pp. 182-191). IEEE.

Yuan, Y., & Wang, F.-Y. (2016). Blockchain: The state of the art and future trends. *Acta Automatica Sinica*, 42(4), 481–494.

Zhang, Y., & Wen, J. (2015). The IoT electric business model: Using blockchain technology for the internet of things. *Peer-to-Peer Networking and Applications*, 10(4), 983–994. DOI: 10.1007/s12083-016-0456-1

Zhao, F., Wu, Z., Xu, W., & Jin, Y. (2019). Application of blockchain technology in smart home systems. *IEEE International Conference on Consumer Electronics (ICCE)*, 1-4.

Chapter 12
Vehicle to Infrastructure Routing Protocols:
AI and Finance Perspectives

Hothefa Shaker
Modern College of Business and Science, Oman

Zeyad T. Sharef
https://orcid.org/0000-0003-0571-5788
Ninevah University, Iraq

Seemaa Abbas
Ninevah University, Iraq

Shahnawaz Khan
Bahrain Polytechnic, Bahrain

ABSTRACT

Vehicular Ad-hoc Network (VANET) is a unique wireless Mobile Ad-Hoc Network (MANET) with high node mobility and fast topology changes. VANETs have developed into an exciting research and application region, especially in the presence of Artificial Intelligence. This kind of technology has a significant impact on Finance. Progressively, vehicles are being furnished with inserted sensors, preparation, and wireless communication capabilities. This vehicle development is accelerating in the world of technology, especially in providing more relaxation and comfort to change the established concept of driving exhaustion. These technologies range from passenger to vehicle and emergency communications, and the future carries many technologies that enhance comfort and relaxation in the vehicle. In addition, Intelligent Transportation Systems (ITS) appear to have a highly dynamic and intermittently connected topology. This paper will present the challenges and perspectives

DOI: 10.4018/979-8-3693-2157-7.ch012

of VANETs and their relation to AI and Finance, focusing on their communication and application challenges. There is a detailed discussion of the different categories of VANET applications and the vehicle-to-infrastructure protocol stack. However, it is considered a particular case of smart cities in V2I.

1. INTRODUCTION

Recently, communication has become necessary in the information society. Everyone can get information anywhere quickly, even in navigation environments, using different devices and networking techniques. From this vision, vehicles are another place where users spend long periods, especially in the context of increasing vehicle and traffic congestion (Mounce & Nelson, 2019). Indeed, distinctive vehicle and network applications can bring added value to the comfort of drivers and passengers, including safety applications, driving efficiency while moving vehicles, traffic fluency and environmental conservation (Pallavi Agarwal, 2017). Therefore, these networks are characterised by solid dynamics, high-dynamic vehicles and specific topology patterns. These characteristics are affecting the performance and feasibility of vehicle applications. Nowadays, the proper operation of vehicular applications remains a significant challenge related to routing protocols in the environmental infrastructure of vehiculars (H. Peng et al., 2018). VANETs are a network that connects directly to the vehicles through a direct connection and does not need equipment for routing and coordination between vehicles, which are utilized to give interchanges Vehicle to Vehicle (V2V) or Vehicle to Infrastructure (V2I). Moreover, a leading component of Intelligent Transportation Systems (ITS) includes radio-controlled vehicles moving towards centres as mobile nodes, and the foundation is moving towards settled centres (Awang et al., 2017). Vehicle-to-infrastructure (V2I) is a protocol for communication that enables vehicles to share data between vehicles and the environmental infrastructures (Liang et al., 2015). At the same time, there are similarities to other specially VANETs, for example, short-range radio broadcasting, self-association, self-management, and low data transfer capability (Domingos et al., 2016). They are associated with one another through wireless networks with predictable portability, quick evolving topology, high computational capacity and variable network thickness. Infrastructure to-vehicle (I2V), Vehicle to Infrastructure (V2I), and Vehicle to Vehicle (V2V) frameworks are empowered by VANETs. Vehicle to Infrastructure (V2I) is a wireless trade of security and operational information among vehicles and roadway infrastructure, expected to keep vehicles away from engine vehicle collisions significantly. Whenever at least two vehicles are in radio correspondence, it results in programmed association and establishment of an ad hoc network, which empowers the sharing of position, speed, and heading information (Patel, 2016).

Recent developments in mobile communications provide ad hoc networks (VANETs) for the deployment of vehicular networks in highways and urban and rural environments, which supports many applications with different quality of service requirements [78]. The objective of a VANET architecture is to permit communication among nearby vehicles and vehicles(Lai et al., 2019). Roadside construction equipment can be categorized into three levels, as shown in Figure 1.

Figure 1. VANET Architectures

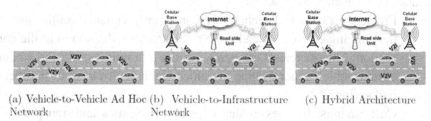

(a) Vehicle-to-Vehicle Ad Hoc Network   (b) Vehicle-to-Infrastructure Network   (c) Hybrid Architecture

i.   Vehicle-to-Vehicle Communication (V2V): a system designed to allow direct vehicular communication without relying on infrastructure support between vehicles to facilitate warnings and can be mainly employed for safety, security, and dissemination applications to drivers concerning impending crashes(Harding et al., 2014).

ii.   Vehicle-to-Infrastructure Communication (V2I): vehicles can communicate with the roadside infrastructure to collaborate and exchange information and data-gathering applications to ensure the safety and comfort of drivers and passengers (Challenges, 2019).

iii. Infrastructure-to Infrastructure (I2I): This kind is combines between both Vehicle-to-Vehicle (V2V) and Vehicle-to- Infrastructure (V2I). In this scenario, the vehicle can communicate with the infrastructure on the side of the road, either in a single-hop or multi-hop pattern, depending on the distance, for example, if it can or can not have direct access to the unit on the side of the road. It can communicate over long distances to the Internet or far away cars (Alves Junior & Wille, 2018).

2. IMPACT OF V2I COMMUNICATIONS ON FINANCE

The Vehicle to Infrastructure (V2I) Routing Protocol is a part of the larger Vehicle-to-Everything (V2X) communication framework. It allows automobiles to communicate with road infrastructure, including traffic lights, road signs, and toll booths. The objective of V2I is to optimize traffic flow, ensure safety, and alleviate congestion through the real-time interchange of data between vehicles and infrastructure (Terry et al, 2019). The following are the main points that show the impact of V2I Communications on finance whether directly or indirectly:

a. Reduced Congestion and Fuel Savings:
    - Efficiency Gains:V2I technology can greatly enhance traffic flow by maximizing efficiency, leading to a substantial reduction in traffic congestion. This increased efficiency results in a reduction of the amount of time vehicles spend idling in traffic, which in turn leads to significant fuel savings.
    - Cost Savings: Businesses that depend on logistics and transportation can achieve lower operational expenses and increase profitability by reducing fuel use.
b. Investment and upkeep of infrastructure:
    - Initial Costs: The implementation of V2I systems necessitates a significant expenditure on intelligent infrastructure, which includes sensors, communication networks, and data management systems.
    - Long-term Savings: Although the initial costs may be substantial, the potential long-term savings resulting from decreased maintenance charges, reduced accident rates, and enhanced traffic management can outweigh these expenditures. Governments and municipalities have the ability to allocate funds in a more efficient manner, thereby improving the utilization of their budgets.
c. Insurance and liability:
    - Reduced Insurance Premiums: Insurance companies may decrease the cost of insurance for vehicles equipped with V2I technology due to improved safety features and a decrease in the number of accidents.
    - Risk management can be enhanced by utilizing real-time data on driving patterns and traffic conditions. This enables insurers to evaluate risks with greater accuracy, resulting in the development of more tailored and equitable pricing models.
d. Economic productivity which refers to the measure of how efficiently resources are used to produce goods and services in an economy:

- Time savings: V2I technology can enhance productivity by minimizing commute time. Reduced travel time for workers leads to increased productivity, resulting in positive economic outcomes.
- Optimizing the effectiveness of the supply chain: Enhanced routing and decreased delays have a positive impact on supply chains, resulting in expedited delivery times and decreased expenses in logistics.

e. Market Opportunities and Employment:
- Technological Advancements: The progress and implementation of V2I technology generate fresh market prospects for technology companies that specialize in hardware, software, and data analytics.
- Employment Generation: V2I systems deployment stimulates employment creation across several sectors such as construction, IT, and engineering, hence fostering economic expansion.

f. Ecological Consequences and Long-Term Viability:
- Emission reductions: This can be achieved by efficient traffic management, which is in line with global sustainability objectives. Decreased pollution can result in financial savings on healthcare expenses and enhanced quality of life.
- Green Investments: V2I systems are in line with green investment programs, which makes it attractive to get money from environmental grants and investors who prioritize sustainable technologies.

The Vehicle to Infrastructure Routing Protocol is a highly advanced technology that offers extensive economic advantages. V2I, or Vehicle-to-Infrastructure technology, has a favorable impact on several financial elements, such as business profitability and public sector budgeting, by improving traffic efficiency, reducing operational costs, and strengthening safety. As technology advances and becomes more widely adopted, the financial advantages are expected to increase, leading to a more efficient, productive, and sustainable economy.

3. THE APPLICATION OF AI IN ROUTING PROTOCOLS AND ITS EFFECT ON FINANCE

The use of Artificial Intelligence (AI) in routing protocols, namely within network and transportation systems, leads to notable progress in efficiency, cost reduction, and risk mitigation (Khan et al, 2022). These enhancements have significant financial consequences for enterprises, governments, and consumers (Bharadiya et al., 2023)

a. Artificial Intelligence in Routing Protocols

- Efficient Network Traffic Management:

Dynamic Routing: AI algorithms can adapt routing patterns in response to real-time data, thereby improving the flow of network traffic and minimizing latency. This is especially advantageous for extensive data centres and internet service providers.

Predictive Maintenance: Artificial intelligence can anticipate and forecast possible network faults, allowing for proactive rerouting of traffic. This proactive approach minimizes the occurrence of downtime and ensures uninterrupted service continuity. This guarantees the stability of operations and minimizes the expenses related to network disruptions.

- Optimized Transportation Systems:

AI-powered routing protocols in transportation systems, such those implemented in smart cities, can enhance traffic flow optimization by processing real-time data from several sources, including traffic cameras, sensors, and vehicle-to-infrastructure (V2I) communication.

Route Planning: AI can offer efficient route optimization for logistics and delivery services, considering factors such as traffic conditions, weather, and other variables. This results in decreased fuel usage and delivery times, resulting in cost reductions.

b. Monetary Consequences

- **Financial savings:**

Operational efficiency is boosted by the use of AI-enhanced routing protocols, which effectively decrease delays, optimize resource allocation, and minimize downtime. This results in substantial cost reductions for businesses and service providers.

Fuel and Maintenance Costs: Optimized routing in transportation minimizes fuel use and vehicle deterioration, resulting in reduced maintenance expenses and prolonged vehicle longevity.

- **Increase in income:**

Enhanced network performance and reliable transportation systems contribute to improved service quality, resulting in increased customer satisfaction, higher customer retention rates, and revenue growth.

Potential areas for expansion in the market: The utilization of AI in routing creates new market prospects for technology businesses and service providers, stimulating expansion in industries including autonomous vehicles, smart cities, and advanced logistics.

- **Management of potential hazards and uncertainties:**

Predictive Analytics: Artificial Intelligence utilizes predictive analytics to anticipate possible disruptions, such as network outages or traffic congestion, enabling proactive actions that reduce risks and avert expensive disasters.

AI enhances the security of routing protocols by promptly identifying and addressing cyber threats, hence safeguarding financial data and minimizing the likelihood of fraudulent activities.

- **Potential avenues for investment:**

Technological advancements, such as the integration of artificial intelligence (AI) into routing protocols, are attracting investments in technology and infrastructure. Companies at the forefront of these breakthroughs are receiving growing investments from venture capital and private equity organizations.

Collaboration between the public and private sectors: Governments and private entities allocate resources to infrastructure projects powered by artificial intelligence, fostering public-private partnerships that promote economic expansion.

- **Advantages for the environment and society:**

Sustainability: By implementing optimized routing strategies, we may minimize idle time and fuel usage in transportation, hence reducing carbon emissions. This aligns with global sustainability goals and has the potential to attract environmentally aware investors (Qader et al, 2021).

Social Impact: Enhanced transportation systems have a positive effect on people's lives by decreasing travel time and improving the efficiency and dependability of public transit.

Implementing AI in routing protocols is a major technological advancement that offers substantial cost advantages. AI-driven routing protocols optimize network and transportation systems, resulting in cost savings, increased income, and improved risk management. These innovations enhance operational efficiency and customer satisfaction, while also generating new investment opportunities and supporting environmental initiatives (Khan et al, 2020). The ongoing advancement of

AI technology will inevitably lead to its increased influence on routing protocols and finance, fostering additional innovation and generating economic advantages.

4. .IMPACT OF URBAN ENVIRONMENTS ON V2I COMMUNICATIONS

It is worth reminding that the number of vehicles that use the present road network infrastructure in urban locations has seen massive growth. A primary consequence of this collapse is management problems, ranging from traffic overcrowding control to driving safety and environmental impact. In recent years, researchers from both industry and academia have been focusing on improving sensing, communications, and dynamic adaptive technologies to make the Traffic Management System (TMS) more effective concerning smart city issues. One of the most critical consequences of road overcrowding for traffic management is related to delaying emergency services, like police and rescue operations, fire, or medical services(Masek et al., 2016).

Vehicle emissions(Mounce & Nelson, 2019) are the by-products of the engine fuel-burning process and the volatility of the fuel, including unburned Hydrocarbon (HC), Nitrogen Oxides (NO), Sulfur Oxide (SO), Volatile Organic Compounds (VOC), Carbon Monoxide (CO), and Particulate Matter (PM) (Ullah et al., 2019; Khan et al, 2021a). Several studies have shown that exposure to these emissions may lead to dangerous health impacts and extreme environments. Many studies have confirmed that vehicle emissions are responsible for a few adverse environmental effects, like acid rain, global warming, and photochemical smog. Acid rain may change the Polycyclic Aromatic Hydrocarbons (PAH) value of waterways and earth, thereby suffering the organisms that depend on these resources. Smog can prevent plant growth and cause the spread of damage to products and forests. Global warming will increase the average temperatures worldwide, create extreme weather events, and cause global climate shifts. Although carbon dioxide does not harm human health directly (Alamri, & Khan, 2023), it may contribute to global warming when the amount released by human activities is more than the natural absorption system (Sorial & Hong, 2014; Khan et al, 2021b).

5. VANETS VERSUS MANET

Over the past years, research has pointed to rapid developments in wireless communication technologies. The increase in road users has led to a decrease in vehicles, contributing to the rise in vehicle accidents. Intelligent Transportation Systems (ITS) have contributed to finding appropriate solutions for transport safety

(Awang et al., 2017). Intelligent Transport Systems aims to improve transport systems' quality and safety and support two types of wireless communications. Long-range wireless communications rely on communications on infrastructure networks such as cellular networks. Short-range wireless communications, which rely on emerging technologies such as mobile and fixed-line variables, are called vehicular ad-hoc networks (VANETs) (Jindal & Bedi, 2016).

VANETs can be used to reduce road traffic, improve road safety, provide emergency services and serve the interests of its users. In VANETs, the security is one of the crucial issues. It is focused on a critical point in developing a robust VANET system. There are no constraints on its movement, so the nodes move freely. Every node will stay connected when it changes its location; as an outcome, VANETs have a highly dynamic topology. Nodes are contacting with each other in single-hop or multi-hop. Every node in VANETs is either a vehicle or a Road Side Unit (RSU) (Lai et al., 2019). Connection in VANETs is divided into Vehicle-to-vehicle (V2V) communication and Vehicle Infrastructure (V2I) communication. The connections among nodes are made using radio signals, and the range of these signals can reach up to 1 KM. Connections among nodes that have distance override the signal range and request messages to hop across multiple nodes. An RSU does routing. RSU plays as a router among vehicles. Every vehicle connected with RSU should be supported by an onboard unit (OBN) to use radio singles. Tamper Proof Device (TPD) is a device that carries all the vehicle secrets like speed, position and driver identity (Awan et al., 2019).

MANETs are self-configured wireless in an ad-hoc network of mobile nodes that can change locations and configure themselves. It depends on the nodes' location, service detection ability, strength to search, and whether path messages use the nearest or closer nodes. Also, it depends on their connectivity to connect the various networks, which can be a standard Wi-Fi association or another medium, for example, a cell or satellite transmission (Jindal et al., 2016).

The attributes of MANETs are abilities to route the data, discover the neighbour for picking up the data and carriage, change route paths, network flexible architecture, no access point demand, connectivity peer-peer, wireless connectivity limited range, saving caching data and collection and requests to solve open or hidden problems. VANETs can be an emerging area of MANETs in which vehicles represent the mobile nodes inside the network and belonging to a wireless telecommunication network area. The target of VANETs is to increment user road safety and the comfort of passengers (Reema, 2017). This allows a user to access the data when driving the vehicle continually and has three components: Vehicles, RTA and RSUs [3].

The MANET have three types as following:

(i) Intelligent vehicular ad hoc networks (InVANETs): These are used ad hoc networks for intelligent vehicular to synthetic intelligence to tackle unforeseen vehicle clashes and accidents [77].

(ii) Vehicular ad hoc networks (VANETs): This type of network can communicate effectively and directly with other vehicles in the same way and helps communicate with equipment and cars parked on the side of the road.

(iii) Internet-based Mobile ad hoc networks (iMANET) help to connect stable as well as mobile nodes (Qureshi & Abdullah, 2013).

The main differences between the MANETs' and VANETs' routing are topology network, patterns of mobility, vehicle density at different times, demographics, and fast changes in vehicles arriving and leaving the VANETs. Meanwhile, VANETs include a small, homogeneous network with applications focused on safety and traffic efficiency. Recently, large-level and homogeneous networks in VANETs have been inserted to provide more safety information and services, as shown in Figure 2 [5].

Figure 2. Heterogeneous network structure in IoV

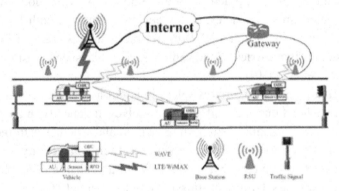

6. VANETS APPLICATION

Productivity and well-being are two essential prerequisites for arranging VANET applications, dependent on their primary role. In any case, effectiveness and security are not isolated from one another. Despite what might be expected, those different angles should be viewed together in the structure of VANET applications (Bhat, 2018). For example, a motor disappointment or an accident involving at least two vehicles can prompt congested driving conditions. A message announcing this occasion passes on well-being cautioning for close-by drivers who use it to expand their mindfulness. A similar message may trigger the calculation of an elective path for a vehicle that wants to go through the mishap area, yet it isn't near that point yet (Bhoi & Khilar, 2016). For this situation, the objective is to expand the vehicle proficiency for individual vehicles. Moreover, contingent upon various factors, for example, the significance of the mishap area, the vehicle framework may figure and propose an elective path to an expansive arrangement of vehicles considering a more extensive perspective on the traffic requests to lessen the effect of this occasion to locales not near the mishap. For this situation, the objective is to expand the general transport proficiency. Note that in the two cases, an early occasion warning can support a driver or a traveller to choose to take an alternate path, utilize an alternate method for transport, or even remain at the ebb and flow area if there should be an occurrence of a genuine traffic issue. For this situation, an extra objective is to furnish an individual with helpful data in arranging a movement identified with the vehicle framework. VANET applications will monitor different types of data, such as car conditions, surrounding roads, approaching vehicles, road surfaces and weather conditions, to make the infrastructure secure and more efficient. Once this data is available, vehicles communicate across wireless communication networks with other vehicles, sharing relevant information for different purposes (Begum, 2016).

Figure 3. VANET Applications

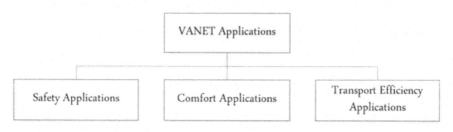

This paper arranges the applications of vehicles through technological communication between vehicles on the road. Previous research has summarized that there are major applications in VANET: security applications, transport efficiency applications, and comfort applications, as shown in Figure 3 (K. Ghafoor, 2016).

i) **Comfort Applications:** Comfort applications relate to giving appropriate comfort to passengers, like traffic data systems, weather data, and areas of a few focuses of administration, like gasoline stations and eateries (Domingos et al., 2016).

ii) **Safety Applications**: These are concerned with enhancing the safety of passengers (vehicles) along the way. This application depends on switching trust between vehicles and remote base stations (IVC). Such as the vehicle receives warning messages about the emergency alarm at a certain distance from the road, like a flood of water or accidents at a certain distance from the road, and the path of traffic must be changed to another direction of vehicles (H. Peng et al., 2018)(Bhat, 2018).

iii) **Transport Efficiency Applications**: contribute to the optimal use of traffic and road traffic, as well as help reduce vehicle collisions and facilitate traffic congestion (K. Z. Ghafoor et al., 2013)[26].

7. ROUTING PROTOCOLS IN VANETS

Current researchers found that vehicle routing protocols are placed in two categories: Topology-based, Position-based routing, Geo-Cast-based routing, Broadcast-based routing and Cluster-based routing (Awang et al., 2017). There is a classification of VANETs routing protocols shown in Figure 4:

Figure 4. Classification VANETs routing protocols

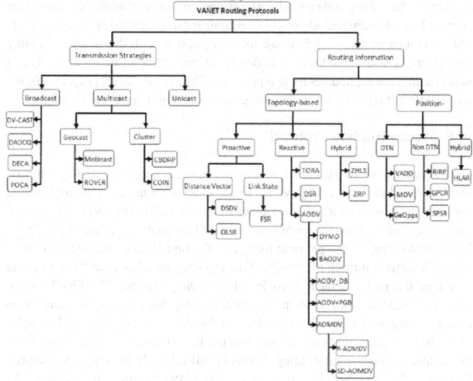

The routing protocols of MANET are not suitable for use in the VANET network. If they use it, they will not be able to deliver the required because the ad hoc network is fast changing [6]. The routing protocols in vehicular ad hoc networks VANETs are divided into topology-based and position-based routing. A routing protocol provides the way that vehicle-to-vehicle communicates with each other entity to exchange data. This procedure contains the decision of forwarding to the establishing vehicles and the safety from any routing failure through the infrastructure environment around the vehicles (Cheng et al., 2015) [75].

5.1 Topology-based routing protocol

A topology routing-based protocol is used to send the packets of data from the source to the purpose. Use the existing link's information in the present net to forward the packet. The categories of this topology are the proactive route and the Reactive route(Patel, 2016). It is a dependent routing scheme for VANETs based on the algorithm of the Bellman-Ford. Also, it fixes the routing loop problem. Each entrance in the routing table includes a sequence number; the sequence numbers are even if a link is present and others add. The number was generated by the destination, and the emitter needs to send out the following update with this number. Routing information is distributed between nodes by sending entire refuse infrequently and minimal incremental updates more repeatedly (Cheng et al., 2015) [74]. This figure shows different types of VANET routing protocols (topology-based Routing).

A. Proactive Routing Protocol

In a proactive routing protocol, each node constantly maintains routing information forwarded in the next step, which routes to all other nodes in the background irrespective of the network of communication requests. This protocol type has low latency because it stores the route from source to destination (Awang et al., 2017). In this route type, by the periodic messages, the node keeps updating its routing table. The stature routing protocol and the topology broadcast can be seen in the optimized link based on the Reverse Path Forwarding Protocol (TBRPF). To maintain a consistent network environment in network topology, use one or more tables to store routing information changes during table drive routing protocol. Examples of methods of protecting position information in a high-risk environment are the Distributed Bellman-Ford Routing Protocol (DBF), Highly Dynamic Destination-Sequenced Distance Vector routing protocol (DSDV), Secure Position Aided Ad hoc Routing protocol (SPAAR)(Ema et al., 2014).

B. Reactive Routing Protocol

Reactive Routing is open only when there is a need to send a packet to its destination for a node to contact each other. It maintains only the current routes in use since the destination became inaccessible over all paths from the source, so in that case, it reduces the burden of the network (Awang et al., 2017).

C. Hybrid Position-based Routing Protocol

It is specially designed to address the issue of connection breakages between the vehicles by leading to a high increase in the routing processing time and a retreating in network scalability.(Cheng et al., 2015) The features of this protocol incorporate on-demand routing with position-dependent geographic routing in a manner that efficiently uses all the position information available. Also designed this protocol is designed to gracefully wind up to on-request routing as the position information reaches a low level (Reema, 2017).

5.2 Broadcast Routing Protocol

Broadcast routing is one of the VANET routing protocols, and it is used for road situations between vehicles, delivering advertisements and announcements, sharing, traffic, weather, and emergencies. Broadcasting is used when multiple hops are used when messages need to be spread to the vehicles beyond the sending range (Reema, 2017). In broadcast routing, changing the light brake on both sides (right/left) and the turn indicator lights by the communication devices will deliver signal messages like images or audio to other vehicles. The driver will drive safely until receiving a warning message. In most emergencies, the SMS has to be quickly delivered and efficiently. Also, it is used for distributing the information to vehicles out of the transmission range with the help of multi-hop transmission. The message is delivered to vehicles within the communication area from the broadcast route. In addition, it shifts the messages to all vehicles in the network. The significant disadvantages of this routing protocol are the unobserved node problem and the high possibility of clashes in the messages, as shown in Figure 5 (Patel, 2016).

Figure 5. Interest Broadcast Storm

```
- - - ▷   Consumer broadcasts the interest packet to its neighboring nodes.
───────▷   In case of no available content, all neighbor vehicles further rebroadcast the interest
           packet with in its vicinity and cause interest broadcast storm.
───────▷   Interest broadcast storm.
```

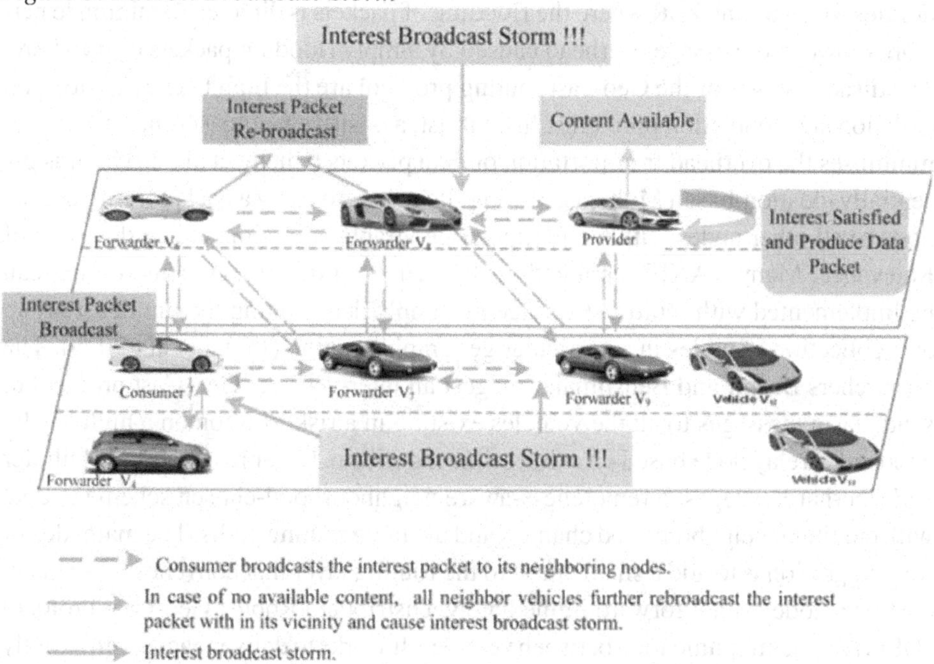

5.3 Position Routing Protocol

Position Routing uses the location services to determine the correct position of the source, neighbour, and destination nodes. It maintains the position information by using the Global Positioning System (GPS) to nodes and determines the correct coordinates of the nodes in all locations (Granda et al., 2018). It gets the location coordinates of the purpose when the source nodes are ready to transmit a packet—the need to determine service because of shortcomings of position routing. The most important advantages of the position route are required discovery and management, Scalability and harmony with high node mobility. Examples of position routing are V2V Protocols and V2I Protocols (A. Kumar & Tyagi, 2014).

5.4 Geo-Cast Routing Protocol

Geo-cast routing uses location-based multicast routing with the primary objective to deliver the packet from the source node to other nodes within a particular geographical area Zone of Related (ZoR). To avoid unnecessary hasty reactions, the vehicle outside ZOR is by geo-casting routing. It has a particular geography that defines a forwarding ZoR where the flooding of packets is directed to minimize network crowd and message overhead caused by simply flooding packets everywhere. The disadvantages of the Geo-cast routing protocol are the high latency period and collision and contention problems. In contrast, a positive Geo-cast routing protocol minimises the overhead transportation of data packets (Cheng et al., 2015). It is essentially location-based Multicast routing. Its goal is to carry a packet from a source node to all other nodes within a particular geographical region, called the Zone of Relevance. Many VANET applications benefit from this router. This routing can be implemented with multicast service by simply determining the multicast group as a collection of nodes in a particular geographic region (Jindal et al., 2016). The researchers Bachir and Benslimane suggest an inter-vehicles Geo-Cast protocol to send alarm messages to all the vehicles existing in a risk location on a highway by choosing a relay node based on a defer time algorithm. Other researchers, Maihöfer and Eberhardt, suggest a remoteness-aware neighbourhood-chosen scheme to deal with continual neighbourhood changes and unstable routing paths. The main idea of this suggestion is to add a small cache to the routing layer that convenes those packets that a node cannot forward immediately. Distributed Robust Geo-Cast Protocol (DRG) is for communication between vehicles. It works to deliver packets efficiently in a heavy network, and it ensures a high allocation ratio in a sparse network at the pension of increased overhead. This protocol can be helpful in traffic lights and in making decision processes for VANETs services (Cheng et al., 2015), as shown in

Figure 5 the message transporter region between the source and destination geocast region in Geo-Cast Routing Protocol.

Figure 6. Geo-Cast Routing Protocol

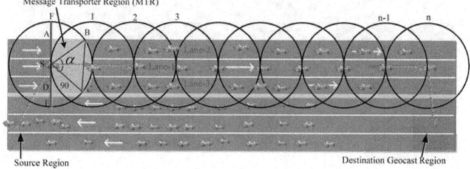

5.5 Cluster Routing Protocol

Cluster Routing is establishing a cluster among vehicles/nodes. A cluster is categorized as a group of nodes. Each cluster has one unique cluster head, responsible for intra and inter-cluster connection. To communicate within the cluster an immediate link is set among the nodes and inter-cluster communication is only possible on the specific cluster heads. To get improved results and scalability for an extensive network of nodes, the cluster head should broadcast the packet to all the nodes in the cluster even when the network is late and overhead is growing for high mobility advantages of VANETs (Cooper et al., 2017).

Figure 7. Cluster-Based Routing

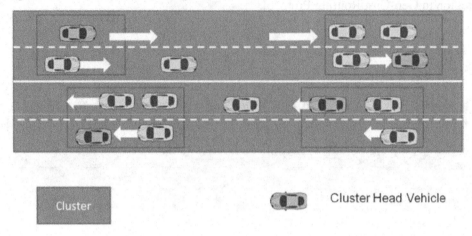

Cluster

Cluster Head Vehicle

8. AD-HOC ROUTING PROTOCOLS PROPERTIES

Ad hoc networks have many unique properties that make them suitable for civilian and commercial purposes. This section will mention a set of essential properties as a criterion for evaluating the flexibility of custom routing protocols, such as:

i. **Distributed process**: the protocol must be distributed. It must not be dependent on a centralized controlling node. This is the case even for stable networks. The difference is that the nodes in an ad-hoc network can get in or leave the network very easily, and because of mobility, the network can be divided (Reema, 2017).

ii. **Loop-free:** to improve the overall performance, the routing protocol must confirm that the routes supplied are loop-free. This will avoid any misuse of CPU consumption or bandwidth (Jahir et al., 2019).

iii. **Demand-based operation**: this protocol must interact just when needed and must not periodically broadcast control information. This way will help to minimize the control overhead in the network and so don't misuse the network resources (S. Zhang et al., 2017).

iv. **Unidirectional link support:** The radio environment can propose forming unidirectional links. Employment of these links and not only the bidirectional links improves the routing protocol execution (Cen et al., 2019).

v. **Security:** Ad-Hoc Routing protocols need security measures to protect the radio environment from impersonation attacks. We need encryption and authentication. These sorts of security will distribute the keys between the nodes in an ad-hoc network (Rahim et al., 2018).

vi. **Power conservation: We need to use some standby mode to save power because there may be** limited battery power in laptops and thin clients around the ad-hoc network (Reema, 2017).

vii. **Multiple routing:** is used to reduce the number of responses to topological changes and congestion. If one route is invalid, another route can be saved and could still be valid, consequently storing the routing protocol from initiating another route discovery procedure (U. A. Khan & Lee, 2019).

viii. **Quality of Service Support**: quality service is necessary in the routing protocol. The quality service will help to find what kind of network will be used (Awan et al., 2019).

9. VEHICULAR COMMUNICATIONS IN VANETS

Vehicles are communicating with other vehicles to make a network. The communications between vehicles are executed using the On-Board Unit (OBU), which will be equipped in vehicles by the industrialist. There are three phases of proposed protocol registration: mutual authentication and certificate authority tracking. First, in registration, Road Side Units (RSUs) and On-Board Units (OBU) OBUs will register themselves to certificate authority. The registration certificate authority will generate and send individual certificates to register RSUs and OBUs. The next step includes creating mutual authentication among V2R and V2V. Certificate authority tracking returns the real ID of OBUs and RSUs from their certificates. It provides effective V2R and V2V authentication at low cost, and hence, it is appropriate for realistic vehicular networks (Friginal et al., 2014).

Connection Breakage Ad hoc on-demand Distance Vector (CBAODV) routing protocol acts as a hotspot among the vehicles to avoid breakage in communication. CS-CBAODV routing protocol is a new interactive-based routing which stores the routing data in a node forever and can be reused this type of concept when the route maintenance fails (N. A. Kumar & Raj, 2015). VANET routing protocols have been developed to forward data packets using route relay vehicles to specific aims. Routing in VANETs can be categorized in many ways: based on packet storing and forwarding, transmission type, delay in the packets and Routing Information(Awang et al., 2017) (Elbery et al., 2015).

Vehicles can communicate using radio waves to share data among them in their suitable network. Any vehicle can compose a temporary network at any cross to send data to closer vehicles. Vehicle traffic can disrupt communication between vehicles. And it causes delays in data transmission. To solve the breakage, a vehicular node can store routing-based data constantly to decrease the link breakage in VANETs. The result will help to reduce data loss and to reduce network delay. The vehicular communications must be executed securely. When transmitted, messages between vehicles should be traced by the certificate authority to get their original identity back. Vehicle environments present strange communication characteristics on roadways. Like distribution ranges of heterogeneous traffic from a large to a smaller number of vehicles, with the high mobility of vehicles (Nwizege et al., 2014).

7.1 Mode of Communication

Day by day, the number of vehicles is increasing at high speed through wireless communication. Also, vehicles have become technological and electronic. They are developing and widening traditional traffic controls to brand-new traffic services (Patel, 2016).

Figure 8. Communication Modes Types in VANETs

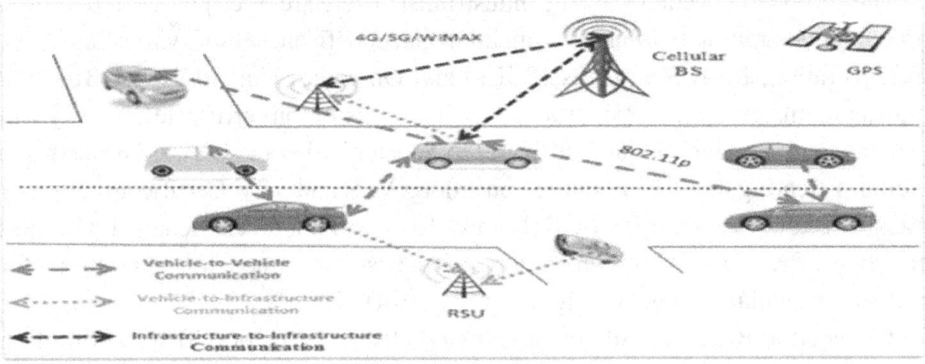

There are different types of communication modes, as shown in figure7:

a) **Road Side Unit (RSU):** is equipped with a system for short-range communication using IEEE 802.11p radio protocol technology. It is generally situated on the roadside and other locations like parking spaces and junctions, which are provided to promote range communication and another routing strategy of VANETs(Lai et al., 2019). The main procedures and functions associated with the RSU are:

i. Extending the range communication of the ad hoc net while redistributing the data on other OBUs and sending the data to other RSUs to send it to other OBUs (**Onboard units**).
ii. Operation safety applications like low bridge alarms, work zones, or accident warnings use I2V (Infrastructure to Vehicle) connections and act as an information source.
iii. Providing connectivity Internet to OBUs (**On Board Units**).

b) **On Board Unit (OBU):** the main tasks of OBU are data security, transfer message reliability, access wireless radio, ad hoc and routing-based position, and network overcrowding control. The OBU included a vehicle from memory, the interface of the user, RPC (Resource Command Processor), and short-range device communication(Awan et al., 2019).

c) **Application Unit (AU):** it can be a specialist device for application safety or a standard device like a PDA (personal digital assistant) for the internet. Also, they communicate with the network via the OBU, which takes responsibility for all network and mobility functions(Elbery et al., 2015).

10. SECURITY OF VANET

The security of VANET has a major impact and plays a significant role. An example of one security parameter is the way a message needs to be sent; in this case, the message that is being transmitted between vehicles must be followed by the certificate authority to get back its original identity (U. A. Khan & Lee, 2019). Security matters in V2I and VANETs, in general, are critical subjects. Without considering security, VANETs, specifically V2I communication can lead to catastrophic results. Security is a crucial topic in V2I and VANETs. VANETs, particularly V2I communication, can have disastrous consequences if security is not considered. A security vulnerability could enable an attacker to tamper with network data, leading to inaccurate information regarding road conditions, traffic congestion, speed limits, accidents, etc. Implementing V2I protocol and VANET protocols must effectively address potential security threats. Key security aspects like authentication, integrity, confidentiality, availability, non-repudiation, privacy protection, and access control are crucial for effective implementation in V2I [40]. Examples of potential attacks in Vehicle-to-Infrastructure (V2I) communication include:

i. **Injection of wrong data:** In the injection of a wrong data attack, the perpetrator sends malicious data into the network to provide vehicles or drivers with false information. This could include directing a driver to travel in the wrong direction, intentionally causing an accident, or creating traffic congestion. To minimise the possibility of an attack or provide protection against it, the integrity of the data unit in V2I must be handled with care. Data integrity, when well-designed, safeguards against unauthorised data modifications and can be applied at either the network or application layer. Integrity can utilise a new hashing function deemed secure, such as SHA-2 and SHA-3 [41].

ii. **Denial of Service**: attacks include overwhelming network resources with bogus requests, causing significant latency and bandwidth consumption, ultimately preventing actual nodes from accessing network services. To prevent this, establish a system to track the origin of requests and identify a high volume of requests from one source as a potential attack. The high rate level must be determined beforehand, and the method to determine the source, whether it is an IP address, MAC address, or any other suitable identifier, must be clearly defined. This is beneficial in a Denial of Service attack, where an attacker attempts to compromise multiple authentic nodes in the network to transmit a large volume of requests. Requests in this scenario originate from several sources and are directed to diverse destinations, making it challenging to rely solely on monitoring a single IP address for frequent requests. This form of attack is called Dynamic Denial of Service (DDoS) [42].

iii. **Attack of the revelation of identity and geographical position of a vehicle**: The attacker intercepts the victim's radio signals to track the movement and determine the route of the victim's vehicle [20].

Furthermore, other common assaults on VANET need to be addressed, such as the timing attack that aims to introduce a delay in message delivery and the crucial importance of physical security in V2I. Access Points (AP) located in the road environment must be safeguarded from threats such as theft, heat, water, and rain [39].

A. Vehicle to Infrastructure Security Requirements

In a communicated vehicle environment, vehicles can reach internal, like vehicle-to-sensor (V2S) and foreign environments, like V2V and V2I, comprehensive RSUs (roadside units) that use Dedicated Short-Range Communication (DSRC). An OBU (On-Board Unit) inside the vehicle transfers information to the surrounding environment. RSUs gather data from vehicles and applications installed in an RSU to transmit the requested service (Rawat et al., 2015). All security solutions concerning V2I and V2V must focus on three substance elements, according to CVRIA. And they are integrity, availability and confidentiality(Islam et al., 2018).

i. **Integrity:** To ensure the accuracy, reliability, and trustworthiness of the messages, the messages exchanged among a vehicle and infrastructure must be protected from any unauthorized alteration or modification. It must preserve every security solution from unintentional modifications or unauthorized intentional. Loss of integrity can affect the declination of services provided by a V2I environment (Islam et al., 2018).

ii. **Availability:** Availability guarantees that systems and information are accessible and usable to authorized personnel. All RSUs must be available in a V2I environment at all times. For example, the critical latency for an interchange inconsistency warning must be less than 100 milliseconds. Also, all security solutions must provide an operational system despite mistakes or risky status (Islam et al., 2018).

iii. **Confidentiality:** The content of the messages must be kept confidential when exchanged in the V2I environment. Confidentiality is not allowed by anyone with no authorized and unintended users to access the content of messages. However, most messages in a connected vehicle environment are general, especially the exchanged messages among vehicles and infrastructure. Message confidentiality and Data confidentiality need to be taken into observance when laying out a secure V2I environment (Mejri et al., 2014).

iv. **Reliability:** The reliability of V2I is influenced by the same factors that impact its continuity. Reliability is influenced by numerous key aspects [42]. Availability and security are crucial for achieving V2I reliability. The availability ensures that nodes have access to resources whenever needed. A failover strategy is essential, with standby equipment in place to replace and cover any failures in the critical V2I components. Integrating the Common Address Redundancy Protocol (CARP) into the V2I protocol can enhance availability. Furthermore, security factors are crucial for ensuring reliability, as previously stated. An attacker can execute a Denial of Service attack to diminish or halt the operation of the network. These hazards must be managed effectively to achieve a satisfactory level of dependability [46].

B. Cyber Attacks in Vehicle to Infrastructure (V2I)

Security attackers are categorized as internal or external based on membership functionality. Activity levels define whether the attackers are passive or active. Assessment of intention or cause for an attack has categorized attackers as malicious or rational. The cyber-attacks that are probable to happen in the interface of V2I are based on the vulnerability of integrity, availability and confidentiality, with a projected probability of an attack ranked as LOW, MODERATE and HIGH (Mishra, 2016; Sachdeva et al, 2022).

C. Emerging Technologies

Nowadays, many new technologies have emerged to make communication networks more secure, more scalable, and more capable of obtaining fine-grained control. In the following sections, I will discuss the usage of these emerging technologies in security solutions of V2I (Islam et al., 2018).

i. **Edge Computing:** It is a technique where the data is processed close to the data secure. It submits proper resource allocation, low latency, and dynamic content management. It guarantees high bandwidth by distributing the computational tasks to several edges. Security modules of V2I need to be near the data source for faster processing, which can be completed by edge computing(Ahmed & Ahmed, 2016).

ii. **Software-defined networking (SDN):** Traditional network management is brittle, complex and fault-prone. The powerful coupling of the data level and control level occasions those problems. The data level is used for forwarding data, and the control level is used for routing packet management, routing logic and access control. By isolating the control level and data level, and inserting programmability, SDN facilitates the network management functions and supplies more flexibility concerning data allocation. In a CV environment, SDN can dynamically reroute the data to various purposes as necessary. It shows an example of SDN benefits to supply more flexible protection strategies and better resource management in the defence of cyber-attacks while reducing network overcrowding and user-perceived latency. We believe that SDN can help build V2I threat protection systems(AT&T, 2016).

iii. **Network Functions Virtualization (NFV):** Network functions such as firewalls and IDSs (intrusion detection systems) are now implemented in specialized hardware like field-programmable port arrays (FPGA). Although specialized hardware gives the best performance, it also leads to high cost, servicing complexity, and lack of flexibility. NFV has emerged to overcome these issues. NFV minimises cost and supplies new opportunities in the scalability and implementation of network jobs in commodity hardware with fine-grained control. NFV and SDN could play a prime role in securing the CV environment shortly, as leading industry players are using these new technologies (AT&T, 2016).

D. CV application-level impact under Distributed Denial of Service (DDoS) attack

With various attackers, the performance of an RSU was evaluated depending on the data receiving average by the application. As the attackers were flooding the RSU, a significant amount of data from rightful vehicles was missing. As shown in Figure 3, with the growing number of attackers, DRR by the application was reduced due to the DDoS attack (Rajan et al, 2022). For example, if the SSGA application manufactures incorrect output, the conflict among vehicles might have a negative result, and conflict can lead to a crash. In testing, a conflict occurred when two vehicles were near a time headway of less than 1.5 seconds (Laaki et al., 2019).

11. VEHICULAR NETWORK ARCHITECTURES WITH SCSS

This article initially presents another sort of 5G-enabled on-road base station, specifically self-sustaining caching stations (SCSs) (SCSs), to improve vehicular system limit cost-effectively. In particular, the SCSs have three highlights: (1) controlled by a sustainable power source rather than power framework, (2) associated with the centre network using millimetre wave (mmWave) backhauls, and (3) cache-enabled for proficient substance conveyance(Y. Zhang et al., 2019).

A. Cellular-Based Vehicular Networks

With the fast development of information and communication technologies, huge advanced on-road applications like argument reality, autonomous driving, infotainment services and other area-based road services are emerging. Improving the ability of vehicular networks is an urgent issue because the data-hungry applications will bring a surge of wireless traffic. For this purpose, we need to deploy road base stations. Due to the requirements of power source supply and backhaul transmission are connected the wired in traditional style in based stations. The requirements caused problems because traditional stations depend on lines power and wired to work, the resulting inflexible deployment mostly in areas with rudimentary power lines or fibre connections like in highways and village areas. Also, the large power consumption can cause high operational costs as well as environmental anxiety. Moreover, the traditional stations only providing connectivity may fail to offer satisfaction because they bring files consume time from remote service as shown in the figure (Shen et al., 2019).

Figure 9. Cellular-Based Vehicular Networks

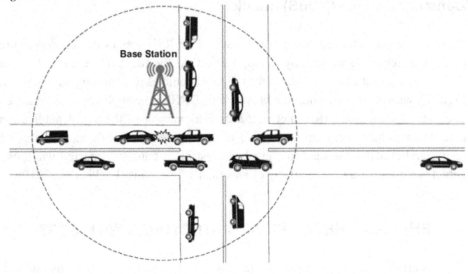

A. Caching Stations of Self-Sustaining

To enhance vehicular network space cost-effectively, need to use useful 5G technologies and suggest deploying SCSs in addition to the use of cellular networks. Equipped with wind turbines or solar panels, SCSs can harvest renewable energy and the power to work in a self-sustaining style without power support as shown in Figure 10 of Vehicular network architecture with self-sustaining caching stations. The efficiency of network energy is expected to be improved by 1000 times when exploiting renewable energy like supplementary or alternative power sources plus, it can liberate network deployment from power lines when renewable energy is harvested. mmWave wireless communication technologies can be used to support wireless backhaul. unlicensed large bandwidth,mmWave bands can obtain broadband wireless communication based on the huge multiple input multiple outputs (MIMO) and beamforming technologies (di Pietro et al., 2019). Therefore, SCSs, which collect both mmWave back techniques and power harvesting can be deployed in a "drop and play" style without wired constraints (Y. Peng et al., 2019).

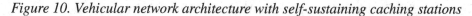

Figure 10. Vehicular network architecture with self-sustaining caching stations

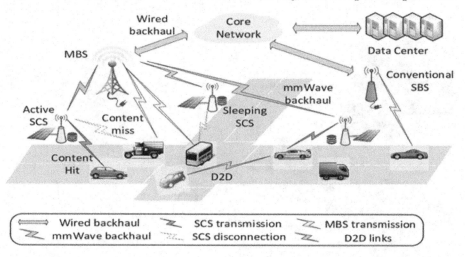

B. 5G-Enabled Heterogeneous Vehicular Network Architecture

Formed a heterogeneous vehicular network architecture when integrated with SCSs, as shown in Figure 11. The traditional macro base stations and mini cell base stations are communicated with high-speed wired backhauls and are powered by traditional energy networks, which mainly provide grid coverage and control for reliability. At the same time, the SCSs are violently deployed for abilities enhancement and fundamentally provide high-speed data access based on stored contents(S. Zhang et al., 2017).

Figure 11. 5G-Enabled Heterogeneous Vehicular Network Architecture

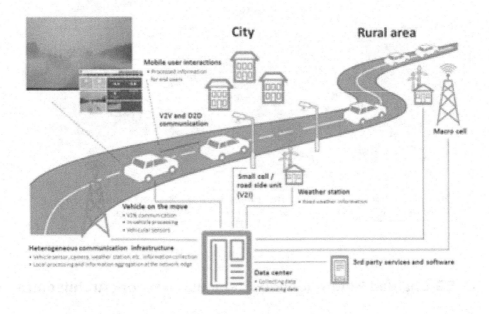

12. HIERARCHICAL NETWORK MANAGEMENT FRAMEWORK

A. Management of Hierarchical Network

To resolve challenges, suggest a Management framework of a hierarchical vehicular network. The suggested framework fundamentally includes three components power management, traffic steering and content caching. Further, network management is proceeding with different strategies in both small and large balances as shown in Figure 10 of the Management framework of hierarchical vehicular network (S. Zhang et al., 2017)(Classification, 2019).

B. Management Challenges

i. *Network Heterogeneity*: Macro Base Stations (MBSs) and Small Cell Base Stations (SCSs) offer distinct features with content access, respect to coverage, user capacity etc. MBSs warranty ubiquitous coverage with a big cell radius (e.g., several kilometres), and hence the connected users can enjoy less handover when moving at a high speed. However, the large coverage radius may also bring huge communications to every MBS (S. Zhang et al., 2017). MBSs can just supply limited radio resources to every vehicle user at a low transmission rate. On the inversion, each SCS covers a comparatively smaller area and serves fewer vehicle users at high transmission rates. Also, the SCS user can reduce end-to-end delay by getting files without backhaul transportation. Nevertheless, SCSs fundamentally target popular file transfer, and their small coverage radius may cause repeated handover issues. In addition, network infrastructures are heterogeneous, with a wide range requiring heterogeneous QoS requirements of vehicular services (Domingos et al., 2016). For instance, messages and safety control occupy limited radio resources because they are delay sensitive, but applications safety-related require big bandwidth like social network on the map and wheel downloading but they can afford longer delays. The traffic demand and heterogeneity of network resources should to taken regarding management resources and user association(Rawat et al., 2015).

ii. **Highly Dynamic Traffic Demand**: Wireless traffic is highly dynamic on the road in all time and locative domains due to the difference in vehicle intensity. May network management face big challenges when the traffic is not uniform. The services cut off when the traffic burst in rush hours cause of limited network resources. At the same time cannot fully use network resources(Alves Junior & Wille, 2018). Also, there may be an imbalance in the locative traffic because of congestion in some cells and while resources are underutilized in other cells, the result will degrade both service quality and network efficiency. Despite traffic volume differences and popularity division of different contents varies by time. So SCSs need to update their content cache to preserve a high content hit rate (S. Zhang et al., 2017).

iii. **Supply Intermittent Energy**: Different *from the* traditional power grid, renewable power arrives at random in an intermittent method, which has the potential to mismatch with traffic demand. Should the network fully use the heterogeneous network resources to provide authoritative on-request services, thus, as to reduce operational costs while meeting differentiated QoS requirements of on-road mobile applications? The challenges of Supply Intermittent Energy are the SCS solar energy system cannot provide service after sunset. Also, the off-balance power required and supply can cause energy failure as well as battery overflow degrading system ability and leading to energy waste (Moreau et al., 2019).

Figure 12. Management framework of hierarchical vehicular network

13. DRIVING HETEROGENEOUS VEHICULAR NETWORKS

Shortly, An abnormal Vehicle (AVs) will gradually prevail on the roads because autonomous vehicles will be a fast development, performing in scenarios where manually driving vehicles and AVs move on the road together (Design, 2019). To achieve information participation between autonomous vehicles and manual driving, a driving heterogeneous vehicular network is needed, and its realization faces the following challenges. Cooperative driving with ADVNETs is a committed technology to improve the efficient safety driving of AVs especially in intersection scenarios. For example, it can be designed to help AVs cross the intersection without traffic lights safely in, through velocity, sharing real-time positions, cooperative-based safety driving patterns and desired driving lane information between AVs within the same platoon. When we need to cross the interactions safely, there should be manual control driving vehicles and the human factors will control the vehicles manually. So, designing an appropriate and efficient connection scheme, to achieve efficient cooperative driving is desired for some scenarios like intersections, we just need to schedule which type of information should be shared by which vehicle. The result in complex message structure in both message types and QoS requirements will happen in cases of different information requirements in manually driven vehicles, AV and HDVANET(Awang et al., 2017). A novel beacon scheduling algorithm has been suggested guaranteeing the trustworthy and timely dissemination of two kinds of beacon messages in HDVNETs, periodic beacon messages for cooperative driving of AVs and event-driven safety messages for manually driving vehicles. However, most of the messages are more complex than that one has been considered. for example, when a special infotainment service is required for event-driven safety messages, periodic messages, video information need to be shared, and vehicles in platoon-based HDVNETs to guarantee the string constancy of platoon while ensuring the QoS requirement of this infotainment service. So it needs different efficient message dissemination schemes for various HDVNET scenarios(Awang et al., 2017)(Scholar, 2014).

14. DEPLOYMENT OF INFRASTRUCTURE FOR VEHICULAR NETWORK

Vehicular networks provide communication between vehicles and between vehicles and Traffic Management Authorities(S. Zhang et al., 2017). Vehicular networks contain communication between Vehicle to Infrastructure (V2I) and Vehicle to Vehicle (V2V). It has established itself in the last few years in a short time because it is one of the most hopeful fields of research within the larger context of metropolitan swarm wireless networks. Infrastructure usage to improve the abilities of communication, which are very important for safety applications, where should the applications to warring messages arrive to the authorities. Also, the message of accidents vehicles and damaged vehicles(Fogue et al., 2018). In addition, it is used for traffic surveillance and planning like warning of clashes, driving support quick response to drivers' mistakes, and useful for priority traffic assistance like noticing ambulances. Vehicle-to-infrastructure (V2I) communication is used to supply localization services to vehicles(Song et al., 2019).

i. **Roadside Units (RSUs)** are infrastructure connection points in vehicular networks. RSUs are important functions in vehicular connections due to their ability to carry important information to the vehicular, transmit received messages to final receivers or provide network access to the vehicular. Usage of RSUs is deployed to improve network performance in vehicular networks and to extend vehicle coverage (Fogue et al., 2018). Vehicle connection abilities highly build on the number of RSUs deployed and their coverage. However, RSUs are generally costly to install and maintain(Fogue et al., 2018). The deployment policies of RSU have been suggested in many works, including several approaches to determine the number of RSUs required to supply a functional RSU deployment in terms of communication within a given scenario(Fogue et al., 2018).

ii. **Dedicated Short-Range Communication (DSRC)**: these techniques use V2I connection and RSU. The vehicle should be equipped with suitable DSRC devices to allow wireless connection and exchange information positions among vehicles and RSU(U. A. Khan & Lee, 2019).

The vehicles can communicate with each other and communicate with different types of infrastructures by using fundamental components, and they are the Internet of Things, vehicle network and 5G network (Muhammad & Safdar, 2018; Alrubaiei et al, 2022). But when marge the vehicle network with the Internet of Things and 5G network, is emerged three challenges. The first challenge is the vehicle network is enabled by services of the 5G network and the Internet of Things. Like 3D map navigation is dependent on authoritative communication, however, the links of vulnerable wireless caused by the high mobility of vehicles and complex traffic scenarios lead to a dangerous drop in-vehicle network connectivity(Shi et al., 2018). The second challenge is not allowing coverage of infrastructures that particular implementation inadequate of vehicle network(Muhammad & Safdar, 2018). The third challenge is the reduction of spectrum resources still a dangerous challenge in vehicle networks. To solve this challenge of reduction of the spectrum, have been suggested to use TV white space band or cognitive radio for some research works (Song et al., 2019). The Internet of Things is one of the fundamental components of the infrastructure. And it has elements such as drones. Drones include communication devices and dedicated sensors. It can do several services like monitoring low altitudes, rescue from post-disaster, logistics application and communication help. Also, drones can support broadband wireless communications(Song et al., 2019).

15. PROMOTING FLEXIBILITY FOR INFRASTRUCTURES

Some major works influence to deployment of the drone's dynamic ability to support ground infrastructures. By sending drones to cover traffic burst areas or holes on request. Also, vehicles can communicate with drones and access infrastructures during drone relay. One of the features of drones is bring flexibility to Vehicular to Infrastructures (V2I) communications (Shi et al., 2018)

16. VEHICLE TO INFRASTRUCTURE (V2I) IN SMART CITIES

Smart cities are areas where invention is supported out of applications and digital networks. It's often called connected, digital or sustainable cities. The goals of converting the city into a smart environment are to relieve the problems output from civilization and increase the urban population. Also, a smart city is a civil area that provides the conditions for sustainable economic increase and quality of life. The smart solutions in the cities are such as green building, traffic crowding avoidance, and modern industrial control systems, some of the technologies can make civil sustainability. A smart city embraces to use of technology to improve how people live, share information and commute. One of the main aspects of a smart city is the vehicles including new sensing, communication and social abilities as a part of the wider internet (Song et al., 2019). The main fundamental to making smart cities a reality is providing mobile wireless sensing and communications, vehicles can ease access to data. There are three main categories of wireless networks that can be divided. The first one is the infrastructure wireless network, which depends on a central station coordinating all communication. The second category is unstructured networks or ad hoc networks give equal function to all stations in the network. The third category is hybrid networks joins the first two categories (Wagner et al., 2016). Use ad hoc networks for communication among vehicles and infrastructure networks, like Wireless Local Area Networks and Cellular Systems for communication (WLANs) with an essence network(Prasan & Murugappan, 2016). The smart technologies and components used in cities are:

i. Self-driving

The goal of self-driving cars is to drive independently without human activation and to navigate the street safely to decrease traffic accidents. According to the report from KPMG, the self-driving may eliminate 90% of accidents. There are six accreditation levels of self-driving as the industry defined, Level 0, the driver controls the vehicle by him/herself, even the vehicle includes different warning systems and interventions. Level 1, the driver will be in full control of the vehicle. This level may include warning applications like blind spot detection. At level 2, the vehicles have a low level of automatic, including an assisted braking system and lane detection. In level 3, the vehicles join two functions for crowded traffic, they are automatic speed reduction and driving in a straight line. At level 4, in this level, the driver just allows limited automatic drive due to consistent monitoring on the road in chosen environments that to give up when control is required. In level 5, the vehicle can reach any place without human interaction [(Wagner et al., 2016). Examples of vehicles that have features of self-drive: Mercedes S-Class 2014, which has auto-parking, lane keeping, automated acceleration/braking and fatigue monitoring and clever steering. Also, the BMW i3 2014 in traffic jams, can speed autonomously and reach 30 miles per hour. Audi A7 2015 in traffic jams, provides autonomously breaking. There are challenges to applying self-drive are need to use some specific advanced networks to improve the vehicle and make it suitable for self-drive. And the advanced networks are not available in all countries. Also, using advanced technologies in vehicles will not keep them in all people's hands so not anyone can buy the technologies vehicles to practice self-drive (Song et al., 2019).

ii. Safety drive

The goals for making vehicles safe to drive are to reduce accidents, and injuries, and to keep the status zero accident. To achieve this goal of zero accidents vehicle network application, that will provide drivers and travellers with a wide range of information. Such as the application explains to use of V2I communication to reduce the arrival time of emergency services(Y. Peng et al., 2019).

iii. Driving of Social

Vehicles combine on the fly to be a part of a social network that contains neighbouring vehicles. The vehicles can be shared the same interests, move towards the same direction/ destination, and locations, or be part of existing relationships. There are smart tools, the drivers use them to help choose the best road. Such as the Google Maps Application(Wagner et al., 2016). Also, some companies use private applications to serve their customers, like Uber and Lyft company. During these applications, the users can share their location with other people (Wang et al., 2019).

iv. Electric Vehicles

Many people are interested in using fully electric, hybrid and zero-emission vehicles. Most people like to use electric vehicles in highly populated locations and at slow speeds. Also, these types of vehicles help to contribute to protecting the environment(Wang et al., 2019).

17. CONTEXT-AWARENESS OF VEHICLE

During the improvements in data and communication advances in the zone of Intelligent Transportation Systems (ITS) especially in the VANETs zone, numerous scientists and industry experts have moved toward becoming pulled into the new field which is known as context-aware vehicular ad-hoc networks. It is another procedure (context-aware technique) that acquaints created arrangements with VANETs' difficulties by utilizing contextual information. This kind of data helps in portraying the circumstance of the driving which is additionally alluded to as driving setting data. The setting data can be the position, heading, speed, and increasing speed of the vehicle, traffic and climate data. All the setting data can be utilized by the directing conventions to expand their execution (Shaibani & Zahary, 2019).

Internet of Vehicles (IoV) is used to enable vehicles to be context-aware of the circumstances that exist around the vehicles, with that particularly related to it (M. F. Khan et al., 2019). There are three main subsystems to providing context awareness in vehicles: sensing, reasoning and acting.

1. **Sensing:** the sensing subsystem combines contextual information from several sensors integrated with the vehicle's OBU. There are different types of sensors according to the vehicle's requirements. Such as sensors for location, or for infrared or ultrasound(Wagner et al., 2016).

2. **Reasoning:** the reasoning processes the primary data to extract high-level contextual information, like the situation of the driver. A single sensor can extract contextual information, determine particular contextual information, or take away from multiple sensors, to determine uncertain contextual information(Granda et al., 2018) (Wagner et al., 2016).

3. **Acting:** the acting subsystem provides services for users or drivers. This subsystem sends warning messages and alerts in vehicles and smart parking, these are considered high applications, that are used to avoid accidents and reduce road crowded (Rahim et al., 2018).

Alhammad et al. created a VANET on-street context-knowing smart parking supporting system, deploying the idea of the centralized Info-Station to determine and reserve parking (Wagner et al., 2016). This reservation process is ordered by the driver's priorities. All the parking area includes Info-Station which acts as a station and provides wireless coverage by Dedicated Short-Range Communications (DSRC) as shown in Figure 11(Mehmood et al., 2017).

Figure 13. On-street parking system scenario

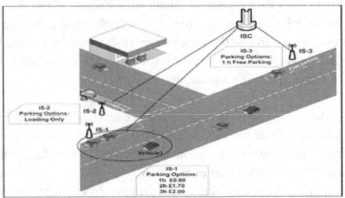

Wan et al. offered a dynamic parking service, this service provides planning for traffic authorisation. Also, provide a service of parking reservation, also allow the drivers to park their vehicles beside the road for short periods. This service provides considers contextual information for the drivers like time and road conditions. Traffic authorities can organize this service dynamically and effectively decrease parking problems in a smart city (Shaibani & Zahary, 2019). Cunha et al. display that vehicles tend to show comparable behaviour and routines in terms of mobility. Vehicle mobility can be mapped as a social network, following the same basic laws of degree distribution and range among nodes. To improve the power of communication protocol services can be applied on vehicular networks (Reema, 2017). The are some challenges to applying V2I in smart cities as the following (Masek et al., 2016)(Ang et al., 2019)(Jindal & Bedi, 2016):

i.   Need to use some specific advanced networks to improve the vehicle and make it suitable for self-drive. And the advanced networks are not available in all countries.
ii. Using advanced technologies in vehicles, will keep them not in all people's hands so not anyone can buy the technologies vehicles to practice self-drive.
iii. In self-drive should the driver be wake up for in case to avoid any electronic fault?
iv. Updating the network of the application to keep up to date with the newest roads and paths.
v.   The sensors cost more money for maintenance and the sensors need to be pre and after-maintenance.
vi. Network applications are sometimes affected by climatic conditions and physiography.

vii. Providing electric points to charge electric vehicles.

18. CHALLENGES AND PERSPECTIVES IN VANETS

The set of standards most commonly implemented in wireless local area networks (WLAN) is IEEE 802.11. Another version of these standards has been created to suit Vehicular Environments, known as IEEE 802.11p [59]. The last-mentioned standard is an enhancement of EEE 802.11 designed for vehicular wireless communication. It is designed to facilitate both vehicle-to-vehicle (V2V) and vehicle-to-infrastructure (V2I) connections [45].

Examples of traffic challenges include safety issues and congestion. Many studies and recommendations have been proposed to address or minimise the effects of these issues. Wireless communication techniques are utilised in Intelligent Transport Systems to facilitate information transmission among cars and between vehicles and infrastructure. The primary focus of this research is V2I. Implementing V2I protocols must address issues such as the Doppler effect, continuity, reliability, and security [69].

i. **Doppler Effect:** The Doppler effect is the variation in wavelength or frequency of a wave concerning an observer who is moving relatively to the source of the wave. In V2I the observer is represented by the infrastructure components, and the source is the moving vehicle. When the moving vehicle tries to send data (a wave signal) to the infrastructure, the infrastructure component must take into consideration the Doppler effect on the received signal. In that case, the frequency of the received signal differs from the real frequency from the source and this is because the source has a velocity (is moving)(Sangodoyin et al., 2019)(G. Noh et al., 2019).

ii. **Continuity:** Continuity in Vehicle-to-Infrastructure (V2I) communication is hindered by increased mobility, posing challenges for seamless hand-offs between infrastructure components and moving vehicles. The data transmission rate is significantly influenced by the frequency of hand-offs. Some solutions focus on minimising connection instability, with many of them depending on Rayleigh fading channels. Other proposed solutions rely on calculating the number of Access Points in the nearby infrastructure to change the data rate. When there are few access points (APs), use a higher data rate for transmission. Conversely, when there are many APs, use a lower data rate (Lin & Tang, 2019)(S. K. Noh et al., 2016).

19. CONCLUSION

This paper presented a comprehensive overview of VANETs. It discussed the Impact of urban environments on V2I communications and routing protocols in VANETs, and existing security mechanisms for safety in vehicular environments. In addition, it discussed in detail the ad-hoc network (VANETs) routing protocols properties and vehicular communications in VANETs. Moreover, it explained the security and desired features and characteristics of VANETs. Furthermore, it highlighted directions for 1) vehicular network architectures with SCSS, 2) hierarchical network management framework, 3) driving heterogeneous vehicular networks, 4) deployment of infrastructure for vehicular networks, and 5) promoting flexibility for infrastructures.

Finally, for future research in VANETs such as vehicle to infrastructure (V2I) in smart cities and context-awareness of Vehicles.

The contribution of this paper is that it offers an overarching overview of connected vehicle technology, its applications, its security mechanisms, open challenges, and potential areas of future studies.

20. FUTURE RECOMMENDATION

Nowadays, vehicles are increasing, so the danger of accidents is increasing, and people are facing harm to their lives. Not all of them have the same ability to drive with full awareness. So the high requirements to the companies of vehicles are supply more safety in the vehicles. Such as the vehicle body will be strong and include advanced sensors. Also, should the traffic authorities build advanced infrastructure including sign directions and cautions?

1. This paper suggests, that advanced vehicles need to connect with the application of a wide-range network and make a survey around 100 meters to inform the driver of the states of vehicles with their total speed. This suggestion will help the driver to be careful when he/she drives and avoid some vehicles that are not illegal to drive. So, I do not agree with some vehicle services, like parking the vehicle beside the road, as Wan et al offered, even the parking for a short period.

2. This paper does not agree with some vehicle services, like parking the vehicle beside the road, as Wan et al offered, even the parking for a short period. Parking vehicles beside the road will cause a traffic jam and more accidents and the drivers who drive on the road can't see the people who cross the street. Also, the driver will get a sensor alarm when driving near vehicles beside the

road and the driver will not pay attention properly to driving. The data between vehicles to infrastructure should be confidential and to reach that, we should design a secure vehicle to Infrastructure. That will avoid exchanging messages in public between V2I.

3. Necessary to providing fast developments in wireless technologies can be used in the improvement of the driving environment by taking into consideration allowing road safety, infotainment and efficient transportation. Providing technological improvement will avoid the causes of increasing accidents and deaths.

4. Data gathering and sensing prioritise the efficient acquisition of road information from numerous diverse sources. The existing systems used by traffic management businesses collect data in various formats, time ranges, and levels of detail. The systems were installed at different times, each with limited functionality for exchanging data between them. This paper suggests that future utilisation of TMSs should adhere to traffic-related information-gathering principles outlined by city authorities to pinpoint areas where new communication technologies and systems could be implemented to enhance the accuracy, timeliness, and cost-effectiveness of data collection. Current trends in TMS development involve utilising advanced communication and sensing technologies like mobile sensing, Wireless Sensor Networks (WSNs), Cellular Networks, and Social Media Feeds to overcome the constraints of existing systems in the future Smart Cities era.

5. Embedded devices, acting as small sensors, are widely deployed in road networks to collect data using wireless technology. These devices can be placed on vehicles, roadside units (RSUs), or even under the pavement to detect and communicate unexpected events. Embedded in-vehicle sensors monitor and measure parameters associated with the vehicle's operations. Furthermore, the data is sent to the vehicles closer in proximity and/or the Roadside Units (RSUs). In embedded systems, sensors are mostly utilised to measure the speed of passing cars, traffic volumes, or other environmental characteristics. This study suggests that modern TMS should prioritise novel methods that allow for data gathering from a specific area under certain time limits while reducing costs and spectrum utilisation, and maximising system efficiency.

6. Wireless sensors have been widely used in various environments to efficiently and accurately track dangerous events. They are already being used for data collection and monitoring in tasks such as real-time control of traffic lights, adjusting them based on road congestion levels, and managing urban parking. Nevertheless, deploying Wireless Sensor Networks (WSNs) in the road environment encounters additional hurdles in addition to the well-recognised concerns. This paper suggests selecting an appropriate routing protocol that can effectively handle certain needs to ensure dependable and efficient Medium Access Control (MAC) functionality and data forwarding methods.

7. Moving on forward, and based on the details of this research, the security side in implementing V2I must have a high priority. It is recommended to add more studies and focus on the prevention and detection parts taking into consideration the privacy and safety of users. This is because users will not feel confident integrating their vehicles into a system that doesn't have a guaranteed level of privacy and safety. Privacy ensures the user that his movement is not under spying nor traced for malicious purposes. In addition to that, the safety factor is what makes the system practical and it is one of the main reasons for creating such a system. So, avoiding errors and attacks that might lead to accidents is extremely important and a recommended field for further research.

REFERENCES

Agarwal, P. (2017). Technical Review on Different Applications, Challenges and Security inVANET. *JoMTRA Journal of Multimedia Technology & Recent Advancements*, 4(3), 21–30.

Ahmed, A., & Ahmed, E. (2016). *A Survey on Mobile Edge Computing. JANUARY*. DOI: 10.13140/RG.2.1.3254.7925

Alamri, S., & Khan, S. (2023). Artificial intelligence based modelling for predicting CO_2 emission for climate change mitigation in Saudi Arabia. *International Journal of Advanced Computer Science and Applications*, 14(4). Advance online publication. DOI: 10.14569/IJACSA.2023.0140421

Alrubaiei, M. H., Al-Saadi, M. H., Shaker, H., Sharef, B., & Khan, S. (2022). Internet of Things in Cyber Security Scope. In *Blockchain Technology and Computational Excellence for Society 5.0* (pp. 146–187). IGI Global. DOI: 10.4018/978-1-7998-8382-1.ch008

Alves, J.Junior, & Wille, E. C. G. (2018). Routing in Vehicular Ad Hoc Networks: Main Characteristics and Tendencies. *Journal of Computer Networks and Communications*, 2018, 1–10. DOI: 10.1155/2018/1302123

Ang, L. M., Seng, K. P., Ijemaru, G. K., & Zungeru, A. M. (2019). Deployment of IoV for Smart Cities: Applications, Architecture, and Challenges. *IEEE Access : Practical Innovations, Open Solutions*, 7, 6473–6492. DOI: 10.1109/ACCESS.2018.2887076

AT&T. (2016). *ECOMP (Enhanced Control, Orchestration, Management & Policy) Architecture White Paper. 0*, 31.

Awan, K., Sherazi, H. H. R., Iqbal, R., Rizwan, S., Khan, Z. A., & Imran, M. A. (2019). A Heterogeneous IoV Architecture for Data Forwarding in Vehicle to Infrastructure Communication. *Mobile Information Systems*, 2019, 1–12. DOI: 10.1155/2019/3101276

Awang, A., Husain, K., Kamel, N., & Aissa, S. (2017). Routing in Vehicular Ad-hoc Networks: A Survey on Single- and Cross-Layer Design Techniques, and Perspectives. *IEEE Access : Practical Innovations, Open Solutions*, 5, 9497–9517. DOI: 10.1109/ACCESS.2017.2692240

Begum, R. (2016). *A Survey on VANETs Applications and Its Challenges*. 1–7. DOI: 10.2307/1170533

Bharadiya, J. P., Thomas, R. K., & Ahmed, F. (2023). Rise of Artificial Intelligence in Business and Industry. *Journal of Engineering Research and Reports*, 25(3), 85–103. DOI: 10.9734/jerr/2023/v25i3893

Bhat, C. (2018). *Cybersecurity Challenges and Pathways in the Context of Connected Vehicle Systems. February*.

Bhoi, S. K., & Khilar, P. M. (2016). VehiHealth: An Emergency Routing Protocol for Vehicular Ad Hoc Network to Support Healthcare System. *Journal of Medical Systems*, 40(3), 1–12. DOI: 10.1007/s10916-015-0420-2 PMID: 26696419

Cen, N., Jagannath, J., Moretti, S., Guan, Z., & Melodia, T. (2019). LANET: Visible-light ad hoc networks. *Ad Hoc Networks*, 84, 107–123. DOI: 10.1016/j.adhoc.2018.04.009

Challenges, G. (2019). *Vehicle-to-Vehicle/Vehicle-to-Infrastructure Control*.

Cheng, J., Cheng, J., Zhou, M., Liu, F., Gao, S., & Liu, C. (2015). Routing in internet of vehicles: A review. *IEEE Transactions on Intelligent Transportation Systems*, 16(5), 2339–2352. DOI: 10.1109/TITS.2015.2423667

Classification, P. (2019). *(12) Patent Application Publication (10) Pub . No . : US 2019 / 0034587 A1. 1*.

Cooper, C., Franklin, D., Ros, M., Safaei, F., & Abolhasan, M. (2017). A Comparative Survey of VANET Clustering Techniques. In *IEEE Communications Surveys and Tutorials* (Vol. 19, Issue 1). DOI: 10.1109/COMST.2016.2611524

Design, P. (2019). Guest Editorial Special Issue on IoT on the Move [IoIV]. *IEEE Internet of Things Journal*, 6(1), 1–5. DOI: 10.1109/JIOT.2019.2896750

di Pietro, N., Merluzzi, M., Strinati, E. C., & Barbarossa, S. (2019). *Resilient Design of 5G Mobile-Edge Computing Over Intermittent mmWave Links*. 1–31.

Domingos, F., Cunha, D., Villas, L., Boukerche, A., Maia, G., Viana, A. C., Mini, R. A. F., & Loureiro, A. A. F. (2016). Data Communication in VANETs: Survey. *Applications and Challenges. Elsevier*, 44, 90–103. DOI: 10.1016/j.adhoc.2016.02.017

Elbery, A., Rakha, H., Elnainay, M., Drira, W., & Filali, F. (2015). Eco-Routing Using V2I Communication: System Evaluation. *IEEE Conference on Intelligent Transportation Systems, Proceedings, ITSC, 2015-Octob*(September), 71–76. DOI: 10.1109/ITSC.2015.20

Ema, R., Akram, A., & Hossain, M. (2014). Performance Analysis of DSDV, AODV AND AOMDV Routing Protocols based on Fixed and Mobility Network Model in Wireless Sensor Network. *Global Journal Of, 14*(6).

Fogue, M., Sanguesa, J., Martinez, F., & Marquez-Barja, J. (2018). Improving Road-side Unit Deployment in Vehicular Networks by Exploiting Genetic Algorithms. *Applied Sciences (Basel, Switzerland)*, 8(1), 86. DOI: 10.3390/app8010086

Friginal, J., De Andrés, D., Ruiz, J. C., & Martínez, M. (2014). A survey of evaluation platforms for ad hoc routing protocols: A resilience perspective. *Computer Networks, 75*(PartA), 395–413. DOI: 10.1016/j.comnet.2014.09.010

Ghafoor, K. (2016). Video Streaming over Vehicular Ad Hoc Networks: A Comparative Study and Future Perspectives. *ARO (Koya)*, 4(2), 25–36. DOI: 10.14500/aro.10128

Ghafoor, K. Z., Mohammed, M. A., Lloret, J., Bakar, K. A., & Zainuddin, Z. M. (2013). Routing Protocols in Vehicular Ad hoc Networks: Survey and Research Challenges. *Network Protocols and Algorithms*, 3(7), 39. DOI: 10.5296/npa.v5i4.4134

Granda, F., Azpilicueta, L., Vargas-Rosales, C., Celaya-Echarri, M., Lopez-Iturri, P., Aguirre, E., Astrain, J. J., Medrano, P., Villandangos, J., & Falcone, F. (2018). Deterministic propagation modeling for intelligent vehicle communication in smart cities. *Sensors (Basel)*, 18(7), 2133. Advance online publication. DOI: 10.3390/s18072133 PMID: 29970826

Harding, J., Powell, G., Yoon, R., Fikentscher, J., Doyle, C., Sade, D., Lukuc, M., Simons, J., & Wang, J. (2014). *Vehicle-to-vehicle communications: Readiness of V2V technology for application (Report No. DOT HS 812 014). August*. DOI: 10.1109/SysEng.2015.7302741

Islam, M., Chowdhury, M., Li, H., & Hu, H. (2018). Cybersecurity Attacks in Vehicle-to-Infrastructure Applications and Their Prevention. *Transportation Research Record: Journal of the Transportation Research Board*, 2672(19), 66–78. Advance online publication. DOI: 10.1177/0361198118799012

Jahir, Y., Atiquzzaman, M., Refai, H., Paranjothi, A., & LoPresti, P. G. (2019). Routing protocols and architecture for Disaster Area Network: A survey. *Ad Hoc Networks*, 82(August), 1–14. DOI: 10.1016/j.adhoc.2018.08.005

Jindal, V., & Bedi, P. (2016). Vehicular Ad-Hoc Networks: Introduction, Standards, Routing Protocols and Challenges. *International Journal of Computer Science Issues*, 13(2), 44–55. DOI: 10.20943/01201602.4455

Jindal, V., Mahavidyalaya, K., & Bedi, P. (2016). Vehicular Ad-Hoc Networks: Introduction, Standards, Routing Protocols and Challenges. *International Journal of Computer Science Issues*, 13(2), 44–55. DOI: 10.20943/01201602.4455

Khan, M. F., Aadil, F., Maqsood, M., Bukhari, S. H. R., Hussain, M., & Nam, Y. (2019). Moth flame clustering algorithm for internet of vehicle (MFCA-IoV). *IEEE Access : Practical Innovations, Open Solutions*, 7, 11613–11629. DOI: 10.1109/ ACCESS.2018.2886420

Khan, S., Al-Dmour, A., Bali, V., Rabbani, M. R., & Thirunavukkarasu, K. (2021a). Cloud computing based futuristic educational model for virtual learning. *Journal of Statistics and Management Systems*, 24(2), 357–385. DOI: 10.1080/09720510.2021.1879468

Khan, S., Qader, M. R., Thirunavukkarasu, K., & Abimannan, S. (2020, October). Analysis of business intelligence impact on organizational performance. In *2020 International Conference on Data Analytics for Business and Industry: Way Towards a Sustainable Economy (ICDABI)* (pp. 1-4). IEEE. DOI: 10.1109/ICDA-BI51230.2020.9325610

Khan, S., Syed, M. H., Hammad, R., & Bushager, A. F. (Eds.). (2022). *Block-chain technology and computational excellence for society 5.0*. IGI Global. DOI: 10.4018/978-1-7998-8382-1

Khan, S., Thirunavukkarasu, K., AlDmour, A., & Shreem, S. S. (Eds.). (2021b). *A Step towards Society 5.0: Research, innovations, and developments in Cloud-based computing technologies*. CRC Press. DOI: 10.1201/9781003138037

Khan, U. A., & Lee, S. S. (2019). Multi-Layer Problems and Solutions in VANETs: A Review. *Electronics (Basel)*, 8(2), 204. DOI: 10.3390/electronics8020204

Kumar, A., & Tyagi, M. (2014). Geographical Topologies of Routing Protocols in Vehicular Ad hoc Networks – A Survey. [IJCSIT]. *International Journal of Computer Science and Information Technologies*, 5(3), 3062–3065.

Kumar, N. A., & Raj, E. G. D. P. (2015). RS-CBAODV: An Enhanced Reactive Routing Algorithm for VANET to Reduce Connection Breakage using Remote Storage Concepts. *International Journal of Information Technology and Computer Science*, 7(10), 74–83. DOI: 10.5815/ijitcs.2015.10.09

Laaki, H., Miche, Y., & Tammi, K. (2019). Prototyping a Digital Twin for real time remote control over mobile networks: Application of remote surgery. *IEEE Access : Practical Innovations, Open Solutions*, 7, 1–1. DOI: 10.1109/ACCESS.2019.2897018

Lai, Y., Lin, H., Yang, F., & Wang, T. (2019). Efficient data request answering in vehicular Ad-hoc networks based on fog nodes and filters. *Future Generation Computer Systems*, 93, 130–142. DOI: 10.1016/j.future.2018.09.065

Liang, W., Li, Z., Zhang, H., Wang, S., & Bie, R. (2015). Vehicular Ad Hoc networks: Architectures, research issues, methodologies, challenges, and trends. *International Journal of Distributed Sensor Networks*, 2015(8), 745303. Advance online publication. DOI: 10.1155/2015/745303

Lin, Z., & Tang, Y. (2019). Distributed Multi-channel MAC Protocol for VANET: An Adaptive Frame Structure Scheme. *IEEE Access : Practical Innovations, Open Solutions*, 7, 1–1. DOI: 10.1109/ACCESS.2019.2892820

Masek, P., Masek, J., Frantik, P., Fujdiak, R., Ometov, A., Hosek, J., Andreev, S., Mlynek, P., & Misurec, J. (2016). A harmonized perspective on transportation management in smart cities: The novel IoT-driven environment for road traffic modeling. *Sensors (Basel)*, 16(11), 1872. Advance online publication. DOI: 10.3390/s16111872 PMID: 27834796

Mehmood, Y., Ahmad, F., Yaqoob, I., Adnane, A., Imran, M., & Guizani, S. (2017). Internet-of-Things-Based Smart Cities: Recent Advances and Challenges. *IEEE Communications Magazine*, 55(9), 16–24. DOI: 10.1109/MCOM.2017.1600514

Mejri, M. N., Ben-Othman, J., & Hamdi, M. (2014). Survey on VANET security challenges and possible cryptographic solutions. *Vehicular Communications*, 1(2), 53–66. DOI: 10.1016/j.vehcom.2014.05.001

Mishra, R. (2016). *VANET Security : Issues, Challenges and Solutions*. 1050–1055.

Moreau, V., Dos Reis, P., & Vuille, F. (2019). Enough Metals? Resource Constraints to Supply a Fully Renewable Energy System. *Resources*, 8(1), 29. DOI: 10.3390/resources8010029

Mounce, R., & Nelson, J. D. (2019). On the potential for one-way electric vehicle car-sharing in future mobility systems. *Transportation Research Part A: Policy and Practice, 120*(November 2018), 17–30. DOI: 10.1016/j.tra.2018.12.003

Muhammad, M., & Safdar, G. A. (2018). Survey on existing authentication issues for cellular-assisted V2X communication. In *Vehicular Communications* (Vol. 12). DOI: 10.1016/j.vehcom.2018.01.008

Noh, G., Kim, J., Chung, H., & Kim, I. (2019). Realizing Multi-Gbps Vehicular Communication: Design, Implementation, and Validation. *IEEE Access : Practical Innovations, Open Solutions*, 7, 1–1. DOI: 10.1109/ACCESS.2019.2896598

Noh, S. K., Kim, P. J., & Yoon, J. H. (2016). Doppler effect on V2I path loss and V2V channel models. *2016 International Conference on Information and Communication Technology Convergence, ICTC 2016, 1*, 898–902. DOI: 10.1109/ICTC.2016.7763324

Nwizege, K. S., Bottero, M., Mmeah, S., & Nwiwure, E. D. (2014). Vehicles-to-infrastructure communication safety messaging in DSRC. *Procedia Computer Science, 34*(DPNoC), 559–564. DOI: 10.1016/j.procs.2014.07.070

Patel, D., Faisal, M., Batavia, P., Makhija, S., & Mani, M. (2016). Overview of Routing Protocols in VANET. *International Journal of Computer Applications*, 136(9), 975–8887. DOI: 10.5120/ijca2016908555

Peng, H., Liang, L., Shen, X., & Li, G. Y. (2018). Vehicular Communications: A Network Layer Perspective. *IEEE Transactions on Vehicular Technology*, 1, 1–32. DOI: 10.1109/TVT.2018.2833427

Peng, Y., Li, J., Park, S., Zhu, K., Hassan, M. M., & Alsanad, A. (2019). Energy-efficient cooperative transmission for intelligent transportation systems. *Future Generation Computer Systems*, 94, 634–640. https://doi.org/https://doi.org/10.1016/j.future.2018.11.053. DOI: 10.1016/j.future.2018.11.053

Prasan, U. D., & Murugappan, S. (2016). An analysis on vehicular ad-hoc networks: Research issues, challenges and applications. *International Journal of Applied Engineering Research: IJAER*, 11(6), 4569–4575.

Qader, M. R., Khan, S., Kamal, M., Usman, M., & Haseeb, M. (2021). Forecasting carbon emissions due to electricity power generation in Bahrain. *Environmental Science and Pollution Research International*, ●●●, 1–12. PMID: 34661842

Qureshi, K. N., & Abdullah, A. H. (2013). Topology based routing protocols for VANET and their comparison with MANET. *Journal of Theoretical and Applied Information Technology*, 58(3), 707–715.

Rahim, A., Kong, X., Xia, F., Ning, Z., Ullah, N., Wang, J., & Das, S. K. (2018). Vehicular Social Networks: A survey. *Pervasive and Mobile Computing*, 43, 96–113. DOI: 10.1016/j.pmcj.2017.12.004

Rajan, K., Kumar, K. S., Kannapiran, T., Khan, S., Al-Dmour, A., & Sharef, B. T. (2022, June). Intelligent Traffic Management System for Smart Cities Utilizing Reinforcement Learning Algorithm. In *2022 ASU International Conference in Emerging Technologies for Sustainability and Intelligent Systems (ICETSIS)* (pp. 170-177). IEEE. DOI: 10.1109/ICETSIS55481.2022.9888885

Rawat, D. B., Bajracharya, C., & Yan, G. (2015). Towards intelligent transportation Cyber-Physical Systems: Real-time computing and communications perspectives. *Conference Proceedings - IEEE SOUTHEASTCON, 2015-June*(June). DOI: 10.1109/SECON.2015.7132923

Reema, M. (2017). *Performance Evaluation and Study of Routing Protocols : MANET vs VANET. 6495*(4), 204–208.

Sachdeva, S., Ali, A., & Khan, S. (2022). Secure and privacy issues in telemedicine: Issues, solutions, and standards. In *Telemedicine: The Computer Transformation of Healthcare* (pp. 321–331). Springer International Publishing. DOI: 10.1007/978-3-030-99457-0_21

Sangodoyin, S., Mecklenbrauker, C. F., Lerch, M., Zochmann, E., Caban, S., Groll, H., Rupp, M., Prokes, A., Blumenstein, J., Pratschner, S., Bernado, L., Zemen, T., Molisch, A. F., & Hofer, M. (2019). Position-Specific Statistics of 60 GHz Vehicular Channels During Overtaking. *IEEE Access : Practical Innovations, Open Solutions*, 7, 1–1. DOI: 10.1109/ACCESS.2019.2893136

Scholar, P. (2014). *Position Based Protocol with QOS Parameters in VANETs *1,2. 3*(1).

Shaibani, R., & Zahary, A. (2019). Survey of Context-Aware Video Transmission over Vehicular Ad-Hoc Networks (VANETs). *ICST Transactions on Mobile Communications and Applications*, 0(0), 156089. DOI: 10.4108/eai.13-7-2018.156089

Shen, X., Chen, J., Wosinska, L., Ou, J., Li, J., Chen, L., & Van, D. P. (2019). Service Migration in Fog Computing Enabled Cellular Networks to Support Real-time Vehicular Communications. *IEEE Access : Practical Innovations, Open Solutions*, 7, 1–1. DOI: 10.1109/ACCESS.2019.2893571

Shi, W., Zhou, H., Li, J., Xu, W., Zhang, N., & Shen, X. (2018). Drone Assisted Vehicular Networks: Architecture, Challenges and Opportunities. *IEEE Network*, 32(3), 130–137. DOI: 10.1109/MNET.2017.1700206

Song, H., Liu, W., Liu, A., Li, X., Huang, B., & Wang, T. (2019). Deployment Optimization of Data Centers in Vehicular Networks. *IEEE Access : Practical Innovations, Open Solutions*, 7, 1–1. DOI: 10.1109/ACCESS.2019.2897615

Sorial, G. A., & Hong, J. (2014). *Environmental Science and Edited by.*

Terry, J., & Bachmann, C. (2019). Quantifying the potential impact of autonomous vehicle adoption on government finances. *Transportation Research Record: Journal of the Transportation Research Board*, 2673(5), 72–83. DOI: 10.1177/0361198119837218

Ullah, A., Yaqoob, S., Imran, M., & Ning, H. (2019). Emergency Message Dissemination Schemes Based on Congestion Avoidance in VANET and Vehicular FoG Computing. *IEEE Access : Practical Innovations, Open Solutions*, 7, 1570–1585. DOI: 10.1109/ACCESS.2018.2887075

Wagner, I., Maglaras, L., Janicke, H., He, Y., & Al-Bayatti, A. (2016). Social Internet of Vehicles for Smart Cities. *Journal of Sensor and Actuator Networks*, 5(1), 3. DOI: 10.3390/jsan5010003

Wang, H., You, F., Chu, X., Li, X., & Sun, X. (2019). Research On Customer Marketing Acceptance for Future Automatic Driving — A Case Study in China City. *IEEE Access : Practical Innovations, Open Solutions*, 7, 1–1. DOI: 10.1109/ACCESS.2019.2898936

Zhang, S., Zhang, N., Fang, X., Yang, P., & Shen, X. S. (2017). Self-Sustaining Caching Stations: Toward Cost-Effective 5G-Enabled Vehicular Networks. *IEEE Communications Magazine*, 55(11), 202–208. DOI: 10.1109/MCOM.2017.1700129

Zhang, Y., Lopez, J., & Wang, Z. (2019). Mobile Edge Computing for Vehicular Networks [From the Guest Editors]. *IEEE Vehicular Technology Magazine*, 14(1), 27–108. DOI: 10.1109/MVT.2018.2885367

Chapter 13
AI Predictive Maintenance in CIoT Using Blockchain

Kuldeep Singh Kaswan

Galgotias University, India

Jagjit Singh Dhatterwal

Koneru Lakshmaiah Education Foundation, Vaddeswaram, India

Kiran Malik

Department of Computer Science and Engineering (AIML), GL Bajaj Institute of Technology & Management, Greater Noida, India

ABSTRACT

Artificial Intelligence (AI) together with Blockchain technology has the ability to revolutionise the areas of predictive maintenance in Connected Internet of Things (CIoT). It is a preventive strategy that involves the ideal use of real time data in a bid to avoid equipment breakdowns, which definitely makes operations to run efficiently. With the application of AI and Blockchain in CIoT, the proper implementation of maintenance policies and strategies available are made efficient and effective through the use of advanced machine learning algorithms and the decentralised system of Blockchain. This chapter looks at the extent of applying AI-Predictive Maintenance, focusing on how machine learning and deep learning enhance the sophistication of models as well as the decision-making steps. It explores the function of Blockchain in data protection and transparency and how it applies to CIoT systems and practices discuss the seminal idea, advantages, and specializations of Blockchain. We can address many issues such as security for data through the application of AI with Blockchain, modification of maintenance scheduling, and work the functional reliability for organizations. The main objective of this chapter is therefore to define the integration of AI and Blockchain and how they are shap-

DOI: 10.4018/979-8-3693-2157-7.ch013

ing predictive maintenance. It offers the framework on how the two components of smart contracts and blockchain measures can be integrated, and how they can solve the issue of data security and privacy. It also considers various cases in industries including manufacturing, energy, and transport; examining actual applications and the problems as well as the possible approaches to overcome faced within the industries. This chapter ends with regards to future trends where attention is directed towards the 4M's and anticipated advancement in the intelligent CIoT systems and predictive maintenance.

1. INTRODUCTION

Distributed data processing is, in many ways, changing how CIoT systems handle and protect the information. Data, in CIoT systems, is produced and required at various points in the numerous devices and networks. Central data management approaches have some specific issues on scalability, security and data integrity. These problems are solved with the help of decentralized systems based on the principles of blockchain technology, as global data are distributed among different nodes. The decentralization of ledgers helps in reducing the cases of data fiddling and promotes transparency through register's no alterability (smith, 2022).

Overview of Predictive Maintenance

The baseline concept of predictive maintenance is to anticipate equipment failures and implement manageable solution before the failures happens. It is therefore an efficient technique that entails the use of historical and current data to estimate when an equipment may likely develop a fault. Weibull distribution is one of the statistical models for dealing with failure time data and identifying when maintenance is required (Jones & Brown, 2021). For example, the Weibull probability density function (PDF) is expressed as:For example, the Weibull probability density function (PDF) is expressed as:

$$f(t; \lambda, k) = \frac{k}{\lambda} \left(\frac{t}{\lambda} \right)^{k-1} \exp\left(-\left(\frac{t}{\lambda} \right)^{k} \right)$$

where λ is the scale parameter and k is the shape parameter. This function helps in understanding the failure distribution and planning maintenance schedules accordingly.

Role of AI in Predictive Maintenance

AI makes Predictive Maintenance better with the use of Artificial learning algorithms enabling massive data analysis. For example, methods such as linear regression can then be used to predict equipment failure from a number of factors. The linear regression model is given by:The linear regression model is given by:

$$y = \beta_0 + \beta_1 x + \epsilon$$

where y is the dependent variable (e.g, time to failure), x is the independent variable (e.g., senson readings), β_0 is the intercept, β_1 is the slope, and ϵ is the error term. AI models can also leverage deep learning techniques to handle complex data patterns and improve prediction accuracy.

Importance of Blockchain in CIoT

In CIoT, blockchain is useful for integrating controlling functions that maintain the availability and immutability of the data. Through its consensus mechanism, blockchain has the ability to fulfill the aspect of data integrity in CIoT systems (Taylor, 2023). Some of these include; the proof of work (PoW) where the solver is required to work out a contraction problem in order to validate a transaction. The function for PoW can be represented as:The function for PoW can be represented as:

$$H(x) = SHA256(x)$$

where $H(x)$ is the hash of the input x, and SHA256 is a cryptographic hash function. Blockchain's immutability and transparency help in maintaining accurate records and preventing tampering or fraud.

2. FUNDAMENTALS OF PREDICTIVE MAINTENANCE IN CIOT

Predictive maintenance relates to the management of equipment or machinery maintenance by forecasting failure so that adequate action may be taken prior to such a failure occurring. The CIoT (Connected Internet of Things) in turn by using sensors and IoT devices, for the real-time monitoring of equipment performance for the kind of Predictive maintenance (Lee et al., 2014).

Definition and Key Concepts

Depending on the characteristics of real-world systems, all this data is processed with the help of sophisticated algorithms that enables predictive analysis of possible failures and their optimal timing. The core idea is based on gathering data from equipment over time and real time, performing statistical analysis and using predictive models in order to estimate future health states of equipment (Li & Zhang, 2017).

Example: If a machine's vibration levels exceed a threshold value, predictive algorithms can forecast potential failure based on historical data. The vibration data $x(t)$ can be modeled using a function such as $x(t) = A\sin(\omega t + \phi)$, where A is amplitude, ω is angular frequency, t is time, and ϕ is phase shift. Anomalies in this function can signal impending equipment issues.

Benefits and Challenges

The advantages of the predictive maintenance include; Less down time, longer equipment life and less cost in maintenance. This way, organisations can be able to avoid circumstances where they have to carry out costly rectifications and or work interruptions (Zhang & Yang, 2019). Nevertheless, there are issues like quality of inputs, system integration issues and very high initial cost of implementation. For instance, interfacing, improving, and employing IoT devices with other systems and also checking the reliability of the data adds more cost and needs a specialist's attention.

Example: Self-predicting maintenance cuts down the downtime by 30% compared to what is achieved by the reactive maintenance strategies. An instance is where a manufacturing plant records a loss of 100 hours of production a year because of equipment breakdowns; predictive maintenance can cut the time lost to 70 hours resulting in improved productivity.

Use Cases in Various Industries

Predictive maintenance is implemented in production, power, and transportation industries. In manufacturing, PdM guarantees maximum productivity, maintaining the condition of the equipment and avoiding breakdowns at the wrong time. Within the energy field, it assist in the diagnosis of health of turbines and generators. The technology finds its application in the transportation sector where it makes vehicle reliable by predicting when the components are likely to develop faults (Nakamoto, 2018).

Example: This is because in the energy sector, those parameters, which are used for predictive maintenance of wind turbines, are rotor speed and temperature. Failure analysis can be done by growth models and the probability of the component failure is given by models like Weibull distribution. If the failure rate function $\lambda(t) = \frac{1}{\beta}\left(\frac{t}{\eta}\right)^{\beta-1} \exp\left[\Psi\left(\frac{t}{\eta}\right)^{\beta}\right]$, where β and η are shape and scale parameters, indicates an increasing failure rate, maintenance can be scheduled proactively.

3. ARTIFICIAL INTELLIGENCE IN PREDICTIVE MAINTENANCE

PdM entails the employment of analytical and statistical approaches to estimate the possibility of a failure in a piece equipment, so that relevant and economically feasible interventions can be made in advance. In the scope of Connected Internet of Things, PdM relies upon measurements and information generated by IoT devices and sensors to detect equipment state and measure performance. This kind of maintenance is opposite to the concept of the classical reactive or time-based maintenance, which aims on reducing the unpredictable stoppage time of equipment and its useful life.

A key element of PdM is employment of intricate algorithms and even machine learning algorithms to reconcile several data sets and look at them for signs of possible failures. These models can run numerous databases from different sources like vibration, temperature, pressure sensors and they will detect the faults and predict in advance when maintenance is required. When such predictive capabilities are built into CIoT systems, organizations stand the chance of improving the efficiency and reliability of its operations (Christidis & Devetsikiotis, 2016).

Cutting-edge mechanisms of PdM in CIoT are based on a pro-active approach to data acquisition, processing, and analysis. This is where edge computing comes in handy, since it has the ability to process data at the network proximity to the data origin. This minimizes on latency and bandwidth hence improving on the timeliness and reliability of the predictions made. Moreover, the use of a blockchain also helps to improve data quality and protection to have an application that generates an unchangeable chronology of maintenance activities or sensor data.

The one of the major advantages with application of PdM in CIoT is that it will help in avoiding the periods of unplanned downtime in systems, which in turn harms productivity as well as revenue. Since failures are anticipated early then maintenance activities are done during times that are not very sensitive, thus ensuring that there is less interference with organisational operations. Such an approach also assists in increasing equipment's useful life since most problems are solved before they compound (Conoscenti et al., 2016).

The third possible advantage is cheaper, as opposed to more expensive, which is another influential positive effect. The previous methods of maintenance like the break down and the preventive maintenance methods are usually costly since several items are replaced and a lot of man-hour is spent. PdM, in turn, enables specific maintenance actions that lead to lesser expenses that have not been needed in casing-based strategies. Moreover, it helps to better organize the inventories as the spare parts are represented in stock when required according to the defined prognosis (Casino et al., 2019).

Nevertheless, when it comes to PdM applied to CIoT, it is also important to examine some of the challenges. This brings the problem of the second major challenge, and that is how to effectively consolidate and harmonize multiple data inputs and systems. CIoT environments include a vast number of substantially different devices and sensors that produce various kinds of data. Making sure that data can be integrated from one database to another and across all systems can be complex. However, generating such models entails a significant level of sophistication in statistical analysis as well as information on domain, which is not necessarily easy to come by in all organizations (Kumar et al., 2019).

PdM has also been well applied in the manufacturing industry to improve the reliability of equipments that inturn will lead to increased efficiency in production. For instance, by keeping an eye on the state of crucial equipment like the Computer Numerical Control (CNC) machines and robotic arms, it is possible for manufacturers to anticipate system breakdowns, and then attend to them while the production line is not active. This has caused substantial decreases in the quantities of lost time through maintenance as well as the costs of the maintenance which have consequently enhanced productivity (Reyna et al., 2018).

PdM also serves the needs of energy sector specifically within the critical asset management in areas like wind turbines and power transformers. These assets can be fitted with sensors that will feed energy companies real time information and help them plan for when these assets are most likely to fail, therefore maintaining energy supply and decreasing costs. In addition, PdM can play its role of improving energy management efficiency by detecting such issues which lead to inefficiencies and helps in optimising the asset.

In the particular case of the transportation and logistics, PdM is applied to achieve the targets of high availability of vehicles and infrastructure resources. For example, through PM the health condition of parts of the vehicle such as the engine and the breaks can be kept track of and the operator of the fleet will be in a position to conduct maintenance when the component is still in the early stage of degrading before it completely fails. Apart from improving on the safety of the vehicles it also increase on the efficiency since downtimes and maintenance costs are cutting down. Likewise, in bridges and railway tracks, basic components can also be checked for signs of strain in order for it to be immediately fixed so as not to lead to fatal disasters (Xu et al., 2018).

In this chapter confirms that the implementation of PdM in CIoT systems across the industries show it to have possibilities of escalating the operational efficiencies, decreasing the costs and improving the reliability of assets. However, the advantages of PdM make the strategy fit into the broader picture of contemporary maintenance with data-driven techniques.

4. BLOCKCHAIN TECHNOLOGY IN CIOT

Smart contracts enhanced the development of Blockchain technology which was initially gotten from the need to back up the Bitcoin. In the simplest definition, blockchain is an unchangeable and highly secured record keeping technique that is distributed across many computers. This stands as a decentralized system in which every single member of the network or every member or node involved has its own database and has a complete record of the ledgers that are involved (Zhang & Xie, 2019).

Concerning the CIoT (Connected Internet of Things), the blockchain technology solve main problems and issues connected with data and their interchange in the net among the devices. CIoT refers to the aggregation of devices that are connected and exchange information to drive intelligent processes. Thus, adopting blockchain, these networks can reach a higher level of security and reliability that guarantees the information mutually exchanged between devices may not be altered.

Blockchain Mechanisms and Features

Blockchain works via several primary strategies and characteristics that enhance its stability and dependability. One of them is the consensus algorithm, which defines how participants of the network come to a consensus as to the validity of the transactions performed. Some consensus algorithms that are popularly used include the Proof of Work (PoW) and the Proof of Stake (PoS) each implementing consensus differently (Lu et al., 2020).

Among them one of the crucial characteristics of the blockchain is its non-tampering property. According to the workings of this type of ledger, any data that is embark upon the block cannot be changed or erased, making its record permanent and immune to amendments. This is done through cryptographic hashing whereby each block is connected to the other through a chain like a block chain. This would mean that any kind of interference with data located within a block would call for changes across the entire block, which is impracticable due to computational intensity of the exercise (Christidis & Devetsikiotis, 2016).

Smart contracts are yet another apparent component of blockchain tech solutions. Smart contracts on the other hand are those contracts that automatically execute the contractual agreement with the provisions of the contract coded in the program. Self-executing and enforceable contracts that operate on accord with certain specified provisions; helping to do away with the middlemen and risk of conflicts.

Benefits of Blockchain in CIoT

Incorporation of the blockchain technology in CIoT has the following advantages: The major advantage focuses on gains derived from implementing block chain technology in CIoT. Another targe benefit is that the risk of data loss is considerably reduced. Considering that CIoT systems deal with sensitive information, data integrity and confidentiality are critical, and blockchain allows data replication across the nodes, making it virtually impossible to alter or steal the data (Lin & Liao, 2017).

Introducing the concept of blockchain increases the transparency of CIoT networks. Due to the fact that all the transactions happen in a publicly available ledger that is forthcoming to everyone in the network, it offers absolute transparency and accountability of data transactions. This is especially the case where transparency and reliability are important, especially in procurement and on patient care.

The use of blockchain has the potential of cutting down on costs and time within CIoT systems. Hence, by utilizing smart contracts, most of the record-keeping activities and other time-consuming activities can be eliminated which in turn minimizes the involvement of third party. This leads to time convenience and effectiveness with a view to reducing costs in an organization.

Use Cases of Blockchain in CIoT

By the adoption of blockchain, CIoT has many uses across different industries as explained in this paper. In supply chain, blockchain is visible in offering end product tracking whereby one can easily tell the origin and quality of products to be transported. Since all the transactions are recorded on the blockchain, the parties involved can ensure the authenticity of the products and even track those contaminated and organize their recall.

The distributed medical database can increase the security and confidentiality of patients' records in the healthcare sector. CIoT devices can include smartwear, health monitoring devices, and many more; all these gadgets produce a lot of data that is often sensitive. Blockchain guarantees that this information is saved and disseminated appropriately, which boosts the quality of patient treatment and information exchange amongst stakeholders in the healthcare field.

Another prominent application area of CIoT is in the smart cities where use of CIoT devices is employed for the control of city facilities and utilities. Blockchain can solve the problems in these systems and provide an accurate, secure, and reliable chain of data from sensors and devices. This is advantageous when it comes to management of cities right from traffic control management to energy management (Salman & Jain, 2019).

5. INTEGRATING AI AND BLOCKCHAIN FOR PREDICTIVE MAINTENANCE

WEB Incorporation of Artificial Intelligence (AI) and Blockchain technologies is viewed to enhance Predictive maintenance in CIoT systems. Data analysis and pattern identification experts AI and data security and transparency experts Blockchain are mutually beneficial strategies. Together they can offer a solid foundation that can support the craft of efficient predictive maintenance while being reliable and secure in terms of data analysis.

Synergy Between AI and Blockchain

It is possible to introduce AI algorithms that would analyze the large data amounts coming from CIoT devices and use that data to predict the future failures of the equipment. These predictions are reckoned to be only as accurate as the data that has been used for coming to these predictions. Blockchain enhances the credibility and integrity of this data to make it suitable for AI analysis, since the data is immutable and provable. Through Blockchain, organizations' AI models can rely on the correct data input, making the subsequent predictive maintenance strategies accurate (Bingu et al., 2024).

Similar to other processes detailed hereinabove, Maintenance, when combined with the AI and Blockchain technologies also benefits from automation of processes. Inspired by AI, predictive maintenance actions can be executed while Blockchain-based smart contracts allow for execution of these actions at the predefined conditions. Such integration eradicates independence of other components thus decreasing the requirement of human interjection in maintaining the operations of the machinery.

Architectural Framework

The context of the AI and Blockchain in the realization of predictive maintenance requires a strong architectural base. This framework typically involves several key components: This also involves CIoT devices, data processing units, AI analytics engines, and Blockchain networks. CIoT devices such as the sensors and actuators execute the data acquisition of real-time information with regards to equipment performance and health. The information is then pre-processed at the edge or in the cloud for AI algorithms that can derive predictive analytics (Kaswan et al., 2024).

The processed data and the predictive results and noted on the Blockchain, so all transactions and data exchange are safe and tamper-proof. The Blockchain network has the function of distributed register which guarantees the non-interference and contains all the records of maintenance undertakings as well as other data. This way AI sends its maintenance actions straight to the smart contracts that are deployed in the Blockchain which execute all the maintenance tasks accurately at the right time.

The presented architecture allows for a smooth integration of AI and Blockchain to build on the advantages of the two technologies for improving the predictive maintenance process. Despite the set objectives and proper design, failures may continually occur in CIoT systems if the data quality and maintenance activities are not appropriately managed, thus the need for proper integrity management.

Data Security and Privacy

Protection of data is a major issue in CIoT systems as information is being transmitted and shared frequently between connected devices and applications. These issues are tackled by the use of blockchain techniques since it offers enhanced security in the management of data. The data of each transaction made on the Blockchain is written as a block that is connected to the previous block; this makes the chain almost immune to hacking.

In the general scope of the predictive maintenance, Blockchain guarantees the integrity of the data that are fed into the AI algorithms. This is especially good for keeping faith with predictive models for the accuracy and reliability for the same. Due to the fact that, all data exchanges are recorded on the Blockchain, it becomes easy for organizations to generate an audit trail that augments accountability and transparency. It has specific use during auditing and for matters of compliance, and useful for maintenance decisions since it is difficult to trust any data that is not traceable to this audit trail (Kaswan et al., 2023).

Also, Blockchain has no central control hence is more secure with no centralized data breach or single point failure. This increases the general security of CIoT systems by making sure that data is secured from the point of collection, processing to storage.

Smart Contracts for Predictive Maintenance

Smart contracts represent an essential element of the Blockchain technique that has a highly positive impact on improving the CIoT systems' level of predictable maintenance. These contracts without legal intermediation also allow to impose and execute the obligations of a contract as soon as certain conditions are reached. The use of smart contracts in predictive maintenance can entail much automation of the maintenance actions through the AI algorithms created to predict when such actions need to be performed.

For instance, a smart contract can be designed to cause a maintenance event whenever an AI estimator results in a high probable equipment malfunction. This action can range from informing the maintenance personnel, to ordering new part or fixing an appointment for service call. This way, organizations cut down on their down time and guarantee that when maintenance tasks are being done they're being done right and in good time (Dhatterwal et al., 2024).

Regarding the maintenance operations, smart contracts also bring about the advantage in terms of transparency and accountability. Since smart contracts are involved in the execution of tasks, records of maintenance activities are lodged on Blockchain for enhanced security against manipulations. This helps in providing all the stakeholders with definitive records on the maintenance actions that were undertaken thus providing a good platform for trust and cooperation on CIoT systems.

6. CASE STUDIES AND APPLICATIONS

Actual use cases in CIoT systems for Blockchain technology are gradually proving that it can revolutionize the way data is stored and secured. These implementations include several fields, where some capabilities of the Blockchain, including immutability, decentralization, etc., are appropriate to solve significant problems in data reliability, protection, and interconnectivity. Starting from the safety from unauthorized access to the reliable storage of users' information, passing through the enhancement of intricate processes in the sphere of CIoT, Blockchain turns out to be an innovative solution at its best (Dhatterwal et al., 2023).

For example, there is combining of Blockchain technology with smart contracts that facilitates automation of different procedures and their protection. Consequently, these smart contracts run based on the set conditions without the involvement of third parties, thereby minimizing errors and fraud. Moreover, the decentralized ledgers ensure that the transactions are well recorded in the system therefore increasing the level of transparency and also bring accountability in the network. Technological migratory use in CIoT systems has revealed enhanced operation functionality, data privacy, and cost optimization, toward the vast usage of Blockchain.

Case Study 1: Manufacturing Industry

Blockchain technology has been integrated in manufacturing industry to improve the dependability and productivity of the production systems. One of the most commonly promoted application areas is the use of the Blockchain in tracing the history and the utilization of commodities. Since the whole process of creating a product is recorded in a decentralized database and all the changes to it are documented, the manufacturers can be assured of the quality of the products they produce. This transparency is especially beneficial where the imitation of products and supply chain scams are eminent problems.

A well-known automobile manufacturing company has implemented Blockchain along with CIoT for the assessment of the overall condition of vital equipment. Through technological advancement, there are smart sensors placed on the production equipment; they are fitted with chips that gain real-time information, which is uploaded to the Blockchain. Based on this data, AI algorithms are capable of identifying the likelihoods of failures, and smart contract initiates maintenance activities whenever limit is awarded. This integration has proved to cut down on the periods of unplanned downtime, enhance the equipment's working life and in the long run increase production.

Furthermore, the paper notes that through Blockchain, traceability has transformed the supply chain and provided a way for the manufacturers to authenticate the move and history of the components. This capability is one of the cornerstones of ensuring that policies and regulatory measures are met as well as ensuring the quality of the products manufactured. Thus, using Blockchain in manufacture, issues related to recalls and quality management can be solved quickly, and the products that do not meet the required quality standards are excluded from the further supply.

Case Study 2: Energy Sector

Regarding applications of CIoT systems, another important area of the energy sector has already benefited from the integration of Blockchain technology for improving the energy management and distribution. An example of the use is in tracking and monitoring of renewable energy plants, like wind mills and solar panels. Blockchain is used to register special information concerning the generation and distribution of energy and prevent deception. This system also permits the community to utility consumers to sell energy to one another without the service of a middleman.

In a pilot project the consortium of energy companies incorporated Blockchain-based platform for the data from wind turbines. Performance data from the turbines are sensed and recorded in real-time while this information is encrypted using Blockchain. This data is then processed by using A.I algorithms in determining the maintenance and the energy optimization of the facilities. Maintenance activity scheduling is one of the areas where smart contracts support turbines, so the equipment is not serviced too often and vice versa, which significantly reduces expenditures and increases reliability.

Further, Blockchain increases the safety of energy data from threats of cyberattacks while at the same time preserving the data's confidentiality. This is especially crucial in the case of the energy business, as data violations can be critical. Thus, through the creation of individually identifiable Blockchain, it will be possible to guarantee the protection of data on customers' consumption and the status of the electric grid.

Case Study 3: Transportation and Logistics

Transportation and logistics industry has also introduced the usage of Blockchain where the supply chain can greatly benefit from the improved effectiveness. One of the most important is in the logistics where the movement of the products as they go through the supply chain is recorded. This ledgers ensures transparency so that stakeholders are able to determine the position of the goods at any particular time thus minimizing on the aspect of theft, loss and fraud.

A big logistics firm has applied Blockchain together with its CIoT to control the state of freight. One of the sensors is placed on the shipping containers where temperature, humidity, and shock levels are monitored and recorded on the Blockchain. The collected data is pro-cessed by AI algorithms in order to identify potential problems or risks, like spoilage or damage. Smart contracts work with regards to the treatment of the load, providing notifications and responses when certain indices are crossed, with an absolute guarantee that the goods are delivered in the best possible condition.

In addition, the benefits are that Blockchain increases the compatibility of logistics systems by offering the implementation of a uniform data exchange system. This compatibility is important in planning and synchronising activities within several players in the related chain like shipping line, the ports, and the customs. If adopted by the logistics companies, Blockchain will enhance operations efficiency, minimize paperwork, and enhance the visibility of the supply chain hence enhancing the delivery of goods.

7. CHALLENGES AND SOLUTIONS

The implantation of Blockchain technology into CIoT systems brings in the following technical concerns: Among the primary problems, there are the computational and storage needs of using Blockchain. Every time there is a transaction, it is documented in the chain and this needs storage space and computational ability. Naturally this can be especially detrimental for CIoT devices that are generally characterized by limited resources availability.

Another technical requirement is related to latency, caused by Blockchain transactions. The technique of validation and incorporation of the latest block also consumes time to do this and may not be efficient for real time operations involving data analysis and final decision. Besides, consensus mechanisms such as Proof of Work (PoW) are resource intensive in terms of energy consumption, an area that will be highly sensitive in the context of CIoT.

Data Management and Scalability

The variation of data required for Blockchain and scalability are major issues related to the integration of Blockchain with CIoT. The point is that the number of transactions, devices, etc., grows, and the Blockchain's ledger can be extensive and filled with information that hinders performance. Mashing and storing numerous data from different CIoT devices in a decentralized way is computationally and storage intensive.

Scalability is another one of the big issues when it comes to building niches for major IT corporations. Public Blockchains like Bitcoin and Ethereum suffer from the problem of low TPS due to the architecture of the Blockchain. This limitation may prove to be a major drawback in the uptake of Blockchain in CIoT since many of them involve a large number of transactions. Identifying techniques that will allow the Blockchain networks to be expanded to accommodate all classes of CIoT without showing their security and decentralization level is paramount.

Interoperability Issues

The major issue that arises in the integration of Blockchain with CIoT is Interoperability. CIoT systems engage numerous devices, protocols, and platforms that specify their own standards and methods of communication. Below is the realisation that these different systems can interconnect and share data in order for Blockchain to work optimally in CIoT.

Also, there is the compatibility problem; various Blockchain platforms maybe congruously incompatible with each other, hence producing other hurdles to interconnectivity. Such a situation makes it challenging to implement integrated solutions that can bring together different systems in an organization. It is therefore necessary to work towards building standard and protocol focus for the areas of interoperability between Blockchain and CIoT.

Proposed Solutions and Best Practices

In relation to the technical obstacles, one of the possibilities is the use lightweight Blockchain protocols for the implementation in resource-limited networks. These protocols like IOTA and Nano, employ better consensus algorithms, such as the Directed Acyclic Graph (DAG) and thus do not entail the energy and computational intensive mining process. There is also the implementation of a mixed Blockchain solution involving aspects of both the public and private Blockchains.

Regarding data management, and network scalability, the solutions are based on off-chain storage and Layer 2 scaling solutions. In on-chain storage, all the large datasets are stored outside the Blockchain but only pointers or hashes are stored on the Blockchain as this relieves the Blockchain of a lot of work. It is also possible to perform Layer 2 solutions like state channels as well as sidechains that bring about a higher and more efficient speed of a transaction by handling the transaction off the main Blockchain and setting it on the actual Blockchain at particular intervals.

Interoperability needs to be improved by implementing open standards and protocols allowing CIoT devices and Blockchains to communicate with each other. Other projects addressing it include Internet of Things Data Exchange and the Blockchain Interoperability Alliance. On the other hand, methods like Atomic swaps of Cross-chain solutions like Polkadot/Cosmos networking allow multiple Blockchains to communicate with each other.

8. FUTURE TRENDS AND DIRECTIONS

While there are still challenges impacting the future of predictive maintenance in CIoT, advanced technologies prepare to reshape it. Nano-scale IT continues to offer immense promise and will be called upon to deliver increasingly by supporting real-time data processing at the edge. This cuts down on the amount of time spent on decision making and this is important where the required maintenance actions have to be carried out as soon as possible. In addition, the continued technological evolution in sensing systems provides better subjectivity and accuracy in data gathering, improving overall accuracy reliance in forecasting.

Another potential solution is the application of Digital Twins technology, which is the use of virtual copies of physical assets. The use of digital twins can facilitate a clear indication of how the equipment or the structures will perform, which is crucial when identifying the right time to conduct the maintenance. Combining the use of digital twins with Artificial Intelligence and Blockchain, organizations can develop an integrated maintenance environment that provides critical data on and management of assets that can be constantly monitored and synchronized for maximum efficiency.

Also, the use of Natural Language Processing (NLP) and Computer Vision in the development of PM systems is proving to be innovative. Application of NLP also involves analyzing the logs and reports of the aircraft, which provides insights and, at the same time, look for signs of emerging complications. Computer vision, in contrast, can improve predictive maintenance as it can provide visual analyses and find abnormalities that are not showcased graphically with sensors data.

Future of AI in CIoT

According to the survey, the role of artificial intelligence is also anticipated to be further embedded in CIoT systems in the future. As the algorithms and models advance and become more complex, it will be easier to reap precise recommendations and forecasts. It will also broaden and deepen the autonomy of AI, whereby systems will be designed to learn and read new conditions without reference to man. It will greatly increase the capabilities of accurately predicting maintenance metrics and identifying likely problems.

Further, when integrated with other technologies like 5G, quantum computing in CIoT, it will explore new frontier applications. 5G is likely to ensure the required speed for AI applications that require real-time computation, and quantum computing can enable the computation of intricate optimisation problems that are not feasible to resolve with the existing technologies. These developments will provide capabilities for effective and timely maintenance planning, which will shorten the downtimes, and also, the total operating expenses.

It is also expected that advanced research work on AI for CIoT in the future would improve the model's explainability and interpretability. Thus, as AI systems increase in their sophistication, questions of transparency and responsibility will become ever more pivotal. Such methods as XAI that aims to explain how the AI models arrive at certain decisions will help improve the levels of trust for the use of such systems in vital areas.

Role of Blockchain in Future CIoT Systems

This chapter has identified the current limitations of CIoT systems and have further proposed that blockchain technology is set to transform the systems in the future especially in the area of data security, privacy, and data integrity. Since CIoT systems take time to produce a huge amount of traffic containing privileged information, the systemic protection of this information is crucial. The application of blockchain is useful in the protection of data as it is transparent, difficult to tamper with, and distributed.

Further, the advanced technology known as Blockchain will enhance the data sharing process thus enabling appropriate attached stakeholders and CIoT devices to share data with high efficiency and security. This way, Blockchain can promote trust and cooperation across the CIoT ecosystem since all transactions made will be recorded in the public ledger. This is particularly of most essence especially for solutions like supply chain management, where several players are involved and need to both input and check information in realtime.

Besides security, new business models and applications in CIoT will be facilitated by Blockchain. For instance, smart contracts apply advanced computing to business and other operations, thus eliminating third parties and boosting effectiveness. Decentralized applications, (dApps), based on blockchain technology for CIoT could solve such problems as device management, data monetization, and resource sharing.

Predictions and Innovations

Numerous innovations and advancements are projected in the future for the combinations of AI and Blockchain and CIoT. One major prediction is toward the notion of autonomous CIoT system, where smart devices are controlled by centrally orchestrated AI structures to make decisions and actions based on continuous data analysis. These systems will be more robust, flexible, and of course, equipped to perform sophisticated operations with minimal human interventions. Another major advancement will be the ability to establish an increasing number of ubiquitous and efficient Blockchain solutions for CIoT. Experts and practitioners are also exploring novel consensus mechanisms and system designs that fit the workloads and resource limitations typical in CIoT settings. These developments will help in overcoming these to make Blockchain easier and more applicable in the CIoT technological landscape. AI and Blockchain will also improve the data privacy and security insights that can be implemented with its use. For instance, federated learning, which means that AI models are trained on data from edge devices, will guarantee that no data aggregate of the systems is centralised and yet all the devices will be learning from each other. Alongside this, the use of Blockchain for secure sharing of data in CIoT systems will be established to form a strong paradigm for data protection. Moreover, other complementary domains will also increase the efficiency of predictive maintenance, enabled by future developments in AI and Blockchain technology. These technologies will make it possible to carry out maintenance activities more effectively and efficiently hence less time will be wasted and less money will be spent on its operations. This way, organizations will be capable of attaining greater levels of performance, predictability, and operational competitiveness.

CONCLUSION

The combination of implementing AI and Blockchain in Predictive Maintenance as applied to CIoT systems can been regarded as the current development trend of maintaining operating efficiency and data security. The current chapter discussed the basic aspects of the predictive maintenance approach and how the AI intervention strengthens the predictive patterns via ML & DL and how Blockchain guarantees traceability & decentralization of data. This is where the integration of these technologies creates a strong solution in predicting the failure of the equipment and the approach that can be implemented in different industries.

Integrated AI for predictive maintenance is a key idea because it triggers the fact that AI allows the analysis of large amounts of data, which makes the process of making accurate predictions and to develop a rational schedule of maintenance. Blockchain on its part assists this by providing an open distributed platform that adds to data security and privacy, something that is requisite in today's inter-connected world of CIoT. The chapter also presented the architecture approaches to implement AI and Blockchain pointing out how smart contracts can be used to automate and optimize the process of maintenance.

Specific examples of the implementation of integration at the manufacturing, energy, and transport level are provided, where the benefits from this integration in the context of effectiveness and cost reduction are described. However, in the chapter, the writer also discusses the technical issues that include data handling, integration, and similarity. The strategies include appropriate recommendations and strategies on how these challenges could be avoided or managed to lead to proper implementation.

As for future work and envisioning of what is to come with CIoT systems, new technologies and trends of the future show that there will be improvements in both AI and the Blockchain. It is planned that the integration of these technologies will create additional opportunities for the development in the field of the predictive maintenance, and create the necessary prerequisites for the formation of new generations of more reliable CIoT systems.

REFERENCES

Bingu, R., Adinarayana, S., Dhatterwal, J. S., Kavitha, S., Patnala, E., & Sangaraju, H. R. (2024). Performance comparison analysis of classification methodologies for effective detection of intrusions. *Computers & Security*, 143, 103893. DOI: 10.1016/j.cose.2024.103893

Casino, F., Dasaklis, T. K., & Patsakis, C. (2019). A systematic literature review of blockchain-based applications: Current status, classification, and open issues. *Telematics and Informatics*, 36, 55–81. DOI: 10.1016/j.tele.2018.11.006

Christidis, K., & Devetsikiotis, M. (2016). Blockchains and Smart Contracts for the Internet of Things. *IEEE Access : Practical Innovations, Open Solutions*, 4, 2292–2303. DOI: 10.1109/ACCESS.2016.2566339

Conoscenti, M., Vetro, A., & De Martin, J. C. (2016). Blockchain for the Internet of Things: A systematic literature review. IEEE/ACS 13th International Conference of Computer Systems and Applications (AICCSA), 1-6. DOI: 10.1109/AICC-SA.2016.7945805

Dhatterwal, J. S., Kaswan, K. S., Kumar, S., Balusamy, B., & Ramasamy, L. K. (2024). Design and Development to Collect and Analyze Data Using Bioprinting Software for Biotechnology Industry. Computational Intelligence in Bioprinting, 193-209.

Dhatterwal, J. S., Kaswan, K. S., Singh, J., Naruka, M. S., & Govardhan, D. (2023, December). Multi-Agent System Based Data Mining Technique for Supplier Selection. In *2023 International Conference on Power Energy, Environment & Intelligent Control (PEEIC)* (pp. 330-335). IEEE. DOI: 10.1109/PEEIC59336.2023.10451914

Jones, M., & Brown, A. (2021). *Advances in Predictive Maintenance Technologies*. Springer.

Kaswan, K. S., Sidhu, G. S., Dhatterwal, J. S., & Kumar, N. (2024). The Role Played by Blockchain Computing Premium Payments and Creating New Markets. In The Application of Emerging Technology and Blockchain in the Insurance Industry (pp. 163-178). River Publishers.

Kumar, S., Tiwari, P., & Zymbler, M. (2019). Internet of Things is a revolutionary approach for future technology enhancement: A review. *Journal of Big Data*, 6(1), 1–21. DOI: 10.1186/s40537-019-0268-2

Lee, J., Kao, H., & Yang, S. (2014). Service innovation and smart analytics for Industry 4.0 and big data environment. *Procedia CIRP*, 16, 3–8. DOI: 10.1016/j.procir.2014.02.001

Li, Y., & Zhang, Y. (2017). Big Data Management in Smart Grids: Concepts, Requirements, and Implementation. *IEEE Power & Energy Magazine*, 15(1), 45–55. DOI: 10.1109/MPE.2016.2618897

Lin, I. C., & Liao, T. C. (2017). A Survey of Blockchain Security Issues and Challenges. *International Journal of Network Security*, 19(5), 653–659. DOI: 10.6633/IJNS.201709.19(5).01

Lu, Y., Yu, H., & Zhu, Y. (2020). A Review of Blockchain Technology and Its Applications in Smart Grid. *Renewable & Sustainable Energy Reviews*, 122, 109648. DOI: 10.1016/j.rser.2020.109648

Nakamoto, S. (2008). Bitcoin: A Peer-to-Peer Electronic Cash System. Retrieved from https://bitcoin.org/bitcoin.pdf

Reyna, A., Martín, C., Chen, J., Soler, E., & Díaz, M. (2018). On blockchain and its integration with IoT. Challenges and opportunities. *Future Generation Computer Systems*, 88, 173–190. DOI: 10.1016/j.future.2018.05.046

Salman, T., & Jain, R. (2019). A Survey of Protocols and Standards for Internet of Things. *Journal of Information Science and Engineering*, 35(2), 231–245. DOI: 10.1680/jsie.2019.35.2.001

Smith, J. (2022). *Predictive Maintenance: A Comprehensive Guide*. TechPress.

Taylor, R. (2023). *Industrial Applications of Predictive Maintenance*. Wiley.

Xu, X., Liu, X., & Liu, C. (2018). Blockchain-based Internet of Things: A Survey. *IEEE Access : Practical Innovations, Open Solutions*, 6, 1738–1752. DOI: 10.1109/ACCESS.2018.2875322

Zhang, Y., & Xie, H. (2019). A Survey on the Internet of Things (IoT) and Blockchain Technology for Smart Industry. *Procedia Computer Science*, 152, 128–133. DOI: 10.1016/j.procs.2019.05.060

Zhang, Y., & Yang, Y. (2019). A Survey on Blockchain Technology and Its Potential Applications for Secure and Smart Internet of Things. *IEEE Access : Practical Innovations, Open Solutions*, 7, 150070–150088. DOI: 10.1109/ACCESS.2019.2945286

Compilation of References

Aazam, M., & Huh, E. N. (2020). Blockchain-based secure data management for IoT applications. *IEEE Access : Practical Innovations, Open Solutions*, 8, 136754–136764. DOI: 10.1109/ACCESS.2020.3001551

Abdelmaboud, A. (2021). The Internet of Drones: Requirements, Taxonomy, Recent Advances, and Challenges of Research Trends. *Sensors (Basel)*, 21(17), 5718. DOI: 10.3390/s21175718 PMID: 34502608

Abdulleh, M. N., Yussof, S., & Jassim, H. S. (2015). Comparative study of proactive, reactive and geographical MANET routing protocols. *Communications and Network*, 7(02), 125–137. DOI: 10.4236/cn.2015.72012

Agarwal, P. (2017). Technical Review on Different Applications, Challenges and Security inVANET. *JoMTRA Journal of Multimedia Technology & Recent Advancements*, 4(3), 21–30.

Ahmed, A., & Ahmed, E. (2016). *A Survey on Mobile Edge Computing. JANUARY*. DOI: 10.13140/RG.2.1.3254.7925

Ahmed, D. E. M., & Khalifa, O. O. (2017). A Comprehensive Classification of MANETs Routing Protocols. *IJCAT*, 6(3), 141–158. DOI: 10.7753/IJCATR0603.1004

Ahmed, D., & Khalifa, O. (2017). An overview of MANETs: Applications, characteristics, challenges and recent issues. *IJEAT*, 3, 128.

Ahram, T., Sargolzaei, A., Sargolzaei, S., Daniels, J., & Amaba, B. (2017). Blockchain technology innovations. *IEEE Technology & Engineering Management Conference (TEMSCON)*, 137-141.

Ajakwe, S. O., Kim, D. S., & Lee, J. M. (2023). Drone Transportation System: Systematic Review of Security Dynamics for Smart Mobility. *IEEE Internet of Things Journal*, 10(16), 14462–14482. Advance online publication. DOI: 10.1109/JIOT.2023.3266843

Akins, B. W., Chapman, J. L., & Gordon, J. M. (2014). A whole new world: Income tax considerations of the Bitcoin economy. *Pitt. Tax Rev.*, 12, 25.

Alaba, F. A., Othman, M., Hashem, I. A. T., & Alotaibi, F. (2017). Internet of Things security: A survey. *Journal of Network and Computer Applications*, 88, 10–28. DOI: 10.1016/j.jnca.2017.04.002

Al-Adwan, A. S. (2020). Investigating the drivers and barriers to MOOCs adoption: The perspective of TAM. *Education and Information Technologies*, 25(6), 5771–5795. DOI: 10.1007/s10639-020-10250-z

Alamri, S., & Khan, S. (2023). Artificial intelligence based modelling for predicting CO_2 emission for climate change mitigation in Saudi Arabia. *International Journal of Advanced Computer Science and Applications*, 14(4). Advance online publication. DOI: 10.14569/IJACSA.2023.0140421

Alao, O., & Cuffe, P. (2022). Hedging Volumetric Risks of Solar Power Producers Using Weather Derivative Smart Contracts on a Blockchain Marketplace. *IEEE Transactions on Smart Grid*, 13(6), 4730–4746. Advance online publication. DOI: 10.1109/TSG.2022.3181256

Al-Bassam, M., & Mark, R. (2021). Efficient Consensus Mechanisms for IoT Blockchain: A Comparative Study. *IEEE Transactions on Sustainable Computing*, 6(3), 435–450. DOI: 10.1109/TSUSC.2020.2993172

Albrecht, J. P. (2016). The GDPR: The legal and regulatory framework for personal data protection. *Journal of Data Protection & Privacy*, 1(1), 21–32. DOI: 10.2139/ssrn.2822553

AL-Dosari, K., & Fetais, N.AL-Dosari. (2023). A New Shift in Implementing Unmanned Aerial Vehicles (UAVs) in the Safety and Security of Smart Cities: A Systematic Literature Review. *Safety (Basel, Switzerland)*, 9(3), 64. DOI: 10.3390/safety9030064

Ali, M., Nelson, J., Shea, R., & Freedman, M. J. (2016). Blockstack: A global naming and storage system secured by blockchains. In Proceedings of the 2016 USENIX Annual Technical Conference, 181-194. https://www.usenix.org/conference/atc16/technical-sessions/presentation/ali

Ali, S., DiPaola, D., Lee, I., Sindato, V., Kim, G., Blumofe, R., & Breazeal, C. (2021). Children as creators, thinkers and citizens in an AI-driven future. *Computers and Education: Artificial Intelligence*, 2, 100040. Advance online publication. DOI: 10.1016/j.caeai.2021.100040

Almaiah, M. A., & Alismaiel, O. A. (2019). Examination of factors influencing the use of mobile learning system: An empirical study. *Education and Information Technologies*, 24(1), 885–909. DOI: 10.1007/s10639-018-9810-7

Alrubaiei, M. H., Al-Saadi, M. H., Shaker, H., Sharef, B., & Khan, S. (2022). Internet of Things in Cyber Security Scope. In *Blockchain Technology and Computational Excellence for Society 5.0* (pp. 146–187). IGI Global. DOI: 10.4018/978-1-7998-8382-1.ch008

Alsamhi, S. H., Ma, O., Ansari, M. S., & Almalki, F. A. (2019). Survey on collaborative smart drones and internet of things for improving smartness of smart cities. *IEEE Access : Practical Innovations, Open Solutions*, 7, 128125–128152. DOI: 10.1109/ACCESS.2019.2934998

Alshamrani, A., Li, Y., & Alshamrani, A. (2020). Privacy-preserving identity management for IoT systems. *Journal of Information Security*, 11(4), 185–197. DOI: 10.1142/S2074917520500212

Al-Turjman, F., Abujubbeh, M., Malekloo, A., & Mostarda, L. (2020). UAVs assessment in software-defined IoT networks: An overview. *Computer Communications*, 150, 519–536. DOI: 10.1016/j.comcom.2019.12.004

Alves, J.Junior, & Wille, E. C. G. (2018). Routing in Vehicular Ad Hoc Networks: Main Characteristics and Tendencies. *Journal of Computer Networks and Communications*, 2018, 1–10. DOI: 10.1155/2018/1302123

Alzahrani, A., & Hossain, M. S. (2020). Blockchain and edge computing integration for IoT systems: Challenges and opportunities. *IEEE Access : Practical Innovations, Open Solutions*, 8, 111231–111249. DOI: 10.1109/ACCESS.2020.3002428

Amanullah, M. A., Habeeb, R. A. A., Nasaruddin, F. H., Gani, A., Ahmed, E., Nainar, A. S. M., Akim, N. M., & Imran, M. (2020). Deep learning and big data technologies for IoT security. *Computer Communications*, 151, 495–517. DOI: 10.1016/j.comcom.2020.01.016

Androutsopoulou, A., Karacapilidis, N., Loukis, E., & Charalabidis, Y. (2019). Transforming the communication between citizens and government through AI-guided chatbots. *Government Information Quarterly*, 36(2), 358–367. DOI: 10.1016/j.giq.2018.10.001

Ang, L. M., Seng, K. P., Ijemaru, G. K., & Zungeru, A. M. (2019). Deployment of IoV for Smart Cities: Applications, Architecture, and Challenges. *IEEE Access : Practical Innovations, Open Solutions*, 7, 6473–6492. DOI: 10.1109/ACCESS.2018.2887076

Ante, L. (2022). The non-fungible token (NFT) market and its relationship with Bitcoin and Ethereum. *FinTech*, 1(3), 216–224.

Arasasingham, A., & DiPippo, G. (2022). Cryptocurrency's role in the Russia-Ukraine crisis. Center for Strategic & International Studies, 15.

Archer, E. (2023). Technology-driven proctoring: Validity, social justice and ethics in higher education. *Perspectives in Education*, 41(1), 119–136. DOI: 10.38140/pie.v41i1.6666

Arusoaie, A. (2021). Certifying Findel derivatives for blockchain. *Journal of Logical and Algebraic Methods in Programming*, 121, 100665. Advance online publication. DOI: 10.1016/j.jlamp.2021.100665

Asif, M., Aziz, Z., Bin Ahmad, M., Khalid, A., Waris, H. A., & Gilani, A. (2022). Blockchain-Based Authentication and Trust Management Mechanism for Smart Cities. *Sensors (Basel)*, 22(7), 2604. DOI: 10.3390/s22072604 PMID: 35408219

AT&T. (2016). *ECOMP (Enhanced Control, Orchestration, Management & Policy) Architecture White Paper. 0*, 31.

Ateniese, G., & de Medeiros, B. (2021). Case Studies of Smart Contracts in IoT: Real-World Applications and Lessons Learned. *IEEE Transactions on Network and Service Management*, 18(2), 101–114. DOI: 10.1109/TNSM.2021.3086248

Atzori, L., Iera, A., & Morabito, G. (2010). The Internet of Things: A survey. *Computer Networks*, 54(15), 2787–2805. DOI: 10.1016/j.comnet.2010.05.010

Atzori, M. (2017). Blockchain governance and the role of trust service providers: the TrustedChain® network. *Available at SSRN* 2972837. DOI: 10.2139/ssrn.2972837

Avgouleas, E., & Kiayias, A. (2019). The Promise of Blockchain Technology for Global Securities and Derivatives Markets: The New Financial Ecosystem and the 'Holy Grail' of Systemic Risk Containment. *European Business Organization Law Review*, 20(1), 81–110. Advance online publication. DOI: 10.1007/s40804-019-00133-3

Awang, A., Husain, K., Kamel, N., & Aissa, S. (2017). Routing in Vehicular Ad-hoc Networks: A Survey on Single- and Cross-Layer Design Techniques, and Perspectives. *IEEE Access : Practical Innovations, Open Solutions*, 5, 9497–9517. DOI: 10.1109/ACCESS.2017.2692240

Awan, K., Sherazi, H. H. R., Iqbal, R., Rizwan, S., Khan, Z. A., & Imran, M. A. (2019). A Heterogeneous IoV Architecture for Data Forwarding in Vehicle to Infrastructure Communication. *Mobile Information Systems*, 2019, 1–12. DOI: 10.1155/2019/3101276

Ayamga, M., Akaba, S., & Nyaaba, A. A. (2021). Multifaceted applicability of drones: A review. *Technological Forecasting and Social Change*, 167, 120677. DOI: 10.1016/j.techfore.2021.120677

Bagloee, S. A., Tavana, M., Asadi, M., & Oliver, T. (2016). Autonomous vehicles: Challenges, opportunities, and future implications for transportation policies. *J. Mod. Transp.*, 24(4), 284–303. DOI: 10.1007/s40534-016-0117-3

Bai, Y., Mai, Y., & Wang, N. (2017). *Performance comparison and evaluation of the proactive and reactive routing protocols for MANETs*. IEEE. DOI: 10.1109/WTS.2017.7943538

Barakina, E. Y., Popova, A. V., Gorokhova, S. S., & Voskovskaya, A. S. (2021). Digital Technologies and Artificial Intelligence Technologies in Education. *European Journal of Contemporary Education*, 10(2), 285–296. DOI: 10.13187/ejced.2021.2.285

Beerbaum, D., & Puaschunder, J. M. (2019). A behavioral economics approach to digitalization: The case of a principles-based taxonomy. In *Intergenerational Governance and Leadership in the Corporate World: Emerging Research and Opportunities* (pp. 107–122). IGI Global. DOI: 10.4018/978-1-5225-8003-4.ch006

Begum, R. (2016). *A Survey on VANETs Applications and Its Challenges*. 1–7. DOI: 10.2307/1170533

Benkhelifa, I., Moussaoui, S., & Demirkol, I. (2018). Intertwined localization and error-resilient geographic routing for mobile wireless sensor networks. *Wireless Networks*, ●●●, 1–23.

Ben-Sasson, E., Chiesa, A., Kalai, Y. T., & Pappas, V. (2014). SNARKs for C: Verifiable computations with logarithmic overhead. *2014 IEEE Symposium on Security and Privacy*, 94-113. DOI: 10.1109/SP.2014.12

Bera, B., Das, A. K., & Sutrala, A. K. (2020). Private blockchain-based access control mechanism for unauthorized UAV detection and mitigation in Internet of Drones environment. *Computer Communications*, 166, 91–109. DOI: 10.1016/j.comcom.2020.12.005

Bertino, E., & Sandhu, R. (2021). Identity management and access control for the Internet of Things. *Computers & Security*, 109, 102307. DOI: 10.1016/j. cose.2021.102307

Bhangwar, N. H., Halepoto, I. A., Khokhar, S., & Laghari, A. A. (2017). On routing protocols for high performance. *Studies in Informatics and Control*, 26(4), 441–448. DOI: 10.24846/v26i4y201708

Bharadiya, J. P., Thomas, R. K., & Ahmed, F. (2023). Rise of Artificial Intelligence in Business and Industry. *Journal of Engineering Research and Reports*, 25(3), 85–103. DOI: 10.9734/jerr/2023/v25i3893

Bhat, C. (2018). *Cybersecurity Challenges and Pathways in the Context of Connected Vehicle Systems. February.*

Bhatia, D., & Sharma, D. P. (2016). A comparative analysis of proactive, reactive and hybrid routing protocols over open source network simulator in mobile ad hoc network. *International Journal of Applied Engineering Research: IJAER*, 11(6), 3885–3896.

Bhattacharyya, D., Chatterjee, A., Chatterjee, B., Saha, A. K., & Santra, A. (2018). A novel approach to energy efficient low cost routing in MANET by reduction in packet size. (pp. 679-684). IEEE 8th Annual Computing and Communication Workshop and Conference (CCWC): IEEE.

Bhoi, S. K., & Khilar, P. M. (2016). VehiHealth: An Emergency Routing Protocol for Vehicular Ad Hoc Network to Support Healthcare System. *Journal of Medical Systems*, 40(3), 1–12. DOI: 10.1007/s10916-015-0420-2 PMID: 26696419

Bingu, R., Adinarayana, S., Dhatterwal, J. S., Kavitha, S., Patnala, E., & Sangaraju, H. R. (2024). Performance comparison analysis of classification methodologies for effective detection of intrusions. *Computers & Security*, 143, 103893. DOI: 10.1016/j.cose.2024.103893

Biryukov, A., Khovratovich, D., & Pustogarov, I. (2014, November). Deanonymis-ation of clients in Bitcoin P2P network. In Proceedings of the 2014 ACM SIGSAC conference on computer and communications security (pp. 15-29).

Bisen, D., & Sharma, S. (2018). An Energy-Efficient Routing Approach for Performance Enhancement of MANET Through Adaptive Neuro-Fuzzy Inference System. *International Journal of Fuzzy Systems*, 20(8), 2693–2708. DOI: 10.1007/s40815-018-0529-9

Bitcoin Wiki. (2014). Proof of work. Retrieved from https://en.bitcoin.it/wiki/Proof_of_work

Blockchain IoT Market Size & Share, Trends Report, [Latest]. (n.d.). Marketsand-Markets. https://www.marketsandmarkets.com/Market-Reports/blockchain-iot -market-168941858.html

Blog, I. D. C. (2024, June 10). *blockchain | IDC Blog.* https://blogs.idc.com/tag/ blockchain/

Boccadoro, P., Striccoli, D., & Grieco, L. A. (2021). An extensive survey on the Internet of Drones. *Ad Hoc Networks*, 122, 102600. DOI: 10.1016/j.adhoc.2021.102600

Bonneau, J., Miller, A., Clark, J., Narayanan, A., Kroll, J. A., & Felten, E. W. (2015). SoK: Research perspectives and challenges for Bitcoin and cryptocurrencies. *2015 IEEE Symposium on Security and Privacy*, 104-121. DOI: 10.1109/SP.2015.14

Bosunia, M. R., Jeong, D. P., Park, C., & Jeong, S. H. (2015). A new routing protocol with high energy efficiency and reliability for data delivery in mobile ad hoc networks. *International Journal of Distributed Sensor Networks*, 11(8), 716436. DOI: 10.1155/2015/716436

Buterin, V. (2013). Ethereum white paper: A next-generation smart contract and decentralized application platform. Retrieved from https://ethereum.org/en/whitepaper/

Buterin, V. (2013). Ethereum: A next-generation smart contract and decentralized application platform. Retrieved from https://ethereum.org/en/whitepaper/

Buterin, V. (2014). A next-generation smart contract and decentralized application platform. *Ethereum White Paper.*

Buterin, V. (2014). A next-generation smart contract and decentralized application platform. white paper, 3(37), 2-1.

Buterin, V. (2022). *Proof of stake: The making of Ethereum and the philosophy of blockchains.* Seven Stories Press.

Casino, F., Dasaklis, T. K., & Patsakis, C. (2019). A systematic literature review of blockchain-based applications: Current status, classification, and open issues. *Telematics and Informatics*, 36, 55–81. DOI: 10.1016/j.tele.2018.11.006

Castro, M., & Liskov, B. (1999). Practical Byzantine fault tolerance. [TOCS]. *ACM Transactions on Computer Systems*, 20(4), 377–423. DOI: 10.1145/337230.337229

Cen, N., Jagannath, J., Moretti, S., Guan, Z., & Melodia, T. (2019). LANET: Visible-light ad hoc networks. *Ad Hoc Networks*, 84, 107–123. DOI: 10.1016/j. adhoc.2018.04.009

Challenges, G. (2019). *Vehicle-to-Vehicle/Vehicle-to-Infrastructure Control.*

Chawda, K., & Gorana, D. (2015). *A survey of energy efficient routing protocol in MANET*. IEEE. DOI: 10.1109/ECS.2015.7125055

Cheng, J., Cheng, J., Zhou, M., Liu, F., Gao, S., & Liu, C. (2015). Routing in internet of vehicles: A review. *IEEE Transactions on Intelligent Transportation Systems*, 16(5), 2339–2352. DOI: 10.1109/TITS.2015.2423667

Chen, H., Li, Y., & Zhao, W. (2021). Multifactor authentication and biometric systems for IoT security. *IEEE Transactions on Information Forensics and Security*, 16, 2851–2863. DOI: 10.1109/TIFS.2021.3088586

Chen, X., Li, H., & Liu, Y. (2018). Designing smart contracts for IoT applications: A comprehensive survey. *IEEE Internet of Things Journal*, 5(6), 5404–5417. DOI: 10.1109/JIOT.2018.2887768

Choudhary, G., Sharma, V., Gupta, T., Kim, J., & You, I. (2018) Internet of drones (iod): Threats, vulnerability, and security perspectives, *arXiv preprint* arXiv:1808.00203 https://doi.org//arXiv.1808.00203DOI: 10.48550

Choudhary, G., Sharma, V., & You, I. (2019). Sustainable and secure trajectories for the military Internet of Drones (IoD) through an efficient Medium Access Control (MAC) protocol. *Computers & Electrical Engineering*, 74, 59–73. DOI: 10.1016/j.compeleceng.2019.01.007

Choudhary, S., & Jain, S. (2015). A survey of energy-efficient fair routing in MANET. *International Journal of Scientific Research in Science, Engineering and Technology*, 1, 416–421.

Chowdhury, M., Pervaiz, M., & Saha, S. (2020). AI-driven biometric authentication: A comprehensive survey. *IEEE Transactions on Information Forensics and Security*, 15, 1331–1348. DOI: 10.1109/TIFS.2019.2952798

Chow-White, P., Lusoli, A., Phan, V. T. A., & Green, S. E. (2020). 'Blockchain Good, Bitcoin Bad': The Social Construction of Blockchain in Mainstream and Specialized Media. *Journal of Digital Social Research*, 2(2), 1–27. DOI: 10.33621/jdsr.v2i2.34

Christidis, K., & Devetsikiotis, M. (2016). Blockchains and Smart Contracts for the Internet of Things. *IEEE Access : Practical Innovations, Open Solutions*, 4, 2292–2303. DOI: 10.1109/ACCESS.2016.2566339

Clack, C. D. (2018). A Blockchain Grand Challenge: Smart Financial Derivatives. *Frontiers in Blockchain*, 1, 1. Advance online publication. DOI: 10.3389/fbloc.2018.00001

Classification, P. (2019). *(12) Patent Application Publication (10) Pub . No . : US 2019 / 0034587 A1. 1.*

CoinGecko. (2022, October 18). *2021 Yearly Cryptocurrency Report.* CoinGecko. https://www.coingecko.com/research/publications/2021-yearly-cryptocurrency -report

Colombo, A., Bellomarini, L., Ceri, S., & Laurenza, E. (2023). Smart Derivative Contracts in DatalogMTL. *Advances in Database Technology - EDBT, 26*(3). DOI: 10.48786/edbt.2023.65

Conoscenti, M., Vetro, A., & De Martin, J. C. (2016, November). Blockchain for the Internet of Things: A systematic literature review. In *2016 IEEE/ACS 13th International Conference of Computer Systems and Applications (AICCSA)* (pp. 1-6). IEEE. DOI: 10.1109/AICCSA.2016.7945805

Conoscenti, M., De Martin, J. C., & D'Agostino, G. (2016). Blockchain-based identity management. *2016 IEEE/IFIP International Conference on Dependable Systems and Networks Workshops (DSN-W)*, 556-557. DOI: 10.1109/DSN-W.2016.57

Cooper, C., Franklin, D., Ros, M., Safaei, F., & Abolhasan, M. (2017). A Comparative Survey of VANET Clustering Techniques. In *IEEE Communications Surveys and Tutorials* (Vol. 19, Issue 1). DOI: 10.1109/COMST.2016.2611524

Cretarola, A., Figà-Talamanca, G., & Grunspan, C. Blockchain and cryptocurrencies: economic and financial research. Decisions Econ Finan 44, 781–787 (2021). https://doi.org/doi:10.1007/s10203-021-00366-3

Croman, K., Decker, C., Eyal, I., & Gencer, A. E. (2016). On scaling decentralized blockchains. *2016 3rd Workshop on Bitcoin and Blockchain Research*, 106-125. https://doi.org/DOI: 10.1145/2994369.2994377

Cui, L., Yang, S., Chen, F., Ming, Z., Lu, N., & Qin, J. (2018). A survey on application of machine learning for Internet of Things. *International Journal of Machine Learning and Cybernetics*, 9(8), 1399–1417. DOI: 10.1007/s13042-018-0834-5

Cunha, P. R. D., Soja, P., & Themistocleous, M. (2021). Blockchain for development: A guiding framework. *Information Technology for Development*, 27(3), 417–438. DOI: 10.1080/02681102.2021.1935453

Dakakni, D., & Safa, N. (2023). Artificial intelligence in the L2 classroom: Implications and challenges on ethics and equity in higher education: A 21st century Pandora's box. *Computers and Education: Artificial Intelligence*, 5, 100179. Advance online publication. DOI: 10.1016/j.caeai.2023.100179

Das, S., & Pal, S. (2019). Analysis of Energy-Efficient Routing Protocols in Mobile Ad Hoc Network. In C. a. In Advances in Computer (Ed.), Advances in Computer, Communication and Control (pp. 285-295). Singapore: Springer. DOI: 10.1007/978-981-13-3122-0_27

Dawaliby, S., Aberkane, A., & Bradai, A. (2020) Blockchain-based IoT platform for autonomous drone operations management. *Proceedings of the 2nd ACM MobiComWorkshop on Drone Assisted Wireless Communications for 5G and Beyond, London, UK*, pp. 31–36. DOI: 10.1145/3414045.3415939

Deebak, B., & Al-Turjman, F. (2020). A smart lightweight privacy preservation scheme for IoT-based UAV communication systems. *Computer Communications*, 162, 102–117. DOI: 10.1016/j.comcom.2020.08.016

DeFiPulse. (2023). Total Value Locked (TVL) in DAOs. Retrieved from DeFiPulse DAO Stats.

Deloitte. (2023). Integrating IoT and blockchain to ensure cyber safety. In *A Middle East Point of View - Summer 2023*. https://www2.deloitte.com/content/dam/Deloitte/xe/Documents/About-Deloitte/mepovdocuments/ME-PoV-issue-41/cyber-safety_mepov41.pdf

Design, P. (2019). Guest Editorial Special Issue on IoT on the Move [IoIV]. *IEEE Internet of Things Journal*, 6(1), 1–5. DOI: 10.1109/JIOT.2019.2896750

Dewey, R., & Newbold, C. (2023). The Pricing And Hedging Of Constant Function Market Makers*. SSRN *Electronic Journal*. DOI: 10.2139/ssrn.4455835

Dhatterwal, J. S., & Kaswan, K. S. (2023). Role of Blockchain Technology in the Financial Market. In *Contemporary Studies of Risks in Emerging Technology, Part A* (pp. 93-109). Emerald Publishing Limited. DOI: 10.1108/978-1-80455-562-020231007

Dhatterwal, J. S., Kaswan, K. S., Kumar, S., Balusamy, B., & Ramasamy, L. K. (2024). Design and Development to Collect and Analyze Data Using Bioprinting Software for Biotechnology Industry. *Computational Intelligence in Bioprinting*, 193-209.

Dhatterwal, J. S., Kaswan, K. S., & Chithaluru, P. (2024). Agricultural cyber-physical systems: evolution, basic, and fundamental concepts. In *Agri 4.0 and the Future of Cyber-Physical Agricultural Systems* (pp. 19–35). Academic Press. DOI: 10.1016/B978-0-443-13185-1.00002-2

Dhatterwal, J. S., Kaswan, K. S., & Johri, P. (2024). IoT Sensor Communication Using Wireless Technology. In *Wireless Communication Technologies* (pp. 66–81). CRC Press. DOI: 10.1201/9781003389231-4

Dhatterwal, J. S., Kaswan, K. S., Singh, J., Naruka, M. S., & Govardhan, D. (2023, December). Multi-Agent System Based Data Mining Technique for Supplier Selection. In *2023 International Conference on Power Energy, Environment & Intelligent Control (PEEIC)* (pp. 330-335). IEEE. DOI: 10.1109/PEEIC59336.2023.10451914

di Pietro, N., Merluzzi, M., Strinati, E. C., & Barbarossa, S. (2019). *Resilient Design of 5G Mobile-Edge Computing Over Intermittent mmWave Links*. 1–31.

Ding, Y. Z., Xu, M. Z., Tian, Y., Li, H. Y., & Liu, B. X. (2016). A ber and 2-hop routing information-based stable geographical routing protocol in manets for multimedia applications. *Wireless Personal Communications*, 90, 3–32.

Diro, A. A., & Chilamkurti, N. (2018). Distributed attack detection scheme using deep learning approach for Internet of Things. *Future Generation Computer Systems*, 82, 761–768. DOI: 10.1016/j.future.2017.08.043

Domingos, F., Cunha, D., Villas, L., Boukerche, A., Maia, G., Viana, A. C., Mini, R. A. F., & Loureiro, A. A. F. (2016). Data Communication in VANETs: Survey. *Applications and Challenges. Elsevier*, 44, 90–103. DOI: 10.1016/j.adhoc.2016.02.017

Dua, V., Rajpal, A., Rajpal, S., Agarwal, M., & Kumar, N. (2023). I-FLASH: Interpretable Fake News Detector Using LIME and SHAP. *Wireless Personal Communications*, 131(4), 2841–2874. DOI: 10.1007/s11277-023-10582-2

Dutra, A. C., Tavares, J. M. R. S., & Silva, L. F. (2018). A blockchain-based approach for supply chain traceability in the automotive industry. *2018 International Joint Conference on Neural Networks (IJCNN)*, 1-8.

Dutta, S. (2024). Framing the Landscape of Technological Enhancements: Artificial Intelligence, Gender Issues, and Ethical Dilemmas. In *Signals and Communication Technology: Vol. Part F1803* (pp. 109–123). Springer Science and Business Media Deutschland GmbH. DOI: 10.1007/978-3-031-45237-6_10

Elbery, A., Rakha, H., Elnainay, M., Drira, W., & Filali, F. (2015). Eco-Routing Using V2I Communication: System Evaluation. *IEEE Conference on Intelligent Transportation Systems, Proceedings, ITSC, 2015-Octob*(September), 71–76. DOI: 10.1109/ITSC.2015.20

Ema, R., Akram, A., & Hossain, M. (2014). Performance Analysis of DSDV, AODV AND AOMDV Routing Protocols based on Fixed and Mobility Network Model in Wireless Sensor Network. *Global Journal Of, 14*(6).

Entriken, W., Shirley, D., Evans, J., & Sachs, N. (2018). "ERC-721 Non-Fungible Token Standard." Retrieved from https://eips.ethereum.org/EIPS/eip-721

Er, J. K., & Er, G. S. (2017). Review study on MANET routing protocols: Challenges and applications. *International Journal of Advanced Research in Computer Science*, 8(4).

Esposito, C., Santis, A. D., & Tortora, G. (2018). Blockchain-based edge computing: A review of applications and challenges. *Journal of Computer Networks and Communications*, 2018, 1–12. DOI: 10.1155/2018/5979512

Faozi, M., & Gustanto, E. S. (2022). Kripto, Blockchain, Bitcoin, dan Masa Depan Bank Islam: Sebuah Literatur Review. *Quranomic: Jurnal Ekonomi Dan Bisnis Islam, 1*(2).

Farell, R. (2015). An analysis of the cryptocurrency industry. *Wharton Research Scholars*, 130, 1–23.

Fesakis, G., & Prantsoudi, S. (2021). Raising Artificial Intelligence Bias Awareness in Secondary Education: The Design of an Educational Intervention. In F. Matos, I. Salavisa, & C. Serrao (Eds.), *3rd European Conference on the Impact of Artificial Intelligence and Robotics, ECIAIR 2021* (pp. 35–42). Academic Conferences and Publishing International Limited. https://doi.org/DOI: 10.34190/EAIR.21.039

Fogue, M., Sanguesa, J., Martinez, F., & Marquez-Barja, J. (2018). Improving Roadside Unit Deployment in Vehicular Networks by Exploiting Genetic Algorithms. *Applied Sciences (Basel, Switzerland)*, 8(1), 86. DOI: 10.3390/app8010086

Foroglou, G., & Tsilidou, A. L. (2015, May). Further applications of the blockchain. In 12th student conference on managerial science and technology (Vol. 9). Athens University of Economics and Business, Athens, Greece.

Fotouhi, A., Qiang, H., Ding, M., Hassan, M., Giordano, L. G., Garcia-Rodriguez, A., & Yuan, J. (2018). Survey on UAV Cellular Communications: Practical Aspects, Standardization Advancements, Regulation, and Security Challenges. *IEEE Communications Surveys and Tutorials*, 21(4), 3417–3442. DOI: 10.1109/COMST.2019.2906228

Friginal, J., De Andrés, D., Ruiz, J. C., & Martínez, M. (2014). A survey of evaluation platforms for ad hoc routing protocols: A resilience perspective. *Computer Networks, 75*(PartA), 395–413. DOI: 10.1016/j.comnet.2014.09.010

Fullan, M. (2013). Stratosphere: Integrating technology, pedagogy, and change knowledge. *The Alberta Journal of Educational Research*, 62(4), 429–432.

Fütterer, T., Fischer, C., Alekseeva, A., Chen, X., Tate, T., Warschauer, M., & Gerjets, P. (2023). ChatGPT in education: Global reactions to AI innovations. *Scientific Reports*, 13(1), 15310. Advance online publication. DOI: 10.1038/s41598-023-42227-6 PMID: 37714915

Gallego-Madrid, J., Molina-Zarca, A., Sanchez-Iborra, R., Bernal-Bernabe, J., Santa, J., Ruiz, P. M., & Skarmeta-Gómez, A. F. (2020). Enhancing Extensive and Remote LoRa Deployments through MEC-Powered Drone Gateways. *Sensors (Basel)*, 20(15), 4109. DOI: 10.3390/s20154109 PMID: 32718087

Ghafoor, K. (2016). Video Streaming over Vehicular Ad Hoc Networks: A Comparative Study and Future Perspectives. *ARO (Koya)*, 4(2), 25–36. DOI: 10.14500/aro.10128

Ghafoor, K. Z., Mohammed, M. A., Lloret, J., Bakar, K. A., & Zainuddin, Z. M. (2013). Routing Protocols in Vehicular Ad hoc Networks: Survey and Research Challenges. *Network Protocols and Algorithms*, 3(7), 39. DOI: 10.5296/npa.v5i4.4134

Gharibi, M., Boutaba, R., & Waslander, S. L. (2016). Internet of Drones. *IEEE Access : Practical Innovations, Open Solutions*, 4, 1148–1162. DOI: 10.1109/ACCESS.2016.2537208

Ghosh, J. (2019). The blockchain: Opportunities for research in information systems and information technology. *Journal of Global Information Technology Management*, 22(4), 235–242. DOI: 10.1080/1097198X.2019.1679954

Godara, A. (2015). Energy Efficient Routing in Clustered Mobile Ad Hoc Network (MANET) (Doctoral dissertation).

Granda, F., Azpilicueta, L., Vargas-Rosales, C., Celaya-Echarri, M., Lopez-Iturri, P., Aguirre, E., Astrain, J. J., Medrano, P., Villandangos, J., & Falcone, F. (2018). Deterministic propagation modeling for intelligent vehicle communication in smart cities. *Sensors (Basel)*, 18(7), 2133. Advance online publication. DOI: 10.3390/s18072133 PMID: 29970826

Granić, A., & Marangunić, N. (2019). Technology acceptance model in educational context: A systematic literature review. *British Journal of Educational Technology*, 50(5), 2572–2593. DOI: 10.1111/bjet.12864

Gubbi, J., Buyya, R., Marusic, S., & Palaniswami, M. (2013). Internet of Things (IoT): A vision, architectural elements, and future directions. *Future Generation Computer Systems*, 29(7), 1645–1660. DOI: 10.1016/j.future.2013.01.010

Guo, L., Li, P., Jin, J., & Mou, J. (2018). Energy-Balanced Routing Protocol with QoS Constraints in Ad Hoc Network. In *International Conference in Communications, Signal Processing, and Systems* (pp. 992-999). Singapore: Springer.

Gupta, L., Jain, R., & Vaszkun, G. (2016). Survey of Important Issues in UAV Communication Networks. *IEEE Communications Surveys and Tutorials*, 18(2), 1123–1152. DOI: 10.1109/COMST.2015.2495297

Gupta, R., & Patel, P. (2016). An improved performance of greedy perimeter stateless routing protocol of vehicular adhoc network in urban realistic scenarios. Int. J. Scientific Res. Comput. Sci. *Eng. Inf. Technol.*, 1(1), 24–29.

Hamal, O., El Faddouli, N.-E., Alaoui Harouni, M. H., & Lu, J. (2022). Artificial Intelligent in Education. *Sustainability (Basel)*, 14(5), 2862. Advance online publication. DOI: 10.3390/su14052862

Hamamreh, R. A., Haji, M. M., & Qutob, A. A. (2018). An Energy-Efficient Clustering Routing Protocol for WSN based on MRHC. *International Journal of Digital Information and Wireless Communications*, 8(3), 214–223. DOI: 10.17781/P002465

Hao, M., Qian, K., & Chau, S. C. K. (2023). Blockchain-enabled Parametric Solar Energy Insurance via Remote Sensing. *E-Energy 2023 - Proceedings of the 2023 14th ACM International Conference on Future Energy Systems.* DOI: 10.1145/3575813.3576880

Harding, J., Powell, G., Yoon, R., Fikentscher, J., Doyle, C., Sade, D., Lukuc, M., Simons, J., & Wang, J. (2014). *Vehicle-to-vehicle communications: Readiness of V2V technology for application (Report No. DOT HS 812 014). August.* DOI: 10.1109/SysEng.2015.7302741

Hardjono, T., Smith, N., & Shrier, D. (2019). Self-sovereign identity frameworks and blockchain ecosystems: A comprehensive review. MIT Connection Science & Engineering. https://doi.org/DOI: 10.2139/ssrn.3309174

Haryanto, S. D., & Sudaryati, E. (2020). The Ethical Perspective of Millennial Accountants in Responding to Opportunities and Challenges of Blockchain 4.0. *Journal of Accounting and Investment*, 21(3). Advance online publication. DOI: 10.18196/jai.2103159

Hassan, M. H., & Muniyandi, R. C. (2017). An Improved Hybrid Technique for Energy and Delay Routing in Mobile Ad-Hoc Networks. *International Journal of Applied Engineering Research: IJAER*, 12(1), 134–139.

Hassan, M., & Hossain, M. A. (2022). A VR based children formula feed preparation training simulator with AI-enabled automated assessment features. *International Conference on Software, Knowledge Information, Industrial Management and Applications, SKIMA, 2022-December*, 303–308. DOI: 10.1109/SKIMA57145.2022.10029659

Hassoun, A., Garcia-Garcia, G., Trollman, H., Jagtap, S., Parra-López, C., Cropotova, J., Bhat, Z., Centobelli, P., & Aït-Kaddour, A. (2023). Birth of dairy 4.0: Opportunities and challenges in adoption of fourth industrial revolution technologies in the production of milk and its derivatives. In *Current Research in Food Science* (Vol. 7). DOI: 10.1016/j.crfs.2023.100535

Held, A. (2023). Crypto Assets and Decentralised Ledgers: Does Situs Actually Matter? In *Blockchain and Private International Law*. DOI: 10.1163/9789004514850_010

Helen, D., & Arivazhagan, D. (2014). Applications, advantages and challenges of ad hoc networks. *JAIR*, 2(8), 7–453.

Hileman, G. (2016). State of blockchain q1 2016: Blockchain funding overtakes bitcoin. *CoinDesk, New York, NY*, (May), 11.

Höhne, S., & Tiberius, V. (2020). Powered by blockchain: Forecasting blockchain use in the electricity market. *International Journal of Energy Sector Management*, 14(6), 1221–1238. DOI: 10.1108/IJESM-10-2019-0002

Hölbl, M., Kosba, A., & Jovanović, J. (2020). Blockchain technology in healthcare: A comprehensive review and directions for future research. *Health Information Science and Systems*, 8(1), 1–15. DOI: 10.1007/s13755-020-00314-7 PMID: 31867102

Hou, K. M., Diao, X., Shi, H., Ding, H., Zhou, H., & de Vaulx, C. (2023). Trends and Challenges in AIoT/IIoT/IoT Implementation. *Sensors (Basel)*, 23(11), 5074. Advance online publication. DOI: 10.3390/s23115074 PMID: 37299800

Hrouga, M., Sbihi, A., & Chavallard, M. (2022). The potentials of combining Blockchain technology and Internet of Things for digital reverse supply chain: A case study. *Journal of Cleaner Production*, 337, 130609. DOI: 10.1016/j.jclepro.2022.130609

Huang, H., Savkin, A. V., Ding, M., & Kaafar, M. A. (2019). Optimized deployment of drone base station to improve user experience in cellular networks. *Journal of Network and Computer Applications*, 144, 49–58. Advance online publication. DOI: 10.1016/j.jnca.2019.07.002

Huang, Y., Wang, Z., & Zhang, Y. (2021). Dynamic scalability in CIoT identity management systems. *IEEE Access : Practical Innovations, Open Solutions*, 9, 14578–14586. DOI: 10.1109/ACCESS.2021.3052074

Hughes, D., & Schwenk, J. (2020). Developing and Deploying Smart Contracts: Best Practices and Tools. *ACM Transactions on Computational Logic*, 21(3), 1–27. DOI: 10.1145/3374136

Hussain, F., Hussain, R., Hassan, S. A., & Hossain, E. (2020). Machine Learning in IoT Security: Current Solutions and Future Challenges. *IEEE Communications Surveys and Tutorials*, 22(3), 1686–1721. DOI: 10.1109/COMST.2020.2986444

Iacovelli, G., Boccadoro, P., & Grieco, L. (2020) An iterative stochastic approach to constrained drones' communications, *Proc. of IEEE/ACM 24th International Symposium on Distributed Simulation and Real Time Applications (DS-RT) (DS-RT'20), Prague, Czech Republic.* DOI: 10.1109/DS-RT50469.2020.9213645

Iche, A. H., & Dhage, M. R. (2015). Location-based routing protocols: A survey. *International Journal of Computer Applications*, 975, 8887.

Indapurkar, A., & Patil, R. (2017). Analysis of Energy Routing Protocol with Power Consumption Optimization in MANET. [IJEMR]. *International Journal of Engineering and Management Research*, 7(1), 100–106.

Islam, M., Chowdhury, M., Li, H., & Hu, H. (2018). Cybersecurity Attacks in Vehicle-to-Infrastructure Applications and Their Prevention. *Transportation Research Record: Journal of the Transportation Research Board*, 2672(19), 66–78. Advance online publication. DOI: 10.1177/0361198118799012

Ito, K., Shibano, K., & Mogi, G. (2022). Predicting the Bubble of Non-Fungible Tokens (NFTs): An Empirical Investigation. arXiv preprint arXiv:2203.12587.

Jagadev, N., Pattanayak, B. K., Singh, D., & Sahoo, S. (2018). A Survey on Bandwidth Management in MANET. *IACSIT International Journal of Engineering and Technology*, 7, 38–41.

Jahir, Y., Atiquzzaman, M., Refai, H., Paranjothi, A., & LoPresti, P. G. (2019). Routing protocols and architecture for Disaster Area Network: A survey. *Ad Hoc Networks*, 82, 1–14. DOI: 10.1016/j.adhoc.2018.08.005

Jaiwani, M., Gopalkrishnan, S., Kale, V., Chatterjee, A., Khatwani, R., Kasam, N., & Mitra, P. K. (2023). The Blockchain Revolution: Disrupting Derivative Markets with Smart Contracts. *2023 IEEE International Conference on Technology Management, Operations and Decisions, ICTMOD 2023.* DOI: 10.1109/ICTMOD59086.2023.10438145

Jayeola, O. (2020). Inefficiencies in trade reporting for over-the-counter derivatives: Is blockchain the solution? *Capital Markets Law Journal*, 15(1), 48–69. Advance online publication. DOI: 10.1093/cmlj/kmz028

Jiang, Q., Li, K., Zhang, Y., & Jiang, L. (2021). AI and blockchain integration: A comprehensive survey and future directions. *IEEE Transactions on Emerging Topics in Computing*, 9(1), 124–137. DOI: 10.1109/TETC.2020.2970990

Jindal, V., & Bedi, P. (2016). Vehicular Ad-Hoc Networks: Introduction, Standards, Routing Protocols and Challenges. *International Journal of Computer Science Issues*, 13(2), 44–55. DOI: 10.20943/01201602.4455

Jin, X., Zhang, Q., & Zhang, J. (2019). Secure data sharing in healthcare IoT using blockchain technology. *IEEE Access : Practical Innovations, Open Solutions*, 7, 170128–170139.

Johnson, D., Menezes, A., & Vanstone, S. (2001). The elliptic curve digital signature algorithm (ecdsa). *International Journal of Information Security*, 1(1), 36–63. DOI: 10.1007/s102070100002

Jones, M., & Brown, A. (2021). *Advances in Predictive Maintenance Technologies*. Springer.

Kamalakshi, N., & Naganna. (2021). Role of blockchain in agriculture and food sector: a summary. In Convergence of Internet of Things and Blockchain Technologies (pp. 93-107). Cham: Springer International Publishing.

Kamalakshi, N., & Naganna. (2021). Role of blockchain in tackling and boosting the supply chain management economy post COVID-19. In Convergence of internet of things and blockchain technologies (pp. 193-205). Cham: Springer International Publishing.

Karaarslan, E., & Konacaklı, E. (2020). Data Storage in the Decentralized World: Blockchain and Derivatives. In *Who Runs the World: Data*. DOI: 10.26650/B/ET06.2020.011.03

Karthikeyan, L. (2015). Comparative study on non-delay tolerant routing protocols in vehicular networks. *Procedia Computer Science*, 50, 252–257. DOI: 10.1016/j.procs.2015.04.052

Kaswan, K. S., Dhatterwal, J. S., Kumar, N., Balusamy, B., & Gangadevi, E. (2024). Cyborg Intelligence for Bioprinting in Computational Design and Analysis of Medical Application. *Computational Intelligence in Bioprinting*, 211-237.

Kaswan, K. S., Sidhu, G. S., Dhatterwal, J. S., & Kumar, N. (2024). The Role Played by Blockchain Computing Premium Payments and Creating New Markets. In The Application of Emerging Technology and Blockchain in the Insurance Industry (pp. 163-178). River Publishers.

Kaswan, K. S., Malik, K., Dhatterwal, J. S., Naruka, M. S., & Govardhan, D. (2023, December). Deepfakes: A Review on Technologies, Applications and Strategies. In *2023 International Conference on Power Energy, Environment & Intelligent Control (PEEIC)* (pp. 292-297). IEEE. DOI: 10.1109/PEEIC59336.2023.10450604

Kaur, H., Singh, H., & Sharma, A. (2016). Geographic routing protocol: A review. *International Journal of Grid and Distributed Computing*, 9(2), 245–254. DOI: 10.14257/ijgdc.2016.9.2.21

Kaur, H, Singh, H., & Sharma, A. (n.d.).

Kazachenok, O. P., Stankevich, G. V., Chubaeva, N. N., & Tyurina, Y. G. (2023). Economic and legal approaches to the humanization of FinTech in the economy of artificial intelligence through the integration of blockchain into ESG Finance. *Humanities & Social Sciences Communications*, 10(1), 167. DOI: 10.1057/s41599-023-01652-8

Khalifa, A. R., Sadek, R. A., & Al-Shora, M. A. (2016). Performance Analysis Of DSR, SEA-DSR And Modified DSR Routing Protocols. *International Journal of Computer Science and Mobile Computing*, 5(7), 204–209.

Khan, M. F., Aadil, F., Maqsood, M., Bukhari, S. H. R., Hussain, M., & Nam, Y. (2019). Moth flame clustering algorithm for internet of vehicle (MFCA-IoV). *IEEE Access : Practical Innovations, Open Solutions*, 7, 11613–11629. DOI: 10.1109/ACCESS.2018.2886420

Khan, R. U., & Alghamdi, A. (2020). A comprehensive survey of blockchain-based edge computing systems for IoT. *IEEE Access : Practical Innovations, Open Solutions*, 8, 84234–84248. DOI: 10.1109/ACCESS.2020.2992871

Khan, S., Al-Dmour, A., Bali, V., Rabbani, M. R., & Thirunavukkarasu, K. (2021a). Cloud computing based futuristic educational model for virtual learning. *Journal of Statistics and Management Systems*, 24(2), 357–385. DOI: 10.1080/09720510.2021.1879468

Khan, S., Qader, M. R., Thirunavukkarasu, K., & Abimannan, S. (2020, October). Analysis of business intelligence impact on organizational performance. In *2020 International Conference on Data Analytics for Business and Industry: Way Towards a Sustainable Economy (ICDABI)* (pp. 1-4). IEEE. DOI: 10.1109/ICDABI51230.2020.9325610

Khan, S., Syed, M. H., Hammad, R., & Bushager, A. F. (Eds.). (2022). *Blockchain technology and computational excellence for society 5.0*. IGI Global. DOI: 10.4018/978-1-7998-8382-1

Khan, S., Thirunavukkarasu, K., AlDmour, A., & Shreem, S. S. (Eds.). (2021b). *A Step towards Society 5.0: Research, innovations, and developments in Cloud-based computing technologies*. CRC Press. DOI: 10.1201/9781003138037

Khan, U. A., & Lee, S. S. (2019). Multi-Layer Problems and Solutions in VANETs: A Review. *Electronics (Basel)*, 8(2), 204. DOI: 10.3390/electronics8020204

Khiem, H. G., Huong, H. L., Phuc, N. T., Khoa, T. D., Khanh, H. V., Quy, L. T., Ngan, N. T. K., Triet, N. M., Kha, N. H., Anh, N. T., Tyong, V. C. P., Bang, L. K., Hieu, D. M., & Bao, T. Q. (2023). A Comprehensive System for Managing Blood Resources Leveraging Blockchain, Smart Contracts, and Non-Fungible Tokens. *International Journal of Advanced Computer Science and Applications*, 14(10). Advance online publication. DOI: 10.14569/IJACSA.2023.01410101

Khurma, O. A., Ali, N., & Hashem, R. (2023). Critical Reflections on ChatGPT in UAE Education Navigating Equity and Governance for Safe and Effective Use. *International Journal of Emerging Technologies in Learning*, 18(14), 188–199. DOI: 10.3991/ijet.v18i14.40935

Khuwaja, A. A., Chen, Y., Zhao, N., Alouini, M. S., & Dobbins, P. (2018). A survey of channel modeling for UAV communications. *IEEE Communications Surveys and Tutorials*, 20(4), 1–1. DOI: 10.1109/COMST.2018.2856587

Kim, D. S., & Tran-Dang, H. (2019). MAC Protocols for Energy-Efficient Wireless Sensor Networks. In Industrial Sensors and Controls in Communication Networks (pp. 141-159). Springer. DOI: 10.1007/978-3-030-04927-0_11

Kim, H. a. (2015). A New Energy-Aware Routing Protocol for Improving Path Stability in Ad-hoc Networks.

King, S., & Nadal, S. (2012). Ppcoin: Peer-to-peer crypto-currency with proof-of-stake. self-published paper, August, 19(1).

King, S., & Nadal, S. (2012). PPCoin: Peer-to-peer crypto-currency with proof-of-stake. *Self-published paper*.

Koletsi, M. (2019). Radical technologies: Blockchain as an organizational movement. *Homo Virtualis*, 2(1), 25. DOI: 10.12681/homvir.20191

Korth, H. F., & Silberschatz, A. (1991). *Database system concepts* (3rd ed.). McGraw-Hill.

Kosba, A., Miller, A., Shi, E., Wen, Z., & Papamanthou, C. (2016, May). Hawk: The blockchain model of cryptography and privacy-preserving smart contracts. In 2016 IEEE symposium on security and privacy (SP) (pp. 839-858). IEEE.

Kosba, A., Miller, A., Shi, E., Wen, Z., & Papamanthou, C. (2016). Hawk: The blockchain model of cryptography and privacy-preserving smart contracts. *In2016 IEEE Symposium on Security and Privacy (SP)* (pp. 839-858). IEEE. DOI: 10.1109/SP.2016.55

Koubaa, A., Qureshi, B., Sriti, M.-F., Allouch, A., Javed, Y., Alajlan, M., Cheikhrouhou, O., Khalgui, M., & Tovar, E. (2019). Drone map planner: A service-oriented cloud-based management system for the internet-of-drones. *Ad Hoc Networks*, 86, 46–62. DOI: 10.1016/j.adhoc.2018.09.013

Krichen, M., Ammi, M., Mihoub, A., & Almutiq, M. (2022). Blockchain for Modern Applications: A Survey. *Sensors (Basel)*, 22(14), 5274. DOI: 10.3390/s22145274 PMID: 35890953

Kumar, A., & Mehta, P. L. (2021). *Internet of drones: An engaging platform for iiot-oriented airborne sensors*. Smart Sensors for Industrial Internet of Things., DOI: 10.1007/978-3-030-52624-5_16

Kumar, A., Shwe, H. Y., Wong, K. J., & Chong, P. H. (2017). Location-based routing protocols for wireless sensor networks: A survey. *Wireless Sensor Network*, 9(1), 25–72. DOI: 10.4236/wsn.2017.91003

Kumar, A., & Tyagi, M. (2014). Geographical Topologies of Routing Protocols in Vehicular Ad hoc Networks – A Survey. [IJCSIT]. *International Journal of Computer Science and Information Technologies*, 5(3), 3062–3065.

Kumar, N. A., & Raj, E. G. D. P. (2015). RS-CBAODV: An Enhanced Reactive Routing Algorithm for VANET to Reduce Connection Breakage using Remote Storage Concepts. *International Journal of Information Technology and Computer Science*, 7(10), 74–83. DOI: 10.5815/ijitcs.2015.10.09

Kumar, R., Tripathi, R., & Joshi, S. (2020). Blockchain-based architecture for secure and efficient IoT supply chain management. *Sensors (Basel)*, 20(17), 5129. PMID: 32825335

Kumar, S., Hsu, S., & Yadav, P. (2023). Automating identity management with blockchain-based smart contracts. *Blockchain Research and Applications*, 14, 100065. DOI: 10.1016/j.bcra.2022.100065

Kumar, S., Tiwari, P., & Zymbler, M. (2019). Internet of Things is a revolutionary approach for future technology enhancement: A review. *Journal of Big Data*, 6(1), 1–21. DOI: 10.1186/s40537-019-0268-2

Laaki, H., Miche, Y., & Tammi, K. (2019). Prototyping a Digital Twin for real time remote control over mobile networks: Application of remote surgery. *IEEE Access : Practical Innovations, Open Solutions*, 7, 1–1. DOI: 10.1109/ACCESS.2019.2897018

Lai, Y., Lin, H., Yang, F., & Wang, T. (2019). Efficient data request answering in vehicular Ad-hoc networks based on fog nodes and filters. *Future Generation Computer Systems*, 93, 130–142. DOI: 10.1016/j.future.2018.09.065

Lakshmi, G. R., & Srikanth, V. (2015). Location-Based routing protocol in wireless sensor network-A survey. *International Journal of Advanced Research in Computer Science and Software Engineering*, 5(4).

Lamport, L., Shostak, R., & Pease, M. (1982). The byzantine generals prob-lem. *ACM Transactions on Programming Languages and Systems*, 4(3), 382–401. DOI: 10.1145/357172.357176

Larchenko, V., & Barynikova, O. (2021). New technologies in education. In Rudoy, D., Olshevskaya, A., & Ugrekhelidze, N. (Eds.), *E3S Web of Conferences* (Vol. 273). EDP Sciences., DOI: 10.1051/e3sconf/202127312145

Latham, A., & Goltz, S. (2019). A survey of the general public's views on the ethics of using AI in education. In S. Isotani, E. Millán, A. Ogan, B. McLaren, P. Hastings, & R. Luckin (Eds.), *Lecture Notes in Computer Science (including subseries Lecture Notes in Artificial Intelligence and Lecture Notes in Bioinformatics): Vol. 11625 LNAI* (pp. 194–206). Springer Verlag. DOI: 10.1007/978-3-030-23204-7_17

Lee Kuo Chuen, D. (Ed.). (2015). *Handbook of Digital Currency* (1st ed.). Elsevier. https://EconPapers.repec.org/RePEc:eee:monogr:9780128021170

Lee, D., & Kwon, H. (2020). Smart contracts for cognitive IoT: Applications and challenges. *Journal of Blockchain Research*, 2(4), 112–124. DOI: 10.1007/s41615-020-00122-7

Lee, J., Kao, H., & Yang, S. (2014). Service innovation and smart analytics for Industry 4.0 and big data environment. *Procedia CIRP*, 16, 3–8. DOI: 10.1016/j.procir.2014.02.001

Liang, W., Li, Z., Zhang, H., Wang, S., & Bie, R. (2015). Vehicular Ad Hoc networks: Architectures, research issues, methodologies, challenges, and trends. *International Journal of Distributed Sensor Networks*, 2015(8), 745303. Advance online publication. DOI: 10.1155/2015/745303

Lian, Y., Tang, H., Xiang, M., & Dong, X. (2024). Public attitudes and sentiments toward ChatGPT in China: A text mining analysis based on social media. *Technology in Society*, 76, 102442. Advance online publication. DOI: 10.1016/j. techsoc.2023.102442

Lin, H.-C., Ho, C.-F., & Yang, H. (2022). Understanding adoption of artificial intelligence-enabled language e-learning system: An empirical study of UTAUT model. *International Journal of Mobile Learning and Organisation*, 16(1), 74–94. DOI: 10.1504/IJMLO.2022.119966

Lin, I. C., & Liao, T. C. (2017). A Survey of Blockchain Security Issues and Challenges. *International Journal of Network Security*, 19(5), 653–659. DOI: 10.6633/ IJNS.201709.19(5).01

Lin, Z., & Tang, Y. (2019). Distributed Multi-channel MAC Protocol for VANET: An Adaptive Frame Structure Scheme. *IEEE Access : Practical Innovations, Open Solutions*, 7, 1–1. DOI: 10.1109/ACCESS.2019.2892820

Li, Q., Zhang, S., & Li, Z. (2019). Security and privacy in smart contracts: A survey. *IEEE Access : Practical Innovations, Open Solutions*, 7, 105453–105468. DOI: 10.1109/ACCESS.2019.2934697

Li, S., Xu, L. D., & Zhao, H. (2021). Industrial IoT: Challenges and solutions for blockchain integration. *Journal of Industrial Information Integration*, 21, 100191. DOI: 10.1016/j.jii.2020.100191

Liu, T., & Chen, X. (2022). Practical Case Studies of Consensus Mechanisms in IoT-Based Blockchains. *Journal of Blockchain Research and Applications*, 8(2), 67–82. DOI: 10.1016/j.jblock.2022.05.001

Liu, Y. (2023). The role of online technology in quality course design. In *The Impact and Importance of Instructional Design in the Educational Landscape* (pp. 178–206). IGI Global., DOI: 10.4018/978-1-6684-8208-7.ch007

Liu, Y., Wu, F., & Wu, J. (2021). Cellular UAV-to-device communications: Joint trajectory, speed, and power optimisation. *IET Communications*, 15(10), 1380–1391. DOI: 10.1049/cmu2.12104

Li, Y., Li, K., Li, H., & Wang, X. (2020). Security and Privacy Issues in the Internet of Things: A Survey. *IEEE Communications Surveys and Tutorials*, 22(4), 2656–2695. DOI: 10.1109/COMST.2020.2993542

Li, Y., Xu, L. D., & Zhao, X. (2020). A survey on scalability and performance of blockchain technology. *IEEE Access : Practical Innovations, Open Solutions*, 8, 66400–66417. DOI: 10.1109/ACCESS.2020.2982257

Li, Y., & Zhang, Y. (2017). Big Data Management in Smart Grids: Concepts, Requirements, and Implementation. *IEEE Power & Energy Magazine*, 15(1), 45–55. DOI: 10.1109/MPE.2016.2618897

Luttrell, R., Wallace, A., McCollough, C., & Lee, J. (2020). The Digital Divide: Addressing Artificial Intelligence in Communication Education. *Journalism and Mass Communication Educator*, 75(4), 470–482. DOI: 10.1177/1077695820925286

Lu, Y., Yu, H., & Zhu, Y. (2020). A Review of Blockchain Technology and Its Applications in Smart Grid. *Renewable & Sustainable Energy Reviews*, 122, 109648. DOI: 10.1016/j.rser.2020.109648

Ly, S., Reyes-Hadsall, S., Drake, L., Zhou, G., Nelson, C., Barbieri, J. S., & Mostaghimi, A. (2023). Public Perceptions, Factors, and Incentives Influencing Patient Willingness to Share Clinical Images for Artificial Intelligence-Based Healthcare Tools. *Dermatology and Therapy*, 13(11), 2895–2902. DOI: 10.1007/s13555-023-01031-w PMID: 37737327

Majdkhyavi, N., & Hassanpour, R. (2015). A Survey of Existing Mechanisms in Energy-Aware Routing In MANETs. *International Journal of Computer Applications Technology and Research*, 4(9), 673–679. DOI: 10.7753/IJCATR0409.1007

Makarov, I., & Schoar, A. (2020). Trading and arbitrage in cryptocurrency markets. *Journal of Financial Economics*, 135(2), 293–319. DOI: 10.1016/j.jfineco.2019.07.001

Makhdoom, I., Abolhasan, M., Abbas, H., & Ni, W. (2019). Blockchain's adoption in IoT: The challenges, and a way forward. *Journal of Network and Computer Applications*, 125, 251–279. DOI: 10.1016/j.jnca.2018.10.019

Malik, K., Dhatterwal, J. S., Kaswan, K. S., Gupta, M., & Thakur, J. (2023, December). Intelligent Approach Integrating Multiagent Systems and Case-Based Reasoning in Brain-Computer Interface. In *2023 International Conference on Power Energy, Environment & Intelligent Control (PEEIC)* (pp. 1632-1636). IEEE. DOI: 10.1109/PEEIC59336.2023.10450496

Malik, R. F., Nurfatih, M. S., Ubaya, H., Zulfahmi, R., & Sodikin, E. (2017). Evaluation of greedy perimeter stateless routing protocol on vehicular ad hoc network in palembang city. In *2017 International Conference on Data and Software Engineering (ICoDSE)* (pp. 1-5). IEEE. DOI: 10.1109/ICODSE.2017.8285873

Malinova, K., & Park, A. (2023). Tokenized Stocks for Trading and Capital Raising. SSRN *Electronic Journal*. DOI: 10.2139/ssrn.4365241

Mannonov, K. M. U., & Myeong, S. (2024). Citizens' Perception of Blockchain-Based E-Voting Systems: Focusing on TAM. *Sustainability (Basel)*, 16(11), 4387. DOI: 10.3390/su16114387

Marcel, G. and Vetrivelan. (2015). Evaluating The Effects of the Energy Management's Issues on the MANET's Performance Using Two Native Routing Protocols against a Power-Aware Routing Protocol. [IJCST]. *International Journal of Computer Science Trends and Technology*, 3(5).

Martha, G. I. R., Warnars, H. L. H. S., & Prabowo, H., Meyliana, & Hidayanto, A. N. (2023). Semantic Literature Review on Non-Fungible Token: Expansion Area of Usage & Trends. *Proceedings of 2023 International Conference on Information Management and Technology, ICIMTech 2023*. DOI: 10.1109/ICIMTech59029.2023.10277808

Masek, P., Masek, J., Frantik, P., Fujdiak, R., Ometov, A., Hosek, J., Andreev, S., Mlynek, P., & Misurec, J. (2016). A harmonized perspective on transportation management in smart cities: The novel IoT-driven environment for road traffic modeling. *Sensors (Basel)*, 16(11), 1872. Advance online publication. DOI: 10.3390/s16111872 PMID: 27834796

Mathieson, K., Leafman, J. S., & Horton, M. B. (2017). Access to digital communication technology and perceptions of telemedicine for patient education among American Indian patients with diabetes. *Journal of Health Care for the Poor and Underserved*, 28(4), 1522–1536. DOI: 10.1353/hpu.2017.0131 PMID: 29176112

Matsumoto, H., Sakai, T., & Yamazaki, Y. (2021). The Decentralized Identity Foundation: Overview and key initiatives. *Journal of Cyber Security Technology*, 5(1), 63–80. DOI: 10.1080/23742917.2021.1892247

Mehmood, Y., Ahmad, F., Yaqoob, I., Adnane, A., Imran, M., & Guizani, S. (2017). Internet-of-Things-Based Smart Cities: Recent Advances and Challenges. *IEEE Communications Magazine*, 55(9), 16–24. DOI: 10.1109/MCOM.2017.1600514

Mejri, M. N., Ben-Othman, J., & Hamdi, M. (2014). Survey on VANET security challenges and possible cryptographic solutions. *Vehicular Communications*, 1(2), 53–66. DOI: 10.1016/j.vehcom.2014.05.001

Merkert, R., & Bushell, J. (2020). Managing the drone revolution: A systematic literature review into the current use of airborne drones and future strategic directions for their effective control. *Journal of Air Transport Management*, 89, 101929. DOI: 10.1016/j.jairtraman.2020.101929 PMID: 32952321

Mesko, B. (2023). The ChatGPT (Generative Artificial Intelligence) Revolution Has Made Artificial Intelligence Approachable for Medical Professionals. *Journal of Medical Internet Research*, 25, e48392. Advance online publication. DOI: 10.2196/48392 PMID: 37347508

Miller, C., Moini, A., & Rodriguez, A. (2022). Self-sovereign identity in IoT systems: Opportunities and challenges. *IEEE Internet of Things Journal*, 9(5), 3882–3894. DOI: 10.1109/JIOT.2022.3155723

Mirabelli, G., & Solina, V. (2020). Blockchain and agricultural supply chains traceability: Research trends and future challenges. *Procedia Manufacturing*, 42, 414–421. DOI: 10.1016/j.promfg.2020.02.054

Mishra, R. (2016). *VANET Security : Issues, Challenges and Solutions*. 1050–1055.

Mishra, P., Varadharajan, V., Tupakula, U., & Pilli, E. S. (2019). A Detailed Investigation and Analysis of Using Machine Learning Techniques for Intrusion Detection. *IEEE Communications Surveys and Tutorials*, 21(1), 686–728. DOI: 10.1109/COMST.2018.2847722

Mittal, V.; Pokhriyal, S.; Srivastava, H.; Vashist, S. and Verma, M. (2018). Location based protocols in WSN: A Review. IIOAB Engineering Technology, ISSN, 0976-3104.

Mizera-Pietraszko, J., & Pająk, M. (2022). Privacy-Preserving Techniques in Blockchain Systems: A Comprehensive Review. *ACM Computing Surveys*, 55(2), 1–36. DOI: 10.1145/3475996

Moreau, V., Dos Reis, P., & Vuille, F. (2019). Enough Metals? Resource Constraints to Supply a Fully Renewable Energy System. *Resources*, 8(1), 29. DOI: 10.3390/resources8010029

Morrison, K. (2021). *The Future of Decentralized Identifiers*. Springer Nature.

Mougayar, W. (2016). *The business blockchain: promise, practice, and application of the next Internet technology*. John Wiley & Sons.

Mounce, R., & Nelson, J. D. (2019). On the potential for one-way electric vehicle car-sharing in future mobility systems. *Transportation Research Part A: Policy and Practice, 120*(November 2018), 17–30. DOI: 10.1016/j.tra.2018.12.003

Moussa, I., Obaidat, M. S., & Ibrahim, I. (2022). Blockchain-based smart home security systems: A survey and future directions. *IEEE Transactions on Network and Service Management*, 19(2), 1787–1802. DOI: 10.1109/TNSM.2022.3155723

Mugo, D. G., Njagi, K., Chemwei, B., & Motanya, J. O. (2017). *The technology acceptance model (TAM) and its application to the utilization of mobile learning technologies.*

Muhammad, M., & Safdar, G. A. (2018). Survey on existing authentication issues for cellular-assisted V2X communication. In *Vehicular Communications* (Vol. 12). DOI: 10.1016/j.vehcom.2018.01.008

Mukherjee, A., Dey, N., & De, D. (2020). Edge Drone: QoS aware MQTT middleware for mobile edge computing in opportunistic Internet of Drone Things. *Computer Communications*, 152, 93–108. DOI: 10.1016/j.comcom.2020.01.039

Mukhopadhyay, U., Skjellum, A., Hambolu, O., Oakley, J., Yu, L., & Brooks, R. (2016, December). A brief survey of cryptocurrency systems. In 2016 14th annual conference on privacy, security and trust (PST) (pp. 745-752). IEEE.

Nakamoto, S. (2008). Bitcoin: A peer-to-peer electronic cash system. *Bitcoin White Paper.*

Nakamoto, S. (2008). *Bitcoin: A peer-to-peer electronic cash system.* Retrieved from https://bitcoin.org/bitcoin.pdf

Nakamoto, S. (2008). Bitcoin: A Peer-to-Peer Electronic Cash System. Retrieved from https://bitcoin.org/bitcoin.pdf

Nakamoto, S. (2008). *Bitcoin: A peer-to-peer electronic cash system.* Satoshi Nakamoto.

Narayanan, A., Bonneau, J., Felten, E., & Miller, A. (2016). *Bitcoin and Cryptocurrency Technologies: A Comprehensive Introduction.* Princeton University Press.

Narayanan, U., Paul, V., & Joseph, S. (2022). Decentralized blockchain based authentication for secure data sharing in Cloud-IoT: DeBlock-Sec. *Journal of Ambient Intelligence and Humanized Computing*, 13(2), 769–787. DOI: 10.1007/s12652-021-02929-z

Na, Y., Wen, Z., Fang, J., Tang, Y., & Li, Y. (2022). A Derivative PBFT Blockchain Consensus Algorithm With Dual Primary Nodes Based on Separation of Powers-DPNPBFT. *IEEE Access: Practical Innovations, Open Solutions*, 10, 76114–76124. Advance online publication. DOI: 10.1109/ACCESS.2022.3192426

Nayyar, A., Nguyen, B.-L., & Nguyen, N. G. (2020) The internet of drone things (IoDT): Future envision of smart drones, *First International Conference on Sustainable Technologies for Computational Intelligence*, 563–580. DOI: 10.1007/978-981-15-0029-9_45

Nemoto, T., & Fujimoto, T. (2023). A Classification and Analysis Focusing on Attempts to Give a Computer a Personality: A Technological History of Chatbots as Simple Artificial Intelligence. In T. Matsuo, T. Fujimoto, & L. G. F (Eds.), *Lecture Notes in Networks and Systems: Vol. 677 LNNS* (pp. 59–70). Springer Science and Business Media Deutschland GmbH. DOI: 10.1007/978-3-031-30769-0_6

Nikolopoulou, K., Gialamas, V., Lavidas, K., & Komis, V. (2021). Teachers' readiness to adopt mobile learning in classrooms: A study in Greece. *Technology. Knowledge and Learning*, 26(1), 53–77. DOI: 10.1007/s10758-020-09453-7

Noh, G., Kim, J., Chung, H., & Kim, I. (2019). Realizing Multi-Gbps Vehicular Communication: Design, Implementation, and Validation. *IEEE Access : Practical Innovations, Open Solutions*, 7, 1–1. DOI: 10.1109/ACCESS.2019.2896598

Noh, S. K., Kim, P. J., & Yoon, J. H. (2016). Doppler effect on V2I path loss and V2V channel models. *2016 International Conference on Information and Communication Technology Convergence, ICTC 2016, 1*, 898–902. DOI: 10.1109/ICTC.2016.7763324

Nomura Research Institute. (2016). Survey on blockchain technologies and related services.

Nouacer, R., Hussein, M., Espinoza, H., Ouhammou, Y., Ladeira, M., & Castiñeira, R. (2020). Towards a Framework of Key Technologies for Drones. *Microprocessors and Microsystems*, 77, 103142. DOI: 10.1016/j.micpro.2020.103142

Noyes, C. (2016). Bitav: Fast anti-malware by distributed blockchain consensus and feedforward scanning. arXiv preprint arXiv:1601.01405.

Nwizege, K. S., Bottero, M., Mmeah, S., & Nwiwure, E. D. (2014). Vehicles-to-infrastructure communication safety messaging in DSRC. *Procedia Computer Science, 34*(DPNoC), 559–564. DOI: 10.1016/j.procs.2014.07.070

Olson, G., & Singer, R. (2018). Exploring Creative Frontiers of AI for ME Production and Distribution. *SMPTE*, 2018, 1–10. Advance online publication. DOI: 10.5594/M001817

Onaolapo, S., & Oyewole, O. (2018). Performance expectancy, effort expectancy, and facilitating conditions as factors influencing smart phones use for mobile learning by postgraduate students of the University of Ibadan, Nigeria. *Interdisciplinary Journal of E-Skills and Lifelong Learning*, 14(1), 95–115. DOI: 10.28945/4085

Organization, W. H. (2017). *WHO | Global data on visual impairment*. WHO.

Panarello, A., Tapas, N., Merlino, G., Longo, F., & Puliafito, A. (2018). Blockchain and IoT integration: A systematic survey. *Sensors (Basel)*, 18(8), 2575. DOI: 10.3390/s18082575 PMID: 30082633

Paolini, A. (2020). The Disruptive Effect of Distributed Ledger Technology and Blockchain in the over the Counter Derivatives Market. *Global Jurist*, 20(2), 20190048. Advance online publication. DOI: 10.1515/gj-2019-0048

Patel, D., Faisal, M., Batavia, P., Makhija, S., & Mani, M. (2016). Overview of Routing Protocols in VANET. *International Journal of Computer Applications*, 136(9), 975–8887. DOI: 10.5120/ijca2016908555

Pea, R. D., Biernacki, P., Bigman, M., Boles, K., Coelho, R., Docherty, V., Garcia, J., Lin, V., Nguyen, J., Pimentel, D., Pozos, R., Reynante, B., Roy, E., Southerton, E., Suzara, M., & Vishwanath, A. (2022). Four Surveillance Technologies Creating Challenges for Education. In *AI in Learning: Designing the Future* (pp. 317–329). Springer International Publishing. DOI: 10.1007/978-3-031-09687-7_19

Pegrum, M. (2019). Mobile AR Trails and Games for Authentic Language Learning. In Handbook of Mobile Teaching and Learning: Second Edition (pp. 1229–1244). Springer Nature. DOI: 10.1007/978-981-13-2766-7_89

Peltoniemi, T., & Ihalainen, J. (2019). Evaluating Blockchain for the Governance of the Plasma Derivatives Supply Chain: How Distributed Ledger Technology Can Mitigate Plasma Supply Chain Risks. *Blockchain in Healthcare Today*, 2, 1–13. Advance online publication. DOI: 10.30953/bhty.v2.107

Peng, H., Liang, L., Shen, X., & Li, G. Y. (2018). Vehicular Communications: A Network Layer Perspective. *IEEE Transactions on Vehicular Technology*, 1, 1–32. DOI: 10.1109/TVT.2018.2833427

Peng, Y., Li, J., Park, S., Zhu, K., Hassan, M. M., & Alsanad, A. (2019). Energy-efficient cooperative transmission for intelligent transportation systems. *Future Generation Computer Systems*, 94, 634–640. https://doi.org/https://doi.org/10.1016/j.future.2018.11.053. DOI: 10.1016/j.future.2018.11.053

Pereira, E., & Silva, M. (2022). Blockchain and Security Solutions for IoT: A Comprehensive Overview. *IEEE Access : Practical Innovations, Open Solutions*, 10, 22357–22376. DOI: 10.1109/ACCESS.2022.3144421

Peters, G. W., Panayi, E., & Chapelle, A. (2015). Trends in crypto-currencies and blockchain technologies: A monetary theory and regulation perspective. arXiv preprint arXiv:1508.04364.

Ponsam, J. G., & Srinivasan, R. (2014). A survey on MANET security challenges, attacks and its countermeasures. [IJETTCS]. *International Journal of Emerging Trends & Technology in Computer Science*, 3(1), 274–279.

Prasan, U. D., & Murugappan, S. (2016). An analysis on vehicular ad-hoc networks: Research issues, challenges and applications. *International Journal of Applied Engineering Research: IJAER*, 11(6), 4569–4575.

Prinsloo, P., Slade, S., & Khalil, M. (2023). Multimodal learning analytics—In-between student privacy and encroachment: A systematic review. *British Journal of Educational Technology*, 54(6), 1566–1586. DOI: 10.1111/bjet.13373

Pullagura, J. R., & Rao, D. V. (2017). Simulation based performance evaluation of energy efficient protocols in ad hoc networks. Journal of Advanced Research in Dynamical and Control Systems. *Special*, (02), 1141–1149.

Qader, M. R., Khan, S., Kamal, M., Usman, M., & Haseeb, M. (2021). Forecasting carbon emissions due to electricity power generation in Bahrain. *Environmental Science and Pollution Research International*, ●●●, 1–12. PMID: 34661842

Qureshi, K. N., & Abdullah, A. H. (2013). Topology based routing protocols for VANET and their comparison with MANET. *Journal of Theoretical and Applied Information Technology*, 58(3), 707–715.

Qushtom, H., Misic, J., Misic, V. B., & Chang, X. (2023). A Two-Stage PBFT Architecture With Trust and Reward Incentive Mechanism. *IEEE Internet of Things Journal*, 10(13), 11440–11452. Advance online publication. DOI: 10.1109/JIOT.2023.3243189

Rabah, K. (2017). Convergence of AI, IoT, big data, blockchain, and robotics. *The 8th International Conference on Information Technology*, 157-163.

Radanovic, I., & Lio, M. (2021). Privacy and Security in Blockchain Systems: A Review. *ACM Computing Surveys*, 54(1), 1–31. DOI: 10.1145/3402994

Rahim, A., Kong, X., Xia, F., Ning, Z., Ullah, N., Wang, J., & Das, S. K. (2018). Vehicular Social Networks: A survey. *Pervasive and Mobile Computing*, 43, 96–113. DOI: 10.1016/j.pmcj.2017.12.004

Rahman, M. M., Rahaman, M. S., Moral, I. H., & Chowdhury, M. S. (2022). Entrepreneurship Education and Entrepreneurial Intention of Business Graduates: Does Artificial Intelligence Matter? In Hossain, S., Hossain, M. S., Kaiser, M. S., Majumder, S. P., & Ray, K. (Eds.), *Lecture Notes in Networks and Systems* (Vol. 437, pp. 109–123). Springer Science and Business Media Deutschland GmbH., DOI: 10.1007/978-981-19-2445-3_8

Rajan, K., Kumar, K. S., Kannapiran, T., Khan, S., Al-Dmour, A., & Sharef, B. T. (2022, June). Intelligent Traffic Management System for Smart Cities Utilizing Reinforcement Learning Algorithm. In *2022 ASU International Conference in Emerging Technologies for Sustainability and Intelligent Systems (ICETSIS)* (pp. 170-177). IEEE. DOI: 10.1109/ICETSIS55481.2022.9888885

Rajasekar, S. and Subramani, A. (2016). A review on routing protocols for mobile Adhoc networks. i-manager's Journal on Mobile Applications and Technologies, 3(1), 39.

Ramanathan, N., Kumar, R., Banerjee, S., & Padmanabhan, S. (2023). Proof of Real-Time Transfer: A Consensus Protocol for Decentralized Data Exchange. *2023 IEEE International Conference on Blockchain and Cryptocurrency, ICBC 2023.* DOI: 10.1109/ICBC56567.2023.10174877

Ramdani, R. M., Sumarwan, U., & Hermadi, I. (2023). Analisis Faktor-Faktor yang Berpengaruh terhadap Sikap Pengguna Aset Digital Non-Fungible Token Berbasis Blockchain pada Komunitas NFT Indonesia. *Jurnal Manajemen Dan Organisasi,* 14(3), 268–286. Advance online publication. DOI: 10.29244/jmo.v14i3.46793

Rathore, M. M., Ahmad, A., & Zhang, Y. (2018). Blockchain technology for secure data management in smart factories. *IEEE Transactions on Industrial Informatics,* 14(9), 3930–3938. DOI: 10.1109/TII.2018.2851171

Ratnakaram, S., Chakravaram, V., Vihari, N. S., & Vidyasagar Rao, G. (2021). Emerging Trends in the Marketing of Financially Engineered Insurance Products. In Tuba, M., Akashe, S., & Joshi, A. (Eds.), *Advances in Intelligent Systems and Computing* (Vol. 1270, pp. 675–684). Springer Science and Business Media Deutschland GmbH., DOI: 10.1007/978-981-15-8289-9_65

Ravi, G., & Kashwan, K. R. (2016). Power Efficient Routing by Load Balancing in Mobile Ad Hoc Networks. In *Intelligent Systems Technologies and Applications* (pp. 147–157). Springer. DOI: 10.1007/978-3-319-23258-4_14

Ravi, R. R., & Jayanthi, V. (2015). Energy efficient neighbor coverage protocol for reducing rebroadcast in MANET. *Procedia Computer Science,* 47, 417–423. DOI: 10.1016/j.procs.2015.03.225

Ravishankar, K., Jeyaprabha, B., Moideen Batcha, H., & Sagunthala, V. R. D. (2018). Intention and awareness on digital media and E-learning solutions among management students in education. *International Journal of Pure and Applied Mathematics,* 120(6), 8101–8114.

Rawat, D. B., Bajracharya, C., & Yan, G. (2015). Towards intelligent transportation Cyber-Physical Systems: Real-time computing and communications perspectives. *Conference Proceedings - IEEE SOUTHEASTCON, 2015-June*(June). DOI: 10.1109/SECON.2015.7132923

Reema, M. (2017). *Performance Evaluation and Study of Routing Protocols : MANET vs VANET. 6495*(4), 204–208.

Regner, F., Urbach, N., & Schweizer, A. (2019). NFTs in practice–non-fungible tokens as core component of a blockchain-based event ticketing application.

Rehman, W., Zainab, H., Imran, J., & Bawany, N. Z. (2021, December). NFTs: Applications and challenges. In 2021 22nd International Arab Conference on Information Technology (ACIT) (pp. 1-7). IEEE.

Rehman, A., Paul, A., Ahmad, A., & Jeon, G. (2020). A novel class based searching algorithm in small world internet of drone network. *Computer Communications*, 157, 329–335. DOI: 10.1016/j.comcom.2020.03.040

Rejeb, A., Rejeb, K., Simske, S., & Treiblmaier, H. (2021). Humanitarian Drones: A Review and Research Agenda. *Internet of Things : Engineering Cyber Physical Human Systems*, 16, 100434. DOI: 10.1016/j.iot.2021.100434

Rekik, M., Mitton, N., & Chtourou, Z. (2015). Geographic greedy routing with aco recovery strategy graco. In *International Conference on Ad-Hoc Networks and Wireless* (pp. 19-32). Cham: Springer. DOI: 10.1007/978-3-319-19662-6_2

Reyna, A., Martín, C., Chen, J., Soler, E., & Díaz, M. (2018). On blockchain and its integration with IoT. Challenges and opportunities. *Future Generation Computer Systems*, 88, 173–190. DOI: 10.1016/j.future.2018.05.046

Rezvy, S., Luo, Y., Petridis, M., Lasebae, A., & Zebin, T. (2019). An efficient deep learning model for intrusion classification and prediction in 5G and IoT networks. In 2019 53rd Annual Conference on Information Sciences and Systems (CISS) (pp. 1-6). IEEE.

Rojas, C. R. (2018). Artificial Intelligence, Blockchain and the Platforms of the Future. *Blockchain and the Platforms of the Future (March 22 ....* Rosa, J. L. de la, Torres-Padrosa, V., El-Fakdi, A., Gibovic, D., O, H., Maicher, L., & Miralles, F. (2017). A survey of Blockchain Technologies for Open Innovation. *World Open Innovation Conference 2017, November*.

Ronaghi, M. H. (2021). A blockchain maturity model in agricultural supply chain. *Information Processing in Agriculture*, 8(3), 398–408. DOI: 10.1016/j.inpa.2020.10.004

S. K. S. M. (2023). Application of Blockchain in Supply Chain Management. *International Journal For Multidisciplinary Research*, 5(2), 2216. DOI: 10.36948/ijfmr.2023.v05i02.2216

Saberi, A., Dastjerdi, A. V., & Buyya, R. (2020). A blockchain-based access control model for the internet of things. *Future Generation Computer Systems*, 108, 664–675.

Sachdeva, S., Ali, A., & Khan, S. (2022). Secure and privacy issues in telemedicine: Issues, solutions, and standards. In *Telemedicine: The Computer Transformation of Healthcare* (pp. 321–331). Springer International Publishing. DOI: 10.1007/978-3-030-99457-0_21

Sadeghi, A., Wachsmann, C., & Wachsmann, A. (2020). Blockchain technology for the Internet of Things: A comprehensive review. *IEEE Access : Practical Innovations, Open Solutions*, 8, 43167–43182. DOI: 10.1109/ACCESS.2020.2975126

Saeidnia, H. R., & Lund, B. D. (2023). Non-fungible tokens (NFT): A safe and effective way to prevent plagiarism in scientific publishing. In *Library Hi Tech News* (Vol. 40, Issue 2). DOI: 10.1108/LHTN-12-2022-0134

Saleem, S., & Omar, R. M. (2015). Measuring customer based beverage brand equity: Investigating the relationship between perceived quality, brand awareness, brand image, and brand loyalty.

Salman, T., & Jain, R. (2019). A Survey of Protocols and Standards for Internet of Things. *Journal of Information Science and Engineering*, 35(2), 231–245. DOI: 10.1680/jsie.2019.35.2.001

Sangodoyin, S., Mecklenbrauker, C. F., Lerch, M., Zochmann, E., Caban, S., Groll, H., Rupp, M., Prokes, A., Blumenstein, J., Pratschner, S., Bernado, L., Zemen, T., Molisch, A. F., & Hofer, M. (2019). Position-Specific Statistics of 60 GHz Vehicular Channels During Overtaking. *IEEE Access : Practical Innovations, Open Solutions*, 7, 1–1. DOI: 10.1109/ACCESS.2019.2893136

Santos, P. A., Rodrigues, R. N., & Albuquerque, C. (2022). Security issues in IoT-based identity management systems. *Computer Networks*, 191, 108022. DOI: 10.1016/j.comnet.2021.108022

Satyanand, K. B., & Karthik, P. (2018). A survey on edge computing and its applications. *Journal of Computer Networks and Communications*, 2018, 1–11. DOI: 10.1155/2018/7327465

Savirimuthu, J. (2019). Blockchain and the Law: The Rule of Code. *Script-ed*, 16(1), 95–102. Advance online publication. DOI: 10.2966/scrip.160119.95

Schär, F. (2021). Decentralized finance: On blockchain-and smart contract-based financial markets. *Review - Federal Reserve Bank of St. Louis*, 103(2). Advance online publication. DOI: 10.20955/r.103.153-74

Schaub, F., Paik, M., & Hsiao, J. (2021). Verifiable credentials and decentralized identifiers in practice. *The Journal of Privacy and Confidentiality*, 11(2), 41–62. DOI: 10.29012/jpc.843

Scholar, P. (2014). *Position Based Protocol with QOS Parameters in VANETs *1,2. 3*(1).

Shafiq, M., Tian, Z., Sun, Y., Du, X., & Guizani, M. (2020). Selection of effective machine learning algorithm and Bot-IoT attacks traffic identification for internet of things in smart city. *Future Generation Computer Systems*, 107, 433–442. DOI: 10.1016/j.future.2020.02.017

Shaibani, R., & Zahary, A. (2019). Survey of Context-Aware Video Transmission over Vehicular Ad-Hoc Networks (VANETs). *ICST Transactions on Mobile Communications and Applications*, 0(0), 156089. DOI: 10.4108/eai.13-7-2018.156089

Sharma, V., & Kumar, R. (2017). Cooperative frameworks and network models for flying ad hoc networks: A survey. *Concurrency and Computation*, 29(4), 1–36. DOI: 10.1002/cpe.3931

Sharples, M., & Domingue, J. (2016). The blockchain and kudos: A distributed system for educational record, reputation and reward. In Adaptive and Adaptable Learning: 11th European Conference on Technology Enhanced Learning, EC-TEL 2016, Lyon, France, September 13-16, 2016 *Proceedings*, 11, 490–496.

Shen, X., Chen, J., Wosinska, L., Ou, J., Li, J., Chen, L., & Van, D. P. (2019). Service Migration in Fog Computing Enabled Cellular Networks to Support Real-time Vehicular Communications. *IEEE Access : Practical Innovations, Open Solutions*, 7, 1–1. DOI: 10.1109/ACCESS.2019.2893571

Shin, D., & Ibahrine, M. (2020). The socio-technical assemblages of blockchain system: How blockchains are framed and how the framing reflects societal contexts. *Digital Policy. Regulation & Governance*, 22(3), 245–263. DOI: 10.1108/DPRG-11-2019-0095

Shi, W., Cao, J., Zhang, Q., Li, Y., & Xu, L. D. (2016). Edge computing: Vision and challenges. *IEEE Internet of Things Journal*, 3(5), 637–646. DOI: 10.1109/JIOT.2016.2579198

Shi, W., Zhou, H., Li, J., Xu, W., Zhang, N., & Shen, X. (2018). Drone Assisted Vehicular Networks: Architecture, Challenges and Opportunities. *IEEE Network*, 32(3), 130–137. DOI: 10.1109/MNET.2017.1700206

Silveira, F. A., & Camilo, S. P. de O. (2023). A blockchain-based platform for trading weather derivatives. *Digital Finance*. Advance online publication. DOI: 10.1007/s42521-022-00071-9

Sirait, T. H., Gamayanto, I., & Ramadhan, A. (2023). Blended Learning Technology during Disease Outbreak: A Systematic Literature Review. *2023 International Conference on Data Science and Its Applications, ICoDSA 2023*, 65–70. DOI: 10.1109/ICoDSA58501.2023.10276457

Smith, J. (2022). *Predictive Maintenance: A Comprehensive Guide*. TechPress.

Sompolinsky, Y., & Zohar, A. (2018). Secure high-throughput broadcasting in blockchain systems. *2018 IEEE European Symposium on Security and Privacy (EuroS&P)*, 209-224. DOI: 10.1109/EuroSP.2018.00028

Song, H., Liu, W., Liu, A., Li, X., Huang, B., & Wang, T. (2019). Deployment Optimization of Data Centers in Vehicular Networks. *IEEE Access : Practical Innovations, Open Solutions*, 7, 1–1. DOI: 10.1109/ACCESS.2019.2897615

Sookhak, M., & Gani, A. (2019). A Survey on Security and Privacy Issues in the Internet of Things. *Journal of Network and Computer Applications*, 130, 66–92. DOI: 10.1016/j.jnca.2019.01.012

Sookram, P. C. (2023). Blockchain and crypto exchange-traded funds. In *The Emerald Handbook on Cryptoassets*. Investment Opportunities and Challenges., DOI: 10.1108/978-1-80455-320-620221011

Soputro, S. G., Imron, A., & Saiban, K. (2023). Consumer Protection in Commodity Futures Trading Transactions in the Physical Crypto Asset Market. *International Journal of Social Science Research and Review*, 6(12), 54–62. Advance online publication. DOI: 10.47814/ijssrr.v6i12.1707

Sorial, G. A., & Hong, J. (2014). *Environmental Science and Edited by*.

Statista. (2021). Number of connected Internet of Things (IoT) devices worldwide from 2015 to 2025. Retrieved from Statista IoT Growth.

Statista. (2024, May 17). *DeFi TVL of multiple blockchains combined as of November 17, 2023*. https://www.statista.com/statistics/1272181/defi-tvl-in-multiple-blockchains/

Sultan, S., Ruan, Y., & Wang, Y. (2020). Decentralized identity management: Architecture, use cases, and challenges. *Future Generation Computer Systems*, 108, 295–307. DOI: 10.1016/j.future.2020.01.039

Sumak, B., Polancic, G., & Hericko, M. (2010). An Empirical Study of Virtual Learning Environment Adoption Using UTAUT. *2010 Second International Conference on Mobile, Hybrid, and On-Line Learning*, 17–22. DOI: 10.1109/eLmL.2010.11

Suman, S.; Agrawal, E.A. and Jaiswal, A.K. (2016). EPARGA: A Resourceful Power Aware Routing Protocol for MANETs. International Journal of Advanced Research in Computer Engineering \& Technology (IJARCET), 5(5).

Sumra, I. A., Sellappan, P., Abdullah, A., & Ali, A. (2018). Security issues and Challenges in MANET-VANET-FANET: A Survey. *EAI Endorsed Transactions on Energy Web and Information Technologies*, 5(17), 1–6. DOI: 10.4108/eai.10-4-2018.155884

Surujnath, R. (2017). Off The Chain! A Guide to Blockchain Derivatives Markets and the Implications on Systemic Risk. *Fordham Journal of Corporate & Financial Law, 22*(2).

Swan, M. (2015). *Blockchain: Blueprint for a new economy*. O'Reilly Media, Inc.

Swan, M. (2015). *Blockchain: Blueprint for a New Economy*. O'Reilly Media.

Swan, M. (2018). In blockchain we trust. *Computer*, 51(2), 82–84.

Swan, M. (2018). *Tokenomics: A Business Guide to Token Usage, Utility, and Value*. O'Reilly Media, Inc.

Swan, M. (2019). DAOs, Democracy and Governance. In *Encyclopedia of Blockchain and Cryptocurrencies* (pp. 209–213). Academic Press.

Symantec Security Summary – February 2021. (2021, March 1). Symantec Enterprise Blogs. https://symantec-enterprise-blogs.security.com/feature-stories/symantec-security-summary-february-2021

Szabo, N. (1997). Formalizing and securing relationships on public networks. *First Monday*, 2(9). Advance online publication. DOI: 10.5210/fm.v2i9.548

Taha, A., Alsaqour, R., Uddin, M., Abdelhaq, M., & Saba, T. (2017). Energy efficient multipath routing protocol for mobile ad-hoc network using the fitness function. *IEEE Access : Practical Innovations, Open Solutions*, 5, 10369–10381. DOI: 10.1109/ACCESS.2017.2707537

Tama, B. A., Kweka, B. J., Park, Y., & Rhee, K. H. (2017). A critical review of blockchain and its current applications. *International Conference on Electrical Engineering and Computer Science (ICECOS)*, 109-113. DOI: 10.1109/ICECOS.2017.8167115

Tanenbaum, A.S., & & H. (2014). Modern operating systems (4th ed.). Pearson.

Tang, Y., Xiong, J., Becerril-Arreola, R., & Iyer, L. (2019). Ethics of blockchain: A framework of technology, applications, impacts, and research directions. *Information Technology & People*, 33(2), 602–632. DOI: 10.1108/ITP-10-2018-0491

Tapscott, D., & Tapscott, A. (2016). *Blockchain Revolution: How the Technology Behind Bitcoin Is Changing Money, Business, and the World*. Penguin Random House.

Taylor, R. (2023). *Industrial Applications of Predictive Maintenance*. Wiley.

Terao, Y., Phoummavong, P., Utsu, K., & Ishii, H. (2016). *A proposal on void zone aware Greedy Forwarding method over MANET. In 2016 IEEE Region 10 Conference (TENCON)*. IEEE.

Terry, J., & Bachmann, C. (2019). Quantifying the potential impact of autonomous vehicle adoption on government finances. *Transportation Research Record: Journal of the Transportation Research Board*, 2673(5), 72–83. DOI: 10.1177/0361198119837218

Thamilarasu, G., & Chawla, S. (2019). Towards Deep-Learning-Driven Intrusion Detection for the Internet of Things. *Sensors (Basel)*, 19(9), 1977. DOI: 10.3390/s19091977 PMID: 31035611

Tian, Y., Yuan, J., & Song, H. (2019). Efficient privacy-preserving authentication framework for edge-assisted Internet of Drones. *J. Inf. Secur. Appl.*, 48, 102354. DOI: 10.1016/j.jisa.2019.06.010

Torrieri, D., Talarico, S., & Valenti, M. C. (2015). Performance comparisons of geographic routing protocols in mobile ad hoc networks. *IEEE Transactions on Communications*, 63(11), 4276–4286. DOI: 10.1109/TCOMM.2015.2477337

Tschorsch, F., & Scheuermann, B. (2016). Bitcoin and beyond: A technical survey on decentralized digital currencies. *IEEE Communications Surveys and Tutorials*, 18(3), 2084–2123. DOI: 10.1109/COMST.2016.2535718

Ullah, A., Yaqoob, S., Imran, M., & Ning, H. (2019). Emergency Message Dissemination Schemes Based on Congestion Avoidance in VANET and Vehicular FoG Computing. *IEEE Access : Practical Innovations, Open Solutions*, 7, 1570–1585. DOI: 10.1109/ACCESS.2018.2887075

Vaneeta, M., Deepa, S. R., Sangeetha, V., Naganna, K., Vasisht, K. S., Ashwini, J., & Srividya, H. R. (2023). Tamper Proof Air Quality Management System using Blockchain. *International Journal of Advanced Computer Science and Applications*, 14(2).

Veerasamy, V., Singh, S., Murshid, S., Nguyen, H. D., & Gooi, H. B. (2023). Blockchain-Based Microgrid Frequency Control and Energy Trading to Incentivize EV Aggregator. *2023 IEEE 3rd International Conference on Sustainable Energy and Future Electric Transportation, SeFet 2023*. DOI: 10.1109/SeFeT57834.2023.10245092

Verma, S. (2021, February 17). *Looking past the industrial future with AI, IoT and blockchain - IBM Blog*. IBM Blog. https://www.ibm.com/blog/looking-past-the -industrial-future-with-ai-iot-and-blockchain/

Verma, K. (2016). Multicast routing protocols for wireless sensor networks: A comparative study. *Int. J. Comput. Netw. Commun*, 1(1), 1–11.

Vermesan, O., Eisenhauer, M., Sundmaeker, H., Guillemin, P., Serrano, M., Tragos, E. Z., ... & Bahr, R. (2022). Internet of things cognitive transformation technology research trends and applications. Cognitive Hyperconnected Digital Transformation, 17-95.

Vermesan, O., Friess, P., Guillemin, P., Serrano, M., Bouraoui, M., Freire, L. P., . . . van der Wees, A. (2022a). IoT digital value chain connecting research, innovation and deployment. In *Digitising the Industry Internet of Things Connecting the Physical, Digital and VirtualWorlds* (pp. 15-128). River Publishers. DOI: 10.1201/9781003337966-3

Vidhya, R., Sandhia, G. K., Jansi, K. R., & Jeya, R. (2022). A predictive model emotion recognition on deep learning and shallow learning techniques using eeg signal. In *Principles and Applications of Socio-Cognitive and Affective Computing* (pp. 43–50). IGI Global., DOI: 10.4018/978-1-6684-3843-5.ch004

Voshmgir, S. (2018). Fungible Tokens vs. Non-Fungible Tokens. Retrieved from https://blockchainhub.net/blog/blog/nfts-fungible-tokens-vs-non-fungible-tokens/

W3C. (2020). Decentralized Identifiers (DIDs) v1.0. World Wide Web Consortium. Retrieved from https://www.w3.org/TR/did-core/

Wagner, I., Maglaras, L., Janicke, H., He, Y., & Al-Bayatti, A. (2016). Social Internet of Vehicles for Smart Cities. *Journal of Sensor and Actuator Networks*, 5(1), 3. DOI: 10.3390/jsan5010003

Walden, V. G. (2021). Digital holocaust memory, education and research. In *Digital Holocaust Memory, Education and Research.* Springer International Publishing., DOI: 10.1007/978-3-030-83496-8_1

Wang, Q., Li, R., Wang, Q., & Chen, S. (2021). Non-fungible token (NFT): Overview, evaluation, opportunities and challenges. arXiv preprint arXiv:2105.07447.

Wang, H., Gupta, S., Singhal, A., Muttreja, P., Singh, S., Sharma, P., & Piterova, A. (2022). An Artificial Intelligence Chatbot for Young People's Sexual and Reproductive Health in India (SnehAI): Instrumental Case Study. *Journal of Medical Internet Research,* 24(1), e29969. Advance online publication. DOI: 10.2196/29969 PMID: 34982034

Wang, H., You, F., Chu, X., Li, X., & Sun, X. (2019). Research On Customer Marketing Acceptance for Future Automatic Driving — A Case Study in China City. *IEEE Access : Practical Innovations, Open Solutions,* 7, 1–1. DOI: 10.1109/ACCESS.2019.2898936

Wang, L., Zhang, X., Wang, Y., Wang, L., Wang, Q., Zang, X., Li, R., Xu, Y., Li, Z., & Chen, Q. (2022). Femtosecond Laser Direct Writing for Eternal Data Storage: Advances and Challenges. *Zhongguo Jiguang. Chinese Journal of Lasers,* 49(10). Advance online publication. DOI: 10.3788/CJL202249.1002504

Wang, Q., Yu, G., Fu, S., Chen, S., Yu, J., & Xu, X. (2023). A Referable NFT Scheme. *2023 IEEE International Conference on Blockchain and Cryptocurrency, ICBC 2023.* DOI: 10.1109/ICBC56567.2023.10174865

Wang, W., Xu, J., & Zhao, Z. (2019). Key management for blockchain-based identity management systems. *IEEE Access : Practical Innovations, Open Solutions,* 7, 48915–48926. DOI: 10.1109/ACCESS.2019.2903431

Wang, X., Zhang, J., & Wang, S. (2020). Cryptographic techniques for blockchain-enabled edge computing. *IEEE Access : Practical Innovations, Open Solutions,* 8, 28220–28230. DOI: 10.1109/ACCESS.2020.2973458

Wang, Z., Zhang, X., Liu, Z., & Zhao, Y. (2019). A blockchain-based security framework for the Internet of Things. *IEEE Internet of Things Journal,* 6(5), 8081–8090.

Wazid, M., Das, A. K., & Lee, J.-H. (2018). *Authentication protocols for the internet of drones: taxonomy, analysis and future directions.* J Ambient Intell Human Comput., DOI: 10.1007/s12652-018-1006-x

Weng, L., Zhang, Y., Yang, Y., Fang, M., & Yu, Z. (2020). A mobility compensation method for drones in 5G-eIoT. *Digital Communications and Networks,* 7(2), 196–200. DOI: 10.1016/j.dcan.2020.07.011

Westerlund, M. (2019). The emergence of deepfake technology: A review. *Technology Innovation Management Review*, 9(11), 39–52. DOI: 10.22215/timreview/1282

Williams, R. B., Asim, M., Park, Y., Shin, D., & Stylos, N. (2022). How does the blockchain find its way in the UAE The blockchain as a sociotechnical system. *International Journal of Technology Management*, 90(1/2), 122. DOI: 10.1504/IJTM.2022.10048640

Wood, G. (2014). *Ethereum: A secure decentralised generalised transaction ledger*. Retrieved from https://ethereum.github.io/yellowpaper/paper.pdf

Wu, K. (2023). Digital Transformation in the FinTech Sector. *Highlights in Business. Economics and Management*, 10, 243–248. Advance online publication. DOI: 10.54097/hbem.v10i.8047

Xiao, L., Wan, X., Lu, X., Zhang, Y., & Wu, D. (2018). IoT Security Techniques Based on Machine Learning: How Do IoT Devices Use AI to Enhance Security? *IEEE Signal Processing Magazine*, 35(5), 41–49. DOI: 10.1109/MSP.2018.2825478

Xu, X., Pautasso, C., Zhu, L., Gramoli, V., Ponomarev, A., Tran, A. B., & Chen, S. (2019). The blockchain as a software connector. *In 2016 13th Working IEEE/IFIP Conference on Software Architecture (WICSA)* (pp. 182-191). IEEE.

Xu, L., Chen, L., & Gao, Z. (2020). Smart contract-based access control for the internet of things. *IEEE Internet of Things Journal*, 7(3), 1902–1912.

Xu, M., Chen, X., & Kou, G. (2019). A systematic review of blockchain. *Financial Innovation*, 5(1), 27. DOI: 10.1186/s40854-019-0147-z

Xu, M., Weber, I., & Staples, M. (2020). *Blockchain technology for smart cities: Use cases and challenges*. Springer., DOI: 10.1007/978-3-030-42424-2

Xu, X., Liu, X., & Liu, C. (2018). Blockchain-based Internet of Things: A Survey. *IEEE Access : Practical Innovations, Open Solutions*, 6, 1738–1752. DOI: 10.1109/ACCESS.2018.2875322

Xu, X., Weber, I., & Staples, M. (2019). Architecting the blockchain for the Internet of Things: A case study. *IEEE Transactions on Engineering Management*, 66(4), 574–585. DOI: 10.1109/TEM.2017.2722467

Yaacoub, J.-P., Noura, H., Salman, O., & Chehab, A. (2020). Security Analysis of Drones Systems: Attacks, Limitations, and Recommendations. *Internet of Things : Engineering Cyber Physical Human Systems*, 11, 100218. DOI: 10.1016/j.iot.2020.100218 PMID: 38620271

Yahuza, M., Idris, M. Y. I., Ahmedy, I. B., Wahab, A. W. A., Nandy, T., Noor, N. M., & Bala, A. (2021). Internet of Drones Security and Privacy Issues: Taxonomy and Open Challenges. *IEEE Access : Practical Innovations, Open Solutions*, 9, 57243–57270. DOI: 10.1109/ACCESS.2021.3072030

Yamini, K. A. P., & Arivoli, K. S. T. (2018). CHALLENGES ON ENERGY CONSUMPTION IN MANET—A SURVEY. *International Journal of Pure and Applied Mathematics*, 119(12), 13735–13741.

Yang, C., Xu, Y., & Liu, Q. (2023). Privacy-preserving techniques in IoT: A survey and future directions. *IEEE Communications Surveys and Tutorials*, 25(1), 230–259. DOI: 10.1109/COMST.2022.3208387

Yang, L., Li, X., & Li, Y. (2020). Blockchain-based secure access control for smart homes. *Journal of Computer Security*, 89, 102515. DOI: 10.1016/j.jocs.2020.102515

Yao, J., & Ansari, N. (2019). QoS-aware power control in internet of drones for data collection service. *IEEE Transactions on Vehicular Technology*, 68(7), 6649–6656. DOI: 10.1109/TVT.2019.2915270

Yli-Huumo, J., Ko, D., Choi, S., Park, S., & Smolander, K. (2016). Where Is Current Research on Blockchain Technology?—A Systematic Review. *PLoS One*, 11(10), e0163477. DOI: 10.1371/journal.pone.0163477 PMID: 27695049

Yuan, Y., & Wang, F.-Y. (2016). Blockchain: The state of the art and future trends. *Acta Automatica Sinica*, 42(4), 481–494.

Zaidi, S., Atiquzzaman, M., & Calafate, C. T. (2020). Internet of Flying Things (IoFT): A survey. *Computer Communications*, 165, 53–74. DOI: 10.1016/j.comcom.2020.10.023

Zhang, H., Lee, I. A., Moore, K. S., & Shah, S. A. (2023). Board 279: Ethics in Artificial Intelligence Education: Preparing Students to Become Responsible Consumers and Developers of AI. *ASEE Annual Conference and Exposition, Conference Proceedings*. https://www.scopus.com/inward/record.uri?eid=2-s2.0-85172111599&partnerID=40&md5=81fb62c6b3d6b7a9ac46405fa4ab6305

Zhang, Y., & Wen, J. (2015, February). An IoT electric business model based on the protocol of bitcoin. In 2015 18th international conference on intelligence in next generation networks (pp. 184-191). IEEE.

Zhang, L., Wang, X., & Wang, S. (2021). Challenges and solutions in blockchain-based edge computing: A comprehensive review. *Journal of Network and Computer Applications*, 187, 103104. DOI: 10.1016/j.jnca.2021.103104

Zhang, L., & Zhang, Z. (2019). Edge computing for IoT: A survey. *IEEE Access : Practical Innovations, Open Solutions*, 7, 80846–80864. DOI: 10.1109/ACCESS.2019.2924248

Zhang, S., Xu, Y., & Li, S. (2020a). Advances in Self-Sovereign Identity and decentralized identity management. *IEEE Access : Practical Innovations, Open Solutions*, 10, 35287–35298. DOI: 10.1109/ACCESS.2022.3165167

Zhang, S., Zhang, N., Fang, X., Yang, P., & Shen, X. S. (2017). Self-Sustaining Caching Stations: Toward Cost-Effective 5G-Enabled Vehicular Networks. *IEEE Communications Magazine*, 55(11), 202–208. DOI: 10.1109/MCOM.2017.1700129

Zhang, X., Chen, W., & Wu, D. (2020b). Blockchain interoperability: A survey and research directions. *IEEE Access : Practical Innovations, Open Solutions*, 8, 116560–116573. DOI: 10.1109/ACCESS.2020.3003195

Zhang, X., Li, D., Wang, C., Jiang, Z., Ngao, A. I., Liu, D., Peters, M. A., & Tian, H. (2023). From ChatGPT to China' Sci-Tech: Implications for Chinese Higher Education. *Beijing International Review of Education*, 5(3), 296–314. DOI: 10.1163/25902539-05030007

Zhang, X., Zhang, X., Zhang, X., Sun, W., Meng, R., & Sun, X. (2023). A Derivative Matrix-Based Covert Communication Method in Blockchain. *Computer Systems Science and Engineering*, 46(1), 225–239. Advance online publication. DOI: 10.32604/csse.2023.034915 PMID: 37155222

Zhang, Y., Lopez, J., & Wang, Z. (2019). Mobile Edge Computing for Vehicular Networks [From the Guest Editors]. *IEEE Vehicular Technology Magazine*, 14(1), 27–108. DOI: 10.1109/MVT.2018.2885367

Zhang, Y., & Wen, J. (2017). The IoT electric business model: Using blockchain technology for the internet of things. *Peer-to-Peer Networking and Applications*, 10(4), 983–994. DOI: 10.1007/s12083-016-0456-1

Zhang, Y., Wu, J., & Liu, X. (2021). Blockchain-Based Security Solutions for IoT Networks: A Survey. *IEEE Internet of Things Journal*, 8(5), 3472–3487. DOI: 10.1109/JIOT.2020.3032878

Zhang, Y., & Xie, H. (2019). A Survey on the Internet of Things (IoT) and Blockchain Technology for Smart Industry. *Procedia Computer Science*, 152, 128–133. DOI: 10.1016/j.procs.2019.05.060

Zhang, Y., & Yang, J. (2019). Enhancing IoT security and privacy with blockchain and edge computing. *IEEE Internet of Things Journal*, 6(3), 4476–4486. DOI: 10.1109/JIOT.2018.2888258

Zhang, Y., Yang, J., & Zhang, Z. (2020). Blockchain-based edge computing for secure and efficient data management in IoT systems. *IEEE Access : Practical Innovations, Open Solutions*, 8, 24334–24347. DOI: 10.1109/ACCESS.2020.2969086

Zhang, Y., & Yang, Y. (2019). A Survey on Blockchain Technology and Its Potential Applications for Secure and Smart Internet of Things. *IEEE Access : Practical Innovations, Open Solutions*, 7, 150070–150088. DOI: 10.1109/ACCESS.2019.2945286

Zhao, F., Wu, Z., Xu, W., & Jin, Y. (2019). Application of blockchain technology in smart home systems. *IEEE International Conference on Consumer Electronics (ICCE)*, 1-4.

Zheng, K., Zheng, L. J., Gauthier, J., Zhou, L., Xu, Y., Behl, A., & Zhang, J. Z. (2022). Blockchain technology for enterprise credit information sharing in supply chain finance. *Journal of Innovation & Knowledge*, 7(4), 100256.

Zheng, Z., Xie, S., Dai, H. N., Chen, X., & Zhang, C. (2018). Blockchain for internet of things: A survey. *IEEE Internet of Things Journal*, 5(6), 5497–5506. DOI: 10.1109/JIOT.2018.2857256

Zheng, Z., Xie, S., Dai, H., Chen, X., & Wang, H. (2018). An Overview of Blockchain Technology: Architecture, Consensus, and Future Trends. *IEEE International Congress on Big Data*, 557-564. DOI: 10.1109/BigDataCongress.2017.85

Zhou, H., Wu, Z., & Sun, J. (2021a). Scalable identity management in IoT: Challenges and solutions. *IEEE Internet of Things Journal*, 8(12), 9392–9404. DOI: 10.1109/JIOT.2021.3063567

Zhou, J., Huang, C., & Sun, X. (2021b). Blockchain and AI integration for smart contract management: A survey. *IEEE Transactions on Knowledge and Data Engineering*, 33(5), 1744–1762. DOI: 10.1109/TKDE.2020.2991334

Zhou, L., & Zhang, J. (2022). Consensus Mechanisms for IoT Blockchain: A Survey. *IEEE Internet of Things Journal*, 9(4), 1234–1248. DOI: 10.1109/JIOT.2022.3204567

Zhu, X., & Liu, Y. (2021). Case Studies of Blockchain Applications in IoT: From Theory to Practice. *Journal of Computer Networks and Communications*, 2021, 1–12. DOI: 10.1155/2021/5555577

Zhu, Y.-P., & Park, H.-W. (2022). Use of Triangulation in Comparing the Blockchain Knowledge Structure between China and South Korea: Scientometric Network, Topic Modeling, and Prediction Technique. *Sustainability (Basel)*, 14(4), 2326. DOI: 10.3390/su14042326

Zohar, A. (2017, August). Securing and scaling cryptocurrencies. In *IJCAI* (pp. 5161-5165). DOI: 10.24963/ijcai.2017/742

Zohar, A. (2015). Bitcoin: Under the hood. *Communications of the ACM*, 58(9), 104–113. DOI: 10.1145/2701411

Zyskind, G., Nathan, O., & Pentland, A. (2015). Decentralizing privacy: Using blockchain to protect personal data. *2015 IEEE Security and Privacy Workshops*, 180-184. DOI: 10.1109/SPW.2015.27

About the Contributors

Adarsh Garg received Ph.D degree in Information Technology from GGSIP university, Delhi. With 24 + years of teaching, corporate and research consultancy in Systems and Data Analytics, she has worked with organizations like WIPRO Tech, GE, IMT Ghaziabad, Punjabi University, Patiala, Galgotias University, prior to joining GLBIMR, She is currently supervising 8 Ph.Ds; published over 50 research papers in refereed international/national journals and Conference proceedings. 5 books Information System Development –A Software Engineering Approach; Environment Sustainability-A true value of IT; Global Health Disaster- Predicting the unpredictable with emerging technologies- AAP, CRC, USA; Reinventing Technological Innovations with Artificial Intelligence, Bentham Books; Advances in Technological Innovations in Higher Education: Theory and Practices, CRC, Taylor & Francis; She is a member of various professional bodies like Computer Society of India, Member ACM-Computer Science Teachers Association. She is on editorial board of reputed journals and a reviewer of articled for various journals of repute.

Fadi Al-Turjman is a professor and research center director.

Shahnawaz Khan received his PhD in Computer Science from Indian Institute of Technology (Banaras Hindu University), India. He has been associated with multiple universities as lecturer, course coordinator and program coordinator. He has co-founded 2 IT companies and has served as chief technical officer. He has always emphasized on bridging the gap between academics and industry keeping in mind the growing IT industry in terms of futuristic technologies. Under his leadership many modernized laboratories came into existence. He has been a key player during the accreditation process of the universities. He has delivered several invited/keynote talks at workshops/seminars in India & abroad. He has been editor of special issues of several journals and has edited several peer-reviewed books. He is an active researcher in the field of Machine learning, NLP, Blockchain and FinTech. He has published multiple patents and more than 50 peer reviewed research articles.

***

|Bipllab Chakraborty - Contributing Author|M-Tech(Gold Medalist) Ph.D. Scholar(National Institute of Technology, Rourkela) Department of Mechanical Engineering

Jagjit Singh Dhatterwal is presently working as an Associate Professor with the Department of Artificial Intelligence & Data Science, Koneru Lakshmaiah Education Foundation, Vaddeswaram, Andhra Pradesh, India. He has supervised many UG and PG projects of engineering students. He is also a member of the Computer Science Teacher Association (CSTA), New York, USA, International Association of Engineers (IAENG), Hong Kong; IACSIT (International Association of Computer Science and Information Technology, USA); a professional member of the Association of Computing Machinery, USA; IEEE; and a life member of the Computer Society of India. His areas of interest include Artificial Intelligence, BCI, cyborgsand Multi-agent Technology. He has number of publications, such as Books/Book chapters/Journal papers and conference papers.

Shashi Kant is an Assistant Professor, College of Business and Economics, Department of Management, Bule Hora University, Ethiopia.

Kaushik Kumar holds a Ph.D. in Engineering from Jadavpur University, India, an MBA in Marketing Management from Indira Gandhi National Open University, India and a Bachelor of Technology from Regional Engineering College (Now National Institute of Technology), Warangal, India. For 11 years, he worked in a manufacturing unit of Global repute. He is currently working as an Associate Professor in the Department of Mechanical Engineering, Birla Institute of Technology, Mesra, Ranchi, India. He has 22 Years of Teaching and Research Experience. His research interests include Composites, Optimization, Non-Conventional Machining, CAD / CAM, Rapid Prototyping and Quality Management Systems towards product development for societal and industrial usage and has received 29 patents for them. He has published 55+ Books (including 31 Edited Book Volume) (They are referred as Text Books and Reference Books by 40+ Universities / Institutes in their academic curriculum), 80 Book Chapters and 200+ Research Papers in peer-reviewed reputed national and international journals. Kaushik has also served as Editor–in–Chief, Series Editor, Guest Editor, Editor, Editorial Board Member and Reviewers for International and National Journals. He has been felicitated with many awards and honours including DISTINGUISHED ALUMNUS AWARD for PROFESSIONAL EXECELLENCE 2023 under Academic and Research from his Alma Matar National Institute of Technology, Warangal,

India. He has also received Sponsored Research and Consultancy Projects of more than 1 Crore from Govt. of India and abroad. Kaushik has delivered expert lectures as Keynote Speaker at International & National Conferences, Resource Person at Various Workshops, FDP's and Short-Term Courses. He has guided many students of Doctoral, Masters and Under Graduate programmes of his home and other institutions in India and abroad. He also has served as Reviewer and Examiner of Doctoral and Masters dissertation for institutes in India and abroad.

Moideen Batcha Having 23 years of Academic experience with specialization of HR.Produced one doctoral candidate and two candidates are in pipeline.Published nearly 20 research papers in Scopus,WoS and Emerald publishing. Complete Doctorate of Philosophy from Madurai Kamaraj University and possesing SLET certificate.

Sabyasachi Pramanik is a professional IEEE member. He obtained a PhD in Computer Science and Engineering from Sri Satya Sai University of Technology and Medical Sciences, Bhopal, India. Presently, he is an Associate Professor, Department of Computer Science and Engineering, Haldia Institute of Technology, India. He has many publications in various reputed international conferences, journals, and book chapters (Indexed by SCIE, Scopus, ESCI, etc). He is doing research in the fields of Artificial Intelligence, Data Privacy, Cybersecurity, Network Security, and Machine Learning. He also serves on the editorial boards of several international journals. He is a reviewer of journal articles from IEEE, Springer, Elsevier, Inderscience, IET and IGI Global. He has reviewed many conference papers, has been a keynote speaker, session chair, and technical program committee member at many international conferences. He has authored a book on Wireless Sensor Network. He has edited 8 books from IGI Global, CRC Press, Springer and Wiley Publications.

Chikesh Ranjan is a highly accomplished Mechanical Engineer, PhD in Mechanical Engineering at the Department of Mechanical Engineering, Birla Institute of Technology Mesra, Ranchi, Jharkhand. He holds a Master of Engineering (M.E) degree in Mechanical Engineering with a specialization in Design of Mechanical Equipment from the same institution. He also holds a Bachelor of Engineering (B.E) in Mechanical Engineering from Marathwara Institute of Technology, Aurangabad, Maharashtra, achieving First Class with distinction upon graduation. Presently, he is serving as a Project Engineer at the National Institute of Technology Rourkela, Sandergarh, Odisha, where his innovative contributions have been recognized through the publication of 15 journal papers, 10 authored books, and 6 book chapters. He has also been actively involved in various workshops, conferences, and webinars, organizing 7 workshops and 8 events, and coordinating 13 events. Additionally, he has participated in 31 training/FDP programs and attended 34 national/international workshops, seminars, and webinars. He has been granted 10 design patents and 5 foreign patents, demonstrating his dedication to advancing mechanical design and technology. With 8 years of Teaching & Research experience, his areas of teaching and research interest are Composites, Non-conventional machining, CAD / CAM Drone Technology, and Robotics. He is a proud member of the Institution of Engineers, India, and has received 7 prestigious awards and honors for his remarkable contributions to the field of Mechanical Engineering.

B. Tripathy Reddy Has 19 + years of Experience as an academician, researcher & administrator. Served in various administrative positions as a Head of the Department - Artificial intelligence & Data Science, Head of the Department - School of Competitive Coding, Head of the Department - Communication & Soft Skills at KL University. also served as Professor In charge for Placements Training for the Department in LBRCE, Instrumental in making the students meeting the industry expectations and having dream start for their professional careers from the campus itself. Has strong Inclination towards research and development. Is doing active research in the area of cloud computing, Artificial Intelligence, Machine learning and Cloud security. Has Published more than 50 articles in referred national and international journals.

Deepak Ranjan Sahoo is a expert in the field of Accounting and Finance, offering a robust combination of academic and corporate experience. With eight years in academia and two years in the corporate sector, he provides a comprehensive perspective that enhances his professional contributions. Dr. Sahoo is currently an Assistant Professor of Finance at MIT Arts Design and Technology University, where he is committed to advancing knowledge and fostering innovation among his students. He holds an M.Com in Corporate Accounting and Financial Management, M.Phil in Business Administration, and PhD in Business Administration. His academic credentials underpin his extensive expertise in key areas of finance, including Financial Modelling and Business Valuation, Fintech, Environmental, Social, and Governance (ESG), Sustainable Development, Behavioral Finance, Derivatives, Risk Management, Fundamental and Technical Analysis, and Capital Market Operations.

Vaishali Deepak Sahoo is an expert in the field of Accounting and Finance, offering a robust combination of academic experience. With eight years in academia, she provides a comprehensive perspective that enhances her professional contributions. Dr. Vaishali is currently an Assistant Professor of Finance at Vishwakarma University, where she is committed to advancing knowledge and fostering innovation among her students. She holds an M.Com in Corporate Accounting and Financial Management, an M.Phil. in Business Administration, and a PhD in Accountancy and Auditing. Her academic credentials underpin her extensive expertise in key areas of finance, including, Financial Management, Environmental, Social, and Governance (ESG), Sustainable Development, Behavioural Finance, Taxation, Risk Management and Capital Market Operations. Her profound understanding of these subjects enriches her teaching and informs her research and professional activities.

J.Srinivas is working at Department of Mechanical Engineering, NIT Rourkela. His topics of interest include: Robotics and control, Drone technologies, Condition monitoring and diagnostics.

Rajalakshmi Vel is a management educator with 20 years of teaching experience at the post graduate level in reputed institutions. Her teaching and research interests are in the area of Learning and Development, Sustainability and health care. She has won best paper award for her research work at International Conference on Sustainable Development Goals and Gender Perspective hosted by SVNIT (2021) and a Case Study at International Communication Management Conference (ICMC, 2020) at the prestigious Mudra Institute of Communications, Ahmedabad. She is also a trainer for NCFM, Mutual Fund modules and also has jointly conducted training programs on Accounting for Sales Tax Officers' Ahmedabad. She has completed Teachers Training Program conducted by Intel Computers and Academia acclaimed Faculty Training Program at ICFAI, Hyderabad. She is well acquainted with the case method of teaching for accounting courses. She has designed certification programs in cross-functional areas of FinTech and Financial Modelling for Business Valuation. She serves as an external expert of the Research Advisory Committees.

Index

Symbols

802.11p 360, 377

A

Adversarial attack 8, 13
AI 1, 2, 18, 19, 20, 22, 23, 24, 25, 26, 27,
    28, 31, 32, 34, 35, 38, 39, 40, 41, 44,
    49, 51, 77, 78, 79, 80, 83, 85, 87, 107,
    108, 109, 110, 112, 129, 271, 273, 312,
    316, 335, 336, 339, 341, 342, 345, 346,
    347, 348, 389, 391, 397, 398, 399, 400,
    401, 404, 405, 406, 407
AI in Education 109
and Energy aware 194, 225
artificial intelligence 1, 19, 28, 31, 34, 37,
    51, 58, 62, 77, 86, 87, 90, 91, 92, 107,
    108, 109, 110, 111, 112, 251, 271,
    299, 304, 327, 341, 345, 346, 347,
    381, 382, 389, 393, 397, 404
Attack Vectors 73

B

block Chain 15, 50, 73, 75, 117, 125, 130,
    229, 230, 236, 246, 258, 267, 269,
    270, 271, 279, 280, 281, 284, 320,
    329, 395, 396
Blockchain 20, 21, 23, 25, 28, 37, 53, 54,
    57, 58, 59, 60, 61, 62, 63, 65, 67, 68,
    69, 70, 71, 72, 73, 74, 75, 76, 77, 78,
    80, 81, 82, 83, 88, 113, 114, 115, 116,
    117, 118, 121, 122, 123, 124, 125,
    126, 127, 128, 129, 130, 131, 132,
    133, 134, 229, 230, 231, 232, 233,
    234, 235, 239, 240, 246, 247, 248,
    249, 250, 251, 252, 253, 254, 255,
    256, 257, 258, 259, 260, 262, 263,
    264, 265, 266, 267, 268, 269, 270,
    271, 272, 273, 274, 275, 276, 277,
    280, 281, 284, 285, 289, 292, 293,
    294, 295, 296, 298, 299, 300, 301,
    302, 303, 304, 305, 306, 307, 308,
    309, 310, 311, 312, 316, 317, 318,
    319, 320, 321, 322, 323, 329, 333,
    334, 335, 336, 338, 339, 340, 381,
    384, 389, 390, 391, 393, 395, 396,
    397, 398, 399, 400, 401, 402, 403,
    404, 405, 406, 407, 408, 409
Blockchain Technology 20, 21, 23, 28, 59,
    60, 61, 62, 65, 67, 74, 75, 76, 78, 80,
    81, 82, 114, 115, 116, 117, 121, 122,
    126, 127, 128, 130, 132, 133, 229,
    230, 231, 232, 233, 234, 239, 246,
    247, 248, 253, 257, 259, 260, 263,
    264, 267, 269, 270, 271, 272, 273,
    277, 280, 289, 300, 301, 302, 303,
    305, 307, 308, 310, 311, 316, 317,
    318, 321, 335, 338, 340, 381, 384,
    389, 390, 395, 396, 399, 400, 401,
    402, 405, 406, 409

C

CIoT 1, 2, 3, 4, 5, 6, 12, 13, 14, 15, 17,
    18, 19, 20, 21, 22, 23, 24, 25, 26, 27,
    28, 31, 32, 33, 34, 35, 36, 38, 39, 40,
    41, 44, 45, 49, 50, 51, 52, 57, 58, 59,
    60, 63, 64, 65, 67, 68, 69, 70, 76, 77,
    78, 80, 113, 114, 115, 116, 130, 131,
    253, 254, 255, 258, 259, 263, 264,
    265, 266, 267, 268, 269, 270, 271,
    272, 273, 274, 301, 302, 303, 304,
    305, 306, 307, 308, 309, 310, 315,
    316, 317, 318, 319, 320, 321, 322,
    323, 325, 326, 327, 328, 329, 330,
    331, 332, 333, 334, 335, 336, 337,
    389, 390, 391, 393, 394, 395, 396,
    397, 398, 399, 400, 401, 402, 403,
    404, 405, 406, 407
Cloud Computing 2, 114, 118, 119, 240,
    246, 384
Cognitive Internet of Things 1, 2, 6, 13, 14,
    17, 20, 25, 28, 31, 33, 34, 35, 36, 38,
    39, 44, 50, 69, 301, 302, 304, 305, 307
Cryptocurrencies 76, 230, 232, 261, 262,
    275, 279, 286, 298, 312, 313
Crypto-Currencies 279, 280, 281, 282,
    286, 287, 288, 296, 297, 300

Cryptographic 58, 67, 69, 71, 72, 73, 78, 117, 122, 126, 129, 133, 232, 233, 234, 239, 260, 264, 306, 329, 385, 391, 395

Cyber-Attacks 49, 363, 364

D

data analysis 2, 114, 119, 271, 391, 397, 402, 405

Decision Making 36, 119, 129, 224, 317, 404

Derivative 229, 230, 237, 238, 248, 249, 250, 252

Digital Divide 86, 102, 103, 109

Dynamic Topology 135, 137, 138, 349

E

Economy 82, 276, 281, 283, 287, 288, 298, 299, 312, 344, 345, 384

Edge computing 2, 4, 19, 28, 37, 49, 55, 113, 114, 115, 116, 118, 119, 121, 122, 123, 124, 125, 126, 127, 128, 129, 130, 131, 132, 133, 134, 272, 318, 325, 364, 381, 382, 388, 393

Educational Technology 85, 86, 92, 105, 108, 111

ethical consideration 51

Ethical Considerations 25, 27, 28, 33, 34, 35, 38, 39, 44, 45, 50, 51, 52, 78, 269, 274

F

Finance 61, 229, 230, 231, 236, 246, 247, 251, 262, 279, 282, 286, 289, 290, 299, 300, 341, 342, 344, 345, 348

Financial Crisis 279, 280, 281, 284, 286, 297

G

Geographic 5, 139, 140, 141, 143, 158, 162, 165, 167, 170, 171, 172, 173, 174, 175, 176, 212, 214, 216, 217, 218, 220, 221, 222, 263, 354, 356

Governance Paradigm 301, 302, 305, 307, 308

H

Healthcare 5, 19, 22, 23, 24, 26, 61, 72, 75, 78, 80, 109, 122, 125, 128, 250, 262, 271, 285, 302, 307, 316, 317, 320, 326, 329, 332, 336, 338, 345, 382, 387, 396, 397

I

Industrial IoT 75, 78, 128, 133, 263, 325, 327, 332

Industrial Security Drones 34, 35, 38, 39, 41, 42, 44, 45, 46, 47, 48, 49, 50, 51, 52

Interconnected Systems 28, 234, 304, 336

Internet of Things 1, 2, 6, 13, 14, 17, 19, 20, 25, 28, 29, 30, 31, 33, 34, 35, 36, 38, 39, 41, 44, 50, 51, 53, 55, 56, 57, 62, 69, 79, 81, 82, 115, 132, 133, 134, 248, 250, 254, 258, 269, 271, 272, 273, 275, 276, 277, 299, 301, 302, 304, 305, 307, 311, 312, 313, 315, 316, 321, 327, 329, 335, 337, 338, 339, 340, 372, 381, 382, 389, 391, 393, 395, 403, 408, 409

Internet of Vehicle 384

ITS 2, 8, 11, 13, 23, 31, 36, 49, 57, 58, 60, 61, 63, 72, 76, 78, 86, 91, 92, 98, 99, 100, 101, 110, 111, 115, 119, 123, 126, 129, 130, 133, 136, 137, 139, 141, 142, 143, 144, 145, 146, 152, 153, 154, 155, 156, 158, 159, 161, 162, 164, 165, 169, 170, 171, 173, 174, 175, 177, 178, 180, 184, 185, 187, 188, 190, 194, 195, 196, 199, 202, 205, 207, 209, 212, 217, 219, 220, 224, 225, 229, 230, 232, 235, 236, 237, 240, 241, 243, 244, 247, 249, 252, 256, 258, 263, 265, 269, 270, 272, 273, 279, 280, 281, 282, 283, 284, 285, 287, 288, 295, 297, 298, 302, 303, 304, 318, 321, 323, 329, 333, 339, 341, 342, 345, 348, 349, 354, 356, 361, 363, 370, 374, 378, 381, 391, 392, 393, 394, 395,

398, 400, 401, 406, 409

M

machine learning 1, 2, 4, 6, 7, 8, 9, 11, 12, 13, 14, 15, 16, 17, 20, 21, 22, 23, 25, 27, 29, 30, 31, 32, 40, 41, 44, 47, 57, 58, 77, 78, 304, 305, 306, 335, 389, 393

MANET 135, 136, 137, 138, 139, 140, 178, 182, 188, 196, 212, 213, 214, 215, 216, 217, 218, 224, 341, 348, 349, 353, 386, 387

N

NFT's 281, 288

P

Probability Density Function 390
Proof of Work 61, 73, 76, 79, 117, 118, 233, 234, 235, 258, 261, 262, 335, 391, 395, 402

R

Routing Protocols 135, 136, 137, 138, 139, 140, 141, 143, 144, 152, 160, 161, 163, 165, 178, 180, 181, 182, 188, 204, 207, 212, 213, 214, 215, 216, 217, 218, 219, 220, 221, 223, 341, 342, 345, 346, 347, 348, 352, 353, 354, 355, 358, 359, 378, 382, 383, 384, 386, 387

Russia 279, 280, 281, 282, 285, 286, 287, 288, 289, 290, 294, 295, 296, 297, 298

S

security challenges 6, 17, 21, 22, 23, 24, 28, 46, 54, 217, 385

Smart Contract 57, 71, 77, 79, 83, 125, 128, 132, 235, 236, 246, 251, 259,

260, 262, 266, 275, 298, 306, 308, 317, 318, 320, 321, 322, 323, 325, 326, 327, 329, 330, 332, 333, 334, 335, 336, 338, 340, 399, 400

Smart Contracts 58, 59, 65, 71, 72, 74, 77, 78, 80, 114, 115, 117, 122, 125, 129, 132, 133, 230, 231, 232, 235, 236, 240, 241, 242, 244, 245, 246, 248, 249, 254, 258, 259, 260, 264, 266, 267, 270, 271, 273, 275, 299, 301, 303, 304, 305, 306, 308, 315, 316, 317, 318, 319, 320, 321, 322, 323, 325, 326, 327, 328, 329, 330, 332, 333, 334, 335, 336, 337, 338, 339, 390, 395, 396, 397, 398, 399, 400, 401, 405, 406, 408

Societal Impact 27, 34

T

Technological Innovation 34, 51, 315
Transparency and accountability 23, 396, 399

U

Ukraine 279, 280, 281, 282, 283, 284, 285, 286, 287, 288, 289, 290, 291, 294, 295, 296, 297, 298

V

Value Chain 237, 313
VANETs 341, 342, 343, 348, 349, 350, 352, 353, 356, 357, 359, 360, 361, 374, 377, 378, 381, 382, 384, 387

W

War 137, 279, 281, 282, 285, 286, 287, 288, 290, 296, 297

Printed in the United States
by Baker & Taylor Publisher Services

Printed in the United States
by Baker & Taylor Publisher Services